THE ROUTLEDGE COMPANION
TO COMMEDIA DELL'ARTE

From Commedia dell'Arte came archetypal characters that are still with us today, such as Harlequin and Pantalone, and the rediscovered craft of writing comic dramas and masked theatre. From it came the forces that helped create and influence Opera, Ballet, Pantomime, Shakespeare, Moliere, Lopes de Vega, Goldoni, Meyerhold, and even the glove puppet, Mr Punch.

The Routledge Companion to Commedia dell'Arte is a wide-ranging volume written by over 50 experts that traces the history, characteristics, and development of this fascinating yet elusive theatre form. In synthesising the elements of Commedia, this book introduces the history of the Sartori mask studio; presents a comparison between Gozzi and Goldoni's complicated and adversarial approaches to theatre; invites discussions on Commedia's relevance to Shakespeare, and illuminates re-interpretations of Commedia in modern times.

The authors are drawn from actors, mask-makers, pedagogues, directors, trainers and academics, all of whom add unique insights into this fundamental pillar of western theatre. Notable contributions include:

- Donato Sartori on the twentieth century Sartori mask
- Rob Henke on the Form and Freedom in Commedia Improvisation
- Anna Cottis on Carlo Boso
- Didi Hopkins on *One Man, Two Guv'nors*
- Kenneth Richards on acting companies
- Antonio Fava on Commedia dell'Arte
- Joan Schirle on Carlo Mazzone-Clementi and women in Commedia
- M. A. Katritzky on Commedia Iconography.

Judith Chaffee is Associate Professor of Theatre at Boston University, and head of movement training for actors. She trained in Commedia with Antonio Fava, Julie Goell, Stanley Allen Sherman, and Carlos García Estévez.

Olly Crick is a performer, trainer and director, having trained in Commedia under Barry Grantham and Carlo Boso. He is founder of The Fabulous Old Spot Theatre Company.

Pablo Picasso: Three Musicians, 1921
Artwork © Succession Picasso/DACS, London 2014
Image © Philadelphia Museum of Art / CORBIS

THE ROUTLEDGE COMPANION TO COMMEDIA DELL'ARTE

Edited by
Judith Chaffee and
Olly Crick

Routledge
Taylor & Francis Group

LONDON AND NEW YORK

First published in paperback 2017

First published 2015
by Routledge
2 Park Square, Milton Park, Abingdon, Oxon OX14 4RN

and by Routledge
711 Third Avenue, New York, NY 10017

Routledge is an imprint of the Taylor & Francis Group, an informa business

British Library Cataloguing in Publication Data
A catalogue record for this book is available from the British Library

Library of Congress Cataloging in Publication Data
A catalog record for this book has been requested

ISBN: 978–0–415–74506–2 (hbk)
ISBN: 978–1–138–22499–5 (pbk)
ISBN: 978–1–315–75084–2 (ebk)

Typeset in Sabon
by Saxon Graphics Ltd, Derby

This book is dedicated to Christopher Cairns, Stephen Knapper, Ninian Kinnier-Wilson, Jacques Lecoq, Franca Rame, Donato Sartori and Giorgio Strehler who walked in the footsteps of the Gelosi, carrying the torch and keeping the spirit of Commedia vibrantly alive.

CONTENTS

CONTENTS

CONTENTS

ACKNOWLEDGEMENTS

We thank the many colleagues, professionals, and experts in Commedia who assisted in the process of researching, contributing, shaping, collating, and editing this volume. Thanks also go to Talia Rodgers and Ben Piggott for supporting us along the way; and special acknowledgements to Pete Wishnok, and to Holly, Daisy, and Rose Tarplee-Crick for their love, patience, and tolerance in seeing this project to completion.

Foreword

AVNER EISENBERG
(AVNER THE ECCENTRIC)

I have long been fascinated and haunted by Commedia. When I was a student at the Lecoq school in the early 70s, Commedia dell'Arte was one of the units of study in the second year. We explored the characters from the point of view of their idiosyncratic movements; their relationship to barnyard society; and the comic archetypes of the stingy old miser, the scheming servants, the bloviating pseudo expert, and the innocent young lovers.

As with so many things taught by M. Lecoq, the importance of studying Commedia did not become clear until years later when I began teaching physical comedy myself and realised that in Commedia training I had the blueprint for timeless comedy. The movement, gestures, and timing of each character are explicitly tied to the breath: the breath of the character, and not the breath of the actor who is perhaps fearful of not being funny. The Commedia characters are not trying to be funny. Theirs is a world of life and death decisions, crime and punishment, war and peace, and hunger. There is always hunger, not just for food, but also for wealth, sex, and power.

Commedia has been largely defined by the postures and poses of the Callot etchings. But Commedia was bawdy and raucous, as alive and immediate as any theatre ever was. From Callot we have but a snapshot of comedy from the heyday of Commedia dell'Arte without realising its debt to theatre that went before and its enormous influence on what came after. As Carlo Mazzone-Clementi defines it, Commedia was the comedy of a known character reacting to an unknown situation.

In donning the mask we learn to instantly inhabit the character. We unambiguously fall into status relationships with our fellow actors, settings, and props, and all without the psychological complications of modern actor training. Commedia is a folk art. Its concepts and techniques are learned by apprenticeship, by example, and, above all, by doing. Moment to moment awareness, simple vulnerability, the development of a vocabulary of little comic turns, or *lazzi*, a sense of the musicality of the play, and the ever changing status relationships are the wheels and cogs of Commedia training and performance.

Commedia dell'Arte of the sixteenth century took from its past and projected its techniques for comedy and its brilliance into the future. To see what Commedia looked like in the 1500s look to Callot. To see what it looks like today look no further than YouTube, boxed sets of DVDs of the classic comedies, and the comedy blogosphere. In the Marx Brothers films we see Groucho as Dottore, Harpo as Pedrolino, Chico as Brighella, and Zeppo as the hapless Inamorato.

In modern television we find the descendants of the Commedia characters alive and well in all their glory. The techniques, sensibilities, and comic structure of Commedia have been passed down through the ages and are alive and well in many modern situation comedies. In fact Commedia was called, *Commedia a situazione* by its contemporaries. It was the sitcom of the sixteenth century. Here are but a few examples:

The Honeymooners
Ralph Kramden – Brighella
Alice – Franceschina
Norton – Arlechino

Fawlty Towers
Basil Fawlty – Brighella or Capitano
Manuel – Arlechino/Pedrolino
Sybil – Franceschina
Polly – Columbina

Sgt. Bilko
Sgt. Bilko – Brighella

All in the Family
Archie Bunker – Pantalone

Training in the style of Commedia, the modern actor gains competence in the craft of these great modern-day descendants of the Commedia's archetypal characters. Read these chapters and think about what Commedia can do for you as an actor. Some of the best practitioners and scholars of Commedia Dell'Arte in the world today have contributed to this volume. Write to them and ask your questions, and above all take a workshop or enrol in a course and learn first-hand the magic of Commedia.

CONTRIBUTORS

Michele Bottini, a graduate of the Scuola D'Arte Drammatica Paolo Grassi in Milan, is currently Artistic Director of the Accademia dell'Arte in Arezzo, Italy, where he teaches Commedia and movement. From 1997 to 2000 he played the title role of Arlecchino with the Piccolo Teatro in Milan, in Giorgio Strehler's *Arlecchino servitore di due padroni*, replacing the legendary actor Ferrucio Soleri. He continues to explore his artistry as a stage and film actor and director, including recent collaborations with Dario Fo.

Linda L. Carroll is Professor of Italian at Tulane University, and author of *Angelo Beolco (Il Ruzante)* (1990) and *Language and Dialect in Ruzante and Goldoni* (1981). She translated a volume of passages from the diaries of the Venetian Marin Sanudo (2008), and *La Prima Oratione* by Angelo Beolco (2009). She has been in receipt of, amongst others, a Fulbright study grant.

Judith Chaffee is Associate Professor of Theatre at Boston University, head of movement training for actors. A professional dancer, actor, and director, her training and research have focused on movement modalities of dance, Commedia dell'Arte, improvisation, Viewpoints, centering techniques, meditation, and devising theatre.

Anna Cottis is a French-based actor, workshop leader, and director. She performed as a traditional clown before switching to Commedia dell'Arte. She now performs internationally with the Compagnie du Mystere Bouffe, and teaches Commedia, grommelot and mask technique at Carlo Boso's Academie des Arts du Spectacle and elsewhere. Her current research is in neurobiological audience reactions to theatre, particularly mask work.

J. Douglas Clayton is Professor Emeritus of Russian at the University of Ottawa (Canada). His scholarly interests include Chekhov and Russian theatre. He is the author of the book *Pierrot in Petrograd: Commedia dell'arte/Balagan in Twentieth-Century Russian Theatre and Drama* (1994).

Olly Crick is a freelance educator, researcher and performer, and is co-author of *Commedia dell'Arte, A Handbook for Troupes* (2001). He performs a history of comedy solo show *From Street to Salon, Solo*, and is Artistic Director of the Fabulous Old Spot Theatre Company. He has trained with Carlo Boso, Barry Grantham, Phillipe Gaullier and John Wright. Currently he is teaching and researching at Edge Hill University.

Nancy L. D'Antuono is Professor Emerita of Italian at Saint Mary's College, Notre Dame, Indiana. She is an authority on the Spanish novella and Lope de Vega; the connections between Spanish Golden Age theatre and the Commedia dell'Arte; its literary antecedents; and also the impact of the Spanish theatre on the Italian scripted theatre and *dramma per musica*.

Avner Eisenberg (Avner the Eccentric) is a world-renowned clown, juggler, teacher, and performer from buffoonery in Paris, to Broadway, to film. Avner is probably best known for his endearing portrayal of The Jewel, the loveable holy man, in *The Jewel of the Nile*, co-starring Michael Douglas and Kathleen Turner. He was also featured in the film *Brenda Starr* and the television series *Webster* and *Mathnet*. Avner is a certified Ericksonian Hypnotist, an NLP Master Practitioner, the artistic director of *Phyzgig*, an annual festival of physical comedy, and a celebrated teacher of physical comedy.

Carlos García Estévez is an actor, stage director, theatre researcher and pedagogue inspired by Jacques Lecoq. He founded his theatre group Teatro Punto in 1998. Recently he has been working as an actor with Simon McBurney and as a researcher and pedagogue with Donato Sartori. He is an associate artist at the LEM (Laboratory for the Study of Movement – École Jacques Lecoq), and, with his theatre laboratory Manifesto Poetico, he performs and devises shows internationally.

Mark Evans is Professor of Theatre Training at Coventry School of Art and Design, Coventry University. He trained in theatre and movement in Paris, with Jacques Lecoq, Philippe Gaullier and Monika Pagneux. He has taught for over twenty years and is currently editing *The Actor Training Reader* (2015) and is writing a book on performance, movement and the body for Palgrave Macmillan.

Antonio Fava is an actor, director, Maestro of Commedia dell'Arte and author of *The Comic Mask in the Commedia dell'Arte* (2007) (*La Maschera Comica nella Commedia dell'Arte*). He directs the School of the Comic Actor in Reggio Emilia, Italy, and designs and makes leather masks for use in his school and performances.

Giulia Filacanapa holds a PhD from the University Paris 8 Saint-Denis on Néo-Commedia dell'Arte and Giovanni Poli and received her Master's Degree in Theatre History from the University of Pisa. She contributes to the European theatre periodicals *Annuario Internazionale della Commedia dell'Arte* and *Atti & Sipari* and has published *Le paroxysme linguistique de Dario Fo* (2012). She has also worked as a teaching assistant for Carlo Boso and Stefano Perocco.

Tim Fitzpatrick recently retired from the Department of Performance Studies at the University of Sydney, which he co-founded, has published on Italian theatre (particularly Pirandello and the Commedia dell'Arte), and more recently on Elizabethan and Jacobean staging practices and the architecture of the second Globe playhouse. He is currently working on an Australian Research Council-funded project examining historical rehearsal processes from the mid-sixteenth to the mid-nineteenth centuries.

Brian Foley has taught Clown and Commedia dell'Arte at New York University and Arizona State University. He was Associate Artistic Director of the World Clown Festival held in China, and, as a co-founder of Bambouk Clown Theatre, he has toured internationally and won both a Golden Nose Award and a Sherman Brothers Award for clowning. Brian received his MFA in Directing for the Theatre from Arizona State University in 2014.

Kathy Foley is Professor of Theatre Arts at the University of California, Santa Cruz, and the editor of *The Asian Theatre Journal*. She specialises in performance of Southeast Asian Theatre and has also taught at Chulalongkorn University in Bangkok and Yonsei University in Seoul. She is the author of the Southeast Asian material in *The Cambridge Guide to Asian Theatre* (1993), numerous articles, and performs and directs dance dramas, puppetry and other works.

Julie Goell is a performer, writer, musician, and puppeteer. She teaches Eccentric Performance in collaboration with her husband, Avner Eisenberg, at the Celebration Barn in Maine. She writes, directs, and designs for Peaks Island Puppets, and directs Maine Singers' Atelier, training singers for performance careers. Based in Rome for ten years, she toured with La Compagnia I Gesti, teaching Physical Comedy at Teatro Studio. She later taught Commedia Dell'Arte and directed farce in theatre programs throughout the United States.

Elizabeth C. Goldsmith is Professor Emerita of French Literature at Boston University. Her research and publications have focused on conversation, letter writing, memoirs, travel, and literary culture in the early modern period. Her most recent book is a biography of two adventurous women writers and celebrities: *The Kings' Mistresses: The Liberated Lives of Marie Mancini, Princess Colonna, and Her Sister Hortense, Duchess Mazarin* (2012).

Mel Gordon is Professor of Acting, Directing and Theatre History at the University of California, Berkeley. Having taught at the Lee Strasberg Institute, NYU, and Yale, he authored *The Grand Guignol: The Theatre of Horror and Terror* (1997), and *Lazzi: The Comic Routines of the Commedia dell'Arte* (1983), amongst others, including over thirty articles and entries on American, French, German, Italian, Russian, and Yiddish theatre and cinema.

Barry Grantham was trained by Idzikowski of the Diaghilev ballet, the inheritor of many of Nijinsky's roles, and who coached Barry in the Harlequin role from *Carnaval*. Barry worked with Massine and Helpmann in *The Red Shoes* and *Tales of Hoffmann*, also performing as a solo mime. He has taught Commedia at the Oval House Theatre and the City Literary Institute in London. He founded The Intention Commedia Company and teaches throughout Europe. He is the author of the best-selling *Playing Commedia* (2000) and of *Commedia Plays* (2006), and is launching a quarterly online journal *Zannizine* devoted to Commedia dell'Arte, starting from January 2014.

Andy Grewar graduated with a BA in English Literature from Natal University and then worked as translator and editor at the University of South Africa, where he wrote and staged five masked, improvised plays *à la* Commedia dell'Arte. He

Lectured in English Literature and Language at the University of Fort Hare and is currently an independent academic and scientific copy-editor.

Mike Griffin teaches and directs across Canada. He has taught at the University of Calgary and Mt. Allison University, where he is currently the Crake Fellow in Drama. Mike also actively leads Commedia dell'Arte workshops throughout the country.

Thomas F. Heck gained his PhD in musicology at Yale in 1970 and for most of his career (1978–2000) was Professor and Head of the Music/Dance Library at the Ohio State University. He has received two Fulbright grants and, in 1994–95, a NIAS fellowship to explore the iconography of the performing arts. Amongst other publications he has co-edited and published *A Treatise on Acting, From Memory and by Improvisation (1699)* by Andrea Perrucci (2008), and *The Commedia dell'Arte in Naples: A Bilingual Edition of the 176 Casamarciano Scenarios* (2001), which garnered the Weiss-Brown Award from the Newberry Library.

Robert Henke is Professor of Drama and Comparative Literature at Washington University in St. Louis. The recipient of fellowships from Villa I Tatti, Fulbright, and the National Endowment for the Humanities, he is the author of *Pastoral Transformations: Italian Tragicomedy and Shakespeare's Late Plays* (1997); *Performance and Literature in the Commedia dell'Arte* (2002); and co-editor, with Eric Nicholson, of *Transnational Exchange in Early Modern Theater* (2008).

Franklin J. Hildy is Professor of Theatre History at the University of Maryland, and co-author, with Oscar G. Brocket, of four editions of *History of the Theatre*. He is a member of the Architecture Research Group for Shakespeare's Globe in London, the founding convener of the Theatre Architecture Working Group for the International Federation for Theatre Research and general editor of theatre-finder.org.

Didi Hopkins started life as a classical percussionist, before moving into theatre. She co-founded Beryl and the Perils and now works as an actor, director and international business coach. Didi worked for the National Theatre in London, introducing Commedia to the teacher's inset programme, and subsequently the National Theatre made five instructional films about her training work there. She was Richard Bean's Commedia advisor prior to his writing *One Man, Two Guvnors* in 2011.

Peter Jordan was a founding member of the Fortunati and an actor with TAG Teatro di Venezia. He was for many years Head of Acting at the Hong Kong Academy for Performing Arts. His many directed productions include: Shakespeare's *The Merchant of Venice* and *All's Well that Ends Well*; Molière's *L'Avare* and *Tartuffe*; Goldoni's *La Locandiera* and *La Casa Nova*; and Flaminio Scala's *The Tragic Events*. Currently, he is Assistant Professor (Drama and Literature) at the City University of Hong Kong and is the author of *The Venetian Origins of the Commedia dell'Arte* (2014), also published by Routledge.

M. A. Katritzky is Barbara Wilkes Research Fellow in Theatre Studies in the English Department of The Open University, UK. Recent books include: *Healing, Performance and Ceremony in the Writings of Three Early Modern Physicians: Hippolytus Guarinonius and the Brothers Felix and Thomas Platter* (2012); *Women, Medicine and Theatre 1500–1750: Literary Mountebanks and Performing Quacks* (2007); *The Art of Commedia: A Study in the Commedia dell'Arte 1560–1620 with Special Reference to the Visual Records* (2006), and, co-authored with colleagues in The Open University English Department, *The Handbook to Literary Research* (2010).

Stephen Knapper (1964–2012) was a co-founder of the Kingston University drama department. He studied French and Modern History at Sussex University, and then went to study under Jacques Lecoq, where he became entranced by the idea of theatre as an agent of social change. His chosen mediums to achieve this were Commedia dell'Arte, and later Carnival, and he specialised in the masks of Scaramouche and the Neapolitan Pulcinella. His chapter is a selection of posthumous edited highlights from his PhD on Scaramouche.

Anne MacNeil is Associate Professor of Music at the University of North Carolina, Chapel Hill. She has authored/edited *Selected Poems of Isabella Andreini* (2003), *Music and Women of the Commedia dell'Arte in the Late Sixteenth Century* (2003), and *The New International Dictionary of Music* (1992), and is a fellow with the American Academy in Rome and the American Association of University Women. Her recent research focuses on early modern laments, opera, and use of boats, barges and waterways as venues for music performances in Renaissance Mantua.

Fabio Mangolini graduated in 1987 from The Marcel Marceau Mime School, and performed as Arlecchino for Les Scalzacani Commedia Company. From 1992 to 1994 he collaborated in Tokyo with Kyogen Master Nomura Kosuke. He has been president of both the Ferrara Theatre Foundation as well as The Italian Opera School. He teaches, directs, and performs internationally, from Moscow, through Europe and Japan, to the US.

Scott McGehee, PhD from Boston College in European Intellectual History, moved to Italy as a Fulbright Fellow in 1995. Having taught for over 25 years with a particular interest in the arts and subversive social movements, he is the Founding Director of Accademia dell'Arte in Arezzo, Italy: www.dell-arte.org.

Kate Meehan has been performing and lecturing in Commedia dell'Arte for nearly two decades. She is the Managing Director of La Fenice, a Texas-based Commedia dell'Arte company which produced the first ever Digital International Commedia dell'Arte Festival. She has an MA in Theatre History and Criticism and has delivered several academic papers including 'Immigrants Via Popular Culture: A Study of the Portrayal of Various Immigrant Cultures in Vaudeville' and 'Bannerman in Hand: Puppetry, Pulcinella and the Popular Class'.

Paul Monaghan is a Canadian/Australian-based theatre professional (director, dramaturg and lighting designer) and academic (Honorary Senior Fellow, School of

Performing Arts, Victorian College of the Arts and University of Melbourne). Paul holds a PhD in Theatre Studies/Classical Studies and is also co-convenor of the Dramaturgies Project and co-convenor/co-editor of Double Dialogues (conference and journal): an ongoing project linking academic discourse with arts practice.

Claudia Orenstein is Associate Professor of Theatre at Hunter College and the CUNY Graduate Center. Her publications include *Festive Revolutions: The Politics of Popular Theatre and the San Francisco Mime Troupe* (1998) and *The Routledge Companion to Puppetry and Material Performance* (forthcoming). Her current research focuses on Indian puppetry.

Louise Peacock is a senior lecturer in Drama and Theatre Practice at the University of Hull from where she obtained her PhD. She is the author of *Serious Play: Modern Clown Performance* (2009) and *Slapstick and Comic Performance: Comedy and Pain* (2014). She teaches in the areas of clowning, Commedia, and stage comedy and has written articles for scholarly journals on slapstick, Commedia and stand-up comedy.

Mace Perlman is a classically trained mime and actor who studied and performed under Marcel Marceau in Paris (1982–84), and with Giorgio Strehler at his Piccolo Teatro in Milan (1987–93), where he acted in Goldoni's *Arlecchino, Servant of Two Masters* and Goethe's *Faust*. The recipient of Stanford University's Robert M. Golden award for excellence in combining performance and scholarship, he specialises in the relation between the mask-characters of the Commedia dell'Arte and playing the great texts of the English, French, and Italian repertoire. He is currently working to create an Academy of Renaissance Theatre – a professional company of players together with a school of theatre, language, and Renaissance culture.

Stephano Perocco di Meduna was working as a film technical director until he studied the craft of mask making in Venice in 1977. From then on he has worked in close collaboration with Carlo Boso, and other close members of his team, as mask maker. He teaches leather mask making at international Commedia workshops, as well as making masks for many European theatre companies including Theatre de l' Eveil, La Compagnia Faux Magnifico, The Theatre du Centaure, Il Teatro di Leo and TAG Teatro di Venezia.

Domenico Pietropaulo is Principal of St Michael's College, University of Toronto, and Chair of the Department of Italian studies. He has edited *The Science of Buffoonery: Theory and History of the Commedia dell'Arte* (1988), and *Goldoni and the Musical Theatre* (1995); and authored *Dante Studies in the Age of Vico* (1989). He specialises in the fields of theatre history, dramaturgy, medieval studies, seventeenth and eighteenth century studies, and literary theory.

Artemis Preeshl is Associate Professor at Loyola University, New Orleans where she teaches performance. As a Fulbright-Nehru scholar, she wrote and directed *Pancha Ratna*, which won Honorable Mention at Hollywood's DIY Film Festival. She has directed Shakespeare and Commedia productions in Italy, Bali, Croatia, Kosovo, Malaysia, New Orleans, and at La Mama in New York.

Richard Stockton Rand began his career as a street performer in the Commedia tradition and went on to act on and off Broadway; in regional theatre; and in festivals throughout the USA, Europe and Canada. He is the recipient of an IAC-National Endowment for the Arts fellowship for solo performance and his monologues have been published in numerous collections. He has served as Chair of Purdue Theatre and President of the Association of Theatre Movement Educators and is currently Professor of Theatre at Purdue University.

Kenneth Richards studied at Oxford and London universities, and at the Royal Academy of Dramatic Art. He taught in several European universities, including Ljubljana in Slovenia and Uppsala in Sweden, and has been a research fellow at the European University in Fiesole, Italy. For twenty years he was Professor of Drama at The University of Manchester. He has contributed to many books and journals, including *The Oxford Companion to the Theatre* (1983), *The Revels History of Drama in English*, *The Cambridge Guide to World Theatre* (1988), and *The Oxford International Encyclopaedia of Dance* (1998), was co-editor of *Theatre Research International*, and with Laura Richards is the author of *The Commedia dell'Arte, A Documentary History* (1990).

Davis Robinson is Professor of Theatre at Bowdoin College in Brunswick, Maine and artistic director of the Boston-based Beau Jest Moving Theatre, an award-winning theatre ensemble. Davis studied physical theatre with Jacques Lecoq and Tony Montanaro, and teaches intensive devising workshops each summer at the Celebration Barn Theater in South Paris, Maine. Davis is the author of *The Physical Comedy Handbook* (1999).

Sara Romersberger is Associate Professor of Theatre, Southern Methodist University, Dallas, TX. As a Movement Specialist and Director, she holds the Certificate École Internationale de Théâtre Jacques Lecoq and has worked nationally and internationally choreographing fights, dances and creating physical comedy. Presently she is working on her book, *Wise Enough to Play the Fool: Playing the Clowns of Shakespeare*.

John Rudlin works as an author, dramaturg, role-play specialist and workshop leader. He is author of *Commedia dell'Arte: an Actor's Handbook* (1994), and is an acknowledged authority on Jacques Copeau, publishing *Jacques Copeau* in 1986 (part of the Cambridge University Press's Directors in Perspective series). He also edited *Copeau: Texts on Theatre* (1990). He co-founded the University of Exeter Drama Department and The Common Players theatre company, specialising in community and rural touring.

Donato Sartori, (1939–2016) Venetian artist, began his career from an early age, in the studio of his father, the sculptor Amleto, starting with the creation, study and research of the ancient form of the Italian Commedia dell'Arte. In 1979 he founded, with his wife Paola Piizzi and other collaborators, the Centro Maschere Strutture Gestuali, making masks for theater, film directors and actors around the world, continuing the work not only of theatrical masks but also in multi-disciplinary art: the total masks and Costumes Urbani. He taught *mascherologia* at the University of Padua and held seminars and keynotes at prestigious international universities.

Roger Savage, PhD, was a lecturer in English Literature at Victoria University in Wellington NZ and then at the University of Edinburgh, where he is now an Honorary Fellow. He taught drama studies for many years; has staged several spoken plays and rather more operas; broadcast often on music-theatre; and has published essays on opera production, courtly theatre, libretto-writing and works by Purcell, Rameau, Vaughan Williams and Stravinsky.

Joan Schirle, actor, playwright, director, deviser, teacher of mask, movement, Commedia, and senior teacher of the FM Alexander Technique, is Founding Artistic Director of Dell'Arte International in Blue Lake, CA. A principal performer with the Dell'Arte Company since 1976, her acting was recognised with a 2006 Fox Foundation/TCG Resident Actor Fellowship. She designed Dell'Arte's MFA in Ensemble Based Physical Theatre and has taught at Yale, UCSD, University of Missouri Kansas City, and the Beijing Dance Academy, as well as for the artists of Cirque du Soleil.

Antonio Scuderi (PhD, UW–Madison) is Professor of Italian at Truman State University, where he founded the Italian program in 1997. He is the author of *Dario Fo and Popular Performance* (1998) and *Dario Fo: Framing, Festival, and the Folkloric Imagination* (2011), and co-editor of *Dario Fo: Stage, Text and Tradition* (2000). His interdisciplinary articles on Italian performance traditions have been published in leading journals of theatre, folklore, and literary studies.

Katrien van Beurden is an actress, director and the artistic director of Theatre Hotel Courage. This international company creates contemporary shows based on Commedia dell'Arte. The company explores Commedia in today's society, with or without masks, to create a tragic-comic and poetic theatre. She is well known for training professional actors, directors, and filmmakers.

Wout van Tongeren is dramaturg and artistic coordinator of the musical theatre company VocaalLAB (Zaandam, the Netherlands). He teaches dramaturgy and philosophy at the Theatre Department of the Amsterdam School of the Arts and is a collaborator in Carlos García Estévez' theatre laboratory Manifesto Poetico.

Matthew R. Wilson is Artistic Director of the award-winning Faction of Fools Theatre in Washington, DC, and International Coordinator of the worldwide Commedia dell'Arte Day. He is a union actor/director and author of *A Commedia Christmas Carol* (2012) MFA, Academy for Classical Acting; PhD candidate, University of Maryland.

Translators

Francesca Chilcote (Chapter 49) earned her BA in Theatre from the College of William and Mary in Williamsburg, Virginia and her MFA in Physical Theatre from the Accademia dell'Arte in Italy, where she trained in Commedia with

Michele Bottini and Marcello Bartoli, both from the Piccolo Theatre of Milan. Her thesis work analyses the construction of gender in Commedia dell'Arte. She continues to live in Italy as a freelance theatre artist.

Eileen E. Cottis, (Chapter 39) MA, BLitt (Oxon) was a senior lecturer in French and Drama at the University of North London (now London Metropolitan University) for 32 years. Her research areas are still nineteenth century French and English theatre, and twentieth century European theatre directors. She is Honorary Secretary of the UK Society for Theatre Research.

Michael Grady (Chapter 5) is a writer and educator with an obsession for comic masks.

Peter Jordan (Chapter 15) See contributors' biographies (page xviii).

Samuel Angus McGehee (Chapter 5) was born in Boston and grew up in Tuscany. He has a degree from Sarah Lawrence College and Banaras Hindu University in Music and Philosophy. Currently obtaining an MFA from the Accademia dell'Arte, Samuel's activities range from storytelling to experimental noise, music, teaching and translating.

Brenda O'Donohue (Chapter 13) teaches in the Department of Italian in Trinity College Dublin, and her research interests include translation for theatre, feminism and performance, and Irish and Italian theatre. Brenda is a member of the International Federation for Theatre Research and the Irish Society for Theatre Research.

Mace Perlman (Chapter 11) See contributors' biographies (page xx).

INTRODUCTION

The rise and fall and rise again of Commedia dell'Arte is unparalleled in the annals of theatre history. Originating in the sixteenth century as a popular Italian theatre form in which actors created stock characters, some in half-masks, who improvised dialogue from plot scenarios, Commedia flourished throughout Europe into the eighteenth century. But, due in part to a reputation for debauchery and scatological humour, and by popular comedic performances of less than professional skill and intent, it was relegated to insignificance by theatre artists interested in "serious art". Since the beginning of the twentieth century, however, there has been a resurgence of Commedia dell'Arte. A great many historical, technical, comparative, and philosophical books have been published about Commedia, and many performances using physical theatre and masks claim to be twentieth or twenty-first century versions of the Commedia style. Publications and pronouncements are prolific but are scattered over a wide range of disciplines, from theatre to opera, ballet, and symphonies; from the historical to the sociological and cultural; as well as from techniques of performance, both traditional and modern. Some of the existing histories of the genre are quite old, and hence unavailable to a general reader. Some of the significant modern papers are available only in limited-edition academic papers or in unpublished doctoral theses. Within this volume you will find an overview of this genre, focusing on key aspects and developments, from its defining features and historical roots to contemporary incarnations, giving space to these new researches and theories. These articles are written by academics, practitioners, and enthusiasts, eminently qualified to synthesize both old and new research as well as performance practices. It is not intended to present a correct one-sided view, but rather confront aspects of the genre that define it as a unique and entrancing form of theatre.

Academics cite sources, gravitating toward proven facts and accurate research, believing that hitherto unknown historical "truth" may emerge from the results of their endeavours. Other people may take these cited facts and link them together in webs and strings of possibilities, offering a reader alternative interpretations. A third group offers creative opinions, often un-cited, and often based on personal artistic agendas in the belief that Commedia's "truth" exists only in live performance. The cocktail of facts, training, and fictive myth exists and has relevance only as far as it helps bring a performance to life in front of an audience. Commedia dell'Arte as a performance medium thrives on its practitioners' artistic visions and re-inventions, and sometimes—within all this joyful brouhaha—the concept of historical truth may get lost. Some historical facts have no bearing on contemporary live performance, and similarly some performer's opinions on history are only as interesting as a reader may be interested in that performer. Academics may look down on performers with poor or inaccurate pedagogy, and performers may cherry-pick history to suit their own artistic vision. There is rectitude at both ends, and, however one side may question the other's motives, both approaches have great intrinsic value.

There are several areas of Commedia dell'Arte and its influences that we chose not to include for various reasons. *Commedia Erudita*, the sixteenth century scripted neo-classical comedy from influential Renaissance writers and philosophers, is one of these. While having a great influence on the development of the Commedia plots and characters, as discussed in several chapters here, we chose to focus on the influences of improvised texts from scenarios—plot outlines—of the *Comici dell'Arte*, as Commedia was originally named. Commedia Erudita may be an entire volume in itself.

This is not a "how-to" manual. It is important to recognize that one cannot learn to perform Commedia from a book, but one can certainly perform more intuitively and with greater insight by understanding the relevancy and history of the form.

Another area we considered was offshoots of Commedia: the myriad of contemporary theatre, television, film, and entertainments seemingly influenced by physical comedy, slapstick, and stock characters—again another volume in itself. These include the antics of the Marx Brothers, consistent characters in their "masks" frolicking through slapstick comedy; or *Fawlty Towers*, with its Capitano and Arlecchinoesque characters; or even the Three Stooges, Charlie Chaplin, or Harold Lloyd: masters of physical comedy. What appeared to be a direct link was the 1963 US television series, *Gilligan's Island*, weekly shenanigans of seven castaways, stranded on a small Pacific island. The characters seemed straight out of Commedia, but according to the show's creator, Sherwood Schwartz, Commedia dell'Arte had no influence on the development of the characters or concepts; it was derivative of societal archetypes, with weekly physical comedy in humorously absurd conditions. Good comedy is good comedy.

Like the other Routledge Companions, this collection of essays is aimed at those fascinated by Commedia: acolytes, undergraduates, academics, performers and maestros. If any particular aspect grabs your attention, you will find references, further reading suggestions and other avenues of investigation. The conundrum in understanding Commedia dell'Arte is identifying the context from which one is approaching it. Look for the beautiful and the grotesque and you will find them. Look for masked actors and you will find them, or not. Look for street theatre or opera and you might find both. Look for improvisation or scripted text and you will find both. These apparently conflicting complexities are explored by Chaya Gordon-Bland, Assistant Professor of Theatre at the University of South Dakota, in her paper "Standing on the shoulders of Arlecchino: how variant philosophies regarding the ontology of Commedia dell'Arte support (or undermine) current pedagogical practices and trends". Gordon-Bland poses the following inquiry as to the nature, context, histories, and significance of Commedia dell'Arte:

As a movement teacher in a BFA Acting program, I am conducting this inquiry from a pedagogical point of view, rather than as an "expert" in Commedia dell'Arte. As I strive toward incorporating Commedia dell'Arte into my University's classes, curriculum and production program, I find myself compelled to reflect upon my own values, perspective and belief systems surrounding this magnetic theatrical form. This reflective process seems relevant and vital for any teacher wishing to achieve "best practices" as we attempt to bring Commedia dell'Arte into our students' creative and imaginative lives. As we undertake this evaluation, the first question we are led to ask is why do we teach Commedia dell'Arte? What are the teaching and learning outcomes to be achieved by bringing this 16th century theatrical form into our classrooms and programs? Some of these outcomes might include: physical and vocal freedom; expansiveness and expressiveness; stimulation of the imagination; fostering a playful, inventive spirit; a sense of discovery; the ability to achieve size (physically, psychologically, emotionally) that is grounded in truth; collaboration, connection and complicity with an audience; ensemble playing; giving and receiving; listening and responding; developing trust and confidence in one's self and others; availability, readiness and presence, to name a few. Your answers to these inquiries will necessarily differ depending on the context of your teaching; but they will also differ according to your philosophy regarding the ontology of Commedia dell'Arte. Clear articulation of our desired teaching outcomes requires us to take a step back; we must know what Commedia is to us before we can know why we teach it. It is necessary but not sufficient to know about the stock characters, masks, original staging conditions, history of the troupes, scenarios, lazzi, etc. To truly understand why we teach Commedia dell'Arte, we must know what Commedia dell'Arte is to us in contemporary terms: Is Commedia dell'Arte a concrete, discrete, and complete historical form that experts must teach students how to re-create? And/or is Commedia an art form with roots in 16th century Italy (and earlier) that continues to breathe, develop and evolve in which students can participate as active creative agents? Is it an art form of the past that has been interrupted and is now being resurrected? In our investigations of Commedia dell'Arte are we interested in resurrection, renovation, reconstruction, rediscovery, or reinvention? Our answers to these questions, our beliefs about Commedia dell'Arte's ontology, will necessarily shape why and how we teach it.

(Gordon-Bland 2014)

This book exists to help Professor Gordon-Bland and many others answer these questions. Is Commedia dell'Arte Improvised Theatre, Masked Theatre, Renaissance Total Theatre, a reluctant anachronism dragged for all the wrong, or maybe right, reasons into the present? Is it Political Theatre or Apolitical Theatre, or all of these in various percentages? Here we have a synthesis of the best and up-to-date researches that may define and be an answer to some specific questions. There may be new research, in the fullness of time that renders this research irrelevant. There are also some articles that may open up new avenues of thought and investigation.

Commedia dell'Arte has been classified by UNESCO as an "Invisible and Intangible Cultural Asset", which indicates someone else other than a motley band of performers, academics and theatrical historians is rooting for it. The current that will help this volume flow is two-fold: what we can learn about how this genre operated as live theatre in the past, and, second, how this information can be used by performers, directors, writers and theatre practitioners today.

Judith Chaffee and Olly Crick, April 2014

Part I

THE DEFINING FEATURES
Actors, scenarios, troupes, stock
characters, masks, language and lazzi

ACTORS

1

THE PRE-EMINENCE OF THE ACTOR IN RENAISSANCE CONTEXT

Subverting the social order

Scott McGehee

The sixteenth century represents the summit in the history of laughter...

(Mikhail Bakhtin 1984)

It is commonplace to refer to the Commedia dell'Arte as actor's theatre when considering the centrality of the actor ensemble in creating performance through various modes of improvisation. Dario Fo goes so far as to assert that the Commedia can be distinguished from all other forms of theatre not by the use of the masks or the fixed stereotypes but "by a genuinely revolutionary approach of making theatre, and the unique role assumed by the actors" (Fo 1991: 13). But, if we are to appreciate fully the "revolutionary" quality of the Commedia and its lessons for contemporary theatre, it is important for it to be understood historically as a part of the wider cultural complex of the Renaissance from which it was both an offspring and a cultural force in itself.

Modern attitudes toward the Commedia tend to cluster around two opposing poles. One might be called the pole of naïve exuberance, imagining the masked comedy as the apogee of world theatre; the other pole tends to simply ignore the Commedia with an attitude of benign neglect. In the first instance we get enthusiastic but naïve theatre, in the second we get only a snobbish disregard for a truly extraordinary moment in theatrical history. But the exuberant and the neglectful suffer from the same historical myopia that prevents each from understanding both the depths of the art as well as the extraordinary potential for contemporary theatre that lies buried in its comic form.

It is not by chance that twentieth century theatrical innovators turned to the Commedia as an endless source of inspiration. Gordon Craig, Vsevolod Meyerhold, Yevgeny Vakhtangov, Nikaloi Erdman, Max Reinhardt, Bertolt Brecht and many others saw in the Commedia the protagonist of a renewed theatre, the actor "filled with unconstrained joy, youth, laughter, improvisation, immediacy and closeness with human emotions side by side with irony and humor." (Vakhtangov in Fisher 1992: 139) For all of them, unleashing the creative powers of the actor was the essence of a new theatre. As Max Reinhardt wrote, "Where the actor is also a dramatic writer, he has the power to create a world according to his own image, thus awakening the drama to its highest form of life…" (Fisher 1992: 166) He envisioned a theatre in which the actor would be "at once sculptor and sculpture" (1992: 172). It is at this precise point that we will find the strongest link between the Commedia dell'Arte and the social imaginary of the Renaissance: man as the self-creator, sculptor and sculpture. If we fail to grasp this link, the Commedia will have little of significance to say to us today.

In the post war period a new interest in the Commedia was centered in Milan around the work of Giorgio Strehler, Paolo Grassi, Jacques Lecoq, Ameleto Sartori, Dario Fo and others. They engaged in intense historical research and experimentation in an effort to reinvent the skills of the trade for modern audiences. Their influence spawned a new generation of artists with a deep interest in the Commedia, notably, Théâtre du Soleil, the Bread and Puppet Theatre, the San Francisco Mime Troup, the TAG, etc. Many, if not most, of these artists and groups were also politically engaged activists who imagined theatre generally and Commedia specifically as a potential force in political struggles. Their interest was in utilizing the Commedia to provoke a comic critique of existing power relationships: against war, against racism, fascism, sexism and capitalism itself. The form of Commedia was valuable in that it was structured by social formations of real power relationships between masters and servants. However, attempts to utilize an antique art form in a modern context are fraught with anachronistic dangers and in less capable hands could quickly become naïve and even cartoonish, unwittingly distorting the animating spirit of the sixteenth century.

Mikhail Bakhtin, in his ground-breaking study of Rabelais writes:

> In the Renaissance, laughter in its most radical, universal and at the same time gay form emerged from the depths of folk culture. It emerged but once in the course of history over a period of sixty or seventy years… and entered with its popular language the sphere of great literature and high ideology…. The wall between official culture and non-official culture inevitably crumbled…. This thousand year old laughter not only fertilized literature but was itself fertilized by humanist knowledge and advance literary techniques.
>
> (Bakhtin 1984: 72)

Bakhtin places the Commedia squarely within this historic conjuncture (Bakhtin 1984: 34). To grasp what is most vibrant in the Commedia it is essential to explore what is meant by laughter that is radical, universal and gay or, in Bakhtin's expression, *carnivalesque*. But equally important is to explore the humanist ideology that formed an essential component of Renaissance laughter.

What follows will be an effort to delineate three points of intersection in which the Commedia is embedded with Renaissance culture. The first point will explore the humanist ideal of the self-creating man: an ideal explicitly opposed to the medieval vision of eternal and fixed character-types bound within a cosmic order of ascending

10

values. The second point will explore the structure of contemporary power relations within Renaissance culture from which the Commedia drew its inspiration. It staged a microcosm of conflicting social forces into which the audience was invited to play a conspiratorial role. And finally, the aesthetic technique of "grotesque realism" as a means of "uncrowning" all that is high, abstract and sacred will be recast as a mode of comic subversion. All three of these points of intersection find their embodiment in the free imagination of the actor.

The maker and molder of thyself: sculptor and sculpture

In *The Moving Body* Jacques Lecoq rejects the idea that the Commedia is an expression of a specific place and time believing that a better nomenclature would be *la comédie humaine,* or the human comedy, suggesting that "historically, the social relations of the Commedia are immutable" (Lecoq 2002: 124). Its function is "to shed light on human nature…" and the "timeless elements of the human comedy…" (Ibid.) But Lecoq's idea runs diametrically opposed to the ethos that was emerging in the Renaissance, an ethos that was certainly part of the intellectual culture that profoundly influenced the emergence of the Commedia. Many modern interpreters of the Commedia miss this point and, like Lecoq, revert to the idea of universal *tipi fissi* (fixed types) as if the springs of human action are to be found beyond the individual's control in the primordial character of man. Still others make reference to Carl Jung's concept of human "archetype" and the theory of the collective unconscious where the ancient image, character or pattern of circumstances is considered universal, originating in pre-logical thought, outside of time, space and culture. This distinctly modern and conservative version of Commedia is the inversion of the Renaissance idea of man as a self-creator. Alternatively, the ancient idea of the Platonic archetype, derived from Plato's ideal forms, an idea prevalent during the Renaissance, would also be misplaced as Platonism explicitly excludes man as being modeled from an archetype (Plato 2013: 320d–322a). But, in either case, it implies that the social structure is the product of man's fixed character and that hierarchies of power are natural hierarchies. Thus, only a fool would challenge such hierarchies.

While Bakhtin's study of Rabelais reveals the influence of folk culture on high literature in the Renaissance, another recent study by Robert Henke demonstrates the profound influence that contemporary literature had on the popular theatre where "actors are the full bearers of humanist culture…" (Henke 2002: 109). Among the principle characteristics of Renaissance thought, at its most radical, was the humanist concept of self-creation. That is to say that man was not a *tipo fisso,* nor governed by necessity, as was the case in medieval thought and virtually all official culture. Original sin, manifesting itself in the seven deadly sins, corresponding to character-types within a timeless cosmos of a fixed order was precisely what was being rejected in the Renaissance. For the new humanists, man was mutable, embedded in real time and real space moving forever forward, ever changing. As Ginnazzo Manetti wrote in 1452, "All that surrounds us is our own work, the work of men… seeing such marvels we understand that we can create even better, more beautiful, more refined, more perfect things than hitherto…" (Manetti 1452).

Moreover, man himself was the result of this creative process. In *The Oration on the Dignity of Man*, often referred to as the manifesto of the Renaissance, Giovanni Pico writes, at the moment that God created Adam,

> there was not among his archetypes that from which he could fashion a new offspring....He therefore took man as creature of indeterminate image... saying to his creation, ...constrained by no limits, in accordance with thine free will, in whose hand we have placed thee, shall ordain for thyself the limits of thy nature... so that with freedom of choice and with honor, as though the maker and molder of thyself, thou mayest fashion thyself in whatever shape thou shalt prefer.
>
> (Pico 1981: 478)

Man as self-maker, as the architect of his own being, had its counterpart in popular culture in what Bakhtin refers to as the people's "second world and second life outside officialdom" in which determinant necessity, expressed in the fixed order of official life, is "uncrowned" by the carnival spirit to free "human consciousness, thought and imagination for new potentialities." (Bakhtin 1984: 6, 49) This ideology of mutability and self-creation had its material expression in the very social structure of the Renaissance through the expansion of commercial life and the emergence of a mercantile spirit. Merchants, craftsmen, traders, innovators of every sort needed to loosen the ridged structures of the social order and laughter was but one of their methods. It should not be surprising to note in this context that Machiavelli, the founder of political science, also wrote one of the most important comedies in the Italian Renaissance, *La mandragola*, nor that Galileo, the founder of the new physics, was also known to write scenarios for the Commedia dell'Arte.

It is also logical that among the eight members of the first Commedia group registered in Padua in 1545 there were four members from the artisan class: two shoemakers, one blacksmith and one stonecutter (Henke 2002: 70). Artisans, like merchants, wanted above all, control of their craft. Seeking guild status was an effort to guarantee the integrity and autonomy of their creative production and to find a relative freedom from patronage in the marketplace. Bakhtin describes the Renaissance marketplace as a "world unto itself" with an atmosphere of "freedom, frankness and familiarity.... The marketplace was the center of all that is unofficial; it enjoyed a certain extraterritoriality." (Bakhtin 1984: 153–154) Henke importantly points out that one of the dynamic elements of the Commedia was the creative tension between the centrifugal tendencies of the virtuosic actor originating in the *buffone* and zanni piazza performers and the "well-made plots" based on literary models (Henke 2002: 2). Within this tension—the fusion of high and low, popular and elite–the actor did indeed find the power to create a world according to his own image.

All attempts to depict the Commedia as a comic form that is eternal and immutable, a form that captures the essential archetypes of humanity, and a form that reveals man's eternal essence, runs counter to the spirit of the age. In Renaissance laughter, the fixed and essential nature of the world crumbles to become ambiguous, ever mutating, ever changing, and ever inverting to reveal a world of endless possibilities. This was the spirit of the age and the Commedia was its comic expression.

Subverting the symbolic order: masters, lovers and servants

A great deal has been written about the forms of social power during the Renaissance, a fact notably marked by the publication of Machiavelli's *Prince* in 1513. The subject of this extraordinary text was power itself. It should not be surprising that this should be the focus of many erudite studies at this time as old powers were dissolving and new ones emerging. There was, in a word, a self-conscious reflection of the meaning and modes of power throughout this period. It is worth pointing out that the history of the Commedia dell'Arte roughly bridges the period between the Council of Trent, marking the onset of the Counter Reformation, through the rise of great-centralized nation states and the outbreak of the French Revolution. Understanding the Commedia is inconceivable without considering the contemporary political and social upheavals of the time and in what manner contemporary social power appeared staged before a popular audience.

The very essence of the Commedia (if we can indeed find an essence) is captured by its unique mode of representing contemporary forms of social power. It was, in its origin, a synecdoche that attempted to reveal the flow of power in iconic form. That is to say that each of the characters individually represented a particular social formation and the characters in ensemble represented the whole of society as revealed in the relative distribution of power among each player. Who has power and who does not? How is power deployed and how is it resisted? The Commedia created a kind of tableaux of contemporary life in which various semiotic orders of power operated. Indeed, we can suggest that the masks themselves help to reinforce the appearance of social types. As Carlo Boso correctly points out "each character is the representative of a social class which, by the act of theatre, becomes the magical incarnation of all its class" (Rudlin 2008: 67).

Pantalone is not a merchant because he has a greedy character; rather he is greedy because he is a merchant. In the latter concept, the emphasis is not on the character as a human archetype but rather on the structure of social power relations, which the stock characters incarnate on stage. More specifically as Erhard Stiefel (mask maker for Théâtre du Soleil) put it:

> The mask's revelatory power is not in giving the audience (and the actor) the possibility of constructing a preconceived stereotypical identification, but on the contrary, in giving them the means to see a particular class through the character, with which they can identify.... Thus, society can be unmasked with a mask, which becomes revelatory and makes life's truth, which we have never known how to see, spring forth.... The beauty and precision of its gestures generate a radiance, which reveals and distinguishes the inner workings of society, which denounces them, but at the same time invokes hope of a different life.
>
> (Stiefel 1975)

The early Commedia plots were in themselves quite simple in their basic form, though sometimes maddeningly complex in their execution. But it was not the plots that revealed the structure of social power in the Commedia: there were seldom wars, revolts, ecclesiastical conflicts, or even a depiction of the lives of the great and powerful; rather it was the enigmatic embodiment of power within each small character in their habitual behavior.

Michele Foucault (1991) locates a critical transition in the deployment of power in his studies of early modern Europe drawing our attention to the "micro-physics" of power or how the technics of power are actually imposed on the human body. The first phase he designates as a system of "sovereign power" where power is embodied in the actual person to whom it is identified. An epochal transition occurs when power itself goes into hiding, to become disembodied or anonymous while taking up residence in rules, regulations, organizational techniques, surveillance, etc. For Foucault, this new mode of "disciplinary power" is the principle characteristic of modernity (Foucault 1991). The Commedia however was born into a world of sovereign power where the social hierarchy was always on display and was always deployed between bodies and within bodies. Furthermore, power was performative; it had to be re-enacted continually through the infinite gestures of daily life. But, these gestures were specific to the power structure, not to the whims of the individual or his ancient archetype. Just as costumes were socially coded in a way to make visible the social structure, so, too, were the mores and manners of every individual. It is here that power or its absence deploys itself through the socially coded body. It can be suggested that all of the principle characters of the Commedia, be they masters, lovers or servants, enacted their dramas within the structure of conflicting symbolic orders.

Grotesque realism: Pantalone's two bodies

Sovereign power always operates on two levels, one visibly and the other invisibly. Visibly, it is the power that compels others to act submissively toward the sovereign, whereas invisible power enables the sovereign to act powerfully. The crown and scepter visibly give a king his social aura, but it is the invisible self-knowledge that divine blood runs in his veins that enables him to act royally. The visible and the invisible are formed by systems of images and signs that structure internal and external meaning. Moreover, such systems structure perception itself. Pantalone, for instance, can only see the world mediated by money; everything has its price, whereas Dottore subsumes the world into forms of esoteric knowledge, as Capitano understands the world as a perpetual contest of strength. Such systems constitute competing symbolic orders that give shape to the socially coded body. In the Commedia what is visible almost never coincides with the invisible. Externally and visibly Capitano is full of strength and power, but internally and invisibly, he is cowardly. The focal point of this non-correspondence is the body itself.

Bakhtin characterizes this play between the socially coded body and the natural or "universal" body as a carnivalesque vision of the world that is artistically expressed as "grotesque realism." For Bakhtin, grotesque realism, of which Commedia is a prime example, is characterized by an inversion of stable hierarchies, the dissolution of conceptual boundaries, the degradation or materialization of all that is high, spiritual, ideal and abstract; distinguished overall by "a celebration of the relativity of the symbolic order" (Brandist 1988: 139). It is in the act of revealing the mutability of the symbolic order that we will find the comic genius of the Renaissance actor best displayed.

In his book *On Humour* Simon Critchley suggests that the comic function of the socially coded body's relationship to the natural body is through exploiting "the gap between being a body and having a body, between... the *physical* and *metaphysical* aspects of being human. What makes us laugh... is the return of the *physical* into the *metaphysical*" (Critchley 2008: 43). The Commedia constructs each character by delineating the difference between the socially coded body—Critchley's metaphysical body that one has—to the natural body that one is, in order to "uncrown" any and all symbolic order that imposes submission on what is natural, universal and joyous in man.

We can think of Don Quixote as a perfect example of a physical uncrowning of the metaphysical, in this case with the comic subversion of medieval chivalry. Quixote sees what is not there, as he perceives the world filtered by the symbolic order of chivalry. He imagines himself as a knight, constructed from the fantastic account in his dusty library. He can see only through the knight's eyes. Windmills become giants, sheep become armies, tavern wenches become ladies and nags become chargers. The courageous body of the errant knight confronts the giant and the old man is tossed to the ground by the windmill.

We see a similar uncrowning of the symbolic orders within each of the characters of the Commedia, the uncrowning of romanticism in the absurd pretenses of the lovers who can express carnal desire only in the sublimated form of poetic declarations; the uncrowning of esoteric knowledge by the endless malapropisms and the gluttonous body of the Dottore; the uncrowning of the military aura in the cowardice of Capitano; and the uncrowning of money's power in the impotent body of Pantalone. Sovereign power is always in conflict with itself.

These characters and dozens of variations within the Commedia were the inventions of the actors who understood quite well the reluctance of the body to conform to the socially constructed codes of appearance and corresponding modes of perception. By exaggerating these codes with the use of the mask—understood as the whole character—we quickly see how social relations are unmasked on the stage. Such inventions were certainly the result of the profound sensibility of the actors to the forms of contemporary power, not to mention the virtuosity required in fusing the metaphysical with the physical body. By exposing the social construction of the symbolic orders the audience may recognize the potential freedom to construct others.

Power must have its object: Zanni, Harlequin and Pulcinella

The servants in the Commedia have a different relationship to the various forms of power. Though they are not entirely free of the symbolic order; Zanni is still the Bergamasque peasant, as Pulcinella still expresses all the gestures of Neapolitan life, but as servants they have no investment in maintaining the world of the master. They are not iconic in the same way that the orders of power are iconic. In fact, their unique and crucial role in the comedy is to subvert the various symbolic orders by creating havoc. We must remember that without the servant, the master's world crumbles. A master is only a master if he commands servants. But the deeper truth is that the master is always dependent upon the servant to interpret his orders. This is the true secret of the servant's power. The servant is closer to the universal natural body than to the metaphysical body of the master, as Sancho Panza is in contrast to Don Quixote. The apparent stupidity of the servant is actually the comic refusal– whether intended or not—of the natural body to accept the logic of power itself. The servants are predictably unpredictable as they act typically outside of the accepted codes of behavior imposed by the master, always asserting what is charmingly human in all of us. Dario Fo once stated that he had been playing Harlequin all his life, adding, "Harlequin is a character who destroys all conventions.... He came out of nothing and can transform himself into anything" (Swain 1993: 14). In this sense the servant in the Commedia represents the free creative spirit of the actor to invent the world according to his own image.

If we are to grasp the "revolutionary" quality of the Commedia dell'Arte and breathe its spirit into modern theatre it will not be through dragging masked characters that were born into a world of sovereign powers—characters who in truth have little real resonance today—into a modern world governed by disembodied, impersonal and anonymous powers. Today's social codes do not function in the same way as they did three centuries ago. What is the power of Pantalone when set against the global rule of finance capital that governs through logarithmic functions and is able to bankrupt entire nations overnight? What is the power of Dottore's knowledge when set against technological proliferation, media bombardment or electronic social networks? And what is the power of Capitano against computer driven drones that rain terror from the sky and can enforce submission of whole populations? Today, the old masters are themselves the servants of a vast mechanic process, each desperately seeking to be a reliable cog in an inanimate wheel. But, regardless of what form power takes, in the end it is still the "servant" who must interpret its commands. As long as power imposes itself, there will always be the mischievous Harlequin who will show us that "laughter liberates not only from external censorship but first of all from the great interior censor..." (Bakhtin 1984: 94). The "revolutionary" spirit of the Commedia will show itself in the freeing of the imaginative force of the actor to reinvent the body as it confronts these modern powers. The actor/author "filled with unconstrained joy, youth, laughter, improvisation, immediacy and closeness with human emotions side by side with irony and humor," (Vakhtangov in Fisher 1992: 139) will uncrown these modern forces and remind us that we can once again become the sculptor and sculpture of our own lives.

References

Bakhtin, Mikhail (1984) *Rabelais and His World*. Bloomington, US: Indiana University Press.
Brandist, Craig (1988) *The Bakhtin Circle: Philosophy, Culture and Politics*. London: Pluto Press.
Critchley, Simon (2008) *On Humour*. London: Routledge.
Fisher, James (1992) *The Theatre of Yesterday and Tomorrow. Commedia dell'Arte on the Modern Stage*. Lewiston, US: Edwin Mellon Press.
Fo, Dario (1991) *The Tricks of the Trade*. New York: Routledge.

Foucault, Michele (1991) *Discipline and Punish*. London: Penguin.

Henke, Robert (2002) *Performance and Literature in the Commedia dell'Arte*. Cambridge, UK: Cambridge University Press.

Lecoq, Jacques (2002) *The Moving Body, Teaching Creative Theatre*. London: Methuen.

Manetti, Giannozzo (1452) *De dignitate et excellentia hominis, On the Dignity of Man*. http://it.wikiquote.org/wiki/Giannozzo_Manetti (accessed 19 August 2014).

Plato (2013) *Protagoras*. Translation B. Jowett. Project Gutenberg: www.gutenberg.org (accessed 19 August 2014).

Pico, Giovanni (1485) "The Dignity of Man" (1981) *The Portable Renaissance Reader*. New York: Penguin.

Rudlin, John (2008) *Commedia dell'Arte: An Actor's Handbook*. London, New York: Routledge.

Stiefel, E. (1975) *L'Age d'Or* (teste-Programme). Paris: Stock.

Swain, John (1993) "Creative Contrarieties, the Commedia Heritage" *Theatre Symposium, a Journal of the Southern Theatre Conference. Commedia dell'Arte Performance Context and Contents. Vol. 1* Ed. Philip Hill, C. Castagno, C Frankel and P. Schmitt. Tuscaloosa, US: University of Alabama Press.

SCENARIOS

2

FORM AND FREEDOM
Between scenario and stage
Robert Henke

The some eight hundred Commedia dell'Arte scenarios that survive attest to an art of improvisation that cannily negotiated flexibility and structure. Notwithstanding the professional actors' frequent performance of scripted as well as improvised plays, these curious and controversial texts quintessentially reflect the collaborative nature of an actors' theater, and the paradoxical fact that the performed scenario was both repeated and unique. The scenario provided the perfect textual machine for a theater that had to be constantly on the move, improvising on the entrepreneurial level just as it did in the performative domain. And, although the Italian actors equaled or excelled their English counterparts in internecine hostility, the short form of the scenario lent itself to collaborative dissemination more than did the zealously guarded English playscript. Mostly manuscript collections from the seventeenth and eighteenth centuries, produced by *dilettanti* as well as professionals, the scenarios can tell us important things about how improvisation actually worked, even as they only tell part of the improvisation story and, in most cases, bear marks of literary embellishment. Even in this last respect, however, they are not divorced from the performative world of the Commedia dell'Arte troupes, who freely pillaged conceits, tropes, and themes from Petrarch, Ariosto, Boccaccio, and other authors, simply bringing to the stage the humanist habit of modular, "rhapsodic" composition. The *comici* were, in that respect, humanists in action.

Form and freedom blended at three different levels in Commedia dell'Arte improvisation: an overall plot synchronizing all of the actors; a substructural level telling actors what scenes, character interactions and "speech-acts" were to be performed; and the local, particular level in which those scenes were fleshed out with verbal, gestural, and kinetic enactment. (In the case of Homeric improvisation, this triadic structure would correspond to the general guest reception motif; its substructural division into entrance, seating, and washing; and the verbal realization of dactylic hexameter accompanied by the performing rhapsode's expressions and gestures.) Although the ratio of freedom to form probably increased at the level of Hamlet's "word and action" (the third domain of the triadic structure), even there the individual actor's use of humanist-style training, memory techniques, and rhetorical topoi to "find" pre-studied and pre-used material probably lent Commedia dell'Arte improvisation more structure than is characterized by Second City and other twenty-first century improv. (Crohn Schmitt 2010). The extant scenarios furnish salient details about the general structural and substructural levels, and not much about the third level, although they would have clearly indicated to the actors "insertion points" where they could deploy the speeches, gags, and feats that they had built up over their entire careers and were only too eager to display.

Overall structure

The different scenario collections—Scala, Locatelli, Corsini, Casamarciano, Vatican, Adriano, Correr, and others—vary in the complexity of their plots, but they often derive from the scripted *Commedia Erudita*, with which the highly literate actor-composers of the Arte would have been quite familiar. "Italian comedy" should be understood as a single system comprising both scripts and scenarios, with transformations from one to another working in both directions. Scala made one of his scenarios, "Il finto marito," into a full-length play, and the Correr manuscript has a scenario version of Ariosto's *Suppositi*—the play that George Gascoigne would translate and that Shakespeare would use for his subplot of *The Taming of the Shrew*. The more complex plots of the Scala scenarios, alone in prefacing the scenario proper with a detailed "*argomento*" or background plot, often contain the kind of circum-Mediterranean romance background familiar to readers of Shakespeare: sea voyages of captivity and liberation, wide expanses of space and time, unlucky dislocations and fortuitous reunions and recognitions. The Correr scenarios, apparently the product of seventeenth-century Venetian professional actors, render actions even more schematically than Scala does, perhaps as befitting professional actors, who would have known how to fill in the gaps. The Correr "*Zanni finto morto*" suspends practically the entire cast in a state of wonder and fear at spirits passing before them, only summarily to resolve matters with a simple "*Negromante scopre ogni cosa, e fanno finir la comedia*" (The magician reveals everything, and the play ends. [Alberti 1996: 259] translation Henke). But such range is to be expected in the scenario form, hovering between orality and writing and beyond the reach of normative literary canons.

As part of the greater Italian humanist experiment of reviving classical comedy, Commedia dell'Arte scenario plots animate the generational conflict of New Comedy between father and child, mediated by the slave/servant. But much as with the Commedia Erudita the New Comedy framework is significantly fleshed out by two pairs of lovers embodying a full range of passionate actions and speeches unknown to Plautus or Terence but very familiar to Ariosto, Della Porta, or the collaborative authors of *Gl'ingannati*, the prototype for Shakespeare's *Twelfth Night*. And not unlike the lovers of Shakespeare's comedies, the passions of Arte *innamorati/e* carry them into compelling and various situations well beyond the predictable rhetoric of the figures as they are often performed today. Arte lovers female and male could handle a sword, perform a mad scene, impersonate other characters, don both same-gender and transvestite disguises, cleverly outplot their antagonists, and practice pranks. Generally, in the Commedia dell'Arte dramatic plotting tends to become more complicated, or at least more agonistic, than the hierarchically nestled structures of oral-formulaic epic (e.g., the story of Odysseus' boar hunt and wound enfolded within the foot-washing scene): where there is one zanni plotting to help his *innamorato* master gain his erotic object, there is probably another zanni, or the innamorato's father himself, trying to thwart him.

As with the complex *intreccii* of the scripted comedy, the scenario plots proffered the pleasure of what is difficult: continually testing, or playing, the ratio of complexity to intelligibility. But the general plot, at least in the case of Scala and most of the manuscript collections, could also function to harness in the centrifugal energies of the improvising *parti ridicole*, especially the Capitano, the zanni, and his brother-in-words, the anarchically associative Dottore. Pier Maria Cecchini, who wrote the first major acting treatise on the Arte, worries as much about the plot-distracting dilations of the *parti ridicole* (Marotti and Romei 1991: 85) as Hamlet does about the improvisations of the clown, who carries on off-book. But the scenario, balancing form and freedom, could also be seen as the secret ally of the virtuosic improviser, offering just enough structure and linear propulsion to make room for the ludic dilations of the zanni, the Capitano, and the Dottore.

Alone in Scala's collection, preceding the act-by-act notations, is included an *argomento*, whose function it is to provide the important background plot to the play (occasionally with some overlap with the actions of the play itself). Considerably varying in complexity, the *argomento* quite literally put the actors on the same page, and frequently in the course of the scenario is evoked as an *aide-memoire* (Scala 1976: Day 11, Act II. 124, Marotti Edition). In a dramaturgy constrained by the unities of time, place, and action, the *argomento* could also offer the reading public— explicitly considered an "audience" of the printed scenarios by Scala—the pleasure of greatly expanding the play in space and time, much like Prospero's initial narrative to Miranda in the unity-structured *Tempest*. A list of characters followed the *argomento*, grouped by household. As Richard Andrews has pointed out, this would have been crucial for actors who, in successive performances, might have been in love with Isabella one night and Flaminia the next, or might have had a different parent one evening to another (Andrews 2008: xvii). As Andrea Perrucci makes clear in his 1699 treatise on improvisational acting, it was crucially important for actors to know to which of the two or three houses designated on the stage set they would have belonged—and of course the houses would have corresponded to their family attribution (Richards and Richards 1990: 206).

One important function of the overall structure as revealed in the scenario would have been to limit the number of actors on stage at any given time. This constraint would have enabled the actors' improvisatory freedom for, as Tim Fitzpatrick has observed, improvisation works far better with two speaking characters (Fitzpatrick 1995: 106). But the scenarios also guide improvisation between more than two characters by various means. First, additional characters tend to align themselves with one of the others, as with a servant taking the side of his master. Second, characters might enter serially and perform the same action, as in Scala's "Il cavadente" (Day 12), when one after another figure enters, as part of a prearranged scheme, to tell Pantalone that he has foul breath (Scala 1976: Day 12, Act I. 132–33). Third, one character might perform the same action on several characters, as in

Scala's "Li duo Capitani simili," when the crazed Isabella beats one character after another (Scala 1976: Day 17, Act II. 124). As Anna Maria Testaverde notes, simple stage directions in the scenarios control presence and absence, entrance and departure: "*si ritira/ritirano*," "*parte/partono*," "*via*," "*resta/restono*," or "*in questo*" (Testaverde 2007: xx–xxi). Whatever the degree to which the *capocomico* guided performance, as Perrucci's treatise suggests at the end of the seventeenth century, the Duke of Saxe-Meiningen is still far in the distance, and the scenario did some of the work of the director.

Substructure: scenes, actions, routines, and speech-acts

The scenario provided ample information about the substructural level of plotting: determining what kinds of actions, scenes, speech-acts, and routines the actors would perform. These monological or interactional units, as Richard Andrews has shown in his analysis of the "elastic gag," could expand and contract as the actors saw fit, especially in response to the audience's perceived interest and pleasure (Andrews 1993: 175–82). Even a simple action, no more than a line in a scenario, could provide richly expandable possibilities. To take an example analyzed by Andrews (actually deriving from a piazza/banquet pamphlet), Pantalone's call to Zanni to appear before him could be richly delayed and expanded in ways for the which the scenario importantly provides a location point, without furnishing any of the verbal texture (Andrews 1993: 176–80). (The zanni asks his master if he is really talking to him; if he wishes him to come with his hat; if he means for him to come at just that instant; etc.) And as well as the "insertion point," the scenario would also indicate to the improving actors clear beginning and end points: the improvisatory unit begins when Pantalone calls for his servant, and ends when the servant finally appears before him.

The vast majority of scenario indications, to be sure, refer to the very plot that functioned, in part, to differentiate the professional comedy from the virtuosic but anarchic improvisations of piazza charlatans. About nine-tenths of the following instruction in Scala's "Il cavadente" refers to plot: "Capitano enters, and rants at Arlecchino, who takes him aside and tells him that his mistress has made arrangements with Pedrolino about what he must do to get into her house. The Capitano turns to Pedrolino, and Arlecchino runs away. Pedrolino, knowing nothing about it, suggests off the cuff that he should go and dress in Venetian costume like Pantalone, and he will then take him in. The Capitano is delighted, and goes off to disguise himself" (Andrews 2008: 65). Still, although only the Capitano's "ranting" at Arlecchino provides a clear insertion point for a detachable, pre-performed set piece, this routine may well have taken over a greater proportion of the entire scene than the few words that Scala devotes to it.

Especially if read with an eye to the rich corpus of printed and manuscript poems, dialogues, *contrasti*, *orazioni*, etc. sometimes performed by Arte actors themselves and culturally adjacent to regular company performance, the scenarios can be seen to accommodate many verbal set pieces that constituted the individual actor's repertoire. A fine case of the Bakhtinian "speech genre," the detachable Arte speech-scene viscerally rendered speech as action, in the form of insults, threats, curses, "caresses," praises, denunciations, challenges, mockery, "desperations," complaints, laments, reproaches, amorous declarations, blusterings, supplications, and much more (Bakhtin 1986: 60–102). A quick scan of the above list suggests the deeply binary nature of character interaction in Commedia dell'Arte action, in which allies and enemies were usually clearly distinguished: in one moment, the besotted Pantalone fulsomely praises the virtues of Isabella, and in the next minute acidly fulminates against his dissolute (and perhaps rival) son. (As a spin on this binarism used effectively in contemporary Commedia performance, Pantalone and the Dottore abjectly and excessively praise each other to their faces, then snarl away to the audience to say what they really think about their fellow *vecchio*.) Scanning the scenario would have told each actor where he or she stood with most of the other major characters—whether friend or foe. In this regard, the agonistic tonality that Walter J. Ong has attributed to oral culture and the binary nature of humanist epideictic rhetoric nicely conjoin (Ong 1982: 43–46).

Some "insertable" forms indicated by the scenarios were even more detachable than the "speech genres" listed above, and could threaten to run away with the entire play. In Act I of Scala's "La fortuna di Flavio," the Dottore Gratiano, said to be "chief of all the mountebanks," performs an entire mountebank scene with Arlecchino and other assistants, probably as centrifugal as the oft-cut Scoto of Mantua mountebank scene in Jonson's *Volpone* (a scene explicitly associated by Jonson to the Commedia dell'Arte). (See Scala 1976: Day 2, Act I. 22.) The splendid "Il vecchio geloso," Day 6 in Scala's *Il teatro delle favole rappresentative*, includes the demi-monde of itinerant beggar-musicians, who perform a dance number for their supper. Also in "Il vecchio geloso," Burratino tells the very Boccaccian tale of jealousy and cuckoldry that has structured the scenario itself (Scala 1976: Day 6, Act III. 83). Novellas circulating in both written and oral form would have provided another important source for Commedia dell'Arte material, as appears to be the case in Scala's version of the Romeo and Juliet story, ("I tragici successi" or "The Tragic Events": Day 18 in Scala's collection [Andrews 2008: 111–12] arguably mediated through the Massuccio/Da Porto/Bandello conduit.) Many of the speech genres used in performance, such as the tirade, the lament, the curse, and the supplication, could have inserted material from the piazza-banquet arena fairly seamlessly, but there were also opportunities to perform piazza material more like a detachable set piece, as with the "Tale of Cuccagna" told by two rogues to the starving Burratino in "Le burle d'Isabella" in order to steal his dinner (Scala 1976: Day 4, Act I. 57). (Poems regarding the mythical land of Cuccagna, where one is paid for sleeping and imprisoned for working, and where food fairly drops from the sky, were extremely popular in sixteenth- and seventeenth-century Italy, and could sometimes have a subversive instead of an opiate effect.) And crowd-pleasing fighting scenes, either with or without weapons, are frequently indicated in the scenarios.

The improvisational system of the Commedia dell'Arte was based on the Brechtian notion of function rather than the realist idea of personation. The character system itself could drive the plot; it was based on a tripartite status hierarchy of vecchio (Pantalone and the Dottore), their children (innamorati/e); and the servants, ostensibly serving the vecchi but often subversively intervening on behalf of the younger generation. A play like "Il vecchio geloso" can be seen to reach down into what might be considered a fourth-status level: the underground beggars, rogues, card sharps, itinerant entertainers, thieves, and prostitutes associated with the zanni—obliquely lending the Commedia dell'Arte a social resonance realized today by Dario Fo but too often obscured by the baroque visual trappings through which it is usually viewed.

Verbal and physical enactment

Having scanned the scenario to determine what kinds of scenes or speech-acts he or she would perform in the course of the play, in order to realize its verbal texture the actor could have then drawn largely upon pre-studied and pre-performed material, calling on the full archive of his or her past performance repertoire. Like Renaissance rhetoricians, the actors organized their material according to codified topics, preparing "mental storehouses" for the different scenes that they would play. As the actor-writer Nicolò Barbieri writes, "the actors study and arm their memory with a great farrago of things, like proverbs, conceits, love speeches, reproaches, desperations, in order to have them ready for the occasion, and their study matches the behavior of the persons whom their represent" (Barbieri 1971: 23). The *zibaldoni* or actors' commonplace books, such as the extant example produced by Stefanelo Botarga and Zan Ganassa, were not just post-performance remembrances (such as the *Lettere* and *Fragmenti* of Isabella Andreini so clearly are), they also indicate pre-performance preparation (Ojeda Calvo 2007). As Natalie Crohn Schmitt has aptly demonstrated, the actors drew on techniques of rhetorical *inventio* in order to "find" topics organized in their mental storehouse, including memory techniques such as the use of grids, "places," images, and alphabetical organization (Crohn Schmitt 2010). Familiar topoi recur in the scenarios of Scala and others, such as the relative merits of the scholarly versus the military life (Scala 1976: Day 14, Act I. 151), the praise (or dispraise) of courtesans (Scala 1976: Day 9, Act II. 105), and the reproach of a daughter for not working hard enough (Scala 1976 Day 6, Act I. 78). If, as Brian Vickers has argued, by the early sixteenth century several million Europeans would have had a working knowledge of rhetoric, the educated Commedia dell'Arte actors (of which there were many) would have employed many of its techniques (including those of epideictic and disputational rhetoric) and, even more importantly, its "habits of mind" (Vickers 1988: 256).

At the linguistic and gestural level as well as the substructural level that we have just examined, the Arte character system could have, in effect, generated language: simply put, knowing one's place in the system would have often told one what to say. Characters occupying the same status level (vecchio-vecchio, innamorati/e, servant-servant) tended to share the same world view, lexicon, rhetorical formulae, topoi—and favorite gripes. Pantalone and the Dottore, fluent in the lexicons of finance, parenting, and bourgeois sagacity, would have much to say together about the laziness of servants, the pros and cons of marriage, the perils of courtesans, the need to keep a close eye on nubile daughters, and the dissolution of sons. Pedrolino and Arlecchino, endowed with a rich gastronomic lexicon, would see the world very differently. A historical taste for improvisational wit, elegant wordplay, and poetic conceits deftly deployed would have rendered the amorous exchanges of the lovers much more compelling to early modern audiences than they tend to be to the present-day public. When figuring centrally in a Commedia dell'Arte scenario, as they do in "Le burle d'Isabella," the nether world of tricksters, rogues, and beggars (what I am calling the lowest, fourth-status level), could have engaged more socially and occasionally politically provocative registers than one typically associates with the Commedia dell'Arte.

Cross-status exchanges were rife with drama and conflict, exemplifying the Bakhtinian utterance in which the speech-act is already "shot through" with the anticipated response from the (usually hostile) interlocuteur. Pantalone's smug defense of his largesse and generosity inevitably invited his abject servant's accusation of mortal stinginess. Lofty innamorati/e encomia to the transcendent power of love were parried by the coarser registers of their servants, much as in Shakespeare. The tripartite status level could generate six different kinds of interactive modules (vecchio-vecchio, innamorati-innamorati, servi-servi, vecchio-innamorato, vecchio-servo, and innamorato-servo), with, of course, additional permutations based on gender (an innamorato's cajoling of his servant Pedrolino in order to get him to do something would be different from his rhetorical strategy with Franceschina). Actors modulated decorum and vocal register across status levels, so that Pantalone cursed the Dottore in the high (if effectively ridiculous) style but his servant in *sermo humilis.* Many speech genres could be performed by all of the characters, some, such as the Capitano's *bravura,* were fairly specific to one *maschera.* Commedia dell'Arte improvisation simply brought to the stage the modular habit of thinking practiced in all early modern theater, whether in the "plots" divided among English playwrights working collaboratively, or with the modular units without which Lope de Vega could not possibly have written, at least according to his claim, a thousand plays.

In the early modern age of "secondary orality," when strong traces of residual orality engaged with emerging forms of print culture (especially in the sphere of popular culture), the verbal realization of scenes, topoi, and speech-acts by improvising actors pervasively enlisted techniques of oral composition. The actors relied upon *sound* as a powerful mnemonic aid, captivating their audiences with the "illocutionary power of the voice" (Zumthor 1990: 21). Especially the Dottore, particularly enamored with the materiality of language, and the incantatory lovers frequently used sound play in their "compositions": "*nume solo di nome, per cuit più non spero, ma spiro*" (Oh power [of love] only I name, for which I no longer hope, but breath; Perrucci 1961: 212). The technique of *copiousness* disseminated by Erasmus to increasing numbers of students aimed to create the "orality effect" in writing by means of repetition with extended variation. The technique was easily transferable to the stage, where key words could have provided useful mnemonic anchors. (No rhetorical technique more effectively demonstrates how reciprocal the relationship between orality and writing was in the early modern period.) The Capitano, with a genius for matching subject and predicate, was a particular champion of copiousness, but all characters employed this "compositional" technique. *Additive* or paratactic rather than hypotactic or subordinated construction, eased transitional flow within speeches, as in the Dottore's pseudo-logical elaborations, "stitching together" in the manner of a "rhapsode" the flotsam and jetsam of humanist culture, just as the innamorata stitched together verses of Petrarch and other poets in the bricolage manner of the *centone*. (With the Dottore, it is important to counteract the common view that he speaks pure nonsense: an analysis of the extant speeches of Lodovico de' Bianchi and other Dottori demonstrate the kind of negotiation of sense and nonsense that characterizes Rabelais, the Shakespearean clown, and even the Dottoresque "tirade" of Lucky in Beckett's *Waiting for Godot*.) The actors frequently used *epithets*—words or phrases applied to a given person or thing to describe a given quality, as in Pantalone's invocation of "the counsel of old men, the curiosity of the young, the adulation of ruffians, the gluttony of parasites" (*Capricci* 1601: A3r). Perhaps, and in a parodic manner, the mental storehouses of the improvising actors constituted something like the *encyclopedic* patrimony of the oral performer, whether medieval *giullare* or early modern charlatan.

In all of this, the actors *performed* literature—classical and contemporary, high and low, from the court and from the street, printed and manuscript—but always extracted, digested, and reprocessed in modular forms. Their cultural and literary range, their channeling of deep sources from popular culture, their practical application of rhetorical techniques involving *inventio* and *memoria*, and their skillful melding of form and freedom made them, in Polonius' words, the "best actors in the world" for the law of improvised "liberty."

Additional notes

1 Citations refer to the Marotti edition of Scala (1976), with the day, act number, and page number of Marotti's edition cited. Although Marotti's edition is in two volumes, the page numeration is consecutive, and so I have not noted the volume number. Readers may very well wish to consult Richard Andrews' superb edition and translation of thirty Scala scenarios (Andrews 2008).
2 The connection between Polonius' famous remarks on the itinerant troupe traveling to Elsinore, and the Commedia dell'Arte has been nicely made by Clubb (1989).

References

Alberti, Carmelo, ed. (1996) *Gli scenari Correr. La Commedia dell'Arte a Venezia*. Rome: Bulzoni.

Andrews, Richard (1993) *Scripts and Scenarios: The Performance of Comedy in Renaissance Italy*. Cambridge, UK: Cambridge University Press.

——(2008) *The Commedia dell'Arte of Flaminio Scala: A Translation and Analysis of 30 Scenarios*. Lanham, Maryland, US: Scarecrow Press.

Bakhtin, M. M. (1986) *Speech Genres and Other Late Essays*. Trans. Vern W. McGee. Austin, US: University of Texas Press.

Barbieri, Nicolò (1971) *La supplica discorso familiare a quelli che tratono di comici* (1634). Ed. Ferdinando Taviani. Milan, Italy: Il Polifilo.

Capricci et nuove fantasie alla Venetiana di Pantalone de' Bisognosi (1601). Vicenza, Italy.

Clubb, Louise George (1989) *Italian Drama in Shakespeare's Time*. New Haven, US: Yale University Press.

Crohn Schmitt, Natalie (2010) "Improvisation in the Commedia dell'Arte in its Golden Age: Why, What, How" *Renaissance Drama* n.s. 38: 225–49.

Fitzpatrick, Tim (1995) *The Relationship of Oral and Literate Performance Processes in the Commedia dell'Arte: Beyond the Improvisation/Memorization Divdide*. Lewiston, US: Edwin Mellon.

Marotti, Ferruccio and Giovanna Romei (1991) *La commedia dell'arte e la società barocca. La professione del teatro*. Rome: Bulzoni.

Ojeda Calvo, Maria del Valle (2007) *Stefanelo Botarga e Zan Ganassa. Scenari e zibaldoni di comici italiani nella Spagna del Cinquecento*. Rome: Bulzoni.

Ong, Walter J. (1982) *Orality and Literacy: The Technologizing of the Word*. London: Methuen.

Perrucci, Andrea (1961) *Dell'Arte rappresentativa premeditata ed all'improvviso* (1699). Ed. Anton Guilio Bragaglia. Florence, Italy: Sansoni.

Richards, Kenneth and Laura Richards (1990) *The Commedia dell'Arte: A Documentary History*. Oxford, UK: Blackwell.

Scala, Flaminio (1976) *Il teatro delle favole rappresentative* (1611). Ed. Ferruccio Marotti, 2 vols. Milan, Italy: Il Polifido.

Testaverde, Anna Maria, ed. (2007) *I canovacci della Commedia dell'Arte*. Turin, Italy: Einaudi.

Vickers, Brian (1988) *In Defense of Rhetoric*. Oxford, UK: Clarendon Press.

Zumthor, Paul (1990) *Oral Poetry: An Introduction*. Trans. Kathryn Murphy-Judy. Minneapolis, US: University of Minnesota Press.

3

PARALLEL PROCESSING

Two playwrights: Scala and Shakespeare

Tim Fitzpatrick

Comparisons are odious, particularly when William Shakespeare is one of the terms of comparison. Flaminio Scala is not Shakespeare's equal, though the reasons why I would posit the bard's pre-eminence are very different from those proffered by the academic industry that has dedicated itself to bardolatry: I have argued in considerable detail that, however excellent the poetry spoken by Shakespeare's characters is, his play-texts are also documents that spectacularly demonstrate the playwright's overarching concern for how his words work in performance (Fitzpatrick 2011). By bringing Shakespeare and Scala together I will suggest that teasing out some of the similarities between these two playwrights can be instructive in regard to similarities between the very different theatre industries of which they were a part; instructive of the role and function of the playwright in those industries; and instructive for an understanding of theatre traditions that, while they grew up as local practices marked by significant geographical and processual differences, were possibly processing in parallel – and might even have cross-pollinated.

Scala and Shakespeare were close contemporaries: Scala (1552–1624) was born a decade before Shakespeare (1564–1616), and died a decade after him. Both were active in the late 1500s and early 1600s: Scala's professional career began in 1577 and spanned 20 years; his volume of scenarios was published considerably later in 1611, and a single fully-dialogued play, *Il finto marito*, in 1619 – well after he had given up the profession of travelling player and retired to run his perfume shop on the Rialto in Venice. Shakespeare began his career in the mid-1580s, and in 1613 retired to Stratford to continue a career in real estate; the First Folio of his plays was only published in 1623, seven years after his death.

We know that Commedia dell'Arte companies visited England in the mid-sixteenth century, and clearly Ben Jonson saw performances if the Mountebank scene in his *Volpone* is anything to go by. But there is only vague documentation about Italian players in England during Shakespeare's lifetime.

There was at least superficial borrowing: Elizabethan playwrights stole many of their plots from the Italian players. In Shakespeare's case one need only think of the explicit references to the plot of the play-within-the-play in *Hamlet*; *Romeo and*

Juliet and the 'separated twins' plays such as *Twelfth Night*. In 1967 Henry F. Salerno published an English version of Flaminio Scala's scenarios (Salerno 1967); it is riddled with translation errors, some serious enough to render sections of the scenarios incoherent. Fortunately Richard Andrews has since published an accurate translation of 30 of Scala's 50 scenarios (Andrews 2008). The useful section of the Salerno volume is an appendix where the editor tracks Elizabethan plot borrowings from Scala's scenarios (Salerno 1967: 395–411).

So what were the conditions of theatrical production that might bring these two playwrights, working in different countries, different theatre architectures and different performance genres, into any alignment at all?

For one thing, both were participants in theatre processes that had no such thing as a director to shape the performance; the rise of the modern director is a fruit of theatrical developments in Germany in the nineteenth century. Conventional wisdom places major responsibility for this development on the shoulders of the Duke of Saxe-Meiningen and on Richard Wagner, but Laura Ginters has shown that the process was somewhat more complicated than that (Ginters 2008). It is an undeniable fact that even before the director enters, theatres seem to have managed without any contribution from what is now seen as an indispensable figure. With no one person charged with full oversight of the production, the organisation of performance must have been based on what Evelyn Tribble has identified as 'distributed cognition' (Tribble 2005). This involves in both our cases a decentralised power-sharing arrangement, in which, inevitably, the playwright (in the sense of the 'overall conceiver and projector of storyline and plot sequencing') must be one of the major 'takers of responsibility'. Anthropologist Richard Bauman has succinctly defined performance – even in its broadest terms such as social performance and storytelling – as the 'assumption of responsibility to an audience for a display of communicative competence' (Bauman 1984: 8). With a multi-performer performance it is necessarily shared between a range of participants: actors, musicians, playwright, stage manager and so on.

It is most common for the playwright to have to exercise this responsibility remotely, since he or she has little if any direct control over what happens in the moment of performance; so this responsibility is most obviously exercised through the text – whether that text be fully dialogued as in Shakespeare's case, or merely outlined as is the case with Scala's scenarios. Let us examine two examples of these two playwrights exercising responsibility for performance through their texts.

Day 3, Act 1, of Scala's volume is translated below by the author. Scala's original does not have numbered scenes, and they have been provided for convenience. In scenes 12–13 one of the female characters, Flaminia, appears at a window, giving rise to a piece of set business which depends on the careful positioning of her two suitors on the stage below. Flaminia is being wooed by two brothers, Orazio and Flavio, and first she sees Orazio on stage – but shortly afterwards Flavio enters, unseen by his brother:

> FLAVIO enters so that Orazio is in the middle, with Flavio behind him. Orazio greets Flaminia who, pretending to greet him in return actually greets Flavio (who is the one she's in love with), saying "Dear Orazio, don't be jealous of your brother; it's you I love, not him".

The scene is explicit in its directions, requiring a straight line between Flaminia at the window, for example, upstage left; Orazio centre; and Flavio downstage right. At this point Pedrolino, who in this scenario is the innkeeper rather than a servant, enters and sees immediately what is going on. He then goes up to Orazio and alerts him to the trick:

> PEDROLINO enters, and realizes Flaminia is pretending to talk to Orazio while really addressing Flavio. He goes up to Orazio and quietly asks him whom Flaminia is speaking to. Orazio says it's to him. Pedrolino shows him Flavio, who's standing behind him. Orazio, on seeing him, angrily draws his sword; Flavio does likewise and they exit fighting. Flaminia withdraws and Pedrolino enters the inn, laughing.

Figure 3.1 shows the arrangement the scenario specifies and requires for the routine to work:

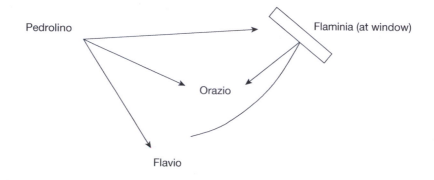

Figure 3.1 The relative positions of the characters on the stage as required for the scene

The scenario's exploitation of the fixity of the character at the window, and its insistence on the straight-line positioning of the other two characters in relation to the window, creates this piece of set business. The playwright is intent on ensuring the physical/visual effect is clear in performance, and the arrangement set out in the scenario has another important function as well: it effectively schematizes the action into a series of binary interactions, avoiding the complexity of a triadic exchange between the three lovers (improvisation is much simpler with two rather than three participants). The scenario structures the scene as a sequence of three binary interactions: Flaminia-Orazio (though Flaminia is really speaking to a silent Flavio), then Pedrolino-Orazio and finally Orazio-Flavio.

Since playwrights such as Scala cannot guarantee they will be there at each performance, they develop remote control methods. This scenario shows Scala as playwright taking the responsibility, via this structuring of the text, for setting up possibilities and ordering interactions in particular ways so as to provide information flow to the audience to keep them up with (or ahead of, or behind) the game. They are led to see the scene from the point of view of Orazio, then of Flavio and Flaminia, then of Pedrolino, and finally again of Orazio.

We see Shakespeare at work with similar logistical issues in a short section of *The Second Part of King Henry VI*. This is the climax of a long scene in which the Queen bids farewell to her beloved Suffolk, banished by her husband the King. Fighting to control her own emotions at the end of a long and intense relationship, the Queen brings Suffolk to the realization that he must choose exile over certain death, and the scene ends with Suffolk's wonderful image of their being torn apart like a ship foundering on the rocks:

QUEEN: Away! Though parting be a fretful corrosive,
    It is applied to a deathful wound.
    To France, sweet Suffolk! Let me hear from thee;
    For wheresoe'er thou art in this world's globe,
    I'll have an Iris that shall find thee out.
    Away!
SUFFOLK: I go.
QUEEN: And take my heart with thee. [*She kisseth him.*]
SUFFOLK: A jewel, lock'd into the woefull'st cask
    That ever did contain a thing of worth.
    Even as a splitted bark, so sunder we:
    This way fall I to death.
QUEEN: This way for me. *Exeunt* [*severally*]
                  (*2 Henry VI*, III. ii. 403–12)

This is extraordinary poetry: the final shared or 'splitted' rhyming couplet is breathtaking in its alliterative and monosyllabic economy. But as poetry on the page it is actually nonsense: what does the repeated 'this way' mean? Some linguists use the term 'shifters' for words like 'this', and for good reason – they shift in meaning according to context. And the meaning of 'this' shifts here, because the characters clearly mean two different 'this' ways: they exit in opposed directions.

It is clear that Shakespeare is thinking practically about the logistics of performance, and that he thinks he has two exit doors to play with – he would only have constructed the repeated and oppositional 'this way' textual pattern if the stage he was envisaging for the performance had two counter-posed exit points that would make it work spatially.

Shakespeare is taking responsibility for the performance here via the dialogue, not via the stage directions: it is the *dialogue* that stresses the opposition between the 'here' of the kingdom and the 'there' of exile, and that cues his actors to create this spatial meaning. The original stage direction '*Exeunt*' is perfectly sufficient, and the '*severally*' that modern editors supply is quite superfluous – Shakespeare's text does not treat its primary readers, his actors, condescendingly.

These examples typify playwrights assuming responsibility for performance in the absence of the yet to be invented director. Much of the director's contribution to modern rehearsal time lies in conducting a process known as 'blocking': working painstakingly through each scene with the actors, elaborating stage positionings and movements, the timing thereof and the characters' underlying motivations – a time-consuming collaborative process which Gay McAuley has identified as being at the centre of the creative exchange between director and actors (McAuley 2012: 75–7, 83–7, 95–8). In the late sixteenth century, with no director and no time to indulge in such laborious practices, one must posit a quite different work process based on 'distributed cognition', a phenomenon exemplified in these two instances. Distributed cognition involves pooled expertise and knowledge that would enable the participants to achieve some organisation (no matter how rudimentary) of the performance by 'distributing' the function of overall spatial organisation of the performance onto the text generated by the playwright, and also onto external (i.e. non-textual, already existing) environmental factors.

How do actors know their entrance and exit points if there's been no rehearsal time in which to plot them punctiliously? There is evidence that Elizabethan playwrights inscribed cues and clues for the actors in their texts, so the cognitive load associated with entrances and exits (and to some extent the blocking of scenes) was taken off the shoulders of the actors and 'distributed' onto the theatre building and the resources of the stage – particularly the two stage doors (Fitzpatrick 2011: 175–96). This involves the emergence of a set of staging conventions shared by playwrights and actors (and audience) that assigned specific values to the stage doors so that actors, 'reading' the text's spatial indications, would know which door to use for an entrance or exit; and so that the audience, seeing the direction of the entrance or exit, would grasp its significance. Not only would the Queen and Suffolk in the excerpt above know they had to exit at different doors; each would also have known which door and why, and the audience would have known what those exits signified.

These shorthand rules that enabled the actors to perform coherently with little rehearsal time were also a means of helping the audience understand what was going on: regularities of use of the doors and other stage resources would enable the audience to build a competence that would help them 'read' the performance. Other more general conventions about theatrical 'genre' would also have assisted them: familiarity breeds expertise, not contempt. A play, for example, that featured a pair of twins (usually separated at birth or by subsequent calamity) would elicit audience expectations precisely because they would immediately recognize it as belonging to the 'lost twins' genre, and would start making projections about where the plot might go. Playwrights could then count on those expectations, and play with the audience (as complicit parties, not as playthings) to achieve particular effects. For example, Shakespeare and the audience have a delicious moment of complicity in *Twelfth Night*. At the beginning of II. ii., it looks to the audience as though Malvolio might be addressing the wrong twin altogether: Olivia has sent him in pursuit of the exiting Viola to return the ring that Olivia says Viola gave her, but the entrance pattern specified by the text for the moment when Malvolio catches up with Viola creates the distinct possibility in the audience's mind that this is instead Sebastian, who has just arrived in Illyria, and that Malvolio is about to make a fool of himself by mistaking him for Viola (see Fitzpatrick 2011: 77–83).

Another commonality between Scala and Shakespeare lies in a mode of theatrical production that was, from a twenty-first century perspective, incredibly fast. The Commedia players were renowned for being able to perform 'at the drop of a hat', and 'off the cuff' (two of the better English translations for '*all'improvviso*', a practice that has nothing to do with post-Stanislavskian 'improvisation').

Even a company of amateurs led by Giovanbattista Fagiuoli, a prominent playwright in late seventeenth century Florence, could create a performance in an afternoon. In the autumn of 1705 Fagiuoli was summoned to the villa of his protector, a Medici cardinal, and one of his scenarios (in manuscript in the Riccardiana Library in Florence) has been retrospectively annotated by the author as follows: 'This scenario was done by me in an hour, on the Cardinal's orders; the roles were then assigned and it was performed the evening of October 20 1705 at Lappeggi.' (Fagiuoli 1705: ms 3472: 305)

It is likely that Fagiuoli annotated the scenario in this way after consulting his diary entry for the date concerned:

> Tuesday October 20: order from His Most Reverend Highness to come to Lappeggi, where on arrival I was ordered by the cardinal to immediately do a scenario for a comedy. This I did; the roles were assigned immediately, and it was performed that evening.
>
> (Fagiuoli 1705: ms 2697)

As for the Elizabethan players in London, we know from Carol Rutter's exploration of Henslowe's papers that the companies performed using a quick turnover of plays in repertory: her analysis shows that in a ten-week period over the summer of 1595 the Admiral's men did 57 performances of 20 different plays, 4 of which were new to their repertory (Rutter 1984: 91). This connotes short rehearsal times, as the one thing we can be sure the Elizabethans had in common with us is that there were then, as now, only 24 hours in the day. Many scholars working from modern theatrical practices tend to go into denial about this brute fact and ignore the logistical impossibility of finely tuned and nuanced productions. Others argue instead for a rough and ready production style in which the words were possibly not well learned and the dialogue 'improvised' – and hence potentially aligned with the practices of the Italian players.

Yet these two high-turnover production processes are clearly working in different ways. If Fagiuoli can think up a detailed plot sequence in an afternoon and get the actors to perform it the same day, he is clearly relying on actors familiar with the sorts of roles required and experienced in performing such roles, and on generic ideas of what the plot outline will consist of (we will return to these three elements – role, experience and agenda – on the following pages). The Elizabethans, on the other hand, worked in a production mode that required substantial time and energy before the actors got their cue-scripts to learn. The text was fully written; it then needed to be partly re-copied multiple times into each of the actors' 'parts' or cue-scripts (more discussion of these to follow). However rapidly the actors might then have managed to learn their scripts, this process from start to finish is not the work of a single afternoon as in Fagiuoli's case.

This, therefore, is where the differences between these two practices begin to manifest themselves. Tiffany Stern's research on what rehearsal involved for Elizabethan actors (Stern 2000) demonstrates that it was indeed not only possible, but was expected by the playwrights as essential, to learn one's lines carefully. She discusses an example from *The Merchant of Venice*, III. iii. of a notorious exchange, where Shylock repeats numerous times his ultimatum to Antonio: he will have his 'bond', the pound of flesh pledged by Antonio for defaulting on his repayment to Shylock. On the page, it looks like a simple exchange between Shylock and Antonio (and to an extent the silent Jailer). The third named character, Solanio, seems a strangely silent and passive onstage presence, whose only function is to call Shylock a dog after the latter has exited:

Enter SHYLOCK, SOLANIO, ANTONIO, *and the jailer.*

SHYLOCK: Jailer, look to him. Tell not me of mercy.
    This is the fool that lent out money gratis.
    Jailer, look to him.
ANTONIO: Hear me yet, good Shylock.
SHYLOCK: I'll have my bond. Speak not against my bond.
    I have sworn an oath that I will have my bond.
    Thou calledst me dog before thou hadst a cause.
    But since I am a dog, beware my fangs.
    The duke shall grant me justice. – I do wonder,
    Thou naughty jailer, that thou art so fond
    To come abroad with him at his request.
ANTONIO: I pray thee, hear me speak.
SHYLOCK: I'll have my bond. I will not hear thee speak.
    I'll have my bond, and therefore speak no more.
    I'll not be made a soft and dull-eyed fool
    To shake the head, relent and sigh, and yield
    To Christian intercessors. Follow not.
    I'll have no speaking. I will have my bond.

Exit SHYLOCK

SOLANIO: It is the most impenetrable cur
    That ever kept with men.
                 The Merchant of Venice, III. iii. 1–19

However, if we 'rewrite' the text so that it represents how the speech would have been broken up in performance, we see immediately that Solanio is by no means silent – and there is a simple reason for this. Elizabethan actors worked from cue-scripts so each actor's 'role' consisted of his speeches in manuscript, prefaced by a word or two – the final words of the preceding speech. It can be suggested that acting therefore consisted of standing on stage in white terror, waiting to hear a couple of key words that were your next cue, and hoping that their utterance by another actor would provoke the appropriate cognitive response that would enable you to utter on cue your next speech.

So, during this speech, Solanio is waiting anxiously for the cue his script is furnished with, which is Shylock's final 'I will have my bond', or more likely just the last two words 'my bond'. Except that, as Stern points out, these two words appear multiple times in the course of Shylock's speeches to Antonio: Shakespeare has deliberately seeded the speech with 'false cues' so that Solanio, prompted by what he thinks is his cue, repeatedly cuts in and starts his speech calling Shylock a dog: 'It is the most impenetrable cur…'

This is how this exchange would have appeared in performance: no longer a flat interaction between Shylock and Antonio, but now a tense triangular exchange as Solanio repeatedly interrupts Shylock's address to Antonio and the Jailer. I have inserted dashes to suggest how Solanio's interjections break up the flow of Shylock's speech:

Enter SHYLOCK, SOLANIO, ANTONIO, *and the jailer.*

SHYLOCK: Jailer, look to him. Tell not me of mercy.
This is the fool that lent out money gratis.
Jailer, look to him.
ANTONIO: Hear me yet, good Shylock.
SHYLOCK: I'll have my bond—
SOLANIO: It is the most impenetrable cur—
SHYLOCK: —Speak not against my bond—
SOLANIO: It is the most impenetrable cur—
SHYLOCK: —I have sworn an oath that I will have my bond—
SOLANIO: It is the most impenetrable cur—
SHYLOCK: —Thou call'dst me dog before thou hadst a cause.
But since I am a dog, beware my fangs.
The duke shall grant me justice. —I do wonder,
Thou naughty jailer, that thou art so fond
To come abroad with him at his request.
ANTONIO: I pray thee, hear me speak.
SHYLOCK: I'll have my bond—
SOLANIO: It is the most impenetrable cur—
SHYLOCK: —I will not hear thee speak.
I'll have my bond.
SOLANIO: It is the most impenetrable cur—
SHYLOCK: —and therefore speak no more.
I'll not be made a soft and dull-eyed fool
To shake the head, relent and sigh, and yield
To Christian intercessors. Follow not.
I'll have no speaking. I will have my bond.

Exit SHYLOCK

SOLANIO: It is the most impenetrable cur
That ever kept with men.

Stern's alerting us to the implications of cue-script performance clarifies the extent to which the text has been structured so as to make this exchange dynamic and complex in performance. Incidentally, it also provides an explanation for Shylock's 'thou call'dst me dog': in the text version this remark seems addressed to Antonio, who (some critics have noted) has not called Shylock a 'dog' either in this or in any previous scene. In the performed version it is not directed to Antonio, but is instead a direct and immediate response to Solanio's repeated calling Shylock a 'cur'. But the more general point to be made is that in writing the scene in this way Shakespeare is relying not only on a Solanio who is expert in picking up his cues and launching (prematurely) into his required speech, but even more so on a Shylock who is line-perfect – so as to deliver the 'false cues', but more importantly so as to ride out the repeated interjections they provoke and continue unfazed to the end of the speech as written, at each interjection rounding on Solanio for interrupting his address to Antonio.

This simple example illustrates that rapid production does not necessarily connote a rough and ready process, poor line-learning and a resort to paraphrase: if Shylock were guilty of any of these, the scene would not work as Shakespeare clearly plans it to: he would not provide the 'false cues' to Solanio, and/or would not be able to maintain the momentum of his speech amidst the unwelcome interruptions.

What this means is that there is a significant difference between 'ad libbing' and 'composition in performance': the latter is an overarching technique which enables the whole performance (even if there are tightly-structured components embedded in it) to be structured quickly and flexibly, so that it can be bent at will to the exigencies of the moment. While an 'ad lib' moment can occur in a fully scripted play, it can only be contemplated when it will not affect the learned structures of text-based performance (or, in modern performance, the computer-controlled lighting and sound cues): it is a parenthesis, an exception that proves the rule. In contrast, what ethnographers call 'composition in performance' (and what I have termed 'flexible performance') is not just an exception but a way of life – and this too in a more general perspective. I have hinted above at the three underlying elements that make composition in performance possible in the Commedia dell'Arte: set roles, aggregated experience in playing those roles, and a clear agenda or outline of what has to happen overall and scene-by-scene.

If we look at these three elements in relation to other broader performance genres, we can begin to see why they might work also in this particular theatrical performance genre. The simple reason is that in most of our interpersonal and social encounters, these three elements are vital to a good outcome. Your effectiveness or the quality of your 'performance' depends on these three: familiarity with the role required in that situation; the experience you have and can bring to bear on the particular issue at hand; and a plan, program, agenda or general aim you are prosecuting in the interaction. This is actually a general model of performance as an endemic interactional structure (Fitzpatrick 1995: 53–75), and it would not be surprising if the actors of the Commedia dell'Arte also found it useful as an underlying structure that enabled them to perform at short notice without a complete script.

We all spend a lot of our time interacting with other human beings in flexible but structured situations, and we do this without written scripts (though we might at times 'rehearse' what we think we might say, or even write ourselves brief notes on which we can base our 'off the cuff' remarks). The Commedia dell'Arte technique is simply an over-coding of this generic interactional structure, and it is fundamentally different from a fully learned, script-based performance that Shakespeare and his fellow-playwrights were used to. The necessary textual traces left by fully scripted theatre, and the undeniable literary greatness of its major exponents, means that Elizabethan theatre has left the Commedia in the shade, looked down on as mere clowning or popular entertainment. Yet it was a massive theatre phenomenon that dominated Europe for 200 years, and fed directly into not only Elizabethan plays, but into the work of Molière and Goldoni, and into the extraordinary Italian operas of Mozart, one of the highest points of European culture.

Both Flaminio Scala and William Shakespeare would have been strangely at home, and would have processed the experience 'in parallel', on the set of a *Hopalong Cassidy* film as described in a syndicated article by Theodore Strauss that appeared in a New Zealand newspaper in 1941 (Strauss 1941). The actor who played Hopalong at the time, and who had done so for the preceding seven years, was William Boyd, described by the reporter as the 'Tom Mix of 1941':

> During these seven years Mr Boyd has made some 36 pictures in the Hopalong series. Now they are made at the rate of six a year. They average a cost of slightly less than 100,000 dollars (roughly £17,000) each and a profit of 100 per cent, which is a better rate of return than that of most super-productions.

This was industrial film-making at its best, with production schedules that are as awesome as those described by Carol Rutter in Elizabethan London:

> Most of the films, Mr. Boyd explained, are made with a location company of at least sixty-five, and they are made fast. Working hours are from sunup to sundown. The average shooting schedule takes two weeks, and that means thirty to forty scenes a day. The shooting is more or less "from the cuff." The script is there, but everybody ad-libs a little and Mr. Boyd usually paraphrases things to suit his own style. After all, by this time he has begun to feel mighty like Hopalong himself.

The practices of ad-libbing and paraphrasing would seem endemic to this sort of production schedule, to the point where it might be argued that they come close to systematic composition in performance, despite the fact that 'the script is there'. Also to be noted is that this flexible approach to dialogue goes hand in hand with specific well-worn roles: Boyd paraphrases because he knows how his character Hopalong talks. Flaminio Scala would recognise a 'mask' and ways of generating dialogue; Shakespeare would see the industrial production processes as akin to those of the King's Men. And both of these commercial playwrights would have been very interested in 'a profit of 100 per cent'.

References

Andrews, Richard ed. (2008) *The Commedia dell'Arte of Flaminio Scala*. Lanham, US/Toronto, Canada/Plymouth, UK: Scarecrow Press.

Bauman, Richard (1984) *Verbal Art as Performance*. Illinois, US: Waveland Press.

Fagiuoli, G. B. (1705) *Amor'aguzza l'ingegno*, Riccardiana Library, Florence, Italy: ms 3472: 305.

Fagiuoli, G. B. (1705) Diary, Riccardiana Library, Florence, Italy: ms 2697.

Fitzpatrick, Tim (1995) *The Relationship of Oral and Literate Performance Processes in the Commedia dell'Arte: Beyond the Improvisation/Memorisation Divide*. Lewiston, US/Queenstown, Canada/Lampeter, UK: Edwin Mellen Press.

Fitzpatrick, Tim (2011) *Playwright, Space and Place in Early Modern Performance: Shakespeare and Company*. Farnham/Burlington: Ashgate Publications.

Ginters, Laura (2008) "Wagner and the Little Ballet Master that Could". *'Being There: After.' Proceedings of the 2006 Annual Conference of the Australasian Association for Theatre, Drama and Performance Studies*, ed. Ian Maxwell. Online refereed publication (no pages given) in collaboration with Sydney eScholarship & Sydney University Press: http://ses.library.usyd.edu.au/handle/2123/2470 (accessed 19 August 2014).

McAuley, Gay (2012) *Not Magic but Work: An Ethnographic Account of a Rehearsal Process*. Manchester, UK: Manchester University Press.

Rutter, Carol (1984) *Documents of the Rose Playhouse*. Manchester, UK: Manchester University Press.

Salerno, Henry F. ed. (1967) *Scenarios of the Commedia dell'Arte*. New York: New York University Press.

Stern, Tiffany (2000) *Rehearsal from Shakespeare to Sheridan*. Oxford, UK: Oxford University Press.

Strauss, Theodore (1941) "'Hopalong' William Boyd – Tom Mix of 1941". *Auckland Star* LXXII Issue 187.

Tribble, Evelyn (2005) "Distributing Cognition in the Globe". *Shakespeare Quarterly* 56/2.

TROUPES

4

THE COMMEDIA DELL'ARTE
ACTING COMPANIES

Kenneth Richards

The defining features of the Italian professional theatre seem to have evolved gradually in the context of formally organised acting companies of many kinds and size. The term 'Commedia dell'Arte' as a definition or broad description of the professional performers was introduced only in the eighteenth century. When we use the term of earlier professional performers we need to recognise the sheer range and variety of Italian players and professional theatre activity in the sixteenth and seventeenth centuries, encompassing as it did companies closely associated with courts, distinguished independent travelling companies, lesser itinerant troupes of various size, and possibly even groups of two, three or more performers, some of whom supported the commercial dealings of mountebanks. We have most information about the great troupes and respected players, who were connected with courts or who appeared at courts or were regularly on the major circuits, and it is on those we will mainly focus here, but we need to be aware of the others, and guard against casually applying what was characteristic of the major companies to the activities of troupes of more modest skills and audience capture.

The gradual evolution of company formations in the middle decades of the sixteenth century is rather obscure, but a significant moment can be noted in a document of 25 February 1545 in which eight individuals in Padua committed themselves contractually for a year to travel and perform as a unit. It could well be that not all early troupes sought legally so to bind themselves, but the advantages of doing so for the smooth operation of what was a commercial undertaking on which individual and family livings depended must have been evident to many. The wording of the document is revealing, noting among other things that the arrangement should legally hold for a year, the members should elect a leader, have a takings cash-box with three keys held by three members of the troupe, that anyone absconding should be financially penalised, and that they should purchase a horse to carry their belongings from place to place (for the full contract and further comment on it see Richards and Richards 1990, pp. 44–6). These details are noted, because they largely held good for more than a century. The requirement of a horse was clearly crucial for a travelling troupe and, along with carts and later, possibly, carriages, was to remain so even for the major companies. No less important was a *capo comico*, to oversee the management of the troupe and exercise authority over members in matters of dispute. Equally important were agreement on regulations to govern the handling of box-office monies, rules to govern the unexpected departure of a member of the company, and the term for which the contract was valid, all crucial matters to a collective business enterprise. Later, the contracts no doubt became lengthier and more sophisticated, but it is likely the elements listed here would have been included for they were calculated to ensure as far as possible the troupe's cohesiveness and camaraderie. This is not the only early contract of which we know, another is dated 29 August 1549 and again in Padua (cited Richards and Richards 1990, pp. 46ff.), and on 10 October 1564 a certain Siennese, Lucrezia, entered into an agreement in Rome to form a company with six males (Taviani and Schino 1982, p. 183). As with the Padua troupe, of how successful these were we have no record, but they probably succeeded if we can judge by the comparative rapidity with which acting companies became successfully established.

What we may loosely call the emerging Italian theatrical profession (the *commedia mercenaria*) drew to itself performers not only with a wide range of abilities, but also from a range of professions and social and educational backgrounds. It inevitably attracted the poor and uneducated, particularly if they were fortunate enough to possess distinctive vocal, instrumental or physical skills exploitable in an entertainment industry at whatever level. But the profession also attracted individuals, both male and female, of education and some social position, and it drew recruits from seemingly quite different fields: Francesco Andreini (1548–1624), the accomplished troupe leader of the Gelosi acting company had been a soldier before turning player. As formations evolved, with some companies acquiring reputations and status among the elite, also attracted to the profession were individuals with literary and physical skills who had initially moved on the artistic and entertainment fringes of the great courts. It is important to remember that while the Commedia dell'Arte has a reputation for improvisation and physical performance, in the Renaissance its literary dimension was important: actors and actresses, at least at the higher levels of the profession, and those who played the roles of lovers, needed to be able to read and write, and so be capable of collecting appropriate literary materials in a *zibaldone* (notebook) for later use where appropriate in stage discourse. Verbally skilful too, and capable of reaching high flights of rhetoric were the stage *vecchi* and the Capitani, and sophisticated witty discourse was by no means alien to zanni (Henke 2002).

The responsibilities of a *capo comico* might include arranging itineraries and bookings, controlling expenditure, coaching young or new players and rehearsing new material. The troupe leader need not necessarily be the lead actor, and indeed some distinguished troupes were led by actresses. The authority of the capo comico and regulation governing conduct may well have become increasingly important in later years when jealousy, amatory entanglements and wounded artistic *amour propre* disrupted the activities of more than one troupe. The personnel structure of companies gradually emerged – probably through trial and error, and certainly determined by performer skills and personalities. The numbers in troupes were doubtless fluid according to the kind and status of the troupe, but by the time the principal companies had become established they ran to about ten or twelve – invariably the half-masked two zanni, or comic servants, two vecchi, a Venetian merchant, Pantalone, and a Bolognese lawyer, Dottore, and the unmasked two or three pairs of male and female lovers (the *amorosi*), a *servetta* or servant girl, and a Capitano or braggart soldier. These were sometimes joined by supernumeraries for bit parts like soldiers, officials, Turks, servants, nurses, etc., and some of them may well have been young or elderly family members of the principal players, for familial links between members of a company were often close, children followed parents into the profession, and in the course of time dynasties of players emerged, like the Andreini, the Biancolelli, the Casanova and the Constantini; the range of their theatrical expertise sometimes embracing the lyric as well as the regular theatre (Rasi 1897–1905, *passim*; Taviani and Schino 1982, *passim*). Although leading troupes in particular could perform scripted as well as improvised pieces, the majority worked for the most part from *scenari*, or action outlines, and the stage space in which these were acted out was invariably a *piazza* backed by two, three or four houses with streets off: in effect a microcosm of a residential quarter of a city – like Milan, Bologna, Padua or Venice. The streets off served for exits and entrances, as did doors in the houses, while practicable windows allowed for contact between interior and street. This unit was superbly flexible: at street level trestle-stage use it required merely a painted backdrop with slits for doors and windows; at its most sophisticated indoors and out; increasingly in the seventeenth century, and later, it could accommodate elaborate machinery and effects.

It is of the major troupes of the 'golden age' (c. 1570–1630) that we know most, some independent, some associated closely with courts, their names reflective of a high culture ambience in being somewhat modelled after the names of the Italian Renaissance Humanist academies. These are the companies, too, with the strongest literary and rhetorical bent in their performances, and prominent in their membership are players who were also poets, dramatist and commentators on the profession. Two of the most distinguished of these in the later decades of the sixteenth century and the early years of the seventeenth – companies much admired by the contemporary commentator Tommaso Garzoni (1584) – were the Gelosi and the Confidenti. The former, which we first encounter in 1568, and which is found acting in Paris as early as 1571, at its peak was led for a time by Francesco Andreini, its star female performer his wife, Isabella Andreini (1562–1604), not only perhaps the most celebrated actress of the age, but a distinguished and widely admired poetess. Andreini broke up the company on his wife's death in 1604, was responsible for gathering and having printed some of his wife's writings, and himself published an illuminating volume of dialogues, *Le Bravure del Capitano Spavento* (1607). The Confidenti we first encounter touring in 1574, for a time it had ties with the Duke of Mantua and later with Don Giovanni de'Medici at Florence. Throughout its long history, to our last record of it in 1639, when it left for Paris, it broke and reformed at least once, included in its complement distinguished players like Tristano Martinelli (1556–c.1630), Niccolò Barbieri (1576–1641), Marc' Antonio Romagnesi (1633–1706), and the actress Marina Dorotea Antonazzoni (1593–1639). From about 1612 to 1620 it was probably led by one of the great figures of the age, Flaminio Scala (between the sixteenth and seventeenth centuries), author of the sole collection of *scenari* published in the period, *Il teatro delle Favole rappresentative* (1611). Other distinguished troupes included the Desiosi, led for a time by the popular actress Diana Ponti (fl. late sixteenth—early seventeenth century), the Uniti, for a time in union with the Confidenti, and the Accesi, which at the turn of the century was headed for a while by one of the most effective actors and valuable commentators on the profession, Pier Maria Cecchini (1563–1645). The Uniti joined several times with the Fedeli troupe, thus having a particularly rich acting complement, and toured abroad to Paris, Vienna, Linz and elsewhere. The Fedeli was, for a long time, led by the son of the Andreini, Gian Battista Andreini (c.1576–1654), a lead actor and one of the most distinguished Italian dramatists of the early seventeenth century, long admired both in the peninsula and in Paris, where we find him in the 1640s, although whether with the Fedeli is not known. His wife, the actress Virginia Ramponi (c.1583–?1630), who acted under the name of La Florinda, was a much admired performer who on one notable occasion took over the lead role in the Rinuccini-Monteverdi opera *Arianna* (in Mantua, 1608). Her accomplishment is a useful reminder that the Italian professionals played an important part in the establishment of *melodramma* on Italian stages (see Lattanzi 2003, *passim*). Finally, an early seventeenth century company worth noting, not least for its English connection, is the Affezionati, seen in Venice in 1632 by the English dramatist Sir Aston Cokain; he reworked one of their scenarios he saw them perform into his play *Trappolino creduto principe* (written 1632–3, pub. 1658). The troupe's players included some of the finest of the 1620s and 1630s, like Silvio Fiorillo and Gian Battista Fiorillo, but of whose dates we know little (see Rasi 1897–1905, *passim*; Taviani and Schino 1982, *passim*).

The fragmentary nature of the extant records of the companies makes it difficult to focus in detail on any one of these troupes with respect to personnel complement at a particular time, as well as on where it acted, the pieces it performed and its reception. We cannot, for example, write as easily about the fortunes of the celebrated Gelosi company in the two decades before it broke up, as we can about a London troupe like the King's Men in the reign of James I. What the brief comments above do indicate, however, is that even lead players could move from one troupe to another (Francesco Andreini and the Martinelli brothers are examples), and that crucial to the success of the troupes, probably at all levels, were actresses, who became stock members of companies from the 1560s onwards. Not only were some of them leaders of troupes, like the Desiosi, for a time also known as the company of Diana, but they were almost certainly in many of them the star players, exhibiting as we have noted a range of performer skills and literary and vocal talents. Indeed, when Diana Ponti left the Desiosi in 1600, and joined the Accesi prior to its departure for Paris, her going may have contributed to the eventual breakup of the company. Rulers on occasion refer to actresses just as if they were heads of companies, for actresses were widely followed not only by the populace, but by the elite. The lead actress Vincenza Armani (c.1530–69), for example, was much admired by the sophisticated members of the Accademia degli Intronati of Siena for her skill in interpreting comedy, tragedy and pastoral (Valerini, cited Taviani and Schino 1982, p. 135). Actresses were adept at cross-dressing and, like other players, at least in the major companies, many could perform both improvised and premeditated, a skill considered important by those putting together acting troupes for touring, for court entertainment, or for royal service abroad.

A given for late Italian Renaissance professional theatre companies was itinerancy. Italy was not unified until the mid-nineteenth century, earlier consisting of a conglomeration of independent states, each with distinctive social, economic and political mores, and often significantly shaped by foreign political and cultural influences. But there were no major towns, save Naples, of the size of London, or Paris, or Madrid capable of providing comfortable economic returns for permanently based companies. Itinerancy, however, laid open a range of state capitals and large towns where travelling troupes could purvey their wares in streets and *piazze*, but more frequently, and increasingly, in enclosed performance places. The advantage of these last was that they allowed performance in any kind of weather and ensured that spectators paid at the box-office. As actors came gradually to contract their skills to companies, so some companies came to hire for periods performance places, whether rooms, or halls, or purpose-built structures. Thus in Venice we find the Accesi in 1622 signing a contract to take a theatre with the owners, the Vendramin, and agreeing to:

> act therein their respectable comedies... They will stay for the whole of next Carnival, which will be the last day of February 1623 More Imperii, will be entitled to all the box-office takings and then at Christmas will be given a gift of three hundred Venetian ducats in cash with the proviso that as long as the players perform they must maintain the lighting, not only on the stage, but throughout the theatre.
>
> (Cited Mangini, pp. 49–50; for the full contract in English see Richards and Richards 1990, p. 104)

Life on the road, however, whether within the peninsula or beyond it, could be hard, as indicated by the actor Domenico Bruni giving a taste of what the neophyte might expect:

> Here today, there tomorrow; sometimes by land, sometimes by sea; and what's worse, forever living in inns where the charges are high and the service is poor. I wish my father had consigned me to another trade, one where I think I could have done better with less trouble.
>
> (Bruni, *Le Fatiche Comiche*, 1623, pp. 6–7, cited in Richards and Richards 1990, p. 218)

Nor was it a profession in which to grow old gracefully, as a caustic remark of the poet Malherbe suggests after he had seen Italian players at Fontainbleau in 1613:

> Arlequin is certainly very different from what he once was, as too is Patrolin: the former is fifty-six years old, and the latter forty-seven, neither of an age any longer appropriate to the stage, where one needs lively temperaments and firm minds, and those one rarely finds in such old bodies as their's.
>
> (Malherbe 1862, p. 337)

His throw-away comment reminds us that life for many players in old age could be harsh.

The great companies of which we know most tended to operate mainly in the northern half of the peninsula, touring on circuits which included the major towns like Bologna, Florence, Ferrara, Mantua, Verona, Cremona, Venice, Padua, Milan and Genoa. But geography and political and cultural affiliations in this peninsula of independent states was conditional. Troupes that operated in southern Italy seem to have cultivated their own territory, sometimes appearing in Rome but frequently active further south in and around Naples and even into Sicily. For periods female players were not permitted in the Papal States, although this was usually no impediment as male actors could assume female roles. Such may also have been the case when Italian acting companies appeared in Elizabethan England, as one did in 1578. As travel conditions improved, the distinction between northern and southern Italy was gradually, although only partly, overcome, as we see in the case of the great seventeenth century actor, Tiberio Fiorilli, who began his career in the Naples region, moved north to Bologna, and was a star attraction in Paris in the 1640s and later with the Comedie-Italienne (for Naples see Prota-Giurleo 1963, *passim*).

The major companies seem to have enjoyed fairly wide social patronage, much depending on where and why they were performing, whether in halls, rooms or the grounds of the social elite, the *stanze* of the main towns on the touring circuits, or open-air in the *piazze*. The cost of entry to closed places, however, almost certainly determined who attended. A report from the early years of the companies suggests a professional audience, for we are told the company of the Roman actress Flaminia in 1567 'performed a beautiful play, it was well attended by many gentlefolk, judges, lawyers, doctors etc.' (D'Ancona 1891, II, p. 445). Their presence does not, of course, exclude those of more modest social standing, and with the development of the companies and circuits their numbers may well have increased. The gender composition of audiences is hard to calculate with confidence. Females certainly attended some elite performances, and doubtless they saw out-door shows, but at least some of the *scenari*, like Scala's *Il Ritratto* (The Picture) seem to indicate a largely male audience (aside from courtesans). How regularly, and in what kinds of performance venue, women attended, as well as the social status of those who did so, may have varied considerably from place to place (for an examination of possibilities see Henke 1997). The kind of work performed may also have conditioned, or been conditioned by, the sort of play a company performed. Plays could include comedies, tragic-comedies, pastorals and even quasi-musical entertainments. Cost of entry to tragedies and pastorals in the seventeenth century seems to have been higher than for comedies, not least because the former often entailed use of scenes and stage machinery. To what extent scripted plays were cut is unclear: when the Gelosi were involved in a production of Tasso's *Aminta* for the Ferrarese Court in 1573, or the Company of the Uniti mounted Guarini's *Il Pastor Fido* with *intermedii* in Bologna on 17 December 1623, we can only speculate as to how much was actually staged (Ricci 1888, p. 32).

Of considerable significance with respect to travelling in search of audiences was the need for companies to satisfy the requirements of city and town administrators and church officials across the range of independent states where they performed.

Permissions were needed to act, for such was one way authorities controlled what the troupes did and what audiences saw. Being itinerants, players were that much more suspect in not being settled residents, and as their performances were invariably by improvisation, the interpolation of unacceptable comment and 'business' was always a fear of officialdom, as was their influence on morals and the young. They could convey unpalatable news from place to place, and might potentially sew or spread dissension and then depart. Again, the skill of some with weapons, swords and daggers in particular, could create an air of potential threat for the suspicious administrator. The London acting companies of the time were obliged to submit scripts to the Lord Chamberlain for approval; but vetting was much more difficult for players performing extempore. The demands of officialdom almost certainly conditioned the subject of stories and the nature of stage action, and players were agile at modifying both according to what they judged permissible from time to time and place to place, for the attitude of state officials, town authorities and local clergy could vary considerably. With respect to the last, at the upper end of the scale Archbishop Carlo Borromeo of Milan, for example, was an important clerical determinant of what in theatre was and was not acceptable, but was not wholly hostile; others, however, like Cardinal Paleotti, could be much more censorious. The players accommodated wherever they could, but were not unwilling to push against the agreed limits. Churchmen and the more straight-laced secular inveighed at times against the reputation and stage conduct of actresses and their sometimes scanty dress, as well as against lubricious stage 'business' and vulgar repartee, although at the same time a degree of bawdiness was invariably present in performances, a liberty characteristic of the age. Much depended on the judgement of the moment, although some things were clearly off limits: it is surely no accident that venial churchmen like Fra Timoteo in Machiavelli's *La Mandragola* are absent from the *scenari*. It may be thought legally binding contracts for the hire of performance places would be of limited utility when troupes moved from state to state, but contracts held across borders and, as troupes were engaged in commercial operations, their existence and that of family members depended on box-office receipts, and to renege on a contract would virtually deny the possibility of return to a key market-place.

Much more than seems to have been the case with the English Elizabethan and Jacobean acting companies of roughly the same period, the Italian troupes appear to have been subject to a fair amount of personnel change, and it is likely there were several reasons for that: first the commitment to itinerancy, not all players being always available for travel; second, the inter-marriage and domestic links between players which might have encouraged both association with a troupe and reason for leaving it; third, the possibility of joining a troupe for foreign travel, although it is likely companies were more stable when working for, or in, the service of a court, native or foreign. A valuable collection of seventeenth century players' letters, *Comici dell'Arte Corrispondenze* (1993), touches on these matters as well as many other aspects of players' lives. In the peninsula a touring season had evolved by the 1560s, even if somewhat flexible. Bologna has been suggested as a possible assembly point for actors by the early to mid-decades of the seventeenth century, and may have been so earlier (Monaldini 1995). Extant material, particularly letters, suggests that changes of personnel were brought about by disputes over money, particularly lavish rewards from princes, as well as by professional jealousies, a hazard later inherited by Italian opera companies both at home and abroad, like the Bartone-Cuzzone quarrels at London's Haymarket Theatre in the early eighteenth century. Hostility between females in particular could extend to extreme lengths, like the plot generated by the actress Margarita to disfigure the face of Angelica, actress wife of Drusiano Martinelli (Smith 1930). Troupes formed, reformed, and sometimes amalgamated, the company names often enduring, their complement occasionally proving more fluid. The early contract cited above bound a player for a year; by the seventeenth century at the latest that may have increased to as much as three or even five years, although most troupes would probably have recognised the futility of holding a player or players who wished to leave. Many kinds of company toured, both in the peninsula and abroad. At the upper end of the market some were put together specifically to serve the entertainment interests of a ruler or member of the nobility and in effect were in the patron's service, sometimes for lengthy periods; great families who supported troupes included the Dukes of Florence, Parma and Modena, and such troupes were employed to provide entertainment at the patron's court. On occasion, companies could be assembled for a special occasion – a wedding, or birthday, or visit of a foreign dignitary – and troupes could be sent on quasi-diplomatic missions to other courts as signs of their patron's munificence, family affection, political friendship and/or hope for support in a political dispute: such were certainly among the reasons why the Duke of Modena's company visited the Court of Charles II in 1678, unhappy as that turned out to be. France and the German states were among the first to receive Italian companies, such visits being fairly common from the early 1570s onwards. Spain, the Low Countries, Denmark and Poland were also attractions, and it was from France and possibly the Low Countries, that some Italian players came into England, as a troupe with the Martinelli brothers did in 1578 (Schricks 1976). Touring, both home and abroad, spawned a rich iconography (Katritzky 2006). Major players invariably led these troupes abroad, and were invited to foreign courts (*Viaggi teatrali*, 1989). Paris was a particular attraction, visiting players occasionally drawing hostility from native actors, as they did in England too after the Restoration when Tiberio Fiorilli and companies of Paris-based actors and actresses crossed the Channel. In 1658 an Italian company was settled permanently in Paris under the monarch's aegis, acting first at the Petit Bourbon with Molière's troupe, before moving to the Hotel de Bourgogne and becoming the Comédie Italienne (Scott 1990). Expelled from Paris in 1697 following a slight to the mistress of Louis XIV, the Italians returned in 1716 under the actor, troupe leader, theatre reformer and historian-theorist, Luigi Riccoboni (de Courville 1943–58). These were the elite players and troupes, but those of lesser standing, including outfits of two, three or four supporting a mountebank, also travelled beyond the peninsula in search of markets. Thomas Platter provides an interesting description of a more modest travelling troupe, that of one Zan Bragetta, that he saw perform at Avignon in 1598. This consisted of four actors and two actresses, and Platter's comments are illuminating of the engaging quality of such a troupe, the variety of skills it displayed, and its flexibility and economic wisdom with respect to performance places:

In the tennis court theatre they took for several weeks they presented on stage some very jolly pieces which frequently ran late into the night – so much so that one was obliged to wind up in candlelight.... They also gave three fine pastorals, in which the Pantalone and the Zani made one die with laughter to see and hear their dialogue, dances, gestures and tumbling..... When they saw that the audience was beginning to fall off, for the cost of the hall was too much, they set up a trestle on the Place au Change.

(Platter 1892, pp. 392–3)

To some extent, the centre of innovative Italian professional activities in the later seventeenth century and in the eighteenth was Paris. Many leading players were attracted there – notwithstanding the suspension between 1697 and 1716 – in large measure because the Italian troupe in Paris had court approval and financial support. In the eighteenth century Italian companies travelled further afield than Western Europe. Russia, particularly, was an attraction, Catherine the Great being one patron who drew to her court Italian dancers, opera singers and actors and acting companies. Venice rather than Bologna seems to have been the formation and departure point for many of these performers. Some of the most important Italian troupes of the late seventeenth century and the eighteenth, however, like those of Pietro Cotta (?–1720) and Antonio Sacchi (1708–88) helped to shape new developments in Italian *teatro di prosa*; Sacchi in particular was a notable performer in *scenari* and plays by the Venetian dramatists Carlo Goldoni (1707–93) and Carlo Gozzi (1720–1806), and is widely considered to be the last of the traditional Commedia dell'Arte troupe leaders, although the spirit and many of the strategies of the improvising players long lived on.

References

Andreini, Francesco *Le Bravure del Capitano Spavento*, Venice, Italy, 1607.

Cokain, Aston *Trappolin Creduto Principe, or Trappolin Supposed a Prince*, London, 1658.

Comici dell'Arte: Corrispondenze, ed. Claudia Burattelli, Domenica Landolfi & Anna Zinanni, under the direction of Siro Ferrone, Casa Editrice Le Lettere, 2 vols., Florence, Italy, 1993.

D'Ancona, A. *Origini del teatro italiano*, 2 vols, Turin, Italy, 1891.

de Courville, Xavier, *Un apotre de l'art du theatre au XVIIIe siècle. Luigi Riccoboni, dit Lelio*, Paris Librairie, E. Droz, 1943-58.

Garzoni, Tommaso *La Piazza Universale, di tutte le professioni del mondo, nobili e ignobili*, Venice, Italy, 1584.

Henke, Robert 'Towards reconstructing the audience of the Commedia dell'Arte', *Essays in Theatre*, vol. 15, No. 2, 1997, pp. 207–20.

Henke, Robert *Performance and Literature in the Commedia dell'Arte*, Cambridge University Press, Cambridge, UK, 2002.

Katritzky, M.A. *The Art of Commedia A Study in the Commedia dell'Arte 1560–1620 with Special reference to the Visual Records*, Rodopi, Amsterdam-New York, 2006.

Lattanzi, A. *Commedia dell'arte e spettacolo in musica tra Sei e Settecento*, EUE, Napoli, Italy, 2003.

Malherbe, François de *Oeuvres de Malherbe*, ed. L. Lalanne, 6 vols, Hachette, Paris, 1862.

Mangini, Nicola *I teatri di Venezia*, Mursia, Milan, Italy, 1974.

Monaldini, Sergio *Il teatro dei comici dell'arte a Bologna*, *L'Archiginnasio*, Nuova Serie, XC, Biblioteca Communale dell'Archiginnasio, Bologna, Italy, 1995.

Platter, Felix and Thomas, *Félix et Thomas Platter à Montpellier*, Societe des Bibliophiles de Montpellier, Montpellier, France, 1892.

Prota-Giurleo, Ulisse *I teatri di Napoli nel Seicento. La commedia e le maschere*, Naples, Italy, 1963.

Rasi, Luigi *I Comici Italiani, Biografie, bibliografia, iconografia*, 3 vols, Bocca, Florence, Italy, 1897–1905

Ricci, Corrado *I Teatri di Bologna nei secolo YVII e XVIII. Storia aneddotica*, Bologna, Italy, 1888.

Richards, Kenneth and Laura *The Commedia dell'arte, A Documentary Account*, Blackwell, Oxford, UK, 1990.

Scala, Flaminio *Il teatro delle Favole rappresentative overo la ricreazione comica, boscareccia e tragica*, Venice 1611; ed. Ferruccio Marotti, 2 vols, Milan, Italy, 1976.

Schricks, Willem 'Commedia dell'Arte players in Antwerp in 1576', *Theatre Research International*, No 2, Oxford University Press, Oxford, 1976.

Scott, Virginia *The Commedia dell'arte in Paris 1644-97*, University of Virginia Press, Charlottesville, US, 1990.

Smith, Winifred *Italian Actors of the Renaissance*, Coward-McCann, New York, 1930.

Taviani, Fredinano and Mirella Schino, *Il segreto della Commedia dell'Arte La memoria delle compagnie italiane del XVI, XVII e XVIII secolo*, La Casa Usher, Florence, Italy, 1982.

Viaggi teatrali dall'Italia a Parigi fra Cinque e Seicento, Costa and Nolan, Genoa, Italy, 1989.

STOCK CHARACTERS

5

YOU MUST HAVE HEARD OF HARLEQUIN...

Michele Bottini
Translated by Samuel Angus McGehee
and Michael J. Grady

One of the most important characters coming out of the Renaissance Commedia dell'Arte was the servant Arlecchino, known in France as Harlequino, and in Great Britain as Harlequin. Coming from the lower valley of the hill town of Bergamo in northern Italy, this zanni was a second level servant who evolved from a clumsy, rather stupid prankster into a spry, mischievous, clever, ever-popular and much-loved character. Written into plays, opera, dance, and the visual arts, the Arlecchino/Harlequin character came to symbolize the essence of Commedia dell'Arte. This chapter will look at how this character has evolved over the centuries and why he is so popular.

I have always hated carnival.

Even since I was a little boy, whenever I would witness people dressing up, putting on masks and transforming, I never found it funny, only quite scary.

And so I always hated carnival.

From among all the masks there was one in particular which bothered me the most, because I could not seem to figure it out: its costume was colorful, much too colorful, with a long stick hanging from the belt, a funny hat, which never seemed to stay in place and a little black mask, which reminded me of the ones that the villains in comic strips wore. It was such an excessive contrast: a character, which showed a joyous side but in truth was hiding something diabolic, a layer of suffering and cruelty.

It was only years later that I began to understand this mask with such a strange name: Arlecchino. Now, I am no longer scared; if anything my relation to Arlecchino is a very tender one, as is my approach to carnival. Now that I know better what it is, or rather what it was, it all has a new meaning.

Arlecchino is the very symbol of carnival; he is the symbol of Commedia dell'Arte, the essence, the soul and the heart.

Arlecchino is revolution.

Let us start from the beginning.

Nothing is created and nothing is destroyed, everything is transformed.

I like to think this is also true for theatre. We have spent rivers of ink trying to put exact dates on the history of theatre and trying to understand the precise origins: when was Commedia dell'Arte born? When and by whom were certain characters created? When exactly did women start to act on stage? And so forth. All this, is an attempt to systematize on to a calendar a long process of sedimentation, which sinks itself into history. It is usual to attribute the birth of Arlecchino to Tristano Martinelli and to his brother Drusiano, in between the second half of the 1500s and the first thirty years of the 1600s. In truth, this is not quite so. What Martinelli and Drusiano have done is to bring together and synthesize a series of already existing elements until finally finding a universal key embodied in a character. Through the interpretation of this character by the great actors, of which Biancolelli, Gherardi, Visentini, Sacchi and, more recently, Moretti and Soleri, Arlecchino has planted deep roots in the hearts of the collective imagination.

But which are these elements that make up such a character?

First we must take a step back and see the sacred representations in medieval Italy. The Church, which had as its language Latin, attempted to spread its religion to a mostly illiterate population by way of images. These sacred images portray an eternal battle between Good and Evil. The evil was represented by devils, and the good was represented by saints and angels. However, in the Bible it is written that 'God created Man in his own image.' And so, the characters who represented Good, i.e. angels, saints or even Christ, would have acted by showing their faces. Characters playing the devil would, by contrast, wear masks. The masks that had been handed down by the Roman tradition of comedy were then placed on these actors of religious propaganda; masks that showed dark faces which were tremendously ridiculous, wildly deformed, and had animalistic features with long noses. The problem for the Church then became that the people ended up recognizing themselves in these diabolical personages who were made to be funny and always on the losing side. These characters had dark and deformed faces like those who have worked in the fields under the sun, who suffer defeat and are always humiliated and beaten down by the 'winning side'; the winning side looking more like the well-kept angel-like ruling class. So, to the spectators, the eternal battle between Good and Evil ended up looking more like an eternal battle between servants and masters.

Arlecchino, therefore, is born from a mix between the figure of the servant who is kept on the lowest rung of the social scale and the devils stemming from creatures of the forests, such as elves and leprechauns. Arlecchino is able to synthesize the desperate character of an unchanging social condition with a sort of concrete intelligence that becomes an animal-like cleverness, a infantile outlook onto reality, perhaps even with a certain objectivity. All these elements come together to give Arlecchino the mantle of champion of the popular masses, who see him as a representation of themselves as well as a hope of change: a hope of revolution as Arlecchino operates his small revolutions and subversions on the stage. Meanwhile, all the other characters, starting with Brighella (his friend\enemy and also a servant—though much more conformist), represent the many vices of the social classes themselves. Arlecchino is the only one who is able to keep an objective and outsider's view by proposing through the comedies the possibility of another attitude in the face of reality. This bewitching talent that Arlecchino has, this instinctive desire for human change, is not born suddenly or by chance, as if it were the invention of a single person or interpreter; this instinctive desire has its roots in humanity.

During the culmination of carnival, the origin of which is too long of a diversion for the moment, the actors whose role it was to interpret the devil became the ones who played the characters of Zanni, and so Arlecchino. These characters were established at the margins of society and maintained their rights—outside of the religious ceremony—to use the priests' or the archbishops' hats and with these, taking all the parameters of that society onto their backs, to deform the face and preach with their own mask. Those were days of revolution, where the world was turned upside-down! The devil was in the church speaking from the pulpit!

However, this practice was tolerated by the powers of the Church all the way into the Counter Reformation. This is partially because the mask had given up its total resemblance to a demon for a more populous face. Because this contained revolution of a sort, it had become an allowance for the masses (peasants who, in spring, were coming out of a stiff winter and about to be put back to work during the productive season) to blow off steam in the form of laughter and 'carnivalesque' festivities. And so there was established a sort of unspoken pact between servants and masters, where the masters allowed to the servants a ritual revolution in exchange for a year of keeping their noses to the grindstone. It is with this backdrop that the mask, which would later be called Arlecchino, becomes the point of reference and the last hope for a social redemption.

Arlecchino drags this function into the *canovacci* of the emerging Commedia dell'Arte, as we understand it. Arlecchino as a servant never has the right or the opportunity to be the protagonist in the technical sense of the story. He is never the character who guides the action of the scene by his choices and desires. The protagonists are always the other characters: Pantalone, Dottore, the Lovers, etc. All those characters that represent power in society can take the liberty of changing the course of events. Not Arlecchino; without this power he plays on the rebound, reacting and being 'victim' of the main events. But it is this very position, where he becomes a loyal mirror of social reality, that permits Arlecchino to become the focal point of all the people who live everyday in that very condition. First Zanni and then Arlecchino in the *mis-en-scène* becomes the mirror of the people who participated in these social rites. Even in the narrative structure this character is marginalized and so enjoys a pure outlook on the central events of the theatrical representation. Also, in the physical sense, onstage the servant always remains a step behind the master, allowing Arlecchino from the back of the stage to reflect to the audience his own account of the events; using techniques like the 'aside' and the 'mask-shot.' Arlecchino is posited as the pure and critical element of a story that is led on by the masters. It naturally follows that such a character would become the star of such representations.

The character of Arlecchino became so loved in the eyes of the public that he was later permitted to abandon the *canovaccio* and, even centuries later, found himself on stages in cabarets and stand-up clubs in a sort of protest role; a similar polemical role that had taken life between Martinelli and Gros Guilliam, another French comedian from the same time, in which they would insult each other from across the square. Martinelli could by that time afford to do this because of the fame and adoration that Arlecchino had warranted throughout the centuries; he had become the embodiment of the essence of the freedom of expression. From the time of Martinelli to the present, Arlecchino has preserved this function, making it indeed a universal critique through gestural and linguistic expression.

Let us take a closer look at this theatrical phenomenon by investigating the name Arlecchino. For centuries it has been argued that the class of actors, which sprung from the masses, were ignorant of culture and simply populist. But when Tristano Martinelli chose the name Arlecchino for his zanni he was well aware of the reference he was making. In the Divine comedy, Alichino is the name of one of the ten devils that accompanies Dante and Virgil in Hell. How could this be considered ignorance? Aside from this reference to high culture we can trace Arlecchino's roots to various figures in different popular traditions throughout Europe, always representing a sort of devilish servant: Hellequin, Arlequin, as well as many other names of the same root, have too much of a direct connection with the zanni's history to be considered chance.

Even Arlecchino's costume helps tie together this multifaceted character. The base that Martinelli used was the typical dress of the servant: dirty rags cut from plain cloth, as color would have been too expensive. However as the costume became more and more ragged it was patched with different colors and random pieces of found material; it is this added brightness that helps exalt the popular side of the poor servant and functions as a throwback to the first sacred iconographies of the colorful devils. Sometimes these patches would have been cut in the shape of leaves as if this zanni was so poor that he had to resort to stitching his clothes from tree leaves! In these cases the accent falls on the wild nature of the zanni who is a creature much more in symbiosis with nature just like peasant masses that lived on the land and with the animals. Martinelli's original costume, despite undergoing changes throughout the years, stayed true to its first essence. Even the wonderful costume created by Franca Squarciapino, which I had the luck and honor to wear in the version of *Arlecchino Servitore di Due Padroni* directed by Giorgio Strehler at the Piccolo Teatro of Milan, is so ragged that almost every inch has been replaced by some piece of mismatched cloth! So multicolored is this outfit that it makes Arlecchino a continuously moving kaleidoscope. Martinelli, however, had given up the baggy pants and big floppy sleeves typical of the peasant fashion, to suit his needs as an acrobat. The costume became much more fitted in order to highlight the body of the actor: showing off the flexibility and wild pirouettes on stage. Martinelli's Arlecchino has an animal side that is preserved in this very aspect of high physicality, translating into theatrical gestures a wild and devilish unpredictability. In the prototype of Arlecchino, costume and gesture become a fixed symbol: a stunning, acrobatic, unpredictable and colorful character who constantly moves on stage; alternating changes in rhythm, form, energy and volume; captivating the attention of spectators both young and old!

The greatest fascination with this character is in fact the physical and gestural expressivity, which in Arlecchino's case becomes a universal language that serves as a sort of counterpoint of mime to all of his words, making his actions highly rhythmical and musical. In modern theatre practice it is often taught that one should not highlight with gestures what one is saying in the lines of the character. Of course, this is quite right, but we must remember that in the birthplace of Arlecchino and in the world where he became such a famous character, verbal communication was most likely more of an obstacle than an adequate mode of expression. In Italy, even today, but much more so in the medieval and Renaissance world, there was no concept of common language, or *koine*. The fall of the Roman Empire, which had made Latin the official language of commerce and law in Europe (much like English is today), caused a geopolitical fragmentation as well as a linguistic fragmentation. To travel from one town to another, even a short distance, often meant a change in language, and sometimes quite a radical difference. It would be the equivalent today of an American traveling to Germany. Of course it goes without saying that the actors of the Renaissance were forced to learn some essentials of the local language to help the audience follow the main events of the plot. However, what became much more important were the ways in which the actors would try to be understood by gestures and mimicry: making the sounds of the words far more expressive than the semantic meaning. This is the seed of what would later be called *grammelot*, a language, which steers away from the general notion of language, where the onomatopoeia becomes the fulcrum of vocal expression.

The actor who would be playing Arlecchino would have been using a northern Italian dialect, usually originating in the region of Veneto serving as a testimony of popular jargon and ignorance. This is such a harsh and radical dialect, strictly tied to a particular territory and so full of linguistic idiosyncrasies, that even to attentive spectators who are familiar with a similar dialect, it would be quite impossible to follow all of the lines. But Arlecchino is above all the character that needs to sustain communication with the audience, so as to serve his function of critic and show his 'objective' eye. Therefore, from the birth of Zanni\Arlecchino, these characters were inventing a new sort of theatrical language, composed in a score of dialectal sounds, made-up or foreign words, onomatopoeic inventions and gesticulations that became woven into the fabric of this very language. This in itself must be one of the principle reasons that Arlecchino became so popular: the audience is invited to abandon a certain mental concentration and attention to concepts, for a far more playful involvement, childlike and, perhaps, pure.

Now it is opportune to pay attention to the mask. A mask made of dark leather with a red knob on its forehead symbolizing a horn reminds us of Arlecchino's province of fallen angel turned demonic. Yet the mask retains a certain childishness to it along with something a little wild. In the middle of the face two spirals open to form wide eyes, always staring in wonder at everything around them. The two cheeks make a frame of hungry sacks as if eternally empty and ready in any moment to eat, like a rodent, all the food in the world! Every proceeding actor has always adapted the mask to fit their personal qualities, trying to find a point of contact with some animal or another; so that the tradition carries with it masks that remind us of a monkey, a cat, a dog, a pig or a mouse. Although the leather mask in itself is fixed, on the actor's face it becomes multiform and violently communicative. One must only slightly nod the mask forward for it to become aggressive, or incline the head back to present a radiant smile, or even slightly cock the head to one side which moves any audience to compassion. The ability of this mask to morph on stage is one more element that contributes to the mighty place that Zanni holds in the world history of theatre! However, even the fixed expression of the mask is something that must not be underestimated. In the Commedia dell'Arte, due to the presence of the mask, the actors had invented a most extraordinary and efficient technique of communication with the audience: the so called 'mask-shot.' Even if this is not the appropriate context for a detour into this technique, the mask-shot refers to the moment when a character, in order to signal an emotional change and to bring the focus to himself before an important reaction, or even simply to communicate befuddlement, turns the mask to the audience to then bring the focus back on to the scene. This is a magical moment during which the audience is asked to personally invest themselves and participate in the action happening on stage provoking hilarity, curiosity and empathy. But during this magical moment, the mask remains as it is, i.e. fixed and immutable. When pointed to the eyes of the audience the mask becomes a sort of mirror: a physical mirror that reflects the audience allowing them to take a look inside. This technique works with all the masks of the Commedia dell'Arte, although especially with Arlecchino. He embodies—as we have discussed earlier in the chapter—the 'social mirror'; thus, this effect is amplified to giant proportions, so much so that every time Arlecchino looks at us we feel an investment by all the refractions of a series of mirrors, which dig their way deep until we release our childishness in a liberating burst of laughter.

As regards the mask, I can clearly remember the precise day on which that item of leather became the window through which I really met Arlecchino. I had already made my performing debut as Arlecchino with the Piccolo Teatro of Milan, my pride and my ego were near bursting in those days. With sufficient hubris, I was concurrently reciting another version of *The Servant of Two Masters* with a troupe from Rome. In fact, with the Rome Company we toured two performances, alternating *The Servant* with *La locandiera*, both by Goldoni. It was a very tough tour, often two or even three shows in a single day: morning, afternoon and evening. We were all exhausted, perhaps I more than others due to the physical and mental demands Arlecchino required for a single show, sometimes more than two and a half hours on stage. Once, after having performed *La locandiera* in central Italy, we departed for Switzerland. With a long journey behind us, we prepared four performances of *The Servant* in less than forty-eight hours! I was terrified at the prospect, and rightfully so. The first day went well enough, but the next day, after the morning's show, our energies were nearing the zero point. When the evening show arrived we attempted to slow the pace a bit, but it was useless. *The Servant* is a theatrical machine that leaves no way out: either you do it in its rhythm or you do not do it at all. In the middle of the show my head was spinning; I recited with my autopilot engaged. I had no more breath; my muscles were drained. The leather mask was so drenched in sweat that it felt soft on the face and through the little holes for the eyes I saw my fellows on stage like fish in an aquarium of murky water. I was tempted to yell, 'Enough, enough, stop everything!' I was tempted to raise the mask, to apologize to audience and leave the show. It was at that moment that something strange happened. I felt as if the mask was becoming animated with life of its own. It seemed to grasp my face and in a quiet voice, the mask said to me: 'Ok, my friend, now follow me...'

Suddenly my tension and my exhaustion seemed to vanish. I regained lucidity and I waited. Arlecchino made a silent pact with me at that moment and I followed. I did exactly what he told me. At that moment my energy returned. I ceased trying to be interesting and entertaining on stage. I was no longer the star of a show. It was the extraordinary feeling that a weight had been lifted; the responsibility for the success of the show it seemed was no longer mine as the actor. I was becoming the servant. I began to take literally what the other characters were saying. I looked at the world with new eyes. Through those two little holes in the leather mask I began to see the world with the eyes of Arlecchino. Everything was suddenly clear, lucid and objective. My eyes had assumed the same childlike purity of the character. The public noticed the change and their laughter became more animated and they ended the show with a standing ovation. It was a triumph and I, jealous of my secret, felt indeed, like a hero.

But Arlecchino is no hero, nor is he a child. There is nothing immediately infantile about him, save perhaps the exaggeration of certain behaviors. Arlecchino has all of the characteristics, desires, dreams and meanness of an adult man: sex, his rapport with work and hardship, food and so on. But Arlecchino is a-moral (not immoral in the etymological sense of the word), in other words, he has a skewed view in his relationship to reality. He looks at the world with pure and ingenuous eyes, uncontaminated by all of the relational superstructures of society. Arlecchino is not a child. We are the ones who see our childishness in him. Or at least, contained within the theatrical space, of a rapid dream of the possibility for our own revolution: to go back and see with more ingenuity and more purity than we are usually able to do.

Arlecchino is Commedia dell'Arte.

Arlecchino is Carnevale.

Arlecchino is Revolution.

6

PANTALONE AND IL DOTTORE
The old men of Commedia
Peter Jordan

The 1565 diary of Prince Ferdinand of Bavaria contains a description of a performance thought to be the first dated evidence of an improvised scenario. The plot follows what would become a typical theme of the Commedia dell'Arte: intergenerational conflict. In this case, it involves two old Venetians vying for the attentions of two young courtesans. They are tricked and thus frustrated in their plans by two young men and the old men's own servants. The play concludes with the marriage of the young couples accompanied by a Venetian dance performed by the old men (Katritzky 1992: 155). From the outset, therefore, the *vecchi*, and their idiotic amorous pretensions were a central feature of the *Commedia all'Improvviso*, driving the plot relentlessly towards their own comeuppance and the triumph of romantic love. The Venetian reference in the diary is not insignificant. The earliest old man of the Commedia dell'Arte, the Magnifico – later evolving into Pantalone de' Bisognosi – was always presented as a citizen of 'The Most Serene Republic'. The character was originally the other half of a comic duo based around the master-servant relationship. As such, the mask can be said to be the archetype of all subsequent masters, including the Dottore, just as Zanni is the ur-servant from which Arlecchino, Brighella, Truffaldino, Pedrolino and others ultimately derive. There are numerous extant status-based duologues of this type, which were in essence the slapstick precursors of more complex narratives developed by the later acting troupes.

With the advent of company formation and the inclusion of multiple characters – masked and unmasked – the conflict of the generations took place within the specific ambit of the family, where the aspirations of the young were subject to the whims of their fathers. The familial element not only bound the characters more closely together in a web of interweaving personal trajectories, but also provided fertile ground for multiple conflicts. The convoluted amorous travails of the principal lovers could now be further exacerbated by the pulls of filial and paternal love. Overturning the brutal financial and legal reality of sixteenth-century intergenerational relationships in a comic and empowering context, the figure of the meddling paterfamilias was endlessly held up for ridicule on the basis of his highly inappropriate, occasionally sentimental, but more often lustful, designs towards young women.

In a piece entitled 'The curse of old men in love' ['*Biasimo de i vecchi innamorati*'], and probably intended for use in one of the Gelosi company's scenarios, Isabella Andreini begins a 'letter' to her antique admirer with the words, 'If this page could laugh, it would' ['*Se questo foglio potesse ridere, riderebbe*']. She then goes on to express her amused incredulity at the machinations of a superannuated Lothario: 'How is it possible that you have not realized that in that wrinkled forehead, those hairy eyebrows and that pasty face there is little, in fact nothing, conducive to love?' ['*com'è possibile che non abbiate scorto che a quella fronte rugosa, a quel ciglio irsuto ed a quella faccia pallida poco, anzi nulla, si convien amore?*']. She goes on to describe his curved back as a pathetic attempt to emulate Cupid's bow with which he forlornly hopes to loose his love into the heart of his beloved, and berates him for wanting to destroy the happiness of others. Finally, she concludes her ruthless mockery of his fumbling attempts at seduction with 'So, give up this enterprise, and be assured that you would do much better to procure a grave rather than a lover' ['*Levatevi dunque dall'impresa, e siate certo che farete molto meglio a procurarvi sepoltura, che amante*'] (Molinari 1999: 977).

Harsh though these words may seem, they are likely to have provoked merciless gales of laughter from a sixteenth-century audience. Old men were not merely unattractive love matches; they were also dangerously powerful obstacles to be overcome. Often, a bridal pair only met for the first time at their wedding, the decision for the union having been arranged privately between their parents without even minimal consultation of the couple concerned. This was particularly so in Venice, a gerontocracy run by a closed group of leading families, where 'connections' were all-important and romantic love was viewed as a pointless un-remunerative and self-indulgent emotion that had no place in the city's endogamous marriage market. Needless to say, such a situation will be a source of tension to those in thrall to it: the young. Comedy thrives on a steady build-up of dramatic tension and a subsequent release thereof, so plots concerning interfering patriarchs (matriarchs do not usually feature prominently), who seem to have the upper hand until an alliance of children and servants finally outwits them, were dependable crowd-pleasers and therefore money-spinners. In the Corsini collection, some seventeen scenarios revolve around an arranged marriage, which is eventually foiled. Many of the other stories involve cantankerous sex-obsessed father-figures, who are sometimes pitted against their own sons in competing for the favourable attentions of a young female.

The roll-call of geriatric masks includes not only the Venetian Magnifico, Messer Pantalone de' Bisognosi and the Bolognese Dottore (Graziano or Balanzone or delle Cottiche), but also less well-known members of the pantheon, such as, Coviello, Cola, Pasquariello, Tartaglia, Pandolfo, Zanobio, Cassandro, Silvio, Ubaldo, and Ceccobimbi. However, it is Pantalone and the Dottore with their frequently symbiotic relationship that now stand out as the leading exemplars of professional senescence in our current conception of the Commedia dell'Arte. Why this should be so is open to question, although one obvious reason is that a great deal of material on these two characters has survived to the present day. Apparently, there are more extant images of Pantalone than of any other Commedia dell'Arte character (Molinari 1985: 21). Whilst not as numerous, there are also plenty of depictions of the Dottore. On the other hand, another comic duo of senior citizens, Ubaldo and Pandolfo, are only known through the Magliabechiano manuscript (now housed in the National Library of Florence), in which they feature in twenty out of twenty-two hand-written *canovacci*. Yet their roles as obstructive and predatory parents are almost identical to those of Pantalone and the Dottore.

The fact of their ubiquity in both the scenarios and the iconography indicates an audience preference for the pair, who survived the entire two-hundred-year duration of the Commedia dell'Arte, traditionally given its *coup de grace* in the mid-eighteenth century, as a result of Goldoni's 'reform' and his insistence on mask-less '*naturalezza*'. However, Goldoni's position is equivocal. He was both the self-appointed nemesis of the Commedia dell'Arte and, in a sense, its defining preserver. In his 1750 play, *Il teatro comico*, he refers disdainfully to the tired, predictable and vulgar '*commedie dell'arte*', thereby unwittingly unifying the early professional theatre under a single title (Goldoni 1983: 13). Furthermore, in his memoirs, he names Pantalone and the Dottore, along with the servants Arlecchino and Brighella, as the four core masks and the 'primary source of the comic situation' ['*la sorgente precipua del comico*'] (Goldoni 1985: 346), thus isolating and elevating these four principal masks in the eyes of posterity. In seeking to consign the '*Commedia delle Maschere*' to oblivion, Goldoni in fact did more than most to shape and preserve our present-day conception of the form and our assumptions about the archetypal vecchi.

Even without Goldoni's help, the evidence points to Pantalone and the Dottore being not only the principal old masters, but also something of a double act. Time and again, they are paired together in the scenarios. This is particularly so in the Flaminio Scala canon, published in 1611, whose plot outlines purport to be the working *canovacci* (with a few allowances for artistic licence) of the celebrated Gelosi company, which contained such contemporary stars as: Francesco Andreini (Capitan Spavento), Isabella Andreini (Innamorata), Victoria Piissimi (Innamorata), Adriano Valerini (Innamorato), Simone da Bologna (Zanni), Silvia Roncagli (Franceschina), Domenico Bruni (Pedrolino), Lodovico de' Bianchi (Graziano) and Giulio Pasquati (Pantalone) (Taviani and Schino 1986: 117). According to a letter of 1584, de' Bianchi and Pasquati, who had both been associated with the Gelosi for at least the previous ten years, were inseparable. In response to a missive from Vincenzo Gonzaga inviting de' Bianchi to perform in Mantua alongside Diana Ponti and the Desiosi, he replied that he would only come if Pasquati came too, explaining that 'without him he would not do anything good' ['*senza di lui non farà cosa buona*']. Cesare Molinari makes the point that this close partnership may itself have spawned one of the most typical scenes in the Commedia dell'Arte, the rapport between the two old men ['*l'incontro fra i due vecchi*'] (Molinari 1985: 114). In the Scala collection they appear together in thirty-four of the forty comedies.

According to the received wisdom, Pantalone is a Venetian merchant and the Dottore is an academic (of sorts) from Bologna. The rationale is sound. Venice was a major commercial trading port and Bologna is the oldest centre of tertiary learning in Europe. Why a merchant and an academic should be intrinsically comic is less clear. It is, perhaps, rather that the two represented two forms of temporal power: money and education. An early commentator, Pier Maria Cecchini, describes Pantalone as 'never inferior in status to a citizen, or at least a wealthy merchant' ['*non essendo mai detto personaggio inferior di conditione Cittadina, o almeno di facultoso mercante*'] (Cecchini 1628: 25–6). One present-day scholar interprets this phrase as meaning that in the course of its evolution, the character declined from noble citizen to that of 'a debased citizen-merchant' (Henke 2002: 19). However, Cecchini's point seems to be more about status. Pantalone's social position should be sufficient to give him the power and authority to meddle in other people's affairs and to obstruct their happiness.

The early scenarios contain only minimal references to either profession and even then, they have little bearing on the plot. In *Il Pedante* [the pedant], Pantalone goes to the Rialto, pretending to be away on business for the night, so that Cataldo, the Tartuffe-like pedant of the title, can be lured into making a play for Pantalone's wife, Isabella, and subsequently only narrowly escaping castration for his pains (Scala 1992: 227–34). By day, the Rialto was a place of informal dealings between merchants, but by night its thriving community of brothels came to life. This lends a certain ambiguity to the precise nature of the old man's 'business'. The above example should also help to distance the Dottore from the image of the pedant, so popular in the plays of the *Commedia Erudita*. As Kathleen Lea has rightly pointed out, such characters were portrayed without family, whereas the Dottore functioned 'to sustain the part of the second father and old rival lover' (Lea 1962: 40).

Indeed, both characters are overwhelmingly parents or 'guardians'. However, of the two, Graziano (the Dottore) is more likely to appear alone and is not necessarily even cast as an academic. In fact, in one scenario, Graziano is another merchant like Pantalone (Scala: 1992: 149). In *La Fortuna di Flavio* [Flavio's fortune], Graziano is a charlatan drawn into the love intrigue (Testaverde 2007: 9–22). Presumably his highly voluble talent for verbosity is here being marshalled for the purpose of selling spurious remedies and the like. Both he and Pantalone are drawn into potentially fatal sword fights with the Capitano, before matters are resolved and Pantalone's son and daughter are married off to their personally chosen paramours. In *Il Vecchio Geloso* [the jealous old man], the Dottore is billed merely as a friend of the family. Despite his failed attempts to bed Flaminia and having been caught trying to assault the wife of Burratino, a grocer, he is spared the deep humiliation reserved for Pantalone, the jealous old man of the title. In an attempt to prevent his much younger wife Isabella from being seduced, he keeps guard outside the room to which she has retired ostensibly to urinate, exhorting others not to disturb her, as she is performing 'a service' ['*servizio*']. Unbeknownst to him, her secret lover Orazio has previously concealed himself in the room. Eventually, Isabella re-emerges soaked in sweat ['*tutta sudata*']. Pantalone gently wipes her with a handkerchief saying that when these desires come, it is best to satisfy them. Later, it transpires that the lovers broke the bed in the throes of their passion, but most gallingly for Pantalone is the discovery that Isabella was a virgin. Their marriage is thus invalid as it has not been consummated and it is now public knowledge that the old man is impotent (Testaverde 2007: 35–45). Why such a specifically located character should be subjected to such unremitting cruelty and deceit indicates that a closer look at the reality of contemporary Venetian society is needed.

After the upheaval of the Protestant challenge to the Catholic Church and the subsequent 'Counter Reformation' spearheaded by the tortuous and longwinded deliberations of the several Councils of Trent, the spiritual parenthood of the papacy was also reflected in a renewed emphasis on filial obedience to the wishes of terrestrial fathers, and the reinforcement of hierarchical authority in general. This was particularly so in Venice's family-based oligarchy, presided over by an endless succession of elderly Doges, who could only arrive at this exalted position after many decades of service to the Venetian patriciate. However, during the course of the sixteenth century the commercial pre-eminence of the city was in terminal decline. As a result, fathers began deliberately to limit the marriage prospects of their children, in order to prevent the dissipation of wealth and prestige. In contrast to the system of primogeniture that existed elsewhere, Venetians might choose any one of their sons as the most suitable repository of the clan patrimony. The remaining sons were condemned to a life of respectable, but politically and financially impotent bachelorhood. For daughters, the choice was starker: marriage or consignment to a nunnery. If an influential and financially favourable match could not be made, then the latter option was taken or, at best, an unmarried daughter might be permitted to live in a semi-servile state with her married sibling. So there was ample motive (and perhaps, need) to deride Venetian fathers in scenarios that cathartically enforced comic law, overturning the oppressive status quo in favour of the underdog, and exchanging the real political impotence of young patricians with the imagined sexual impotence of their fathers.

Whilst the Dottore also often held and exercised parental power, it tended to be less pronounced. Instead, the Dottore seems rather to have been an incarnated lampoon of learning, tending towards long sententious and often nonsensical speeches in a macaronic mixture of cod Bolognese, cod Latin and cod Greek, which were intended to display learning but achieved the opposite. The best example of the Dottore's pompous pronouncements are to be found in Lodovico de' Bianchi's *Le cento e qundici conclusioni in ottava rima del plusquamperfetto Dottor Graziano Partesana da Francolin* [the hundred and fifteen conclusions in octaves of the more-than-perfect Doctor Graziano Partesana of Francolin]. The self-confessed master of logic begins with the following eclectic insights into the nature of reality and the human condition:

> The flowering rose smells good,
> And the man who walks is not dead
> Someone who is always wrong is never right,
> The ship that is on the high seas is away from port,
> He who does not want peace, let him argue,
> And that which is square is not round,
> And he who does not want to be first, should be second.
> [*La Rosa ch'è fiorida, sa da bon,*
> *E l'uomo che mania, non è mort,*
> *Un che sempre abbia stort, mai ha rason,*
> *La nave ch'è in alto mar, è via dal port,*
> *Chi non vol star in pas, faza costion,*
> *E chi non vol andar pian, camina fort,*
> *E quell ch'è fat a quadro, non è tond,*
> *E chi non vol esser al prim, sippa al segond.*]
>   (Molinari 1999: 929–30)

The remaining one hundred and seven 'conclusions' include such deathless nuggets of wisdom as: today cannot be tomorrow, chickpeas are not like beans, someone who is asleep cannot be awake, someone dead can no longer talk, he who does not study cannot become a doctor, someone without legs will have trouble walking, and summer is hotter than winter. The speech is also interspersed with malapropisms known in Italian as *spropositi*, for example exchanging 'conclusion' for 'confusion'. His final caveat is that, 'Whomsoever says that I am not a Doctor, I prescribe shit in his face' ['*Qui diran che mi non sia Dottor, / Rezipe: al sò mostazzo in cagador*'] (Molinari 1999: 930–4). Throughout the *Conclusioni*, there is a carnivalesque *mélange* of supremely trite observations that juxtapose existential concerns with banalities, often related to bodily functions of a scatological nature. Unlike the rather more interactive discourse of his coetaneous sparring partner, the Dottore appears to enjoy nothing better than expressing himself rhetorically to no one in particular and to everyone in general.

The most detailed early Pantalone material is to be found in the anonymous *Capriccii et nuove fantasie alla Venetiana, di Pantalon de' Bisognosi* [caprices and new fantasies in the Venetian manner, by Pantalone de' Bisognosi]. These contain little evidence that the character is a merchant, let alone that his putative profession has any bearing on his comic potential.

On the other hand, the *Capriccii* abound with references to women, seduction and sex. For example, the homily entitled, '*A i mal prattichi, e desfrenai Zoveni*' ['On the bad practices of unbridled youngsters'] begins something like this:

> Considering, contemplating, and conjecturing about your ill-considered, ill-contemplated and ill-conjectured consideration, contemplation and conjecture, by the considering, the contemplating and the conjecturing of considerers, contemplators and conjecturers, who consider, contemplate, and conjecture considerately, contemplatively and conjecturally.
>
> (Anon 1601)

Thus it continues relentlessly through virtually every possible part of speech and permutation of tense and mood. The ultimate aim of the admonition is to coach feckless young men in the subtle art of obtaining the favours of women. After a series of military metaphors, the youth is exhorted to 'plant his standard' ['*pianta 'l stendardo*']. However, if in spite of one's best efforts 'the fortress should surrender easily to some other magnanimous and victorious Captain' ['*la fortezza se rendesse con facilitae a qualch'altro magnanimo e vittorioso Capitanio*'], then there are always prostitutes available. This cynical conclusion lays bare the fact that Pantalone's advice has all to do with sexual conquest and nothing to do with romance, let alone marriage.

Elsewhere in the *Capriccii*, the content is not merely absurd, it is also vigorously ribald. Nautical metaphors in the *Contrasto de tor, e no tor moier, de Pantalon, e Zan Capella* [dispute over whether or not to take a wife, by Pantalone and Zan Capella] contain patent sexual references, as in, 'By nature, her ships want the rudder straight all the time' ['*Le so barche per natura / Vuol da ogni ora el timon dretto*']. Another even more obvious example comes in the *Contrasto de Pantalon, e la so*

Inamorata [dispute between Pantalone and his beloved]. Using a musical analogy this time, Pantalone brags that the 'master expert will enter with his trombone' ['*mistro esperto intrera co'l so trombon*']. To this, the woman replies contemptuously, 'shame on you, you're no expert at keeping the trombone straight' ['*Vergogneve no se esperto / A tegnir dretto el trombone*']. Whilst the notion of keeping a rudder straight has a certain amount of validity in nautical terms, the same expression, '*tegnir dretto*', when referring to a trombone makes no musical sense at all. Furthermore, in view of the fact that the trombone is unique among wind instruments in that its length can be extended, it is impossible to overlook the patent sexual reference in the phrase.

Similar to Pantalone's monetary power, the Dottore wielded, albeit bogus, intellectual influence in a largely illiterate society. Since the actors of the Commedia dell'Arte were careful not to make any direct assaults on the spiritual authority of the Church, an obvious secular target would have been the university academic par excellence from Bologna, the scholar-windbag. However, according to the earliest reports, the Dottore originally hailed from a small locality called Francolino in the Po delta on the borders of Ferrara and Venice, a common staging post for itinerant actors (Molinari 1999: 929). There is even a theory dating from 1594, which claims that the character derives from the curious mannerisms and habits of an old barber called Messer Gratiano dalle Cotiche. It is said that Lodovico de Bianchi took inspiration from this real-life character, (Lea 1962: 39). The suffix '*dalle Cotiche*' [possibly meaning 'codexes' or 'bacon rinds', or both] was probably an invention typical of the early professionals who delighted in mixing reality with artifice, the prosaic and the absurd, such that the dividing line became deliberately blurred. Maybe his association with the university town came later as a logical corollary to his academic pretensions. However, even with the undeniably Venetian Pantalone, some of his most famous interpreters were not from the city. Giulio Pasquati was a Paduan, Giacomo Braga was from Ferrara, and a 1620 letter from Pier Maria Cecchini refers to a 'Francesco Bolognese' playing the role of Magnifico (Ferrone *et al.* 1993: 291–2). Whilst it is normally assumed that the two characters expressed themselves in their respective native dialects, given the diverse origins of the actors playing these roles, it is more likely that they spoke a more generally comprehensible linguistic hybrid. This was perhaps especially so for the Dottore, as the Bolognese dialect is a good deal more impenetrable than Venetian patois. It is more feasible that the actors playing the Dottore reproduced 'a sort of Sprachmischung which would identify a speaker as being from the north of Italy in general, rather than from Bologna in particular' (Clivio 1989: 220).

Finally, unlike the Dottore, whose costume tended to imitate the sober black of academic dress, with its wide-brimmed black hat sometimes counterpointed by a white ruff around the neck, there seems to have been a deliberately comic inappropriateness in Pantalone's tight-fitting red hose and doublet, and prominent codpiece. Rather than marking him out as a merchant his attire bears an uncanny resemblance to the contemporary dress of young patrician members of the Companies of the Hose [Compagnie della Calza], who were at the forefront of the development of secular theatre and who were also, at that time, feeling the effects of the policy of marriage restriction imposed by their fathers. Furthermore, the iconography of Pantalone indicates that the actors playing the role were robustly built and athletic. This fact seems to have been highlighted rather than downplayed. The overlapping ironies would have been powerfully evident: a young man mimicking an old man mimicking a young man.

Such evidence suggests that the old men of the Commedia dell'Arte, as with the other characters, were not neatly and discretely packaged stock characters, but were rather more complex composites that nevertheless reflected contemporary preoccupations. It also testifies to the subversive and transformative power of the mask, a power that the early practitioners harnessed with ruthless efficiency in a profession 'whose end, both at the first and now, was and is to hold, as 'twere, the mirror up to nature' (*Hamlet*, III. ii. 20–22). The challenge for the theatre of today is to find a relevant application of the Commedia dell'Arte that can appeal to contemporary audiences in precisely the visceral way that the flagship vecchi, Pantalone and the Dottore, went to the heart of social tensions engendered by elders – but not necessarily betters – who held sway over the young, the under-educated and the impecunious.

References

Anon. *Capriccii et nuove fantasie alla Venetiana, di Pantalon de' Bisognosi (di novo posti in luce)* (1601) Vicenza, then Brescia, Italy, 1601 [N.B. The original text has no page numbers].

Cecchini, Pier Maria *Frutti de le moderne comedie et avisi a chi le recita* (1628) Padua, Italy: Guareso Guareschi.

Clivio, Gianrenzo 'The languages of the Commedia dell'Arte', in Pietropaolo, Domenico (ed.) *The Science of Buffoonery: Theory and History of the Commedia dell'Arte* (1989) Toronto, Canada: Dovehouse.

Ferrone, Siro, Buratelli, Claudia, Landolfi, Domenica, Zinanni, Anna (eds.) *Comici dell'Arte: Corrispondenze* (1993) Florence, Italy: Le Lettere.

Goldoni, Carlo *Il teatro comico* (1983) Milan, Italy: Signorelli.

Goldoni, Carlo *Memorie* (1985) Milan, Italy: Rizzoli.

Henke, R. *Performance and Literature in the Commedia dell'Arte* (2002) Cambridge, UK: Cambridge University Press.

Katritzky, M. A. 'The diaries of Prince Ferdinand of Bavaria: Commedia dell'Arte at the wedding festivals of Florence (1565)', in J. R. Mulryne and Margaret Shewring (eds) (1992) *Italian Renaissance Festivals and Their European Influence*. New York: Edwin Mellen Press.

Lea, K. M. *Italian Popular Comedy: A Study in the Commedia dell'Arte, 1560–1620: With Special Reference to the English Stage* (1962) New York: Russell and Russell.

Molinari, C. *La Commedia dell'Arte* (1985) Milan, Italy: Mondadori.

Molinari, C. (ed.) *La Commedia dell'Arte* (1999) Rome: Istituto poligrafico e zecca dello stato.

Scala, F. *Scenarios of the Commedia dell'Arte: Flaminio Scala's Il teatro delle favole rappresentative*, trans. H. F. Salerno (1992) New York: Limelight.

Taviani, F. and Schino M. *Il Segreto della Commedia dell'Arte* (1986) Florence, Italy: Usher.

Testaverde, Anna Maria (ed.) *I canovacci della Commedia dell'Arte* (2007) Turin, Italy: Einaudi.

7

THE YOUNG LOVERS

Richard Stockton Rand

First love, be it romantic projection, physical infatuation, or sacred communion is one of the most meaningful and defining experiences in life and a central plot element in innumerable poems, novels, plays, operas, films and television shows. From *Pyramus and Thisbe* to *The Bachelorette*, romantic encounters have been chronicled in primitive cave drawings, Harlequin novels and supermarket magazines. At this moment, stories of young lovers play out in real time on city streets; in parks, restaurants, cafes and bars; and in virtual time on social media, email and Skype. Whether we are watching a movie, soap opera, or Broadway play, we can find young lovers embroiled in melodramas, romantic comedies, farces, tragedies, chick flicks or animated adventures. Interestingly, young lovers in plays from 200 BC share many of the same traits as young lovers in modern day sitcoms. As Kenneth and Laura Richards point out, they also perform a similar function: "Lovers... served to bridge the imagined world of the play and the actual world of the spectators" (Richards and Richards 1990: 121). The connective thread between the lovers and their audience is, of course, the experience of falling in love, a topic that continues to fascinate and entertain audiences.

Philosophers and psychologists have been trying to comprehend the nature of love for eons and the only thing they all agree on is that love is a mysterious and irrational phenomenon. If we are too forceful in the pursuit of love, we will not inspire love; and if we are too passive, intimate exchange is impossible. Love exists in a precarious and indescribable realm between control and surrender, a place of intense communion that seems to have a will of its own. Needless to say, most of us were unprepared for intimacy when we first fell in love but, whatever our experience, the desire to vicariously re-experience falling in love is universal. The Young Lovers of the Commedia dell'Arte (*gli innamorati*) give us an ideal point of entry into this phenomenon.

Commedia Young Lovers were typically highly educated, but all the education in the world could not help them process hormonal reactions and physical sensations, made all the more intense by the sensual deprivation that characterized their cloistered childhoods. These young lovers discover love in an unprecedented head-over-heels encounter that bypasses thoughtful reflection, plunges them into emotional chaos, and leads them to surrender all restraint to the object of their affection. But an analysis of falling in love does not do justice to the palpable experience of a love-at-first sight encounter. For that, we need to hear from a young lover:

> First there came out a lady. What did I say? A Goddess, rather, who, invited by general applause, released her foot to dance to the sound of a violin, and bound all hearts in shackles. Her greetings were arrows, her curtsies assaults, her movements shocks to the soul, her turns circles of enchantment. She showed herself to be a heaven, in beauty as in trepidation. While I, ecstatic, look at her; astonished, watch her; impassioned, contemplate her; and enamored, adore her, I see that she, by I know not what stroke of fortune, is inviting me to dance....I trembled, I froze, I perspired, I became at one and the same time all fire and all ice, and when I felt her soft hand touch mine, I felt my heart forcibly stolen from my breast.
>
> (Perrucci 2008: 116)

You cannot help but marvel at the histrionics of the young lover. At the same time you cannot deny the authenticity of the love-at-first-sight experience. Despite, or perhaps because of, the sensorial hyperbole, we are catapulted back to the re-experience of sensations and emotions from our own time-stands-still experience of love.

Unlike the earthier more primitive stock characters, Commedia Young Lovers are ethereal, impressionable and more vulnerable to the ways of the world. Originating in the cultured province of Tuscany, Commedia lovers were learned children of bourgeois parents. Though they had memorized the poetry of Cavalcanti and Petrarch and studied the philosophy of Ficino and Landino, their education was based more on moral and philosophical principles than real-world experience. Consequently, they believed that life could be mastered through imitation, memorization, and adherence to prescribed codes. Naturally, it could not, and when life experience did not conform to expectation, the resultant contradiction threw them into crisis. Endearing, comical and exasperating, Commedia dell'Arte pokes fun at the naivety and pretentiousness of the Young Lover.

Early iterations of young lovers were based, in large part, on the amateur actors in the *Commedia Erudita* (CE) – a popular Renaissance recitation presentation for sophisticated and wealthy audiences. The poetry of Francesca Petrarca, or Petrarch, was often featured in the CE, and later incorporated into Commedia Young Lover scenarios where it was equally at home. The following excerpt from Petrarch's "Canzoniere" beautifully captures the prototype's mercurial sensibility:

> Love leads me on, from thought to thought...
> now smiles, or weeps, or fears, or feels secure:
> and my face that follows the soul where she leads
> is turbid and then clear,
> and remains only a short time in one mode:

so that a man expert in such a life would say
at the sight of me: "He is on fire, and uncertain of his state."

(Petrarch 2002: Poem 129)

Though written in the fourteenth century, the experience is one we can all understand.

Young lover prototypes

The look and style of the young lover differs significantly from one generation to the next. One need only compare two flower children at a love-in in the 1960s to a couple hooking up at a disco in the 1980s, to be struck by the difference. Even in the early Roman farces of Plautus and Terence we see very different types of young lovers. Though both playwrights were influenced by the quieter domestic comedies of Greek playwright Menander, Plautus wrote broad farces with childish lovers and Terence wrote gentler comedies with sentimental lovers. A range of young lover types were evident in Commedia troupes, as well. The renowned actress, Isabella Andreini, was sophisticated, highly educated and a "symbol of moral virtue" (Perrucci 2008: 92), while the actress, Teodora Ricci, mistress to Carlo Gozzi, was a "capricious platonic flame" (Lee 1978: 283). Shakespeare took many of his young lovers from Commedia scenarios and he has given us a more diverse array of lover prototypes than any other writer. Some, like Phoebe and Silvius, are simple country folk; while others, like Beatrice and Benedick, are educated aristocrats. When playing the Young Lover, actors should first try and discern the essential nature of their young lover prototype. The following list of prototypes will serve as a starting point from which to analyze, categorize, devise, and embody a range of young lovers.

Table 7.1 Young lover prototypes

Delicate	Passionate	Hopeful	Proud	Narcissistic	Elegant	Despairing	Dashing
Fragile	Affectionate	Expectant	Dignified	Peevish	Attractive	Doubtful	Spirited
Insecure	Eager	Bright	Noble	Petulant	Beautiful	Anxious	Jaunty
Tentative	Enamored	Promising	Virtuous	Self-Seeking	Alluring	Distressed	Impetuous
Sensitive	Adoring	Enthusiastic	Courageous	Selfish	Radiant	Depressed	Bold
Dainty	Smitten	Excited	Boastful	Egotistical	Captivating	Forlorn	Daring
Flowerlike	Infatuated	Overeager	Arrogant	Preening	Brilliant	Hopeless	Peacockish
Graceful	Ardent	Joyous	Pompous	Cavalier	Ravishing	Despondent	Flamboyant
Gentle	Overzealous	Jubilant	Triumphant	Ostentatious	Bewitching	Distraught	Inflated
Tender	Inflamed	Exultant	Vindictive	Grandiose	Dazzling	Suicidal	Majestic

Emotions: The beating heart of young love

Let everything happen to you: beauty and terror. Just keep going. No feeling is final.

(Rainer Maria Rilke)

The flow of emotion plays a central role in the Young Lover scenarios. Though Dario Fo describes Commedia as "Theatre of the Pelvis" (Fo 1991: 36), scenes between young lovers might best be described as "Theatre of the Palpitating Heart," for it is an understanding of heartfelt emotion that actors bring to their portrayal of a character Carl Jung considered "the archetype of feeling" (Moore and Gillette 1993: 136).

When playing young lovers, actors may be tempted to caricature the expression of emotion. Instead, actors should allow the full impact of each emotional event to penetrate to the core of their being and affect both subtle shifts and extravagant displays of emotion. Actors cast in the role of young lovers have to be emotional virtuosos. The following table outlines the range and shades of emotion that actors playing young lovers must be able to express.

Table 7.2 The range and shades of emotion for young lovers

Hope	Empathy	Excitement	Love	Heroic	Attraction	Jealousy
Optimistic	Understanding	Eager	Fond	Confident	Desire	Desirous
Anticipatory	Resonating	Enthusiastic	Tender	Courageous	Enamored	Covetous
Expectant	Consentaneous	Delighted	Attracted	Daring	Turned On	Envious
Confident	Of One Mind	Gay	Desiring	Prideful	Yearning	Greedy
Cheerful	Sympathizing	Invigorated	Adoring	Vindicated	Obsessed	Spiteful
On Edge	Of One Heart	Exhilarated	Reverential	Victorious	Infatuated	Invidious
Hope Against Hope	Consensual	Elated	Addicted	Grandiose	Yearning	Vindictive
On Tenterhooks	Synchronizing	Jubilant	Ecstatic	Triumphant	Palpitating	Vengeful
Hope Beyond Hope	Harmonizing	Frenzied	Enthralled	Monomaniacal	Convulsing	Malignant

Anxiety	Desperation	Sadness	Disgust	Anger	Hate	
Concerned	Dismayed	Somber	Displeased	Irritated	Apathetic	
Worried	Needy	Disappointed	Distasteful	Disdainful	Disdainful	
Distressed	Helpless	Lovelorn	Loathsome	Dismissive	Disliking	
Agitated	Powerless	Mournful	Abhorrent	Upset	Antipathetic	
Alarmed	Yearning	Despairing	Repugnant	Rageful	Hurtful	
Anguished	Pleading	Despondent	Repulsive	Wrathful	Condemning	
Panicked	Distraught	Forlorn	Nauseated	Enraged	Despising	
Full of Dread	Apoplectic	Wretched	Repugnant	Livid	Maleficent	
Tormented	Groveling	Woeful	Intolerable	Furious	Demonizing	

The psychology of young lovers

Though they would undoubtedly take issue with some of my comments, the narcissistic young lovers would be thrilled to know that an essay has been written about them; and yet their journey, if it is successful, will take them from narcissistic self-absorption to intimate partnership. Young lovers start out as "educated innocents" who can only philosophize about love. All their schooling has not begun to prepare them for their first all-consuming crush. These young male and female suitors – not yet sweethearts and a long way from being lovers – must take their first shaky steps into the uncharted realm of intimate encounter alone. The terror of losing a "self" they have not yet had time to discover is intensified by gushing sensations and hormonal changes that make it impossible for them to control their own bodies, let alone remember and adhere to prescribed codes of decorum. Their inability to control their own feelings, and the realization that they have little control over their romantic partner's feelings, or any of the miscellaneous outside forces that dictate their destiny, are what characterize their inner crisis. Their needs and fears – conscious and unconscious – are what drive the scenarios. To justify their behavior and motivate their actions, actors would do well to pinpoint when – in a scene or monologue – specific needs and fears arise. The following list is a good starting point.

Needs

- To be the center of attention
- To control other's perceptions and opinions
- To receive special consideration
- To be a paragon of virtue
- To receive praise
- To be loved unconditionally
- To be worshipped

Conscious fears

- Fear of indifference
- Fear of being seen as unattractive
- Fear of embarrassment
- Fear of losing love
- Fear of being demeaned or mocked
- Fear of criticism and blame

Unconscious fears

- Fear of being unlovable
- Fear of intimate physical contact
- Fear of overstimulation
- Fear of losing control of bodily functions
- Fear of inherent worthlessness
- Fear that love will die
- Fear that love is an illusion
- Fear that love does not exist

Contradictory forces

> But no matter what his suffering, the Lover knows the fierce and terrible joy
> at the heart of all things.
>
> (Moore and Gillette 1993: 136)

The beating heart of the young lover is gripped by conflicting impulses and paralyzing contradictions. While attempting to control their emotions and retain some semblance of autonomy, they yearn to shed all restraint and merge with their lover. Unable to tolerate the tension of these opposing forces, the lovers' carefully crafted personas begin to fall apart. Embodying this experience requires the actor to physicalize the whole gamut of young lover impulses and desires. Whether they are swept up in romantic ecstasy, consumed with jealousy, or crushed by perceived betrayal, their emotional swings – *experienced alternately or in rapid succession* – propel the action and make them both heartrending and farcical.

With an understanding of prototype, emotional life, and character psychology, the actor is ready to apply specific rules of comedy to the unfolding action in a Young Lover scene:

The seven rules of comedy

- Action evokes immediate reaction
- Lovers careen from one emotion to another
- Scenes are driven by life and death appeals
- Accusations and attacks cut to the quick
- Words strike straight to the heart
- Contradictory impulses are physicalized: longing and fear/chastity and lust/ eloquence and tantrum/fragile and willful
- Resolution is magical: defenses dissolve, wounds magically disappear, faith is restored, lovers are conjoined

Playing the performance

Commedia troupes were – for all intents and purposes – street performing, and as any street performer will attest, holding one's audience in a crowded marketplace demanded story-telling expertise, on-the-spot invention, and physical and vocal virtuosity. Audiences were, at least initially, Italian, and though Italian audiences differed from one province to another, Italians, as Luigi Barzini notes, share an appreciation for a particular type of performance: "Inevitably Italians are tempted to applaud more those performances which stray dangerously farthest from reality… and still manage to be effective, convincing, stirring or entertaining." (Barzini 1964: 90)

In addition to bringing a daring theatricality to their performances, actors playing young lovers consciously give a dual performance. At the same time that the actor is entertaining the audience, the character is performing for his or her sweetheart; yet neither performance is anything less than genuine. Poetic serenades, emotional displays, and an orchestrated mating dance are consciously designed to be both visual spectacle and heartfelt appeal. Actors playing young lovers bring themselves to both events – the theatrical performance and the romantic encounter – as if they were wholly unprecedented, life-changing, and miraculous.

Physical virtuosity

It is important to remember that most Commedia scenarios were skeletal outlines, giving actors plenty of opportunity to improvise, embellish, and define or redefine a given prototype. All of this was accomplished using one body and one voice. The physical life of Young Lovers was balletic and bird-like, with actors rising, suspending, swooping, inflating, deflating, and impulsively interacting to create a dizzying display of emotions and reactions. The receiving and sending of breath and impulse was the catalyst for emotional engagement, with inhalations lifting them to the heavens and expirations spiralling them down to earth in a parabolic plight of paramours. In the animal kingdom, the mating ritual of the bird of paradise comes closest to the courtship dance of Commedia Young Lovers. To attract a mate, the bird of paradise preens and transfigures itself in a performance that is both riveting and ridiculous. Though each species has its own dance, all the mating dances are desperate, over-the-top performances artfully orchestrated to win a mate.

The vocal life

Let [lovers]… make an effort to master perfect Italian, with a Tuscan vocabulary… / One should also be acquainted with figures of speech and rhetorical tropes… figures to add beauty… figures used to add energy… / That is how he must be – perfectly trained.

(Perrucci 2008: 104)

Unlike other prototypes, actors playing young lovers needed to be well-versed in the poetry and philosophy of love. Research, study and practice were essential: "Those who delight in acting the difficult role of the lover enrich their minds beforehand with a pleasant quantity of noble speeches pertinent to the variety of subjects the stage requires." (Richards and Richards 1990: 126)

Prompt books of romantic conceits and philosophy were invaluable to actors who played young lovers: "The *concetti* with which [an actor] should be equipped… should be collected in a book…under the headings of requited love, contempt, pursuit, rejection, disdain, jealousy, peace, friendship, merit, departure, and so on." (Perrucci 2008: 105)

In addition to having poems and passages at the ready for any occasion, actors playing young lovers needed to pinpoint and master the following rhetorical conceits.

Rhetorical conceits

- Alliteration – the repetition of speech sounds in a sequence of connected words.
- Allusion – a reference to a well-known person, place or event. Allusions may be concrete or abstract, referring to particular persons or things, or to generalized experience.

- Antithesis – contrast or opposition in the meanings of contiguous phrases.
- Assonance – repetition of vowel sound, especially in stressed syllables.
- Exhortation – emotional appeal designed to encourage, motivate or incite.
- Hyperbole – bold overstatement used to express strong feeling or produce a strong impression.
- Interrogation – asking a question as a way of making a person reconsider his or her wrongdoing.
- Invocation – the act of invoking or calling upon God.
- Irony – the pointing out of an incongruity between reality and appearance.
- Metaphor – a word or phrase denoting an action or thing is transferred to a different action or thing.
- Petrarchan conceit – detailed, imaginative comparisons applied to the object of one's affection.
- Prosopopea – representing an abstract quality or idea as a person or creature.

Once performers understand the inner life and master the playing of their young lover prototype, an understanding of archetype and dramatic journey gives their performance resonance and enables them to take their audience on a transformational journey of self-realization and communion.

The lover archetype

The Lover is the archetype of vivid, spontaneous and channeled Libido.
(Moore and Gillette 1993: 135)

Though Commedia Young Lovers were often portrayed as childish and immature, their journey represents a universal rite of passage that needs to be understood in a larger evolutionary context. Commedia lovers are more than cartoon characters. They are mythic archetypes working through fantasies and conflicts in the pursuit of sacred love. Central to the young lovers' quest is their belief that each human being has a soul mate, someone destined to be their partner, someone with whom they can experience wedded bliss and eternal fulfillment. But, as Kierkegaard notes: "Perfect love means to love the one through whom one became unhappy" (Auden 1966: 201). As young lovers see one another's insecurities, flaws, and inherent egotism, their childlike fantasies of love are shattered and they are made miserable by what they believe to be the death of love. Yet it is the destruction of their fantasy that gives them an opportunity to see the whole of one another and find an intimate connection they will need if they are to survive long enough to raise the next generation of young lovers.

Dramatic journey

In any good story the hero grows and changes, making a journey from one way of being to the next: from despair to hope, weakness to strength, folly to wisdom, love to hate, and back again. It's these emotional journeys that hook an audience and make a story worth watching.

(Vogler 1992: 17)

The catalyst for the young lovers' dramatic journey is the life force and interpersonal dynamism generated by the shared fantasy of "true" love. This energy enables the lovers to respond to changing circumstance, overcome obstacles, gain insight into themselves and the world around them, and learn life lessons they will need on their next journey. Though we laugh at their dilemmas and overreactions, Commedia Young Lovers are experiencing the same emotions and are motivated by the same hopes and fantasies that have motivated all young lovers.

The journey of young lovers incorporates elements of both myth and drama, including inciting incident, fantasy or vision, encounter, trial, reversal, rising action, sacrifice, climax and resolution. We can chart their journey by breaking down a scenario into beats and assigning each beat an evocative title that captures that beat's essential action or theme. Reviewing the list of beat titles gives the actor a clear picture of the twists and turns and overall emotional arc of a scenario:

- Love awakened
- Intoxicating feelings
- A match made in heaven
- Flirtation or betrayal
- Recrimination and blame
- Lovers no more
- Bitterness and loss
- Brooding melancholy or hopeless despair
- An overture of reconciliation
- A heartfelt appeal
- Hope revived
- Contrition and forgiveness
- Romance and rapture
- An unexpected trial
- Threatened by outside forces
- All is lost
- Devising a plan
- A glimmer of hope
- Divine intervention
- Love conquers all
- Lovers united
- A communion of souls

The mythic journey of young lovers

the soul cannot exist in peace until it finds its other...

(Campbell and Moyers 1988: 198)

Young lovers embark on a mythic interpersonal journey that, if successful, corrects a basic opposition between female and male and unites the two lovers in a sacred marriage. Supernatural forces play a critical role in this shared rite of passage and, according to Jung, "...the feeling that some supra-personal force is actively interfering in a creative way... in accordance with a secret design" (Jung 1964: 162). Jung believed that "it frequently takes a special crisis in [the lovers'] lives to make them understand it" (Ibid., 134). Schopenhauer described the ritual as the merging of an objective event – the two individual journeys – and a shared subjective event – love. He believed "that both kinds of connection exist simultaneously, and the selfsame event, although a link in two totally different chains, nevertheless falls into place in both, so that the fate of one individual invariably fits the fate of the other..." (Jung 1970: 12) We see the forces of fate made manifest in Perrucci's "Dialogue of Disdain and Reconciliation":

SHE: What spell holds me back?
HE: What unknown power hinders me?
    (Perrucci 2008: 116)

Unconscious forces also lead them to play a dual role in the scenes. In Perrucci's "Dialogue," the young lover knows *unconsciously* that s/he must play the role of the Young Lover: appealing and accusing, demanding and rejecting, and ultimately overcoming threats and obstacles after testing the mettle of a bond that s/he knows must be strong enough to weather the trials of sixteenth century life. Somewhere amidst their impassioned soliloquies; their yes-and-no, act-and-overreact duet; young lovers realize that – in the space between his eyes and hers – lives a truth. They share a destiny. Though they may resist the bold acknowledgment of love, their stichomythic battles are leading them inexorably to a precipice, a climactic trapeze leap, an act of bravery in a dramatic high-wire encounter that, if reciprocated, will seal their bond, change their lives, and place them firmly on destiny's path. In the audience, spectators mirror the invisible neural impulses that they *sense* in the lovers onstage, so if actors onstage believably capture the experience of love, then spectators in the audience will re-experience what they felt when they first "played" the role of lover. So, although we make fun of their courtship rite, young lovers remind us of a time when we were first transformed by love. But the crises of the young lovers must seem real and their struggles genuine for their journey (and our experience of their journey) to be transformational.

> Love is indeed a wondrous master, Sir,
> Whose teaching makes us what we never were,
> And under whose miraculous tuition
> One can suddenly change one's disposition. (Act III, Sc. 4)
>   (Molière 1971: 77)

If the young lovers knew that – as was the case in the sixteenth and seventeenth century – by the time they were thirty they would be aging Pantalones and Pantalonas watching their children fall prey to the same forces that felled them, they might not succumb as readily. As Luigi Barzini reminds us, "...behind the skillful performances, real life... can be sordid, tragic, and pitiless... a mortally dangerous game... always difficult" (Barzini 1964: 101). Love, too, is dangerous. It exerts its mysterious sway upon us and defines the course of our lives, at times, against our will. Once the young lovers have been formally wedded, they will reckon with the harsh realities of life, but they mustn't know that plague is rife, most children die in infancy, and what initially attracted them to one another will fade away in short order. They must not have time to think beyond a heart-throb or question their heartfelt conviction. Whether they are deluded by destiny or unconsciously co-conspiring with some divine force, it matters not. Lovers will continue to play the role of lovers, onstage and off, or life will not go on. Indeed, the actors must play their parts with heartfelt conviction in order to inspire and re-inspire our belief that love conquers all.

Conclusion

Looking back two millennia, the integration of young lovers alongside the masked stock characters of early Roman farces created a more integrated and humanistic form of comedy that evolved into the Commedia dell'Arte. As troupes were embraced by rich patrons and a more diverse audience, scenes and plays of young lovers became more meaningful and more complex, addressing issues of intimacy, autonomy, and identity. Scenarios performed by Commedia troupes were witnessed by Shakespeare, Lope De Vega, Molière, Farquhar and Marivaux, all of whom went on to write plays where young lovers addressed moral and ethical issues that went far beyond anything seen in the Commedia dell'Arte. Many of these same plots and prototypes have been adapted and passed down from generation to generation in countless plays, films, operas, and ballets. We find variations on Commedia Young Lovers in an astonishing range of work, from *Les Liaisons Dangereuses* to *Barefoot in the Park*, *Madame Butterfly* to *Cinderella*, and *Giselle* to Disney's *Brave*. As the world changes so does our view of young love and the way in which it is depicted. It may be difficult to see a connection between Pyramus and Thisbe, Frankie Avalon and Annette Funicello, and Robert Pattinson and Kristen Stewart, but they are all young lovers who faced trials in different cultures at different points in time. Though the canon of dramatic literature is filled with young lovers who meet tragic fates, tragedy has no place in the lives of young lovers in the Commedia dell'Arte. Though they may be blindsided by complications, thwarted by unforeseen threats, and derailed by tragic turns of event, confidants will come to their aid or protectors will arrive at the eleventh hour to magically resolve all disputes and renew our faith in love's ability to overcome all obstacles. It is comedy after all. Young sweethearts must be united, physical and divine energies must be conjoined, and newlyweds must consummate relationships, bear children, rear the next generation of young sweethearts and perpetuate the species. That is their role in the human comedy and they must play it with such passion and grandeur that we all long to be young lovers again.

References

Auden, W. H. (1966) *The Living Thoughts of Kierkegaard*. Bloomington, US: Indiana University Press.

Barzini, Luigi (1964) *The Italians*. New York: Atheneum.

Campbell, Joseph and Bill Moyers (1988) *The Power of Myth*. New York: Doubleday.

Fo, Dario (1991) *The Tricks of the Trade*, Trans. Joe Farrell. New York: Routledge.

Jung, Carl G. (1964) *Man and his Symbols*. New York: Doubleday & Company Inc.

Jung, Carl G (1970) *The Structure and Dynamics of Psyche*, (Collected Works of C. G. Jung, Volume 8), Trans. Gerhard Adler, R. F. C. Hull. Princeton, US: Princeton University Press.

Lee, Vernon (1978) *Studies of the Eighteenth Century in Italy*. New York: Da Capo Press.

Molière, Jean Baptiste Poquelin De (1971) *The School for Wives* Trans. Richard Wilbur. New York: Harcourt Brace Jovanovich.

Moore, Robert and Douglas Gillette (1993) *The Lover Within*. New York: William Morrow.

Perrucci, Andrea (2008) *A Treatise on Acting, From Memory and by Improvisation (1699)* Trans. and Ed. by Francesco Cotticelli, Anne Goodrich Heck, and Thomas F. Heck. Maryland, US: Scarecrow Press, Inc.

Petrarch (2002) *The Canzoniere* Trans. A. S. Kline. Online. Available at: www.poetry intranslation.com/PITBR/Italian/PetrarchCanzoniere123-183.htm (accessed 19 August 2014).

Richards, Kenneth and Laura Richards (1990) *The Commedia dell'Arte, A Documentary History*. Oxford: Published by Basil Blackwell for The Shakespeare Head Press.

Rilke, Rainer Maria (2012) Trans. Anita Barrows and Joanna Macy. Online. Available at: http://exceptindreams.livejournal.com/388734.html (accessed 19 August 2014).

Vogler, Christopher (1992) *The Writer's Journey: Mythic Structure for Storytellers and Screenwriters*. Studio City, CA, US: Michael Wiese Productions.

8

READING AND INTERPRETING THE CAPITANO'S MULTIPLE MASK-SHAPES

Mace Perlman

Who is the Captain, that mask-character of the Commedia dell'Arte whom we may also know as il Capitano? He is the fifth wheel, the odd man out, the loner who appears now and again in the northern Italian theatre, alongside those basic four masks: Pantalone, the Dottore, and the first and second zannis, the ones who have endured through the centuries. Sometimes referred to as a lover, so fixed in his obsessive passion that he has transformed into a mask, he is always an outsider. Whether Spanish in Naples or Neapolitan in Venice, his speech is that of the *forestiere*, or foreigner, an intrusive and mysterious presence, "not from around these parts." While Brighella often assumes a new identity as part of a play's intrigue, the Capitano seems to have generated, and now embodies, a mystery as part of his very being. Francesco Andreini's Capitano Spavento da Vall'Inferna (Captain Fright of Hell Valley), an early and seminal figure in the centuries-long line of Capitani, claims a mythic origin story of a birth in full armor, nursing on hemlock, setting the stage for a lifetime of otherness.

Though we know him to be a soldier, we rarely see him engaged in battle. His military profession provides, more than anything else, a convenient excuse for his being away from home. Whether or not he has ever seen combat—and his stories are always much in question—his military identity means that he need not actually engage himself in any real-world employment. "First into battle and first in retreat," he seeks out confrontation and competitive comparisons, as they are his only guarantee of his own existence; yet he flees them the moment they show any sign of materializing into action.

Scholars and actors alike may easily reduce the Captain to a stereotype of the loudmouth, but cowardly, soldier. Yet there is something deeply moving in the character's need for approval and, when faced with rejection, the refuge he takes in self-aggrandizement. More than any of his fellow mask-characters, the Captain is his mask; the very fact of masking itself describes the essence of the Captain's personality.

All masks seem to hide and protect, on the one hand and, paradoxically, also reveal the wearer's essence. In the case of the Captain, however, this double nature of the mask is uniquely in evidence. In reality, there is no masked servant or masked old man in the streets beyond the walls of the theatre; yet the soldier's armor, and even facial armor such as the visor, protects him from harm and both proclaims and hides the wearer's identity. Of all the Commedia's characters, the Captain, as a professional soldier, most requires a mask; and having donned that piece of self-protection, he discovers that his heart is just as badly in need of a visor as his body. The Captain's mask is more than a mere mask: it is the emblem of a soul-in-armor.

As we read of the Capitani of the Commedia dell'Arte and of their kin in the plays of the early modern theatre, we encounter a long line of "braggarts" from Plautus' *miles gloriosus* to Shakespeare's Pistol, Falstaff, and Parolles; we encounter a number of so-called "liars," protagonists of eponymous plays by Corneille and Goldoni, among others. We also encounter "seducers," most famously in Molière's *Dom Juan* and in Mozart and Da Ponte's *Don Giovanni*, who in turn descend from Tirso de Molina's *burlador* or *Barber of Seville*. Lastly there are the "dreamers," from Don Quixote to Andreini's Capitan Spavento and Shakespeare's Don Adriano de Armado.

These descriptions of braggart, liar, seducer, and dreamer may close us off from the inner need of the all-too-human character they describe. What may seem a true description of character in a play title or epithet begins to melt away in actual performance, if the mask's gaze, illuminating the conscious being within, is willingly and generously offered up by the masked actor. Whether playing for an audience or watching another actor play in the mask, I have experienced and witnessed a kind of empathic sharing occur, wherein judgment is suspended, at least momentarily. When an actor acknowledges and shares with an audience member through moment-by-moment *colpi di maschera* (eye-to-eye "gazes of the mask"), a window is opened directly into the experience of the actor-as-character.

True for all the mask-characters, this is true above all with the Captain: his mask is his protection, allowing him to be truly vulnerable with the audience. Like Hamlet, who can only reveal his true self once the court has left the stage ("now I am alone! / Oh what a rogue and peasant slave am I" (III. i. 549–50), the Captain must remain on guard with the other characters of the play. In the company of his fellows on stage, he must keep up the appearances and rhetoric of one who performs conquests, whether military or amorous; yet when alone with us, his listeners, his "co-mates in exile," he may reveal his true vulnerability. Like Achilles' heel, his eyes are chinks in the armor, through which we may watch the masked actor-in-character's struggle to come to terms with the gap between his own self-image and the outside world's view of him. This is a much more interesting proposition than simply to witness the vain tirades of an overconfident extrovert, which only in any case constitute an outer shell. The mask provides both the exterior shape the character has borrowed or fashioned over the course of a lifetime; and, by way of the actor's gaze, it offers us an amplified view, much like the cinematic close-up, into the interior life of the human being.

I would like to examine three mask-shapes, as offered by the masks of the gifted maskmaker, Renzo Antonello, of Vicenza, Italy; to "read" them as I have read them over the more than twenty-five years I have played in them and watched others play;

and to examine in more depth the character of the Capitano Spavento, which the third form suggests. Together with the reader, I hope to gain some insight into the human character that produced these forms as a response to life, that is, as the result of encounters with other human beings (see Figures 8.1, 8.2, 8.3 and 8.4).

The "crazed" Capitano

Figure 8.1 Example of a "crazed" Capitano mask by Renzo Antonello, from author's collection.

The first shape presents the wide face of a character who appears dog-like, a hound-dog. He is both expansive and explosive, and the jagged staccato energies of his brows and cheeks jut out like fault-lines around the central core of the forward ski-slope of his nose. As in all the half-face masks, the nose at the mask's center presents the fundamental relationship he has with the world. Like the ski-slope, his nose is designed for his ego to achieve peak velocity before jumping out into the unknown space of social interaction. That slope is buttressed, for further support, at the nostrils; yet the impact of his collision with social reality is registered in the quaking of his brows and the shock-lines of his cheeks. Only his sloping nose's first attempt at approaching the world and the bean-shaped ovals of his eyes show a legato flow. All the rest of him is a staccato zigzag of stops and starts as a result of his rigidity, the rigidity of his boasts, his vaunts and tall tales. He is "crazed" like ice, "cracked and crazed" like a mountain caught in the midst of a great earthquake. The hopeful energetic flow of his approach, when met with the world's rejection, has nowhere to go but to splinter into fragments. In Renaissance comedies, he bears names like Spezzaferro (Iron breaker), Frangipietra (Stone fracturer), and Terramoto (Earth shaker) (cf. Boughner 1954: 53–4); yet it seems clear that his threats of extreme destruction echo and mirror injuries sustained to his own being and sense of self. Like Shakespeare's King Lear—brought to the breaking point, and struggling not to weep, not to flow—who threatens, "I will do such things…What they are, yet I know not, but they shall be / The terrors of the earth" (II. iv. 280–2), the Capitano must invent new rhetoric to match the size of his need to be appreciated.

Like Lear confronted with his daughters, the gap between the cracking Captain's own self-assessment and the status accorded him is more than his mind can encompass rationally. Lear's madness, as unique a conception as it is, is not unlike the "crazed" Captain's, the almost inevitable physiological result of enforced rigidity. If weeping is not an option—and here we see a certain idea of masculinity operating in connection with dignity and self-worth—then the slide into madness becomes a very immediate possibility. Continuing with the same speech, "You think I'll weep," says Lear, "No, I'll not weep: / I have full cause of weeping; but this heart / Shall break into a hundred thousand flaws, / Or ere I'll weep. O fool, I shall go mad." (II. iv. 282–6)

Is it his sense of honor that so constrains him? Certainly the Spanish origins of the mask provide ample justification for invoking honor as that which refuses to yield in the Captain. But something more universal is at work as well, which is why the mask may represent any nationality. He may be from any one of a number of nations, yet his sense of belonging to a specific nation is important. He values his connection to his tribe, and he needs his entourage of hangers-on. Lear, deprived of his followers, seems to have lost his ability to command. How does one maintain dignity when confronted with a failure to lead and a failure to impress?

I have introduced Lear into this examination of the Capitano's ever-present potential for madness not only to suggest that the mask-character's struggles may be tragic as well as comic; but also because the shape we are examining, the shifting tectonic plates of this Captain's precarious sense of self, also help us to perceive the comic in Shakespeare's tragic protagonist. When Lear threatens, "I will do such things…What they are, yet I know not, but they shall be / The terrors of the earth" (Ibid.), he is deep into the comic territory of the Captain, who claims superhuman powers, who is a close friend of the Gods and has dined with Death herself.

The intrusive Captain

Figure 8.2 Example of an "intrusive" Capitano mask by Renzo Antonello, from author's collection.

A second shape for the Captain is that of the intruder, aggressive and direct. While the last mask shape was open and expansive, this mask is focused along his barrel of a nose, expressing a core of ever-energized invasive intention. While the last Captain presented only the staccato energies of fire and earth, this mask has more air to fan the flames of his eyebrows. There is also a very noticeable twist to the nose, which speaks of the effort involved in pushing his agenda out into the world. When that agenda is rejected, and, indeed, his nose ends in a flattened space of collision like all three of the Captains we are examining, the eyebrows fly to the heavens, suggesting the plumes of a helmet. When first attempting to bring this mask to life some twenty or so years ago, my imagination seized upon Mitteleuropa as the mask's origin; and no sooner had I chosen a Teutonic register than the tightness of the mask combined with his driving and intrusive intention made it clear that he was feeling squeezed by "de Poland on ze von side... unt ze Franz on ze ozzer... unt all I need is a little LEBEN-STRAAAAUM!"

What continues to amaze me in this mask is the license it affords the wearer to enter into what seems as dangerous territory as the Nazi invasion of Poland, and then to unleash grateful waves of laughter in an audience. Perhaps, just as Lear's denial of weeping invites our tears on his behalf, the more this mask forbids laughter, forbids mockery, the funnier he becomes. Again, in attempting to control that which is uncontrollable—tears, laughter—some deeply human instinct is aroused in us as audience members. The Captain mask lays bare this all-too-human need to control; and by demonstrating its futility and ultimate failure, releases us from its clutches.

This intruder's soaring brows, so different from the mountain crags of the crazed Captain, result from his ego's collision and negotiations with the world. I have always read them as flames of narcissism reaching to the sky: a "feather in his cap," a wave of an overhead arm to a distant lady, a fluttering flag in the wind to announce his entrance. Yet perhaps they may also represent lightning-bolts of energy channeling down from the heavens into the spot between his eyes, a spot that corresponds to the center of the actor's chest, the terribly fragile ego of the Captain.

That wounded and fragile soul at the core of all this bluster takes refuge in another comfort that we have only thus far seen in passing: his vanity. It was there all the time, of course, in the overblown boasts of the *miles gloriosus*. The crazed Captain may take pride in the beauty of his heroic feats, but this Captain, so aggressive in his self-assurance, so single-minded in his intention to seduce, seems fastidious in his attention to detail. The mask's features invite a vertical physicality and a tightness. He is both "up" and "tight" and, in performance, I have discovered that this "up-tightness" seems to invite the idea of a corseted personality. Like the famous Italian poet, playwright, and aesthete Gabriele D'Annunzio, who had a rib surgically removed to afford him a more pleasing bow, there is something of the dandy in the Captain, who will undergo all manner of suffering and deprivation to please the object of his affection. French foot soldiers, marching under Napoleon, soaked their tights the night before battle to better display their fine, muscular legs... and died in great numbers of pneumonia. Tragic or comic? I am reminded of Malvolio's constrictive cross-gartering, and of Cyrano's feasting on a single grape; in the Capitano lies an ascetic as well as an aesthetic impulse.

The visionary Captain

Figure 8.3 Example of a "visionary" Capitano mask by Renzo Antonello, from author's collection.

Deprived of his followers, deprived of his conquests, whether military or amorous, the Captain must resort to his own imagination to produce the world that the outer world has failed to produce for him. This imagination, both in the case of Andreini's Capitano Spavento and Cervantes' Don Quixote, is fueled by literature, which provides examples of earlier heroes and their epic battles. This is where the distinctions between history and myth may blur.

If the long nose of the intrusive Captain may bring to mind Pinocchio, this Captain's nose seems to lift and float as it pushes forward. Rather than colliding with the wall of reality as the tighter mask does, or shattering like the more rigid, crazed Captain, this mask opens into a new reality, a reality of its own creation.

Where does the liar end, and the mythmaker begin? Rather than dedicating precious energy to self-defense, this mask seems to invest its energy into the act of vision itself. With owl eyes, Minerva-like, this Captain gazes into the fog of his own isolation and produces adventures worthy of a hero. If the character's vision is sufficiently luminous, reality may recede to make way for the Captain's waking dream.

Though the Captain has always been a loner of sorts, this Captain risks a more radical isolation, losing touch with the outside world. More than ever, he needs a companion who can translate for him and serve as his bridge to the audience, a servant who can provide an earthy counterweight to his unbound musings, an anchor or tether to the world of the everyday and its practical requirements.

The concentric circles of this Captain's eyes suggest a lack of sleep; and indeed this character may be a burner of midnight oil. Food is generally not of great interest to him, certainly less important than his passion for knowledge. He is a voracious reader of texts and his project is "fabulous" in more than one sense. He is a maker of fables, the greatest of which is himself. Thus, he is fabulous and the world he has created is fabulous as well. Only his servant notices the unpaid bills, the empty larder: the material unsustainability of his project.

Figure 8.4 Example of il Dottore mask by Renzo Antonello—compare to the "visionary" Capitano mask in Figure 8.3.

An interesting parallel can be seen in the features of this mask to that of the Dottore: while he lacks the Dottore's sensuality (together with his bloated center), his eyebrows, like the Dottore's, are great arches, the product of his dreaming. It is by no accident that the energies at work in this mask produced the two parts of Francesco Andreini's *Bravure del Capitano Spavento*, or the two parts of Cervantes' *Don Quixote*, or even the two parts of Goethe's *Faust*. It is as if, having explored a world of his own making, this mask must create other worlds to explore, breaking the very frame of the work and the world he has established. There is a circularity to the Dottore's features and a circularity to his speech patterns and reasoning which keep him revolving and circling back in a closed loop; but the concentric circles of the visionary Captain produce ever-expanding worlds of thought and narrative.

If the comparison between Capitano Spavento and Don Quixote is a natural one since both undertake fantastic journeys of the mind, struggling to maintain a sense of self, caught between the exalted and the mundane, with often comic results, Spavento is, from the very first words of Andreini's text, already fully masked and actively engaged in dialogue with his servant, Trappola. There he remains, as if the one could not exist without the other. His mask may be fully formed; yet from the very first, his identity is unstable and somehow incomplete. We are aware of the herculean effort he must make to maintain his sense of self; and from the outset, it is clearly a problem of vision, both literal and figurative:

> If Mars is the God of battles (as some say), and if I am Mars, by Mars transformed into Mars, why do I not see, far from my person, the war in Flanders, beloved object of mine, and all its events? And why am I not possessed, together with the name, of [that name's] full effect and power?
>
> (Andreini 1987: 13)

For Spavento, names contain numinous magic and utterances are transformative. Simply by pronouncing himself to be the god of battles, he expects to be possessed of all that god's attributes; yet his human senses fail to confirm his imagined powers. Trappola's ready reply must both sooth and rebalance his master:

> What's happening to you is like what happens to someone who, gazing too fixedly at the sun at that hour when it shines most brightly, and blinded by

the splendor of its most refulgent rays, sees not, and knows not. You are so intent on this Mars of yours, and you behold him so fixedly, that clouded over by the splendor of his Deity, you neither see nor know who you are.

(Andreini 1987: 13)

"You are an ignoramus," retorts the Captain, "and know nothing of Philosophy." He then sidesteps any further debate by giving Trappola tasks to accomplish, re-establishing his dominance as the master of his servant. A public display of warriors on horseback is to take place in a few days, and "I must," insists Spavento,

> more than any other, appear superbly armed and furnished, being as I am the Generale generalissimo; go now to Vulcan my armorer, and tell him from me, to make my arms far more shining than the Sun at its brightest so that their splendor may rob the viewers of their vision.
>
> (Andreini 1987: 13)

Trappola must hold the Captain's imagination in check, reminding Spavento who he is. But the Captain is a master of evasion, when his dreams are at stake. He continually returns to the question of his own nature and identity, asking Trappola for confirmation; yet he also refuses Trappola's answers when they fail to meet with his liking. On the one hand, he vaunts his attributes in a manner typical of any "braggart" soldier, insisting that Trappola "keep his eyes and ears intent" on everyone he meets, lest he should encounter some

> hero or demigod burning and sparking with the lit desire to hear of my condition... you shall say that I am the Captain Spavento of Hell Valley, nicknamed the Diabolical, Prince of the equestrian order, Trismegistus, that is, very great defier, very great wounder, very great killer, tamer, and dominator of the universe, son of the Earthquake and the Thunderbolt, Death's relation, and a very close friend to the great Devil of Hell.
>
> (Andreini 1987: 14)

On the other hand, Spavento has even more questions on the topic of Spavento than he has answers. While the *Bravure* begin with the previous tirade of grand defiance ("bravura" in Italian), they also continually play upon Spavento's limitless capacity for wonder.

> I wonder at Nature, who having made for me a heart so great, did not in like manner make me a body to match its greatness, for done had she that, I would have a body larger quite than the globe of the moon.
>
> (Andreini 1987: 255)

Trappola proceeds to show Spavento that he is a giant, but when his master begins to want to pull down stars to serve as buttons for his riding-coat—and strike a blow to the Prime Mover—Trappola turns to convincing him that he is tiny. "But how can this be," asks Spavento, "that I am great and tiny of stature, as you say, and at one and the same time?" (Andreini 1987: 256)

Spavento cannot imagine himself to be both "grande grande" and "picciolo picciolo"; yet of course, he is just that. His very name shows us this dual nature: it is the active verb, "I frighten"; and it is the noun for "fright." Is the Captain the great dominator of all creation, as he broadcasts himself to be, as even the famous tower of Pisa recognized (Andreini 1987: 157), kneeling before him as he passed and remaining, so as to honor him, frozen in that position to this very day? Or is he himself trapped in a mask of Fright, a mask of his own making, locking him into a constant state of startled fear, a fear perhaps of his own inadequacy?

Francesco Andreini published the first part of his *Bravure* in 1607, only three years after the death of his beloved wife and stage-partner, Isabella. His stage career was behind him and his magnus opus represented in large part an attempt to defy death, not only the death of his wife, but the death of his art and the potential death of his renown. Nature, Time, Fortune, Fame, and Death herself figure as major protagonists in the work, whom Spavento both claims as close friends and even lovers, engaging in a kind of celebrity namedropping; and whom he also takes on as his arch-adversaries. In posing Spavento's urgent question, "Am I grande grande or am I picciolo picciolo?" Andreini identifies the core preoccupation of the Capitano, and stands at the threshold of our modern sense of self. Like Hamlet, another dreaming human coping with loss, Andreini's Captain crawls between heaven and earth, part angel, part animal; and for all his humanist culture, we can make out his progeny in Sid Caesar's German doorman, in Seinfeld's Kramer, in Chaplin's dictator, Hinkel… anywhere delusions of grandeur spring from fears of insignificance.

References

Andreini, Francesco (1987) *Le Bravure del Capitano Spavento* a cura di (ed. by) Roberto Tessari, Pisa, Italy: Giardini Editori e Stampatori.

Benini, Enrica (May, 1979) "Un bullo barocco: Capitan Spavento" *Quaderni di Teatro*, vol. 1, no. 4, 128–41.

Boughner, Daniel C. (1954) *The Braggart in Renaissance Comedy: A Study in Comparative Drama from Aristophanes to Shakespeare* Westport, CT, US: Greenwood Press, Publishers.

Shakespeare, William (1974) *The Riverside Shakespeare* (ed. by) G. Blakemore Evans *et al.* Boston, US: Houghton Mifflin Co.

9

LE SERVETTE IN COMMEDIA DELL'ARTE

Julie Goell

> Theater spectacles foster fornication, adultery and prostitution and must therefore be avoided at all costs. To attend is to participate in mortal sin. If it is a sin to do, then it is also a sin to see it done. Their themes are love... not rarely do they mention unmentionable body parts and, shameful to say, prescribe potions which cause virginity to return or bachelors to find a wife.
>
> Destructorium Vitiorum, Allessandro Anglio,
> First Milanese Council (Taviani 1969: 115)

In his book, *The Italian Comedy*, Duchartre (1966) argues that the female roles were underdeveloped due to women being banned from playing onstage for the first sixteen hundred years of Christianity. In the repressive atmosphere of the sixteenth century, it is hardly surprising that little documentation remains of these comediennes. Their contributions were silenced, forgotten, their successes unsung, operating as they did, in the margins of social acceptability and on the wrong side of the law. Proof of their presence may be gleaned in the yellowed list of dramatis personae, like shadows to be shape-shifted only by living actresses—to infuse them again with the voices, flesh and guile for which they were known.

Religious and political forces in the Italian states conspired to ban women's participation in theater. The region was under pressure from the Inquisition, resulting in papal bans against women performing.

The actors who played Arlecchino, Scapin, and Scaramouche, were men of letters who left detailed performance notes called *zibaldoni*. Everisto Gherardi, Luigi Riccoboni, Francesco Andreini, Flaminio Scala, Andrea Perrucci, Tiberio Fiorilli, and Domenico Biancolelli all left detailed records of their theatrical exploits. The actresses who played the servants, Columbina and Franceschina left no such traces. No poetry, ballads, letters, dialogues, scenarios, or personal reflections have been found. Most women of the time neither read nor wrote, but even if they could they were not likely to flaunt their illicit activities on the stage.

One outlier was Isabella Andreini, an accomplished actress who moved with her husband's company, I Gelosi, from Padova to Paris on the wave of the Commedia diaspora as companies fled the restrictions of the Inquisition in Italy. She was a famed woman of letters, who was celebrated in the literary circles of her time. She is best known for her portrayal of the *prima innamorata*, to which she bequeathed the name, Isabella. A literary phenomenon of her time, she challenged notions of what was acceptable for women in the arts, altering perceptions about them forever.

In England—in the time of Shakespeare, Sheridan, and Congrieve—female roles were played by men. The Kingdom of Naples, which included Rome, provinces to the south, Sicily, and Corsica, were under Spanish dominion for two hundred years, coinciding almost to the year with the Golden Age of Improvised Comedy in both countries. The Inquisition accompanied the Spanish occupation and southern Italy was compliant in restraining artistic expression. Laws were issued directly from the Vatican in Rome where, according to Goldoni, women's roles were still played "by beardless youths and clean-shaven men." (Duchartre 1966: 262)

However, in northern Italy, The Inquisition notwithstanding, the Serenissima, The Most Serene Republic of Venice, was lax in its enforcement. There, women had tread the boards since the earliest documented professional company in 1554.

Under the Inquisition women were prohibited from inheriting or owning property, retaining child custody, voting, or being educated. Considered chattel, they were not accorded the rights of citizens. Independent, smart, and outspoken women were burned at the stake. Against this backdrop of sanctioned subjugation, stands the figure of the *servetta*, the diminutive name for the whole class of female servants in Commedia, who were feisty, honest, good-hearted, and smart.

Were we to rate the Commedia characters on an intelligence spectrum from low to high, it might look like this: Pedrolino, Pantalone, Capitano, Dottore, Arlecchino, the Innamorata, Columbina, Brighella, Franceschina. While Franceschina is clearly at the top of the heap, Columbina, with her coy innocence still manages to outwit her male counterparts.

The role of the smart female character in the comic tradition continues to this day. Women in comic roles both then and now are not to be trifled with: Alice Cramden, Sybil Fawlty, Roseanne Barr, and Rosie O'Donnell, to name a few. As in the Commedia dell'Arte they reprimand, threaten, and cajole the master, in words no son, daughter, neighbor, or male servant could get away with.

How is this breach of class accomplished? The servetta is forthright and unafraid to stand her ground for a just cause. She does not hesitate to harangue her master for his vanity, lust, and greed. She lives outside the laws that govern social status and acceptable social behavior. Men shrink before her superior, if rustic, intellect.

The roles, originated in scenario form to be improvised and later fleshed out as full-length plays, are key to unlocking the mystery that continues to shroud the condition and the contributions made by the servette. Ruzzante, Barbieri, Marais, Molière, Beaumarchais, Goldoni, and Gozzi recorded scripts from scenarios of their own devising, working out the details in their own companies. As noted by the theater historian, Eugenio Levi, in his preface to *Il Meglio di Goldoni* (Goldoni 1958), plays of the Commedia and post-Commedia cannon have survived a long practice of being reduced to scenario form, reconstituted into full-length scripts by satirists, from Menander to Ted Hoffman, only to be winnowed down to a basic plot line so some other playwright could retell the story in his own words.

An example of this expansion and contraction of a story line is *Phormio*, by Roman playwright Terence, which was the source for *Les Fourberies de Scapin*, by Molière, and was most recently updated and premiered in London as *Scapino* by Jim Dale. In *The Imaginary Invalid* by Molière, the female servant, Toinette, serves as a fulcrum on which the plot teeters and ultimately resolves. Rarely was a comedienne placed in such a pivotal role. A veritable Scapin in petticoats, she unmasks Argan's vanity, his hypochondria, and restores the family to sanity. One would assume the actress who played Toinette had to have been a seasoned professional.

To discover more about the role of the servetta, boil down *The Imaginary Invalid*, to its bare bones scenario form. From there flesh out the plot and dialogue in your own words. Try it out in a different period, with different genders, and different hotspot issues. This process will place you squarely among the ranks of Commedia practitioners while revealing the foibles and the power of the servetta.

Two monologues

Of the serving women there are two basic types. Columbina, the *seconda innamorata*, is usually embroiled in a parallel love story to that of the prima innamorata. In these proto-*Upstairs/Downstairs* scenarios, Columbina usually serves the prima innamorata, Isabella. Typically, Columbina is young and gullible, flirtatious yet innocent. Romantically paired with Arlecchino, Colombina can be crafty, coy, and smarter than her lover. In *Prologue*, below, she appears under the name Ricciolina.

The other female servant in the zanni family is Franceschina, the housekeeper with seniority and a set of keys to everything. Sometimes called the Bawd, Franceschina has the experience that Columbina lacks and there is not a father she cannot get the better of. Franceschina may be romantically involved with Capitano or one of the Magnifici, one of the socially superior older men. It is interesting to note that a Magnifico may take up with a servant, but for a young Innamorato to choose her, she must be a Lover in disguise, or an unwitting victim of mistaken identity. An Innamorata would not be paired with a serving man unless it were really her lover in disguise, come to test her fidelity.

Following are two entertaining monologues of unknown origin, which allow the two characters to speak for themselves. The speaker in *The Melon Peel* is a Franceschina, older, wiser, and seasoned in the ways of love.

> I know all too well where my mistress is headed: the precipice I toppled over when I lost my virginity. It was all on account of a melon peel! Oh when I think of it, I could die of shame. I can't recall it without streaking my cheeks with tears. Let me bring you up to speed ladies and gentlemen: As a young girl, beautiful, round, and soft as a turtle dove, a certain young Spaniard from my town fell in love with me. With much passion he says to me, "Ahi, querida, que me matais, mi corazon esta perdido. Yo me muero por ella." One day I find myself in a garden, in a white mantle, graceful as a swan, yearning to be tamed. He tries to kiss me, but not as the French do. Putting

my hands up to stop him as he comes toward me I slip on a melon peel and fall supine. The fresh breeze lifts my skirts. My poor lover runs to cover me, but tripping on the same peel, he falls on top of me in such a manner that the thrust makes my belly swell.

I had to leave my village in shame. Imagine my father's disgrace! Fathers everywhere make this same mistake: they marry their daughters off when they want, but daughters marry when they have to. Testimius, the jailed scholar, speaking in his book, On Base Incarnality, finishes with this verse, "Young maiden, winsome, and lithe, who would tempt each passerby, first be a bride, and then a wife."

(*The Melon Peel*, translated by Julie Goell)

The following piece, entitled *Prologue*, is a rant delivered by Ricciolina, a Columbina prototype, about her co-workers in an itinerant company of improvising actors. A more apt title might be 'The Inadvertent Prologue'.

Oh yes I'm angry. Just because I'm your servant doesn't give you the right to treat me like a slave. Not only do I cook your meals, chop your wood, haul your water from the well, go to market, wash your shirts, starch your collars, and stitch your clothes, but now you want me to play the prologue. Hah! I'd rather see seven husbands die first.

Oh my, dear ladies and gentlemen, circumstances have forced me to become a servant to these actors. They led me to believe that life on the road was an adventure; a potpourri of pleasures spiced with happy camaraderie and garnished with delights. They even had me believing that soon I'd be rich, but they and all their glorious promises turn out to be deceivers. Let's talk about the life of the happy comedian: rain, ice, snow, knock-kneed horses, broken wagons, impertinent porters, and insistent coachmen. Enough! As for me, they make me sick. Listen up, in the morning my lady summons me, "Ricciolina, bring me The Lover Fiammetta, I want to study my lines." Lines! Hah! Pantalone: "I told you to fetch me The Letters of Calmo at the post." Fetch! And Zanni: "Hortatio's Vacation and the Hours of Recreation." The Dottore: "The Dictae of the Doctors and the Novus Polianteus." El Capitano: "Ricciolina, te quiero portarme Las Adventuras del Capitano Matamores." And Franceschina wants La Celestina to learn to learn to play the hussy. The Lover: "Ricciolina, bring me The Letters of Plato." It's Ricciolina here, and Ricciolina there. Ricciolina, Ricciolina, all at once and at the same time. And now you want me to play the prologue? To hell with the lot of you! I don't have to do it, and I won't do it. Dear ladies, and gentlemen, I am going in now. If they yell and beat me, someone please come and save me, I beg you. And if that someone needs a maid, I will always serve him faithfully. Goodbye. Goodbye.

(*Prologue*, translated by Julie Goell)

This piece is based on the comedic concept of Prologue by Way of Lament, and was used as an introduction into which the actress could smartly drop in characters from any scenario. By complaining about them, doing cruel imitations and parodies, and poking fun at their literary choices she effectively introduces them to the audience. In the right hands *Prologue* is a tour de force showpiece. From it we may conclude that the performer entrusted with the piece was savvy, funny, competent and sympathetic.

Using the deductive approach suggested by Carlo Mazzone-Clementi and Jane Hill in their article, "Commedia and the Actor" (Mazzone-Clementi and Hill 1974), through the actor's art, one might recreate the barnyard dynamic of the Commedia family of characters. This method is as close as it gets to the Commedia essence that is *improvviso*. If there is no element of improvisation, it lacks the flavor of the form.

As to the growing repository of scholarly resources on the servette, there is now a wealth of source material available online, facsimiles of original editions from the sixteenth century, open-source and free. Recent translations of some of the editions listed below are awaiting analysis and further study in this fascinating and growing body of work relating to the role of women in Commedia dell'Arte.

References

Bouffoneries. Cazilhac, France, 1980–1996. Vol. 3, pp. 47–48 and Vol. 11, p. 41.

Duchartre, Pierre Louis. *The Italian Comedy*. New York. Dover Publications, INC. 1966. pp. 262–86.

Goldoni, Carlo. *Il Meglio*. Milan, Italy. Longanesi & Co. 1958. Introduction by Eugenio Levi.

Mazzone-Clementi, Carlo and Hill, Jane. "Commedia and the Actor" *The Drama Review* 18, Dell'Arte, Inc. 1974.

Taviani, Ferdinando. *La Fascinazione Del Teatro*. Rome. Mario Bulzoni Editore. 1969.

10

CARNIVAL, COMEDY AND THE COMMEDIA

A case study of the mask of Scaramouche

Stephen P. J. Knapper

Adapted from the doctoral thesis of the same title by
permission of the Estate of Stephen Knapper

The mask and carnival

The first depiction of the figure (Scaramouche) appears in Jacques Callot's celebrated series *1 Balli di Sfessania* of 1621. Without doubt this was the iconographical model for George Sidney's 1952 Hollywood version of the stage figure such that Stewart Granger's first appearance is preceded by a frame portraying a poster for the travelling players, depicting Callot's *Scaramucia,* and the first costume he wears as Scaramouche is surely modeled on this, as was Carlo Boso's Scaramuccia in the mask's return to the theatre in 1986. Working from the findings of Anna Maria Evangelista, Sara Mamone has noted the similarity between many of the names of the masked figures and actors from these companies (Gli Uniti, Gli Accesi, I Fedeli and I Confidenti), among them the Neapolitan, Giovan Battista Fiorillo, *in arte* (who played) Scaramuzza, who, in the light of evidence recently discovered, seems likely to have been the model for the engraving subtitled Scaramucia/Fricasso (Mamone 1992: 185). It should be noted that while Scaramucia appears in the engraving with Fricasso, seemingly about to bump into each other in what appears to be a comic duel scene, another engraving in the series has Taglia Cantoni, who seems the double of Scaramucia, facing a Fracasso, again in a duel scene, seemingly the reverse of the former.

Neapolitan anthropologist, musicologist and theatre director Roberto De Simone sees the origins of the mask of Scaramouche in a practice indulged in by young men at carnival time in Southern Italy who would parade beneath the balconies of young women holding a pole suspended from which was a pot to which a rope was attached. When the rope was pulled, a giant phallus would spring out of the pot and frighten the women back into their houses. A folk tale is told of how Sgarra-Muscia, a phallus, finds a uterus on a mountain where she has been abandoned by two testicles who had accompanied her there and left after she had told them they were good for nothing. She offers him a home for life if he will help her but without those *due coglioni*. This primal association between the mask and the phallus is highlighted in De Simone's interpretation of its etymology: "a fusion of the dialect words *sgarrare* (to err in a duel) and *muscia* (a cat, and sixteenth century symbol for a uterus), the compound effect being that of a character failing in the act of love. Further connotations of impotence are indicated by the fact that *muscio* also means soft, and *muzza* means cut off. Here, we have something of a paradox with a carnival practice symbolizing virility juxtaposed with a name signifying impotence. (De Simone interview 1993)

Further complications arise from the word *sgarrare* implying connotations of duelling – albeit in this sense metaphorically – which can also be ascribed to the etymology of the Italian noun *scaramuccia,* sharing the same meaning as the English word *skirmish* and the French word *escarmouche,* all stemming from the Frankish root *skirmjan* (to defend) which is also the origin of the verbs *schermare* and *escrimer* meaning to fence. Indeed the Scaramucia of Callot's engraving is wielding a rapier and a cloak in a very competent *en garde* position about to incompetently collide into the back of Fricasso. There is a paradox inherent in this double image whose binary nature is typical of the Mannerist principle of *discordia concors* – the juxtaposition of opposites in the same form. Callot has been described as one of the last exponents of Northern Mannerism and not only may his images be a potentially rich source for information about outdoor staging but they may also supply us with keys to the origins of the masks in carnivalesque festivities and folk festival. In spite of this a theatre historian who has made a valuable contribution to the artistic context of the early Commedia dell'Arte has found himself so impressed by the power of the images that he is moved to conclude his discussion of them by saying:

> The etchings are intertwined with the identity of the "commedia dell'arte". The prints stand out not only for their excellent technique but also because they represent a different vision of the theatre. The gestures are at once ambiguous and celebrative, energetic but poised, grotesque yet amusing. This is part of the commedia dell'arte that escapes narrative; refusing to be captured by the literary, it eludes meaning.
>
> (Hauser 1994: 212)

What then of the meaning of Callot's Scaramucia, or for that matter De Simone's Sgarra-Muscia, or even of what I have chosen to give the generic name "the mask of Scaramouche" throughout this study? Can they therefore be interpreted at all or is that meaning fundamentally ambiguous and ultimately ironic? The meanings signified by the name Sgarra-Muscia, or Scaramucia, are simultaneously double, moving between the said and the unsaid, creating a third meaning of something between the two – thus a comic effect is obtained. As Sgarra-Muscia may be at the same time virile and impotent, Scaramucia is competent and clumsy. Scaramouche may have two or more different though not necessarily opposed signifieds. Thus the name Scaramouche may connote both skill with a sword and impotence, the further historical irony here being that in a sketch for one of the masques at the Stuart court made by Inigo Jones derived from Callot, there appears "a fantastical lover

Scaramuzo"; and the beatings suffered by the Scaramuzza of *La Lucilla Costante* at the hands of Volpone and Policinello are hardly indications of a mighty swordsman.

The Scaramuzza of the Fiorillo plays is certainly referred to as a parasite, a character with antecedents in *Commedia Erudita*, Roman and Greek Old, Middle and New comedy. Indeed Enid Welsford has identified this figure with the Greek laughter-maker, the origin of the medieval buffoon. New light may be thrown on the Scaramucia of Callot's *Balli di Sfessania* by the probability that the Sfessania dance, referred to in Del Tufo's 1584 poem describing the Neapolitan carnival as having magical powers of healing, was a derivation of a Maltese *moresco* sword dance.

In relation to the scripted plays by the early modern *comici dell'arte* Flaminio Scala and Silvio Fiorillo, the characters of Scaramuccia and Scaramuzza supply us with plentiful examples of grotesque realism in their debasing of official discourse to the realms of food, sex and the body. Similarly, in its ironic movement from significations of potency to impotency (Sgarra-Muscia); martial competence to clumsiness (Scaramucia); man to woman (the transvestite strategies of Scaramuccia in Scala's *Il Finto Manto* and Scaramuzza in Fiorillo's *La Lucilla Costante*); servant to master (Tiberio Fiorilli's Scaramouche), the paradox inherent in the shifting early modern understandings of the mask evokes the dualistic and ambivalent structures of carnival laughter.

The inclusion of the name Memeo Squaquera in Scaramuzza's genealogy is an echo of the traces of the character from Fiorillo's plays and another concrete link with the world of carnival. There is the connection of this Neapolitan mask, which was also figured by Callot in his *Balli di Sfessania* chapter; the Scaramuzza of the Silvio Fiorillo plays is a captain's parasite, typified by devices Bakhtin described as grotesque realism, ambivalence, heteroglossia and carnival laughter. (Bakhtin 1993: 162) In so doing he forms part of a long tradition in Western European theatre stretching back to Aristophanes wherein the servant, or slave, becomes the advocate of the people and has a critical, mocking and levelling relationship with power, personified in these plays by the braggart captains.

The mask in performance: Scaramuccia/Scaramuzza in the scripted plays of the *comici dell'arte*

We can examine the character of Scaramuccia/Scaramuzza as it appears in three fully-scripted and published plays in early seventeenth century Italy: Flaminio Scala's *Il Finto Marito* (1618), Silvio Fiorillo's *Li Tre Capitani Vanagloriosi* (1621) and *La Lucilla Costante/Con le ridicolose disfide e prodezze di Policinella (1632)*. Particular attention will be paid to Fiorillo's plays, examined for the first time in English, as they are the closest evidence of the mask that can be linked to a known actor. It is not until 1618 that the character makes his first entrance onto the pages of the actor Flaminio Scala's, *Il Finto Manto* as a *primo zanni*: the cunning, first servant.

Scaramuccia is an adaptation of Pedrolino from the earlier scenario *Il Marito*, published by Scala in the collection entitled *Il Teatro delle Favole Rappresentative* (1611) (Salerno 1967). Pedrolino appears in all of the scenarios in this collection and is the character with the most verbs attributed to him in the *didascalies* (stage directions), an indication of his importance in the organisation and execution of the action. Tim Fitzpatrick has made a detailed study of the relationship of the scenario to the fully-scripted play in a well-argued attempt to ascribe the oral derivations of Commedia dell'Arte in performance and concludes that the character of Scaramuccia is pivotal to the action of *Il Finto Marito,* devising and resolving the intrigue to the lovers' satisfaction and in the process thwarting the libidinous and mercenary intentions of the old men. In a division of the exposition of the action into four main categories (movement; interpersonal acts flowing from role and plot function; perceptions and communications in the fictional world; and emotional reactions to events in that world) the character of Pedrolino in the scenarios is thus described:

> the preponderance of the sub-category of informing points clearly to his plot-function as facilitator, achieved by means of generating and passing information and instructions to the other characters. His role as enabler (deciding what is to be done and giving orders to bring it about) is also predominant. Correspondingly slight is the emotional dimension, although he too can suffer depression – though it is usually brought on by his plans (rather than his amorous intentions) being thwarted by circumstance or the machinations of the old men.
>
> (Fitzpatrick 1995: 322)

Scala, who collected, notated and published the scenarios nine years before he published the fully-scripted *Il Finto Marito,* was an experienced actor and *capo comico* of several companies between the late sixteenth and early seventeenth centuries. His career spans the "golden age" of the Commedia dell'Arte and he worked with many of the great performers associated with this period.

During the time he worked for the Uniti troupe, he probably first worked with the actor Giovanni Pellesini, *in arte* Pedrolino, who, Siro Ferrone informs us, was one of the last *buffoni di corte* (court jesters). It is not known if Scaramuccia was played by Pellesini or by Giovan Battista Fiorillo. Scala and Silvio Fiorillo played together in the Accesi's tour of France in 1606, evidence of a possible collaboration between the two following publication of the play. It has even been suggested that the organising Scaramuccia is a cipher for Scala himself.

La Lucilla Costante/Con le ridicolose disfide e prodezze di Policinella was Silvio Fiorillo's second scripted play to feature the character of Scaramuzza. The character first appears in the earlier *Li Tre Capitani Vanagloriosi* and is described as a *parasito napoletano* (a long-winded parasite) and serves as a comic foil to the hyperbolic Spanish Capitano Mattamoros, played by Silvio Fiorillo himself. Judging by the information contained in Fiorillo's letters of the time and company lists from theatres in Genoa, Florence and Naples, it is reasonable to assume that Scaramuzza was played by his son Giovan Battista Fiorillo. In an article published in 1882 Achille Neri reports a contract of the Uniti troupe playing in Genoa in 1614 (playing in Florence later that year) including Silvio Fiorillo and his sons Giovan Battista and Girolamo, the former playing the part of Scaramuzza. Ulisse Prota-Giurleo published a contract in 1962 in which it is stipulated that in the 1615 season the Neapolitan Teatro della Porta della Calce was sublet to Silvio Fiorillo and Stefano Castiglione, *in arte* Fulvio, and that the company included Scaramuzza (Neri 1882).

That Giovan Battista was the first actor we can reliably trace to have played the part is backed up by extant primary sources in the letters from Silvio Fiorillo held in the archives which show that he effectively managed Giovan Battista in the early stages of his career before he took on the mask of Trappolino in 1620. (Fiorilli 1619) It was probably then or sometime soon after that his younger brother, Tiberio, took on the mask of Scaramuzza. The only record we have of Giovan Battista's Scaramuzza is in Silvio's first published play, *Li Tre Capitani Vanagloriosi,* while the subtly different Scaramuzza of *La Lucilla Costante* is more likely to be a transcription of Tiberio's early interpretation. The common factor to both their histories is that of their writers, therefore before looking at the mask of Scaramuzza we are obliged to consider the history of its first transcriber, Silvio Fiorillo, *in arte* Capitan Mattamoros and also very probably Policinella.

The prologue for *Li Tre Capitani Vanagloriosi* follows the standard procedure for the scripted plays of the *comici dell'arte* by addressing the readers as spectators. There are a number of examples in the action of what appears to be direct address to an audience in Scaramuzza's speeches. He has a role akin to that of the parasite of classical and renaissance comedy, debunking the hyperbole of the boasting captain while maintaining a symbiotic relationship of support for his master in confrontational scenes with the other captains and servants. His importance to the plot is minimal and yet he appears in the opening scene and closes the comedy with a direct address to the audience. Scaramuzza is the only other character who speaks in Neapolitan which, for the most part, is used to offset the classical allusions of his master's bombastic Spanish. Put in the context of statements by Fiorillo in the prologues of his other works, there seems to be something of the political, albeit covert, in this use of dialect. (In *Li Tre Capitani*) there is an undeniable mocking tone in the asides Scaramuzza gives to the audience after hearing the captain's boastings, indeed the boastings themselves are made more ridiculous by the invention of new words in a hybrid Hispano-Italian.

That Silvio Fiorillo managed to perform *La Lucilla Costante* with Spanish protection, (the play is dedicated to the Spanish governor of Milan) besides performing as the self-parodying Spanish captain Mattamoros is a testament to his ingenuity. The trait obviously ran in the family as his son Tiberio was eventually to combine the roles of captain and parasite and take them to find incredible success in Paris as Scaramouche, finding favour at the French court, not only for his undoubtable skill as a performer, but also because he mocked the Spanish.

The man and the mask: The myth and material history of Tiberio Fiorilli

At the age of eighteen Tiberio Fiorilli was kicked out of the family home to find his fortune on the road, becoming an actor by chance with a company of Commedia dell'Arte players in Fano and finding the perfect mirror of his own gluttonous character in the mask of Scaramouche. Angelo Constantini's disputed biography, *La Vie de Scaramouche* (1695), follows Scaramouche's adventures around Italy from Naples to the North and back again, to Sicily, Rome, Vienna and, finally, Paris.

Tiberio was Silvio's son and Giovan Battista's younger brother. It must be assumed that he began to play the role of Scaramuzza sometime after 1620 when Giovan Battista began to play the mask of Trappolino. There is evidence that he was in Paris in 1644 and may have first gone there in 1639. He developed a relationship with Cardinal Mazarin whose support in the French court matched that from the Medici court. In various stories there is evidence of the actor's wit in gaining favour from his masters and at the same time tricking them into offering some kind of material reward, especially in the court of Louis XIV. A special relationship with Louis XIV was perhaps forged in the early years of his long Parisian sojourn, when we are told that he held the infant king in his arms and was pissed upon for his efforts. According to Constantini, Scaramouche's revenge took many forms over the years, tricking Louis, and even his mother, out of money at any opportunity. (Scott 1995: 85)

Scaramouche's relationship with Cardinal Mazarin in France in 1647–58 is deemed worthy of satire. In a complicated semiotic process of ironical significance it can be seen that comparison (of Mazarin) with the Scaramouche type is intended to denigrate, but the nature of that type still remains unclear. *Les Terreurs de Mazarin* could refer to the pictorial representation of Callot's Scaramucia, but the reference to his harangues at the Petit-Bourbon and Palais Cardinal (Palais Royal) theatres is a clear identification with the interpretation of the actor Tiberio Fiorilli. The fact that Scaramouche is given the title of *Capitaine et Générale,* perhaps provides a clue to the role he played in those theatres, particularly as the harangue was a favoured device of the braggart captain.

The master and the mirror: Scaramouche and Molière

Published in 1670 the engraving by L. Weyen – *Scaramouche enseignant, Molière étudiant* – is perhaps the only image we have of a seventeenth century actor transmitting his knowledge to another by studying his comic grimaces with the aid of a mirror. This particular image is a satirical depiction of two actors and therefore its overriding intention is the denigration of its target, Molière. It represents the culmination of similar attacks on Molière throughout the 1660s. These years marked his consolidation and confrontations with the targets of his satires at the court of Louis XIV after being granted the use of the theatre in the Palais Royal (formerly known as the Palais Cardinal as it had been built by Richelieu) in 1660, to be joined by the returning Italians, led by Tiberio Fiorilli, in January 1662. Citing the performance of May 1659 at the French court in which Scarmouche played alongside Jodelet as evidence of the cross fertilization of French farce and Commedia dell'Arte, it would seem that the conditions for the joint influence of the farceur tradition and of the Italians were indeed present in Paris when Molière began to play there in 1658. Gaston Hall, however, posits that the most discernible influence Fiorilli (and Jodelet) had upon Molière was in the transition of his style of acting from an essentially tragic register to a comic, even buffonesque, one which he dates from his interpretation of Sganarelle in *Le Cocu imaginaire* first performed at the Petit-Bourbon on 28 May 1660. The mocking portrait of Molière in poetic and critical works attribute parts of his costume, his facial appearance, his acting style and even the composition of his comedies to Scaramouche. There is an emphasis on the *naturel* quality of Scaramouche's acting providing its appeal for Molière. We are specifically informed that it was his postures and his grimaces that Molière imitated and striking iconographical evidence of this has already been pointed out in a comparison of two independent portraits of the two actors; the posture of both actors owes much to the feet positions of courtly dance.

It is of course in *Le Medecin volant* that Sganarelle appears in Molière's dramatic canon for the first time. The character is roughly sketched out and was to change substantially in the later plays, *Sganarelle, ou le Cocu imaginaire (1660)*, *L'Ecole des maris* (1661), *Le Mariageforce* (1664), *Dom Juan ou le Festin de Pierre* (1665), *L'Amour Médecin* (1665), and *Le Médecin malgré lui* (1666). Molière himself played all these roles and they represent a movement away from the scheming valet, or *fourbum imperatur,* of the Mascarille type which he had played to great acclaim in *L'itourdi* and *Les Précieuses ridicules* and was only to return to in the *persona* of Scapin in *Les Fourberies de Scapin* in 1670.

There is ample iconographical and documentary evidence to suggest that Scaramouche was indeed the Italian counterpart of Sganarelle, at least for the manner in which he was played. It is however difficult to argue convincingly a direct derivation for the Sganarelle of *Le Médecin Volant* from a similar role Fiorilli may have played as Scaramouche in 1647 in the absence of a tangible text to refer to, and indeed of primary evidence of the performance. Yet the premise served as a particularly inspiring departure for Dario Fo's vibrant production of the play at the Comedie-Francaise in 1990 on the invitation of its then director, Antoine Vitez, wherein the recognition of Scaramouche as the *père de Sganarelle* provided a springboard for a host of acrobatic *lazzi,* musical interludes and improvised additions to Molière's text based upon archival research in what has been termed "l'invention d'un tradition" (Riviere 1991: 8). In the published diagrams Fo used as directorial notes Sganarelle can be seen in the black costume of Scaramouche.

Contending that Sganarelle's disjointed discourse and irrational superstitions can be read as an intentional subterfuge to avoid direct confrontation with his monologic master, he suggests that Molière, in playing the character, uses it as a mask behind which he can resist his authoritarian censors after the banning of *Tartuffe* in 1664. Thus Sganarelle, like the Neapolitan Scaramuza, becomes a representative of the people that his master, like the Spanish captain Matamoros, cuts himself off from. This close proximity surely provided Molière with the opportunity to closely observe Scaramouche's acting and to adapt it for his varied portrayals of Sganarelle, making the latter's influence upon him "more of a commonplace than a point of contention." (Andrews 1989: 142)

The mask and revolution: Sabatini's *Scaramouche*

He was born with the gift of laughter and a sense that the world was mad.
(Sabatini 1921: 1)

The opening line of Rafael Sabatini's 1921 novel, *Scaramouche,* is inscribed on his tombstone in Switzerland as well as on one of the colleges in Yale, and has been used in the obituary of the American student political activist Abbie Hoffman. As a leading screenwriter of historical fiction has remarked, the epithet is typical of Sabatini's skill in commanding the reader's attention from the first lines (Fraser 1988: 128). It describes the protagonist, Andre-Louis Moreau, who is forced to don the mask of Scaramouche in order to seek revenge for the murder of his revolutionary friend at the hands of a reactionary Marquis on the eve of the French Revolution. Publication of the novel in America by Houghton Mifflin and Co. in 1921 brought instant success to Sabatini, the son of an Italian tenor and a Lancastrian soprano who had read widely as a child in a variety of languages having been educated in Portugal and Switzerland while his parents toured the opera houses of Europe. At the age of seventeen, fluent in Italian, Spanish, French, German, Portuguese and English, he started work as a translator for a Brazilian coffee import firm in Liverpool, where his grandfather lived. He was to work there for ten years and during the last three began to write historical fiction in a short story format for Pearson's magazines in London. The model for Machiavelli's *The Prince* was the subject of one of Sabatini's long historical biographies and in it he relates an incident wherein Cesare Borgia donned a disguise to enter into village carnival festivities and wrestle with the rustics in Cesena much to the disapproval of the author of the *Diario Cesenate*. The story is pertinent to our concerns in that it is an instance of the Renaissance nobility indulging in popular festivity and that it is yet another example of one of Sabatini's heroes – in this case the arch-politician – disguising himself to enter the world of carnival (Sabatini 1911: 266-7). The theme was to develop more fully and enjoy unprecedented success with the publication of *Scaramouche*. Rejected by six other publishing houses the manuscript for the novel was read by chance by a commissioning editor at Houghton, Mifflin and Co. and given the go ahead in 1921. In Sabatini's own words:

> Its success was immediate and incredible. Edition after edition was called for. It was filmed. It was dramatised. As a consequence, all the old novels of mine that had been passed over were rushed to the printing presses of Boston; and of *The Sea Hawk* which no publisher in the States would set up when it was offered in 1914, the American sales to date run into something like half a million copies. It was the repercussions here of that American success which at last firmly established me on this side, and threw wide for me the doors at which I had stood humbly, cap in hand.
>
> (Sabatini 1935: 11)

The novel is divided into three parts, 'The Robe'; 'The Buskin'; and 'The Sword', corresponding to the three phases of the protagonist's career as a lawyer, actor and swordsman. Andre-Louis Moreau is a young cynical Breton lawyer who reluctantly becomes involved in the beginnings of the French Revolution after his best friend, Philippe de Valmorin, a seminarist and revolutionary, is killed in an ill-matched duel by the Marquis de la Tour d'Azyr. His attempts to find justice for his friend's murder at the office of the King's Lieutenant in Rennes prove futile and he accidently finds his true vocation as a political agitator when he makes a speech to the crowd of the societies of law students outside decrying Philippe's murder as a flagrant example of the nobility's abuse of privilege. He is forced to flee the law as a result of his political activity and after a fleeting meeting with his childhood sweetheart, Aline de Kercadiou, who, to his displeasure, is being courted by the Marquis, he hides in a barn at night. Upon awakening the next morning he surprises a company of Commedia dell'Arte players rehearsing their improvisations, as he ironically puts it. Joining the company he eventually replaces the actor playing Scaramouche.

The novel contains quite an accurate depiction of the major events of the French Revolution and some of the socio-economic and political forces behind it. A synopsis made for Metro Pictures just after the novel was published concludes with doubts as to its popular appeal: "The public would be interested in the historical sequences but would they care about Andre or Scaramouche?" (Meagher 1921) It was pointed out that the Revolution offered the opportunity for "spectacular effects", although it would be expensive and it was perhaps with the former consideration in mind that a decision was made to start production in 1923. Rex Ingrams, the director of *The Four Horsemen of the Apocalypse* starring Rudolfo Valentino, was assigned to a script by the screenwriter Willis Goldbeck. The script was essentially faithful to the novel in its development of the narrative, and great importance was attached to the revolutionary background. Painstaking care was taken in providing authentic backdrops, a village was constructed in the San Fernando Valley and a set of revolutionary Paris was built in the Metro studios with meticulous attention to detail. The film's star, Ramon Novarro, who was to replace Valentino as Metro's leading man, helped to recruit fellow Mexican immigrants in Los Angeles to be part of the 10,000 extras recruited for the many crowd scenes. By the end of filming it had cost $1,139,014 and was thus the star vehicle of Metro's 1923–4 programme.

Preparations for the remake of *Scaramouche* were begun in earnest in 1946 with a script being prepared by Irmgard von Cube and Allen Vincent. Shooting began in the autumn (of 1951), after the director George Sidney had taken a location crew up to San Francisco's Golden Gate Park for background footage which was also provided by a consignment of film from the Isle of Man and the Channel Islands. Playing Scaramouche had been built into Stewart Granger's contract with MGM but he initially disagreed strongly with producer Carey Wilson's decision to concentrate more on the comedy suggested by George Froeschel and Ronald Millar's free adaptation of Sabatini's story than the dramatic background of the French Revolution. Elizabeth Taylor and Ava Gardner were to play the leading ladies, but due to other commitments were replaced by Janet Leigh as Aline and Eleanor Parker as the fiery actress Lenore. Granger finally agreed to Millar and Froeschel's script and the dancer, producer and writer Mel Ferrer, who had directed Jose Ferrer as *Cyrano* on Broadway in 1946, was announced as the Marquis. The final version has a classic comic ending.

The significance of the mask of Scaramouche was spelled out in von Cube and Vincent's first outline by a Zany, who in the later treatment turns out to be a revolutionary agent, to a bemused policeman: "You see, your honor, Scaramouche is not a man – at least not a single man. He is someone else everyday – he has no substance – he is only an idea – he stands apart – disinterested – impersonal – unattainable – he is Justice." (Von Cube and Vincent 1946: 17)

This equation between the mask and a political and ethical concept is, similarly, not overtly stated in any of the following treatments or scripts. Nevertheless it pervades the final cut as it is through donning the mask of Scaramouche that the protagonist is able to wreak his revenge on the Marquis and thus symbolically champion the cause of the Revolution. The Marquis, like his Sabatinian antecedent, finds Philippe has a "dangerous gift of eloquence" and must be suppressed. This suppression of free speech by force is enacted in the duel between the Marquis, and Philippe. Despite one failed attempt while learning this skill from the Marquis' own fencing master, a revolutionary sympathiser, in which he is saved by Aline, Andre finally humiliates the Marquis (after one of the longest and best duels in cinematographic history) and spares his life. Andre is positively aided and abetted in his quest for revenge by the mask of Scaramouche. Stewart Granger's first appearance on screen as Andre is immediately preceded by a poster, adapted from Callot's engraving, featuring the mask. His disguise is presented to him in the form of a drunken actor wearing a long-nosed mask. For the purposes of the exposition of the plot the mask of Scaramouche is essential and it dominates the rest of the film.

The return of Scaramouche

Sidney's 1952 MGM remake, which a leading expert on stage combat has termed "the perfect swashbuckler" (Ware 1995), spawned enough interest for producers on the continent to back three films loosely based on characters from Sabatini's novel in the 1960s and 1970s: *El Mascara de Scaramouche* (1963), *Los Hijos de Scaramouche* (1975), and *Le Awenture e gli Amori di Scaramouche* (1976). A television series starring Domenico Modugno based on Constantini's biography was launched in 1964. The mask returned to the Italian theatre in the past two decades, through Carlo Boso's *Scaramouche* (1986), Nello Mascia's *Scaramuccia: vita, awenture, amori, morte e resurrezione di un attore immortale* (1990) and Leo De Berardinis' *Il Ritomo di Scaramouche de Jean Baptiste Poquelin e Leon de Berardin (1994)*. The Hispano-Franco-Italian co-production, *El Mascara de Scaramouche*, directed by Antonio Isasi in 1963 was a jolly swashbuckling romp well received under the title, *The Adventures of Scaramouche*, by the English speaking film press. Similarities with Sabatini's plot were confined to the revenge of a wronged aristocrat under the guise of the mask of Scaramouche in an adaptation of an original story by Guido Malatesta. The title song was composed by the popular singer Charles Aznavour, and indeed the link between popular music and the character was strengthened in Italy when the singer Domenico Modugno played Scaramouche as a vagabond adventurer in a television series for the RAI in the 1960s. His theme tune, *Volare*, was reprised in the 1980s by the Franco-Spanish flamenco rock group, The Gypsy Kings, to find European success.

The mask and the millennium

For Nello Mascia (a distinguished Neapolitan actor who has worked with Strehler and Eduardo de Filippo) and Nicola Miletti (a fellow actor) the character of Scaramuccia is inextricably linked to the life of the actor Fiorilli, and in more general terms to the condition of the seventeenth century Italian comic actor. Like De Simone, Mascia sees the character as an original product of the popular carnival culture. Echoes of the character's historical origins in the figure of Memeo Squaquera and the dying moments of carnival resound here. Fiorilli was responsible for transforming a mask of popular descent to a mask of the bourgeoisie – his black costume mirroring that of the doctor or the intellectual. Furthermore, Fiorilli's innovation of dispensing with the mask and adopting the French farceurs' tradition of playing "*enfarine*" can be seen as a betrayal of the "masked comedy" from which he sprang. The decline of the character's importance after Fiorilli's death also mirrors the decline of the *Commedia all'Improvviso* as a whole. Why did the character disappear from the limelight? Why is it not found in the plays of Marivaux, Goldoni or any of the other adaptors of the Commedia tradition? Mascia feels that it was as if Scaramuccia was shat out by the other characters to be eventually eaten up by them again. The diachronic progress through the bourgeois period made by the mask with its incorporation of the master/servant dialectic, diffused through various dialogic strategies, implies that its subversive potential will survive into the next millennium. With a sly smile it awaits, in the wings, its next entrance onto the world's stage.

Stephen Knapper: 1964–2012

To view the entire 286 page thesis: visit the British Library online PhD Ethos website: http://ethos.bl.uk/SearchResults.do and search for Stephen Knapper.

References

Andrews, R. (1989) "Arte dialogue structures in the comedies of Molière", in Christopher Cairns (ed.) *The Commedia Dell'Arte from the Renaissance to Dario Fo*, Lewiston, US; Queenstown, Canada; Lampeter, UK: Edwin Mellen.

Bahktin, M. M. (1993) cit. in *Parody: Ancient, Modern, and Post Modern*, by M. A. Rose.

Constantini, Angelo *La Vie de Scaramouche*, Paris: Barbin 1695.

Fiorilli, S. to Ferdinando Gonzaga and to Ercole Marliani (1619) in *Corrispondenze*, Florence, Italy. pp. 337–8.

Fiorillo, Silvio (1621) *Li Tre Capitani Vanagloriosi. Capricciosa Rappresentazione di Strani Amorati auenimenti*. Naples, Italy: Domenico Maccarono.

Fiorillo, Silvio (1632) *La Lucilla Costante con le ridicolose disfide e prodezze di Policinella*. Milan, Italy.

Fitzpatrick, T. (1995) *Workings of the Commedia dell'Arte: Oral and Literate Performance Processes*, Lewiston, US; Queenstown, Canada; Lampeter, UK: Edwin Mellen.

Fraser, G. M. (1988) *The Hollywood History of the World*, London: Penguin.

Hauser, A. (1994) in P. Castagno (ed). *Early Commedia dell'Arte 1550-1621. The Mannerist Context*, New York: Lang.

Mamone, S. (1992) "Le Miroir de spectacles Jacques Callot a Florence" in P. Chone' (ed.) *Jacques Callot 1592-1635*, Paris: Editions de la Reunion des Muses Nationaux.

Meagher, E. J. (1921, October). *Synopsis of Scaramouche* in MGM Film Collection, Los Angeles, US: USC Library.

Neri, A. (1882, July) "Una Compagnia comici nel 1614" in *Fanfulla della Domenica*, Rome.

Riviere, J. L (1991) "Farcir la Farce" in *Molière-Dario Fo: le Medecin malagre, lui et le medecin Volant*, Paris: Imprimene Nationale.

Sabatini, R. (1911) *The Life of Cesare Borgia: A History and Some Criticisms*, London: Stanley Paul and Co.

——(1921) *Scaramouche*, London: Hutchinson.

——(1935, May). Review of his career in *The Liverpolitan*, Birkenhead, UK.

Salerno, Henry F. editor (1967) *Scenarios of the Commedia dell'Arte: Flaminio Scala's "Il Teatro delle favole rappresentative"*[1611]. New York: New York University Press.

Scala, Flaminio (1618) "Il Finto Marito" in *Commedie dei Comici dell'Arte*, L. Falavolti (ed.). Turin, Italy 1982.

Scott, V. (1995) *The Commedia dell'Arte in Paris 1644-97*, Charlottesville, VA, US: UVA Press.

de Simone, R. (1993, March) Interview.

Von Cube, Irmgard and Vincent, Allen (1946) *Scaramouche*. Outline, September 17, 1946. MGM Collection, Cinema-Television Library and Archives of the Performing Arts, Doheny Library, University of Southern California (USC), Los Angeles, US.

Ware, D. (1995, April) "The Duelist in Fact and Fiction", illustrated lecture at the National Film Theatre.

11

OFFICIAL RECOGNITION OF PULCINELLA

The one who saved the Commedia from extinction by securing its continuity to the present day

Antonio Fava

Translated by Mace Perlman

After the fall of the *Ancien Régime* in France, the Revolution mercilessly dispatched all that was "old and decaying" throughout the Old Continent. One by one, time-worn ways of ruling the state were overthrown or updated. Revolutions often leave deeper marks in a culture's customs than in its forms of government. The restorations that followed the great revolutionary uprisings failed to restore the old usages, now outmoded, as new tastes marched vainly on, heedless of the loss.

Commedia dell'Arte, also known as *Commedia Improvvisa*, or *Commedia Italiana*, was among the victims of this great renovation. It left important, even indelible, traces in all the theatrical arts of Europe, and then, thought to be old, was made to disappear; thrown away with the old rubbish. But how could the Commedia be considered so old despite its ability to update and adapt itself? Its life had already lasted so long, in large part thanks to its self-regenerating qualities. The problem was that the Commedia everywhere was supported by some *ancien régime*, so that it absolutely had to go, along with all the fashions connected with those regimes. Thus its *Arlecchinettini* (insignificant Harlequins), *Pantaloncini* (diminished Pantaloons), *innamoratini* (easily dismissed lovers) and the whole set of its quaint, little masks were dismantled and, apparently, made to disappear – as, it is to be admitted, during the Rococò period everything was reduced to an utterly frivolous and cloying diminutive of its former self. Yet it was only apparently so, because in fact, nothing disappeared. To put it in Darwinian terms, the survival and continuity of Commedia were secured by its own adaptability. Certain theatrical forms are born, or develop, and need ideas. Commedia was born from a powerful gene pool, which imposes, even today, certain fundamental principles on the comic disciplines, including the idea that a character may exist before anyone writes a text for him. The character exists just as people exist, and as with people in real life, his stage life will give him the destiny that he is meant to have.

When the modern circus appears, we see the *infarinato* ("flour-faced" type) from the Commedia, a character who finds a perfect new home in the world of the ring, so different from the world of the stage: can anyone see any actual difference between a so-called "white clown" and an infarinato from the Commedia? So much are the two alike that one of the names of the infarinato, perhaps its most famous and abused, is Bajazzu in its original form, which means "joker" in the Calabrese dialect. Later reduced to the Italian Pagliaccio, after the historical collapse of the "Commedia system"; "pagliaccio" being the very term that the Latin languages use for "clown" (*pagliaccio, payaso, paillasse, palhaço,* etc.).

Pulcinella becomes Polichinelle in France – gloriously so – briefly as a human stage-character, introduced by the great Neapolitan actor Michelangelo Fracanzano; and later as a puppet.

In the seventeenth century, Pulcinella is introduced in England in the form of a puppet, as "Signor Bologna, alias Pulcinella". As Punch, he appears in the masterpiece, *The Tragical Comedy or Comical Tragedy of Punch and Judy*, first published by Routledge in 1860, with the famous and beautiful illustrations of George Cruikshank (Cruikshank 1976).

In England he is a puppet from the beginning, with the name of Punchinello, only Punch later on, and Mr Punch; and together with his wife Judy, the English version of Zezza, he brings to life stories teeming to the brim with comedy and violence. The brutality of this British Pulcinella, Punch, can only be explained through the infantile, and ever-hungry, innocence which is always attributed to the puppet, even when it represents an adult character. Punch is a total hedonist; he only wants his personal pleasure. Anything else is an annoyance, an interference, and must be eliminated. This innocence, ever-present yet undeclared, is what binds him to his Southern Italian origins, in a South where even the worst is never unquestionably guilty.

The nineteenth-century *Pantomime* reuses the infarinato in France, by making him very sad and mute, and he becomes a sort of affected Harlequin in England. From the world of Opera comes the idealization of Commedia, already taken for dead and buried, and therefore worthy of celebration. By the twentieth century, we are over it. Boito's libretto entitled *Basi e Bote* (1881), set to music by Pick-Mangiagalli and finally staged in 1927, shows an irreparably diminished and insignificant vision of Commedia. With *Le Maschere*, Mascagni attempts Goldoni, but in spite of the wonderful music, it has no chance to compete dramaturgically with the great Venetian playwright, who furthermore was not representative of the Commedia but on the contrary, clearly and simply, was its liquidator. Richard Strauss's wonderful *Ariadne Auf Naxos* makes myth of the Commedia, immersing it in classical mythology. The Italian Ferruccio Busoni, residing in Germany, mixes Arlecchino with Dante! And why not? It seems Italian, so it is all right.

A great exception, which is ignored by theatre historians in spite of its great popularity, is Ruggero Leoncavallo's *I Pagliacci*: in spite of its unavoidable "Arlecchinism". It does bear witness to the author's real-life experience in Calabria, in Southern Italy, where Pulcinella rules, and where the masks can still be seen performing in the theatre. In *I Pagliacci*, a "Pulcinellian" and romantic spirit, sentimental and tragic at the same time, is expressed by the real characters and not by the fictional ones. Strangely, the scenic fiction, which is the most insignificant sort of *Arlecchinata*, is purely artificial, while the "real life" in the piece is strongly Pulcinellian. Leoncavallo witnessed a tragedy of jealousy, which occurred in front of a theatre in Calabria, involving a stabbing and much blood. The event inspired his masterwork, for which he wrote the libretto and composed the music.

In *I Pagliacci*, we also see that odd centuries-old confusion between the one who laughs and the one who makes others laugh: the comic character should not laugh, but must instead make people laugh. The ones laughing must be in the audience. But with "Ridi, Pagliaccio" we are faced with the most classic and ancient of confusions: the confusion between the comic performer and the laughing populace. In Victor Hugo's masterwork *L'Homme Qui Rit* (Hugo 1869), we also read about this confusion for hundreds of pages. The Romantic Age is not amenable to the comic in its pure state; it plunges it into the most tragic sorrow, in the process confusing terms and rules.

And so it is that, with the end of Commedia in the north of Italy and in the Continent, the best Commedia comes from the Kingdom of the Two Sicilies, from Napoli and throughout Southern Italy, before Italy was unified in 1861. We speak of Pulcinella.

This greatest of masks has never ceased to exist. The crumbling of Commedia in the rest of Italy, in France, in the North and in the rest of Europe does not concern the almost stable Kingdom of Naples. Pulcinella is not affected by the historical and social upheavals, nor by the very brief republican experience from January to June 1799, nor by the return of the King. It is not influenced by the Murattian period, nor by the new return of the King. It is not even influenced by the definitive dissolution of the Southern Kingdom, when it is integrated in the new, modern, and powerful nation called Italy. Similarly, Naples never stops being a great capital for the theatre.

In Naples there was a flourishing of farces featuring Pulcinella, known as *pulcinellate*. The *guarattella*, which was the travelling hut where pulcinellate with puppets were staged, saw the great Pulcinella performed by Antonio Petito, king of the Teatro San Carlino. Another great artist, Eduardo Scarpetta, who created the character of Felice Sciosciammocca (who is not Pulcinella but keeps on his comic spirit), coincided with the great comedians from the Taranto and Maggio families.

Before the last war, in Calabria, my father Tommaso used to perform his *Purcinedda* and today, *mò mò* – even now – around the whole world, I, myself, perform the same mask. From the "end of the Commedia" until halfway through the twentieth century, Pulcinella was the one and only mask acting in continuity with earlier Commedia dell'Arte on the stages of Europe. This explains the evolution of a world, Pulcinella's world, which has no comparison with that of other masks, nor with the Commedia as it is commonly understood, for while Pulcinella kept on his path, all the rest either became extinct or remained frozen in an unchangeable form. By the end of the eighteenth century, the Commedia dell'Arte was over, as theatre history teaches.

What did the Commedia look like at the moment of its own end? Structurally, it was exactly as it was at the moment of its development. The Commedia reached its maturity in the years following 1560, when the first actress appeared, immediately presenting herself both as a real woman and professional actress. The farcical style of the first Commedia, which appeared in the north of Italy about thirty years earlier, rapidly and radically changed and evolved from a pure farcical theatre of *lazzi* to a dramaturgically structured theatrical form. The mature Commedia was accurately documented in Massimo Troiano's description of the staging of *La Cortegiana* in 1568 (Petraccone 1927), and in Alessandro Scalzi's frescos that illustrated it, also in 1568. On that occasion, the conception and practice of the Commedia reached a level that could be defined as beautiful, magnificent, well-made, prestigious, and highly professional.

The idea of professionalism imposed from the very beginning the principle of a "specialization", which means that an actor was used to playing the same character in all the *fabule* or *commedie*. It is the application of the principle of specialization that explains why we have fixed types. There are four archetypes: the Old Man, the Servant, the Lover, and the Captain, and a number of variants, not always definable but which surely include a paired couple of Lovers of the first type (the idealists); a paired couple of Lovers of the second type (the adventurers); two old men, the Dottore and the Magnifico; and one or more Bravi. The Bravo has nowadays been renamed a Captain due to today's universal confusion between the two: the Captain, historically, was a Lover of the second type, while the disastrous *fanfarone* ("swaggering braggart") with the mask is the Bravo or the Bullo. But our time is full of interpretative blunders of this sort. Finally, we have the servants in the roles of First Zanni (the clever, wily, scheming servant) and Second Zanni (the foolish servant). Pulcinella is up to this moment just a name, one of a hundred names for the Second Zanni. He is a foolish servant. Together with the First Zanni, who in the southern Commedia is systematically Coviello, Pulcinella takes part in the intrigues that in Commedia dell'Arte are necessary to find a solution to a series of problems; problems which always arise from the love troubles of the two (or more) couples of Lovers.

The two consequences that we deduce from the end of the Commedia system are: first, the interruption of any possible formal-poetic-technical development of the Commedia as it was known and as it might be studied and analysed today; and second, the continuation of the evolution of the orphan Pulcinella in a Southern Italy which is conservative and surrounded by revolution, within which ideas are not lacking nor are possibilities for developing them. It is absolutely natural that Pulcinella should happily keep on developing at home. The theatre develops, transforms, proposes and promotes new forms and new ideas, but Pulcinella is always present and is part of it. He can no longer be a Second Zanni, for the new dramaturgies have cancelled those practices and those systems; nonetheless, the existence of Pulcinella as the voice of the people, as the direct expression of a people as lively and spirited as the Neapolitans is never questioned. The nineteenth century masterfully redesigns this character: he is no longer the foolish servant beside the cleverer Coviello, but rather the "human" up to his ears in a world of wily, arrogant, self-interested, and undeservedly "superior" guys. Pulcinella is the expression of a human condition made foolish by those unable, unwilling, and never obligated to recognize dignity as everyone's necessary and common right. Pulcinella, a man without dignity, is nevertheless indispensable to us all: without his foolishness, his ignorance, his extreme credulity and sometimes his aggressiveness, none of his countless "bosses" could ever escape from the awkward tangle of troubles in which they find themselves. Pulcinella is everyone's saviour, saved by no one.

As a social figure, Pulcinella does not engender in us any form of identification or recognition; he is too "low" a human figure in every sense. Pulcinella concerns us all, anyone caught in a moment of weakness, of extreme difficulty, of urgent need, faced with something which requires an immediate leap to escape – right now, *mò mò*. Commedia as a whole could never accomplish this historic step; it has never been allowed to do it. We rediscover Commedia today, but through a "freedom of interpretation" that is nearly always pure interpretative arbitrariness.

No one among the historians has ever realized that there was, and there is, a continuity which is called Pulcinella. The great Neapolitan tradition, ignored and confined to a sort of "cultural backwater", where it by no means belongs! It was overtaken and given a beating by the concept of a "rediscovered" Commedia, a strategy employing the "walking dead", a sort of "theatrical Frankenstein".

Pulcinella appears, by this name, towards the end of the sixteenth century. He had already existed, in a very similar form, under the name of Pascariello, created by Neapolitan companies in order to replace the Bergamask Zanni, who was incomprehensible and unpleasant for the southern audience. Silvio Fiorillo refined, repaired, polished, corrected, and supplied the finishing touches to the old Pascariello, then renamed him Pulcinella (which means "chicken", that is to say, the perfect victim for smarter guys) and put him on the path to everlasting success.

Until the end of the eighteenth century, Pulcinella is an ordinary Second Zanni, no different from any other, as are Arlecchino, Truffaldino, Tabacchino, Traccagnino, Trivellino, Bertolino, Bagattino and so on, (for at least three hundred more instances, as indicated by the current state of my research). But later, left alone, he evolves and originates the *pulcinellata*: the solo pulcinellata, the one for couples, the one for entire families – large families – of *pulcinelli*. Then there is the servant Pulcinella in middle-class Neapolitan houses, who is a kind of lone survivor, the only mask in a world of lower-middle-class and middle-bourgeois stage characters who accurately mirror the audience in the hall. There is the romantic Pulcinella, who is better than any other *buffo* at accepting the morbid side of romanticism. Pulcinella is the one who makes people laugh and cry at the same time, who gives himself over to impossible love-affairs, and is turned down, rejected. He is the ugly one, the horrible, the obscene, *'o scarrafone*, the dirty and smelly, the ignorant, and the indolent. He loves, though is never loved in return, more intensely than anyone. Can one possibly be more romantic than this? Horribly ugly outside and indescribably beautiful within! Only Pulcinella can be this way, for none of the other masks were afforded access and a period of passage through romanticism. For this reason a certain neo-Commedia, an approach that is against my beliefs, is nowadays proposed in an alchemical, artificial, cold, and vaguely mystical manner. This "commediuncula", this "test-tube Commedia", forced back to life beginning at the second half of the last century, is utterly lacking in any breath of the romantic.

Pulcinella possesses a powerful, extraordinary, romantic life-force which is understandable today because he has travelled on foot, tirelessly, from the romanticism of the nineteenth century to the "quick" sentimentalism of today; just as the Opera did; just as the Cinema did as well. Well done, Pulcinella. Very well done indeed. Bravo Pulcinella. Bravissimo.

References

Cruikshank, George (1976) *The Tragical Comedy or Comical Tragedy of Punch and Judy*. London: Routledge & Kegan Paul Ltd. First published in 1860 by George Routledge & Sons, Ltd.

Hugo, Victor-Marie (1869) *L'Homme Qui Rit*. Paris.

Petraccone, Enzo (1927) The *Comedy: History, Technique, Scenarios*. Naples, Italy: Riccardo Ricciardi Publishers.

12

THE MANY FACES OF BRIGHELLA

The knave we love to hate

Artemis Preeshl

Of all the characters of the Italian comedy Brighella is without doubt the most disturbing.

(Pierre Louis Duchartre 1966: 161)

In Carlo Gozzi's 1762 production of *Turandot,* Brighella stands guard at his post. His friend, Calaf, asks, "What is happening?" Brighella says there is no need to be afraid of phantoms. Suddenly, ghosts fill the stage with a cacophony of sound. Thus Vakhtangov appropriately begins his "speech on spectacle" with the drama king, Brighella (Taviani and Schino 1982: 80). An urban legend that haunts Commedia dell'Arte stages, Brighella is often cited as one of the primary northern masks, yet the rogue disappears and reappears through the centuries to our chagrin and delight. Brighella is the quintessential knave, the villain we love to hate. The slick opportunist stops at virtually nothing to achieve his ends. However, if Brighella were merely Machiavellian, the audience and performers would not enjoy his antics so much. Brighella was best known as a valet. This clever servant gathered information through reconnoitering, gossiping, and eavesdropping to solve problems created by his master and his children. Sometimes, Brighella slapped down Arlecchino, the second zanni, who is his usual partner in plot. The quick-witted and loquacious Brighella rose to the status of a *petit bourgeois* in later scenarios. The bossy servant managed an inn, tended bar, cooked, guarded (and/or pilfered) his patron's merchandise, or told fortunes. His flattery instilled confidence in a potential mark. If the price was right, Brighella even killed. The intriguer bullied, cajoled and waxed eloquent to command fear and respect. Despite his skill in throwing his victim off balance, Brighella's love of wine, women and song, and his incorrigible dishonesty, prevented him from bettering his lifestyle. In scenario after scenario, this dominant servant makes fun of our shortcomings at his own expense. Brighella's impudence and knavery accesses our humanity so we can face the truth about our lives through his artistic license.

Brighella Cavicchio da Val Brembana initially played the dominant straight man. Brighella's name arose from "*briga* (trouble), *brigare* (to intrigue or wangle) and *imbrogliare* (to deceive, shuffle, confuse)" (Oreglia 1968: 71). Cavicchio, comes from "*cavillo*" (quibble, protest, chicane) (Rudlin 1994: 84). Angelo Beolco, called Il Ruzzante, popularized Brighella-like characters who spoke in Bergamasque dialect in the 1520s. Although records of sixteenth century performances of Brighella have not been uncovered, according to Nicoll, Carlo Cantu "fully developed" the role of Brighella in the early seventeenth century (Nicoll 1963: 77). According to Kennard, our earliest textual reference to this seductive rogue, occurred in *Maridazzo di M. Zan Frognocola con Madonna Gnignicola* (1618): "Brighella dances with Franceschina" (Kennard 1967: 55). D'Ancona noted in *Corona Macheronica di Zan Muzzina*: "Zan Buffetto, Brighella and Bagattin...lived" (D'Ancona 1932: 455, ff. 2). Brighella reached the zenith of his celebrity in the late seventeenth century. As his popularity grew, the ubiquitous, yet chimeric, servant became more eloquent, and less violent, in theft and seduction.

Brighella sported an olive green or brown mask with a hooked nose and slanted eyes, often accessorized with a beard or mustache. The foxy mask won confidence, but the heaviness of Brighella's nose and lips hinted at his murderous intentions (Nicoll 1963: 77). As befitting a gentleman's servant, green braids or stripes lined his white jacket, pants, and short cape. His lean purse bespoke his greed even as his belted dagger warned potential targets of his malevolent intent. The wily cheat made cunning, rude jokes in a groveling voice, which menaced foolish servants or old men. The brusque or seductive bravo spoke in the Bergamasque dialect. Commedia teacher Barry Grantham (2000) suggested that Brighella was the only contemporary Commedia dell'Arte character who benefitted from an Italian accent because he seemed to be stereotypically Italian. His mellifluous voice inspired confidence in a susceptible mark and seduced reluctant servettas. (Grantham 2000: 195). Yet, Brighella moved differently from the other zanni. Instead of contralateral walking, Brighella's elbow and knee of the one side of the body move toward each other as he walks (Fava 2004). His languid shiftlessness belied his surprising dexterity.

Greek and Roman origins of Commedia dell'Arte have been widely debated. Hunter (2002: 204) linked zanni to the "clownish and low entertainment" of Sannio, the pimp, in Book II of Cicero's antique Roman comedy, *De Oratore*. (See also Disraeli 2012: 123.). In his *Memoires*, Carlo Gozzi cautioned against a direct lineage between Roman theatrical masks of the *Fabula Atellanae* to Commedia dell'Arte; however, he suggested that Maccus was "a Protean fool or Harlequin" and Sanniones gave rise to zanni, "the Bergamasque name for a varlet – Jack" (Gozzi and Gratarol 1797: 39). The rascally servant personified Brighella. Oreglia (1968) likened Brighella to the eponymous character in Plautus's play, *Epidicus, or The Fortunate Discovery* (194 BCE). The servant of the Athenian Periphanes epitomized the many faces of Brighella. He fell in love with a music-girl, passed her off as his master's long-lost daughter, and tricked Periphanes into ransoming her. When Periphanes' real daughter appeared, his ex-wife, Philippa, disavowed the music-girl. Although the master discovered his servant's ruses, Periphanes pardoned Epidicus. The personae of the Latin character as flatterer, lover, and con artist called up characteristics of Brighella's predecessors and descendants.

The power of the Brighella spawned new masks that specialized as a musician, lover, host, or thief. Interpreters of Brighella and his cousins selected aspects of his traits, personalized the mask according to their talents, and renamed the mask as a new character. Consequently, the essence of the generative Brighella endured through his heirs more than in his own name. The zanni mask varied according to the skills of the actor who played a given role. The flexibility of the mask brought out the special brilliance of the actor's interpretation. Numerous authors concur that Brighella's Italian and French forerunners and offspring included Beltramo, Pedrolino, Franca-Trippa, Finocchio, Flauntino, Mezzetino, Pasquariel Scapino, Sganarello, and Frontin (Salerno 1967; Gozzi and Gratarol 1797; Lea 1934; Rolfe 1977). By identifying Brighella in scenarios and plays, the varlet's evolution may be traced over four centuries in Europe.

Sixteenth century

During Italy's political and religious turmoil in the sixteenth century, the role of the unreliable servant played well as comedic social critique. Angelo Beolco acted in and wrote comedies in vernacular Paduan in the early sixteenth century. Il Ruzzante or "jester" created the Bergamask Zanni Tonin in *La Moscheta* (1529) who may be considered kin to Brighella and Arlecchino (Duchartre 1966: 81). By 1570, Commedia dell'Arte actors performed at state events such as the wedding of Lucrezia d'Este (Henke 2002), and the Duke de Nevers's dinner in Paris (Baschet1882). In his work "Le Bal costume sous Charles IX" (1572–4), Porbus the Elder painted a woodcut with Brighella "making free with the maid" (Duchartre1966: 83). Porbus' painting was probably modeled after Zan Ganassa's performance prior to Marguerite de Valois' marriage to Henri de Bourbon, King of Navarre (Palleschi 2005). Maurice Sand (Sand and Manceau 1860) identified Charles IX as the green and white clad Brighella. However, Duchartre categorized Charles IX and the Duc de Guise, beloved of Marguerite de Valois, as inamorati (Duchartre 1966: 83). Regardless of the interpretation, this places Brighella in the first extant picture of Commedia dell'Arte.

According to Lea (1934: 488), a member of I Confidenti's second company performed Brighella onstage in 1638. Despite Brighella's current fame as the first zanni, his character manifested in Brighella-like masks in the first generation of Commedia dell'Arte companies. This can be seen in Gabriello Panzanini's role of Franca-Trippa with I Gelosi in 1577. Also, his baggy, white costume with its draping sleeves anticipated the costume of Pulchinella. Riccoboni noted Brighella's similarity to the southern zanni, "in Neapolitan comedies the Brighella and Arlecchino parts are taken by two Pulchinelli – one sharp, the other stupid" (Kennard 1935: 54). In the 1570s or 1580s, I Confidenti featured Giovanni Pellesini as Pedrolino at the Duke of Ferrara's banquet (Henke 2002: 82). Rossi's preface to *La Fiammella* (1584) identified the *Bergamini*, Arlecchino, Pedrolino and Burattino and "others who imitate similar ridiculous characters" (Lea II 1962: vol. II, 498) in I Gelosi. Although Rossi praised the Bergamask dialect of I Gelosi's Simone da Bologna, and I Confidenti's Battista da Rimini (Lea 1962: 75), Bergamask referred to Arlecchino rather than Brighella. Kathleen Lea (1962) asserted that, in the seventeenth century, the Neapolitan dialect supplanted the Bergamasque dialect of the zanni. Although visual and textual references place Brighella at the Commedia dell'Arte table, Pulchinella spawned Brighella's meanness, Pedrolino lent intrigue, and Burattino carved out his niche as an owner/manager of a small business, which led to Brighella becoming an unscrupulous manipulator and would-be confidante.

In Flaminio Scala's *Scenarios of the Commedia dell'Arte: Flaminio Scala's Il teatro delle favole rappresentative*, Kenneth McKee listed Brighella first among the zanni in his foreword to Salerno's edition. (Salerno 1967: xiv) However, Scala does not feature Brighella in any of the fifty scenarios. Instead, Burattino played the host of an inn (Days 2, 3, 4, 6, 23, 25), servant to the lovers (Days 3, 22, 34, 35, 38, 44, 45), servant to the lovers' fathers (Days 19, 27, 31), servant without a master (Day 28), merchant (Day 37), clown (Day 41), and porter and father (Day 42); Pedrolino started as a servant, but rose in rank to husband, male nurse, and Corporal (Days 3, 5, 6, 19, 22, 23, 25, 27, 28, 34, 35, 37, 38, 41, 42, 44, and 45). However, Brighella's second name, Cavicchio, appeared in Scala's story, "The Fortune of the Solitary Prince" (Day 50), as a resentful, but goodhearted, rustic. Cavicchio discovered the young girl wandering amid haystacks and raised Princess' lost daughter as "Foresta." When Princess recognized her daughter, Cavicchio brought the gold and silver clothing to the Princess to prove his story. In "Four Fake Spirits" (Day 33), the character Nicoletto represented the violent aspect of Brighella. Pantalone ordered Nicoletto, his henchman, to beat up Capitano to dissuade him from marrying Pantalone's ward, Isabella, but Arlecchino warned the Captain. In an exorcism of the lovers' lusty spirits, the henchman came to kill Capitano. Because Pantalone had forgiven the Captain, he refused to let Nicoletto kill him. The furious Nicoletto threatened to kill everyone. However, when the magician warned the henchman that he, too, would become possessed, Nicoletto desisted. Whereas Nicoletto's rage was controlled by the threat of possession, Cavicchio's naive interpretation of Brighella's mask showed his independence from a master.

Several Shakespearean characters recall Brighella's charming and malevolent qualities. Smith (1964) noted the mock-seriousness of the clown Launcelot Gobbo in *The Merchant of Venice* (1596–8) demonstrated his acerbic wit. Allardyce Nicoll (1963) compared Dogberry and Verges in *Much Ado About Nothing* (1598–9) to Brighella and Harlequin. Despite the appropriate first and second zanni pairing, Nicoll (1963) asserted that Shakespeare's realistic setting of *Much Ado About Nothing* in Sicily could not support the anti-realism of the Commedia dell'Arte masks. The extent to which Commedia impacted Shakespeare is visible, but not yet proved.

Seventeenth century

Quintessential interpreters of Brighella's heirs wooed the audience and their ladies eloquently. I Gelosi actor Niccolo Barbieri made the Milanese Beltrame famous. This actor cum author played the Brighella-like role with I Gelosi and I Fedeli in Italy and Paris in the early seventeenth century (Kennard 1935; Zapperi 1964). Parmese actor Carlo Cantù was immortalized as the musical Buffetto in a Parisian engraving in 1646. Seventeenth century Spoletian actor Giovanni Gherardi originated Flautino who made sounds like a flute by delicately adjusting his vocal tract in 1675 (Oreglia 1968). Pier Maria Cecchini played Frittelino, self-proclaimed slave of Flaminia, his real-life wife, for Marie de Medici and Henri IV in 1600 (Duchartre

1966). Rather than identifying Frittelino with the first zanni, Kennard noted Cecchini "acted with applause under this mask in the part of the second zanni" (Kennard 1935:178, ff. 2). Of these characters, Beltrame embodied Brighella's first enduring, and therefore legitimate, heir.

In the next generation, Scapino and Mezzetino led the Brighella tribe. Unlike the brawler Brighella, Scapino lives up to the meaning of his name, *scappare*, which means "to flee." As Scapino, Giovani Bissoni sold potions with a mountebank in the Riccoboni's company in 1716 (Duchartre 1966). Molière immortalized this Francophilic Brighella as a valet in *Les Fourberies de Scapin* in 1671. This clever liar and thief persuaded with wit and wile. Watteau secured the memory of Mezzetino's lute-playing troubadour in his eighteenth century painting (Watteau *c*. 1718–20). Mezzetino was tricky in love and livery as he impulsively serenaded and danced his way into women's hearts. For Gozzi, Mezzettino or *Il Villano* "had the air of" the Fabula's character, Stupidus (Gozzi and Gratarol 1797: 39). His foolishness in love made the amorous suitor capable of "blind devotion" (Duchartre 1966: 171). Angelo Constantini played Mezzetino in Dominico Biancolelli's company in Paris in 1682 (Kennard 1935). For Brighella and his guise as Mezzetino, cheating was justified in the name of love. Arlequino's increasing popularity led to the adoption of Truffaldino and Mezzetino masks over those of Brighella (Lee 1887). Brighella's tricks became subtler to accommodate the emphasis on intellect in the Age of Reason.

Eighteenth century

Cyril W. Beaumont, in his editorial introduction to Gregorio Lambranzi's ballet in the *New and Curious School of Theatrical Dancing: The Classic Illustrated Treatise on Commedia dell'Arte Performance* (Lambranzi 2002), described Brighella as:

> a dangerous rascal…ingratiating manner…confidence trickster…Lively and insolent with women…first to take flight when a difficulty arises or danger threatens…[which] will not prevent…a stab in the back if opportunity permits and necessity require. Skilled in flattery, able to sing, play and dance…mak[es] himself a welcome, if uninvited, guest…a prince of wheedlers.
>
> (Lambranzi 2000: 10)

Yet, the Venetian choreographer Gregorio Lambranzi (1700) omitted Brighella from his ballet. However, Brighella's heirs danced significant roles as Fenocchio, a master of "amorous intrigue"; Mezzetino, a "shrewd lackey," "gay philanderer," a cuckold, or a man having an affair with another man's wife; and Scapino, before a cowardly escape artist (Lambranzi 2000: 10–11). Brighella's troubadour aspect appeared in Mozart's and Beaumarchais' *Figaro*. In Act IV of Beaumarchais' play, the *Marriage*, Figaro woos his fiancée Susanna saying, "In Love's Creed, too much is not even enough," even as he frustrates the Count's attempt to marry Susanna. (Beaumarchais 1784: 4.1)

Although Brighella lost status in his own right, the *lazzi* of the ballet dancers, actors, and opera singers called forth the spirit of the knave.

In *Motti arguti allegorici alla maschera del Brighella*, Atanasio Zanoni (1847) was described as "speaking with elegance, reasoning with good sense, one versed in the sciences and… something of a philosopher" in the company of Antonio Sacchi, the Arlecchino (Nicoll 1963: 77, 195). Kennard praised Zanoni as "one of the best comedians of the eighteenth century" (Kennard 1935: 55). Oreglia summed up Brighella's philosophy in two of Zanoni's quips: "When you tell lies, tell big ones. Lies, steaks, and meatballs must be big or not at all" and "Don't do all you can, don't eat all you want, don't spend all you have, don't tell all you know" (Oreglia 1968: 75–76). To Zanoni's wisecracks, Kennard added: "One ought not to say a thief but a clever mathematician who finds a thing before its owner knows he has lost it" and "things appropriated are property inherited before the death of its owner" (Kennard 1935: 55). Brighella restrained his desires in lean times; but when he gambled, he bet the house.

Carlo Goldoni wrote scripted Commedia dell'Arte characters into more specialized roles. In *The Servant of Two Masters* (1743), five out of ten of the scenes took place at Brighella's inn. In the opening scene, Pantalone asked if Truffaldino is a "fool" or a "knave." In response, translator Edward Dent dubbed Brighella "knave" and Arlecchino "fool." Yet Brighella demonstrated uncommon loyalty as a confidence man. When Beatrice cross-dressed as her deceased brother to dupe Pantalone into cashing her brother's letters of credit, the innkeeper helped Beatrice gain freedom. Beatrice praised Brighella as clever valet to a Turinese nobleman at Pantalone's dinner, which Brighella had prepared. Though Beatrice's servant, Truffaldino, criticized the cook's ability to set a table, since the master Pantalone complimented Brighella's cooking as pleasing to the guests; thus, the host's reputation was unstained. Perhaps Goldoni's popularization of the mask as an innkeeper inspired Italian inns to adopt Brighella as their namesake. Although, with his dubious reputation, it is slightly ironic that contemporary inns and restaurants bear the knave's name. Guiseppe Angeleri was a celebrated interpreter of Brighella in Goldoni's eighteenth century comedies (Duchartre 1966: 164). Goldoni's zanni, including Brighella, occupied middle-class roles such as gondoliers, servants, storekeepers and card-sharks who "could never forget to cry, shout, jabber, jump, scuffle, and tussle together" (Lee 1978: 258). The knave's bestial nature limited his social mobility to a petit bourgeois.

Into the twentieth century and beyond

As styles changed, Commedia dell'Arte performance waned in the nineteenth century's Age of Romanticism. Although nineteenth century accounts are uncommon, scholar and practitioner John Rudlin described a scenario during Roman Carnival in 1826. When Pantalone wanted to remarry, Brighella conned the old pantaloon by showing a young woman to him. Then, he tricked her into giving his clothes for charity. Arlecchino cross-dressed as the young girl. When Pantalone made a pass at the "girl," Arlecchino beat the old lecher (Rudlin 1994: 96). Although Brighella initially dominated Arlequino in the early nineteenth century, Brighella resembled the trusting Auguste clown, duped by Arlecchino (Johnson 2010). At the turn of the century, a seemingly kinder Brighella bowed graciously in an elegant white costume in Henri Reidel's engraving *Brighella* from the Masks and Characters of Italian Theatre edition of *Le Journal des Dames et des Modes* (1914). Following substantial research into Commedia dell'Arte in the twentieth century, Brighella gradually regained his debauchery. Brighella is an unprincipled, cynical dissembler who "thrives on quarrels, intrigues, and secrets" and drinks his money away (Rolfe 1977: 21). Brighella had a "malicious desire for revenge" (Rudlin 1994: 109). This predatory rogue craftily planned his theft and disarmed with charm.

Commedia dell'Arte teacher and performer Mel Gordon stated that lazzi injected humor or covered missed cues, dazzled the audience with special skills, and fulfilled the plot points of the *scenario* (Gordon 1983: 5). In Rolfe's Lazzo 2 (1977), Brighella offered to guard the goods of unwitting travelers (Lazzo 2), stole Columbina's food as she cooked (Scene 7), and tempted Arlecchino to fight with promises of promotion, fame, glory in war (Scenes 15–16). Gordon esteemed Brighella as a "violent and cynical libertine who normally became involved in unlawful seduction and theft" (Gordon 1983: 60). Brighella appeared in Gordon's ladder *lazzo*. When Arlecchino used the ladder as stilts, the mean-spirited Brighella shook the ladder (Gordon 1983: 9). Brighella failed to unseat the dexterous acrobat. In Grantham's rendition, Arlecchino played the master. Brighella tricked Arlequino into climbing a ladder because a "servant would not be higher than the master" (Grantham 2000: 198).

Grantham considered Brighella as a "bravo" dressed as a bandit (Grantham 2000: 161) and created entire plays based on Flaminio Scala's *Scenarios* in which Brighella was a "macho" known for his "devious" and "covert violence" (Grantham 2006: xvi). As spy and salesman, Brighella laid in wait until he pounced on his next victim. In *Duchess Mislaid*, Brighella revealed his motive to find Pantalone's "hidden hoard" in his asides. Pantalone's manservant woke his master with verbal abuse and circuitous misdirection. The master's upcoming hunt with Dr. Graziano, his putative future in-law, was more important than the dead body that Brighella found, and frisked, on the doorstep. During the hunt, the servants enacted the "Bee lazzi" as they slept and snored. Capitano Spavento's servant, Torolino, capitalized on Brighella's thieving reputation. When Torolino led Brighella to believe that the Captain's chest was filled with money, Brighella enlisted Padella, servant of the innkeeper, Burattino, to steal the would-be key from Torolino. When Padella discovered that the key did not work, Brighella pried open Spavento's chest. When Burattino accused Brighella and Padella of theft, he found only bricks and rags in the chest. Pantalone pulled Padella and Brighella's ears as a punishment. Thus, Grantham emphasized Brighella's role as valet and thief.

In the twentieth century, Brighella's comic aspect joined with his violent deception. On Teatro Piccolo's American tour, David W. M. Kelch performed Brighella. In an interview with Rachel Bykowski, Kelch (2011) compared the "loveable misanthrope and thug" to Truffaldino. On the rung of the ladder between servant and master, Brighella tried to better himself by "conning someone or putting a knife in someone's back... with a smile on his face and song in his heart." (Kelch 2011) From Brighella's dangerous beginnings in the sixteenth century, the knave evolved into a clever thief and bourgeois manager in the seventeenth century. In the eighteenth century, Brighella and his kin defended themselves verbally rather than physically as a poet, astrologer, and gentleman's gentleman. Though the first zanni usually instigated jokes, he sometimes received his comeuppance. Brighella's smarmy flattery and boastful swagger frequently extricated the unrepentant rake from his misdeeds. Although documentation of a performer in Brighella's mask has not been uncovered prior to the seventeenth century, Brighella's celebrity commands a central place in Commedia dell'Arte, "its lively crackling of the dialogue and quips remained: Arlecchino, Pantalone, Columbina, Brighella and their ancestors, reigned for a long time on all stages" (D'Ancona 1964, Book 3: 196). His knavery both appalls and delights us. Brighella does and says things that we might want to do or say, but cannot or will not, to maintain our social status. This first zanni reminds us that we all have good and bad inside of us. Brighella, his predecessors and his heirs live on as the trickster. In our human dramas, in life and onstage, the Brighelle do the dirty work that society makes run so that we may laugh at our misanthropic inclinations and keep our hands clean.

References

Baschet, Armand (1882) *Les Comediens italiens à la cour de France*. Lieu d'édition, Paris. Année d'édition. In MacNeil, Anne. (2003) *Music and Women of the Commedia dell'Arte in the Late Sixteenth Century*. Oxford: Oxford University Press.

Beaumarchais, Pierre-Augustin Caron (1784) *The Follies of a Day; or, the Marriage of Figaro. A Comedy, as It Is Now Performing at the Theatre-Royal, Covent-Garden*. From the French of M. de Beaumarchais. Thomas Holcroft (tr.) London: G.G. & J.J. Robinson.

D'Ancona (1964) [1932]. *The Italian Theatre. Book Three. Appendix II*: Il Teatro Mantovano nel Secolo XVI. New York: Benjamin Blom.

Disraeli, Isaac and Benjamin Disraeli (2012) *The Works of Benjamin Disraeli: Earl of Beaconsfield*. Vol. 2. Forgotten. Central: Hong Kong.

Duchartre, Pierre Louis (1966) *The Italian Comedy*. London: Dover.

Fava, Antonio. Personal communication, Philadelphia (2004) and Reggio Emilia (2005).

Goldoni, Carlo (1928) [1743] *The Servant of Two Masters*, Edward Dent (tr.) with Introduction, "The Comedy of Masks" by Edward J. Dent. London: Cambridge University Press. www.gutenberg.ca/ebooks/goldonident-twomasters/goldonident-twomasters-00-h.html (accessed 20 August 2014).

Gordon, Mel (1983) *Lazzi: The Comic Routines of the Commedia dell'Arte*. Performing Arts Publications Journal.

Gozzi, Carlo and Piero Antonio Gratarol (2010) [1797]. *Memoirs of Count Carlo Gozzi*. John Addington Symonds (tr.) [EBook #33225] www.gutenberg.org/files/33225/33225-h/33225-h.htm (accessed 20 August 2014).

Granthan, Barry (2000) *Playing Commedia: A Training Guide to Commedia Techniques*. Portsmouth, NH, US: Heinemann Drama.

——(2006) *Commedia plays: Scenarios, Scripts, Lazzi*. London: Nick Hern.

Henke, Robert (2002) *Performance and Literature in the Commedia Dell'Arte*. Cambridge, UK: Cambridge University Press.

Hunter, Richard (2002) "Acting Down: the ideology of Hellenistic performance." In *Greek and Roman Actors: Aspects of an Ancient Profession*, ed. Easterling, Pat and Edith Hall. Cambridge, UK: Cambridge University Press.

Johnson, Bruce "Charlie" (2010) "Creating Happy Memories that Last a Lifetime: History and Philosophy". March/April. History Column. *Clowning Around*. World Clown Association. www.charliethejugglingclown.com (accessed 20 August 2014).

Kelch, David W. M. (2011) "Commedia Character Shorts: Lesson 5 – Brighella". Videography: Rachel Bykowski. www.youtube.com/watch?v=IBcf7ZH7jQc (accessed 20 August 2014).

Kennard, Joseph Spencer (1935) *Masks and Marionettes,* New York: Macmillan.

——(1967) *Goldoni and the Venice of his time.* New York: Benjamin Blom.

Lambranzi, Gregorio (2002) [1700] *New and Curious School of Theatrical Dancing: The Classic Illustrated Treatise on Commedia dell'Arte Performance.* Preface by Cyril W. Beaumont (ed.) Plate by Johann Georg Puschner, Derra de Moroda(tr.) Mineola, NY, US: Dover.

Lea, Kathleen (1962) [1934] *Italian Popular Comedy: A Study in the Commedia dell'Arte, 1560–1620 with Special Reference to the English Stage.* Vols I & II. Oxford, UK: Clarendon.

Lee, Vernon (1978) [1887] *Studies in the Eighteenth Century in Italy.* London: Da Capo.

Molière (1671) *Les Fourberies de Scapin.* www.gutenberg.org/ebooks/8776 (accessed 20 August 2014).

Nicoll, Allardyce (1963) *The World of Harlequin: A Critical Study of the Commedia dell'Arte.* London: Cambridge University Press.

Oreglia, Giacomo (1968) The *Commedia dell'Arte.* London: Methuen.

Palleschi, Marino (2005) "In the name of Auguste Vestris: The Commedia dell'Arte: Its Origins, Development and Influence on Ballet". www.balletto.net/ (accessed 20 August 2014).

Plautus, T. Maccius (194 BCE) *Epidicus, or The Fortunate Discovery.* http://archive.org/stream/jstor-289424/289424_djvu.txt (accessed 13 September 2014).

Porbus the Elder, Paul, (or Frans Porbus) (1570–2) Oil on canvas. Museum of Bayeux.

Reidel, Henri (1914) "Brighella" from the Masks and Characters of Italian Theatre Edition of *Le Journal des Dames et des Modes* Color litho. www.bridgemanart.com (accessed 20 August 2014).

Riccoboni, Luigi (1969) *Histoire du Théâtre Italien.* Facsimile edn Paris: Ovens.

—— (1973) [1728]. *Discorso della commedia all'improvviso. Scenari inediti.* New York: Il Polifilo.

Rolfe, Bari (1977) *Commedia dell'Arte: A Scene Study Book.* Oakland, CA, US: Persona.

Rossi, Bartolomeo (1584) *La Fiammella.* Paris: A. Angeliero. In Lea, Kathleen. 1934. *Italian Popular Comedy: A study in the Commedia dell'Arte, 1560–1620 with Special Reference to the English Stage.* Vol. II. Oxford, UK: Clarendon.

Rudlin, John (1994) *Commedia Dell'Arte: An Actor's Handbook.* New York: Routledge.

Salerno, Henry F. (ed. tr.) (1967). *Scenarios of the Commedia dell'Arte: Flaminio Scala's Il teatro delle favole rappresentative.* New York: New York University.

Sand, Maurice and Alexandre Manceau (1860) *Masque et Bouffons: Comédie Italienne.* Paris: Michel Lévy Frères.

Smith, Winifred (1964) *Commedia dell'Arte.* New York: Columbia University Press.

Taviani, Ferdinando and Mirella Schino (1982) *Il segreto della Commedia dell'Arte: La memoria delle compagnie italiane del XVI, XVII and XVIII secolo.* Artemis Preeshl (tr.) Florence, Italy: Casa Usher.

Watteau, Antoine. Oil on canvas. (*c.* 1718–20) The Metropolitan Museum. www.metmuseum.org/collections/search-the-collections/110002379 (accessed 20 August 2014).

Zanoni, Atanasio (1847) *Motti arguti allegorici alla maschera del Brighella di Atanasio Zanoni.* Venice, Italy: Sebastiano Tondelli. In Nicoll, Allardyce. (1963) *The World of Harlequin: A Critical Study of the Commedia dell'Arte.* London: Cambridge University Press.

Zapperi, Ada (1964) *Dizionario-Biografico degli Italiani.* Vol. 6. www.treccani.it/enciclopedia/niccolo-barbieri/

MASKS

13

A MASK MAKER'S JOURNEY

Stefano Perocco di Meduna

Translated by Brenda O'Donohue

This story, the story of the reinvention of Commedia dell'Arte's leather masks, has its beginnings in a 'historical' encounter: a meeting, between director Gianfranco De Bosio, mime *virtuoso* Jacques Lecoq, and sculptor Amelto Sartori which took place in the University Theatre of Padua, and marked the start of an experience that would bring about the rebirth of the theatrical mask. The outcome of this momentous experience was the liberation of the mask; freeing it from the glass cases of a museum and returning it to the stage. The encounter took place in Padua in 1948, and in order to fully understand its context, one must look to the historical backdrop against which it was set. The war had recently ended, and the memory of thousands of dead still dogged the collective consciousness. The world of culture had also suffered its losses – in Padua, the ruins of the Eremitani Church were still smoking, and the treasured Mantegna frescoes had been blown to smithereens. Despite all this, however, there was a tremendous desire for a new theatre. Through founding a university theatre, and an affiliated acting school, De Bosio, Lecoq and Sartori set in motion a series of experiments that became the hothouse in which the seeds of renovation and renewal flourished and then grew. Mime, the rediscovery of Commedia dell'Arte, the exploration of the Pirandellian mask's symbolic value, the remodelling of the mask that began with an investigation into the profound depths of the human psyche – all of these elements were combined in the crucible with the intention of reanimating contemporary Italian theatre, and making it an integral part of the post-war European cultural awakening. And, thanks in large part to the renown of Amleto Sartori's masks, the mask's presence onstage gained a new significance.

The years passed and the University Theatre of Padua passed the baton to the Piccolo Teatro in Milan. The path of renewal continued right up to the 1970s, with Strehler's experiments, the revisiting of Goldoni's plays, and Donato Sartori's reworking of the legacy he inherited from his father Amleto.

The dynamism produced by this flurry of activity worked as a catalyst. Its energy was easily discernable in Italy and was channelled into a series of manifestations that converged in the key concept of 'decentralization'. Decentralization means moving culture away from the center and into the periphery; moving it out of the closed spaces of traditionally recognized cultural institutions (museums, libraries, theatres) and into open public spaces where cultural experiences and the enjoyment of artistic resources can be shared. In 1976, the Venice Biennale, influenced by this renewed awareness of art's social quality, organized a busy schedule of engagements throughout the Venetian province exploring the theme across the artistic spectrum – from the visual arts, to cinema, to theatre – under the name, 'Biennale Decentralized'. This desire to open up cultural experience to its social dimension developed in parallel to a more generalized widening of horizons in the form of a new receptiveness to other cultures. And so our experience was enriched, firstly through knowledge, and later through understanding and exchange of the aesthetic and sacred aspects of theatre forms originating in the East, which ranged from Indian Kathakali to Japanese Noh theatre. Indeed, it was an encounter with a young Japanese maestro and student of Lecoq, Kuniaki Ida, in 1977 that would launch my adventure as a mask maker. The intrinsic symbolic value of the Japanese mask; its particular gift for crystalizing forms (almost distilling their essence into a moment outside time) and its capacity to draw form and content together; these were the unique impulses which formed the base on which my artistic creative project would be built. Kuniaki was not the only artist the Biennale called to Mirano. Alongside him was Donato Sartori and his masks. It seemed magical to me that I could touch these long-admired objects; I could place my hands on them and feel an unfamiliar material: leather. The project developed by Donato, and the cultural groups from Mirano and Scaltenigo, followed the themes of pollution and factories. Imagination embodied the mummy of a labourer, equipped with protective masks and gas-masks, that an imagined future archaeologist would uncover. Dramatic and violent forms were created in leather, which were repeated at the University of Pavia and, subsequently, in the Atelier on Group Theatre in Bergamo, directed by Eugenio Barba. Then the turning-point: Donato put forward a project for Venice, and there, in May 1977, the spark that would transform the project into reality was lit.

My defining encounter, however, was to be with Carlo Boso, a theatre actor who was drawn into directing after an intense collaboration with Giorgio Strehler at the Piccolo Teatro. The basic idea was to create a spectacle that told a traditional Commedia dell'Arte story from a new perspective; to revisit the servant-master theme and its evolution over time. The title, 'Report on Servants and Masters in the Commedia dell'Arte', made the project's intention explicit from the outset. In reality, it was a spectacle that travelled two paths, or if you prefer, was divided into two separate representations. Firstly, the preparatory phase, in the form of an open workshop, was presented to the public as a representation of how a show is produced. This was then followed by a final *mise-en-scène* in which the same audience witnessed the transformation of the work-in-progress into its final form as a finished product. This could be described as a return to the classical formula of 'a play within a play', but reformulated in the form of (physical) projection of the spectacle outside the confines of the theatre, and then on its return to the stage. The actors in rehearsal, the creation of the masks, the preparation of the costumes, the dressing of the set, the artistic creative process that goes before the staging – all carried out under the open skies of Campo del Ghetto – revealed the genesis of theatrical representation and the process of artistic creation to the eyes of curious passers-by. There were five apprentices in the workshop, directed by Donato Sartori, and all were driven by a great energy and enthusiasm, beginning with the preparation of *Bilora* by Ruzante, and, simultaneously, the construction of the wooden mask matrixes

After that experience, which was a kind of beginning for me, years of intense and continuing collaboration with Carlo Boso followed. The preparation of shows was accompanied by a profound exploration of the themes and potentiality of Commedia dell'Arte. This collaboration often took place in the context of training courses for young French actors. Their approach to this form of theatre, characterized as it was by the enthusiasm of novices, helped us to draw out Commedia's latent potential, which we came to define primarily as a capacity for shrewd and novel readings of contemporaneity.

My encounter with Leo de Berardinis was a milestone in my career, marked by elements of the new, as well as aspects of tradition. I met Leo at the beginning of the 1990s. Naturally, we spoke of masks, about their 'place' in our theatrical system, and the reasons why the Italian theatrical tradition was so proud of this object that nobody truly understood. Why were Italian actors so connected to the mask tradition that they felt (and continue to feel today) a kinship with it? And why, then, were they so disinclined to put on the mask and identify with it? We tried to formulate answers to these questions, deciding that perhaps it was the result of the Italian actors' training, a question of schooling. If we had similar training to that available in Paris, maybe we would experience less difficulty in reinventing ourselves and taking on the semblances of a piece of leather that has monstrous features?

I do not know if this first encounter awakened his curiosity, but I know for certain that Leo went on to discuss Commedia dell'Arte with Sylvie (Bobette) Levesque and Eugenio Allegri. A few months later, I received a phone call. Francesca Mazza wanted a witch's mask for a new show, *Il ritorno di Scaramouche*. The idea came about during a workshop led by Eugenio Allegri, which was attended by the actors of Teatro di Leo. My masks had been used during the workshop. Francesca wanted one of my masks at all costs, while the other actors were less enthusiastic about the idea! So it was that on my return from Montpellier where I had put up an exhibition, I brought some masks to Bologna. The masks were stored in a voluminous cardboard box that I placed on the floor of the rehearsal room. As soon as I began to root around looking for Francesca's mask, the magic began. A hundred hands appeared in front of me and voices could be heard, 'Would you lend this one to me? Can I? And what about this one? Oh, I'll try this on! I'll try that one again!' At that moment, a metamorphosis began; each actor rethought their role, reinterpreting it in line with the mask they were wearing. *Il ritorno di Scaramouche* was reborn, this time as a performance in mask!

Leo wanted a Pantalone mask for himself. I created the hooked profile of a nocturnal bird, a kind of elderly tawny owl, that conferred an unprecedented tragic dimension on that Pantalone from 'Castellamare di Scabbia', who spoke with an improbable half-Venetian and half-Neapolitan accent. Immediately afterwards came *King Lear*. Leo requested a mask whose creation proved to be equally arduous, and which had to be remade several times. Quite the challenge! The brief was difficult;

I was asked to mix the physiognomic features of the faces of Leo and Beckett, to create a blend of both faces, in order to intensify their expressive strength without falling into the trap of caricature. The mask was produced in three different colours; light natural leather, red with gold leaf in parts, and black. It made its debut during the previews in Salerno in its first incarnation in natural leather, while all three versions would feature in Urbino for the first run of *King Lear no. 1*. The transition of the mask from one colour to another induced the spectator to move from one existential and emotional state to another. Then a brilliant insight prompted Leo to transform the mask's mutability into a theatrical mechanism. The mask's capacity to be an agent of transformation became a dramatic principle, causing the implosion of what is traditionally and superficially presumed to be theatre's fixity and immobility. Performances known to us all, such as *Lear Opera*, *Prova di Don Giovanni*, *Past Eve and Adam's*, and *Come una rivista*, grew out of this insight of Leo's. I still feel a sense of regret at not having been able to pursue a path that promised to bestow many other similarly stimulating experiments on Italian theatre. (Leo De Berardinis died from the effects of an anaesthetic, which put him into an irreversible coma).

Naturally, Carlo and Leo were not the only directors I worked with, but they are certainly the ones who influenced my mask-making the most. Their particular visions of theatre were quite dissimilar, however. Carlo considers theatre to be a folk ritual, ostensibly light-hearted and carefree, while carrying a strong social message. Theatre, for Carlo, is engaged in a continuous dialogue with the public, and is always careful to acknowledge their moods, desires and suffering. Apart from the obvious 'political' content pervading his productions, Leo's direction followed a rigorous aesthetic investigation. With untiring tenaciousness, Leo pursued the shadow of aesthetic perfection through an uninterrupted process of refinement and inexhaustible attention to scenic elements. This made his shows inimitable, because they were the fruit of a magnificent and alchemic combination of force and poetry. However, both directors had one thing in common, and this was the most important lesson I was to learn; they both placed the actor at the centre of theatrical work. In the process of devising the spectacle, both conceived the various scenic elements in relation to the actor. Scenography, lights, costumes, music, movement, texts and masks became instruments, almost weapons, in the actor's hands, with which he could go out and conquer the world. The masks became artifices through which the vital energy of the character was channelled. The human figure took on the semblances of an animal, so that the public could read its deepest essence. This transformation, miraculous in its own way, had the courage to transmute a piece of leather into a god, a lay god if you will, a pagan god, but a god in any case.

This divinity always has, more or less obviously, animal attributes, because theatrical masks have their origins in animals. Indeed, my research has led me into the representation of animals, retracing the evolution of interpretative systems with which the human eye and mind have refigured and codified the animal mode. I patiently explored old books on physiognomy and more modern books on psycho-morphology. I searched for elements of interaction and exchange between man and animals, the metamorphosis, symbolism and genesis of monsters in Greek and Eastern mythology. I ventured into the territory of making unusual parallels and hazardous comparisons. Pulcinella's sex was ambiguous and she was born from an egg. Then on to the scene came a set of quadruplets, Helen, Clytemnestra, Castor, and Polydeuces, who also hatched from an egg and whose paternity was uncertain. Saints Pantaleon and Nicolas became thaumaturgic saints, near contemporaries of Pantalone and Santa Claus. They were reborn in the form of two old fogeys dressed in red and decked out in clothes of faded luxury – the vestiges of an ancient power stripped of its authority and prestige. Arlecchino instead, the untameable and wild spirit of the popular capacity to survive, had a solid kinship with the *chiarivari* gangs. Gozzi's Truffaldino met the Stag King, and an unprecedented relationship was born. And so on.

Many coincidences tie our experiences to ancient rituals, and they are hidden in our most profound memories. The mask helps us to rediscover them.

14

MASK PERFORMANCE FOR A CONTEMPORARY COMMEDIA DELL'ARTE

Carlos García Estévez

Introduction and interview by Wout van Tongeren

The half masks used in Commedia dell'Arte force the actor to refrain from the techniques (or tricks) that might have great success in naturalistic theatre. There is no place for meaningful looks or elaborated psychological processes behind a mask: it demands clarity, decisiveness and immediacy. However, this does not mean that the acting should become entirely a matter of *form*. This is perhaps the biggest difficulty: someone playing the masks is easily inclined to focus fully on the exterior form whilst losing the inner life of the character. Subsequently, what could be deeply moving or hilarious, becomes a rather embarrassing performance, or, at best, a display of empty virtuosity. Here lies a fascinating feature of mask acting: it should be both 'formally elaborate' and 'internally animated' to convince any audience.

Carlos García Estévez has a particular way of dealing with the formal aspects of Commedia dell'Arte, in which the mask is of elementary importance. One could say that Carlos 'draws' the figure and gestures of a character from the mask. This process begins by looking through its simple expressive features (snub nose, pronounced eyebrows, curled moustache, etc.) and discovering its structural or 'spatial' qualities. These qualities are not only the lines and planes out of which the mask is made but also those which it 'projects' outwards, in several directions. This way, the mask becomes a great source of information for the actor who is going to play with it. To give a simple example: a mask that contains many strong, straight, outgoing lines will demand from the actor a way of moving and speaking that is equally strict and forceful. Even the temporal qualities, like the rhythm of a character's movements might be learned by the careful study of a mask.

With this approach, an actor will have to learn another technique for every mask, though of course certain fundamental techniques can be used across masks. If the performer lacks the appropriate technical precision, the mask simply will not come to life. Sometimes people wonder whether the high 'formality' of this type of acting is not limiting the actor's expressive possibilities. But this would be the same as asking whether a person is limiting his musical capacities when he decides to commit himself to a particular instrument. The commonplace expression that the actor's body and voice are his instruments is in fact not precise enough. It is more accurate to say that an actor's body is merely the bare material out of which s/he still has to *build a particular instrument* (or a few particular instruments). For the process of building this instrument (i.e. mastering a certain acting style or even a particular character) many hours of specific training are required. The actor should be an artisan as much as a creative artist. Thus viewed, it is not surprising that some actors who are very successful in naturalistic plays, struggle immensely when trying to do Commedia dell'Arte; it is a matter of different instruments for which, at least to a certain extent, different talents are required. One thing should be stressed here: for García Estévez the great technical demands should never obliterate the *playfulness* of the performer. During the training he keeps stimulating and teasing his actors to keep the work light and joyful, however difficult it is. Even the most technical little exercise can be grasped as an opportunity to play, to be creative.

With its emphasis on concepts like lines, planes, forces and directions, Carlos García Estévez's approach is rather abstract. In his current theatre laboratory, Manifesto Poetico, this abstract approach has been even extended to research into the theatrical space as such. This does not mean, however, that a theatre which results from such research is vague and conceptual. It is García Estévez' view that abstraction helps us get to the essence of everything we perceive. The actor abstracts from the 'imprecision' of daily behaviour to purify and clarify his actions. Thus, the result is very concrete: a performance that is well-defined, recognizable, *essential*.

What, according to Manifesto Poetico, do the masks from the Commedia dell'Arte represent?
The masks of the Commedia dell'Arte represent the tempers, customs, classes, professions, passions and vices of the common people. They represent a universal human *commedia*. Those masks and characters, at a certain point in the history of Commedia dell'Arte, became so popular that something changed about them and something got lost. A popular spirit probably got lost as soon as those characters started to be a kind of fashion and they became more of a cliché, an idea, losing their original engine and passions. In the twentieth century some people (most notably Jacques Lecoq) tried to regain the original intensity by working with masks and avoiding the stereotyped movements that had become attached to them.

If the characters from the Commedia dell'Arte lose their universal sense they will be emptied of their essential content. The characters will become silly, commercialized, divided from each other: the Commedia will be weakened. It will abandon its real path and it will lose its purpose. It will stop speaking from the point of view of the common people and become sterile and unfruitful.

What would be the main starting point for the study of a contemporary mask?
Before I look at the mask itself, my starting point is the study of the foundations of movement: the space, rhythm and forces. It is fundamental to discover the space where the engine of the character and its forces can circulate with the correct directions and its concrete rhythm. I see this study as something abstract that we could bring to life through what I understand of mask mimo-dynamics. This abstract

study allows me to create a journey that goes from the abstraction of that mask to the concreteness of the mask. Obviously, I do not simply remain on that abstract layer; I also explore the concrete study of the mask. I find myself looking at the mask in two different ways: a naturalistic mask which shows the archetype and a mimo-dynamic mask that personifies its forces.

Jacques Lecoq describes mimo-dynamics very precisely and exactly. When you are finding the mimo-dynamic you are not miming the form but miming its dynamic and that means miming the invisible part of it. Within the meaning of the word 'dynamic' we can find three elements: rhythm, space and forces. These elements can be appreciated when we analyse the conflict that results between the movements 'push' and 'pull'. So, there is a collision between two opposite forces, contrary and complementary, that exists, as we know, in the nature of all things. When there is a movement on one side, there is another that happens on the other side. If this does not occur there will be disequilibrium, a rupture.

When we talk about discovering the space, what do we mean by this?
We could imagine that a mask is composed like an architectural space. We analyse the mask so as to bring its space to life through links that are not measurable but are, nonetheless, rhythmic links. In our research we can implement a circuit, a structure of feelings and of emotions. This circuit and/or structure can be inscribed/designed in the space. This is something that, in a similar way, we explore at the LEM (Laboratory of Movement Study) at the Ecole Internationale de Théâtre Jacques Lecoq in Paris (see Figure 14.1).

Figure 14.1 Study of 'Body of the mask'. LEM (Laboratory of Movement Study) at the Ecole Internationale de Théâtre Jacques Lecoq, Paris.

We can say that in an architectural space, we can see feelings or passions. They have their concrete place in the space. For example, if we asked someone on the street: where would you place yourself if you were very afraid, at the centre or at the periphery of the space? He would probably answer: 'at the periphery'.

Why should we study the Commedia dell'Arte masks from this abstract point of view rather than from what we know as 'traditional' methods?
The Commedia dell'Arte masks reveal a historic charge and I think, in the present time, this is often not known or understood. This misunderstanding encourages the artist to reproduce human types that do not represent today's people for today's audiences. It is very common to see actors trying to reproduce a theatre of the past, a *theatre of yesterday*, which I appreciate, but I want to look forward to a theatre that resonates more truthfully today. I think that the dell'Arte actor should be committed to making a theatre of today that can talk about tomorrow.

With this commitment, it is important to be aware of the past and concreteness of the 'popular tradition', the fundamental element for the continuation of the Commedia dell'Arte. I do not think, however, that it is fundamental to observe the traditional Commedia from its clichés and stereotypes of human typologies – 'Arlecchino used to do it like this, Pantalone was like that…' – but I do think that it is fundamental to look at the tradition from its essence and from its concrete permanencies. What were the engines that made those characters move at that time in history? How do passions like love, envy, jealousy and fear make people move? It is obvious that human passions are a constant over history and they are, and were, the engines of our existence.

On the other hand, the way we communicate and express ourselves today is totally different from how we did so 400 years ago. It is clear that certain things have to be reconceived for the times whilst accepting the permanencies and essences that we can still see today from the popular tradition. And from there we could start to look for a continuity of the Commedia dell'Arte. In the process of working on the research, I strive to access this continuity. I ask the question: 'How can the Commedia dell'Arte exist today?'

What would be the first step for this research?
A part of the study of movement is the study of the masks from the Commedia dell'Arte; but not the masks that we find in books and museums. My research is based on the masks that were re-invented and adapted for the modern stage by Amleto Sartori in the late 40s and the masks that have been composed following similar influences. With the arrival of those new contemporary masks the actor must start to rethink Commedia dell'Arte for today. The contemporary masks are different from the ancient masks and therefore demand that the actor finds a different way to carry the mask. This new way of knowing, wearing, playing the mask is often not being contemplated in the profession.

How would we have an actor approach a contemporary mask? Or, specifically, how would you approach a contemporary mask as an actor?
I observe the masks of the Commedia dell'Arte imagining that I do not know anything of their past or background; and without trying to interpret what kind of

characters they could be. I simply observe them as if they were sculptures and architectonic forms. I like to look for what is hiding behind those forms, their abstractions, and from that point of view, try to understand them as expressive forms that propose behaviours in the space. Also, I like to research the masks from their outer space and their inner space. From the outer space I can identify a naturalistic mask and from the inner space, I can identify a mimo-dynamic mask (non-naturalistic mask). A mimo-dynamic mask is the inner structure of the naturalistic mask and it governs the behaviour of the form. It has composition and, in its structure, a system of forces that put the form out of balance.

What is the difference between one and the other?
The naturalistic mask shows the basic human types and the non-naturalistic mask (mimo-dynamic mask) personifies the forces and the inner structure of those human types. In our laboratory of research, Manifesto Poetico, we are interested mainly in the mimo-dynamic mask. We are searching for the abstraction of the mask as a starting point for the training of the actor and for the creation of archetypical contemporary characters.

What would be a brief description for each of these ways of seeing the mask: the naturalistic mask and the non-naturalistic mask?
The naturalistic mask describes everything that the audience can identify at a glance, as something concrete, physical. It is what contains the character. It is a container.

The mimo-dynamic mask represents everything that the audience cannot identify at a glance. It is the abstraction of the form, its sensorial aspects and its character content. To see the mask in its imaginative territory and to see all the qualities that make it human but which are not measurable at a glance. It is the *content* of the character.

These two aspects (physical and sensorial) are also used for the composition of the mask. See the technique of mask-sculptor Donato Sartori (Sartori 2003): *Il sentimento e il suo contrario* (feeling and its opposite).

With the mimo-dynamic mask, how can we measure those aspects that we cannot see by simply viewing, or looking at, the mask?
The mask, like an ecosystem, is composed of many interrelated different parts. Like an architectural form, those parts are in constant harmony and in perfect balance with each other. This harmony appears because there is simplicity. The mask is well structured and in correct proportion. Here we are purely talking about geometry.

How do I measure the things that you do not see? I enjoy the investigations and in my research I do not really know how to measure what I cannot see, but I can give them a *measure*. This measure has to be inside the parameters of equilibrium that are defined by the law of gravity. This geometrical point of view is, for me, the first tool for discovering the space, the structure and matter that lies behind the form.

We can say that the movement of the human being comes from the centre of the body, let us say the pelvis, which is also the centre of gravity. We then search for the centre of the mask and, from there, initiate the movement of the mask. We can also measure any physical space and find its centre. In my work with the masks I always find myself with these three constant points: the centre of the body, the centre of the mask and the centre of the dramatic space. To me they are three fixed points.

I find this interesting because these three fixed points are also present in nature. It is enough to know the location of those points and understand them in order to be able to change them and create with them like painters, filmmakers, magicians, architects, etc.

Then, how would the actor be at the service of the mask?
Like any structure, the mask has a centre of gravity that keeps it in balance. For me, a mask that works on the stage is the one that, being suspended in the space, stays in balance. It projects itself on the space through the conflict of its forces that are pushing and pulling it. Within this conflict of forces the mask has to re-establish the balance by itself. It is fundamental for the study of the mask that the actor knows how to identify the centre of the mask and its system of forces that come from that centre.

From the centre of the mask we can see a combination of lines projected on the space. The system of forces of each mask suggests a different way of getting out of balance and a different way of behaving in the space. This essential behaviour of movement is, for me, the seed, the core of the character. With this knowledge we can begin to create a contemporary character (see Figures 14.2 and 14.3).

Figure 14.2 Scene from 'The Moon of Santiago' from Solo dell'Arte. Performed by Carlos Garcia Estevez. The mask is Capitano Matamoros by Donato Sartori.

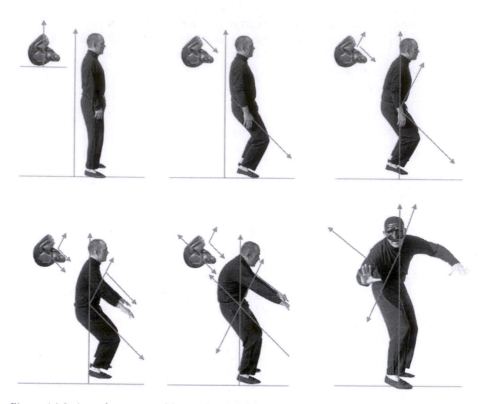

Figure 14.3 A study system of forces for the character Paco Lopez de Baranda. Performed by Carlos Garcia Estevez. The mask is Pantalone by Den Durand.

What is the importance of the masks of the Commedia dell'Arte in the physicality of a contemporary theatre and for a contemporary actor?
Researching the work of the actor is fascinating; as is, of course, the work of the three dimensional masked performer. Here the actor projects himself and creates an impact on the space. The mask gives us this possibility in a very concrete way.

For example, if we look at the mask from a rhythmic point of view we discover that the mask forces the actor to simultaneously apply three different aspects of rhythm. The actor must enter into the rhythm proposed by the form, the rhythm of its musicality and the rhythm of its meter and find a way of talking (which cannot at all be an ordinary way of talking, but rather must be in the world of the mask).

Is it the case that only by observing the mask can we see the high level work necessary for the actor?
Well, yes, at the Manifesto Poetico laboratory we aim to grasp the scope of the mask not only by looking at it, but also by looking beyond it. In order to master the mask as a character, it is very important that the artist knows how to uncover the surface of the form and investigate the machinery of it. Once done, we understand the high level of skill required for this art form. Unfortunately, often the quality of the mask is highly underestimated and the importance of a well-designed mask is very much misunderstood.

It should be obvious that we cannot reach a high level of performance with masks that do not work, that are not expressive or well made. A professional musician cannot produce virtuosity with the kind of violin that is sold in a souvenir shop in Vienna.

I can only know how far and how high a level I can reach if I have a good mask and I know all the qualities that are hidden in the form. So yes, there is a high level of training necessary for the actor to make it work well. Playing the mask is an art in itself. Being an actor does not mean that you can perform with a mask. Mask training is another chapter.

Both the mask and the player must be of the highest level.

When, at the laboratory, we talk about three dimensional work, do we also talk about a three dimensional actor?

I talk about an actor who offers to an audience a three dimensional experience and not a two dimensional, flat experience. I am talking about an experience made in an empty space, the actor and a mask. No scenography, technological elements, costumes, etc. For this, the audience has a fundamental role because they must remember the imaginary state of their childhood where they could create everything possible with just their imagination. The only thing that the mask does is to activate that universe. I think this is the door to that access, a way of seeing the theatre. It is fundamental for a theatre of tomorrow.

The masks of Commedia dell'Arte are an archetypical reference that is recognizable in a universal way and therefore they are an apt gateway for the audience to enter this three dimensional universe. This archetypical reference has permanency for our time.

The actor can, in an empty space, suggest and make us believe we are in a concrete location, one that is already constructed architectonically with concrete directions, depth and perspective. The mask helps the audience enter this theatrical dimension, which is able to show the reality of things in a way that we could not or did not see before, as poetry does with verses and images. I like to think that the mask performer is like an architect of the imagination. The mask in that case would be like a fixed point in the space where the imagination of the audience can be projected. The mask would be as a vanishing point where the audience can project their imagination to the infinite.

Lecoq used to talk about the different aspects of analysing movement. He talked about mechanic, dynamic, dramatic and poetic aspects. Very often we can see propositions that reach a dramatic aspect, but reaching a poetic language is always very difficult. We must show the audience those things that we *do not* see but that *do* exist; the things that we do not yet know about our existence; and what makes us dream. I think the mask is there to accomplish this function and remind us of where we come from in a way that goes beyond reason.

When we talk about inner space, we talk about inner structure. From the point of view of our research, where in space would we place the sensorial and imaginary aspects that we were talking about before? Would we also place them within the inner space?

For a long time I thought that the mask had to be projected towards the space and the audience. I always understood it this way. When I started deeper research about space I realized that it is the audience who projects themselves into the mask, and it

137

is the actor who receives this impact from the audience; he then takes it and he sends it back, already transformed. The form – that is, the mask – receives information from the audience; it uses its sensorial and imaginative universe to transform it within its poetic universe and then performs it. For me, one of the purposes of the mask is to be a kind of mirror for the audience, a sort of filter. The extraordinarily difficult thing for the actor to do is to articulate this inner space in a very sharp way in order for the expression to be sent back to the audience – a transformed, suggestive, provoking and poetic expression. That means that, for me, the mask tells the story depending on the audience's state of being, ambience, atmosphere and characteristics. Sometimes what the actor receives from the audience is not concrete: a kind of energy, the way they breathe, their reactions to what they see, gestures, etc. In my view, this dialogue between the inner and the outer space (push and pull) that exists between the mask and the audience is a passionate game, and it is only possible to play it if the actor possesses the madness, the playful spirit and the seriousness of a child playing. We can find the same spirit in popular tradition: a festive and celebratory spirit: the spirit of the collective.

Reference

Sartori, Donati (2003) *Le Maschere nell'antichita, Storia, modi e metodi della maschera dell'arte*. Villa Pacchiani, Italy: Centro Maschere e Strutture Gestuali.

15

NEW ROLES FOR THE MASK IN TWENTIETH CENTURY THEATRE

Donato Sartori

Translated by Peter Jordan

If we were to trace the history of the theatrical mask in the last century of the second millennium, we should first refer to the adventure that the English director and set designer Edward Gordon Craig (1872–1966) had both with the theatre and with the theatrical mask – virtually unknown in the late nineteenth century – which he somehow resurrected from the limbo of a distant past. The son of Ellen Terry – one of the greatest British actresses of all time – he was one of the major scenic innovators of the twentieth century, and the only one to come directly from a stage background.

Critical of the hyper-realism that was all the rage at the time, he proposed, in the framework of a set reduced to its essentials, but enriched with massive architectonic shapes, an *übermarionette* actor who, as in ancient Greece, had a face covered by a mask. In Florence, in 1908, he began publishing the magazine *The Mask*, where he states:

> Used by the savages when making war at a time when war was looked upon as an art; used by the ancients in their ceremonies when faces were held to be too weak and disturbing an element; used by those artists of the theatre, Æschylus, Sophocles and Euripides; found essential to their highest drama by the Japanese masters of the ninth and fourteenth centuries; rejected later on in the eighteenth century by the European actors, and relegated by them to the toy shop and the fancy-dress ball, the Mask has sunk to the level of the Dance, of Pantomime and of the Marionette. From being a work of art carved in wood or ivory and sometimes ornamented with precious metals or precious stones, and later made in leather, it has frittered itself away to a piece of paper, badly painted or covered with black satin.
>
> (Craig 1920: 98–110)

In later life, Craig was an instructor at the Academy of Fine Arts in Florence, teaching young people a theatre of pure movement, where it is possible that he had some influence on the young Amleto Sartori, a student of sculpture at the same institute. The ball was now rolling: curiosity about this extraordinary tool-object, the mask, would pervade the theatrical world for the entire century.

A few years later, in 1912 Germany, the then twenty-four-year-old Oskar Schlemmer, one of the fathers of the Bauhaus movement in Weimar, formulated his first ideas for dance, costume and mask projects, which later became known as the Triadisches Ballett, or Triadic Ballet. Almost simultaneously, in France, a young dramatist, Jacques Copeau, who also established himself as a director, actor and author, opened a small theatre on the Left Bank: the Théâtre du Vieux Colombier. The adjoining drama school was attended by some of the best-known (and not only French) theatrical figures of the century. These events unfolded between 1913 and 1924 and resonated throughout Europe, not only for being a real and actual workshop for theatre artists, but also for the application of a new scenic system and the choice of the mask as a means of theatrical expression. From then on, it took on a role of primary importance for research and the training of actors who would claim theatre as a fundamental dimension of their own lives.

Copeau was considered by many as the forefather of a new way of making theatre through the creative self-immersion of the performer in the text and the theatrical event, in a spirit of exultation. This approach was taken up by the most innovative and iconic figures of the French stage: from Charles Dullin; to Louis Jouvet (whom Copeau first met in 1910); to Georges Pitoëff; and a young Jean Vilar, who later created two major theatrical institutions, the Avignon Festival and the Théâtre National Populaire.

The cultural ferment of those years was also stimulated by a strong push, from researchers and theatre historians in search of their lost roots, to return to the origins of that popular theatre from the early Renaissance onwards: the Commedia dell'Arte – for well over two centuries, the undisputed protagonist of the European stage. The initial impetus came from a young critic and historian of Russian theatre Konstantin Miklaševskij (1886–1944), who in 1915 published in St. Petersburg a work entitled: 'La Commedia dell'Arte or the Theatre of the Italian Comedians of the XVI, XVII and XVIII Centuries'. This text appeared in the Russian journal, *The Love for Three Oranges*, edited by Meyerhold, and is of undoubted documentary historical value. It is in itself of relevant interest, as it provides tangible evidence of a revivalist period and a focus on the techniques, themes and masks of the Commedia dell'Arte in the Russian avant-garde.

This publication, the subtitle of which was *The Journal of Dr. Everywhere*, a.k.a. Dr Dappertutto (Meyerhold's nom-de-plume), and which appeared for nine editions, fought under the banner of the Commedia dell'Arte and the work of Gozzi, against the psychological and naturalist theatre in vogue at that time. The first appearance of Italian comedians was at the court of Tsarina Anna Ivanovna in 1731. From this date on, many companies took the chance to advance into Russian territory, spreading the Commedia dell'Arte throughout the country, as far as Siberia.

From the very beginning of his theatrical journey, Copeau studied and shared his longstanding love for Commedia masks with Leon Chancerel, an outstanding man of the theatre who opened up to him a vast documentary repertoire of figures and characters. This included Maurice Sand's *Masques et Bouffons*, illustrated with the exquisite polychrome etchings of A. Manceau (Sand 1860). It was against this background that Konstantin Miklaševskij (who took the pseudonym "Mic" when his book was published in France in 1927) made Copeau's acquaintance, marking the beginning of a firm friendship and long collaboration. It was in fact Copeau's belief that "the masked actor has greater power than the one whose face is visible to the public." After a long series of diverse theatrical projects, the French actor and director, Charles Dullin (1885–1949), decided to join forces with Copeau at the Vieux Colombier. In 1921, he founded his own school, attended, among others, by Antonin Artaud, Jean-Louis Barrault and Étienne Decroux.

At the outbreak of World War I, on a train to Paris were two young men who had decided to enlist in the 22nd regiment of Dragoons. They were Pierre Louis Duchartre and Charles Dullin (See the interview with P. L. Duchartre mentioned in *Art of the Mask in the Commedia dell'Arte* (1983) by Sartori and Lanata.) This meeting convinced Duchartre to immerse himself in the strange and unfamiliar world of that theatre, to which he did not belong, but for which he had a visceral fascination. In fact, once the war was over, he dedicated himself to researching the origins of theatre and the masks of the Commedia dell'Arte. In 1925, he published the first draft of *La Comédie Italienne*, which would become one of the most sought-after cultural references for actors, directors, scholars and theatre aficionados (Duchartre 1925).

Among the many students of Copeau's Vieux Colombier School, one in particular, Étienne Decroux, emerged specializing in the use of the body as a theatrical tool, so much so that he would go on to champion mimetic forms which attracted many emerging performers of the time, including Jean-Louis Barrault and Marcel Marceau.

"Remove the face to rediscover the body" was the defining aim of the school's pedagogical methodology and would become the motto of Decroux, who believed in concealing the actor's facial expressions from the audience's sight. To this end, he developed his own original mask technique. In fact, he used an extremely light fabric, similar to a veil, which enveloped the actor's head, while still allowing relative visual clarity and unrestricted breathing (see Figure 15.1).

At the Vieux Colombier School, on the other hand, cardboard masks were manufactured according to Copeau's own experimental technique. These consisted of pieces of newspaper, superimposed in layers, and cemented with glue made from wheat starch and the addition of a sugar cube. This recipe was a trade secret of Copeau's and added to the mystery of the mask.

The vaguely anthropomorphic masks had to be completely expressionless, so as to task student actors with expressing the various emotions solely through a mimetic use of the body. It should be noted that Copeau's masks were only used for training purposes, never for public performance. This particular teaching tool was known as the "noble" or "calm" mask for the aloof lack of expression that characterized it. Eventually, at the end of World War II in Padua, it took on the name of "neutral mask" (see Figure 15.2).

The vehicle of transmission was Jean Dasté, pupil and son-in law to Copeau, having married his daughter Marie Hélène. After the experience of the Vieux Colombier, Dasté decided to follow the master, who moved to Burgundy in 1924, where he organized a group of actors: the Copiaus.

Figure 15.1 Étienne Decroux with a mask.

Figure 15.2 Jacques Lecoq with a male neutral mask by Amleto Sartori: Lesson-Performance
Tout Bouge by and with Jacques Lecoq 1970.

In 1945, Dasté and Marie Hélène founded their own company, Les Comédiens de Grenoble, named after the city in which they put into practice the theories, teachings and mask work learned from Copeau. This was where the young Jacques Lecoq made his first appearance as a professional actor-mime, having recently completed a course in the study of dramatic art under Charles Dullin and Jean-Louis Barrault.

For the young twenty-four-year-old mime, working in the Grenoble group signalled his first encounter with the mythical Copeau, the pedagogical tradition of the Vieux Colombier and above all with the experience of the Copiaus.

Through Dasté, Lecoq would discover the *jeu du masque* and above all many tricks of the trade, with regard to both the use and creation of papier-mâché masks.

Returning to Paris in 1945, Lecoq was hired by the recently founded EPJD (Education par le jeu dramatique) school, directed by Jean-Louis Barrault. It was here that he discovered his vocation as a teacher, rather than as an actor. It was also here that he met the Venetian director Gianfranco De Bosio and his associate Lieta Papafava dei Carraresi who were in Paris – thanks to a grant from the University of Padua – for a theatrical refresher course at the EPJD. De Bosio – assistant to the poet Diego Valeri, then director of the Faculty of Arts – worked hard to change the prescribed course of academic theatre; at that time it was extremely conservative and pervaded by traditionalist currents that did not reflect the sense of cultural euphoria spanning Europe in the immediate post-war period. In fact, in that enthusiastic climate, the university produced – under the guidance of distinguished academics and young people who had participated in the Resistance – a series of cultural initiatives, including one to found its own university theatre.

On his return from Paris, De Bosio took over the leadership of the Teatro dell'Università and founded the adjoining school, where, among those invited to teach, were: Lecoq, for movement; Lieta Papafava, for acting and text; Ludovico Zorzi, theatre history; and Amleto Sartori, art history and mask-making.

A few days after his arrival, Lecoq made his first demonstration to the actors of the company, and immediately showed what he could do. In particular he demonstrated the famous walking-on-the-spot mime, invented in the thirties by Decroux. There was ironic appreciation from an actor who blurted out: "Great, but where are you going?" (*bravo... ma dove va?*). This led Lecoq to the realization that pure mime, intended as an independent genre, as performed by the likes of Decroux and Marcel Marceau, was far removed from the *mime dramatique* open to the theatre.

Lecoq was not carrying masks of any sort when he arrived in Padua. The only one he had, given to him by Dasté, was foolishly lent to a dancer for a demonstration in Germany: "I arrived in Padua with the technique for the construction of a neutral mask in my head, and the idea of working this mask in the school."

De Bosio suggested he contact the sculptor Amleto Sartori, who had already made masks for a performance of *poesia Negra* (Afro-Cuban poetry) mounted by the University of Padua. Other masks followed for productions that the University Theatre staged from 1948 to 1951. Among these was an extraordinary production of *Six Characters in Search of an Author*, directed by Gianfranco De Bosio, with Giulio Bosetti in the role of the child. Sartori's involvement in the Pirandello project gave him the chance to explore the depths of the human psyche, producing a series of character-masks in multi-coloured papier-mâché which gave a decidedly modern feel to the whole production.

The die was now cast. The fame of Amleto's masks spread quickly, not just in Italy but throughout Europe during the post-war cultural re-awakening. Naturally gifted in portraiture, Amleto was intrigued by Lecoq's request for masks to be used in the drama school. After noting the complete inability of students to model the neutral faces of the masks, he proposed an extremely effective solution. As Lecoq recounts:

> moulding the clay was the most difficult thing for the students to accomplish. The results were very unsatisfactory. The masks were only neutral in name... Sartori observed our efforts with great respect and with some compassion. Then, with the opening of my first masked mime, *Seaport*, inspired by the port of Chioggia, Amleto came to the expert and authoritative decision that the masks would have to be made by him, as ours were too ugly. No one ventured to oppose his decision, nor did I expect anyone to: a heavy weight had been removed from our shoulders. So, with neutral masks of papier-mâché and glue, Sartori began his adventure with masks and, for me, it was the beginning of a long collaboration and a great friendship.
> (Sartori and Lanata 1983 [Taken from J. Lecoq, "The geometry at the service of emotion" in *Art of the Mask in the Commedia dell'Arte*])

In fact, the fame of the leather masks created by the Italian artist reached Jean-Louis Barrault in Paris, who initially wanted to experiment with the masks of the Commedia dell'Arte for a production at the Théâtre Marigny (1951) and later for the characters of Ruzante's *Vaccaria*.

These productions were a great success in Paris. The audience was enthralled and was soon treated to a new production that Barrault would stage for the International Festival of Bordeaux (1955) and subsequently at the Odeon Theatre in Paris, Aeschylus' complex trilogy, the *Oresteia*, with some seventy-five leather masks sculpted by Amleto Sartori (see Figure 15.3).

Those were the years of my early childhood memories of theatre and masks, a period that in the eyes of a boy were seen as a game. I remember long sleepless nights, due to the presence of actors and theatre people who frequented my home in Riviera Paleocapa, from whose windows I could see the majestic grandeur of the Observatory.

I remember the frenzied rantings of Agostino Contarello, an extraordinary Paduan actor-author, who came over to rehearse his theatrical characters, before performing them at the University Theatre. During the endless nights of wakefulness (I slept in a room next to the kitchen, the only heated room in the house, where the gatherings took place), dozens of people would meet to discuss theatre or just to drink a good few glasses of wine with friends, often until morning. The friendship between my father and Jacques Lecoq (later joined by Marcello Moretti, Strehler's extraordinary Arlecchino) was such that the two often disappeared for whole days in search of distinctive characters and faces, real human masks that could only be found in certain parts of the city or its environs.

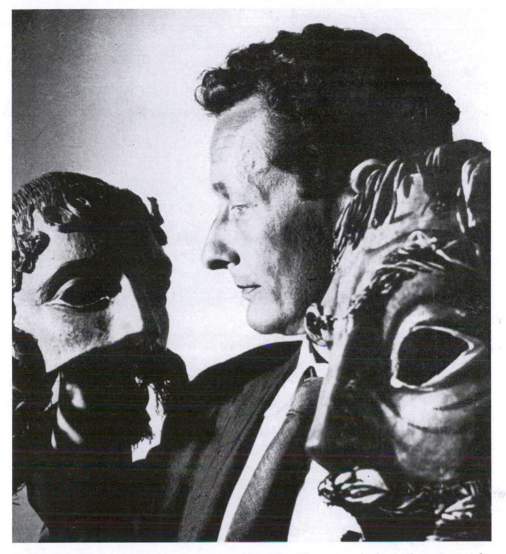

Figure 15.3 Actor and Director Jean Louis Barrault with two masks by Amletto Sartori for *the Oresteia* by Aeschylus, 1955.

The market for fruits and herbs, under the Great Hall in the old town, with its colourful stalls and fragrances, teeming with picturesque popular fauna, was an inexhaustible source of inspiration for typically Paduan Ruzantian masks. Amleto loved these places and often came with Lecoq in search of inspiration, like a curious, enraptured child. He was discovering the true, popular essence of Italy: the Italy of the *Commedia all'Improvviso*. The Italy of Beolco's plays was here, alive with his real characters, with the typical yelling and shouting of the street markets.

Like all the best fairy tales, the adventure of the University Theatre of Padua came to an end. The first signs of a crisis gripping it brought Giorgio Strehler closer.

Together with Paolo Grassi, he had successfully launched the Piccolo Teatro in Milan some years previously. The first meeting between Sartori and Strehler took place on a sunny day at the end of 1951, in a cafe fronting the Teatro Olimpico in Vicenza, where the Piccolo Teatro was staging Sophocles' *Electra* directed by Strehler and choreographed by Lecoq.

The partnership between Amleto and the Piccolo continued until his death, and saw the creation of, among other things, the first leather masks for *Arlecchino, Servant of Two Masters*. Subsequently, the collaboration with Strehler continued with the creation of other masks made by me, including my 'Cat' Arlecchino for Ferruccio Soleri, which still prevails on stages all over the world. From this moment on, the future of Amleto Sartori was dedicated to research on the theatrical mask. Unfortunately, he did not have the chance see the fruits of so much work. Cancer took him away, aged just forty-six, after a brave but futile struggle against the disease. It fell to me to learn from his still living hands, thereby assuring the continuance of his extraordinary research, in the work of his apprentice-son, who had been raised from a very young age in the daily routine of a workshop that had a vague whiff of the Renaissance about it. These were very hard times when I struggled with the choices to be made, and a direction that was not just the slavish continuation of a path already marked out. But shortly thereafter, the cultural avalanche of 1968 in Paris engulfed me. The excitement of this extraordinary landmark event pushed me to take a risk with choices and decisions, which even today I do not regret.

The combining of theatre with the visual arts, music with gesture and dance, colour with form, launched me into a new multidisciplinary dimension, allowing me to embark on extraordinary adventures and experiments that took me to every corner of the planet.

In 1979 the first nucleus was formed under the title: The Masks and Gestural Structures Centre (Centro Maschere e Strutture Gestuali). It was composed of myself; Paolo Trombetta, then a young designer with previous theatre experience; and the neo-architect, Paola Piizzi; and my wife. A few years ago we were joined by our daughter, Sarah Sartori.

This interdisciplinary body, that to this day still confines itself within the ambit of the mask, was later divided into three strands or core areas of investigation and study:

- the ethno-anthropological mask;
- the theatrical mask, from antiquity to the present day;
- beyond the mask.

The latter strand focused on recent interdisciplinary research regarding urban disguise and gestural structures. Despite the long and arduous journey, begun with so much effort and uncertainty, through many ups and downs, and extraordinary artistic ventures, we are still together after more than thirty years of association.

For the entire course of that first year there was a constant wandering across Europe between educational research activities and mounting ever more complex and significant shows, including the production of new masks for new theatrical productions, designs for urban masquerades, and outdoor "happenings". Often the seminars were accompanied by a wide variety of collaborations with actors, performers or visual artists. Among the many participants, the actor Mario Gonzales – a veteran of the recent extraordinary experiment of the Théâtre du Soleil, *L'Age d'Or*, directed by Arianne Mnouchkine – revealed a real talent for the interpretation of characters from the Commedia dell'Arte.

The collaboration continued in a long string of seminars in Brussels, and more in Como, organized by the Piccolo Teatro of Milan. In a later series in Greece, more specifically the island of Zakintos, we had the good fortune to have the extraordinary participation of the Minister of Culture, the actress Melina Mercouri, who performed versions of several female masks. After a gruelling tour to the most iconic capitals of Eastern Europe: Bucharest, Warsaw, Prague, Budapest and Belgrade, word of our activities came to Italy and made its way through the bureaucratic maze of the 1980 Biennale of Venice Theatre. The then director, Maurizio Scapparo, whose ambitious initiatives transformed the city into one big stage, sent for me because he wanted to present a coherent plan conceived as a completely new and novel approach to this event. He wanted to revive the ancient Venetian carnival, dormant for centuries, to re-invest it with a character that was not only playful, but also theatrical and cultural. What better time to show off the new mask than for a new carnival that would soon open a new era for the city of Venice?

I proposed a project that would cater to Maurizio Scapparo's needs but that would also break out of the specific theatre context allocated to me. I and my colleagues proceeded to take possession of the little theatre situated on the north side of the ancient Palazzo Grassi. We cleared it of its old seats, thus opening up an extraordinary space for experimentation.

Together with the new staff of the Abano Terme Centre, we held a series of meetings at the Academy of Fine Arts, with the intention of selecting collaborators from among its teachers and students. From Poland, we brought over the Osmego Dnia Orkiestra, one of the musical groups of the Polish avant-garde that we had heard during our recent tour of Eastern Europe. We also engaged a theatre group from the Venetian hinterland (Teatro Modo) and a modern dance company (Charà). All in all, we were able to count on the participation of around sixty collaborators.

We named our operation, Ambienteazione, a term which left no doubt as to the nature of the project. We worked day and night creating architectural reliefs of particular zones of the city, then proceeded to conduct some historical enquiries, drawing up maps suitable for identifying the routes most amenable to itinerant spectacle.

The stage and all the interior space were used daily for theatre and dance rehearsals, or for finding the most viable methods of installing acrylic fibre in the most emblematic parts of Venice. As we approached the date set, our anxiety increased proportionally to the remaining time available for completing all our preparations. In the last forty days, to save time, the theatre became a huge camp where we ate frugally and slept in sleeping bags. The days leading up to Mardi Gras were used by the group to envelop the alleys, little squares, piazzas, bell towers, bridges and historic buildings with this white fibre, which took on the appearance of a giant spider's web. Along the way, the invasive acrylic material created spaces suitable for theatrical events and performances, which added the human element within an aesthetic framework, bringing it to life through gesture and dance. On the morning of the fateful Tuesday, it was dull and damp. To the first pedestrians hurrying by, Piazza San Marco appeared to be completely transformed, cloaked under a huge weave of white threads that covered the sky with a dome of air, a billowing cocoon that swelled and swooped with the sea breeze, in a sort of ethereal dance.

The square began to fill up quickly with a crowd of onlookers, tourists, and participants who attended the day's theatre, dance and artistic entertainments, specially arranged for the occasion. However, a miracle occurred in the evening, when an overflowing crowd filled the entire piazza; something that even I and my colleagues had not foreseen.

Under the vast floodlights installed by RAI (Italian Radio and Television), to the moving sound of complex musical instruments used by the Polish group, something happened which I never would have expected. The unanticipated magic of the moment and the effect of the sound spreading across the square to a rhythm imposed by the wind on that enormous blanket of air, set off an explosion of participatory energy in the crowd that, up to that point, had remained latent. So it was that this immense audience of eighty-five thousand people began to play with us, taking possession of the threads billowing in the wind, which were then used for a collective game played by tens of thousands of hands waving in the air intent on catching, pulling and unravelling the web that now covered all those present in the piazza. In this way, the first day of carnival was celebrated without masks, but covered by one single immense masking that set the ball rolling for an endless succession of novel and resurgent Venetian carnivals (see Figure 15.4).

Figure 15.4 Urban Mask by Donato Sartori and Centro Maschere e Strutture Gestuali, Venice, Piazza San Marco Theatre Biennale, culminating moment of the nocturnal performance, Ambienteazione, 1980.

The old Venetian carnival had endured for centuries until the fall of the Republic to Napoleonic forces, in 1797. If, for Venice, this masking was the beginning of the modern carnival, for the Mask Centre, in collaboration with Ambienteazione, it was the beginning of a successful series of seminars, performances and urban maskings that within a few years of activity reached other major Italian cities: Genoa, Trieste, Naples, Padua, Milan and later Bologna and Florence. These events, far from being equivalent to theatrical plays, required particular and specific plans for each site, incorporating social, cultural and architectural differences from one place to another.

The 1980s and 1990s saw an increasing number of projects in Europe, including touring exhibitions, educational activities, installations and urban maskings. These were also sought after in other parts of the world, including Latin America, the United States, the Middle and Far East. They were busy years for the design and construction of new themed exhibitions which, through the promotion of the Italian Ministry of Foreign Affairs, took us on tour to Africa (Nigeria, Tanzania, Ghana and Cote d'Ivoire); to other capitals such as Paris, Moscow, Tokyo and Beijing (where we saw the vicious repression of the student uprising in Tiananmen Square); then to Houston in the United States; to Rio de Janeiro, where we created a spectacular urban masking in the central Cinelandia Square; and then to San Paulo, Brasilia as well as many other cities in North-East Brazil.

Each activity in the various parts of the world allowed us to mingle radically with the cultural fabric of different countries. We took advantage of this opportunity to collect materials, documents and artefacts that would serve an idea taking shape with increasing urgency: The House of Masks.

In the ensuing years, we divided our time between the home laboratory of Abano Terme, a spa town situated between Padua and Venice, and long stays abroad. Among the various activities to emerge in the mid-1990s was a request from a prestigious theatre, the Folkteatern Gävle in Sweden, run by Peter Oskarson, to resurrect from the depths of a distant past, medieval Nordic masks: a legacy of the Viking epics (see Figure 15.5).

The ambitious World Theatre Project took advantage of the resources of a Swedish theatre body that provided, among other facilities, a fully equipped studio-workshop, Maskverkstaden. I ran it, for nearly ten years, as a centre for historical research, experimentation and creation of sculptures, masks, tools and objects deployed within the complex structure of international theatre. The World Theatre Project also took advantage of collaborations with international groups, including the Peking Opera of Shanghai directed by Ma-Ke; the Natana Kairali centre for Kathakali and Kuttyattam dance, directed by Gopal Venu, in Kerala, India; the African war dances of Teatro Avenida, Mozambique; Folkteatern Gävle, Sweden; and the Mask Centre at Abano Terme.

In the same context, the extraordinary production of the complex Aeschylus trilogy, the *Oresteia*, directed by Peter Oskarson, was brought to life. This allowed us to make several study trips to sites for historical research and for the staging of this Greek opus – to India, Mozambique and many places in Greece – in order to get to know the locations, theatres and religious places mentioned in it. To develop the one hundred and forty masks, made according to new typologies and construction techniques, we experimented in depth with the imagined acoustics for the Greek

Figure 15.5 Donato Sartori, Hellequin, diabolic leader of Nordic mythology, World Theatre Project, directed by Peteer Oskarson, Shadow Puppet in untreated elk leather, Sweden 1999.

chorus. We were thus able to compare them with those made over fifty years ago by my father, under the direction of J. L. Barrault for the same tragedy created by the Odeon Theatre in Paris.

The new millennium seems to have brought a renewed interest to Italy in relation to indigenous cultural impulses, shifting a natural passion for foreign things that, for a long time, has been orientated towards a pro-American globalisation. In this setting, a historic advisory meeting, in Abano Terme, decided unanimously to assign and dedicate an ancient Venetian villa, conveniently restored and refurbished as a museum, to the research and activities of the Sartoris (see Figure 15.6).

This is a new House of Masks, a living museum, not set in stone, where the interests can converge not only of scholars in the field, but also of those involved with theatre, music; in short, the expressive arts. It is for everyone who wants to learn about cultural origins, which confer on Italian culture a historic role that places it at the forefront of the most extraordinary artistic sites on the entire planet.

Figure 15.6 Venetian Villa Trevisan Savioli, owned by the municipality of Abano Terme: site of the Museo Internazionale della Maschera Amleto e Donato Sartori.

These last years were devoted mainly to this ambitious museum project, a culmination of many years of collective work by the members of the centre. Finally, it seems to be approaching its completion, thus permitting us to concentrate all the resources and privileges acquired over nearly seventy-five years, on Venetian territory, the natural historical seat of the mask, be it theatrical, carnivalesque or recreational.

Here, after many decades of gruelling artistic and cultural activity, of research around the world, after propagating through a capillary effect the sense of the Italian theatrical mask, a focal point has been created, on which to merge attention on one of the most diffuse communication tools in every epoch, for as long as man has existed: Amleto and Donato's International Museum of the Mask (Internazionale della Maschera Amleto e Donato Sartori), opened in 2005 by Franca Rame and Nobel Prize winner Dario Fo with a show created especially for the occasion, *Masks, Puppets and Painted Men* (*Maschere, Pupazzi e Uomini Dipinti*). (See Figure 15.7.)

I give notice that in 2015 there will be many international cultural activities (exhibitions, conferences, seminars, etc.) on the occasion of the centenary of the birth of Amleto Sartori, the thirtieth birthday of Mask, Gesture, Narration (Maschera Gesto Narrazione) at the International Seminar on the Art of the Mask in the Commedia dell'Arte (Seminario Internazionale Arte della Maschera nella Commedia dell'Arte).

Figure 15.7 Donato Sartori (left) with Nobel Prize winning playwright Dario Fo (2005).

References

Craig, Edward Gordon (1920) 'A Note on Masks' in *The Theatre Advancing*. Boston, US: Little, Brown and Company, pp. 98–110.

Duchartre, Pierre Louis (1925) *La Comedie Italienne*. Paris: Librarie de Franca.

Miklaševskij, Konstantin (1915) 'La Commedia dell'Arte or the Theatre of the Italian Comedians of the XVI, XVII, and XVIII Centuries' in *The Love of Three Oranges* (ed. V. Meyerhold). Moscow: L'Académie Impériale des Sciences de Russie.

Sand, Maurice (1860) *Masques et Bouffons*. Paris: A. Levy Fils.

Sartori, Donato and Lanata, B. (1983) *Art of the Mask in the Commedia dell'Arte*. Florence, Italy: House of Usher.

LANGUAGE

16

GROMMELOT

John Rudlin

Grommelot is the supposedly gibberish or nonsense language invented by the *comici dell'arte* for use in rehearsal and performance. I say 'supposedly' because gibberish is meaningless, whereas grommelot is meaningful. Nonsense can be resorted to anytime and anywhere, often to obscure, whereas grommelot is context specific and comprehensible. Michel Saint-Denis called it 'the music of meaning': not nonsense at all, but the distillation of sense into onomatopoeic vocalisation (Saint-Denis 1982). Antonin Artaud was fascinated by it, finding as he did that words were a barrier to meaning rather than an intensifier of it. Other orthographies for this made-up language are 'grammelot' or 'grumelot'; sometimes with one 'm', sometimes with two; sometimes in the singular, sometimes the plural. My preference for 'grommelot' is based on the following etymology:

In vulgar Latin there was a word *grumellu*s from which modern French derives *grumeau* meaning a small particle, e.g. of salt. And *grumeller* is to sprinkle with the above. In Italian a *gremolada* is a mixture of chopped garlic and parsley traditionally sprinkled on Milanese osso bucco and a *grumelo* is a small lump. On the other hand, *grommeler* in French is to mutter under one's breath. According to Larousse, *grommeler* is 'from the ancient German, *grummelu*, Swedish *grymta*, English *to grumble*, words formed from the prefix *ge*, from which nothing has remained except the first letter, and a primitive which signifies to tumble or to mutter, to make a muffled or muted sound' (1865).

The earliest recorded instances given are from 1547. The Oxford English Dictionary also has 'to gromme' as being to growl like a beast, probably from the Dutch *grommelen*. Either 'grumelot' or 'grommelot' would seem to be etymologically correct, therefore, if we admit that sounds can be sprinkled as if on food, or muttered between the teeth or growled. Zanni's ever grumbling stomach would argue for the former, the animal origins of individual Masks for the latter. I think we may discount 'grammelot' as a misnomer based on the supposition that a language must have something to do with grammar.

Dario Fo prefers 'grammelot', however: in his Nobel Prize acceptance speech he stressed the importance of its contribution to his work, originating, he supposed, in the plays of the early sixteenth century playwright Angelo Beolco, a.k.a. Ruzante. For Fo, the latter was 'the true father of the Commedia dell'Arte' who, furthermore:

> constructed a language of his own, a language of and for the theatre, based on a variety of tongues: the dialects of the Po Valley, expressions in Latin, Spanish, even German, all mixed with onomatopoeic sounds of his own invention. It is from him, from Beolco Ruzante, that I've learned to free myself from conventional literary writing and to express myself with words that you can chew, with unusual sounds, with various techniques of rhythm and breathing, even with the rambling nonsense-speech of the grammelot.
> (Fo 1997: Nobel Prize for Literature acceptance speech)

In addition, Maurice Sand in his *The History of the Harlequinade* states that: 'In truth Ruzante was the first to open the doors of comedy to popular dialects. All his characters speak different languages from Paduan, Bergamese, Bolognese, Venetian and Tuscan to Latin, Italianised Spanish and modern Greek' (Sand 1915: 283).

As Commedia spread throughout Europe in the sixteenth and seventeenth centuries its polyglot nature was a strength rather than a weakness. One could even argue that grommelot was unnecessary to it, since most of its languages would have been locally incomprehensible, even in Italy itself. The high-heeled boot has always been an obvious geographical entity, but it was not until 1860, after the efforts of Mazzini, Cavour and Garibaldi, that it became a political and linguistic one. In the *seicento* each Mask spoke the dialect of its region of origin. These dialects were as various as there are as there are kinds of pasta. In his *Treatise on Acting* Andrea Perrucci says of Pantalone, for example, that 'whoever plays this role must have perfected the Venetian tongue, with all its dialects, proverbs and vocabulary' (Perrucci 2008: 131). In Neapolitan comedy there was a *vecchio* called Pangrazio il Bisccglicse. Bisceglia is a little town in Apulia whose dialect, with its whining intonation, had the Neapolitans in stitches whenever they heard it. Apparently audiences laughed as soon as Pangrazio entered and hooted with ridicule as soon as he opened his mouth. Pantalone's avian cackle would be similarly derided throughout Italy.

Another class for pan-Italian ridicule was the professional. The Doctor, the know-nothing know-it-all, can extemporise on medicine, jurisprudence, astronomy, rhetoric, *et cetera, ad infinitum*. This was known as his *sproloquio*. 'Il Dottore Gratiano', Perrucci says, has to have 'perfect Bolognese'. But what was perfect Bolognese? According to Giarenzo Clivio:

> As the rest of the Gallo-Italic dialects, Bolognese shows the well-known tendency to drop unstressed vowels, but even more markedly so than Milanese or Piedmontese, so that its phonemic economy differs drastically from Italian and southern dialects, and even Venetian: abundant heterorganic consonant clusters, a complex metaphonic system affecting the surviving tonic vowels ... contribute to making genuine Bolognese a very difficult language to other Italians.
>
> (Clivio 1989: 219)

The actor Pier Maria Cecchini recommended making the Doctor more comprehensible by 'Tuscanising' his Bolognese, preferably incorrectly. Add to that Gratiano's propensity for peppering his speech with misquoted Latin tags, his lisp and his persistent insobriety and one wonders whether comprehensibility was a *sine qua non*.

As a despised mercenary, Il Capitano could speak Spanish, Neapolitan, or even Sicilian. The first zanni spoke in his dialect of regional origin, Bergamese in the case of Brighella, for example or, in the case of Coviello, Neapolitan; the second zanni in mountain Bergamese or Neapolitan again in the case of Pulcinella. The Lovers, according to Perrucci, 'should study in order to have perfect knowledge of the Italian language, with its Tuscan vocabulary' (Perrucci 2008: 194). This was not modern Italian, however: they addressed each other in a bookish, rather archaic and stilted language that no one actually spoke outside the literary academies.

Did the early *comici dell'arte* really add grommelot to this salmagundi on their tours round the republics and city states of Italy: Savoy (Turino), Genoa, Lucca, Milano, Parma, Mantua, Padua, The Venetian Republic (Venice,) Ferrara, The Papal State (Bologna, Urbino, Rome), Toscano (Florence, Sienna), and Napoli, not to mention Corsica, Sardinia, and Sicilia? If they did, it could only have been in order to simplify rather complicate the task of comedic communication, affording the Masks at least one language in common, at the same time as inviting the audience to be complicit in their communality. As their range spread as far Germany, Russia and Denmark, it may have become even more important to their vocabulary.

With grommelot we are looking at, or rather hearing, an oral tradition which may date back as far as the Roman *mimes,* cast adrift to tour Europe in search of a living after the closure of the amphitheatres in the fourth century AD. The carnality of the late Roman stage left the early Christian Fathers no option but to create, agree and promulgate a doctrine which condemned both theatre itself (as an alternative public congregation to the mass) and the *mimes* who performed its profane rituals. In 306 AD the Council of Elvira compelled actors to abandon their calling before being received into the Christian Church, and those who did not do so became pariahs. All over the former Roman Empire outlawed actors thus took to the road and had to compete for a living with jugglers and rope-dancers. Under the Goths, spoken Latin fell into disrepair and strolling players perhaps found themselves in need of a new *lingua franca* with which to communicate with their audiences. By the time of the crusades there was one such to hand, or rather to tongue: the Lingua Franca! This was a commercial pidgin based on several Mediterranean languages and used extensively in seaports up until the late eighteenth century in order for different nations to be able to bargain and trade. Only fragments of it remain and there is no way of knowing to what extent, if any, it related to grommelot. It is, however, worth noting that actors were not the only ones to find need of such pan-European lines of communication. In *Mistero Buffo* Dario Fo consciously re-created such a language from archaic Po Valley dialects and phonemes from Latin, Spanish and German as well as onomatopoeic sounds for international consumption. The Canadian globe-trotting Cirque du Soleil call their version Cirquish but admit that is just their word for grommelot. However, anyone wishing to hear true grommelot in international action can do no better than listen to Pingu, the modelling clay penguin boy, as voiced by Carlo Bonomi, an Italian clown and comic actor. Bonomi dubbed all the different voices for the original made-in-Sweden animation series without a script, *all'improvviso*. The seemingly nonsensical language he used is sometimes called Pinguish or Penguinese by the numerous world-wide adult aficionados of the programme. But Bonomi was in fact using grommelot. The original *Pingu* series ended in 1998, but the rights were bought six years later by a British company who produced a further fifty-two five minute programmes. Bonomi was considered too old for the new series and he was replaced by Marcello Magni, a founder member of Complicité and David Sant, a London-based Spanish actor and clown. Both had learned *grummelotage* at the Paris school of Jacques LeCoq. LeCoq learned it from Jacques Copeau's son-in-law Jean Dasté when he was at the Comédie St. Etienne. Charles Dullin, Leon Chancerel and Michel Saint-Denis also used it in their schools and all acknowledged that it sprang from the work initiated by Copeau and Suzanne Bing in the Vieux Colombier School, where Dasté was a pupil. Copeau, I suspect, gleaned it from watching the Fratellini Brothers clowning at The Circus Medrano in Paris, to which he was a frequent visitor; he subsequently invited them to teach clowning at his new school.

So where did the Fratellinis get it from? Paris, 14 May 1697, letter to the lieutenant general of the police: 'The King has dismissed his Italian actors and His Majesty orders me to write to you to close their theatre forever' (Scott 1990: 326). The King was Louis XIV who, as a boy, had adored the Commedia performers, Scaramouche in particular. Aged five, the Dauphin is supposed to have laughed so much at the funny faces pulled by the latter that he disgraced himself. The story (told by the Riccoboni the elder) may be spurious, but the fact that it became so current points to an underlying truth, most of it on Fiorilli's knee... Later, as King, he handled the company's subsidy personally and even became godfather to one of the sons of Domenico Biancolelli, the Arlequin of the troupe. Why, then, did Louis now turn against *Les Italiens*? The answer usually accepted is that they were proposing to perform (although there is no firm evidence that they actually did so) a piece entitled *La Falsa (Finta) matrigna – La Fausse Prude* in French – which was supposed to contain calumny against his morganatic wife, Madame the Marquise de Maintenon. In fact the writing had been on the wall for some time, if only the Italians had paused to read it. That they had been in great favour the beginning of the century was partly due to a fashion imposed by Italian queens who imparted a taste for their native tongue to their French entourages. For fifty years anyone of consequence spoke fluent Italian, but after Louis XIV attained majority, the mood and the *mode* changed. Despite their performing more and more in French, sometimes dialogue, then whole scenes and finally even entire plays, the audiences for *comédies à l'italienne* had been falling off. Now, to counter public criticism of the licentiousness of his reign, Louis wished it to be known that Le Roi Soleil would not permit onstage allusions to current events, depiction of political personages or obscenity. But, as ever, the Italians improvised round the problem and Mezzetin in particular was noted for the scurrility of his *lazzis*.

Other historians point to the fact that Louis was fighting wars on several fronts at the time and that the treasury was empty. The closure of La Comédie Italienne was to save the royal coffers 18,000 livres per annum... The Italians appealed, but to no avail and they were given one month to leave the country. In fact very few of them returned to Italy since most were French citizens either by birth or naturalisation, or were married to French citizens. Like the *mimes* after the fall of the Roman Empire, they went to ground and joined with the acrobats, tightrope walkers and other fairground showmen who were already performing playlets, often written by well-known authors. The Italian repertoire was thus added to that of the *théâtres de la foire* at Saint-Germain and Saint-Laurent. Their spectators came with them and the proprietors of the fairground booths soon reckoned it commercially viable to build permanent theatres to accommodate their appreciating audiences. Such professionalising of theatrical entertainment at the *foires* began to worry the Comédie-Française, which did not like such box office competition (it even went dark at one time due to lack of bums on seats), and tried every means to preserve its privileges. After many proceedings brought before the law courts and the *parlement*, they achieved the outright prohibition of performances of plays and farces at the *foires* in 1703. The Italians accordingly replaced plots with detached scenes separated by *intermezzi*. All dialogue was prohibited in the following year, so they next used monologues with responses shouted from the wings, alternating tirades or talking to animals and imagining their responses. Pulcinella wrote what he wanted to say with his right forefinger on to the palm of his left hand, which would then be read out loud by the actor he was addressing. In 1707 all speech was banned; the Italians resorted to singing, but this was outlawed as well, this time thanks to the intervention of the Opéra (Académie Royale de la Musique). The 'legitimate' French actors next took the law into their own hands and sent in carpenters and bailiffs who demolished and burned the wooden fairground theatres. They were, however, judged to have exceeded their rights and were made to pay 6,000 livres in damages, more than enough for the *thétres forains* to be rebuilt. In 1710 Arlequin, Mezzetin, Pierrot, *et al.* were reduced to tossing scrolls into the audience for them to read out loud; then they tried silent parody, then used marionettes, then '*la pièce à ècritaux*'. This last was pantomime embellished with music, ballets and lavish changes of decor. The text was written on placards which the actor pulled from his pocket or which were dropped down from the flies. From 1711 text in prose was replaced by verses on canvas rolls which the audience sang to well-known tunes, led by professional singers planted in their midst.

However, the device for circumventing dialogue that the Italians made use of which is most relevant to the current quest for grommelot is, according to Emile Campardon, that they 'invented a form of jargon evoking a sort of low Latin but which did not compete with the French language of which the Comédie-Française claimed exclusive use'. Just for once we do have a written example of this low Latin 'jargon' from *Arlequin Barbet, Pagode et Mèdecin, pièce chinoise en deux actes, en monologues, mêlée de jargon*, performed in February 1723 at the Foire Saint-Germain. Arlequin, disguised as a medical doctor but hungry as ever, has the following non-dialogue with a certain Le Colao, the Emperor of China's prime minister.

ARLEQUIN: So, he's going to have dinner?
LE COLAO: Va dinao.
ARLEQUIN: And we are going to do the same?

LE COLAO: Convenio, demeurao, Medecinao regardao dinao L'Emperao.
ARLEQUIN: What, my job obliges me to watch him eat?

Le Colao mutters in his ear.
In order to make sure there's nothing wrong with it? And what happens to me if he overeats or dies of something dodgy?

LE COLAO: Ho! Ho!

Le Colao mutters in his ear.

ARLEQUIN: That would make him happy? How do you mean?

Le Colao mutters in his ear.
Well then! Supposing the king died?

LE COLAO: Pendao le Medicinao.
ARLEQUIN: You'll hang the doctor? Mercy!

Obviously adding 'ao' on the end of recognisable words is not true grommelot, Chinese or not, but the muttering in the ear certainly was, and Arlequin's translations of this 'jargon' constitute a comedic as well as an expedient device. Also, the use of dog Latin root syllables in Le Colao's chinoiserie is interestingly close to surviving Lingua Franca vocables...

The origins of grommelot are, therefore, almost as various in possibility as the etymology and orthography of the term itself. A best guess would be that the Italians in Paris had been using it before their banishment, while still at the height of their popularity, in order not to further alienate Francophones in their audience; that it was then already in their property basket, left over from their touring days round the city states of Italy; that it had some, though not total, correspondence with the Lingua Franca and that it then survived in the Parisian *foires* until re-adopted by Italian circus clowns and garnered from them by Jacques Copeau for transmission on into the twentieth century via the schools of Saint-Denis in England and North America, and thence to Jacques LeCoq via Jean Dasté and passed on by LeCoq to Dario Fo, who re-invented it for his own comedic repertoire, which includes but is not exclusively, Commedia. But, and it is a big 'but', since he never underwent any formal training and had probably never heard of Commedia dell'Arte, the French clown and director Jacques Tati makes extensive use of grommelot in his films: the hapless postman in the 1949 film *Jour de Fête*, for example, mutters continuously under his breath in significant speechlessness. It is perhaps relevant, though, that Tati's real name was Tatischeff – his father was Russian and his mother Dutch, so perhaps double Dutch came naturally to him...

However circuitous the route of grommelot's survival and re-invention, its function in training and performance in present-day practice is unambiguous. It frees the apprentice actor from mental pre-occupation with intelligible verbalisation, enabling, indeed obliging, a gestural intensification to take place in the body of the mask wearer. Commedia dell'Arte is a grotesque form. 'Grotesque' is defined in the Concise Oxford Dictionary as having both the sense of 'comically or repulsively ugly or distorted' and as a 'style of decorative painting or sculpture consisting of the interweaving of human and animal forms'. In learning to play a Mask (as opposed to act in a mask), it can be helpful to find the animal form before addressing the grotesque human one. The trainee is then, necessarily, in a pre-linguistic mode, and animal sounds can evolve towards recognisable vocables as the gestural interpretation appropriate to each Mask develops. The Mask's intention passes directly from the cerebral cortex via the cerebellum into the actor's body, modified by acquired physical practices. From the body, sensations then flow back to the speech centre of the cerebral cortex, which, unable to find linguistic equivalents, allows grommelot to emerge. Il Capitano, for example, can bark like a mastiff long before he can deliver any rodomontade; il Dottore may squeak like a pig before achieving *sproloquio*; Pantalone squawks before he can deliver tirades; Colombina coos before finding the voice of sweet reason, etc. What can thus be avoided is the Mask's intention passing first within the actor's cerebral cortex to the centre of verbal articulation and only thence to the body, which consequently lacks gestural immediacy as if illustrating the bubbles of speech in a cartoon. Open vowel sounds come first, followed by diphthongs, all modified by the mouth shapes suggested by the requirement of fitting the flexible human physiognomy of the lower face to the fixed upper jaw outline of the half mask.

Interaction between Masks in training or rehearsal is also facilitated by grommelot since neither Mask will struggle to keep up an end in an improvised dialogue. Like knocking up at tennis or ping-pong, it is in the interests of both parties to keep the ball in play – indeed the use of a ball tossed back and forth may help the development of stichomythic patterns. It is important, however, that this does not become merely mechanical: one is not juggling clubs and the Masks must always be aware of the context and significance of what they are 'grommeloting' as if it were obvious. Only then can the musical aspect of the 'music of meaning' be fully played out. In my teaching I find the use of terms from music scoring to be instrumental to this end:

Pace *(tempo)*

Accelerando	Getting faster
Adagio	Slowly
Calando	Dying out (combination of *diminuendo* and *rallantando*)
Incalzando	Hastening on
Largamente	Slow and dignified
Lento	Slow
Lesto	Quickly
Lestissiomo	Very quickly
Presto	Quick
Rallantando	Slowing down
Ravivando	Becoming faster and more animated
Ritenuto	Sudden slowing down
Slentando	Getting slower

Volume

Appena	Barely audible
Crescendo	Getting louder
Decrescendo	Getting quieter
Incallando	Getting faster and louder

Tone

Addolendo	Becoming *dolce*
Affabile	In a gentle, pleasing manner
Affretando	Gaining in urgency
Agitato	Stormily
Allegro	Briskly, in a lively manner
Andante	Moving along, flowing
Animando	Becoming *animato*
Animato	Animated
Capriccioso	Lively and whimsical
Desto	Wide awake, sprightly
Estinto	As softly as possible
Discreto	Discretely
Dolce	Sweetly
Elevato	Elevated
Facilemente	Easily, fluently
Fastoso	Pompous
Fluido	Fluidly
Gemendo	Moaning
Generoso	Generous, lofty
Grandioso	With grandiloquence
Imperioso	Imperiously
Impetuoso	Impetuous
Indeciso	Hesitantly
Lontano	Faint, distant
Lusigando	In a coaxing, intimate manner
Moderato	Moderate
Netto	Clearly
Pesanto	Heavy
Piano	Soft
Pianissimo	As quietly as possible
Sciolto	Unfettered, free and easy
Scherzo	Playful, vigorous, bustling
Sfogato	Light and easy
Sonoro	Sonorous
Sostenuto	Sustained
Spandendo	Expanding in power
Spiccato	Clear articulation syllable by syllable

Spiritoso	With spirit
Stirando	Drawn out
Strepitoso	Noisy, forceful
Subito	Suddenly
Superbo	Proudly
Tempestuoso	Tempestuously
Tenendo	Sustainedly
Tinto	Colourful, expressive
Tondo	Rounded
Tremendo	Tremendous

Emotion

Addolorato	Sadly
Amoroso	Lovingly
Appassionato	Passionately
Appenato	Tormentedly
Arditamente	Boldly
Concitato	Roused up, stirred
Calmato	Calmed down
Calore	Warmth, passion
Declamando	Declaiming
Delicato	Delicate
Devoto	With devotion
Disperato	Desperately
Divoto	Devout
Dolente	Sorrowful
Freddo	Cold, indifferent
Doloroso	Pained
Furioso	Furious
Lacrimoso	Tearful
Lagnoso	Doleful
Lamentando	Lamenting
Languido	Languid
Lieto	Joyful
Lietissimo	Very joyful
Luttuoso	Mournful
Pacato	Placid
Raddolcendo	Calming down
Riposo	With a feeling of repose
Schietto	Sincere
Sgambato	Weary
Smaniato	Frenzy
Tenero	Tender
Tepido	Lukewarm
Torvo	Grim

One or more indications can be agreed upon before improvising a scene, or the coach can shout out changes which must immediately be adopted. In advanced playing one Mask can be using one tempo, for example, and the other a different one. Commedia is essentially a dialogue form and the more variety and flexibility that can be brought to it, the less an audience is likely to suffer ennui. A final pre-linguistic development might be the adoption of a regional dialect or national accent as a vocal basis; getting together an international troupe can be a great advantage here, since the over and undertones need to be effortless.

Moving on to performance, one is continually confronted with the problem that one has to educate a modern audience in the style and comedic values of Commedia at the same time as affording them an enjoyable experience. Indeed, the latter is dependent on the former, but an unsugared pill is not likely to be swallowed. The sense of complicity referred to above becomes essential. Some Masks, such as Pulcinella and Colombina, have this possibility built in, but others will find grommelot most helpful.

There is a self-reflexivity implicit in grommelot where it becomes a performative game of meta-language in which the actor allows the audience to 'win' by guessing his meaning. While the audience and actor have words for the images performed, they are simultaneously aware of the word they would normally use to designate something, and of the distance between that and the sound the performer actually uses within his grommelot to designate the same thing. Thus, the pleasure of grommelot results from the inventiveness of the actor as well as from the audience's awareness of this inventiveness.

Grommelot should, however, be used sparingly, kept in reserve even, for moments of disaster, otherwise, like Tartaglia's stammering, it can hold up the action and become too much of a good thing.

Buon bais v'la shay poo di sa key discare apopo poopah indigament saggimetto.

References

Clivio, Gianrenzo P. (1989) 'The languages of the commedia dell'arte'. *University of Toronto Italian Studies 3, The Science of Buffoonery: Theory and History of the Commedia dell'Arte*, ed. Pietropaolo. Dovehouse Editions Inc.

Fo, Dario (1987) *Manuale Minimo dell'Attore*. Turin, Italy: Einaudi, translated Farrell, Joe (1991) *The Tricks of the Trade*. London: Methuen.

——Nobel Prize for Literature Acceptance speech (1997) www.nobelprize.org/nobel_prizes/literature/laureates/1997/fo-lecture.html (accessed 20 August 2014).

Larousse's Grand dictionnaire universel, Vol. 8. (1865) Paris: Administration Du Grand Dictionnaire Universale.

Perrucci, Andrea (2008) *A Treatise on Acting, from Memory and by Improvisation* (1699), (bilingual edition edited and translated by Francesco Cotticelli, Anne Goodrich Heck and Thomas Heck) Maryland, US; Toronto, Canada; Plymouth, UK: The Scarecrow Press Inc.

Saint-Denis, Michel (1982) *Training for the Theatre: Premises and Promises*. London: Heinemann.

Sand, Maurice (1915) *The History of The Harlequinade*. London: Secker.

Scott, Virginia (1990) *The Commedia dell'Arte in Paris 1644-1697*, Charlottesville, US: Virginia University Press.

LAZZI

17

LAZZI

Mel Gordon

The Commedia dell'Arte (1550–1750) is often cited as the progenitor of modern acting in Europe. From its beginnings, the itinerant Italian troupes presented themselves as professional ensembles with long-established reputations. They usually consisted of two or three extended families and almost always included both female and child performers. Since their productions rarely highlighted sophisticated plotting, extensive dialog, or complex visual effects, the Commedia spectators focused their attentions on individual actors and their comic interplay.

Costumed as recognizable types and/or masked, the Italian players appeared to be living outside the confines of prepared scripts as they unstintingly improvised their madcap banter and scenic antics. Sometimes actors broke standard theatrical convention to directly address their audiences. For the most part, the performers were not judged by their fidelity to any dramatic text or set roles but by their unremitting ability to garner laughs.

Each Commedia company featured a stable of archetypical characters: straight Young Lovers and a vast assortment of wily servants, duplicitous fathers, confidence men, vainglorious masters, and vagabond child-men. This second category provided the welcomed social satire, grotesque humor, hare-brained schemes, and frequently obscene interludes that audiences came to expect from the Commedia panorama. These recurring comic routines, which were episodically disconnected from the overall scenarios and percolated from show to show, were known by the players and historians as *lazzi*.

From the beginning of Commedia scholarship, there has been a deep concern with the derivation of the word "lazzi." Luigi Riccoboni in his *Histoire du Théâtre Italien* (1728) wrote that it was a Lombard corruption of the Tuscan word *lacci*, which meant cord or ribbon. The term "lazzi," Riccoboni reasoned, alluded to the comic business that tied together the performance. Of course, the practical reality was quite different; lazzi functioned as standalone numbers that, more often than not, disrupted or obscured the Commedia stories or performance unity. Possibly the metaphor of an extraneous ribbon or the actual use of ropes and ribbons in the isolated comic enactments was the origin of the word.

A. Valeri proposed another etymological theory in a series of articles published in the 1890s. Lazzi, according to Valeri, was only the simple corruption of *l'azione* (the action), referring to the activities between the plotted scenes. Still other linguistic theories suggest parallels between the word "lazzi" and the Hebrew *latzon* (trick), the Swedish *lat* (gesture), and the Latin *lax* (fraud).

Whatever the origins of the word, the definition of lazzi is relatively standard: "We give the name *lazzi* to the actions of Arlecchino or other masked characters when they interrupt a scene by their expressions of terror or by their fooleries," declared Riccoboni (1728). In *Dell'arte Rappresentativa Premeditata e All'improvviso* (1699), Andrea Perrucci simply defined the *lazzo*, a single lazzi, as "something foolish, witty, or metaphorical in word or action." (Perrucci 1699: 192) Nineteenth-century scholars described lazzi as "stage tricks" or "comic stage business."

Clearly, the word had a multiplicity of meanings, even for the Commedia performers themselves. It co-existed with the Roman expression *trionfi* (triumphs), *azzi,* (actions), *burla,* (joke) and the French word *jeu* (play). Generally, lazzi referred to zany scenic enactments that were planned or unplanned and that could be performed in any one of dozens of plays. Put another way, lazzi alluded to any discrete comic and repeatable activity that guaranteed laughs for its participants.

The earliest books on the Commedia provided the reader with a vast iconography of lazzi scenes. But the drawings, mezzotints, and paintings of perverse sexual play, nudity, vomiting, defecation, and all sorts of activities involving enemas and chamber pots – capturings of typical lazzo routines – were almost never described in the texts themselves. For instance, in the authoritative Pierre Duchartre history, *The Italian Comedy* (1966: 56–7), where captions accompanied most of the pictures, a drawing of the Doctor administering an enema to Arlecchino's exposed buttocks was described as showing an "injection" with a "syringe." In other books, the authors completely ignored this visual documentation. In fact, the Commedia's celebrated lazzi, or comic bits, were rarely discussed in more than a couple of paragraphs. Most writers seldom referred to the obscene lazzi, which made up a good portion of the whole. It was as if these scholars, publishing in the early twentieth century, were psychologically or morally inhibited from accurately documenting the Commedia's best-known performance innovation.

Function of lazzi

Constant Mic in *La Commedia dell'Arte* (1927) maintained that the use of lazzi fell into three categories: 1) when, in fact, they arose out of the scenic occasion – for instance, when the audience became restless or bored during the performance, when the actors tried to comically cover dropped lines or cues, when the performers attempted to inject new and irrelevant amusements at the conclusion of a scene; 2) when the lazzi were an expected and welcomed event for the spectators, who came to see the lazzi as high points or specialty acts in the performance; and 3) when the lazzi were actually written into the Commedia texts as contrived business. [When a lazzi became overly extended or integrated into the plot development, it was called a *burla* or *jeu*.]

How the lazzi were initiated on the stage seems to be a point of contention among historians, but again the answer may lie in a variety of approaches. Some were obviously used whenever a scene appeared to drag on too long and were totally improvised by one actor. Others, involving stage properties and several actors, had to be intricately pre-planned. Some lazzi could be instigated by a single performer, which forced his unsuspecting partners to improvise around him.

An example of a lazzo being both improvised and contrived can be seen in the "Lazzo of Nightfall." If, in the middle of a performance, the Commedia manager noticed that the audience, which frequently did not understand Italian, was not responding well, he, in the character of Arlecchino, could begin a monologue, such as "Time flies at the pace of a snail on the floodwater current that has just stopped. Why Midnight, you hourglass thief ..." This would cue his actors to start setting up the "Lazzo of Nightfall," where all the actors suddenly pretend that darkness has descended over them. The same lazzo with its fixed or semi-fixed routines, of course, could be decided on before the performance began.

Sources of lazzi

Although several thousand performers enacted Commedia scenarios during its heyday, except for a single manuscript deposited at the library of Perugia, no detailed lists of lazzi are extant. Most of what is known of lazzi is from descriptions, performers' autobiographical statements, and notations of lazzi sequences – sometimes no more than titles – in Commedia plot outlines or scenarios that were posted on the wings of the stage or appeared in the Commedia texts that were intended for publication.

Why the lazzi were never made public can be explained in several ways. While the Commedia troupes could not patent their routines, they were not anxious to have their best work copied or read by a theatre-going public. If much of the Commedia was obscene, as is suggested by the visual and fragmented written evidence, then writing down the explicit details could only jeopardize the troupes, which, like many itinerant performers, were sometimes only a step or so ahead of the legal authorities. Finally, it is possible that it simply never occurred to many Commedia troupes, like so many popular performers, to write out and preserve their lazzi.

The lazzi categories

Below is a short assemblage of lazzi and brief descriptions of the actions and the characters who performed them. This list was created from various Commedia company inventories and texts. They are categorized according to their overall comic appeal.

Acrobatic and mimic lazzi

1) *Lazzi of Falling*: Arlecchino falls from a high ladder or wall after being shaken off, shot, or gravitationally abandoned. The humor involves Arlecchino's desperate attempts not to fall. This lazzi can also refer to Pulcinella's ridiculous

falling fits when he attempts to run away from danger and Arlecchino's pratfalls over furniture, often into a bathtub.

2) *Lazzo of Binding Them*: Arlecchino and another Zanni, both famished, are tied up and bound back-to-back. A bowl of ricotta cheese is placed at their feet. When one bends down to eat it, he lifts the other into the air, and vice versa.

3) *Lazzo of the Statue*: Arlecchino is brought in as a statue or an automaton. He plays tricks on the other characters when their backs are turned, always returning to the statue position when they face him.

4) *Lazzo of Falling into Unconsciousness*: Arlecchino continually falls into a deadly state of unconsciousness, without regard to his surroundings.

5) *Lazzo of Catching a Flea*: Arlecchino, twisting his body into impossible positions and bent backwards with his head between his legs, catches an invisible flea. He celebrates his victory with a series of double back-springs.

6) *Lazzo of the Hands Behind the Back*: Arlecchino, attempting to hide behind another character, places his arms around him, making all the hand gestures for him. In this way, Arlecchino torments the other character by slapping his face, pinching his nose, and so forth. Arlechino and the other character also play the guitar using four hands.

Comic violence/cruel behavior

1) *Lazzo of the Tooth Extractor*: Dottore [or Arlecchino disguised as a dentist] fools Pantalone into thinking that rotten teeth are causing his bad breath. Using oversized or ridiculous tools, Dottore extracts two or more good teeth from Pantalone's mouth.

2) *Lazzo of the Innocent By-Stander*: Arlecchino and another Zanni meet each other face-to-face and are armed to the teeth. They heap abuse on each other, relying on others to hold them back physically. Finally, when Capitano seeks to separate them, they strike out at each other with Capitano receiving most of the blows.

3) *Lazzo of the Cuff*: At the conclusion of an argument, the male lover is hit by the female lover, who then exits. Pantalone, who happens to wander by at that moment, is struck by the male lover, who then departs. Pantalone then beats a newly arrived zanni character, who in turn strikes another zanni, who beats yet another zanni character, who hits Zanni himself, the last arrival.

4) *Lazzo of Counting*: Directed to beat Zanni [or Arlecchino] ten times, Capitano loses count repeatedly. As he flogs Zanni, Capitano counts, "One, two, three.... What comes after three?" Zanni shouts, "Ten!" Capitano begins again, "One, two, three.... No, four comes after three." He starts the count again.

5) *Lazzo of Killing*: Zanni and another servant decide to kill Pantalone. To demonstrate to the other how he would kill Pantalone, Zanni says, "You be Pantalone" and he begins to strangle the other servant. With his last breath, the other servant says, "No, you be Pantalone," and he begins to beat Zanni. This continues in tandem.

Food lazzi

1) *Lazzo of Kissing the Hand*: Instructed by Capitano to give a bowl of macaroni to another zanni, Arlecchino finds the other zanni character weeping. Accepting the dish, the other zanni explains that something awful happened to his wife. The second zanni begins eating and crying. Saddened, Arlecchino also begins to eat the macaroni and cry. A third zanni enters and begins to eat and cry as Arlecchino and the second zanni tell him the tragic story.

2) *Lazzo of Hunger*: Arlecchino [or Pantalone] relates how hungry he is after a shipwreck. He demonstrates his hunger by chewing on his shoes or any property on the stage.

3) *Lazzo of the Royal Taster*: The sacrificial king, Arlecchino is treated to a sumptuous banquet. But just before Arlecchino can feast on each course, the royal physician, Dottore, grabs each dish from him, explaining that it causes apoplexy: loss of consciousness from a blockage in a vein or artery. Finally, Arlecchino pushes a plate of food into Dottore's face.

Illogical lazzi

1) *Lazzo of Begging*: Arlecchino tips his hat to Cinthio, asking for a handout for an impoverished, mute beggar. Cinthio inquires whether Arlecchino is mute. "Yes, sir," replies Arlecchino. "But how can you be mute, when you just answered my question?" asks Cinthio. Arlecchino explains that it would have shown poor upbringing had he not answered Cinthio's question. Realizing his mistake now, Arlecchino claims that he meant to say that he is deaf, not mute. When Cinthio refutes that claim, Arlecchino explains that in fact he is blind. When Arlecchino ducks Cinthio's jab, Arlecchino claims that he is a lame beggar instead.

2) *Lazzo of the Tempest Survived*: One character describes a story of a ship in a tempest and how he was saved from it. One of the zanni repeats the story, but in a ridiculous way. Finally seeing that he is not believed, the zanni character explains that in the middle of the storm he went ashore, entered a city, and found a marketplace. There he bought two bladders, which he affixed to his arms before returning to the sea. These kept him afloat and thus he saved himself.

3) *Lazzo of "Have You Eaten?"*: Two characters come to a zanni, who is a doctor, to bring him to Capitano's daughter. The zanni character responds by asking them if they have eaten. They say, "yes." The zanni character repeats the question several times and they beat him.

4) *Lazzo of "Put on Your Hat!"*: Capitano requests one of the zanni for his doctoral skills. Capitano bows and the zanni character responds by asking him to put on his hat. Realizing that his hat is already on his head, Capitano becomes confused. The zanni character repeats his command.

5) *Lazzo of "I Am Not a Doctor!"*: One of the master characters accuses one of the zanni characters of not being a doctor. The zanni replies that he is not a doctor, as if he was disagreeing with the other character. This is repeated.

Sexual/scatological lazzi

1) *Lazzo of the Chamber Pot*: The servant-girl empties a pot filled with disgusting water, out the window. It hits Pantalone as he serenades the female lover.

2) *Lazzo of Vomit*: At the beginning of a performance, or just after drinking some of Dottore's medicine, Arlecchino vomits.

3) *Lazzo of Hiding*: Arlecchino and the female lover [or Colombina] are alone in her room when knocking is heard. The female lover tells Arlecchino to hide since that knock can only belong to Pantalone. Finding no place to hide, Arlecchino is persuaded to become a chair. Throwing a sheet over Arlecchino, whose arms have formed the arms of a chair, and his knees the seat, the female lover calls in Pantalone. Unheeding of the lover's warning, Pantalone sits in the Arlecchino-chair.

4) *Lazzo of the Waiter*: Dressed as a waiter, Arlecchino serves all the food, the salad, an omelets, and so forth, by pulling them out of his breeches. When a customer complains about a dirty plate, Arlecchino cleans it by rubbing it on the back of his pants.

5) *Lazzo of Enlarging the Legs*: Pulcinella hides under Tartaglia's smock. The movement of Pulcinella's head gives the appearance of Tartaglia's genitals bulging.

6) *Lazzo of the Pellegrina*: The lovers, supplicating Coviello, fall to their knees. Coviello, bending to speak to one, sticks his ass in the other's face.

Social-class rebellion lazzi

1) *Lazzo of Silence*: A zanni character becomes dumbfounded when his master shouts at him for doing what the zanni character thought was a duty that his master had requested. Other characters enter the stage, each with a ridiculous reason for scolding the zanni character. All this time, the zanni character is silent. When Capitano pinches the zanni character to see if he is awake, the zanni gives out a frightened cry that scares the other characters. The zanni calmly exits.

2) *Lazzo of Rage*: After being yelled at by Capitano, Zanni and another servant silently take his abuse and scolding. As soon as Capitano leaves, they show complete mimic of rage, mocking Capitano. When Capitano returns, they resume their first silent, bland attitudes.

3) *Lazzo of "Not This, That!"*: Pantalone screams at Arlecchino to hand him his clothing, but no matter which piece Arlecchino gives him, Pantalone shouts, "Not this, that!"

4) *Lazzo of Making Him Lower*: Arlecchino, disguised as an official, signals those bowing to him to bow lower still. Arlecchino forces them to do this until they fall over.

Stage/life duality lazzi

1) *Lazzo of the Chase*: With a drawn sword, Capitano chases one of the zanni characters. They remain on the stage in a stationary position as they mime running, each slightly out of reach of the other. As they run, each begins to acknowledge the audience's response.

2) *Lazzo of Make Believe*: While describing his intense hunger or thirst, Arlecchino takes a piece of bread or a container of water out of his pocket and consumes it. He returns to his pathetic monologue.

3) *Lazzo of the Interruption*: In the middle of the performance, actors walk into the audience while other actors are speaking on the stage. The off-stage actors begin to shout ridiculous and irrelevant phrases, like, "Be quiet, the hen is laying the egg," or "The pot won't boil."

4) *Lazzo of Searching*: The lovers search for one another. But each time one leaves the stage, the other appears. This is repeated several times.

5) *Lazzo of the Dead*: After one of the characters is killed and put in a coffin, he pops up several times during the performance to tell the audience not to disturb the dead.

6) *Lazzo of the Script*: Arlecchino tells a joke, which does not get a laugh from the audience. He tells it again this time more slowly. Receiving no response from the audience, Arlecchino pulls out a script from his sleeve and reads the joke. Again Arlecchino receives no laughs. He tells the audience from now on he will tell his own jokes, not those of the playwright.

Stage properties as lazzi

1) *Lazzo of the False Arm*: Using a false or wooden arm, Gratiano [or a thief] allows himself to be held by suspicious characters. When they begin to beat him, he escapes, leaving the bewildered characters with the wooden arm.

2) *Lazzo of the Tables*: Just as two characters are about to indulge in an elaborate feast, the tables suddenly arise and walk away. Or, part of the table settings arise and chase Arlecchino from the table.

3) *Lazzo of the Zig-Zag*: Arlecchino uses and expanding hinged apparatus to deliver a letter across the stage, or to pick Dottore's pocket.

Stupidity/inappropriate behavior lazzi

1) *Lazzo of Cowardice*: Pantalone and Zanni [or Arlecchino] search for the man who has beaten them. They practice dueling. But when Capitano appears, they suddenly forget how to hold their swords in their fright. Pantalone and Zanni attempt to persuade the other to fight, pushing the other toward Capitano.

2) *Lazzo of the Chairs*: A zanni character is guarding another character while they both sit in chairs. Attempting to escape, the second character moves his chair slightly. The zanni character follows. The second character drags his chair halfway across the stage with the zanni character in pursuit. They smile at each other. This continues.

3) *Lazzo of Counting Money*: Zanni divides Pantalone's money in the following way: He counts, "One for Pantalone, two for me. One for Pantalone, two for me." In this way, he divides the money giving Pantalone one each time and giving himself two each time.

4) *Lazzo of the Dispute*: A common routine that revolves around an endless and frequently pointless argument between two or three characters: (a) Zanni and another servant argue over who should be the first to eat the macaroni, the one who brought the flour or the one who brought the cheese. (b) Zanni and another servant character argue over which the nobler beast, the goat or the sheep, is. (c) The lovers argue over whether it is possible to have love without pain, or whether it is better to love or hunt. Often, each character will convince the other of the correctness of his views and the dispute will continue with the situation reversed.

5) *Lazzo of Friendship*: Zanni is hired by Pantalone and a second servant character is hired by Dottore to fight their old feud. When Zanni and the second servant character meet, ready to battle, they discover that they are long lost friends and embrace and salute each other to the dismay of Pantalone and Dottore.

Transformation lazzi

1) *Lazzo of Nightfall*: Using candles and lanterns, the characters signify that the scene is taking place at night or in darkness. The characters grope around the street, climb ladders into various houses, falling, bumping into objects and people, discovering what they think are bloody corpses, mistaking identities and conversations.

2) *Lazzio of the Nymph*: To disguise himself, one of the zanni characters dresses as a nymph. He practices walking and talking like a woman. He also becomes concerned that men and gods will fall in love with him.

3) *Lazzi of Fear (or Terror)*: This involves the extreme manifestation of fear, usually as a result of a slow realization of real or bogus danger: (a) Satyrs [or living characters thought to be ghosts] frighten Zanni and Pantalone [or Arlecchino or Dottore] into extreme hysteria; they run about and knock into each other. (b) Sitting down to mourn the death of his master, Arlecchino does not notice that another character, in an attempt to scare Arlecchino, has put his hands beside Arlecchino's and his foot between Arlecchino's feet; counting the number of hands and feet, Arlecchino becomes seized with terror.

4) *Lazzo of Laughter into Tears*: Arlecchino begins to laugh hysterically. Slowly his laughter turns into weeping and tears.

Trickery lazzi

1) *Lazzo of Bamboozling*: Zanni, offering Pantalone secrets of amorous speech, teaches him a thousand ridiculous sayings. Then, with Zanni egging him on, Pantalone repeats them to his beloved.

2) *Lazzo of the Country of Cuccagna*: Two thieves enter to tell Zanni about a magic land, Cuccagna. As one spins tales about the good life in that land, the

other wolfs down Zanni's meal. The second then begins to lament about the difficulties of life as the other eats from Zanni's basket.

3) *Lazzo of the Card Game*: A thief teaches Zanni a new card game. Zanni loses everything since the thief keeps making up new rules as it suits him.

4) *Lazzo of the Multiple Thieves*: Pantalone hands Zanni a gold collar for safekeeping. Watching from the side, a third character disguises himself as a devil and scares Zanni out of the collar. A fourth character watching from the other side of the stage, dresses as a ghost and frightens the third character out of the prize. Witnessing this whole scam, Pantalone and a servant enter, dressed as policemen, and take the gold collar from the fourth character.

5) *Lazzo of the Shoe*: The guards have come to arrest one of the zanni characters. He says that first he must tie his shoe, and bending down, he grabs one of the ankles of each of the two guards, trips them up, and runs off.

6) *Lazzo of the Living Corpse*: Arlecchino picks up a slumbering character, whom he takes for a corpse. Arlecchino's sword drops and the character grabs it and strikes Arlecchino's rear. Arlecchino sets the other character down and turns around to look for the source of the hit. The second character then kicks Arlecchino in the rear. Arlecchino falls and gets up, starting again to carry the character away. He leans the second character against the wings of the right side of the stage. While Arlecchino looks out over the audience, the character runs to the other side of the stage and leans against the wings there in the same position.

Word play lazzi

1) *Lazzo of the Third*: The lovers have quarreled. They call on Pulcinella. The man says to Pulcinella, "Tell her she's an ingrate!" Pulcinella goes to the woman, "He says that he'll grate you!" She replies, "Tell him he's a tyrant (*tiranno*)!" Pulcinella returns to the man and says, "She hopes that you get the plague (*il malanno*)!" He replies, "Tell her she's a barbarian (*barbara*)!" Pulcinella relays, "He says you should shave (*ue facci la barba*)!" The woman tells Pulcinella, "He's disloyal (*disleale*) and he betrayed me (*mi ha tradita*)!" Pulcinella returns to the man, "She said, 'Make a serving dish (*serueale*) of boiling water (*acqua bollita*)." The man replies, "She is a temperamental tyrant (*tiranna stizzosa*)!" Pulcinella tells the woman that for one year the man has found her hairy (*tiene pelosa*).

2) *Lazzo of "I Don't Believe It!"*: Confused by the other characters' reactions to him, not aware that he is being mistaken for his double, Zanni repeats endlessly, "I don't believe it!"

3) *Lazzi of Replying Only By Monosyllables*: Weeping, Arlecchino enters the stage. Dottore and another character question him as to his behavior, but Arlecchino only answers in monosyllables. Alternatively, Arlecchino's master questions him while Arlecchino is eating. Concerned about a widow, the master asks increasingly complicated questions about her, while Arlecchino always manages to answer in a monosyllable as he gobbles down the food.

4) *Lazzo of the List*: The German innkeeper reads from a shopping list. Everything is mispronounced. So, "four chickens" becomes "four broken pillars." And so forth.

References

Duchartre, Pierre Louis (1966) *The Italian Comedy*. New York: Dover Publications, Inc.

Mic, Constant (1927) *La Commedia dell'Arte Ou Le Theatre Des Comediens Italiens Des XVIe, XVIIe & XVIIIe Siecles*. Paris: Librairie Teatrale.

Perrucci, Andrea (1699) *A Treatise on Acting from Memory and by Improvisation*. Bilingual Edition in English and Italian. Translated and edited by Cotticelli, F., Heck, A. G. and Heck, T. F. Lanham, (2008) Lanham, Maryland, US; Toronto, Canada and Plymouth, UK: The Scarecrow Press, Inc.

Riccoboni, Luigi (1728) *Histoire du Théâtre Italien*.2 vols. Paris: Pierre Delormel.

Valeri, A. (1894) "Gli Scenarie inediti di Basilio Locatelli" in *Nuova Rassegna*. Vol. 2. Rome: Tipografia Folchetto. pp. 441–456 and 523–537.

18

PRINCIPLES OF COMEDY FOR COMMEDIA DELL'ARTE

Brian Foley

Comic players have access to a rich history of effective tools and techniques, and a student of Commedia is well served by exploring as many of them as possible. While it is important to differentiate Commedia dell'Arte from its predecessors and its descendants, the performer of the human comedy may benefit from approaching Commedia as a segment, significant nonetheless, of a broader history of comedic performance. For it is true that some jokes and references are fleeting, and tied to a specific moment in time and place. But a student of the history of comedy will recognize that from Plautus to the medieval Troubadour, from Chaplin to Friends, there have been commonalities in many of the subjects, situations, and performance techniques that have inspired laughter. Lowell Swortzell, who has researched the history of comedic performers, writes that they have been "performing many of the same routines (and even telling many of the same jokes) for several thousand years." (Swortzell 1978: 4) And as to whether the techniques of the first Commedia players were adapted from Roman comedy or developed independently, K. M. Lea notes, "the comic possibilities of a great nose, a bald head, a ragged garment, or a protruding stomach might occur to any buffoon though he never came into contact consciously or unconsciously with Maccus, Pappus, or the mimus centunculus." (Lea 1962: 228)

Antonio Fava rightly differentiates Commedia from mime, dance, pantomime, circus clowning, and street performance, though he does note that the genre "includes all the techniques and disciplines of the varied forms of theater." (Fava 2007: xiv) And while the original troupes' repertoires included comedies, tragedies, and pastorals, the word "Commedia" certainly connotes comedy to many of its contemporary scholars, practitioners, and most importantly, its audiences. Mel Gordon writes of Commedia's accessible energy recalling "the most popular entertainments of the first part of the twentieth century" including "Charlie Chaplin, W.C. Fields, Bert Lahr, the Marx Brothers, Jack Benny, or Laurel and Hardy," all of whom are comedians. (Gordon 1983: 3) If players are to once again find a living audience for this "popular entertainment," then we see the value in exploring the living tradition of comedy that clowns, street performers, burlesque comedians and vaudevillians have preserved in their repertoires for hundreds of years. These are the techniques discussed in this chapter.

These techniques are to be practiced in tandem with the other requirements particular to Commedia dell'Arte such as mask, mime, and acrobatics. They are not intended to supersede, rather to partner these other techniques, and help the player achieve the synthesis of performance skills demanded by this challenging and rewarding genre of theatre.

Tension and breath

One way to discuss comedy is to examine the repeated building and release of tension in a performance. One established technique for players to explore this is via working with breath. Much can be observed about breath, including the obvious association of tension with the holding of breath, and that to produce laughter one must release the breath. The audience can be manipulated via the performer's use of breath: the natural tendency of the human being to imitate and empathize with what they see and hear can result in the audience holding breath when a performer does so, and then releasing breath as the player does in kind. But if the performer cannot or will not release the breath, the audience will be more inclined to hold their breath, which preserves rather than releases tension, and discourages laughter. (Iacoboni 2009: 659)

A free breath relieves physical tension in the performer: tension that is understood to block a player's expression, communication, and emotion. Avner Eisenberg, a student of Jacques Lecoq and former instructor at the Dell'Arte School, states emphatically, "Tension is your enemy. It produces emotional, mental and physical numbness." (Eisenberg 2013) Master acting teacher Carol Fox Prescott focuses much of her work on the breath. She writes, "when my body is free to breathe without unnecessary tension, I can respond freely to any circumstances, real or imaginary" (Prescott 2011). The playful, improvisatory feel of Commedia resists too much tension, and welcomes a free, flowing breath. My own students provoke the most laughter from their classmates when side-coached to simply look at the audience and breathe.

Encountering the audience and telling the truth

The theatre's invisible fourth wall was a nineteenth century development which did not exist in the period of Commedia dell'Arte's first triumphs. In lecture-demonstration, Fava declares that the fourth wall is "back there!" tossing his hands toward the rear wall of the auditorium. In Commedia dell'Arte, like contemporary street performance, the player and the audience exist in the same space, and they are able to communicate with each other.

How can a comic performer make use of that freedom to communicate? Eisenberg performs a hat juggling routine in his show. He begins by placing the hat on his head with a simple flourish. Often the audience responds with applause, in which case he gives the audience a look as if to say, "Oh, you enjoyed that? I will do some more." And he continues performing hat tricks, continuing to validate the increasing audience response.

If, however, the audience neither laughs nor claps after the first hat flourish, he gives the audience a look that implies he was expecting some kind of response. In that case, he removes his hat and performs progressively more impressive and difficult manipulation to get the biggest response possible. Eisenberg says, "Either way it builds. And because you're validating whatever they did, it's almost like validation therapy. I think it lets them relax and ultimately laugh." (Eisenberg 2013) Note his link between relaxation (release of tension) and laughter.

Patricia J. Campbell interviewed dozens of street performers and noted, "Breaking the fourth wall is necessary to keep people from falling into their television-viewing attitude—inert, not reacting aloud or rewarding the performer." (Campbell 1981: 213) Audiences in the period of Commedia's initial prominence had no television-viewing attitude, for obvious reasons, but contemporary audiences do. And as audiences spend more time in cars, in cubicles, and before the rectangular screens of their phones, tablets, and computers, the simple act of reminding the audience that the performer can see and hear them as easily as they can see and hear the performer not only builds more tension (for if the performers can see and hear the audience, what prevents the craziness that exists onstage from jumping over the footlights?) but also exists as an invitation for the audience to play along with the performers on stage. (Izzo 1997: 6–7)

How is the audience expected to play along with Commedia's performers? Barry Grantham writes that the audience shares in the pretense that a wooden sword is, in this fictional world, sharpened steel, or that a high-back chair is in fact a horse to be ridden across the countryside. The audience is complicit in the imitative play—it is their role in the game to preserve the illusion the performers establish. But the objective truth is kept on display as well, to keep the fantasy in balance—the wooden sword is revealed as not truly thrust through a character's chest, but merely resting under a player's arm. The particularly tall back of the chair is acknowledged as an absurdly long neck for this unusual horse. (Grantham 2000: 12) The player builds tension by creating an easily broken fantasy world, and then breaks that tension with the acknowledgement of the absurdities or contradictions in the creation of the fantasy. To that end, Avner has codified a principle of clown work that may be applicable to Commedia—"Use mime to create fantasy, not to re-create reality." The truth must remain objective, and in contrast to the mimetic fantasy. (Eisenberg 2007)

To ensure that the rules of this game of make-believe are understood and agreed upon by the audience, Larry Pisoni, founder of the Pickle Family Circus, teaches his students to "Set the stage for comedy." At the moment of each performer's first entrance, the character regards the audience with an inner dialogue of, "Are you ready?" or "Will you play along with me?" This first invitation to a friendly game that audiences and performers play together, can create a tone of complicity that will exist between performer and audience for the remainder of the performance.

Games and narrative

Fava compares Commedia favorably to soccer, insofar as both have specific and rigid rules that are obeyed by the players and understood by the spectators. Once the rules are clearly put forth, the players may play the sport for the enjoyment of the spectators. (Fava 2007: 109) Grantham uses the term "game," rather than sport, reminding us that it is a game of imagination into which the audience is invited to play with the performers. (Grantham 2000: 12) The word "sport" suggests competitive play, while "game" suggests imitative play; in either case, establishing the rules of the game clearly and early is paramount.

The games must not be overly complicated, as the rules must be understood quickly. Lecoq wrote:

> The themes we use are very simple: "Someone calls for someone" can become a major theme, provided, of course, that the person who is called for never comes! Between the call of one and the arrival of the other there is room for all the theatre in the world.
>
> (Lecoq 2001: 111)

"All that theatre" is the playing of the game. It is the discoveries that alter the call, or prevent the calling completely (a case of hiccups, for example). It is the character being called for entering the stage from the opposite wing, and joining the first character in the calling. The multiple assumptions associated with a character calling for another—that the character called for will eventually come, that the character called for is different from the character already onstage, and that the character called for is a human and actually exists; these assumptions can be toyed with, delayed, and shattered once they are recognized.

John Wright observes:

> The more you declare the game, the more distanced we'll feel from you as a character, and the closer we'll feel to you as a person. If we see that what you're doing is a game, we'll see you playing a game rather than you playing somebody else. Our interest will lie more in what happens in the game rather than what happens in the dramatic situation. Your action will look deliberately comic, clown like, or parodic, or, quite simply, theatrical.
>
> (Wright 2006: 47)

As a half-mask is present in Commedia to act as both an element of character and an alienating artifice of theatricality, the declaration and playing of a game is an effective comedic technique to allow the player to straddle the line between the imaginary world and the reality of the theatrical construct. Using the example of the high-backed chair as horse, one player works to create the fantasy of horse through imitative play. As a second character deconstructs the fantasy via an acknowledgement of the differences between the real chair and the imagined horse, we have the opportunity for a bit of competitive play. The first player attempts to preserve the illusion, while the second works to destroy it. The first player stays in the game by modifying the description of the animal to remain compatible with the chair as described by the second player. The game defines rules and sets up expectations that may be broken with surprising reveals and shattered with unexpected punch lines—how might Capitano justify his horse's lack of a mane to his Zanni servant?

Expectations and surprise

Perhaps the response from Capitano in that situation that might inspire the loudest laughter from the audience would also be the most surprising response. Bruce "Charlie" Johnson writes of surprise in comedy, "You cause the audience to expect one thing, and then surprise them by doing something else." He offers as by way of example, the following joke with a clear set-up and punch line:

Q: Tell me how long cows should be milked?
A: The same as short ones.

The expectation is that the answer will refer to the length of time it takes to milk a cow, but the reader is surprised to find reference to the physical length of the cow. (Johnson 1988: 7) Therefore, leading the audience away from the punch line should lead to greater surprise, and a bigger laugh. Note that in the punch line, "The same as short ones," the reveal, or the word that, according to Scott Meltzer of Comedy Industries, "shatters" the assumptions of the audience, is put near the end of the punch line sentence. Meltzer elaborates:

Always place the reveal as close to the end of the punch as possible. If it is placed in the middle of the punch, the audience will start laughing and you will continue to talk. The audience will shut up to hear what you are saying. Don't talk past the reveal. You don't want to step on your laughs unless you've got a very good reason. When you talk past your reveal you're training your audience not to laugh.

(Meltzer 2001)

Meltzer uses violent words like "punch" and "shatter" to remind him to be bolder in his comedic writing and to create greater contrast between the set-up and the reveal. This boldness extends to the very consonants in the words chosen in the punch. Neil Simon records the lore of the vaudeville comedian in the play, The Sunshine Boys. The character Willie notes, "Words with a 'K' are funny." (Simon 1973:15) Plosives like K, T, and P assault the ear and, Meltzer says, heighten the impact of the punch. One may experiment with choosing percussive consonant sounds versus nasal or fricative consonant sounds in the text of a punch line. Contrasting the softer sounds of a set-up with the percussive sounds of a punch line will not only heighten the impact of the comedy, but can help a player specify language choice as related to character and situation.

Timing

The appropriate rhythm and tempo of the set-up and the punch line is what is referred to as comic timing. Johnson defines timing thusly: "You give the audience enough time to... develop expectations; but not enough time to guess what the surprise will be." (Johnson 1988: 8) Fava adds:

An effect is comic only when it satisfies opportune requirements, when it falls at the exact moment for its maximum efficacy, so as to provoke a chain of laughter. Too late or too early, even the slightest misstep, can compromise the effect.

(Fava 2007: 162)

Jacques Lecoq wrote of timing and rhythm, "Tempo is geometrical, rhythm is organic…. Rhythm is the result of an actor's response to another live performer." I note that a rhythm may also be developed between performer and audience. Lecoq continues, "To enter into the rhythm is, precisely, to enter into the great driving force of life itself." (Lecoq 2001: 32)

A technique that combines rhythm, timing, and the shattering of assumptions is commonly referred to as the "Rule of Three." This "rule" in comedy has often been defined: "things are funny when done three times." Repetition is certainly a technique of comedy, but repeating something three times, seven times, eleven times, or thirty times over the course of a theatrical event could be effectively comedic depending on context, rhythm, tempo, and the successful misdirection in the set-up. The Rule of Three actually refers to the smallest number of occurrences it takes to establish and then break a pattern. Once a pattern has been established by performing an action twice, or speaking a line of text twice, the audience carries expectations, or what Meltzer would call "assumptions." The third action or line of text shatters those expectations via a reveal—a physical, verbal, or rhythmic difference.

By way of example, Johnson describes a comedy juggling *lazzo*—a performer juggles three balls, and tosses one high, allowing it to fall and bounce off the floor, returning the juggling sequence. This action is repeated exactly, creating a pattern. The third time a ball is tossed high in the air, the audience expects a similar bounce, but this ball lands with a thud, as it is, in fact, made of clay. (Johnson 1988: 7–8) The Rule of Three may be spread across more than one performer or character. In a duo, the comic will offer a set-up, the "straight man" will repeat the set-up, and the comic will break the pattern with the punch line. In a trio, the first character can establish an action and the second character may repeat it, in which case the third will shatter the assumption of her repeating the action by performing a different one. Sometimes the character with the highest status will establish the action, and the characters of lower status will repeat, mock, and subvert it. However, in an action like carefully stepping over a slippery spot on the stage, it may be funnier to allow the character with the highest status to break the pattern and take the fall.

Status and stakes

Status relationships, such as the one found in the duo of "straight man" and "comic," are another essential key to help unlock the comedic potential of Commedia. In each character relationship there is an opportunity to discover a status differential. Whether driven by social class, wealth, gender, romantic appeal, knowledge, or hunger, the gap in status between two or more characters provides opportunities for their players to find something over which to compete. And the stakes of the competition are absurdly high, requiring bold tactics from the characters to stay in the game. If, as

182

Fava suggests, the constant undercurrent for all of Commedia's characters is the "permanent emergency of survival itself," we seek games in which one player's urgent desire is in conflict with the urgent desire of another player. (Fava 2007: xv) Performer and director Adam Gertsacov suggests that if players do not feel like their characters' actions, if performed out in the real world, would get them arrested, then they must make bolder choices. (Gertsacov 2014) The cartoonish violence of a slapstick hit is an example of a high-stakes response to almost any provocation.

The status differential also feeds the tension. In an art developed in an age when corporal punishment of servants was accepted practice, the servants' desires must be shared with the audience, but concealed from the masters onstage. This creates many high-stakes opportunities to mock, to steal, to cheat, or simply goof off without getting caught. When a character is caught in a status transgression, either a quick snapping back into the prescribed status relationship, or the total disregard for social norms and exploring the tension in a status reversal are some ways that have been proven effective to explore the comedy in status and stakes.

The comic vision

Geoff Hoyle, a former Pickle Family Circus clown observes:

> You can deduce certain rules empirically from what you observe and by doing it. But beware: comedy is about breaking rules. If you work in comedy you have a comic vision or you don't…. People who successfully work in comedy have a comic take on life.
>
> (Robinson 1999: 117)

Johnson offers several different ways to develop the comedic perspective. After defining various techniques of comedy (i.e. Reversal, Delayed Anticipated Action, and Imagined Predicament), he challenges the reader to identify the techniques in play in various examples from silent film, the early days of television, and jokes. (Johnson 1988: 41) These techniques, once identified, can become the foundation of a process of creating comedic material not bound to pop culture or contemporary comedy's multi-layered meta-references.

My own students explore classic Commedia dell'Arte *lazzi* through the lens of Johnson's list of techniques of comedy, putting a name to what classic comic techniques are in play. In creating new material, they use Meltzer's approach to listing the multiple assumptions inherent in any action that can be shattered by a verbal or visual punch line. In this way, their comedic creations are rooted in a classic tradition of popular comedy that is based on the observation of absurdities in shared human existence. Once the assumptions and foundational comedic techniques are clear, they next use the approaches of Grantham and Wright to translate this information into a game that they can play on stage; optimally, one that includes both performers and audience. This has proven to be a useful process for creating comic lazzi that are simple, direct, playful, and immediate. Anachronistic references are kept to a minimum, and at its most successful, it has yielded work that preserves the classic tradition without sacrificing contemporary laughs.

References

Campbell, Patricia J. (1981) Passing the Hat. New York: Delacorte Press.

Eisenberg, Avner (2007) "Avner the Eccentric—Eccentric Principles." Avner the Eccentric. Online. www.avnertheeccentric.com/eccentric_principles.php (accessed 01 November 2013).

——(2013) Interview by Jim R. Moore. "Interview with Avner the Eccentric: 'Exceptions to Gravity.'" Vaudevisuals.com. 02 March 2013. Online. www.youtube.com/watch?v=r3sZv-WN6Os (accessed 01 November 2013).

Fava, Antonio (2007) The Comic Mask in the Commedia dell'Arte: Actor Training, Improvisation, and the Poetics of Survival. Evanston, US: Northwestern University Press.

Gertsacov, Adam (2014) "Commedia Techniques." Message to Brian Foley. 07 March 2014. Personal e-mail.

Gordon, Mel (1983) Lazzi: The Comic Routines of the Commedia dell'Arte. New York: Performing Arts Journal.

Grantham, Barry (2000) Playing Commedia. London: Nick Hern Books.

Iacoboni, Marco (2009) "Imitation, Empathy, and Mirror Neurons." Annual Review of Psychology 60: 653–70. Online. www.adineu.com.ar/IMITATION%20EMPATHY%20AND%20MIRROR%20NEURONS%20IACOBONI.pdf (accessed 01 November 2013).

Izzo, Gary (1997) The Art of Play: The New Genre of Interactive Theatre. Portsmouth, US: Heinemann.

Johnson, Bruce "Charlie" (1988) Comedy Techniques for Entertainers. La Crosse, US: Visual Magic.

Lea, K. M. (1962) Italian Popular Comedy: A Study in the Commedia dell'Arte, 1560–1620 with Special Reference to the English Stage. Vol. 1. New York: Russell & Russell, Inc.

Lecoq, Jacques (2001) The Moving Body (Le Corps Poetique): Teaching Creative Theatre. New York: Routledge.

Meltzer, Scott (2001) "A Dozen Ways to Improve Your Jokes." Motionfest. The Laughter Arts Foundation. Baltimore, US. 09 November 2001. Lecture.

—— (2012) "Be Funnier with Scotty Meltzer: Creationism." eJuggle. 21 April 2012. Online. http://ezine.juggle.org/2012/04/21/be-funnier-with-scotty-meltzer-creationism/ (accessed 01 November 2013).

Pipkin, Turk (1989) Be A Clown! New York: Workman Publishing Company, Inc.

Prescott, Carol Fox. "Acting Is...." Carol Fox Prescott. 2011. Online. http://carolfoxprescott.com/acting-is/ (accessed 01 November 2013).

Robinson, Davis Rider (1999) The Physical Comedy Handbook. Portsmouth, US: Heinemann.

Simon, Neil (1973) The Sunshine Boys. New York: Random House.

Swortzell, Lowell (1978) Here Come the Clowns: A Cavalcade of Comedy from Antiquity to the Present. New York: The Viking Press.

Wright, John (2006) Why Is That So Funny? London: Nick Hern Books, Ltd.

19

SLAPSTICK AND COMIC VIOLENCE IN COMMEDIA DELL'ARTE

Dr Louise Peacock

Slapstick and comic violence are so central to both Commedia scenarios and *lazzi* that they are impossible to ignore, contributing as they do so much to the audience's enjoyment of the performance. It is, therefore, worth considering how comic violence is presented to the audience and the ways in which that presentation guides their response to it. Exploration of the purpose of comic violence is also relevant. Sometimes it serves as a structural device: as a way to punctuate the performance; at others it allows the performers to pass comment on the society and times in which they live and work. Beyond these considerations it is important to analyse how slapstick violence might have been performed on the traditional Commedia stage.

The performance frame of Commedia, marked as it is by the traditional raised stage with its stylised backdrop, use of masks, acrobatics and gesture, goes some way towards making physical violence and pain acceptable and even entertaining because the action is distanced from reality. What is more significant is the comic and even absurd tone of many Commedia scenarios and lazzi. In Commedia fantastical things happen which cue the audience into an expectation of the absurd and the unreasonable. Examples of this can be found in Gordon's *Lazzi* (1983) where a number of the lazzi demand acts by the performers which are physically impossible. In one, Arlecchino must transform himself into a piece of broccoli; in another he must eat himself. It is this wild and glorious comic imagination which renders the impossible feasible in a way which provokes the audience to laugh by that which, in everyday life, would make us wince or flinch.

Audience response is guided by the way the masks on stage respond to the pain inflicted on them. If the response is unrealistic through exaggeration (Arlecchino is tumbled over by somebody blowing on him) or understatement (Arlecchino is hit around the head with his own slapstick but barely reacts) then the audience is reminded of the performance frame because we recognise that the performer's response is artificial.

In establishing this unreal world, so different from the one inhabited by the audience, the masks and physical stylisation of the performance support comic identification. When we watch Arlecchino we can laugh because we are identifying with him as a type rather than as an individual. His mask, costume and stance indicate to us that here is Arlecchino and he is not of our world. With Arlecchino in particular, the skill of the performer also serves to remove him further from our everyday reality. When he turns a somersault without spilling any wine from the glass he is holding he renders himself 'other' because he can achieve things which the audience could not.

A range of techniques support the audience's response to slapstick and to comic violence. Elsewhere I have asserted that 'Pantalone and Arlecchino represent a seminal double act' (Peacock 2011:64) and the presence of this double act makes a vital contribution to the way in which comic violence can be performed. In the hands of this duo, contrasting as they do in terms of age, agility and status, the comic violence is rarely motivated by individual malice. Instead it is used as 'a social instrument either to confirm or subvert the usual status quo' (ibid., 64). When Pantalone hits Arlecchino he does not do so out of any individual hatred towards Arlecchino, he does so because as the master it is his right. On the occasions when Arlecchino gets his own back the audience are entertained by the reversal of the status quo which allows Arlecchino to be superior however momentarily. In addition to the double act, Commedia performers make use of the threat of pain, anticipation, reversal, repetition and escalation. It is also significant that the performed pain is clearly unreal and without consequence. This is why Arlecchino's *batocchio* or slapstick is so important. It allows for a blow to be struck with a sharp sound but with minimal physical impact. Thus, the noise signals that the blow has occurred and the victim can perform a comical reaction to it without having been hurt. As Gordon's book demonstrates the use of stage props is significant in Commedia performance and props are particularly important in the depiction of slapstick and comic violence.

The two most common forms of slapstick violence in Commedia are deliberately inflicted pain and accidental pain. A range of examples of the ways in which this violence might work can be found in the lazzi listed in Gordon's book. There they are helpfully categorised according to the nature of the lazzi whereas here I will consider lazzi drawn from a range of Gordon's categories in relation to the kind of pain depicted or the techniques used in the depiction.

Threat of pain and anticipation are closely connected. For example, in the Lazzo of the Tooth Extractor when Arlecchino (disguised as a dentist) approaches Pantalone to extract his teeth using over-sized or ridiculous tools the audience is aware of the threat of pain long before any performed pain occurs. The extended nature of the action up to the moment of extraction builds the audience's sense of anticipation. This can be enhanced by the use of looks to the audience by Arlecchino. He may ask for their support, seeking approval to continue. Whilst all this is taking place Pantalone's fear can be seen on his face and may be heard as whimpering, pleading or screaming.

Repetition and escalation whilst closely connected and often occurring together are not the same thing. Examples of repetition can be found in a number of lazzi including the Lazzo of the Cuff. This *lazzo* usually begins with two masks arguing. At the conclusion of the argument one mask hits the other. One of these masks leaves and another mask enters. The new mask is hit by the existing mask. This pattern of exit, entrance, and blow can be repeated until all the masks in the troupe have been involved. Here repetition clearly builds a sense of anticipation which is fulfilled. None of the blows is hard enough to convey real malice so the audience is free to laugh at the blow and the response of the recipient. The same pattern of expectation through repetition is established in the Lazzo of the Counting. In this lazzo, the Capitano is told to beat Arlecchino ten times (perhaps because Pantalone does not have the energy to do so). The Capitano keeps losing count. Each time he loses count Arlecchino shouts 'ten' hopefully only for the Capitano to begin again at one. This lazzo, like so many others, can be extended according to the response from the audience. The first time through the audience does not know the Capitano will lose count but each subsequent repetition builds both anticipation and fulfilment. The comic nature of the pain can be increased by the way the blows are performed and the ways in which Arlecchino reacts. Whilst both of these lazzi rely heavily on repetition, neither necessarily includes any escalation (though the second could be performed with increasing blows). The Lazzo of Killing however provides an excellent opportunity for escalation. In this lazzo a pair of masks (Zanni and the Capitano) decide to kill a third mask (Flavio). They each demonstrate to the other how they intend to kill him. These methods for killing Flavio become more and more extreme as they each take turns to demonstrate. The comedy for the audience lies in the exaggerated and increasingly complex methods which may be shown.

The Lazzo of the Shampoo and the Lazzo of the Stones both rely on the use of props to provide the comedy. In the first of these lazzi, 'Arlecchino attempts to clean Pantalone's hair with an overlarge rake' (Gordon 1983: 15). The over-sized nature of the prop contributes to the comedy, emphasising the lack of reality in the performance and highlighting Arlecchino's stupidity because he has not realised how inappropriate his chosen tool is. Thus the pain inflicted is accidental rather than maliciously intended. The audience may laugh at the ridiculousness of the situation. If the action prior to this lazzo has encouraged the audience to sympathise with the lowly servant then they will laugh at this moment of payback. Pantalone's reactions both facial and vocal can be used to reinforce the humour. In the second lazzo the pain is once again unintentionally inflicted but this time it is self-inflicted. Arlecchino is so hungry and so stupid that he thinks eating stones may assuage his hunger. Instead, they cause him pain because they 'seemingly break his teeth and cut his throat' (ibid., 18). Once again the comedy can be enhanced by Arlecchino's reactions which can be played directly out to the audience and which may include 'asides during which he gives his full attention to the spectators before returning to complete absorption in the action' (Rudlin 1994: 79).

Some lazzi also reflected issues which were relevant to contemporary audiences. Grantham suggest that 'the horrors of contemporary medicine seem to have held a particular fascination for Commedia dell'Arte' (Grantham 2006: 223). Performances including depictions of enemas, tooth extractions, operations and dismemberments provide rich opportunities for slapstick performance resulting in comic pain (if not exactly comic violence). Duchartre includes a sequence of illustrations depicting

'The Marvellous Malady of Harlequin' and the fifth plate (Duchartre 1966: 56-57) shows Arlecchino receiving an enema (Duchartre primly describes it as an injection). In performance the comic potential of such action is huge. Effectively, this would occur as a lazzo or a sequence of lazzi within the scenario. Anticipation would be built by the Dottore readying his syringe and by Arlecchino's reluctance to expose his bottom. Once the enema is being applied the source of comedy becomes dual. Doubtless the performance of Arlecchino's reactions would provoke laughter from the audience and some sections of the audience would also have found the grossness of the action, supported as it could have been by an over-sized prop and appropriately coloured liquid, hilarious and, perhaps, pleasantly shocking.

Another popular device in Commedia, which was both thematic and structural, was the fight which was commonly used to close either the first act, the second act or both, and which came about as a result of an argument or the presence of Il Capitano. The fights could be sword fights or fist fights involving two or many masks. Grantham recognises that 'unarmed fights give excellent comic possibilities, including blows that don't land home or blows resulting in acrobatic falls, rolls and flips' (Grantham 2006: 271). Both sword and fist fights present opportunities for all of the techniques identified above. First, as the participants draw their swords or raise their fists the audience recognises the threat of pain and their sense of anticipation is awakened. It could be reversed or unfulfilled at this point by one of the combatants running away. If the fight begins, then the performers become involved in a sequence of repetition and escalation. Humour can be extracted from blows which land as intended, and from blows which miss. The nature of the sound effects will depend on the props being used. Grantham even suggests that the actors might add vocal sound effects to increase the comedy value of the fight.

The lazzi demonstrate how central the performance of pain and violence was to Commedia. This recognition inflects the way we read the scenarios. Andrews acknowledges the centrality of violence in the performance of Commedia thus: 'a statistical survey (however approximate) of set pieces in Scala which would demand some rehearsal, would show that by far the most common single activity is that of fighting' (Andrews 2008: xlv).

Fights being used to conclude acts can be seen in a range of scenarios including Day 1, The Two Old Twins; Day 2, Flavio's Luck; Day 16, The Mirror; Day 17, The Two Identical Captains; and Day 33, The Four Fake Spirits. This list is not exhaustive but it indicates the prevalence of violence and as Andrews suggests 'most of the fighting has a comic context, and the low life punch ups would be milked... for cartoon violence' (Andrews 2008: xlv). Usually it is the male characters involved in the violence, but in The Two Identical Captains, Flaminia and Franceschina exchange blows over whether Isabella (Franceschina's mistress) should pursue her love for Orazio. This fight is relatively short in duration and is followed by a fight between Isabella and Flaminia. When Pantalone, Flaminia's father, enters Flaminia tells him that she was fighting with Isabella who is crazy. When she hears this 'Isabella says that she is the one who is crazy and, enraged, throws herself at Flaminia hitting her and hitting everyone else on the stage' (Andrews 2008: 99). The potential for comedy lies in the relative rarity of the women's centrality to the violence. Additionally, the scenario makes use of both repetition and escalation in the number and intensity of the fights. Andrews describes the fight between Isabella and Flaminia as 'an entertaining collapse in decorum for the two actresses concerned' (ibid., 105). Doubtless the audience would find the sight of the two usually demure actresses attacking each other with energy on the stage highly entertaining.

What remains is to consider in detail the ways lazzi might sit within a scenario, what their function might be and how they might be performed. It is well established that the existing scenarios are only an outline of what occurred and as such they do not indicate how the fights and chases would have been performed. Therefore, when we read the scenario we must imagine how it might have been played to create comedy. Day 35, The Fake Friend, of Flaminio Scala's scenarios as translated by Salerno provides us with plenty of opportunity to stretch our imagination in this way. When the scenario opens, Pantalone is beating his son Flavio 'because he found him trying to break into his money chest' (Salerno 1967: 259). Here Flavio and Pantalone represent an oppositional double act, mismatched in terms of age and status. If Pantalone is played as elderly and infirm then much comedy can be extracted from his attempts to beat his son without over-exerting himself. It is possible to imagine a sequence of events in which Pantalone gradually readies himself to slap his son or to throw a punch at him only to have Flavio duck or pull back so that the blow misses. If Pantalone has attempted to slap Flavio, the natural consequence of the miss is that the force of the swing of his arm would spin him round. At this point he could end up facing Flavio, wondering why Flavio is not hurt or facing away from Flavio which could lead to confusion as to where Flavio has gone. The next action is that Pantalone refuses to give Flavio his hat and cape so Flavio tries to tear them from him. This provides a perfect opportunity for Pantalone to end on his back; as Rudlin suggests: 'like a beetle he cannot then right himself' (Rudlin 1994: 94). The comic violence then escalates as more masks become involved. Both Pedrolino and Burattino enter carrying the bar from a door. The comic potential of planks or pieces of wood is well established in slapstick and physical comedy now so it seems reasonable to assume that a contemporary audience might have similar expectations to a modern day audience when presented with the sight of two not very bright characters holding potential weapons. When two zanni enter, each carrying one, this should raise the audience's expectation of further pain. In fact that anticipation is subverted because, according to the scenario, what takes place is not anybody being hit by a plank. Instead 'Franceschina, Isabella's servant, comes to the window and throws a pan of dishwater on Flavio's head' (Salerno 1967: 259). There is plenty of comic opportunity here. The moment can be elongated if Franceschina delays throwing the water until she has been in the window long enough to build anticipation. The comedy can be highlighted by Flavio's reaction, which could include screaming, shouting, wringing out his hat or shaking his head to rid it of excess water. Additionally the audience response can be encouraged by the reactions of those present as an onstage audience. If some or all of Pantalone, Pedrolino and Burattino laugh and enjoy Flavio's misfortune, then the audience is more likely to laugh. The next example of comic violence occurs shortly after this when Isabella 'enters beating Franceschina for soaking Flavio' (ibid., 259). Here the violence is used as a form of punishment and reinforces the usual status roles of the characters involved. All of the comic violence described here takes place in the first twenty lines

189

of the scenario. The audience would, therefore, have been bombarded with examples of comic pain very quickly. This may have served the purpose of attracting and holding the attention of an audience early in the performance. Doubtless the physical violence meted out would have been matched by the sounds of screams and shouting, offering an aurally explosive and eye-catching start to the performance. The first act does not end with a fight or a chase, as is so common elsewhere, perhaps because of the level of violence earlier in the scenario. Spavento and Oratio have their swords drawn, about to fight as the act closes, but actual violence is averted by Isabella intervening and telling them to part on friendly terms if they really love her. The second act contains violence early on and this may be another reason why the usual fight does not take place at the end of Act 1. The fight or violence at that point usually provides a rousing end to the act but, given the violence early in Acts 1 and 2, it may be that some variation of pace and action is necessary. As Act 2 opens, Flavio (dressed as Oratio) is talking to Flaminia. Isabella sees this and thinks that Flavio (who she loves) is in love with Flaminia. In a rage 'she climbs out through the window, jumps on Flavio, and begins to hit him without giving him a chance to speak' (ibid., 261). The comic potential of this sequence is huge. It could be played so that when Isabella lands on Flavio he is knocked to the floor so that she can sit on him and hit him. Alternatively she could land on his back, cover his eyes with one hand so that he staggers around whilst she hits him with the other. The audience may have been particularly entertained to see a young man being beaten by a woman. As soon as he can, Flavio runs off and the violence continues as Isabella and Flaminia fight. No sooner has Oratio arrived and separated the women than Pedrolino enters and accuses Franceschina of being a thief. This provokes a fight between him and Franceschina. The variety of violence in this scene adds to the entertainment. First a higher status woman, Isabella, attacks a higher status man (Flavio), then two higher class women, Flaminia and Isabella, fight, then the two servants of the houses fight (one male and one female). This ensures that the three fights, occurring so close together, can be played in different ways using different fighting techniques and different blows. The next step is that Spavento enters and parts Pedrolino and Franceschina. Oratio then challenges him to a duel and Pedrolino challenges Arlecchino, Spavento's servant, to a duel also. The violence, therefore, is only ended by the threat of more violence to come. Once again this would increase the audience's anticipation of more comic pain and violence to come. The second act ends with an argument between Pantalone and Flavio, which is interrupted because Franceschina empties a chamber pot on them. The audience would enjoy the repetition seeing Franceschina soak Flavio again. The third act opens with Oratio and Spavento duelling, demonstrating the relentless nature of the violence in this scenario (which is described as a comedy so we know that, for the most part, the violence will be played for laughs). In a repetition of the intervention in Act 1, Arlecchino comes between them, wielding the bar from the door. It is possible that Arlecchino could stop the fight by coming between them in the way that might be expected but, given Arlecchino's usual combination of stupidity and acrobatic ability, it is also possible that he could cause chaos by coming between them then spinning round to talk to one or the other, endangering or hitting whoever is behind him. This could be played so that each time he spins round with the bar swinging behind him Oratio and

Spavento manage to avoid being hit, giving the audience the pleasure of both anticipation and enjoyment of their skill in avoiding being hit. Alternatively, they could each be hit by Arlecchino as a result of his well-intentioned incompetence. Sequences such as this demonstrate the range of possibilities open to a skilled Commedia troupe.

Another scenario which provides useful examples of how pain and violence could be deployed for comic effect is Day 29, The Faithful Friend. This scenario provides us with an example of violence which reverses the usual status relationships between the characters because, as Andrews acknowledges, the fact that Pedrolino can beat his master is 'totally implausible in real social terms' but it certainly adds to the 'general mayhem' (Andrews 2008: 180). This action may have been particularly entertaining for an audience because of its impossibility in everyday life. The comedy could be enhanced by the way in which Pedrolino disguises his voice, by Pantalone's reactions, by the nature and variety of the blows Pedrolino rains down on him and by the reactions of Arlecchino who is so scared that he falls off his ladder. The fall also provides a counterpoint to the beating so that the audience is provided with examples of both deliberately inflicted pain and accidental pain. Pedrolino's pleasure is emphasised by the fact that he laughs as he exits. The positioning of the beating at the end of the act also ensures that the violence serves its common purpose of punctuating the structure of the scenario so that the act ends on a high point. This is mirrored, to some extent by the fight which concludes Act 2. Here the two *vecchi* Graziano and Pantalone fight 'They come to blows and weapons, and exit fighting along the street' (ibid., 177). The two combatants are of equal status but there should be a striking physical contrast because Pantalone is traditionally thin and scrawny in comparison to the girth of the Dottore, consequently the audience would be likely to enjoy the physical contrast of this temporary double act. The example of violence in the final act of this scenario highlights the comic nature of the violence and also demonstrates how props could be used to support the comedy. In the list of properties for the comedy it lists 'blood and paste to make up a wound' and 'plenty of linen strips and bandages to bind a wounded head' (ibid., 172). Halfway through the third act there is uproar because the policemen try to take Isabella by force against Flavio's wishes. In the struggle Flavio is hurt 'on the head with a wound which bleeds copiously' (ibid., 178). It is not clear exactly how the paste and wound would have been used but one possibility is that the wound was concealed in one of Flavio's hands so that he could fix it to his head as he slumped from the sword blow or it could be hidden under his hat. This demonstrates the readiness of Commedia troupes to use special effects to support the impact of the violence they were performing. A comic contrast to the wound suffered by Flavio is presented when Spavento enters 'all bandaged up and walking with crutches' (ibid., 178). His arrival facilitates a comic dénouement for the sequence. Pantalone calls for a chair and unwinds layer after layer of bandage. There is much comic possibility in the playing with bandage and becoming tangled in it. There is also a comic repetition in the other characters repeated expectation that each layer will be the layer that reveals the wound, only to be disappointed. When it is discovered that Spavento is not wounded at all, 'Arlecchino gives him a good beating with a stick' (ibid., 178) and Spavento runs away. Elsewhere Rudlin (1984) has described the comic potential of

Capitano's run, and this could be used to good effect here but not before the audience have had the pleasure of seeing the servant Arlecchino beating one of his superiors without any fear of consequence. There is blatant comic irony here: that these two scenarios which focus so much on the nature of friendship also provide such a range of examples of characters injuring and harming each other.

As I have illustrated, the slapstick violence so popular in Commedia lazzi is carefully contrived by means of framing, masks, physicality and by structural devices such as the double act, repetition, anticipation, escalation, excess and embodiment to make the violence not only acceptable but also vicariously and viscerally enjoyable.

References

Andrews, Richard. (2008) *The Commedia dell'Arte of Flaminio Scala: A Translation and Analysis of 30 Scenarios.* Maryland, US: Scarecrow Press.

Duchartre, Pierre Louis (1996) *The Italian Comedy* (tr. Randolph T Weaver) Toronto and London: Dover Press. (Originally printed in 1929 by George C. Harrop, London).

Gordon, Mel. (1983) *Lazzi: The Comic Routines of Commedia dell'Arte.* New York: Performing Arts Journal.

Grantham, Barry. (2006) *Commedia Plays: Scenarios, Scripts, Lazzi.* London: Nick Hern.

Peacock, Louise. (2011) "Conflict and Slapstick in Commedia dell'Arte – the double act of Pantalone and Arlecchino". *Comedy Studies.* Vol. 4, no. 1: Intellect.

Rudlin, John. (1994) *Commedia dell'Arte: An Actor's Handbook.* Routledge: London.

Salerno, H. F. (1967) *Scenarios of the Commedia dell'Arte: Flaminio Scala's Il Teatro delle favole rappresentative.* New York: New York University Press.

Part II

HISTORICAL CONTEXT
What we know from whom, about what, and why it matters

20

ARISTOCRATIC ARCHEOLOGY

Greco-Roman roots

Paul Monaghan

The notion that an "unbroken line" links ancient Roman comic performance forms and the Commedia dell'Arte has been largely discarded in recent decades due to a lack of evidence. But debate continues to rage over the degree to which the "improvised" ancient mimes and Atellan farces, and the "fully scripted" third- and second-century BC comedies of Plautus and Terence, provided the structural and stylistic foundations of the Commedia dell'Arte. Scholars from around the mid-sixteenth century, such as Antonio Minturno (*Arte Poetica* 1563) and Niccolo Rossi (*Discorsi Sulla Commedia* 1589) (see Smith 1964: 22), were certain of the influence of their ancient forbears, but as both Smith (ibid.) and Richards and Richards (1990: 11) point out, Renaissance writers were always keen to situate themselves in an ancient lineage, regardless of the facts. Even those, however, who largely dismiss the "origins" of Commedia dell'Arte in Roman comic genres, and who argue instead for the more immediate influence of Italian Renaissance entertainers and carnival traditions, Boccaccio's *Decameron*, and/or the improvisational genius of professional comic actors, agree that the Commedia dell'Arte drew a great deal from its scripted older sibling, the *Commedia Erudita* (plays written in imitation of Plautus and Terence). And since, as Radcliff-Umstead has amply demonstrated, there existed an extensive "rapport of mutual inspiration and reinforcement" (1989: 33) between the Commedia Erudita and the improvised comedies that developed around the middle of the sixteenth century, arguments *against* the strong influence of Roman comedy on the development of the Commedia dell'Arte seem somewhat superfluous. At a minimum, terms such as genealogy, theatrical milieu, and "transformative adaptation" of "antecedents" are appropriate. If the innovative brilliance of the Commedia dell'Arte is thought to be reduced by ascribing to it a superb earlier model, then Shakespeare and many others are also so reduced.

Rather than continuing the "origins" argument here, this essay focuses on the comedies of Plautus and their ancient performance as antecedents to the Commedia dell'Arte. To a lesser degree, it also focuses on Atellan farce, Roman mimes, and the comedies of Terence. I suggest that, however it came about, key aspects of Commedia dell'Arte bear a strong resemblance to what is known and can reasonably be inferred of Roman – and especially Plautine – comedy *in performance*, despite its predominantly "scripted" nature. Marshall rightly points out that the distinction between "improvised" and "scripted" can be exaggerated, and is often misunderstood (2006: 245ff). These terms exist on a continuum that ranges from pure improvisation, in which nothing is predetermined in any way, and performance in which there can be no variation whatsoever (if that were actually possible). Few performance traditions exist at either end of this continuum. Like the Commedia dell'Arte, it is highly likely that, in antiquity, forms like Atellan farce and mime were "scripted" in the broad sense that pre-selected scenarios provided a narrative framework within which both "set pieces" and spontaneous (or pre-planned, "as-if spontaneous") performer elaborations were common. Marshall also believes the comedies of Plautus were "blended" in this way (2006: 261ff); his argument, although unconvincing in my view, serves to focus our attention on the skills required of the ancient performers of Plautine comedy. To the extent that I am able to contribute to those who have written elsewhere on this topic, I offer my own experience performing in and directing numerous Plautine comedies (in Latin and English), an extensive professional theatre practice, and my ongoing scholarship on the performance of ancient drama, both in antiquity and the modern world.

The Roman comedies of Plautus, Terence, and a collection of others (now largely lost) – referred to as *comoedia* in their own time, but *comoedia palliata* later in reference to the "Greek dress" worn by their characters – were themselves adaptations of fourth-century BC Greek plays referred to as "New Comedy". These ancient "sit-coms", focusing on more domestic themes with a certain "realism" compared to other ancient forms, owed their form and content as much to Euripidean tragedy as to the more fantastical and political "Old Comedy" of Aristophanes and his contemporaries. The robust comedies of Plautus, almost certainly influenced by both the mimes and Atellan farce, were highly popular in the late-third, second, and first centuries BC, but suffered later from Christian disapproval. Nicolas Crusanus rediscovered sixteen Plautine comedies in 1425, bringing the total number of his plays in circulation at that time to twenty (Erasmi 1989: 9). The more polished and genteel Terence was less popular during his own time, but admired by Cicero, Horace, and later Roman writers. He survived the Middle Ages intact, with his six plays "widely studied as models of style from the ninth century onwards" (Axton 1974: 24). Most famously, a tenth-century canoness, Hroswitha of Gandersheim, composed Christian comedies, in Latin, in the style of Terence's plays (Denard 2007: 159). New editions of the complete works of both playwrights were published in Italy in the early 1470s, and with the help of the newly invented printing press (1450), the plays of Plautus and Terence were being read and performed all over Italy from 1476 until well into the sixteenth century (Erasmi 1989: 9–10). Alongside and in imitation of these, writers in learned circles were writing their own Commedia Erudita, in five acts, for performance by amateur groups. Roman comedies had no act divisions, but later ancient grammarians had produced editions with scene divisions based on the entrances and exits of characters. Horace, whose work was enormously influential in the Renaissance, had recommended in his *Ars Poetica* (line 189: see Horace 1971) that plays should have five acts, and the writers of Commedia Erudita took Horace's advice to heart.

The ancient performance environment:
Atellan farce and Roman mime

Denard reminds us that, in both Greece and Rome, tragedy and comedy "were surrounded on all sides by an extended family of other theatrical forms... festive mockeries, mythological burlesques, satires, farces, comical tragedies, history plays and dance dramas." In addition, there were "a host of other performance activities" by entertainers of all kinds (2007: 139). When Greek New Comedy was adapted and – in the case of Plautus far more than Terence – transformed in Rome during the third and second centuries BC, it naturally drew from this environment. Northern Italy, dominated by the Etruscans who had themselves been influenced by Greek culture for centuries (Manuwald 2011: 23), left to Rome many cultural practices, including festival processions, dance, and gladiatorial games. In the central Italian town of Atella (between Naples and Capua), masked and improvisational farces performed in Oscan were well established by the time they were imported into Rome during the third century BC. Thereafter they were performed in both Oscan and Latin, and eventually only in Latin. Mimes, which may have originated in Greece but were also popular in Alexandria (Beacham 1991: 129), seem to have made their way into Rome via Southern Italy, which had likewise been colonized by Greek settlers from at least the seventh century BC. Called "Magna Graeca" by the Romans, Southern Italy had a flourishing theatrical culture consisting of what were formerly referred to as "phlyax" plays, but are now known to have been a Greek comic form that was shifting between Old and New Comedy (Csapo 2010: 52ff). Interestingly, while Latin terms for the practicalities of performance, like *histrio* (actor), *persona* (mask, character), and *scaena* (stage) seem to have derived from Etruscan, Latin terms for genres, like *fabula, comoedia, tragoedia,* and *mimus* (mimes), derive from Greek (Manuwald 2011: 24–25).

Despite the fact that both the Roman mimes and Atellan farce have frequently been linked to Commedia dell'Arte, very little is known about either. The two genres may have been performed on the same temporary, wooden stages (Marshall 2006: 32, 47) as the comedies of Plautus and Terence (Manuwald 2011: 175). Both started out as "improvised" forms, but at some point, probably during the first century BC when the *comoedia* were in decline, became "scripted" and were performed as short after-pieces, or *exodia* (ibid., 170). Ancient sources suggest gesture was important for both forms (ibid., 174), but no detail survives.

Atellan farce was performed by male actors wearing full-face, heavily-etched masks, and involved the interactions of a small number of stock characters with strongly defined qualities, drives, or appetites. Northrop Fry describes such character types as having an excess of a certain "humour", whose "dramatic function is to express a state of what might be called 'ritual bondage'." The character is "obsessed by his humour, and his function in the play is primarily to repeat his obsession" (Frye 1981: 87). Henri Bergson described such characters as driven by "that mechanical element which resembles a piece of clockwork, wound up once and for all and capable of working automatically" (1956: 156; cf. 179–80). The five known Atellan characters, most of whom shared a great appetite for food, are: Maccus, a clown, Bucco, a braggart, Papus, an old man (sometimes a lusty one), Dossennus, a trickster, and Manducus, who had large jaws and was presumably even more of a glutton than the others (Manuwald 2011: 172; Fantham 1989: 24; Denard 2007: 147; and Beacham 1991: 6). These appetite-driven *personae*, whose interactions were shaped by plots concerning family and rural life, love affairs and the like, seem to have left a strong trace on Roman – or at least on Plautine – comedy. Atellan farce is frequently described as "primitive" by modern scholars, who usually allude to more "sophisticated" forms that superseded it. But as Hornby warns us, "the approach to acting at a given time is simply the one that is appropriate to it" (1992: 148), and teleological judgments are misplaced. Moreover, the fact that Atellan performers were able to preserve their social rank and continue to serve in the army suggests they may have been of a higher social standing than other performers, who could not (Manuwald 2011: 174).

Roman mimes, unlike the modern, silent variety, involved speaking performers (called both *mimus* and *planipes*, or "barefoot") who, unusually for both Greece and Rome, were unmasked and both male and female. Titles and brief descriptions from antiquity suggest the scenarios tended to focus on relationships, family conflicts, love, and sexual intrigues; the "cuckold mime" appears to have been popular (Reynolds 1946), and female performers sometimes appeared naked. But scenarios could also draw on myth; and allusions to current politics also appear to have been common (Beacham 1991: 131). Denard suggests that mime "annexed all the popular theatrical and paratheatrical influences it could," including songs, dance, acrobatics, and magic tricks (2007: 34). The costume for the mimes included an item called the *centunculus*, a colorful patch-work tunic which some have been tempted to associate with Arclecchino (Fantham 1989: 26). (The Etruscan dance-figure, Phersu, who seems to have been involved in a spectacle involving public executions, and whose name is the origin of the Latin word for mask and character, *persona*, also wore a colorful patch-work costume: Olivova 1984: 158–9). The fact that the faces of mime actors were visible suggests facial expression may have been a feature, and there seems to have been a school for mime artists during the first century BC (Beacham 1991: 135). Although Christian emperors tended to ban the mimes, they survived until at least the seventh century AD (Beacham 1991: 138).

It is worth pointing out that, while the well-defined nature of the *Atellanae* masks would perhaps have allowed for variation in scenarios designed to generate amusing interactions between their "humors," the more standardized mime scenarios would perhaps have allowed for variation and subtlety of characterization.

Plautus (and Terence) in performance

A similar differentiation seems to have developed between the more subtle *personae* of Greek New Comedy and Plautus' adaptations of them (Wiles 1991: 135). In the fourth century BC, Aristotelian theories linked the *psyche* (soul) with physicality, breath, vocal quality, and the face, and it was through a man's choices and actions that his *ethos* (moral quality, character) was revealed. In a work known as the *Tractatus Coislinianus*, which may be a summary of the lost section of Aristotle's *Poetics* which dealt with comedy (Janko 1987: 170), and elsewhere in Aristotle (*Ethics* II.7.1108a 21ff: see Aristotle 2000; *Rhetoric* III.18.1419b 6ff: see Aristotle

2007), four comic types are envisaged: *bomolochos* (buffoon), *eiron* (ironical man), *alazon* (braggart), and *agroikos* (the rustic). Aristotle's pupil and successor, Theophrastus, wrote a compendium of comical *personae* that could be found in the *agora*. The new theories of perception, linking the exterior appearance of a person to his inner self, forged new possibilities for the use of the mask in theatre (Wiles 1991: 24). In the second century AD, a Roman grammarian named Julius Pollux of Naukratis, drawing on an earlier Hellenistic source, set out a system of masks for New Comedy (*Onomastikon* IV.143–54: see Csapo and Slater 1994: 393–402). The forty-four mask types are arranged into four genera: old men, young men, slaves, and women. Each mask, which covered the entire head, is inscribed with contrary polarities. The theatrical mask maker's art lay in his ability to produce relatively finely graded masks capable of expressing the required subtleties of *ethos,* and the special skill of the actor was to adapt his physicality and movement in such a way as to present different aspects of the mask to the audience in order for them to perceive these subtleties. Menander, the paradigmatic writer of Hellenistic New Comedy and a contemporary of Aristotle, wrote his comedies for this integrated system of masks (Wiles 1991: 85ff, 218ff).

But the transition from Greece to Rome involved a loss of subtlety and the development of more heavily defined features in the masks. As Webster reports, "nuances were lost as mask-types were amalgamated or abandoned; there was a progressive stylization and unrealistic elaboration of particular features" (Webster *et al.* 1995: 41; cf. Wiles 1991: 138). It is also clear from the plays themselves that Plautine comic *personae* were driven by a "ritual bondage" almost as tight as that which existed in Atellan farce. Plautus' full Roman name, Titus Maccius ("son of Maccus") Plautus ("flatfoot"), suggests he had at some point been an actor of *Atellanae*, and he would certainly have been familiar with Roman mimes. Everything about Plautine *personae*, including their costumes and props, loudly proclaims their pre-formed natures as soon as they appear, and their humors are the driving forces behind the varied plots of his comedies. Terence consciously modeled his more polite comedies on Menander – Julius Caesar criticized him for being a "half-Menander" (Radice 1976: 17) – and perhaps because of this, his plays proved more resilient during the medieval Christian shutdown of ancient theatre.

The *servus callidus* (clever slave) is the leading trickster, although at times he is successful only by the skin of his teeth. His mask consists of a larger head with an asymmetrically fierce appearance, reddish hair, a large, funnel-shaped open mouth, open eyes and raised, asymmetrical eyebrows drawn together in the middle. His legs and feet stand apart, and his knees turn outward – the opposite of what was considered decorous. He has a large potbelly, ample buttocks, thick calves and large feet (see Figures 20.1 and 20.2).

The *servus callidus* dismisses the threat of punishment as a necessary by product of his comic job description, and dares his masters to make the accomplishment of his trickery as difficult as possible. The *bonus servus* (good slave), on the other hand, sometimes also an *agroikos*, fears punishment, is fiercely loyal to his master, and doggedly sticks to his duties like the automaton that Bergson described. The *adulescens* (young man), with his pallid complexion, a full head of hair, and lowered eyebrows, is of course hopelessly in love. He frequently bemoans that his life is not

Figure 20.1 Servus Callidus of Roman comedy (left) with virgo and adulescens. From the house of Casca Longus, Pompeii.

Figure 20.2 Scene from Plautus' Mostellaria, directed by Paul Monaghan, Canberra, 1981. The image shows the servus callidus, Tranio (left), senex iratus, Theopropides, and a moneylender, Misargyrides.

worth living because the object of his heart's desire, a *virgo* (unmarried young woman), *meretrix* (courtesan), *tibicina* (flute-girl), or *ancilla* (female slave) is in the clutches of a *leno* (pimp), *lena* (madame), or *miles* (soldier). The *senex iratus* (angry old man), often an irascible skinflint who would have his clever slave flogged daily if he could, has a bald head, beard, gloomy eyes with the right eyebrow raised, and a hooked nose. He walks with the aid of a stick, and sometimes lusts after a *virgo* or *ancilla*, even if she is the object of his own son's affections. The *leno* (pimp) is either fully bald or has curly hair at the back of his head, with a thick beard, slight grin, and clenched eyebrows; he also has a paunch. The pimp in Plautus' *Pseudolus*, Ballio, walks sideways like a crab, is driven by his love of money, will sell his own parents if there is a profit to be made, and is outrageously callous in the face of young love. The *miles gloriosus* (braggart soldier) is typically in love with his own good looks, believes he is God's gift to women, and brags about his incredible (and impossible) military exploits, all the while shrinking in terror from the slightest threat, especially to his manhood. His mask has a stern complexion and curly hair that moves when his head does. He struts about the stage, with his sword no doubt providing evidence of his *immense* virility... until it shrivels. The *parasitus* (toady) scrounges from everyone, and the *coquus* (cook) is a sometimes outrageously self-important but clever addition to the cast.

Amongst the women, the "beautiful" *virgo* has a clear, pale complexion, smooth hair, and straight brows. The *matrona* (wife), snub-nosed and fierce-looking, could also be fierce in behavior, at least towards her wayward husband. An *ancilla* (female slave) sometimes participates in duping whoever is the butt of the plot's assault, but it is the mature prostitute (*meretrix*), with her reddish complexion, curls around the ears, and a "sexually-enhanced" body-suit, who is fiendishly clever and provocative, especially when called on to help punish a *leno*, *senex iratus*, or *miles gloriosus*.

That training in physical and vocal precision appropriate to these *personae* was important, and that actors, who were professionals but of low social status (whether slaves or free), tended to perform particular *personae* as suited to their abilities, is indicated in ancient literary and visual evidence (Webster *et al.* 1995; Beacham 1991: 136; Manuwald 2011: 73–4). The first century actor Quintus Roscius Gallus, for example, famous for his performance as Ballio, was in demand as an acting teacher, and also wrote a treatise on the use of gesture in comedy and in daily life. It was said that he never used a gesture on stage that he had not already rehearsed beforehand (Garton 1972: 183; cf. Dutsch 2013: 419). Writing in the mid- to late-first century AD, Quintilian (*Inst. Orat* 11.3.179–80: see Quintilian 2001) compares two famous comic actors: Demetrius and Stratocles. The former was known for his hand gestures, his seductive voice, "the skill with which he would make his dress seem to puff out with wind as he walked, and the expressive movements of the right side..." Stratocles, on the other hand, was known for "his nimbleness and rapidity of movement... [and] the way in which he sank his neck into his shoulders." Such details are sure signs of a precise comic physicality.

PAUL MONAGHAN

Ludi and *ludificatio*

In many Plautine comedies, the term *ludificatio* can be given to the comic process involved in punishing those *personae* whose humors deserved such treatment. The Roman Republican aristocracy's emphasis on the virtues of *gravitas* (solemnity) were "embodied in a unique series of restrictive, moralistic ordinances" (Segal 1987: 10). Since Romans did not have weekends off work, and like many other cultures in which the "injury to personality caused by bondage to work" required recuperative outlets limited to festival time (Caillois 1961: 32), this *gravitas* was set aside to some extent during state-organised religious festivals, called *ludi* ("games"). Theatrical performances, called *ludi scaenici* ("scenic games"), took place during such festivals. The comic process I am calling *ludificatio* was tantamount to converting the everyday Roman "bondage to work" into a temporary festive spirit, and since Roman comedies were adaptations of earlier Greek models, this involved Romans (or at least Roman comic actors) letting go and "being Greek" for a while – *pergraecari* is the verb used by Plautus. The process involved specific steps driven by the appetites or humors observed in the Roman system of masks. Blocking agents like the *senex*, *leno*, *servus bonus*, or *miles* are marked for attack because, dedicated as they are to their workaday occupations, their very natures constitute an unsatisfactory situation that must be corrected. The plot functions to heighten and then deflate and punish the appetites of these *personae*, who must not only suffer a reversal of their original position, they must also become the agents of their own downfall and be forced to admit to the crime that their humors constitute.

The *Miles Gloriosus* clearly displays this process of *ludificatio* in two iterations. As a *servus bonus*, and therefore already "a worthless man" (line 145: see Plautus 1996), Sceledrus is the guardian of the *virgo* (Philocomasium), who belongs to the *miles* (Pyrgopolynices). She is, of course, in love with the *adulescens* (Pleusicles), and it is the job of the *servus callidus* (Palaestrio) to help the girl escape the soldier's clutches. Like all *servi boni*, Sceledrus is fiercely loyal to his master, fears punishment, and does his duty with a supremely punishable certainty and moral fervor. By just over one third of the way through the play, Sceledrus has been threatened with severe punishment, accused of perpetrating *ludificatio*, and forced to admit his crime. He leaves the play a shriveling wreck of confusion. But the archetypical *alazon*, Pyrgopolynices, is the major target. His obsession with his own wealth, military magnificence, and prodigious sexual prowess are on display in the brilliant opening scene of the play where, with the encouragement of his *parasitus* (Artotrogus), the *miles* claims he puffed away the legions of Neptune's grandson with a single breath and killed 7,000 soldiers in battle in a single day. He boasts that Venus is his grandmother, and believes himself so irresistible to women that thousands are on fire for him. Through the machinations of the *servus callidus*, Pyrgopolynices loses his money and the girl, and is lured into a trap whereby, instead of enjoying the voluptuous *meretrix* (Acroteleutium), he is confronted with a *senex iratus* armed with a stick. Mercilessly beaten, he is threatened with the removal of his testicles, striped of all his symbols of wealth, valor, and beauty, and under the threat of even more punishment he admits to his crime and leaves the stage a deflated wimp.

Terence is more interested in introducing his new "double plot" to Roman comedy than in this process of *ludificatio*. In keeping with his desire (as stated in his prologues) to write more subtle plays in the spirit of Menander, Terence's *personae* display more layers and foibles than the two dimensional – yet far more memorable – Plautine figures. The cleverness of Plautus' *servus callidus* has been largely transferred in Terence's pays to other characters, who are for the most part no longer slaves (for example, Phormio in *Phormio*, and Aeschinus in *The Brothers*). Contrasting pairs such as the profligate and the sensible *adulescens*, or the *senex iratus* and *senex lenis* (in *The Brothers*), who turn out to have a surprising alternative side to them, have gained praise over the centuries as gentle depictions of actual human behavior.

Language, meter, music... and performance

While the trademark of Plautine comedy is his brilliant comic use of language and rhythm, Terence is known for his clean, "pure" Latin and fine sentiments. The texts of both writers consist of colloquial Latin with an enormous number of elisions when spoken aloud. In one sense, this was the language of the audience, which would have helped to set up a sense of collusion with them. But all Roman comedy was written in verse, and ancient evidence (see Moore 2008) divides the plays into *deverbium* (unaccompanied) and *canticum* (accompanied by the *tibicen* playing a twin-piped instrument called the *tibia*). *Canticum* sections are divided into *cantica recitativa* (longer but regular meters) and *cantica mixtis modi* or *mutatis modis* (consisting of a variety of shorter meters, which changed frequently). Although the nature of the *tibicen's* music and exactly how each kind of *canticum* was delivered are unknown, they are commonly referred to as "recitative" and "song." Ancient evidence suggests both were more heightened and rhythmical than the *deverbium* sections (Moore 2008: 28). The arrangement of the three verse types commonly follows a rhythmic pattern of *deverbium-mixtis modis-recitativa*, although variations certainly occur (Marshall 2006: 203–44, 280–4).

As the "spoken" meter, *deverbium* sections are mostly devoted to exposition (Duckworth, 1952: 373), and hence are standard for opening scenes and for the communication of important plot information (Moore 2008: 17). *Deverbium* sections tend to stay focused on the fictional world of the play, with infrequent asides or allusions to the world of the audience. Sections in *cantica recitativa* are primarily concerned with the development and presentation of the more animalistic humors of Plautine *personae*, and are therefore the sections in which the procedures of *ludificatio* are more fully prepared and perpetrated. They contain by far the most numerous asides to the audience, thus creating a kind of dual playing field (on stage and in the auditorium). There is also a far greater sense, or rather *pretense*, of improvisation, especially by the *servus callidus*, who is commonly forced to dig deep into his store of "improvisatory skills" in order to accomplish his tasks. It would seem reasonable to suggest that the influence of Atellan farce and mimes on these very "Plautine" sections is significant, especially as there are also a greater number of allusions in them to Roman life and customs. It is difficult to precisely gauge the effect of the *mixtis modis cantica* with so little knowledge of how they were delivered, but they seem to have required the skills of an expert composer (Moore 2008: 25).

Plautus employs these heightened theatrical "numbers" with great comic zest. They are commonly "entrance songs", and mostly solos (or solos which become duets) in which certain *personae* "strut their stuff". In *Pseudolus*, for example, in the first section of *mixtis modis cantica* (ll.133–264: see Plautus 1991), Ballio presents himself as the delectably ugly arch pimp, ordering his chattels about, threatening horrible punishments, and demanding to be pampered on this, his birthday. It establishes him as the principal foe, both for rapport with the audience and on the level of *ludificatio*. These sections are far more presentational than representational, and we can be sure that they were very much for the benefit of audience enjoyment.

Conclusion

Wiles rightly asserts that Plautine comedy was "not an imitation of an action, but… an action in itself" (1991: 7), and it was this very *theatrical* quality that increasingly attracted scholars, imitators, and the public in Italy during the very period when the Commedia dell'Arte was developing. Plautus was not "improvised" in the same way that Commedia dell'Arte was, although a *sense* of improvisation was ever-present. But what Plautus offered the New Comedy, in addition to his dazzling use of language and a cast of vivid *personae* whose humors were expressed both physically and in their behavior, was pre-eminently a comedy that was expressed *in and by means of performance* and the abilities of expert performers. Moreover, we do not need to posit any kind of direct transmission of the traditions of Atellan farce and Roman mime through to the sixteenth century and beyond, because key aspects of these forms were retained within the comic license of Plautine comedy. As Hardin notes, at the turn into the sixteenth century, following Horace's advice in *Ars Poetica* (268–74: see Horace 1971) that Plautine comedy was suitable only for foolish plebeians, "classical comedy… meant Terence alone" (2007: 789), especially after the commentaries on Terence by the Roman grammarian Donatus were rediscovered in 1433 (Webber 1956: 196). During the following decades, however, despite continuing scholarly suspicion of anything that pleased the crowds, the increasing prominence of Plautus posited "a model of classical (therefore, significant) comedy that violated Terentian decorum, bringing the highest standards of comic art uncomfortably close to those of low, clownish, popular comedy" (Hardin 2007: 813) – the kind of comedy, in other words, that the new professionals of the Commedia dell'Arte would excel in.

References

Aristotle (2000) *Ethics*. David Bostock (tr.). Oxford and New York: Oxford University Press.
Aristotle (2007) *On Rhetoric*. George A. Kennedy (tr.). New York: Oxford University Press.
Axton, Richard (1974) *European Drama of the Early Middle Ages*. London: Hutchinson.
Beacham, Richard C. (1991) *The Roman Theatre and its Audience*. Cambridge, Mass., US: Harvard University Press.
Bergson, Henri (1956) "Laughter". *Comedy*. Wylie Sypher (ed.). New York: John Hopkins University Press, pp. 61–192.
Caillois, Roger (1961) *Man, Play and Games*. Meyer Barash (tr.). New York: The Free Press.

Csapo, Eric (2010) *Actors and Icons of the Ancient Theatre*. Chichester, UK: Wiley-Blackwell.

Csapo, Eric and William J. Slater (eds) (1994) *The Context of Ancient Drama*. Ann Arbor, US: University of Michigan Press.

Denard, Hugh (2007) "Lost Theatre and Performance Traditions in Greece and Rome". *The Cambridge Companion to Greek and Roman Theatre*. Marianne McDonald and J. M. Walton (eds). Cambridge, UK: Cambridge University Press, pp. 139–60.

Duckworth, George (1952) *The Nature of Roman Comedy: A Study in Popular Entertainment*. Princeton, US: Princeton University Press.

Dutsch, Dorita (2013) "Towards a Roman Theory of Theatrical Gesture". *Performance in Greek and Roman Theatre*. George W. M. Harrison and Vayos Liapis (eds). Leiden, The Netherlands and Boston, US: Brill, pp. 409–31.

Erasmi, Gabriele (1989) "The *Commedia dell'Arte* and the Greek Comic Tradition". *The Science of Buffoonery: Theory and History of Commedia dell'Arte*. Domenico Pietropaulo (ed.). Ottawa: Dovehouse Editions, pp. 9–22.

Fantham, Elaine (1989) "The Earliest Comic Theatre at Rome: Atellan Farce, Comedy and Mime as Antecedents of the *Commedia dell'Arte*". *The Science of Buffoonery: Theory and History of Commedia dell'Arte*. Domenico Pietropaulo (ed.). Ottawa: Dovehouse Editions, pp. 23–32.

Frye, Northrop (1981) "The Mythos of Spring: Comedy". *Comedy: Meaning and Form*, Robert Corrigan (ed.). New York: Harper and Row, pp. 84–99.

Garton, Charles (1972) "How Roscius Acted Ballio". *Personal Aspects of the Roman Theatre*. Toronto, Canada: A. M. Hakkert Ltd, pp. 169–88.

Hardin, Richard (2007) "Encountering Plautus in the Renaissance: A Humanist Debate on Comedy". *Renaissance Quarterly* 60 (3) (2007), pp. 789–818.

Horace (1971) *Horace on Poetry: The Ars Poetica*. C.O. Brink (tr.). London: Cambridge University Press.

Hornby, Richard (1992) *The End of Acting: A Radical View*. New York: Applause Theatre Books.

Janko, Richard (1987) *Aristotle: Poetics I with the Tractatus Coislinianus: a Hypotheitcal Reconstruction of Poetics II; the Fragments of the On the Poets*. Richard Janko (ed.). Indianapolis, US: Hackett Publishing Co.

Manuwald, Gesine (2011) *Roman Republican Theatre*. Cambridge, UK: Cambridge University Press.

Marshall, C. W. (2006) *The Stagecraft and Performance of Roman Comedy*. Cambridge, UK: Cambridge University Press.

Moore, Timothy J (2008) "When Did the Tibicen Play? Meter and Musical Accompaniment in Roman Comedy". *Transactions of the American Philological Association* 138 (1) (Spring 2008), pp. 3–46.

Olivova, Vera (1984) *Sports and Games in the Ancient World*. D. Orpington (tr.). London: Orbis Publishing.

Plautus (1991) "Pseudolus". *Plautus: Three Comedies*. Peter L. Smith (tr.). Ithaca, US: Cornell University Press.

Plautus (1996) "The Braggart Soldier" (*Miles Gloriosus*). *Plautus: Four Comedies*. Eric Segal (tr.). Oxford, UK: Oxford University Press.

Pollux, Julius (1994) "*Onomasticon 4.99-154*". *The Context of Ancient Drama*. Eric Csapo and William J. Slater (eds). Ann Arbor, US: University of Michigan Press, pp. 393–402.

Quintilian (2001) *The Orator's Education (Institutio Oratoria)*. Donald Russell (ed., tr.). Cambridge, Mass, US: Harvard University Press.

Radcliff-Umstead, Douglas (1989) "The Erudite Comic Tradition of the *Commedia dell'Arte*". *The Science of Buffoonery: Theory and History of Commedia dell'Arte*. Domenico Pietropaulo (ed.). Ottawa: Dovehouse Editions, pp. 33–58.

Radice, Betty (1976) "Introduction". *Terence: The Comedies*. Betty Radice (tr.). Harmondsworth, UK: Penguin Books, pp. 11–29.

Reynolds, R. W. (1946) "The Adultery Mime". *The Classical Quarterly* 40 (3-4) (July 1946), pp. 77–84.

Richards, Kenneth and Laura Richards (1990) *The Commedia dell'Arte: A Documentary History*. Oxford, UK: Blackwell.

Segal, Eric (1987) *Roman Laughter: The Comedy of Plautus*, 2nd edn. New York: Oxford University Press.

Smith, Winifred (1964) *The Commedia dell'Arte*. New York and London: Benjamin Blom.

Webber, Edwin (1956) "The Literary Reputation of Plautus and Terence in Medieval and Pre-Renaissance Spain". *Hispanic Review* 24 (3), pp.191–206

Webster, T. B. L., J. R. Green and A. Seeber (1995) *Monuments Illustrating New Comedy*, vols. 1 and 2, (3rd edn.) London: Institute of Classical Studies.

Wiles, David (1991) *Masks of Menander: Sign and Meaning in Greek and Roman Performance*. New York: Cambridge University Press.

21

THE RISE OF COMMEDIA DELL'ARTE IN ITALY

A historical perspective

Kate Meehan

The birth of the phenomena known as Commedia dell'Arte was in the vanguard of the rebirth of professional theatre in Europe and owes a great deal to the restoration of urban societies and the development of a class of people with some measure of disposable income. The preceding centuries, commonly known as the medieval period, sowed the seeds for its birth and ensured that a performance style similar to Commedia dell'Arte was a cultural inevitability. From the rise and fall of the Roman Empire to the similar fate of the Venetian Republic, this urban revival went through several phases, each contributing to the tropes employed in Commedia dell'Arte.

The birth of Commedia dell'Arte is inextricably tied to the history of the Italian Peninsula. In the third century BCE, the Roman Republic seized control of the southern portion of the Italian Peninsula where Greek-founded city-states, including Naples, stood. Hellenistic Greece's New Comedy focused on domestic stories of the middle class featuring conventionalized characters and standard plot devices. Atellan farce, from Atella near Naples, elaborated on the fixed characters and incorporated standardized masks and costumes (Brocket and Hildy 2003: 37–45). Whether these comedic styles directly influenced Commedia dell'Arte or not, they established a formula for "Italian" comedy rooted in domestic and social stereotypes.

In 476, Odovacer, a Roman general of "barbarian" parentage, seized control of Rome. In 493, he was overthrown by the king of the Germanic Ostrogoths, Theodoric. In 553, the Eastern Roman Emperor, Justinian, re-conquered the Italian Peninsula in an attempt to restore the Roman Empire to its former glory. Three years after his death in 565, the Lombards invaded Italy and within the year had conquered the majority of northern and parts of southern Italy. They renamed this conquered land the "Kingdom of the Lombards," and divided it into thirty-six duchies. Over the next century, they expanded their territory, eventually securing Ravenna in 751 and alienating the papacy. In 773, Pope Adrian I requested the aid of Pepin's son, Charlemagne, who conquered Lombardy and became the King of Italy. In 800, Charlemagne was crowned by Pope Leo III and became the "Emperor of the Romans." This potted history of violent regime change serves to highlight that the

Italian Peninsula continued its Roman tradition as a melting pot of varied cultures, each scrambling to lay claim to the Roman Imperial legacy.

With Charlemagne's conquest came the import of nobility and feudalism, which was heavily infiltrated and influenced by the Church. Members of the new nobility kept entertainers of all sorts, most often individuals or small groups who specialized in juggling and other physical feats, along with trained animal acts. Church edicts during the ninth century banning secular performance near churches indicate that these performers were accessible to the laity as well, though unwelcomed by the religious (Brocket and Hildy 2003: 74).

During the tenth and eleventh centuries, communities called Communes developed, characterized by oaths of self-governance and self-protection (Waley and Dean 2010: 10). While in the countryside, people were divided into tidy categories: the *maiores*, or land owners, and the *minores,* or town-dwelling peasantry; such simple classifications within the Communes were impossible. By the end of the thirteenth century, two thirds of the heads of urban households owned land. A very high proportion of people in cities were engaged in both agrarian production on their own land and some other form of commercial or industrial trade. (ibid., 12–13). This is germane to the development of Commedia dell'Arte because the development of cities created a new demographic – tradespeople with money, capital, the potential for social mobility and a shared perspective.

In addition, Communes nurtured the development of trade guilds, which controlled the practice of various trades within the city. These guilds provided training through apprenticeships, set quality standards, and regulated the number of practitioners within a city. Later, these guilds would collaborate to produce elaborate plays based on biblical stories, called Mystery Plays. They are of particular importance here because they represented communities gathering in open spaces for entertainment. The guilds often competed with each other to create increasingly fantastic scenes, making full use of medieval technology to create some impressive special effects.

The administration of these cities is also credited with the development of universities. For the first time in centuries, persons able to read, write and tally figures were required on a large scale. Universities began to appear all over Europe, the first being the University of Bologna (1088), followed by the University of Paris (1150) and the University of Oxford (1167). More appeared over the next two centuries. While they were generally well distributed throughout Europe, a concentration of universities developed in Italy, which flourished as a mid-way point for trade from the East to the rest of Europe as well as a gathering point for European armies during the Crusades, beginning in 1195 and continuing intermittently whenever it was politically expedient.

Divergent opinions among the new urban societies and traditional ecclesiastical learning created political friction between the Communes and the Church. The position of the Notary, an individual who kept the records of the city, became an important position that could wield significant political influence. Scholarship from the East, which had preserved the ancient Greek texts, fueled a renewed interest in antiquity and its philosophers. These scholars multiplied and would become the basis of the Dottore character, known for his dubious knowledge of Greek or Latin and little common sense. It is notable that the character of Dottore traditionally hails from Bologna, the site of the oldest university in Italy and a city known for its large number of notaries; Bologna employed as many as 2,000 by the end of the twelfth century. (Ducharte 1966: 196; Waley and Dean 2010: 16).

The transport of goods across long distances, especially by ship, was an expensive and risky process though the rewards of success were high. Money lenders began to form partnerships and corporations to mitigate individual losses should ships sink or caravans be attacked by bandits. Men brave enough to stake their lives for potential fortune invested themselves and piloted the trade ships for a share of the profits. Some of these money lenders developed long-lived familial dynasties like the Medici and Borgia, and rose to positions of great power. Often, cities turned to these families in times of trouble or public anarchy, offering their cities up to their exclusive, hereditary rule under the assumption that they would restore order. Cities run by powerful families or individuals were called *Signoria*, and throughout the late medieval period, many of the Communes converted to this model. Leaders of several of the earliest *Signoria*, such as Venice (organized as a *Signoria* in about 700 CE), Genoa and Amalfi, took the title of Doge. Magnifico, one of the earliest Commedia characters, is also an honorific given to the noblemen of Venice. The Mask of Pantalone is based on these early money lenders and merchants, and reliable sources state that the role itself originated in Venice, which, in addition to being controlled by a Doge, was an extremely competitive hub of international trade (Ducharte 1966: 179).

The year 1315 marks a turning point in the evolution of the West. Across Europe, the weather changed dramatically. For a few years, harvests had not been good, driving up the cost of grain. In May of 1315, an unusually cold summer coupled with subsequent heavy rains in the fall, destroyed cereal crops and caused widespread flooding (Lucas 1930: 346). Disease followed and, beginning in 1317, an epidemic swept the sheep and cattle populations, killing off herds across Europe (Kershaw 1973:14). Reports of cannibalism, though hotly contested among historians, indicate how dire the situation was. Conditions remained devastating until the harvest of 1325, though failures and livestock epidemics continued for the next two decades. Society, weakened by malnutrition and population loss, was primed for disaster in the face of the plague.

In October 1347, twelve Genoese galley ships arrived in Sicily carrying fleas infected with the *Yersinia pestis* bacteria, known commonly as the Bubonic Plague, which killed the host in a matter of days. By January 1348, the epidemic had reached Venice, and shortly thereafter arrived in Pisa. By June, plague outbreaks were recorded in Spain, Portugal, France and England.

The plague affected Italy harder than other areas, with death tolls in some cities as high as 75 percent of the population over a span of four years. In the wake of such a catastrophe, the entire social structure of Italy changed dramatically. Wealthy homes were left empty without surviving heirs to claim them. Fields were left unplowed. Plague survivors who previously worked as field hands found their labor in particular demand. For the first time in recorded history, they could set their own price for their efforts if they decided to return to the fields at all. The structure of feudal society was in peril, and laws were rapidly passed capping wages for agricultural labor. For a time, unscrupulous individuals were able to take advantage of the widespread death, and some were able to secure positions of moderate power by seizing assets and positions in the vacuum left by the tragedy.

As communities struggled to cope with what surely felt like the apocalypse, scholars in Italy wrote feverishly about what it meant to be human. In Tuscany, Petrarch began writing poetry and various philosophical and self-help books. Dante wrote his *Divine Comedy*, an allegory on Christian theology that reflected a shift towards intellectualism. Boccaccio wrote the *Decameron*, a novel about a group of people fleeing the plague and amusing themselves with short stories that range from moral lessons to erotic fantasies. These authors, considered the fathers of Humanism, all focus to some extent on new ideals of quick wit, sophistication and intelligence. They lived or worked in Tuscany, and the dialect in which most of them wrote, Tuscan, became the Italian equivalent of Standard American or the Queen's English. Their Lovers' roles strove to epitomize the refinement and wit established by the Humanists, and they spoke in the Tuscan dialect to reflect their sophistication.

In 1423, a series of wars broke out between the Republic of Venice and Duchy of Milan and their various allies over control of the fertile Po Valley. This valley provided the only land-trade route from the Italian Peninsula to the rest of Europe. None of these states maintained an army. Instead, they hired mercenaries, called *condottieri*, to fight for them. Among the most famous of these condottieri was Francesco Sforza, who is mentioned in Machiavelli's *The Prince* as both the ultimate military general and a warning against using mercenaries. He switched sides often and, through a series of shrewd political and martial maneuverings, was eventually named Duke of Milan.

Sforza's fourth son, Ludovico, inherited the Duchy, and, through political blundering, initiated a series of wars known collectively as The Italian Wars in an attempt to retain his title. During these wars, France, Spain, the Holy Roman Empire and the *condotierri* of most of the Italian city-states fought, slashed, burned and pillaged their way up and down the Italian Peninsula off and on for sixty years. These *condotierri* inspired the mask of Il Capitano, who is often played with foreign accents, usually Spanish, and is portrayed as either terrifying and deadly or foppish and impotent.

In 1475, chroniclers began noting "Great Winters," which were colder, lasted longer, and killed crops and animals (Alfani 2010: 5). Glaciers in the Alps expanded every year into the Po Valley, sealing farmable land under a thick layer of ice. Throughout the end of the fifteenth and beginning of the sixteenth centuries, the combination of bad weather and poor harvests caused a series of localized famines. Mercenaries and foreign armies, despoiling farmland and pillaging as they went, compounded the effect of these famines. A letter to the Pope in 1527 from the city of Parma indicated:

> All around in the countryside, up to six miles from the city, there is no bread, no wine… especially where our soldiers were and are billeted, no food reserves, no barrels, but everything has been burned…. Many beasts great and small are eaten by the soldiers, who are openly robbing us.
>
> (Alfani 2010: 9)

In the wake of the war, droves of dispossessed rural people fled from both the marauding armies and starvation into the safety afforded by the walled Italian city-states, creating a new class of people at the lowest end of society. These refugees inspired the role of Zanni, who in his earliest stages was desperate, hungry and utterly ignorant of urban life. Over time, the role of Zanni as a single individual split into variations on the lower classes. The first zanni became the mouthpiece of the skilled working classes while masks like Arlecchino and Pulcinella represented the second zannis, the immigrant or lowest class in the North and South of Italy, respectively.

The society of the time created circumstances that impacted on women. Women in polite society were married with dowries paid in currency, rather than land which was the custom in northern Europe. Between 1450 and 1550, Italian dowries tripled (Robin *et al.* 2007: 94). This reduced the number of daughters a typical family could afford to marry off. Women were disallowed from marrying below their social status, a restriction not suffered by men, creating smaller pools of eligible bachelors from which a suitable husband could be found (Sperling 1999: 28). Convents, which required a significantly smaller dowry, became a convenient repository for third and fourth daughters. By the end of the sixteenth century, over 60 percent of upper class women joined convents, and only a fraction did so voluntarily.

Upper class men, particularly in Venice, were marrying later in life, but pre-marital affairs were out of the question for well-bred women. This created a need for women outside the patriarchal inheritance structure. Industrious women used this demand to develop an elaborate courtesan culture (*cortigiane*) providing a sexual outlet without stigma. These *cortigiane* also specialized in developing musical and literary abilities, knowledge of current politics and world history, and social refinement befitting wealthy patrons. The additional services came at a price, and a new class of wealthy, well-connected, independent women developed. The *cortigiane* of Venice became so famous they became one of the chief tourist attractions at the busy trade port. At one point, the city boasted 10,000 *cortigiane* for their 100,000 inhabitants, and directories of the most famous were provided to visiting nobility and wealthy merchants (Griffin 2001: 13). Other Italian cities record *cortigiane* among their citizens, but Venice certainly topped the league, in both quality and quantity. Records indicate that *cortigiane* provided musical interludes at events hosted by their sponsors or for the general public (Feldman and Gordon 2006: 20).

The earliest records of females in the Commedia dell'Arte indicate they performed as the *cantarina*, whose sole purpose was to provide music. The role was always performed by a "prostitute," and required both musical and dancing abilities (Ducharte 1966: 263). From there, it was an astute business decision to include women in performance roles. These were first recorded in 1566 by the troupe Zan Ganassa, though earlier sources discuss the presence of women on stage.

The *cortigiane* became valuable assets to early Commedia dell'Arte troupes, both as performers and troupe members, bringing their pre-existing patronage from foreign and domestic nobility and wealthy merchants. In addition to securing upper class patronage for the troupes, they also possessed the refinement to portray the female lover with cosmopolitan panache. The inclusion of females on the stage expanded roles for women, developing female equivalents of the first and second zanni.

By the sixteenth century, there were two classes of people in the Italian city-states with time and money to spend on entertainment. The largest and most accessible group was the working class, and by performing in the busy markets of the piazza, entrepreneurial artists were able to access them directly. The constraints of performing in crowded markets informed the physical style of their performances, requiring broad, articulate gestures and a reliance on body language and easily recognizable character types. This ensured their narratives were understandable across the distance and throng of a piazza and accommodated audience members who spoke in dialects and languages other than that of the performers. Masks, in addition to helping the audiences identify these characters, provided the actors with some measure of anonymity for the anti-authoritarian satire that would endear them to their working class audiences. Performing improvised scenarios in which the protagonists and antagonists of the working class schemed, cajoled, satirized, loved and lost, positioned these performers as spokespersons of the largest demographic in the city.

In 1545, the first professional contract between individual performers was signed in Padua by Ser Maphio and several others. This marked a major development in theatre being viable as a profession with an early version of Commedia as its artistic incarnation. Professional theatre had arrived that was popular with both the rulers and the ruled and possessed a narrative tailored specifically to meet the demands of the contemporary audience. The wealthy were purchasing performances as a commodity with the assumption that it had commercial value. This also meant that formal and pre-planned entertainment was something ordinary people could financially support. Performances had shifted from their initial place as the provenance of the privileged to a developed commercial entity to which all elements of society had access. Early modern commercial theatre had arrived in Italy.

References

Alfani, Guido (2010) *Climate, Population and Famine in Northern Italy: General Tendencies and Malthusian Crisis, ca. 1450-1800.* Dondena Working Paper No. 27, Carlo F. Dondena Center for Research on Social Dynamics, Universita Bocconi, Italy.

Brockett, Oscar and Hildy, Franklin J. (2003) *History of the Theatre*, 9th Edition, Allyn and Bacon, Boston, US.

Ducharte, Pierre Louis (1966) *The Italian Comedy*, Dover, New York.

Feldman, Martha and Gordon, Bonnie (2006) *The Courtesan's Arts: Cross Cultural Perspectives*, Oxford University Press, New York.

Griffin, Susan (2001) *The Book of the Courtesans: A Catalogue of their Virtues*, Broadway Books, New York.

Kershaw, Ian (1973) "The Great Famine And Agrarian Crisis In England 1315–1322," *Past and Present*, vol. 59, no. 1, pp. 3–50.

Lucas, Henry S (1930) "The Great European Famine of 1315, 1316, and 1317," *Speculum*, Vol. 5, No. 4, pp. 343–77.

Robin, Diana, Larsen, Anne R. and Levin, Carole (2007) *Encyclopedia of Women in the Renaissance: Italy, France and England*, ABC-CLIO Inc, Santa Barbara, US.

Sperling, Jutta Gisela (1999) *Convents and the Body Politic in Late Renaissance Venice*, University of Chicago Press, London.

Waley, Daniel and Dean, Trevor (2010) *The Italian City-Republics*, Pearson Education, Harlow, UK.

22

THE GREAT RUZANTE

Linda L. Carroll

Cultural context

Modern theater developed in the early years of the sixteenth century in central and northern Italy, where various festive genres rooted in pre-Christian rituals delighted the populace and vernacular literature based on dialogue flourished, and where courts and humanists revived Roman and Greek comedy.

At the heart of these developments lay Padua with its ancient university. While Latin and Greek learning made Padua a natural home for the revival of the plays of Terence, Plautus, and Seneca, of Aristophanes and Euripides, it was also a lively center of vernacular traditions. A Roman theater in Prato dalla Valle had continued to host popular entertainments such as the Wild Man, while the Roman Arena staged dramatic works. Students entertained themselves with original works, including in "maccheronic" Latin (filled with student errors) and in the *mariazo* tradition (plays staged at peasant weddings in which two suitors contend for the bride).

Life and performances

Born in Padua in about 1494, Angelo Beolco was an illegitimate, or natural, son. His father, the scion of a noble Milanese family that had turned to commerce, was a university student enamoured of Tuscan humanism, and his mother a servant, likely of peasant origin. He probably spent periods on the family's country properties near Pernumia, the home of his paternal grandmother's family, and Montagnana, where his father had purchased some former Este feudal property. In both locales Paduans and Venetians were neighbors, enjoying their summers and overseeing the peasants who cultivated their land. Pernumia also lay on the route connecting Padua and Ferrara, transited by numerous performers who entertained both city and country dwellers with music and dance, as well, likely, as rudimentary theatrical performances. Montagnana was a fortified town with a large garrison and the home of Beolco's stepmother.

Out of this mix of country and city, of popular and learned cultures, Beolco created some of the first vernacular comedies of the Italian Renaissance, building them around a peasant character whom he played and who usually bore the name Ruzante. Many of the plays, following the *mariazo* tradition, center on the conflict over a desirable young woman. The usual contenders are Ruzante and his friend and rival Menato, played by the Paduan noble Marc'Aurelio Alvaroto.

Little is known about Beolco's early career, and the dating of his plays is complicated by rewritings. His first surviving datable full play is *La Pastoral*, set in Padua at the close of the wars of the League of Cambrai (1516 or 1517), in which Venice had first lost and then regained much of its mainland state. Written in Tuscan and Paduan country dialect, the play juxtaposes aristocratic students playing Arcadian shepherds suffering from unrequited love with a peasant character, Ruzante, distracted from his farm duties by his own love troubles and an autocratic father. Through his practical powers of observation, Ruzante saves the life of an Arcadian character and the play culminates in a general dance to the sound of pipes.

Beolco caught the attention of Venetian aristocrats, always seeking fresh, piquant carnival entertainment. As recorded by Venice's chronicler, the patrician Marin Sanudo (Italianized as Marino Sanuto), Beolco staged a peasant-style comedy as part of the vast festivity given during Carnival 1520 by the patrician festive group Immortali (Immortals) for the new marquis of Mantua, Federico II Gonzaga. *La Pastoral*, likely that comedy, was copied in Padua the following year by Stefano Magno, the son of the city's *capitanio* or military governor. Through 1526, Beolco is recorded by Sanudo as performing at least once every carnival in Venice. In 1521, for example, he entertained at the home of patrician Piero Pesaro at a party given by a noble *condottiero* (army officer) to thank another aristocratic festive company, the Ortolani or Farmers, for including him. Numerous high-ranking guests attended, including the Prince of Sanseverino, on his way home from the imperial court. Beolco's 1522 performance occurred in the same year that Machiavelli's play about an impotent Florentine doctor, generally identified as the *Mandragola*, was performed in Venice, perhaps for the first time. Another high point in Beolco's career occurred in 1523, when, before a public composed of high government officials, he staged his carnival comedy at the Ducal Palace in May for the wedding of the doge's grandson to the daughter of a wealthy banker. Sanudo condemned the choice as inappropriate for such a dignified occasion. Ever more daring, Beolco chose a play for Carnival 1525 about wifely infidelity whose bad language so shocked the women attending that it was substituted between the rehearsal and the official performance. His final recorded Venetian performance occurred the following year during a festivity at which the French king Francis I, who had been captured in battle by the forces of Holy Roman Emperor Charles V, was mocked in the form of a mutilated rooster (*gallo*, also "Gallic" in Italian usage).

Subsequently Beolco performed in Padua and its countryside, where he had continued to perform during his Venetian years, and in Ferrara. In 1528 he gave an oration to celebrate the cardinalate of Francesco Cornaro, the brother of the Cardinal Marco whose 1521 entrance as bishop of Padua he had gladdened with a comic oration. Also in that year, he was included in the wedding festivities of the Ferrarese heir-in-waiting Ercole d'Este and French princess Renée, and was subsequently included in several Ferrarese Carnival festivities. At least one was coordinated with the great playwright and man of letters Ludovico Ariosto. In 1532 the theater in the Este palace burned down. Two months later in Padua at the home of his patron Alvise Cornaro, Beolco staged his *Vaccaria*, adapted from Plautus's *Asinaria* and probably originally planned for a Ferrarese performance. Attending was another military governor, Andrea Marcello, possibly the uncle of a member of the Immortali. This was the last recorded Beolco performance.

By the early 1530s times had changed, putting an end to free-wheeling comedies. The 1530 Peace of Bologna concluded the Italian Wars and signaled Charles V's control of most of the Italian peninsula and the end of Venetian expansion. The terrifying 1527 Sack of Rome, attributed to the Lutherans in Charles's army, together with the growth of Protestant sects reinforced a religious and behavioral conformism within the Catholic Church that would soon lead to the Council of Trent and the Inquisition. Beolco developed a career managing the agricultural properties of several Paduan religious institutions. In July of 1533 Ariosto died; the Este Theater, in which he had been staging comedies since 1507, was never reconstructed. Beolco's last known work is a version of the melancholy *Letter to Alvarotto* (his friend and theatrical companion) written in either 1536 or 1537. He died early in 1542 while rehearsing for a performance of Sperone Speroni's tragedy *Canace*.

Plays

Unlike most works of the time, Beolco's plays, which are set either in the country or in the marginal areas of cities, center not on upper class characters but on peasant men and women who actively seek solutions for the problems that they face. The men participate in local government and, when that is not enough, they appeal to Venetian authorities. When they feel cheated, they act to even the score. In orations to ecclesiastical figures they ask for improvements to their living conditions. The women have their own farms and their work brings them relative prosperity. When war strikes, however, it upends their lives and causes enormous suffering. Another brutal factor is famine, which stalks the countryside with regularity. Together these factors force many peasants into the cities, where they work as servants. Research has shown that Beolco's plays follow the historical developments of his times accurately.

In *La Pastoral* Padua is still feeling the effects of the wars, during which it had been besieged by the enemy and filled with Venice's troops. The Prologue recalls that war prevented the students from studying in the university and the peasants from farming the countryside. When Ruzante thinks that his mate Zilio wants to borrow his cow, he reminds him that German soldiers stole her. Yet the war is over and the countryside peaceful enough to permit students acting as Arcadian shepherds to enunciate the sorrows of unrequited love. Return to cultivation has brought Ruzante enough prosperity that he can concentrate more on pursuit of Betia than food. In a contrast that will characterize their entire interaction, Ruzante, rather passive and something of a loser, hopes to win her through courtship, while his more aggressive and prosperous friend and enemy advises him to take her by force. Before the question can be decided, Ruzante's curmudgeonly father dies, an event that fills him with joy. Paying the Bergamasque doctor from whom he sought treatment for his father, Ruzante calls the pipers to play a concluding dance and chooses his partner from the women of the audience.

Women and the value of their work to peasant life emerge in the two plays dating largely from the peaceful period of 1518 to the early 1520s. In the *Prima oratione* (First Oration), which Beolco wrote possibly as early as 1518 and certainly by 1521 (Beolco 2009), the orator Ruzante addresses Cardinal Marco Cornaro, the new bishop of Padua. Elected representative by his village council, Ruzante praises the fertile Paduan farmland and glorifies the region's women, who are not only beautiful but so strong that they easily wield even the heaviest farm tool, carry triplets, and take on any man. Urging the cardinal to prefer living pleasures to statues and coins, he describes the joys of the hunt in the *pavan* (Paduan territory). The orator concludes by proposing to the bishop as local religious authority seven laws to make the peasants' lives more pleasant, equitable, and secure. These include the freedom to enjoy a Sunday outdoors rather than attending Mass, a dispensation to gather crops on Sunday if they are threatened by bad weather, a choice for priests to be either castrated or married to resolve the inequity of peasants having to support priests' children, and the permission for country men and women to have four spouses each, which will both cause the city people to rush to become peasants and produce a bumper crop of strong babies to defend the region from future invaders. When this oration was delivered on the Cornaro estate near Asolo, the public may have included local peasants.

Possibly delivered as wedding entertainment, *La Betia* centers on a young peasant woman and her choice of suitors. After an initial act in which characters argue about the nature of love in a send-up of university debates, the play brings the issues to life. Zilio, the Ruzante-style character, dreams of Betia but despairs of winning her. His friend Nale, the Menato-style character, advises him to do as he did while courting his wife, impress her by spending lots of money on entertainment and treats at the fair. Zilio reminds him that he is a poor day laborer. When Betia appears, she rejects Zilio as unable to satisfy her after an exhausting day of work. After his exit, Nale slyly offers himself as second husband, a proposition that Betia eagerly accepts. Such an irregular arrangement requires elopement, which Betia effects by lying to her mother Menega, who runs their farm. The plot is almost spoiled by the large amount of clothing and personal effects that Betia packs but the threesome finally gets away. Nale then contends that Betia is his, Zilio objects, and the two almost come to blows. Donna Menega organizes a party to fetch her daughter and attempts to convince her that Zilio is not good enough. Betia insists and Menega is persuaded by the *degan* (mayor) to agree to the wedding. Menega gives her daughter away with the customary *elogio della sposa* (speech praising the bride) but fills it with double-entendres: Betia is a hard worker who prospers by raising silkworms, cultivating robust vegetables and serving soldiers. After the ceremony, Nale presses his suit so hard that Zilio knifes him and Nale falls to the ground. Nale's wife Tamia laments the loss of such a hardy lover and worthy citizen. Nale, realizing his advantage, assumes the identity of a ghost and teases her with tales of the underworld, until she leaves to take up with a waiting lover. Not wanting done to him what he does to others, Nale quickly comes back to life and proposes an open marriage between the two couples as equalizer, a solution readily accepted by the other three. The play closes on a sour note, however, as the excluded lover vows that he will be included even though he has no wife to contribute. A farewell soliloquy adapts Boccaccio's defense of his work against a critique of inappropriate sensuality. The prologues demonstrate that *La Betia* was performed in Venice and the Paduan countryside; stage instructions telling Nale to give two speeches "*verso il populo*" (toward the people) prove that the play was given on at least some occasions to an audience with some popular participation.

During Carnival 1524, Ruzante paraded through Venice with the Ortolani, everyone carrying farm implements. It is assumed that he recited his brief soliloquy *Una lettera qual scrive Ruzante a una so*, usually known as the *Lettera giocosa* (A Letter that Ruzante Writes to a Beloved; Playful Letter), possibly also performed that year for the wedding of the daughter of Padua's *capitanio*. Mocking those who write love notes in highfalutin language, Ruzante offers instead to cultivate the farm of the young woman with his sturdy tools and make it produce. A final paragraph asks her to save him a place on top of the bell tower of St. Mark when the water rises, a reference to a prophecy of catastrophic flooding in 1524. The work closes with the only explicit reference to a living patrician, Francesco Donò (Donà, Donato), probably the one who had recently returned from governance duties in Padua.

The *Seconda oratione* (Second Oration) and three short dialogues, *Dialogo facetissimo* or *Menego* (Very Jokey Dialogue; Menego), *Parlamento de Ruzante* or *Reduce* (Ruzante's Speech; The Veteran; Ruzante Returns from the Wars), and *Bilora* (Weasel) in their current form probably date to the late 1520s (Beolco 1958, 1968, 1995). The dialogues, at least the latter two, are likely to have been performed in Ferrara. All deal with the extremely harsh conditions of those years of war, famine, plague and their aftermath. The oration was probably delivered in summer or fall 1528, after Francesco Cornaro's elevation to the cardinalate and before his departure for Rome. Ruzante assures him that he has abandoned everything to come tell the cardinal that the starving inhabitants of the Paduan countryside are happy that he has been made a cardinal because they trust him to take care of them. After alluding to the appeal of Lutheranism to the local population and to the savage sacking of Rome by Lutherans the preceding year, Beolco asks for a law that, instead of being on city people's side like the current ones, favors the peasants Menego, Nale, and Duozo.

Staged in the country in hunting season in 1528 and with a sad content belying its title, the *Dialogo facetissimo* recounts the terrible sufferings that famine is inflicting on the peasants. A starving Menego offers his beloved Gnua a loaf of bread but Nale steals her without Menego's lifting a hand. Having learned from his friend Duozo that he was not assailed by the many he claimed but by one, Menego decides to commit suicide by eating himself. He figures that this way he will be full and blame will fall on Nale, who will be banished. Duozo tells him of the priest of Diana, who can set everything right. The two visit the priest, who strongly resembles Alvise Cornaro, believed to have rewritten parts of the play. He puts them in contact with friends who have died, restores Gnua to Menego, and re-establishes the friendship between Menego and Nale.

Often viewed as a pair, the other two dialogues are inspired, respectively, by works of Erasmus and of Lucian of Samosata. In the first, Ruzante, enrolled as a foot soldier to improve his financial condition through pay and plunder (part of military pay), flees the unbearable violence of the front. He arrives in Venice in search of his wife Gnua, where he encounters Menato, also looking for her, his former lover, now attached to a strongman. Seeing Menato's shock at his poor condition, Ruzante recounts the hardships of the front and the contempt of Venice's French allies for the peasant foot soldiers. Worst of all is the terrifying danger of the battlefield: to save himself from it he ran, barefoot, from Cremona to Venice in three days. Catching sight of Gnua, Ruzante prepares to join her but she explains that she would return to him only if he could provide her with food every day. Her new man appears, beats the cowering Ruzante, and leaves with Gnua. Ruzante proclaims with braggadocio that he was assailed by one hundred men. Refusing Menato's eye-witness testimony that there was only one, he fantasizes a revenge in which he ties the couple together, comparing the scene to comedies and wedding entertainment.

Bilora, which concludes with an on-stage murder, marks Italian Renaissance comedy's darkest moment. The peasant protagonist Bilora was not played by Beolco but by Castegnola, perhaps the Zaccaria Castegnola who married Beolco's widow. Like Ruzante in *Reduce*, Bilora arrives in Venice in search of his wife Dina. But it is no longer wartime; instead she has left his abuse to be the pampered beloved of a well-to-do Venetian businessman, Andronico. Bilora cannot live without her, nor can he suffer the blow to his pride that her loss to an impotent old city man represents. Looking for Dina, he encounters his friend Pitaro, who sees trouble brewing and counsels a courteous approach. Bilora does so with Dina, but she puts him off and gives him money for refreshments at the tavern. Bilora, inebriated, returns and accompanies Pitaro to Andronico's house, where the old man puts the question of returning to her husband directly to Dina. Her demurral and Andronico's insults send Bilora into a rage. He waits at Andronico's door and, when the old man comes out, stabs him. Reversing the roles of the previous two plays, Bilora, the wronged husband, stands over the lover explicating his right to justice: "Give me my woman back. You should have left her alone... I warned you."

Reduce's love quadrangle is fully explored in Beolco's masterpiece, *La Moschetta* (an untranslatable title with multiple references including to the incorrect Italian of dialect speakers and to the flies to which the character Ruzante refers; Beolco 1993). It was rewritten several times; the printed version probably dates to the early 1530s. Menato opens the play with a soliloquy cursing love, which has led him to betray his friend Ruzante and sleep with his wife Betia. It has also hooked him so badly that even after she rejects him in her ambition to rise socially, he follows the couple to Padua, where they have settled in the *borghi* on its outskirts. Ruzante, who wants a comfortable life without much work, steals some money from the soldier Tonin and does not look too closely at the source of the money brought in by his wife. Betia has set herself up in the oldest profession in the world in a town with many bachelor soldiers and students. Tonin has his eye on her, figuring that he will extract repayment in kind. Menato plots his revenge, convincing Ruzante to test his wife's virtue by dressing as a student and propositioning her. When she accepts, Ruzante flies into a rage, providing her with the perfect excuse to seek refuge at Tonin's house, where their erotic encounter occurs. Ruzante's blustering efforts to persuade her to return to him having failed, he joins forces with Menato, who approaches Tonin courteously.

Tonin agrees to give up Betia, but only after payment of half of the stolen sum; Ruzante being without means, Menato supplies it. Humiliated by Tonin's insults, Ruzante plans a night attack on Tonin's house. Menato instead shrewdly guides him to Ruzante's own house. Surreptitiously entering it, Menato pretends to be an angry citizen mistakenly awakened by Ruzante's assault and beats him. Betia pleads for peace and the threesome enter their home.

Clearly in the *mariazo* tradition is country-set *Fiorina* (Fiore's Play), in which Ruzante and Marchioro fight over the title character. After Marchioro wins their battle and her love, Ruzante forces her to marry him by kidnapping her. The fathers keep the peace by convincing Marchioro to marry Ruzante's sister instead.

Two Plautine adaptations come next. *La Piovana* (The Girl from Piove, The Piove Comedy), based on Plautus's *Rudens*, is set in Chioggia, south of Venice, and written in Paduan dialect. Action centers on the conflict over Nina between her beloved and a pimp who has stolen her. A happy ending comes when the couple is allowed to marry because a treasure, which is awarded to the servants who helped save her, proves that Nina is of good station. *La Vaccaria* (The Cow Comedy) moves toward established values, with the set of higher-ranked characters speaking Tuscan and following official norms of conduct contrasted with the servants, who speak dialect and act spontaneously. Fiorinetta, the beloved of a respectable young man, Flavio, is forced to work as a prostitute by the woman believed to be her mother, who demands a large sum to allow Flavio a year of her time. Flavio's sympathetic father Placido sets the servant to finding the money, at the price of spending the first night with her himself. When Placido's wife hears this, she pretends that Flavio will marry the girl; a horrified Placido objects because of her low status and lack of dowry.

Perhaps Beolco's last full comedy, but bearing signs of an early origin, is *L'Anconitana* (The Woman from Ancona, The Ancona Comedy; Beolco 1994). Three southern Italians, ransomed by a Venetian merchant from Turkish captors, arrive in Padua to repay the ransom by working as beauticians. Gismondo, actually Isotta dressed as a man, becomes the love object of the wife of the Venetian businessman Tomao, himself planning a rural getaway with a courtesan. Gismondo is also pursued by the Anconitan widow Ginevra, in male disguise. Tomao's servant Ruzante discovers the true identities of Isotta and Ginevra, who discover they are sisters and plan an open marriage with the two ransomed men. Tomao and the courtesan, accompanied by Ruzante and Bessa, his beloved and the courtesan's servant, leave for the country, freeing Tomao's wife to meet with her lover. The hypocrisy of the higher-ranked characters' lip service to moral values is contrasted with the honesty in word and action of the servants.

Beolco's final work is a version of the extensive soliloquy entitled *Lettera all'Alvarotto* (Letter to Alvarotto) bearing the date of January, 1536 (in the Venetian dating system corresponding to 1537). Rejecting high culture, Ruzante finds happiness on the imaginary farm of Lady Mirth, where Joy, Wisdom, Laughter, and Play flourish and from which that nasty baby Cupid and his companions Jealousy, Troubles, and Curses are excluded.

Influence on the future of theater

Beolco either initiated or made great strides in a number of pivotal developments in the history of Western theater. Basing himself on the archetypes of country genres and on the revived classical plays and the vernacular plays inspired by them, he created standing characters that would serve as the basis for Commedia dell'Arte stock characters. At least one of his plays was performed before a large public audience. His constant re-writing and adapting of his texts and his antipathy to having them fixed on the printed page opened the way for the *canovaccio*. One of several contemporary actors who became known by the name of his character, Beolco was the first modern actor to become famous as an actor. Including women among the performers at least as singers, he developed the acting troupe, which would be formalized with the first contract in Padua in 1545.

References

Beolco, Angelo (Ruzante) (1958) "Ruzzante Returns from the Wars" in *The Classic Theater*, Eric Bentley (ed.), Angela Ingold and Theodore Hoffman (tr.), Garden City, US: Doubleday.

——(1968) "Bilora" in *Masterworks of World Drama*, Anthony Caputi (ed. and tr.), Boston, US: Heath.

——(1993) *La Moschetta*, Antonio Franceschetti and Kenneth R. Bartlett (tr., intro. and notes), Ottawa: Dovehouse.

——(1994) *L'Anconitana/The Woman from Ancona*, Nancy Dersofi (tr., intro., and notes), Berkeley, US: University of California Press.

——(1995) *The Veteran (Parlamento de Ruzante) and Weasel (Bilora)*, Ronnie Ferguson (tr., intro., notes), New York: P. Lang.

——(2009) *La prima oratione/The First Oration*, Linda L. Carroll (ed. and tr.), London: Modern Humanities Research Association.

23

THE COMING TOGETHER

Olly Crick

Commedia dell'Arte developed from a wide variety of sources: the artistic impulses of the Renaissance, carnival and folk theatre, emergent amateur humanist theatre, a burgeoning class of professional entertainers, and the cultural peculiarities of Venice, the city of its origins. Each element brought something unique of itself which, when combined by the forces of history and change, created a theatre form far greater than the sum of its parts. What is extraordinary is that this form burst fully formed on the scene between 1568 and 1601 (a very short period of time). Before those dates there existed theatre with some of the attributes of Commedia but certainly not all. During and after these dates, over seven famous companies came into existence, as if from nowhere, as well as many less renowned ones. A European professional theatre, based on fixed types and improvised dialogue, had appeared.

Its cocktail of performance virtuosity and dramatic narrative ensured that it not only survived, but flourished almost everywhere it went; influencing and affecting indigenous theatre wherever it toured. The question is always why it did so, and what it was about the synergy of its elements that gave it such vitality and longevity.

In its simplest terms, Commedia was created at the crucial juncture between an economic and an artistic renaissance. Representatives from the educated aristocratic and mercantile classes joined forces on stage with professional lower class performers. All brought their specializations and skills to the party and this combination then evolved together. This particular combination became a highly significant factor ensuring its longevity and theatrical success.

The re-establishing of trade routes throughout Europe in the late Middle Ages created a more stable society with a financial surplus, which in turn was partly responsible for the development of the Renaissance. Financial security, even for a small elite, had amongst its many side effects two elements highly significant for both artists and the Arts.

The first was that a ruler could now surround himself with the Arts in their broadest sense. This functioned as both luxury on a personal level, as well as civic manifestations of their munificence and power. Artistic largesse was displayed, not as an altruistic act by these rulers, but as a display of wealth and power. The

Performing Arts fitted into both these categories and, with patronage, benefitted financially, grew and developed.

The second important factor was that wealth bought an education, and also the leisure time with which to practice its benefits. A contemporary neo-classical education brought its students face to face with, amongst other studies, Roman and Greek comic playwrights such as Plautus and Menander. The plays were not only studied by scholars, but were performed by them. They first appeared as educated entertainments in schools or colleges, in the original Latin or Greek. These had limited value, as audience members or patrons without good Latin were excluded from fully understanding the performance. Partly as a consequence of this, plays were then translated into the vernacular for court performances all over Europe. The poet William Warner translated the *Menachmae* of Plautus into English in 1595. It may have been this version that was performed before King Henry VIII.

It was the multi-character and multi-act structures of the rediscovered classical comedies that became the model for the new breed of dramatic entertainment. Everyone who could hold a pen, from Shakespeare to Ruzzante, to the literary societies of Italy (such as the Intronati of Siena) used, or at least adapted, these dramatic structures upon which to hang their tales. These were comedies about man's relationship with man, very different from medieval religious dramas concerned with man's relationship to God.

The scenario writers of the first professional Commedia comedies would certainly have access to this knowledge. The surviving scenarios and *canovaccios*—plot outlines recorded in retirement, such as the Flaminia Scala collection, published in 1611—show a clear understanding of multi-character plot development, and the structural and compositional device of both a three-act and five-act play. A Commedia company could now keep an audience's interest over several hours, by the unfolding of a dramatic story. The key to this was improvising the text and action. These improvisations were then used to adapt to the variety of performance venues and audience types and to change the length and content of each scene. It is possible to postulate that the improvisation skill possessed by these early performers was that of linear-improvisation: being able to embroider as well as expand or contract, upon a predetermined dramatic through-line or character story-arc.

It is an assumption, but I think a good one, that this ability allows the possibility of adapting in real time to the audience response to a performance. To be able to perform a fixed storyline in a way that takes into account the audience, the performance space, the weather, the country, the time of day, as well as any simultaneously occurring event within the body of the audience, is a definite performance strength for any itinerant company. It is also a skill to be developed individually as a performer, and was known to English actors (and much admired by them) as the Italian style of acting. This particular skill was a direct consequence of understanding how dramatic structure functions, and was derived from their neo-classical education.

The "educated" came from two distinct classes: the minor aristocracy and the bourgeoisie. Inheritance laws, designed to keep land or other sources of wealth together, dictated that first sons received the bulk of any estate, It followed that all second, third or fourth sons and daughters, whilst receiving a good education, had poor inheritance prospects and were likely to find themselves as mercenaries, monks, priests, married off or becoming nuns respectively. There was no such thing as an established "career" in this new world of theatre, but an entirely new pathway to wealth, fame and survival had suddenly opened up.

A "good" aristocratic education involved singing, learning to play an instrument, deportment, dancing, rhetoric and sword fighting (or embroidery), in short how to behave like an aristocrat in public. It is a very short step from displaying these attributes in public, to portraying these attributes on a public stage. Whilst being denied the money commensurate with their class by primogeniture, this group certainly had the attributes to live an aristocratic life convincingly on stage. The same inheritance laws would apply to children of traders, merchants and guildsmen.

In Venice the young men of well to do trade families organized themselves into fraternities, (such as the Compagnia dei Sempiterni della Calza) one of whose remits was to provide amateur entertainment. For younger sons, with small prospect of inheritance, and an education matching their aristocratic coevals, professional theatre might just seem like an exciting new business venture. This group brought with them the required vital business acumen.

The third class of people still needed to make up the performance cocktail were those already performing for a living, called *buffone*. Prior to the emergence of the big name troops there were both individuals and smaller groups of part-time professionals plying their trade publically, such as that of Zan Polo in 1532 (Katritzky 2006: 19; Lea 1934: 474–8). These groups and individuals performed in a wide variety of styles: pastorals, recited verse, dramatic prose and rustic farces (*vilaneschas*). Of significance to us is the fact that an emerging new style was appearing, labelled by diarist Sanudo as Bergamask Comedy. He first observed this on 3 February 1532, commenting that "among the players are a woman ('la Michiela'), and a vulgar bravo" (Katritzky 2006:19).

It is also within this time frame that the mask of the Magnifico developed, and became, with his servant Zanni, an integral part of the *Commedia all'Improvviso*. For a more detailed analysis of the Magnifico's first appearance, and subsequent metamorphosis into Pantalone di Bisognosi, refer to Dr Peter Jordan's chapter within this volume.

Katritzky notes that Sanudo's diaries point to collaborations between amateur and professional players. Carlo Boso (Cardiff Laboratory Theatre 1986, workshop and University of Windsor, Canada, Commedia Convention 2013, pers. comm.) states that one of the mechanisms by which these collaborations occurred was performing Plautine adaptations and derivations at court. Court officials initially paid *buffoni* to perform onstage with them in the roles of servants. From the 1530s onwards professional theatre developed in Italy to the point when, on 31 July 1573, the entire Gelosi company was hired to perform Tasso's *Aminta*.

The amateur side of the new drama is exemplified by one play, collectively written by an amateur literary society called the Intronati of Siena. The play was called *The Deceived* and, originally published in 1538, achieved in print immense popularity. It went through twenty Italian editions, and was translated into French, Italian and paradoxically, also into Latin. The literary movement, to which the Intronati belonged, was called the *Commedia Erudita*. Members of this movement may have performed with, and certainly interacted with, the professional performers. The newfound amateur knowledge may have been seen by the professionals as a new way to do "theatre" business and playwrights (dilettante or not) now had better actors to say their words. Exact proof of this developing synergy is hard to pin down, but remains a worthy supposition.

What is fact, however, is that on 25 February 1545 (the exact date being identified by Cesare Molinari, 1985, 66, 70, and now celebrated as Commedia dell'Arte day) "Maphio ditto Zanini" and seven other men contracted to form a fraternal company at the end of Lent for the purpose of performing comedies and making money. They repeated the venture in 1546 and in 1549, as it was clearly a good way to do business. The contract was the legal document used to ensure the signatories stayed "fraternal" until they had made their money.

Katritzky observes that, from an iconographic point of view (Katritzky 1998:104–24), another class of people can be considered to be part of this crossover period: professional mountebanks, and other salesmen of patent cures and medicines. There is strong evidence from traveller's diaries (called *album amicorum*) of, amongst others, a German physician called Thomas Platter, to support this point of view. In detail he describes how a seven strong troop of mountebanks, led by Zanni Bragetta, would have a meal together on a trestle table in public, then perform "an amusing comedy on that same table" (Katritzky 1998: 114), before they opened a trunk of "medicine" and made serious attempts to sell the same to their audience. Platter wrote down, almost word for word, the patter and sales method (including an onstage zanni stooge who vouched for the medicine) used by Bragetta and his team. It is easily recognizable as the same patter used in fairgrounds and carneys the world over.

This team of mountebanks, it is inferred, used the performance of a comedy to attract a crowd from which to extract money: both by taking the hat round for the comedy, and (judging by the detail used by Platter) in this case specifically for the purpose of selling "medicine" to the audience afterwards. Mountebanks, therefore, could and did perform comedy. The pictures of the mountebanks on their trestle stages show both men and women in high fashion, as well as a recognizable masked Commedia Zanni.

Of greater significance, according to Platter (Katritzky 1998: 112), is that the reason Bragetta's troupe was performing outside is that the previous engagement ceased to be profitable. Their unfortunate situation, once again, was faithfully reported by Thomas Platter in his diary:

> They performed for several weeks, on a raised platform in an indoor tennis court... when they noticed that not many people were coming to their comedies any more, even though they still had to pay a high rent for the tennis court, they set up a long table in the market place, called the Place au Change, and after the meal they all stood together on this same table one next to the other, and... played an amusing comedy on that same table for a couple of hours or so... a large crowd of folk had gathered together, from 100 to 500 or even 1000 people.
>
> (as cited in Katritzky 1998: 112)

From this, and other evidence unearthed by Katritzky, it is clear that these mountebanks could and did perform long form dramatic comedy, and had been doing so with some success prior to dwindling crowds rendering it unprofitable. Platter describes within their comedies elements of mime, dancing, comic bird impressions, and accomplished musical passages as well as a noteworthy illusionary beheading of an actress on stage. From the iconographic evidence of the mountebanks, "Grande Tour" diaries such as belonged to Platter, and other *alba amicorum*, the earliest ascribable date to these mountebanks' performances is approximately 1590. This is, unsurprisingly, inside the same time frame as when the more famous companies come into being. A lot of people were taking Plautus and Terence, and their neo-classical antecedents, very seriously.

Documentary evidence from official records gives us many details about the famous companies, but these "supergroups" could not have sprung out of nowhere. Perhaps some of these mountebank companies, finding a comic form and a financial-survival model that worked, achieved the goal any theatrical manager would aspire to: rich and aristocratic patrons. The better and more socially mobile troops, maybe containing aristocratic blood, simply went up in the world. Whilst Bragetta's troop were still selling snake oil in the Piazzas to survive, Drusiano Martinelli was negotiating performance fees with Prince Vincenzo of Mantua (Winifred Smith 1968: 41).

The specific time of year that served as a focus for these performances was Carnival, and its inter-reaction with the following period of Lent. In the Christian calendar Lent is a time of fasting, religious contemplation and abstaining from certain types of food. In the pre-Christian calendar, Carnival is the period of festivities and misrule lasting several weeks, culminating on Shrove Tuesday (Mardi Gras or Pancake Day), preceding Lent. Carnival also roughly corresponded with the Roman Festivities of Saturnalia and Bacchanalia, closely associated with the imminence of a slack period of food production. Lent roughly corresponded to the time of year in Northern Europe where the only food that was generally available was dried and preserved. Meat was off the menu, as cattle and sheep were gestating and poultry had stopped producing eggs: eating the breeders of next year's food supply would have been suicide. Populations survived on what could be safely stored and all food that would spoil had to be eaten as soon as possible. Consequently Carnival became a time of conspicuous consumption when all perishable foods were consumed, and Lent was the time when fasting and abstinence was the order of the day.

The feasting at Carnival may not be just one's last good meal for a while, but also one's last good meal ever if winter delayed the growing of new crops. Any festivities occurring at this highly charged point in the year would naturally reflect this heightened sense of being alive. Theatre and other entertainment produced for this period would also reflect this. It was a time of year of extremes and contrasts and, unsurprisingly, also when Commedia dell'Arte was born.

All the opposites, contradictions, hopes and fears of a population are brought together within this short period of time: a fomenter of emotions and animal instincts that spills, of course, out onto the stage. Any theatrical entertainment wanting to grab the attention of the population at this time of year must not only encompass this vitality, but also reflect it to the audience within a direct, visceral and culturally recognizable form. Where does the life or death quality of a Commedia performance originate? From the battle between life and death embodied within Carnival.

The Renaissance rulers of Venice had a clear attitude to their Carnival: that it must not get out of hand. To prevent this period of license turning into a focus for popular discontent, the Venetian authorities enforced an official strand of state sponsored merrymaking within it including the very popular public bull-baiting. Carried out by specially trained dogs and handlers large, numbers of bulls were set upon, maimed and then "executed" by sword wielding butchers. These displays symbolized a historical Venetian military victory over Patriarch Ulrich of Aquilea (himself a pawn in Holy Roman Emperor Frederick Barbarosa's Imperial expansionism) in 1162, and the collective will of the *Serenissima* (Venetian republic) to protect itself. On another level it was a bloody display of power, and a source of meat to the populace. These events were highly popular, engaged a form of public bloodlust, and had aristocratic sponsors (Johnson 2011: 30–40) who competed to see how many bulls could be slaughtered. Carnival was fundamental in Venetian society, but was never permitted to upset the social order.

In a similar way this new theatrical phenomenon, despite continual castigation by the Church as immoral (and its performers declared anathema), never thought to challenge the social order. It never sought to upset its financial and artistic patrons, and thus ensured its long-term survival.

The use of masks in Commedia dell'Arte can be directly attributed to Venetian culture. There are loose similarities between Commedia dell'Arte and Roman Atellan farce which, although comic in nature and masked, has no proven causal link. It is more likely that masks came from a more popular tradition. Masks were worn in medieval liturgical dramas by the devil characters, and in rustic folk dramas (such as the Swabian-Alemannic devil dramas of the *Fastnacht*) so were not unknown to the general populace. Venice itself had a long tradition of mask use dating back to the thirteenth century. In May 1268, for example, a law was passed in Venice preventing masked men from throwing perfumed eggs at ladies. This was obviously an occurrence that had reached some kind of acceptability threshold, hence the law. Masks were worn commonly in Venetian society, both to maintain a dynamic, though often fictive, form of being socially incognito, and also as disguises proper. Mask wearing by all Venetians reached a climax at Carnival. By the end of the seventeenth century Venetian citizens were wearing masks in public for up to six months a year.

The reasons they did so were not always associated with Carnival. Venice, as both a trading centre and a republic within a monarchical world, developed a culture of self-protection and secrecy. It kept political decisions, and those who made them, secret (Senate votes were taken masked). This cult of the incognito kept the Venetian elite in power and at the same time, during Carnival, ramped up the levels of licentiousness. Masks present a paradox: an external visage that may or may not be the same person underneath. Both men and women, during Carnival, masked their faces, which protected their modesty and identity. Behind these masks lay, despite the tight constraints of Venetian society, the potentially greatest of all liberties: self-expression. In this light it is hardly surprising that the *buffoni* and early actors chose to wear masks to perform in public. They gained the freedom to behave and perform as if they were someone else, which in a sense, they were.

This license, when masked, to behave outside societal limits would certainly fuel a performer's imagination, creating the possibility of extemporized dialogue and the first steps towards dramatic improvisation. The dramatic device of disguising oneself as someone else to achieve a particular goal appeared almost normal behaviour in this society. Add to this the life or death energy of the Carnival-Lent dyad and Venice does appear as a focus for some quite spectacular forces. Felicity Firth (1978: 63) identifies two traits common to all Italian comedy from this period: "one, the preoccupation with the concept of identity; and two, the insistence upon wit or intellectual virtue as the ultimate human value". Human duality had replaced celestial duality in the worn mask. For a human to wear a mask was to demonstrate his dialogue with humanity, not (dressed as a medieval devil) as part of a battle between heaven and hell. The new emerging comedy was neo-classical in form, and very decidedly humanist.

How improvisation became a feature is also unclear, though there are contributory factors, which may have guided the companies in that direction. In a society with a very strong clerical power-base, the absence of written words may have been a way of avoiding moral censorship. Paleotti, in 1578, noted that the comic actors would often add unscripted and rude elements not present in a text (cited in Katritzky 2006: 27). Improvisation would also have avoided political censorship and given the actors freedom to change necessary details, such as which particular patron is to be praised to the skies in this show. Punishment for offending a political or religious body was arbitrary, without appeal, and potentially fatal. Improvisation, though, was noted as a skill and craft associated specifically with Italian performers, and though mention of it is extremely rare before 1620 (Katritzky 2006: 27), the skill was recorded in a written document in 1568 and also in the murdered actress Vicenza Armani's funeral oration in 1569. In the 1580s, though, improvised comedy was still only one aspect of the *comici's* performance repertoire. The companies would perform what was required of them, from new plays on the Plautine and Terentian models to the Vilanesca farces. From the 1620s improvised comedy had evolved to become a featured skill and selling point.

Detailed analysis of the Flaminia Scala scenarios by Tim Fitzpatrick (1995) reveal, despite their apparent complexity, an inherent structure that supports linear (that is to say following a predetermined dramatic narrative) improvisation. The dramas are constructed almost entirely out of two person (or two person initiated) scenes. It is, as a practical matter, much easier to improvise a scene successfully in pairs, than with three or more. The dramatic flow of the piece is kept alive by the simple expedience of one actor leaving the stage as another joins. A Commedia scenario comprises serial dramatic duets. Scala also, helpfully, as well as including the dramatic story to be unfolded for each pair, gives the precise entrance and exit lines. This is for the benefit of the next performer on, as they have an exact cue line upon which to make their entrance. This is vital in maintaining performance momentum and avoiding ugly or embarrassing gaps. The Scala scenarios, as decoded by Fitzpatrick, appear to be a perfect skeleton, which became fleshed out in performance by actors, skilled in improvisation.

The practical implications of only one person leaving or joining the stage, at any given time, are significant. A travelling professional company of performers needs to ensure that their shows can be performed in as wide a variety of venues as possible, from a market square to a banqueting hall, or even the Duke's private rooms. To create dramas that demand multiple entrance and exit points for their success would create unnecessary problems and limit the venues they could perform in. Having merely one entrance and exit means that the actors can focus purely on performance, and not on having to remember from where to make their entrance. The troop, consequently, can perform to its very best in any venue offered. This is, again, a definite advantage for a touring troop.

Commedia, therefore, was a form of theatre that not only made use of the recovered Roman and Greek models of theatre, but sat astride the intellectual revolution of the Renaissance. Humanity started to reinvent itself and man-defined-by-man became the order of the day, not man defined by his relationship to God. This new Commedia was not divine but human, and reflected society from its leaders down to its servants. It was a gigantic leap away from the medieval mindset, and was powered by selected professional *buffoni*, performers, mountebanks, actresses and masked zannis; infused with the life or death struggles present within Carnival. The spring of Commedia was wound up in Venice and Northern Italy and set running throughout Europe and the world. It is still running today.

References

Firth, Felicity (1978) "Comedy in Italy", *Comic Drama: the European Heritage* (ed. W. D. Howarth). London: Methuen.

Fitzpatrick, Tim (1995) *The Relationship of Oral and Literate Performance Processes in the Commedia dell'Arte.* Lewiston, US; Queenstown, Canada; Lampeter, UK: The Edwin Mellen Press.

Johnson, James H. (2011) *Venice Incognito: Masks in the Serene Republic.* California, US: University of California Press.

Katritzky, M. A. (ed.) (1998) "Was Commedia dell'Arte performed by Mountebanks?", *Theatre Research International* Vol 23 Number 2, Belfast: Oxford University Press.

——(2006) *The Art of Commedia: A Study in the Commedia dell'Arte 1560-1620 with Special Reference to the Visual Records.* Amsterdam, New York: Rodopi.

Lea, Kathryn M. (1934) *Italian Popular Comedy, a Study in the Commedia dell'Arte, 1560-1620, with Special Reference to the English Stage.* London, New York, Toronto, Melbourne: Oxford University Press.

Molinari, Cesare (1985) *La Commedia dell'Arte* Milan, Italy: Mondadori.

Scala, Flaminio (1611) *Il Teatro delle favole rappresentative: Scenarios of the Commedia dell'Arte:* Henry F. Salerno (tr.) New York: New York University Press/London University Press (1967).

Smith, Winifred (1968) *Italian Actors of the Renaissance.* New York, London: Benjamin Blom.

24

STAGES AND STAGING PRACTICES IN EARLY COMMEDIA DELL'ARTE

Franklin J. Hildy and Matthew R. Wilson

Although Commedia dell'Arte has been described as "street theatre," historical evidence indicates that Commedia companies utilized indoor stages and that the most prestigious players shunned marketplace theatre. As Antonio Fava has mused, "No actor 'dreamed' of playing in the street" (Fava 2007: 47–8), but versatile *comici* adapted their performance practices for the diverse venues they encountered on tour.

Commedia and the advent of theatre architecture

In an oft-cited contract from 1545, Ser Maphio and seven men from various Italian cities agreed to form an acting company. Ser Maphio used the stage name Zanini, and the others agreed to follow his leadership including "making use of such improvisation as he may command" (Oreglia 1968: 141). This contract is generally considered the earliest formal documentation of a Commedia dell'Arte troupe (see Chapter 4); however, the troupe was not the first professional acting company formed in Italy. Angelo Beolco (*c.* 1495–1542), who used the stage name il Ruzante, had formed a company in Ferrara as early as 1529 and there is evidence of several other companies in between (Chapter 22). The members of Ser Maphio's troupe would certainly have come in contact with some of them and have been influenced by what those earlier companies performed.

Virginia Scott has noted that the earliest known "act of association" involving an acting company in France was signed in Paris in 1544. This mixed company of Italian and French actors (and actresses) agreed to perform "ancient plays, moralities, farces, and other Roman and French plays" (Scott 2009: 61). Their leader, Jehan Anthoine, taught "the art of acting ancient Roman plays" suggesting that his background was in the classical revival and *Commedia Erudita*. Substitute "Italian improvised comedy" for "French plays" in the list above and it gives a good idea of what early companies in Italy were capable of staging. Only gradually did such companies become more specialized. After forming in Padua, Ser Maphio's troupe performed in Venice in 1546 and after reforming on two additional occasions they traveled to Rome, arriving in November of 1549. This is significant because a new public theatre opened in Rome that year. It was located in the Santi Apostoli hall in the Palazzo Colonna but soon moved to the recently remodeled, but no longer needed, church of San Biagio della Pagnotta on the Via Giulia. Eugene Johnson notes that Maphio's Company was present at the right time to perform in the San Biagio theatre (Johnson 2005: 33). This might explain why Giorgio Vasari (1511–74) believed that Commedia dell'Arte was created there (Pallen 1999: 34). Scholars tend to dismiss Vasari's claim, but it is notable that he identified the beginnings of Commedia with performances inside a theatre building.

Indoor stages

K. M. Lea has argued that Commedia dell'Arte was created from the interaction of Commedia Erudita with "indigenous comic talent" and points to the sources of much Commedia dell'Arte material in the scripts of the Erudita (Lea 1962: v.1, 228). Throughout Europe, the development of professional acting companies in the early sixteenth century was paralleled by developments in theatre architecture. Italy was a special case because both its professional theatre and its theatre architecture were applied theatre history projects, that is, they were conscious attempts to create something new from the study of the theatre of the past. Attempts to rediscover the classical theatre of Greece and Rome led to the building of theatres, the writing of new plays, and the reinvention of *Commedia all'Improvviso*. Recent scholarship has described the spread of these practices as a transnational exchange of "theatregrams" (Clubb 1989: 6; Henke 2008: 19–34), and it is notable that the theatregrams circulated in neoclassical academies, Commedia Erudita, and court *intermezzi* emphasized the theatrical venue's capacity to control the performance environment and to showcase stage technology.

Vasari notes that the theatre at San Biagio was beautifully decorated and very well equipped. Its major innovation was the provision of private rooms with shutters from which the clergy could watch a play without being observed. This is a feature copied in other theatres and was especially valuable for Commedia troupes when the clergy wanted to enjoy a performance but did not wish to be seen supporting them. By the time this theatre was built, nearly all the architectural forms that later Commedia dell'Arte troupes would encounter had already been invented. A courtyard at the d'Este palace in Ferrara was converted into a temporary theatre in 1486 to revive a play by Plautus, and a similar structure was built in front of the palace of Cardinal Riario in Rome for a production of a play by Seneca that same year. In 1499 Ercole d'Este had a theatre built into the *Sale Grande* of his palace, with the stage on a long wall, an arrangement copied in Mantua in 1501. In 1504 Ercole ordered the construction of a purpose-built theatre, the Sala dale Comedie; it was never completed but a temporary purpose-built theatre, the Teatro del Campidoglio, was erected in Rome in 1513 (Tuohy 1996: 117–20). A *teatro da sala*, with its stage at one end of a hall, accommodation for audience along three walls and a raised dais in the central open area for select nobility, was built in Urbino in 1513. Another was built within the Palazzo Medici in Via Larga in 1518 for the performance of new plays based on classical models. By 1525 theatres were being built in the homes of the lesser gentry across Italy, and in 1531 the first public theatre was opened above an apothecary shop in Ferrara. A remarkable theatre was built in a garden courtyard at the Palazzo Medici in 1539, which may have featured the first proscenium arch stage (Pallen 1999: 28–32). *Teatri da sala* were built in many cities including Florence and Naples (1536), Vicenza (1539, designed by Serlio), Venice (1542), Rome (1546), and Bologna in 1547. The latter had the distinction of being built in a public building rather than the palace of a local ruler, a model used in Siena in 1555 and in many other cities thereafter. Such theatres were kept in use longer and were more readily available for public performances than those built at courts. As the San Biagio opened in Rome, the first permanent court theatre was being built in Mantua. Whether this was another teatro da sala or a freestanding structure we do not know (Johnson 2005: 26–8). It did not open until 1551, but by 1567 it was being used for public performances by a Commedia dell'Arte troupe. (An alternative to the permanent court theatre, a reusable teatro da sala was built in Florence in 1565. It had a well-documented proscenium arch and employed the first front curtain.) All of these spaces had facilities for scenery— generally perspective scenery—that was used for the classical revival dramas and Commedia Erudita. Many of the theatres also had scene changing equipment and special effects machines for intermezzi. Commedia dell'Arte companies did not need this equipment, but when it was available they often made use of it (Lea 1962: v.1, 325–32).

As Commedia dell'Arte grew in popularity, communities found ways to accommodate them. By 1567, two Commedia dell'Arte companies where performing in Mantua, one in the court theatre and one in a private home converted into a theatre. Even the town hall, the Palazzo della Ragione, was brought into service for performances. That same year "Leone hebreo" petitioned the Duke for permission to build a "stanza" for "those who go about performing for a price." *Stanza*, (pl. *stanze*) simply means "room," but in this case indicates a multi-purpose meeting hall. The following year the city of Genoa authorized the performance of comedy in a local inn (Johnson 2005: 35). The Medici built the Baldracca, a public theatre, outside their court theatre in the Uffizi in 1576, possibly as a bribe to keep the Gelosi Company from returning to Venice (Lea 1962: v.1, 162) but certainly as a venue for professional entertainers traveling to the city. Eventually private boxes with a palace entrance were built here to allow courtiers to watch plays without being seen. Commedia troupes were, on occasion, still invited to play in the palace theatre itself, as they did when it was first used in 1586. By 1580 the city of Venice had become concerned about safety and instituted an inspection regime. This encouraged the building of new theatres with levels of boxes along one or more sides. One of these was occupied by the Gelosi and another by the Confidenti. Venice banned theatre from 1585 to 1607, but, when it resumed, theatres like these were built again. By 1637 they had evolved into the pit, box, and gallery, proscenium arch theatres—the *teatro all'italiana*—that dominated theatre architecture until the nineteenth century. It would be nice to attribute the spread of this design to traveling Commedia players, but it was due to Italy's other great performance export: opera.

Europe's oldest existing post-Roman theatre, the Teatro Olimpico, was built for the academy at Vicenza in 1584 for a production of the Greek tragedy *Oedipus the*

King. But the oldest existing free-standing theatre in Europe, the Teatro all'Antica at Sabbioneta (1588), was built for comedy with a permanent, comic fixed scene: a single vista, forced perspective, urban exterior. Stanley V. Longman has noted that Duke Vespasiano Gonzaga Colonna hired a Commedia troupe, possibly a precursor to the Accesi, to open this theatre in 1590. The Duke intended to have this company in residence for at least two months every year (Longman 1993: 60; Mazzoni and Guaita 1985: 87–8). Unfortunately, the Duke's plans for the theatre, for his resident Commedia company, and for Sabbioneta itself were cut short by his death in 1591.

When Commedia dell'Arte troupes traveled to Europe, they used theatres where they found them, helped create them when possible, and made do without them when necessary. Commedia troupes traveling to France after 1571 generally performed in temporary theatres built in the great hall of noble households. When they arrived in Paris they used the only theatre there, the Hôtel de Bourgogne (Henke 2008: 27–30). Built in 1548, this was the first permanent purpose-built theatre in Europe since Roman times; however, its design had not benefited from the experimentation that was helping perfect Italian theatre architecture, so in 1577 the Gelosi Company performed instead in a teatro da sala that had been recently constructed in the Petit-Bourbon, possibly for them (Howarth 1997: 84). When the Ganassa Company reached Spain in 1574 they became instrumental in the development of corral theatres there (McKendrick 1989: 48).

Outdoor stages

Despite ample evidence that Commedia dell'Arte grew up with and utilized indoor theatrical venues, Commedia companies have long been identified with temporary stages in market squares as evocatively depicted in the visual art of Callot, Scarron, Dujardin, and others. The Renaissance marketplace was inherently "theatrical," a civic center where townspeople "performed" the drama of their everyday lives, where public gathering were held, where merchants competed for the attention of potential customers, and where charlatans staged their demonstrations (Johnson 2000: 436–53; Henke 2002: 6–8); however, a close association between Commedia dell'Arte and "public art of the people" is misleading. There are certainly woodcuts, engravings, paintings, and drawings of masked and costumed characters appearing on market stages, but this iconography is not easy to interpret (see Chapter 30).

In the seventeenth century these images show everything from performers on the ground, to three planks supported by low trestles, to large rectangular or square platforms raised five to eight feet.

One of the latter structures is depicted in two prints from Jacques Callot's collection *Balli di Sfessania* (1621–2). In one engraving, two characters labeled "Razullo" and "Cucurucu" dance in the foreground while a crowd in the background watches a scene staged on a temporary, outdoor platform. The audience members stand around three sides of the stage, with the majority across the front. The stage appears to be elevated by scaffolding to about six feet high. The area underneath the stage is curtained, perhaps allowing for storage or an "off stage" area for actors. The playing space appears to be roughly fifteen feet wide and half as deep. At the back hangs a simple curtain painted with an urban background, similar to a backdrop described in a 1533 Ruzante performance (Ferguson 1999: 149). This curtain also creates a "backstage" area, and one actor is seen peeking out from its right side. The frontispiece for the *Balli* collection depicts a closer view of a modest stage with three masked performers in front of a bare, nondescript curtain. Two other performers—an unmasked woman and a masked man—peak from two slits in the curtains, which could be used to indicate windows or doorways. At stage right, another performer is climbing a ladder from the ground level to the stage.

Scholars have argued that, at best, these images represent one of the less-successful Commedia troupes (Erenstein 2000: 4–6) and that they may not depict Commedia at all. The collection specifically treats, not theatre, but "dances" (*balli*), and almost all of the etchings in the collection showcase fairground performers, minstrels, and acrobats, rather than Commedia actors (Posner 1977: 203–4). Later illustrations from the eighteenth century show much more sophisticated structures with scene changing equipment and boxes for audience seating, but these are most likely illustrations of comic opera. Although numerous paintings and engravings depict performers on market stages, it is not clear whether many of them actually represent Commedia dell'Arte performances.

Pictographic evidence can shed light on the kinds of stages that might have been available, but written reports demonstrate that the most successful troupes preferred to work indoors. This may have been part of "the constant struggle of early *comici* to dissociate themselves from the stigma attached to *buffoni*, street players and mountebanks" (Katritzky 2006: 35), a struggle the *prima donna* Isabella Andreini (1562–1604) illustrated when she complained to the Governor of Milan that "those who mount benches in the public piazza perform comedies and thus ruin them" and petitioned to have them banned (Henke 2002: 234n). When members of a successful Commedia dell'Arte company were seen in a market square, it may have been because they were raising extra funds on the way to perform in another city, because they had been commissioned to perform there, or because they were giving a preview to entice audiences to a ticketed performance elsewhere. It was generally not because they liked to play there.

Staging and performance practices

Ferdinand, the second son of the Duke of Bavaria, Albrecht V (ruled 1550–79), was sent to Florence in 1565 to witness the wedding of Francesco de Medici to the Hapsburg princess, Giovanna d'Austria. He kept a diary, or one was kept for him, documenting his experiences, including witnessing several Commedia dell'Arte performances (Katritzky 2006: 60–72). This is the earliest description we have of such performances, but a fuller, more detailed account is Massimo Troiano's well-known description of a performance he helped create for the marriage between Ferdinand's older brother, William, heir to the Dukedom of Bavaria, and Renata of Lorraine in the spring of 1568 (Lea 1962: v.1, 5–11; Oreglia 1964: 4–10). Both Troiano and his partner in this creation, Orlando de Lasso, were court musicians, as was at least one of the other five actors in the piece. Orlando, it must be noted, was not simply a court musician, but was one of the foremost composers in Europe and in charge of all entertainments for the Bavarian court. Troiano reports that Orlando was given just thirty-six hours to create this production, held near the end of several weeks of entertainments. The three court musicians performed six of the play's ten roles and also provided incidental music. Their considerable involvement is a reminder of the long tradition of minstrelsy in Europe and its close association with the early development of professional theatre. Minstrel companies were hired for their music but could also provide other forms of entertainment, including plays. When specialist companies of actors gradually started appearing across Europe after the 1520s, they used the organizational structures, patronage agreements, and international touring arrangements the minstrels had pioneered for over two centuries. While court musicians no longer thought of themselves as minstrels, it is not surprising that they knew of the latest developments in theatre or that they had the skill to act plays at a level suitable for the Duke's court. They were, as their predecessors had been, professional entertainers with multiple talents.

Troiano's account of this production includes descriptions of early staging practices. Much is said about the costuming (doublets of crimson velvet, black velvet cloaks lined with sable) and the props (armor, daggers, swords, muskets, letters, a necklace, a cloths basket). Some blocking is indicated (Pantalone and Zanni bumping into one another on the street, letters and necklaces being exchanged between characters), and *lazzi* are described (Zanni and Pantalone spinning each other around upon first meeting, Pantalone being beaten with a slapstick, Zanni trying to hide in a sack); and disguises are mentioned (Zanni switches clothing with Pantalone). The doubling and tripling of roles is explained. Improvisation is discussed, as is the actors' abilities to make themselves understood to an audience who did not understand Italian dialects. The door to Camilla's house is heavily used, although its location on stage is not given, while other entrances and exits are simply "off stage." As might be expected, a great deal is also said about the use of music in the performance. Unfortunately, this valuable description by a participant/observer says little about the space where the performance occurred within the Residenz Palace at Munich.

In 1576, Prince William, the future William V (ruled 1579–97), commemorated this production from his marriage celebrations in the famous "Fool's staircase" at his summer home at Trausnitz Castle in Landshut, Germany. Here he had Commedia dell'Arte scenes painted along the walls of thirteen flights of steps as they ascended from ground level to the first and second floors of the building. The frescos do not follow the story described by Troiano and probably reflect only recollections of moments from that event along with additional Commedia figures who had appeared in other entertainments during the wedding celebrations, as well as additional material added to properly fill the spaces. The frescos are nonetheless instructive and are the oldest illustrations of Commedia figures in action. More characters, and therefore more costumes, are illustrated on the staircase than were in the original production, and there are several differences in the props. The frescos also show us the distinctive Commedia dell'Arte masks, which Troiano mentions but does not describe. The frescos depict lazzi that were not in the original production, including a commonly illustrated gag of a donkey being given an enema and an image of a female character throwing the contents of a chamber pot onto Pantalone (see Figure 24.1). The latter is especially interesting as it indicates that second level windows were a feature of Commedia dell'Arte staging whenever they could be made available. Such windows are seen elsewhere on the staircase and in numerous later illustrations. The variety in the depictions of windows is a clear indication of the range of performance conditions all Commedia companies faced.

Figure 24.1 Pantalone, followed by a zanni, enters the stage from the door of Camilla's house. A woman is shown at a window emptying a chamber pot onto them. From The Staircase of Fools (1576), courtesy Trausnitz Castle, Landshut Germany (see Bavarian Palace Department in the References section for website details). Photo by F. J. Hildy.

Commedia on tour

Although Commedia was not intended for the street, it was built for the road, with an emphasis on the company's ability to travel. The players honed an improvised style that showcased the actors' ability to play in any location to any audience, without being tied to the dictates of an author's script or the specifics of a building's design. Commedia players created a transnational appeal by developing a product that was both universal and adaptable. Their vast repertoire of improvised comedies, scripted tragedies, and elaborate pastorals needed to be produced from a finite set of materials. Most of the extant *scenari* call for the same stock properties: trunks, food, serving ware, lanterns, bags, ladders, ropes, swords, musical instruments, and, of course, staffs and slapsticks for comic combat. Companies also limited their collection of costumes and masks, which might be one reason why a Commedia performer would specialize in a single role that he or she would play in every show. The character relationships changed from play to play (e.g., in Flaminio Scala's 1611 collection of scenari, Isabella is sometimes Pantalone's daughter and other times his young wife; sometimes she is Flavio's love interest and other times his sister), but the characterization was roughly the same, allowing performers to insert their pre-existing character into any story so that troupes could stage a multitude of plays with the minimum number of costumes and masks. All of these design materials had to be packed to move with whatever means possible. Ser Maphio's early company came together to purchase a single horse to transport the company's materials, but Goldoni's later *Memoirs* describe a company that traveled on a well-fitted boat and boasted multiple support personnel, families, and a host of animals.

Robert Henke has argued that Commedia dell'Arte grew up as "the perfect transnational machine" (Henke 2008: 19). Armed with universal stories, economically-selected props and costumes, and versatile actors who could perform across linguistic and cultural barriers, Commedia entertained crowds across the Italian peninsula and as far away as London and Moscow. Much of the style we know today as Commedia dell'Arte was specifically developed to meet the diverse demands of all possible audiences and to utilize the wide range of conditions in all possible performance settings. Commedia could flourish on modest market stages, or it could impress in cutting-edge indoor playhouses. By improvising around fixed structures, Commedia players adapted both their stories and their stagings, allowing them to take advantage of the wide range of venues available during the most experimental age theatre architecture has ever known (see Figure 24.2).

Figure 24.2 Young lover (inamorato). In the background an audience is watching a Commedia dell'Arte performance. The artist suggests the stage is outdoors but the stage set is more likely from an indoor production. Courtesy, Library of Congress.

References

Bavarian Palace Department, Trausnitz Castle, "Virtual Tour," www.schloesser-bayern.com/fileadmin/sites/schlbay/pano/nbay/la-trntz/pano-sv.html?pano=eg/kasse/pano.xml&parLanguage=en (accessed 21 August 2014). [Hover over the ground plan on the image or click "show floor plan" in the bottom menu bar; select "half landing 8" in the upper left of the floor plan to enter the "Fool's Staircase."]

Clubb, Louise George (1989) *Italian Drama in Shakespeare's Time*, New Haven, US: Yale University Press.

Erenstein, Robert L. (2000) "The Rise and Fall of Commedia dell'Arte," *500 Years of Theatre History*, 3–20, Lyme, US: Smith and Kraus.

Fava, Antonio (2007) *The Comic Mask in the Commedia dell'Arte*, Thomas Simpson (tr.), Evanston, US: Northwestern University Press.

Ferguson, Ronnie (1999) "Venues and Staging in Ruzante's Theatre: A Practitioner's Experience," *The Renaissance Theatre: Texts, Performance, Design*, 146–59, Aldershot, UK: Ashgate.

Henke, Robert (2002) *Performance and Literature in the Commedia dell'Arte*, Cambridge, UK: Cambridge University Press.

——(2008) "Border Crossing in the *Commedia dell'Arte*," *Transnational Exchange in Early Modern Theater*, Burlington, US: Ashgate.

Howarth, William D. (1997) *French Theatre in the Neo-Classical Era, 1550-1789*, Cambridge, UK: Cambridge University Press.

Johnson, Eugene J. (2000) "Jacopo Sansovino, Giacomo Torelli, and the Theatricality of the Piazzetta in Venice," *Journal of the Society of Architectural Historians* 59, no. 4: 436–53.

——(2005) "The Architecture of Italian Theaters around the Time of William Shakespeare," *Shakespeare Studies* 33: 23–50.

Katritzky, M. A. (2006) *The Art of Commedia*, Amsterdam: Rodopi.

Lea, K. M. (1962), *Italian Popular Comedy*, 2 vols. New York: Russell & Russell.

Longman, Stanley V. (1993) "A Renaissance Anomaly: A *Commedia dell'Arte* Troupe in Residence at the Court Theatre at Sabbioneta," *Commedia dell'Arte Performance: Contexts and Contents*, 57–65, Tuscaloosa, AL, US: Southeastern Theatre Conference and University of Alabama Press.

Mazzoni, Stefano and Ovidio Guaita (1985) *Il teatro di Sabbioneta*, Florence, Italy: L.S. Olschki.

McKendrick, Melveena (1989) *Theatre in Spain, 1490–1700*, Cambridge, UK: Cambridge University Press.

Oreglia, Giacomo (1968) *The Commedia dell'Arte*, Lovett F. Edwards (tr.), New York: Hill and Wang.

Pallen, Thomas A. (1999) *Vasari on Theatre*. Carbondale, US: Southern Illinois University Press.

Posner, Donald (1977) "Jacques Callot and the Dances Called *Sfessania*," *The Art Bulletin* 59, no. 2: 203–16.

Scott, Virginia (2009) *Women on the Stage in Early Modern France, 1540-1750*. Cambridge, UK: Cambridge University Press.

Touhy, Thomas (1996) *Herculean Ferrara: Ercole d'Este (1471–1505) and the Invention of Ducal Capital*, Cambridge, UK: Cambridge University Press.

25

COMMEDIA DELL'ARTE AND THE SPANISH GOLDEN AGE THEATRE

Nancy L. D'Antuono

Originally published in *Theatre Symposium*, V. 1, pp. 28–35, in 1993, and reprinted with kind permission of the University of Alabama

My area of expertise is the relationship between the Commedia dell'Arte and the theatre of Spain's Golden Age. Early in my academic career I began working with the Italian *novella* and its presence in the theatre of Lope de Vega. As I examined the thirty-two Lope plays derived from Italian short stories, I became reacquainted with the Commedia dell'Arte and its role in shaping Lope's dramaturgy in general, and, in particular, the eight plays examined in detail. About twelve years ago, at a conference in Rome, a fellow *comedia* (Spanish – a drama or play that could be either in a serious or comic genre) specialist suggested that I look into the presence of the Spanish *comedia* in Italy during the seventeenth century and its impact on Italian dramaturgy, both as concerns the *Commedia Erudita* or *Sostenuta* and the Commedia dell'Arte. As I proceeded with my research, I ran into a critical stance on the part of Italian scholars which paralleled that of scholars treating Spanish Golden Age plays. Only a few plays met the high standards of these critics as concerned content. Most of the *rifacimenti* (a rewrite of an Italian play or Commedia into Spanish) of Spanish plays were written off as neither fish nor fowl and barely worthy of discussion. As for the Spanish repertory of the Commedia dell'Arte: nary a word. The rigidity of posture reminded me of my undergraduate and graduate courses in Spanish drama in which the same "sacred" plays were discussed over and over again as the masterpieces of Spain's seventeenth-century theatre. Among these were *El Medico de su Honra* (*The Surgeon of His Honor*, Calderón de la Barca 1945) in which a husband has his wife bled to death to prevent his "honor" from being tarnished by the prince's unwelcome attentions; *Fuenteovejuna* (*The Sheepwell*, Vega Carpio 1950) which treats the themes of the responsibility of rulers and the respect for human dignity no matter what the social class; and *La Vida es* sueño (*Life is a Dream*, Calderón de la Barca 1959) which deals with the question of man's comportment in this world if, indeed, it is but a dream. Rarely did we read a comic play. I can recall only one, *Don Gil de las Calzas Verdes* (*Don Gil of the Green Stockings*, Tellez 1944). Yet when one considers the immense popularity of the Spanish *comedia* at home and in Italy (under Spanish domination from 1504 until 1700) and the vast quantity of plays that reached the boards of both nations, how can it be that so few plays emerge as representative masterpieces? If all of the others are, by implication, so imperfect, how do we account for their unqualified success as Spanish stage pieces and their subsequent triumph as Italian *rifacimenti* and Commedia dell'Arte *scenari?* I mention both genres together since I believe them to be one and the same, theatrically speaking, with common roots and much interdependence in the evolution of their form, if not their content.

Performing in Spain between 1574 and 1597, the *comici dell'arte* contributed directly to the evolution of the Spanish *comedia* and to the development of the *gracioso* (the Spanish servant role equivalent to the Commedia dell'Arte zanni role) perfected by Lope de Vega from zanni. Lope's fascination with the Commedia dell'Arte, its masks and its *lazzi* has been well documented. His plays contain numerous references to the masks and antics of Ganassa, Arlecchino, Stefanello Bottarga, Trastullo, and Franceschina. Lope attended the Commedia dell'Arte performances with such regularity that he was once arrested for libel while sitting at a performance of *Los Italianos.* In 1599 we find him in Valencia, leading a Carnival parade dressed in the red and black garb of Pantalone. Having come to Spain when its national theatre was just taking shape, the *comici* (comediens) offered Lope de Vega, and through him all subsequent Golden Age dramatists, those elements that would characterize the Spanish stage offerings of the next hundred years: a three-act dramatic structure, balance and duplication in plot and characterization, and a rapid-moving story line centering on the tribulations of young lovers who, with the help of crafty servants, outwit rivals and elders in order to bring their love to fruition. The Spaniards would repay this debt some fifty years later by providing the *comici dell'arte* with new plots with which to shore up their waning repertory.

Before I discuss the Commedia dell'Arte's approach to the Spanish comedies, some comment is necessary as to the content of the Spanish sources. The dramatic energy of these pieces stems from the playwright's ability to fuse the theatrical novelties of the Italian players to the social, ideological, and religious mandates of his age. The emerging comedies are cohesive units that, while thoroughly entertaining, reaffirm, or at least appear to affirm, three givens: Church, Monarchy, and Honor. I would mention, parenthetically, that the last two elements – the monarchical ideal and the Spanish code of honor – were the components with which Italian *rifacitori* and *capocomici* (the head comics, actor managers or leaders of the acting troupes) had the greatest difficulty. In fact, the subtle logic of the Spanish honor code was to a large degree incomprehensible to the Italians.

The Commedia dell'Arte's unrivaled capacity for revitalization and accommodation brought the actors, out of necessity, to the Spanish *comedia.* By the end of the first quarter of the seventeenth century the Italian repertory had worn thin from repetition (they had, after all, been kings of the boards for over sixty years). Their audience was now being seduced by a competing force: the *comedia* of Lope and his followers as performed by Spanish acting troupes pouring into viceregal Naples and from there to ambassadorial courts in Rome, Florence, Mantua, Milan, and Venice. By

1630 Naples' Via del Teatro dei Fiorentini had already been renamed (at least by reputation) Via della Commedia Spagnola. The *comici* had no choice but to take to themselves what they recognized as the latest craving of their public. The spectators' demands and the *comici's* obeisance kept the Spanish *comedia* on the Italian stage until the end of the eighteenth century. Who better to ensure the longevity of the Commedia dell'Arte than the very art form it had helped shape half a century earlier? They had before them a wealth of plays whose success was undeniable. Lope and his followers offered works that incorporated the best of the Commedia dell'Arte while eliminating the gross language and obscene gestures that antagonized church authorities. How could the *comici* resist?

The Italian players' interest in the Spanish *comedia* went beyond the sudden quest for new material and financial gain. The relationship between the actors of the two nations had been nurtured by mutual esteem for each other's talents. Italian actors felt much could be learned from the Spaniards' execution of serious roles; Spaniards admired the *comici's* ability to create while performing. Spanish and Italian actors had worked side by side since the arrival of the first Spanish performers in 1620. The company of Antonio de Melo, a Portuguese Neapolitan who made his career on the stage as Captino Flegetonte, included two Spanish actors. The positive reaction of the Italian audience to the *entr'acte* (interval or intermission) dancing of Beatriz de Guzman prompted de Melo to offer next Spanish cape-and-sword plays. Both Spaniards and Italians reacted so well that de Melo encouraged Sancho de Paz to form a regular company for the following season. Thus began a symbiotic relationship that was to last at least one hundred years. A contract of 1620 lists two Italian actors with Sancho de Paz. They were Ambrosio Buonhomo (Coviello) and Andrea Calccse (Pulcinella), who played out their well-known *contrasti* (short scenes, often comic, involving opposing characters, and/or contrasting character types) during the *intermezzi*. In 1621 a third Italian joined them: Bartolomeo Ziti, who played a Neapolitan Dottor Gratiano. In 1628 he was still part of the company and traveled to Rome with them. Artistic commonality transcended national and linguistic barriers. The rich professional cross-fertilization and the longstanding respect for one another's art coupled with unequivocal acclaim led naturally to the assimilation of Spanish plots into the Italian repertory. Spanish play texts circulated freely among them, often long before the works were published in Spain. A case in point is the scenario *Sette infanti dell'Ara* (Cotticelli, Heck and Heck 2001: 454–6). A letter by the actress Leonora Castiglione mentions its being performed during the 1634 season, yet the source play, Lope de Vega's *El Bastardo Mudarra*, was not published until 1641.

The absorption of Spanish plays into the Italian repertory brought with it another phenomenon: the translation for publication of Spanish plays by Italian actors and actresses. The earliest on record are those of Marco Napolione, an actor who flourished around the middle of the seventeenth century and was famous for the role of Flaminio. Unfortunately, Napolione's twenty-two translations, the titles of which are recorded in Allacci's *Drammaturgia* (1755), are no longer extant. By 1676 Angela D'Orso, in the service of the Duke of Modena, had translated twelve Spanish plays, four of which are extant. Domenico Antonio Parrino, the actor-turned-publisher (known for the role of Flaminio in late seventeenth-century Naples), printed works translated by fellow actors. There are extant translations by Orsola Biancolelli (wife of the famous seventeenth-century Arlecchino, Domenico Biancolelli), Francesco Manzani, Nicolo Biancolelli, and Francesco Calderoni. The tradition continues in the eighteenth century with the translations of Francesco Bartoli, Luigi Riccoboni, and D. Placido Adriani. As for the reason for these translations, I can only surmise that the actors had probably played the leading roles on stage or translated the work at the request of a noble patron and subsequently decided to publish the translation, thereby legitimizing their function as quasi-*literati* rather than simply as actors and actresses.

The plays most commonly adapted or translated by the *comici* were the light-hearted comedies of intrigue, those which most resembled the typical Commedia dell'Arte offerings. The tripartite structure common to both art forms facilitated the transposition of content *grosso modo* (approximately), but did not preclude adjustments stemming from a particular *capocomico's* dramatic vision. Here, too, the rearrangement was easily accomplished. The *galán* and *dama* of the Spanish original became the *primo innamorato* and *prima donna* of the Italian company. Similarly, the second pair of lovers (if the subplot so demanded) could be passed onto the second lover and second lady. The blocking figure, if a parent, might now be Pantalone or Dottor Gratiano. If the Spanish plot contained an unsuccessful second suitor, the role most often went to the Capitano, The *dama's* female servant found her counterpart in the *servetta;* the gracioso easily reverted back to his progenitor: Zanni and variants thereof. As for the scenario's title, the *comici* simply translated the Spanish into parallel Italian phrases. There was no effort to hide the source. In fact, they banked on the audience's recognition of the piece in order to draw a large crowd, They also knew that plays by Lope de Vega drew the largest audiences and did not hesitate to place his name on their publicity posters even when the work was not his.

The preference for comedies of intrigue did not exclude the occasional adaptation of tragic or serious pieces. The *comici* recognized the dramatic power of these works and of their audience appeal. The adaptations, however, while adhering to the Spanish plot lines, often scene by scene, are testaments to the divergent social values of both nations, For example, in the case of *Il medico di suo honore* (Ms. 4186, Biblioteca Casanatense, Rome, from Calderon's *Medico de su honra,* Calderón de la Barca 1945), the ending of the play was recast twice, pointing to the discomfort of the Italians with the murder (by bleeding) of an innocent wife for the sake of one's "honor." The notion of a husband standing around congratulating himself over the clever manner in which he had avoided defamation was simply more than an Italian audience could tolerate. It could accept the death of an adulterous spouse, but not the premeditated elimination of a guiltless woman, Whereas the king in Calderon's play is reluctant to punish the offending husband, in the first of the Italian revisions the king condemns the man to death, The king subsequently spares him owing to the supplications of many members of the court as well as those of a lady who loves the protagonist. Marked for insertion at the point where the lady and the members of the court plead for the husband's life is a second revised ending: The king now asks for time to reconsider the death penalty. Witnesses, including the man who had attempted to seduce her, come forth to attest to the wife's innocence. Accepting their testimony as fact, the king decides that the husband must die and invites all to attend the execution. Thus the protagonist's execution is an unavoidable act of justice stemming from the rational examination of facts.

By and large, however, the comedies of intrigue that ended with one or more couples happily married were the favorites of the *comici*. To date 104 *scenari* have been traced to Spanish sources. Of these, seven are my own discoveries in the course of my research on the theatres of Calderón and Lope de Vega in Italy. As I worked with the three new pieces deriving from Lope's theatre, an interesting phenomenon emerged. Each of the Spanish plays was derived from an Italian *novella*. Thus we find the Italians recapturing their own literary heritage through a Spanish literary filter. My study confirms that each of the three *scenari* is clearly derived from the Spanish and not from the original *novella*. This finding, in turn, raises another issue. We know that the novella by its very structure lent itself to dramatization and that it is likely that many *novelle* found their way into the Commedia dell'Arte repertory. This fact brings me to a question Tom Heck raised in a personal conversation: How can we be sure that Lope was not inspired in each instance, at least partially, by an earlier Italian scenario? The possibility cannot be discounted. Unfortunately, none of the sixteenth-century pieces have survived. To date I have come across only one play that strongly suggests such a possibility. I refer to Calderón's *El alcaide de si mismo* (*The Jailer of Himself*, Calderón de la Barca, 1960), which subsequently appears as a scenario, *Guardia de se stesso* (1700; Cotticelli, Heck and Heck 2001: 490–3), Although there are Italian nobles in the Spanish play, the most important character seems to be Benito, a country bumpkin who finds a suit of armor (discarded by a fleeing nobleman), puts it on, and is then arrested. His captors believe him to be the Prince of Sicily who has recently killed another Italian nobleman in a tournament. Benito, as "Prince," is detained, and a substantial portion of the remainder of the play centers on the humorous episodes arising from the differing perceptions by the other characters of the uncouth "Prince." In the Naples scenario, Benito is Pulcinella, who differs little from his Spanish predecessor except in his preference for *maccheroni* when offered food. If anything, Calderon's Benito appears to be more of a glutton than Pulcinella himself. In relation to the other characters, Benito's role assumes a great deal more importance than is common in these plays. Although I have not yet been able to pinpoint an Italian source, I remain convinced, since the setting is Naples and the characters are mostly Italian nobles, and in view of the Benito/Pulcinella parallel, that an earlier scenario may indeed have inspired Calderón's play.

The same may be true, though to a much lesser extent, in the case of two Lope plays related to two of the *scenari* under consideration here. Before approaching these, I would like to call attention to Lope de Vega's high regard for Isabella Andreini, *prima donna* of *The Madness of Isabella*, She is mentioned in two of his last plays, *El castigo sin venganza* (Vega Carpio 1632) and *Las bizarrías de Belisa* (ibid. 1634), In the first play the Duke of Ferrara, eager for a night of merrymaking, sets out with his servants to find an appropriate place. They come to a door and hear some actors rehearsing. The Duke comments that if it is Andrelina (a misspelling of "la Andreini") she is an actress of great fame, capable of displaying many extremes of emotion. In the second comedy, the heroine Belisa recites a sonnet. The gentleman with her remarks that it is worthy of "Isabella Andreina," such is its beauty. I have not yet been able to confirm whether Lope actually saw Isabella Andreini perform or whether he knew her only by reputation, possibly through his contact with Italians in Madrid, Seville, or Valencia. There is no record of the Andreinis having performed in Spain, although there is a document in the Archives of Seville that refers to a Spanish company of actors known as Los celosos. Is this name a deliberate attempt to recall I Gelosi? Had the Spaniards seen them perform and modelled their company after theirs? Until more documents surface, the question must remain unanswered.

Lope may have intended to honor Isabella Andreini and also Francesco in an early comedy, *La discreta enamorada* (written between 1606 and 1608, Vega Carpio 1913). It is a play in which the presence of the Commedia dell'Arte is almost palpable, in my opinion. In its comic vitality, its sparkling dialogue, and its swift forward thrust of the action, the work corresponds closely to the kind of intrigues for which the Italian players were famous. The plot advances almost entirely on the basis of deceptions, tricks, and jokes perpetrated by the principal characters on one another. Although the setting is Spanish, there appears to be little concern for the question of honor. The question of the protagonist's nobility, usually inseparable from matters of honor, is conspicuously absent. The characters, the lovers aside, all seem more concerned with the accumulation of wealth than with values of any transcendence. Though Spanish in name, the characters appear to be adaptations of Italian prototypes. Beyond the zanni/gracioso, *innamorati/enamorados* parallels, Lope's Captain Bernardo is a brilliant fusion of the braggart Captain and Pantalone. He is the robust, middle-aged father and retired soldier eager to marry a spirited young girl, Fenisa, young enough to marry his son, whom the girl really loves. The close ties between the role of the Captain and that of Fenisa, who once having accepted his proposal of marriage orchestrates the foolish Captain's every move until she emerges married to the man of her choice, prompts me to think of Francesco Andreini (Capitano Spavento) and of his wife, Isabella, *prima donna* of the troupe. Could not the Italian acting couple and the roles they immortalized have suggested the characterization of the corresponding roles in *La discreta enamorada* (Vega Carpio 1913)? Isabella died in France on 11 June 1605, and shortly thereafter Francesco retired from the stage. Lope's play was written between 1606 and 1608. Had Lope intended to honor their memory in *La discreta enamorada*? I believe so. The fact that Lope pays unmistakable tribute to the famous acting talents of Isabella three decades later in two of his last plays would seem to support the hypothesis.

As for the *scenari*, *The Madness of Isabella* and *Innocence Restored* (Locatelli 1622), these may be connected to two plays by Lope de Vega: *Los locos de Valencia* (*The Mad Ones of Valencia*, written between 1590 and 1595, Vega Carpio 1946) and *Viuda, casada y doncella* (*Married, Widowed and Chaste*, written 1595–1603, ibid. 1930) – though not in the usual linear fashion. Lope seems to have taken the notion of a lady going mad upon finding herself rejected and expanded upon it to include three characters who feign madness to be near the one they love whom they believe to be mad. Beyond the notion of madness caused by abandonment by one's beloved, the plots move in different directions. Interestingly enough, the plot of *Viuda, casada y doncella* has several points in common with *The Madness of Isabella*, yet its title is thematically tied to *Innocence Restored* (Locatelli 1622) and the matter of the lady's gout being cured by one who is "married, widowed, yet a virgin." In both *Madness* and *Viuda* we have a lover who is shipwrecked in Moorish waters. In both, the man becomes attached to a Moorish girl who is willing to betray her master to run off with her new love. In *Madness*, Oratio eventually marries Isabella; in *Viuda*, once the escape has been effected, Floriano tells Fatima that he is married to Clavela and that he cannot marry her. Fatima settles for marrying Celio, Floriano's manservant, when the latter asks for her hand. Oratio's and Floriano's absence encourages the pursuit of their ladies by rivals. The endings, however, veer in different directions. Horatio recognizes his obligation to Isabella and marries her; Floriano arrives just in time to stop the union of Liberio and Clavela and claims Clavela as his wife.

As for the ties between *Viuda, casada y doncella* (Vega Carpio 1930) and *Innocence Restored* (Locatelli 1622), they do not go much beyond the title. Lope's chaste widow has no magic power to cure maladies. Since Lope's play predates the Locatelli scenario – it also predates Verucci's *It Dispettoso Marito* (written in 1612, Verucci 1671) – might Lope's play have inspired Verucci's play or the Locatelli scenario? It would not seem so. Perhaps it would be more appropriate to say, in this instance, that they both deal with a theme common to both the folklore and the *novella* tradition.

References

Allacci, Leone. *Drammaturgia...accresciuta e continuata fino all'anno MDCCLV.* (1755) Giambattista Pasquale: Venice, Italy.

Calderón de la Barca, Pedro. *El Médico de su honra.* Obras completas. *Dramas* II 184–214 (1945) Madrid: Aguilar.

——*El Alcaide de sí mismo. Obras completas .Comedias*, II 801–34 (1960) Madrid: Aguilar.

——*La vida es sueño.* Obras competes. Dramas I 365–87 (1959) Madrid: Aguilar.

Cotticelli, Francesco, Anne Goodrich Heck. Thomas F. Heck. *The Commedia dell'Arte in Naples / La commedia dell' arte a Napoli: a Bilingual Edition of the 176 Casamarciano Scenarios.* (2001) Lanham, Maryland, US: Scarecrow Press.

Guardia di se stesso. Scenario 70, (1700) MS. Raccolta Casamarciano, Biblioteca Nazionale di Napoli, Codex XI.AA.40, 227r–230v.

Locatelli, Basilio. "L'innocenza rivenduta" (Innocence Restored), Scenario 4 *Della scena dei Soggetti comici e tragici di BLR*, Parte Prima (1622) Biblioteca Casanatense, Roma, MS, 1211, cc 31r-36v.

Medico di suo honore. Scenario. Ms. 4186. Biblioteca Csanatense, Roma.

Pazzia di Isabella, La. (*The Madness of Isabella*) Scenario, Pandolfi, Vito. *La Commedia dell'Arte. Storia e Testi.*. V, 220.

Setti infanti del Ara. Scenario 57, Raccolta Casamarciano, Biblioteca Nazionale di Napoli, XI.AA.40, II, 188r–191r.

Tellez, Fray Gabriel (Tirso de Molina). *Don Gil de las calzas verdes.* Comedias escogidas de Biblioteca de Autores Españoles. Nuea edicion. 402–22 (1944) Madrid: Atlas.

Vega Carpio, Lope de. "El Bastardo Mudarra" *Veintiquatro Parte perfeta de la comedias del Fénix de España, Frey Lope Félix de Vega Carpio.* (1641) Zaragoza, Spain: Pedro Verges.

——"La discreta enamorada" *Obras de Lope de Vega.* 395–437 (1913) Madrid: Real Academia Española, XV.

——"Viuda casada y doncella" *Obras de Lope de Vega*, Real Academia Española, Nueva edición. 455–91 (1930) Madrid: Galo Saez.

——"La bizarrías de Belisa" *Teatro Escogido de Lope de Vega*. 346–75 (1934) Paris: Baudry.

——"Los locos de Valencia" *Comedias escogidas de Frey Lope de Vega Carpio*, XXIV, 113–36 (1946) Madrid: Biblioteca de autores espannoles.

——"El Castigo sin venganza" *Comedias escogidas de Frey Lope de Vega Carpio*, Madrid: Biblioteca de autores españoles, XXIV, 567–84 (1946).

——"Fuenteovejuna" *Comedias ascogidas de Frey Lope de Vega Carpio*, 634–50 (1950). Madrid: Biblioteca de autores españoles.

Verucci, Vergilio. *Il Dispettoso marito*. (1671) Roma: Gioseffo Marelli.

26

CELESTIAL SIRENS OF THE COMMEDIA DELL'ARTE STAGE

Anne E. MacNeil

The first descriptions we have of women performing in the Commedia dell'Arte are from July 1567, in the small town of Mantua, Italy, nestled in the delta of the river Po, along its tributary, the Mincio. The Roman Inquisition was in town, interrogating and torturing her citizens for possible religious heresy, and the Duke of Mantua, Guglielmo Gonzaga, commissioned a canon from the cathedral to report on events taking place around the city. So, Monsignor Antonio Ceruto wrote letters nearly every day to the Duke, describing what was going on around town. Despite his august title, Ceruto was a fun-loving man whose charge often centered on descriptions of musical and theatrical entertainments. He seems to have loved attending comedies and concerts, and his letters describe at length performances of comedies, tragedies, and laments by the first-known companies of professional comedians to feature prima donnas. (MacNeil 2012 and forthcoming)

Ceruto's descriptions of performances by Flaminia romana and Vincenza Armani that July form a cornerstone of the literature on the Commedia dell'Arte. Although it is uniquely atypical for any sixteenth-century chronicler to refer to a comedienne by her surname, M.A. Katritzky has identified Flaminia romana as Barbara Flaminia of Rome, sometimes called Ortensia, wife of the comedian and leader of the troupe, Giovanni Alberto Naselli, otherwise known as Zan Ganassa (Katritzky 2006: 201). Vincenza Armani, ostensibly the more famous of the two, was the prima donna of a company led by Adriano Valerini of Verona, which would become known as the Gelosi. In 1567, the two actresses competed with each other, holding all of Mantua in thrall, offering tragic representations of scenes from Lodovico Ariosto's *Orlando furioso* and of noble heroines like Dido, from Virgil's tale of Dido and Aeneas. Indeed, on July 25, Ceruto wrote that all of Mantua was in terror of the Inquisitors and that only the comedies were able to relieve the general atmosphere of fear and anxiety. (MacNeil 2012 and forthcoming)

His descriptions of actresses competing with one another invoke a prominent aesthetic of Commedia dell'Arte performance that prima donnas display a scholarly conception of feminine virtue (indeed, the motto of Vincenza's company, the Gelosi, was "Virtue, fame, and honor: these are the Gelosi"). The crux of each competition centers on the performer's fulfilment of Neo-classical, humanist ideals: her wisdom and wit in selecting and imitating either classical or contemporary models, and her ability to harmonize with the classical ideal of the Music of the Spheres in reciting and singing affective verse. Vincenza and Flaminia challenged each other with tragedies and *intermedii*, with observers making special note of their performances of laments and other passages set to music. Looking to declare a winner, audiences commended Flaminia for her fine laments and for the nobility of her tragedy, and they praised Vincenza for her music-making and beautiful clothes, although the quality of her drama was eventually acknowledged to be inferior. With the debate still raging, on July 5 the companies entered into a contest of intermedi. As described in a letter from Luigi Rogna in Mantua, to [Pietro Martire Cornacchia] on July 6, 1567, Vincenza sang the role of Cupid, who freed the nymph Clori from her Ovidian metamorphosis into a tree, and Flaminia's company introduced into their intermedi satyrs and sorcerers who danced morescas; Flaminia played the part of a nymph. As far as Ceruto was concerned, Flaminia won.

Earlier in the year, about a week before carnival, Flaminia had traveled by boat from Mantua to Venice with two other comediennes and several musicians from the Duke's court and from the Cathedral of S. Pietro. Ceruto's description of their music-making was ecstatic:

> Where on that boat one did not hear other than angelic harmony: it is said that the Po, for delight, turned her waters into perfumed and rosy water: I hear that the Signori Accademici in Vincenza made sonnets for this trip that burn with eternal flame.
>
> (MacNeil 2012)

The following spring, in 1568, Flaminia and Vincenza were again in Mantua, competing for recognition from their audiences. Then, suddenly, in 1569 Vincenza was poisoned and died. Her death rocked the Commedia dell'Arte world, and her fellow actors mourned Vincenza loudly and long. In an oration published in honor of her death, Adriano Valerini placed music high among Vincenza's talents, together with rhetorical eloquence, decorum, improvisation, and *varietà*. He wrote that she sang sonnets and madrigals with the best singers of the time and played a variety of musical instruments with a celestial hand. When she accompanied herself singing, Vincenza caused even the stars to align in the heavens:

> In music, not only did she sing her part securely with the finest singers of Europe, but she composed miraculously in this profession, putting into song those same sonnets and madrigals that she wrote herself, in the manner of a musician and a poet. She played a variety of musical instruments with such grace that it seemed an angelic hand touched their concordant wood, and it appeared almost as if she spoke with her fingers. She accompanied the sweet sound of her melody with such beauty that every sense, however sickly and sad, remained happy and content. And Souls who felt an unheard semblance

of that true harmony that the stars create in their movement, melted with the ineffable sweetness [of the sound], remembering their celestial home.

(Valerini 1570; Marotti and Romei 1991: 33;
MacNeil 2003: 35–6)

Vincenza's company endured for three generations, until the year of the second treaty of the Pax Hispanica, 1604. As far as we know, the genesis of the troupe was guided, together with Valerini, by her, whose talents for oratory, singing, and musical and poetic composition made her the most lauded actress of the 1560s. Vittoria Piisimi reigned over the troupe's next incarnation, and she too brought a lively talent for music, as well as for dancing, to her art. The last generation is that of Isabella Andreini, whose magnificence as an actress, singer, poet, and playwright, came to define the company that died when she did, in Lyons on June 10, 1604. After Isabella's death, the spirit of the Gelosi, together with many of its members, went into the Compagnia dei Fedeli, led by Isabella's eldest son Giovan Battista and his first wife Virginia Ramponi Andreini. Virginia created the title role of Arianna in Ottaviano Rinuccini's and Claudio Monteverdi's tragedy of the same name, performed in Mantua for the wedding celebrations of Francesco IV Gonzaga and Margarita d'Austria in 1608. (MacNeil 2003: 3–5; MacNeil 1999)

Vittoria Piisimi stood at the height of her profession in the 1570s, 1580s and 1590s. She performed with the Gelosi for new king, Henri III of France, in 1574 when he traveled from Warsaw to Paris for his coronation, and the last notice we have of her is October 15, 1595. (Frangipani 1574; Nolhac and Solerti 1890: 133–4, 144, 231) For the presentation of Cornelio Frangipani's *Tragedia* in Venice on July 24, she and her colleagues:

> recited in the manner derived from the ancients: all the performers sang in the softest harmonies, when singing alone, when singing together; and at the end, the chorus of Mercury was of instrumentalists, who had the most various instruments that were ever played. The trumpets heralded the entrance of the gods on stage, which was done with a tragic machine which was impossible to regulate because of the great tumult of people that were there. Neither was it possible to imitate the antiquity of the musical works, which were composed by Sig. Claudio Merulo, who is of such quality that the ancients can never aspire to it. Monsig. Gioseffo Zarlino, who is of the same quality, was occupied with the music played for the King on the Bucintoro, which set some of my Latin poetry, and with the [music for the] church of S. Marco. And he was the director of those [musics] that were made continually at His Majesty's command.

(Frangipani 1574; Nolhac and Solerti 1890 133–4)

Frangipani's description extends the compass of our understanding of comedians' talents and performing repertories. It tells us not only that the Gelosi performed tragic texts set to music, but that they sang music written by one of the great composers of the sixteenth century, Claudio Merulo, in both monodic and polyphonic settings. Moreover, it relates that their singing was suited to the Neo-classical manner favored by Renaissance humanists. Aristocratic members of Giovanni de' Bardi's salon in Florence, known as the Camerata, similarly began to imitate the ancient manner of combining music and rhetoric in the 1570s. (MacNeil 2003: 11–12)

Merulo's settings for Frangipani's tragedy unfortunately share the fate of much music performed on the Commedia dell'Arte stage in that they are not known to survive, and the above description of the 1574 performance—the sole known report of that entertainment—appears only as an addendum to the second edition of Frangipani's text. Indeed, the printed editions of *Tragedia* contain only musical lyrics, leading Nolhac and Solerti to hypothesize that the work more closely resembled a cantata than a play, which would make the employment of Piisimi and company as its performers quite unnecessary (Nolhac and Solerti 1890). It is not clear, though, that the work consisted only of the published text; its performance by professional comedians suggests that additional spoken text would have been improvised, while the music and musical lyrics were composed. The lyrics published in the second edition offer tenuous clues to their musical settings and to the performing styles of those who sang them. Most of the text is set in *ottava rima* (poetry in eight-line stanzas), although Mars and the choruses sing in *versi sciolti* (free verse) of varying stanza lengths and rhyme formations, freely alternating seven- and eleven-syllable lines and concluding each stanza with a rhyming couplet. The musical settings for Mars and the choruses were thus undoubtedly madrigals, some set for solo voice, as indicated above, and some sung in parts. The *ottave* (eight-line stanzas), too, may have been set as polyphonic madrigals, although it is more likely that they were sung over a ground bass in the manner of story-tellers known as *cantastorie*, or sung to an improvised instrumental accompaniment like the songs of thirteenth-century *trobadors* or minstrels. (MacNeil 2003: 12–13; Haar 1986: 76–100)

Pallas Athena, the leading female role in *Tragedia*, and therefore the role Vittoria Piisimi would have performed, sings an affective address to Henri III ("Poi che veggio de Dei questo soggiorno") and then, in the finale, a duet with Mars ("Spargiam piante felici allori, e mirti"). The duet is followed by a chorus that concludes the work. Piisimi's appearance as a goddess in the play implies that her entrance was heralded by a trumpet fanfare, as stated in Frangipani's description, and that she sang Merulo's melodies with the proportional perfection and harmonious manner due to music that "surpasses the ancients in its imitation of antiquity." The rhetorical tropes contained in her opening aria betray its formula, which shows marked similarities to other sung introductory soliloquies of its kind:

Poi che veggio de Dei questo soggiorno
Così illustrarsi, e come de' bei lumi
Celesti adorno farsi tutto Cielo,
Vò discoprirmi, e uscir da quella nube
Che me ha celato a gli occhi de' mortali
Indegni di guardar celesti numi,
Per parlar teco che tuoi detti rei
Potriano tormi tutti gli honor miei.
                    (Frangipani 1574: fol. [3v])

(I make this journey from the gods to give lustre and, with beautiful, celestial lights, to adorn all Heaven. I want to unveil myself and to step down from the cloud that has concealed me from mortal eyes, which are unworthy of looking at the celestial gods, in order to speak with you, so that your kings can grant me all my honors.) (MacNeil 2003: 14–16)

Later musical and theatrical entertainments, including the intermedii for the Medici wedding of 1589 and for the wedding of the Count of Harò in 1594, Claudio Monteverdi's and Alessandro Striggio's opera *Orfeo* (1607), and Francesco Cavalli's opera *La Calisto* (1651) similarly begin with a goddess descending from Mount Olympus, heralding in song her role as messenger and magnifier of the gods, who will watch over the entertainment and ensure its celestial qualities.

One of the truly remarkable aspects of the Gelosi's performance of Frangipani's *Tragedia* is the time allotted to its preparation. On July 10, Aloisio Mocenigo in Venice wrote to Ottaviano Maggi in Milan to request that the Gelosi be sent with all speed in order to perform for the king. Three days later, the comedians requested permission of their patron Don Giovanni d'Austria to leave the city. And on July 21, one week after they left Milan, Vittoria Piisimi and the Gelosi performed Frangipani's *Tragedia*. Did Maggi send Merulo's music together with his request? How long did the comedians' journey take, either over land or along the Po River? Two days? A week? That the comedians learned the music composed for the performance in the space of a week or less, whether they were *en route* or not, is impressive indeed. It also tempers the shock of Antonio Costantini's remark during the winter of 1608 that Virginia Andreini, Isabella's daughter-in-law, similarly learned the role of Monteverdi's *Arianna* in six days before she performed it in Mantua. Clearly, comedians (and especially the prima donnas!) were quick on their feet and could learn new material, be it music, poetry or prose, at a speed that today we find astonishing. (MacNeil 2003: 13)

The nobility and refinement of Vittoria Piisimi's acting over the course of her career were lauded by the cleric Tomaso Garzoni in his 1585 publication of *La piazza universale*, where he depicts the actress as a sorceress and a siren. He accords her the highest praise, figured in Neo-classical terms of proportional perfection, enchantment and harmony, and he suggests that her singing voice was sweet, soft and penetrating:

> But above all, the divine Vittoria, who metamorphoses herself on stage, seems to me worthy of the highest honors; that beautiful witch of love who entices the hearts of a thousand lovers with her words; that sweet siren who bewitches the souls of her devoted spectators with soft incantations, and who without doubt deserves to be heralded as the summation of the art, having proportionate gestures, harmonious and concordant movements, magisterial and welcome acts, affable and sweet words, lovely and cunning sighs, witty and gentle smiles, noble and generous deportment, and in her entire person a perfect decorum that is due to and belongs to a perfect comedienne.
>
> (Garzoni 1585: 737)

Both Vittoria Piisimi and Isabella Andreini performed with the Gelosi in Florence for the Medici wedding festivities of 1589 for Grand Duke Ferdinando de' Medici and Christine of Lorraine. Giuseppe Pavoni, an envoy from Bologna, is the only eye-witness known to have chronicled their comedies for the Florentine wedding, and his diary provides one of the few detailed descriptions of a Commedia dell'Arte performance. (MacNeil 2003: 32–3, 46–76; Saslow 1996; Treadwell 2008) It yields important information, not only about the Gelosi's stagecraft, but in more general terms, about the performance of Commedia dell'Arte plays at court and, in particular, about the practice of performing "*in concorrenza*" or in competition, as Flaminia romana and Vincenza Armani did in 1567. Pavoni's account speaks of the rivalry of the two prima donnas and of the Grand Duke's wishes to hear them perform in competition. Like the ancient orators who vied for superiority in contests at the festival of the Great Panathenaea in Athens, the Gelosi therefore presented two comedies for the wedding festivities: *La cingana* (The Gypsy), starring Vittoria Piisimi, and *La pazzia d'Isabella* (The Madness of Isabella), featuring Isabella Andreini. Once he had seen the performances, Pavoni clearly favored Andreini's *La pazzia d'Isabella*. He described her portrayal of the madwoman in detail, giving the plot, an account of Andreini's acting, singing and parlance in diverse languages, and summarizing the audience's reactions to the performance. *La pazzia d'Isabella* was evidently the court's favorite as well as Pavoni's, and the 27-year-old Andreini the more intriguing of the two actresses: a noteworthy feat, given the praises heaped on Piisimi by both Frangipani and Garzoni for her skill. Andreini expressed her insanity in "elegant and wise style" and thereby demonstrated her "sane and learned intellect." She left her audience abuzz with the marvel of her performance, and inspired Pavoni to confirm the praise written by Garzoni four years earlier, that, "while the world endures, her beautiful eloquence and valor will be praised." In contrast, *La cingana* received little attention from Pavoni, although the words used by the Grand Duke to describe Vittoria's performance call to mind her intellectual valor: "a marvel, let alone the intellect of a woman." (Pavoni 1589: 43–6; Marotti and Romei 1991: 12; MacNeil 2003: 32–3)

> Saturday, which was the sixth, the Gelosi with those two most famous women Vittoria and Isabella, finding themselves in Florence again, appeared before the Grand Duke who asked them, in order to have a good entertainment, to recite a comedy of their own choosing. Upon which, the said women nearly quarreled because Vittoria wanted to recite *La cingana* and the other woman wanted to perform her *pazzia*, entitled *La pazzia d'Isabella*, *La cingana* being the favorite of Vittoria and *La pazzia* the favorite of Isabella. They agreed, however, that the first to be recited would be *La cingana* and that *La pazzia* would be performed another time. And thus they recited the said *La cingana* with the same intermedii that were performed with the high Comedy [Girolamo Bargagli's *La pellegrina*]. But whoever has not heard Vittoria perform *La cingana* has not seen or heard a rare and marvelous thing, which certainly in this Comedy left everyone most satisfied. At another time they performed *La pazzia*, and it came to Isabella

to be the madwoman. Her valor and the loveliness of her conceits are indescribable; her virtues are already noted and manifest to all Italy.

(Pavoni 1589: 29–30)

The Gelosi staged their comedies on consecutive Saturdays, sandwiched between the two performances of the high comedy, Girolamo Bargagli's *La pellegrina*. *La cingana* was given on May 6 and *La pazzia d'Isabella* on May 13 at "the twenty-second hour" or about 4:00pm. All four performances took place on the stage of the Uffizi theater, accompanied by the lavish intermedii designed by Florentine courtiers under the direction of Giovanni de' Bardi. Pavoni's confirmation of performance venue for the Gelosi's comedies and of the accompanying intermedii is unique among the numerous sources documenting the 1589 events: "And thus, the Grand Duke having made his wishes known to the Gelosi, at the twenty-second hour, on the same stage where *La pellegrina* was recited, they performed *La pazzia* with the same intermedii I have already described." (Pavoni 1589: 43–4)

Presentation of *La cingana* and *La pazzia d'Isabella* with Bardi's intermedii on the stage of the Uffizi theater discloses an impressive architecture of performance that helps us to understand the Gelosi's style of homage to their Medici patrons and their contributions to the wedding festivities in 1589. In the absence of a text for either comedy and of any mention of them in Bastiano de' Rossi's commemorative *Descrizione* (1589), a close reading of Pavoni's account yields the only avenue of interpretation for the comedies, for the songs Andreini sang as part of *La pazzia d'Isabella* and for the reasons why Andreini might have won the contest with Piisimi.

The language of Pavoni's diary, and especially his description of Andreini's madness and its cure, alludes to the classical ideals of virtue, valor, and eloquence that govern comediennes' performances *in concorrenza*. Demonstrating her intellectual prowess in a number of languages and in her imitations of other characters, Andreini makes cunning sense out of her nonsensical rantings. Her overabundance of passion when in the guise of the madwoman spills out inevitably in song.

Isabella, in that she found herself deceived by Flavio's insidiousness, and not knowing how to remedy the harm he had done, gave herself over completely to sorrow and thus was overcome by passion. And allowing herself to succumb to rage and fury, she went out of herself and, like a madwoman, went running through the city, stopping now this one, now that one, and speaking now in Spanish, now in Greek, now in Italian, and many other languages, but all without reason. And among other things she set to speaking French and also singing certain canzonettas in the French manner, giving such delight to the most serene bride that she could hardly express it. She then mixed in imitations of the languages of all her comedians, like that of Pantalone, of Gratiano, of Zanni, of Pedrolino, of Francatrippa, of Burattino, of Captain Cardone and of Franceschina so naturally and with so many eccentricities that it is not possible to put into words the valor and virtue of this woman. Finally, by the art of magic, with certain waters they gave her to drink, she returned to her original state and thus, with elegant and learned style explaining the passions of love, and the travails of those who find themselves in similar predicaments, she made an end to the comedy. Demonstrating in the performance of this Madness her sane and learned intellect, Isabella left such a murmur and marvel in her audience, that while the world endures, her beautiful eloquence and valor will be praised.

(Pavoni 1589: 45–6)

Pavoni's description demonstrates the interpretative depth capable of performances that might otherwise be cast as simple amusements for their Florentine audience. His words portray Andreini as an actress familiar with a style of courtly discourse that impressed her listeners with its rhetorical flair and urbane references to humanistic conceits. The chronicler's use of the words *virtù* (virtue) and *valore* (courage) hint at Andreini's erudition and her ability to "order her mind with respect to reason. The songs she sings are audible testimony to this rationality, for the individual notes harmonize with each other, and the harmonies resonate with the order of the universe. Virtue, in addition to resulting from this organization of one's thoughts and emotions, is formed, so writes the Accademia della Crusca in its *Vocabolario* of 1612, by submission to authority, and sometimes it may be ingested in a drink ("*essendo la virtù del beveraggio consumata*"). (*Vocabolario* 1612) This last characterization is particularly apposite to Andreini's performance of the madwoman, for her insanity is cured with magic water. Lodovico Ariosto, too, conceives of virtue as a liquid property, healing Orlando's madness in the *Orlando furioso* with magic water; Andreini exhibits virtue upon virtue in her imitation of such a worthy source. (MacNeil 2003: 46–76)

Francesco Andreini's *Bravure del Capitano Spavento* offers a touching reminder, not only of his love for his wife and of Isabella's widespread fame, but of the celestial attributes ascribed to her in life. A small section of it reads,

Oh! Sacred and venerated stone, break, for pity's sake, and disclose your beloved contents to my eyes! Take these, my sighs, these, my tears, and these kisses as well, and give them to the cold ashes of my dear Phyllis, who in your damp, cold breast lies freezing, so that, if ever her most beautiful spirit will deem them worthy of one solitary glance, she will know that with her death a thousand deaths and a thousand more I suffer for her. And turning again to speak with you, beautiful soul in heaven above, know that when the sun, in mounting its gilded carriage, faded your mortal star, it remained three times in its course, wanting to die, and in the end, to cover your doom with eternal shade. Know, too, that at your death the celestial spheres were heard singing hymns sweet and soft, and that the worldly goddesses who live on Mount Parnassus were seen all dressed in funereal robes, and were heard to sing the most doleful elegies around your honored tomb.

(Andreini 1607: 5)

One needn't mythologize the comediennes who performed with or in competition with the great prima donnas of the sixteenth century to notice how often concepts of facile memory, proportional perfection, an angelic spirit, and celestial harmony are invoked to describe them. When Vincenza Armani sang, "souls that no longer heard that true harmony which makes the stars move, melted in the ineffable sweetness [of the sound], remembering their celestial home," and her rival Flaminia sang in such "angelic harmony" with others that the waters of the Po became like rose-water (MacNeil 2012). Vittoria Piisimi bewitched her audiences with "proportionate gestures" and "harmonious and concordant movements" (Garzoni 1585: 737), and Isabella Andreini, "with an angelic countenance," won over the minds of her listeners (MacNeil 2012). Although often competing with each other for fame and glory, these actresses won the devotion of their audiences with their homages to Neo-classical humanism and with their celestial song.

References

Andreini, Francesco (1607) *Le bravure del Capitano Spavento*. Venice, Italy: Giacomo Antonio Somasco.

——(1987) *Le bravura del Capitano Spavento*, Roberto Tessari (tr.), Pisa, Italy: Giardini.

Frangipani, Cornelio (1574) *Tragedia*. Venice, Domenico Farri.

Garzoni, Tommaso (1585) *La piazza universal di tutte le professioni del mondo, e nobili et ignobili*. Venice, Italy: Gio. Battista Somasco.

Haar, James (1986) *Essays on Italian Poetry and Music in the Renaissance, 1350–1600*. Berkeley and Los Angeles, US: University of California Press.

Katritzky, M.A. (2006) *The Art of Commedia: A Study in the Commedia dell'Arte 1560–1620 with Special Reference to the Visual Records*. Amsterdam and New York: Brepols.

MacNeil, Anne (1999) "Weeping at the Water's Edge," *Early Music* 27: 406–18.

——(2003) *Music and Women of the Commedia dell'Arte n the Late-Sixteenth Century*. Oxford, UK: Oxford University Press.

——(2012) "Monsignor Antonio Ceruto and Music-making in Mantua in the 1560s." Paper presented at the Congress of the International Musicological Society, Rome, Italy.

——(forthcoming) *On Jacopo's Boat*.

Marotti, Ferruccio, and Romei, Giovanna (1991) *La professione del teatro*, vol. 2 of *La Commedia dell'Arte e la società barocca*. Rome: Bulzoni.

Nolhac, Pierre de, and Solerti, Angelo (1890) *Il viaggio in Italia di Enrico III Re di Francia e le feste a Venezia, Ferrara, Mantova e Torino*. Turin, Italy: Roux e C.

Pavoni, Giuseppe (1589) *Diario descritto da Giuseppe Pavoni delle feste celebrate nelle solennissime nozze delli serenissimi sposi, il Sig. Don Ferdinando Medici & la Sig. Donna Christina di Loreno Gran Duchi di Toscana*. Bologna, Italy: Giovanni Rossi.

Rossi, Bastiano de' (1589) *Descrizione dell'apparato e degl'intermedi, fatti per la commedia rappresentata in Firenze, nelle nozze de' serenissimi Don Ferdinando Medici e Madama Christina di Loreno, Gran Duchi di Toscana*. Florence, Italy: Anton Padovani.

Saslow, James (1996) *The Medici Wedding of 1589: Florentine Festival as Theatrum Mundi*. New Haven, US and London: Yale University Press.

Treadwell, Nina (2008) *Music and Wonder at the Medici Court: The 1589 Interludes for La pellegrina*. Bloomington, US: University of Indiana Press.

Valerini, Adriano (1570) *Oratione d'Adriano Valerini Veronese, in morte della divina Signora Vincenza Armani, comica eccellentissima*. Verona, Italy: Bastian dalle Donne & Giovanni Fratelli.

Vocabulario (1612) *Vocabolario degli Accademici della Crusca*. Venice, Italy: Giovanni Alberti.

27

INCIDENTAL MUSIC IN COMMEDIA DELL'ARTE PERFORMANCES

Thomas F. Heck

Originally published in *Theatre Symposium*, V. 1, pp. 7–12, in 1993, and reprinted with kind permission of the University of Alabama

There are intriguing parallels between improvised music such as jazz and improvised theatre such as the Commedia dell'Arte. Both genres require that the performers have a flawless sense of rhythm and style; they must make their entrances on cue and play their parts in character. Most saliently, both art forms stand or fall on the performer's ability to embroider upon some kind of skeletal structure, whether it be a plot outline in a scenario collection or a single melodic line with chord symbols in a "fake book."

The notion of "embroidering" brings to mind a common misconception regarding the meaning of a term frequently encountered in Commedia literature, namely the *canovaccio* (Italian) or *canevas* (French). The terms refer to the plot outline or *scenario* that undergirds a Commedia performance. Well-meaning etymologists in the theatre history community, perhaps having at their disposal a French or Italian pocket dictionary that offers "canvas" as a functional English equivalent, have suggested that the term's theatrical usage derives from the alleged performance practice of taking a scenario and pinning it to the "canvas," that is, the backdrop of the open-air platform stage sometimes used by itinerant Commedia troupes. The actors—as this just-so story goes—would glance at these sheets just before making their entrances, using them as a kind of *aide-mémoire*.

The source of this legend may be traced to various accounts of actors. Riccoboni's *Histoire du théâtre Italien* (of 1728), is the earliest known to me. As relayed in Duchartre's *The Italian Comedy* (1966), Riccoboni once wrote: "Flaminio Scala's plays are not in dialogue, but are set down in simple scenario form. They are not so concise as those we use and *hang upon the wall of the theatre* behind the scenes..." (Riccoboni 1728, author's emphasis)

Another quasi-source for posting scenarios on the canvas backdrops might be Carlo Gozzi's late eighteenth-century *Memorie inutili*:

> The subject which serves as guide for these excellent players is written entirely on a small slip of paper and *posted under a little lamp* for the greater convenience of the troupe. It is astonishing to think that, with such a trifling aide as this, ten or twelve actors are able to keep the public in a gale of laughter for three hours or more and bring to a satisfactory close the argument which has been set for them.
>
> (Gozzi 1797, author's emphasis)

This may sound plausible, but neither witness points to canvas backdrops as such. When one looks up *canovaccio* in several Italian etymological dictionaries, it becomes clear that for centuries the term has had a special significance in embroidery: It means a piece of loosely woven cloth on which a line or pattern has been traced, upon which one embroiders, adding color and texture in the process. The French cognate is *canevas*. We need no longer speculate, therefore, on the presumed practice of pinning scenarios on canvas backdrops. Rather, we can now be satisfied with a perfectly plausible and relevant etymology for *canovaccio* taken directly from the art of embroidery, which fits the nature of Commedia performance much better than the canvas-backdrop theory alone.

In what way does all this relate to music? First, the whole phenomenon of the *basso continuo*—the figured bass, a numeric (actually intervallic) notation for keyboard players commonly found in European scores dating roughly from 1600 to 1760— represents nothing if not a case of musicians embroidering on a line, in this instance a carefully constructed bass line. The resulting sound and texture noticeably enhanced the quality and tone color of the (otherwise monochromatic) bass line. Second, during the sixteenth and early seventeenth centuries dozens of books of guitar tablature were produced, in which not even a musical staff is discernible. Instead, one finds simply a single line (a time-line, as it were) with chord letters and tick marks showing when and how to strum: up or down (samples of such primitive chordal guitar notation can be found in Sanz 1674).

One of the earliest notated dances for the guitar was, in fact, the *folia*. It required that the performers improvise a set of variations over a chord pattern. The harmonic progression in modern chord notation might look and sound rather familiar:

Dm	→	A	→	Dm	→	C
F	→	C	→	Dm	→	A
Dm	→	A	→	Dm	→	C
F	→	C	→	Dm, A	→	Dm

Another such chord pattern popular with street musicians of the sixteenth century was the *ciaccona*, forerunner of the highly stylized baroque *chaconne* of some two hundred years later. Margherita Costa's play *Li Buffoni* (Florence, 1641), recently published in *Commedie dell'Arte*, the anthology of plays by professional Italian actors (Ferrone 1986: 233–357), includes the fully written-out text of a "Canzonetta da cantarsi e ballarsi in ciaccona"—a canzonetta to sing and dance to the strains of the *ciaccona*. It is printed at the back of the play, evidently being intended as something special for the third act, subject to the availability of a suitable performer. One would like to suppose that any reasonably trained actor or actress of the era knew how the *ciaccona* went—it was such a commonplace.

$$\| : C \rightarrow D \rightarrow Em \rightarrow C, D : \|$$

Most entertainers could probably have sung endless vocal "riffs" or take-offs on this chord sequence. Modern-day actors can easily hear examples of the *ciaccona* chord-progression online, but for the sake of the record, a well-stocked music library should have recording of a *ciaccona* by Alessandro Piccinini (1566–1638) available. "Ciaccona in partite variate," performed by Jacob Lindberg, (*Italian Music for Lute and Chitarrone*, BIS LP 226:1983) is a good example. In the example below, chord changes are suggested by the author for one full repetition of the chord pattern over two lines of poetry. The singer would have to improvise a melody consonant with those chords to perform this *ciaccona* convincingly:

CANZONETTA DA CANTARSI E BALLARSI IN CIACCONA INTORNO L'INGABBIATI PERSONAGGI IN SCORNO DELLA CUTTA E PAPPAGALLO NELLA FINE DEL TERZO ED ULTIMO ATTO

C   D
Scenda qua, posi qui
Em   C   D   ‖
Strepitando il córnacchione
(etc.)
Ed al suon del nottolone
Ecco faccia il chichirichì.
Ogni razza buscaina
D'animali pennacchiuti
Degli ucelli la regina
Delle bestie it re saluti.
Oh che scherzo, oh che gióia.

Iconographic sources confirm repeatedly that guitars, lutes, and *colascioni* of various kids were used both on and off stage to accompany songs and dances in Commedia dell'Arte performance (see Figure 27.1). Many examples of this specific iconography can be found in M. A. Katritzky's *The Art of Commedia* (2006).

Those who have worked with Commedia scenarios know that many call explicitly for some kind of music somewhere in the play. Often the specific instruments needed are listed in the *robba* or *robbe*, that is, the "stuff" or props usually itemized at the beginning of each play. Even if instruments are not mentioned up front, it seems quite clear that there were numerous places where musical activity was called for, especially serenades under the windows of prospective lovers. Many such instances are revealed in the accompanying appendix, "Musical Allusions in the Casamarciano *Scenari*."

Figure 27.1 Carlo Cantù (Buffett) plays his guitar in Paris. Stefano della Bella engraving, seventeenth century.

Exotic-sounding incidental music must have been used, too, for exotic scenes. Many *scenari* include a Turk as a protagonist. In the Locatelli *zibaldone*, in the scenario *L'innocentia rivenduta* or *Innocence Restored*, (Lea 1934: 573) we find Rais the Turk. Shakespeare's play, *Cymbeline,* is thought to be derived from this source. Shakespeare's "exotic land" would have been Rome; there are many quick scene changes between England and Rome in *Cymbeline*. But if you are in Italy, your exotic land needs to be a bit further east. In either case, the musical opportunity is, to me, fairly clear. Before the Turk makes his entrance on stage, one might want to play a musical cue for the audience using an exotic-sounding instrument like a *colascione*, a long-necked lute, probably strung with two wire strings, and frequently pictured in Commedia-related engravings (see Figure 27.2). It makes a twanging sound, needless to say. The theatre community knows well that it is easy to add the desired atmosphere to a play with the right kind of incidental music.

There is another easy musical device that could be useful: In the aforementioned scenario *L'innocentia rivenduta*, an oracle addresses the Duke at the beginning of

Figure 27.2 Coviello plays a colascione in this Bertelli engraving of 1643.

Act 1. The oracle's script is the only example of a written-out text in the whole scenario. I suggest that it most probably would have been *intoned* in some way for dramatic effect, rather than simply recited. There is another place, at the beginning of Act 2, where the Duke returns to the oracle, and one might have comparable chanted music there too, even if the oracle does not give the answer that is requested. It is still dramatically appropriate to "refer back" with a musical device, in this case perhaps something as simple as a recitation tone.

Sometimes an eyewitness account of what transpired in a particular improvised comedy can be helpful in understanding the musical practices of a given time, place, and troupe. The actress Isabella Andreini, for example, was famous for her mad scenes, and it appears that she had at least two at her disposal. Besides the scenario, *The Madness of Isabella (La Pazzia d'Isabella)*, the thirty-eighth scenario in the Scala collection (Salerno 1967: 282), there is a May 1589 account of a mad scene of Isabella's in which she, in a frenzy at one point, "began to speak in French, and to sing various songs in the French manner, which gave such pleasure to the most serene bride, that she could hardly express it." (*"si mise a parlar Francese & a cantar certe canzonette pure alla Francese, che diedero tanto diletto alla Sereniss. Sposa, che maggiore non si potria esprimere."*) (Pavoni 1589: 45–6), and then Isabella went on to imitate flawlessly the speech of the other actors in her troupe. It should be noted that the madness of

Isabella in the published Scala edition has no apparent connection to the version in which she performed in 1589, whose description by Pavoni is being discussed here.

What songs might Isabella have been singing "in the French manner"? I can suggest two examples of something Isabella might well have sung. The first is a French *air de cour*—courtly air—usually for voice and lute, sometimes performed also with harpsichord. The *air de cour* involves a declamatory style with special emphasis on the rhythm of the words. The style seems to have been a musical response to Jean Antione Baïf and his circle of French poets, who were greatly concerned with declamation, just as the French language was becoming standardized.

An example of a recorded *air de cour* is "Eau Vive Source d'Amour," by Jacques Mauduit, who was born in 1557 (*Airs from the Courts and Times of Henri IV and Louis XIII*, Turnabout TVS 34316, side 1, band 2).

One cannot beat time to this song because the rhythm is taken from the text itself, each syllable being given its own space. It should be liberating for people in theatre to realize that for centuries vocal music could be flexible in rhythm, not driven by the beats so pervasive today. One should feel free to use flexible musical declamation, in other words, when planning the incidental music for a scenario's revival today.

And yet, there was and is another style of song from around 1600 that does have a dominant musical rhythm, that is to say, it presents a steady beat. We call these songs "dance airs" or "dance tunes" because of their rhythmic regularity. An example from the same period, one that Isabella might have elected to perform, would be "Beaux yeux," or "Beautiful Eyes," by Jean Baptiste Bésard, who was born in 1567 (From the album *Ancient Airs and Dances* Hyperion CDA 66228, track 18). This is the French equivalent of the Italian *canzonetta,* found in many Italian sources. Can we imagine Isabella singing a lilting little dance air like this one on stage, as part of one of her *pazzia* scenes—her famous scenes of madness? I can. She could perform it with a guitar accompaniment, she could clap her hands and do it solo, *or* she could dance and sing—there were many possibilities. In addition, there were a thousand *airs de cour* published between 1600 and 1650. It was an enormously popular genre—the French equivalent of the English lute song.

Another interesting hint as to how Isabella Andreini might have used musical allusions, if not the music itself, is found in the Scala edition of *The Madness of Isabella* (Act 3, scene 8) (Salerno 1967). Our protagonist is described as performing a series of crazy episodes where she appears dressed as a madwoman. The other actors stop to listen as she enters, and she then begins to speak: "I remember the year I could not remember / that a harpsichord joined together a Spanish Pavan with a galliard of Santin di Parma…" and so on. Nonsense? Yes, of course.

But if we take the trouble to check the references, we quickly realize that the outburst is even more absurd than what appears on the surface, because a *Spanish pavane* is a stately dance in double meter and a *gagliarda* is a rapid dance in triple meter. They do not share the same chord progressions; the two just do not work together contrapuntally. Incidentally "Santin di Parma" is a reference to Santino Garci da Parma, who was a notable sixteenth-century lutenist. In the album called *Ancient Airs and Dances,* there is an actual *gagliarda* by Garci da Parma called "La Cesarina." There is also a Spanish Pavan by Ferrabosco.

The reason I mention these real pieces of instrumental music is *not* to suggest that they were interpolated as background music into the mad scene in question, but to propose that the audiences of around 1600 would probably have understood such allusions much better than audiences of today. So it would be important to allow oneself, as a director of a modern Commedia performance, to arrange for the musical and other cultural references to be updated. Humor must be valued and somehow preserved.

Other interesting uses of music in Commedia performance are found in three scripted plays from the second volume of Ferrone's *Commedie dell'arte* (1986). One is seen in Margherita Costa's play mentioned earlier, *Li Buffoni*, and is entitled "*Canzonnetta da cantarsi a tre voci al principio della commedia innanzi il prologo*" (Ferrone 1986: 243). It is a three-voice *canzonetta*. Could there have been multi-voiced, polyphonic music in Commedia dell'Arte performances? Yes, most definitely! There is a famous Fossard engraving that shows three men, a Pantalone with his Harlequin and a zanni, serenading a woman in a tower (Duchartre 1929: 325). Three-voice *canzonette* were very common at this time.

Other scenes demonstrate singing entrances and singing exits. One of them includes an episode in which a person, Tedeschino, goes from dancing to singing, and someone actually hands him a guitar and says, "Here, strum away."

It would be remiss to conclude this chapter without acknowledging the many musical allusions to be found in the Casamarciano collection of Naples—the largest collection of scenarios in Italy. It has been available since 2001 in a modern bilingual edition by this writer and two of his colleagues (Cotticelli, Heck and Heck 2001). Based on the evidence shown in the concluding appendix, one can safely make the following observations:

- The *guitar* (at the time a baroque guitar, with five courses of mostly double-strings) is by far the instrument most called for, although in one place ["Amanti volubili," ii/2] a guitar [is] to be broken in every performance. Guitars have always been sacrificial beasts in the musical world, and still are today when rock musicians bash their guitars on stage for dramatic effect.
- The vast majority of the musical episodes involve *singing*. Of these, about half mention more than one person (i.e. "they sing"), meaning that *duets or trios* could have been performed on stage (see episodes 1, 15, 16, 18, 19, 22, 23, and 29–31).
- Episodes B. 4–7 acknowledge the power of the singing voice to charm the savage beast, in this case a fearsome Basilisk. The same theme—the calmative power of music—was demonstrated in one of the earliest operas, Monteverdi's *L'Orfeo* of 1609, in which Orpheus literally disarms the powers of hell with his songs.
- *Dancing and jumping* onstage are described in episodes B. 1, 9, 18, 19, and 29.
- The *guitar* figures in episodes B. 2, 3, 9, 10, 13, 15, and 21, and is probably implied in 14 and 16.
- The long-necked *colascione*, usually strung with two strings, appears in episodes 2, 18, and 26.
- *Trumpets* are needed in episodes 17, 19, 20, and 27.

- Episode B. 22 calls for "ridiculous musical instruments." There are ample illustrations of *comici dell'arte* playing metal grills as if they were guitars. (Katritzky plates 216, 218, 223, 319) They might even have used a *cupa-cupa* (an obscene-sounding friction drum, long a part of the Neapolitan folk music tradition). Figure 27.3 shows a Neapolitan Pulcinella pumping such an instrument while two others sing. (Cotticelli, Heck and Heck 2001).

Finally, a general question: How does one spot potential musical opportunities in dramatic texts? Usually when I scan a theatrical text looking for musical clues, my eye will gravitate to the shorter-lined poetry within a longer section of prose. One develops this skill when working with opera librettos, because in opera librettos, typically, the arias have the briefest texts of all, yet represent the richest musical events that one will find.

Figure 27.3 A Neapolitan Pulcinella plays a cupa-cupa (friction drum) while two friends sing. Majolica tile painting, Chiostro di Santa Chiara, Naples.

References

Cotticelli, Francesco, Anne Goodrich Heck, and Thomas Heck. *Commedia dell'Arte in Naples: A Bilingual Edition of the 176 Casamarciano Scenarios.* Washington, DC: Scarecrow Press, 2001.

Duchartre, Pierre Louis. *The Italian Comedy* (tr. Randolph T. Weaver) Toronto, Canada and London, Dover Press, 1966 (originally printed by George C. Harrop, London, 1929).

Ferrone (ed.) *Commedie dei comici dell'arte*, UTET,1986. (In Italian—a collection of Commedia texts by Flaminio Scala, Nicolò Barbieri, Silvio Fiorillo, Pier Maria Cecchini and Giovan Battista Andreini.)

Gozzi, Carlo. *Memorie Inutili.* Venice, Italy, 1797.

Katritzky, M.A. *The Art of Commedia: A Study in the Commedia dell'Arte, 1560–1620, with Special Reference to the Visual Records.* Amsterdam and New York: Editions Rodopi, 2006.

Lea, Kathleen M. *Italian Popular Comedy. 2 Volumes.* London: Oxford University Press, 1934.

Pavoni, G. *Diario descritto da Giuseppe Pavoni: delle feste celebtate nelle solennissime nozze delli serenissimi sposi, il sig. don Ferdinando Medici, & la sig. donna Christina di Loreno gran duchi di Toscana,* 15 May1589. Bologna, Italy: Giovanni Rossi, 1589), 45–6.

Riccoboni, Luigi D. *Histoire du Théâtre Italien.* Paris: Pierre Delormel, 1728.

Salerno, Henry F. (ed.) *Scenarios of the Commedia dell'Arte: Flaminio Scala's "Il Teatro delle favole rappresentative."* New York: New York University Press, 1967.

Sanz, Gaspar *Instruccion de musica sobre la guitarra española.* Zaragosa, 1674: folio 16r, 18r, 20r.

Appendix

Musical allusions in the Casamarciano Scenari (Naples, B. N.) Compiled by Thomas F. Heck (Cotticelli, Heck and Heck 2001).

A. Musical "props" needed in performance

Often the information at the head of a scenario will include specific mention of musical instruments, as seen below, where a *colascione* and a guitar are called for among the props.

COVIELLO's PRANKS
["Invenzioni di Covello," i/12]

Dramatis personae	Setting	Properties
Dottore Gratiano, father of Cinzio	[A street in] Naples	A stick, a baboon mask
		A sword, a dog with a rope
Pulcinella, Dottore's servant		A short musket, a traveling trunk
Coviello, Cinzio's servant		A chamber pot, a dish of macaroni

Dramatis personae	Setting	Properties
Isabella		A urinal, things to eat with table
Rosetta, her servant		linens and a sideboard
Two Thieves		A beard, a Spanish captain's outfit
		A courier's outfit, a moneybag
		Bandages to bind up Pulcinella's head with boiled egg white
		A letter and a money order
		A colascione, a guitar
		Two lengths of string, a large knife

(Author's emphasis.)

There are similar musical references to be found in the "props" lists.

1) A guitar ["La Fortuna non Conosciuta," i/15]
2) Some musical instruments ["Chi la fa, l'aspetti," i/28]
3) A guitar ["Il vecchio ingannato," i/30]
4) Two musical instruments ["Le fabriche," i/46]
5) A musician's outfit and a musical instrument for Celio ["Li pittori ladri," i/64]
6) A musical instrument for Coviello ["La Dorina serva nobile," i/76]
7) A guitar ["Il marito più onorato, cornuto in sua opinione," i/86]
8) A musical instrument ["Pulcinella pazzo per forza," i/91]
9) "A guitar to be broken" and "A musical instrument" ["Amanti volubili," ii/2]
10) "Trumpets and drums" and "A colascione and tambourines" ["Nuovo finto principe," ii/11]
11) A guitar for playing, a gun for shooting, a stick for beating ["Veste," ii/35]
12) Two colascioni to play ["Finto cieco," ii/38]
13) Some guitars ["Bastarda impertinente," ii/43]
14) Some musicians ["Il comvitato di pietra," ii/47
15) Instrumental and vocal music ["Figliol prodigo," ii/63]
16) Sound effects (for a tournament) ["Guardia di se stesso," ii/70]
17) Someone singing offstage, accompanied by a spinet ["Non amando amare," ii/89]

B. Some musical episodes described in the 176 surviving Casamarciano Scenari

1) So she makes them sing, and dance, and jump, and do other such things. [Act I, scene 7 of "L'Astutia del mariolo," i/4]
2) A night scene with music, Pulcinella playing the colascione and Dottore playing the guitar under Isabella's window. [Act I, scene 1 of "Invenzioni di Covello," i/12]

3) Pulcinella exits and comes back with a guitar to serenade his lover. He begins to sing. After his song, a jug of water is thrown down on him from the window. [Act III, scene 3 of "La Fortuna non Conosciuta," i/15]

4) By singing [to calm him down], Pulcinella does the lazzo of having [the Basilisk] pick all these things back up. After this scene, Pulcinella goes inside. [Act II, scene 2 of "Il Basilisco del Barnagasso," i/23]

5) Pulcinella has [the notary] read the deed, then tries to give it to the Basilisk, who refuses to accept it. Finally, Pulcinella does the lazzo of singing, and the Basilisk accepts it. [Act III, scene 2 of "Il Basilisco del Barnagasso," i/23]

6) Pulcinella wants him to take back what he has just thrown off. [The Basilisk] refuses, until Pulcinella says it by singing it. Only then does he take all his things back. [Act II, scene 1 of "Il Basilisk del Barnagasso—d'altro modo," i/24]

7) Pulcinella tells the Basilisk to take it, but the Basilisk continues to refuse. Finally, Pulcinella tells him, by singing, to take it, and he takes it. [Act III, scene 2 of "Il Basilisk del Barnagasso—d'altro modo," i/24]

8) Pulcinella will pretend to be crippled. Then he does his lazzi with Fidalma, to teach her how to beg for alms by singing, and they leave. [Act III, scene 3 of "Il Basilisk del Barnagasso—d'altro modo," i/24]

9) With the lazzo of singing, playing and dancing, Coviello begs her, as a prank, to dress as a Moorish woman. [Act I, scene 11 of "Li Finti Turchi," i/25]

10) [Giangurgolo enters] with a guitar. He sings, and then [Rosetta] enters. [Act I, scene 11 of "Il vecchio ingannato," i/30]

11) Pulcinella is inside, singing, but then he comes out, ... [Act I, scene 4 of "Il discenzo," i/43]

12) The women are behind the painting, and cannot be seen. Pulcinella sings. From time to time, the women, now one, now the other, and sometimes both, echo [his song] from behind the painting. Pulcinella does his lazzi, showing his amazement, as he looks around and finds no one. After this scene (which should last a while), during which the women repeat every word, sigh, or anything else that Pulcinella utters, whether in song or not, Pulcinella exits, frightened. [Act I, scene 11 of "La dama creduta spirito folletto," i/68]

(at night – a street in the city)

13) Dottore [enters] with a sword and a lantern, accompanied by Coviello, [who is] carrying a guitar. He says he is coming to this place, as usual, to serenade Flaminia.... [he] tells Coviello to start singing. [Act I, Scene 1, of "Il marito più onorato, cornuto in sua opinione," i/86]

14) Dottore, Tartaglia and Rosalba, holding musical instruments, come up to a spot beneath Ottavia's windows. [The old men] have [her] start singing, and withdraw. When the song ends, she dedicates it to Signor Orazio. At that,

> Orazio, [appearing] at the window, asks who was so bold as to serenade him under his window. [Act I of "Amanti volubili," ii/2]

15) Celindo, wearing a cloak and a helmet, and holding a guitar, [enters] with Pulcinella. They approach Ottavia's windows. [Celindo] does the lazzo of [asking] if [his servant] is armed. [Pulcinella does the lazzo] of saying yes, with

a nod of his head, and [the lazzo] of dusk. They begin to make music. [Act I of "Amanti volubili," ii/2]

16) Orazio, Luzio, and Coviello, dressed as musicians, [do] the lazzi of Orpheus and Amphion. They make the old men play music and sing. [end of Act II of "Aquidotto," ii/4]

17) Drums and trumpets [announce]

The King, Orazio, Dottore, Tartaglia, Coviello, and the Court.

18) Pascariello, Pulcinella, Rosetta, and some peasants [enter], with a colascione and tambourines, playing and rejoicing at the marriage [of Pulcinella and Rosetta]. They all begin to sing and dance. [from Act I of "Nuovo finto principe," ii/11]

19) [Pulcinella] sits down on the throne and calls for musicians to be brought in and for their singing to begin. They [reply] that there are no musicians. He [orders] Coviello and Tartaglia to sing. They refuse. He beats them and makes them sing. Then he orders that the dances begin. [Coviello and Tartaglia] say that there are no dancers. He [orders] Coviello and Tartaglia to dance. Finally, [Pulcinella] orders that two horses be brought in, to ride around on. They [reply] that the horses did not return with him, and the other horses are out to pasture. He asks for two saddles and two bridles, which he puts into Coviello's and Tartaglia's mouths, with the saddles on their backs. He calls for a trumpet and climbs onto Tartaglia's back, pulling up on the bridle and sounding the trumpet, while Rosetta rides on Coviello's back. With these lazzi the second act ends, with [Pulcinella and Rosetta] beating them and causing an uproar. [end of Act II of "Nuovo finto principe," ii/11]

20) The counselors exhort them to be patient, and call Some soldiers, who take them away to prison. Astonished, Tartaglia and Coviello stay behind. At that, Pulcinella, still frightened by the blast of trumpets and instruments of war, … [Act III of "Nuovo finto principe," ii/11]

21) Coviello [enters] with a guitar, [speaking] of his love for Rosetta. He says that he has come before dawn to serenade her, and starts playing. At that, Rosetta [comes out]. They do their love scene. [opening scene of "Veste," ii/35]

22) Orazio [enters] as a blind beggar, with Pulcinella, as a beggar, both carrying ridiculous musical instruments. They do lazzi of singing and begging for alms. [from Act I of "Finto cieco," ii/38]

23) Coviello and Pulcinella [come out], disguised as a choir master and a singer, sheet music in hand. [They do] their lazzi of singing. The old men tear up the music and leave once more to fetch the authorities. [from Act III of "Comedia in comedia," ii/39]

24) Rosetta [comes out,] listens to him, pretends to love him [in return], and says, aside, that she will play a prank on him. She says that, if he wants to get into her house that night, he should come back at two in the morning, playing a musical instrument. The neighbors will believe there are people playing music out in the fresh air, and will not think ill of it. In this way she will get him into her house. Happy, Tartaglia leaves, to get an instrument. [Rosetta] goes inside. [from Act I of "Bastarda impertinente," ii/43]

25) Flaminia [comes out] of her house with a broom. Singing, she sweeps the street. [ibid.]

26) Tartaglia [enters] with a colascione and a lantern, saying that it is time to go to Rosetta's, as arranged. He approaches a corner of the stage and puts the lamp on the ground. He starts playing. [ibid.]

27) Trumpets [sound] The King asks an attendant to see who is coming. [from Act II of "Il comvitato di pietra," ii/47

28) The apprentices ceremoniously sit Pulcinella down on the bench. Timoteo wants to check his voice, and does lazzi of having him sing. They tie [Pulcinella] up. [Pulcinella does] his lazzi, and from time to time calls for Coviello. They are about to castrate him when he realizes what is going on and gets angry. With an uproar the second act ends. [end of Act II of "Soldato per vendetta," ii/56]

29) Coviello and Rosetta are singing and dancing, rejoicing at the wedding of their master and mistress, and wishing them happiness. [Act I of "Diavolo predicatore," ii/66]

30) Coviello orders some musicians to sing. [Pulcinella says] that he wants them to sing the "barile." Coviello [replies] that such indecent gestures are not worthy of a prince like him. [Pulcinella] gets angry. [from Act III of "Guardia di se stesso," ii/70]

31) Some musicians [enter], and sing. Samson falls asleep. [from Act II of "Samson," ii/86]

32) Leonilda tells them that while they are talking, she will go into the next room and sing an aria with her spinet. Ramidoro [says] to go ahead. Leonilda goes inside and sings. They stay behind and listen to her singing (whether they sit down or remain standing is optional). Ramidoro shows his emotions, and Coviello rebukes him. Ramidoro would like to go in where she is singing, but Coviello holds him back. After finishing her song, Leonilda comes back, and asks Ramidoro if he liked the aria. [Act II, scene 15 of "Non amando amare," ii/89]

28

MEETINGS ON NAXOS

Opera and Commedia dell'Arte

Roger Savage

It was Mantua in the spring of 1608, and Duke Vincenzo Gonzaga's court was determined to put on a great show—indeed a sequence of great shows—to celebrate the upcoming wedding of the duke's son to the Infanta Margherita of Savoy. There was to be a play with spectacular 'interludes', a new dramatic ballet and an operatic première. The opera was *L'Arianna*. It would present the legend of the time spent on the island of Naxos by the Cretan princess Ariadne: her desertion there by the hero Theseus (who had eloped to the island with her after she helped him defeat the Minotaur), her desolation and desire to die, and her rescue and translation to a new life and love by the god Bacchus. The libretto was by Ottavio Rinuccini, opera's prime poet since the creation of the form just ten years before the first operatic masterpiece, *La Favola d'Orfeo*. Careful stage preparations for *L'Arianna* had been going on since January, and there were especially high hopes for the eighteen-year-old Caterina Martinelli, who was to sing the leading role. But disaster struck. Martinelli, who had not been well for some time, suddenly died of smallpox, and the opera, only weeks before the great day, was left without a leading lady. What to do? Various names were canvassed without success. Then someone suggested 'La Florinda'. This was the stage name of a twenty-five-year-old actress in a Commedia dell'Arte troupe which toured around northern Italy. Would *she* be up to it? In March the Mantuans decided to take the risk and cast her. As things turned out, this was an inspiration. Florinda, it was said, learned the role in a mere six days, and she was certainly a great success when the première finally came in May. Chroniclers, letter writers and at least one poet reported that her lament and prayer for death as Ariadne—'Lasciatemi morire'—had all the ladies in the noble audience in tears. (Fabbri 1994: 77–87, etc.; MacNeil 2003: Ch.4)

Now it would be tempting to romanticise this (true) story: to imagine Florinda as a counter-cultural figure, an unknown, unwashed soubrette from a rough and ready street-theatre collective who was whisked away Cinderella-like into a world of high-cultural mandarins and proceeded to amaze them all by becoming the belle of the ball, the Great Tragic Discovery from the Back Streets. It is a temptation to be resisted, however. Florinda—in real life Virginia Ramponi—had class. She was a noted *innamorata* with I Fedeli, a sophisticated Commedia troupe which already had strong connections with the Gonzaga court. (Duke Vincenzo himself was its patron.) More, she was the wife of Giovan Battista Andreini, the company's well-connected actor-manager. Giovan Battista wrote plays in all the genres: some wholly his own work, others perhaps assembled by him for publication from the Fideli's improvisations. It had been her performance in 1603 as the unfortunate Queen of Scotland in his first play—the very long, very literary, very melancholy tragedy *Florinda*—which had earned Virginia her stage name. So, not only did Monteverdi and Rinuccini not have to go slumming to find their soprano-substitute; they did not even have to teach her to be a high-serious stage-princess. They could be pretty sure that, provided she could cope with the actual notes, she would have the skills and resources to ensure that Ariadne's lament at her desertion by Theseus would be the long-remembered high point of the show. And cope she did. Only a week after she was cast in the role, report was circulating in Mantua that 'she sings it with such grace and affect that it has made Madame [the Duchess], Signor Rinuccini and the gentlemen who have heard her marvel'. (Fabbri 1994: 83)

The intriguing thing illustrated by the Florinda-Virginia story, then, is not the space between Early Opera and the Commedia dell'Arte, as received opinion about the two modes ('refined' *vs* 'streetwise', 'rarefied' *vs* 'freewheeling', 'elitist' *vs* 'demotic') might assume. Rather, it is their closeness in some areas, which might suggest closeness in others too. There was certainly physical closeness on occasion. Opera from 1598 to 1608—for the following three decades as well—almost always owed its existence to some princely celebration sponsored by a duke or cardinal, or to the initiative of some private 'academy' of court-linked gentlemen. And Commedia too, though less tied to the court and more able to take to the road when it wished, often relied on the patronage of powerful aristocrats: the Mantuan Gonzaga, the Medici of Florence, the Este of Ferrara and so on. So there was a rubbing of shoulders in the corridors of power. Beyond that, it seems that composers and Commedia-troupers tended to like what each other did. Giovan Battista Andreini himself was probably not alone among the actors in his admiration for Marco da Gagliano's *Dafne* and Monteverdi's *Arianna* and *Orfeo*. On the composers' side, that towering mid-sixteenth-century figure Orlandus Lassus had taken the role of Pantalone in an amateur Commedia-style show at his patron Duke Wilhelm V's castle in 1568, later including a madrigalised dialogue between the tetchy Magnifico and a drunken Zanni in his 1581 collection of *Villanelle*. And around the end of the century the madrigal-books of such Venetian *petits maîtres* as Giovanni Croce, Orazio Vecchi and Adriano Banchieri featured vivid musical snapshots of Commedia in performance: one-off settings of comic soliloquies in Croce's *Triaca Musicale* (*The Musical Antidote*, 1595), sequences of sung monologues, dialogues, serenades and dances in Vecchi's *L'Amfiparnaso* (*The Twin-Peaked Parnassus*, 1597) and in Banchieri's double bill celebrating aged folly and youthful prudence: *La Pazzia Senile* (1598) and *La Prudenza Giovenile* (1607).

This rapport was the easier in that both opera and the Commedia dell'Arte were forms of professional music-theatre. Opera of course was all-sung, and although Commedia was mainly spoken, music was often called on to add point, spice and variety, so that it was an asset in a member of one of the more up-market troupes if he or she was able to sing and/or dance and/or play an instrument as well as memorise scripts, develop a character 'line' and improvise verbally and physically. Thus, when the Gelosi troupe staged Cornelio Frangipani's allegorical piece *Tragedia* in Venice in 1574, the author recalled that 'all the performers sang [Claudio Merulo's music] in the softest harmonies, sometimes singing alone, sometimes together; and at the end, the chorus of Mercury was of instrumentalists, who had the most various instruments that were ever played.' (MacNeil 2003: 12, cf. 15–31) It has even been suggested that Commedia's habit of sprinkling spoken plays with little songs was a factor behind the addition—in Monteverdi's *Orfeo* for instance—of catchy strophic canzonettas to the earnest, declamatory mode of recitative-writing that was the staple of the tirades and dialogues in the earliest operas: an addition that marked the beginning of the later, all-conquering operatic aria. As for professionalism, the groups of vocal and instrumental musicians who performed those early *Ariannas*, *Orfeos*, *Euridices* and *Dafnes* were salaried or fee'd masters of their various arts, as were the members of the Commedia troupes that had been criss-crossing Italy since the mid-sixteenth century. And it was a common professionalism that led to a common breakthrough: to their both employing women in leading roles. The Commedia dell'Arte had pioneered the idea of the actress as star performer from the 1560s, which led to tributes like Tommaso Garzoni's in 1585 to the innamorata Vittoria Piisimi: 'that divine Vittoria who creates metamorphoses of herself on the stage, [...] that sweet siren whose melodious enchantments catch the soul of her admiring spectators, [...] the epitome of her profession'. (Nicholson 2013: 376) Piisimi's colleague-cum-rival the great Isabella Andreini of the Gelosi troupe carried on the tradition; so it was apt that it should have been a daughter-in-law of hers, Florinda-Virginia, who was loaned by the Fideli in that emergency in 1608 to create the abandoned and rescued Ariadne and so to become the first *prima donna* in opera.

And the links did not end there. Opera and Commedia occasionally had plot-materials in common. Commedia's principal alternatives to the broad or subtle comedies we tend to associate with it were pastoral plays that stemmed from the same world as those celebrated late-Renaissance Arcadian evocations: Torquato Tasso's *Aminta*, which the Gelosi troupe themselves premièred at Ferrara in 1573, and Battista Guarini's *Pastor Fido*, premièred at Duke Vincenzo's Mantua in 1598. Opera's ground-breaking librettist Rinuccini was something of a disciple of Tasso and Guarini too, so that nymphs and shepherds (Naxos fisherfolk in the case of *Arianna*) mingle with mythical figures in quite a large proportion of the operas of the form's first thirty years. As for comedy itself, in time comical scenes began to make a modest appearance in opera. Though Mantuan and Florentine opera-folk in the 1600s were not much taken with such things, bizarre events and comic characters—servants especially—appear in Roman opera at the Barberini court from the 1620s on. In at least one Roman piece, *L'Egisto* or *Chi Soffre Speri* (*Sufferers May Hope*), a 'Commedia in Musica' to a text by the innovative Giulio Rospigliosi set by Virgilio Mazzocchi and Marco Marazzoli, the hero's perpetually hungry servants, comes straight from the Commedia in the persons (and strong regional dialects) of a Neapolitan Coviello and a Bergamask Zanni. In the show's revival two years after its 1637 première, the two are even sent on a shopping expedition to a bustling fair:

the spectacular and musically complex 'Fiera di Farfa', which had decor by the great Gian Lorenzo Bernini. (Murata 1981: 32–4 and 258–88; Hammond 1994: 226–7 and 235–9) This letting-loose of Commedia characters on elaborate and ambitious scenes was also happening in courtly theatres on the other side of the Alps. Witness the troupe of six Burratines and six Pantaloons who leap from the body of a 'she-monster' to dance in a high-fantastical episode of Ben Jonson's masque before King James *The Vision of Delight* in 1617, and the Air, Chaconne and Rejouissance danced by a Harlequin and two each of Trivelins and Scaramouches in the Italian episode of the 'Ballet des Nations' that ends Molière and Jean-Baptiste Lully's comedy-ballet of 1670, *Le Bourgeois Gentilhomme*. Molière goes one further in the first *intermède* of his collaboration with Marc-Antoine Charpentier on *Le Malade Imaginaire* (*The Hypochondriac*) in 1673: a scene of poor Polichinelle trying to serenade his mistress but being interrupted, first by a band of stroppy violinists and then by a troupe of archers who tweak his nose repeatedly, beat him black and blue, and relieve him of his purse. Like the 'Fiera di Farfa', this is total music-theatre seventeenth-century style, blending (in Molière's case) choral song, speech, instrumental music, *mélodrame*, knockabout and dance.

It was around the time of *Chi Soffre Speri* that the Commedia dell'Arte had a further gift for its young operatic cousin, a crucial one as it turned out. Until then, as we have seen, opera had largely been a matter of one-off creations for a few princely courts; but its increasing spread over Italy and its concern to make a space for itself in the Veneto (the rich republican city of Venice and the lands under its control) raised two questions: could it become more mobile, and could it cut itself off, at least in part, from court connections? Well yes, it could; and it was Commedia that provided the model of the self-sufficient troupe which might tour from city to city or establish itself in one of the commercially run Venetian theatres, tangling there with the new breed of impresarios. Those playhouses with their rentable boxes had first been set up in the 1580s as *stanze delle commedie*, only to be taken down again quite soon afterwards but re-established twenty years later as a permanent feature of the city. (Bianconi and Pestelli 1998: 7–10, 14–17, etc.) Now, in the later 1630s and 1640s, those *stanze* became homes for opera too.

Short comic scenes of one sort and another appear in the most earnest Venetian operas of the mid-seventeenth century and beyond: here a cowardly servant, there a streetwise old nurse—probably played *en travesti*, as Commedia's Franceschina sometimes was (Pirrotta 1984: 355–6). A Commedia trouper visiting one of the city's opera houses would have felt quite at home with the below-stairs life it portrayed, also with the occasional mad (or mock-mad) scene that hinted at a Commedia ancestry and with some of the operas' plot-lines, reminiscent as they could be of Commedia scenarios. Similarly, a member of a Venice-based opera company visiting a show *dell'arte* would have relished its actors occasionally bursting into simple yet telling song. But as the eighteenth century drew closer, arias at the opera house became more complex and virtuosic, and librettos more uniformly high-toned and straight-laced. *Opera seria*, with its penchant for very soberly presented ancient pseudo-history, was becoming all the rage, and *it* had no room for comedy, least of all the Commedia dell'Arte's kind. One of Commedia's responses was to send *opera seria* up rotten in a series of travesties. This, for example, from the cast-list of a cod libretto *circa* 1720: 'NERO: Signor Pantalone de' Bisognosi of Venice, Book-Keeper to the Most Noble Rialto Bridge' (Weiss 1984: 213), which is reminiscent of the burlesque shows put on in Paris in the late seventeenth and early eighteenth centuries by the Théâtre Italien there—*Arlequin Phaëton, Arlequin Persée, Arlequin Atys*—that pulled the rug from under the so-serious French operatic spectacles of Lully and his librettist Philippe Quinault.

In fact, it is not quite accurate to say that *opera seria* provided no space for comedy, for there were the inviting spaces between the acts of its standard three-act structure; and before long these two interval-gaps found themselves playing host to pairs of small-cast comic *intermezzi* (two-handers often) that constituted miniature operas in their own right. Their plot-material more often than not called on a mix of direct social observation and pickings from the rich fruit-salad of traditional comic motifs left by the sixteenth and seventeenth centuries—Commedia motifs among them. Sometimes the title would make the latter connection clear, as with two *intermezzi* from 1728 and 1739 to scores by Johann Adolf Hasse: *Pantaleone and Carlotta Disguised as a German* and *Captain Galoppo and the Servant-Girl Merlina supposed a Widow*. At other times, it would not take more than a few minutes' attention to a piece for the link to become obvious. For instance, the most famous *intermezzo* of all, Giovanni Battista Pergolesi's *La Serva Padrona* (*The Maid-Mistress*) of 1733, to a text by Gennaro Federico—crafty maidservant manipulates moneyed older master into marriage with the help of another servant playing a dumb but dangerous-seeming soldier-boy—is pure Columbina-Pantalone-Zanni in its character-typing.

The related but much more extended *opera buffa* that developed as the eighteenth century went on might use this sort of material too, though in time it could also call on the very personally Commedia-inflected plays of Carlo Goldoni and Pierre de Beaumarchais: notably Beaumarchais' *Barbier de Séville* and *Mariage de Figaro*. (There were also Carlo Gozzi's fantastical, folksy Commedia pieces, but they had to wait till the twentieth century to be discovered by opera.) Beaumarchais' *Mariage* was, of course, the source for Lorenzo da Ponte's libretto to Mozart's *Nozze di Figaro*, and it is striking how the Figaro of *Mariage/Nozze*, from one angle an up-to-date, self-made Enlightenment man of energetic enterprise and radical social attitude, is, from another, the heir to the age-old tribe of bright, inventive Zanni. At least one of the cast-members at the première of *Le Nozze*, Michael Kelly, was determined to do justice to the Commedia connections of another of its characters, the Tartaglia-like stuttering lawyer Don Curzio. Mozart (who himself enjoyed dressing up in his father's Harlequin costume and once wrote a brief dance-pantomime to a Commedia scenario) had wanted Kelly to stutter during his recitatives in *Nozze* but not while singing in the big Act III Sextet. Kelly, though, was determined to be a consistent yet musically sensitive stutterer all the way through, and at curtain-down on the opening night Mozart allowed that he had pulled this off admirably. (Kelly 1975: 132; Abert 2007: 724–5)

The arrival of Revolution and Romanticism meant that opera and Commedia moved further and further apart—as a rule anyway, though it was a rule broken by that brilliant theatrical throwback, Rossini's *Barbiere di Siviglia*, composed as late as 1816. *Barbiere* aside though, the two forms kept their distance through the nineteenth century: a century which saw the Commedia's world as it was mirrored in the other arts sentimentalised nostalgically or internalised nightmarishly. Think of Harlequin,

Columbine, Pierrot and the others as they appear in Robert Schumann's pianoforte sequence *Carnaval*, Paul Verlaine's cycle of lyrics *Fêtes Galantes*, Jules Laforgue's Pierrot poems, the *Pierrot Lunaire* of Albert Giraud (along with the neurasthenic *mélodrame* Arnold Schoenberg derived from it) and the graphic work of Aubrey Beardsley, not forgetting the paintings of Pablo Picasso's early 'blue' and 'rose' periods. It was as this phase was coming to an end that Commedia linked up with opera again. The reunion was heralded by Ruggiero Leoncavallo's *Pagliacci* of 1892 and Pietro Mascagni's *Le Maschere* of 1901, both of which allude in play-within-play mode to the nineteenth-century Commedia tradition, capitalising on its charm (the Harlequinade in *Pagliacci*) and its vivacity (the old Masks updated in *Le Maschere*). Then followed operas with scores by Giacomo Puccini, Ferrucio Busoni and Richard Strauss which evoked Commedia as something more positive, more ebullient, more brightly coloured than the nineteenth century had thought—something more 'realistic' too.

This comes over in a cosy way in the version of Gozzi's Commedia-goes-East fantasy *Turandot* (1762) that Puccini set in the 1920s. In it Gozzi's court functionaries Pantalone, Tartaglia and Truffaldino become the more Pekinese Ping, Pang and Pong: the representatives of 'good sense', as the composer put it, in a dangerous operatic world. (Green and Swan 1993: 218, cf. 216–27) Busoni too wrote an operatic *Turandot*: one rather closer to Gozzi, with the three Masks keeping their original names and harbouring an understandable nostalgia for Venice. Beyond that, he was involved as librettist-composer in the 1910s with two complementary operas: *Doktor Faust*—Teutonic, tragi-comic, metaphysical, visionary—and Faust's antitype, *Arlecchino*, a bright, astringent, quite unsentimental Italianate comedy calling on several traditional Commedia character-types in order to show us 'Things As They Are'. (Jacobs 1993: 235–9) In the same decade, Richard Strauss collaborated with the poet Hugo von Hofmannsthal on a project which took ideas like these further. Their five-year partnership on this was a complex one, resulting in two distinct though overlapping works. We might look at the second of these, a through-sung opera premièred in 1916. Its title: *Ariadne auf Naxos*.

The scene is a grand house in Vienna in the eighteenth century. At first we are backstage of a small private theatre; later we see a show on the stage itself. While the Master of the House wines and dines his guests nearby, last-minute preparations are underway behind the scenes for an *opera seria* to be given after dinner: an Ariadne opera, presenting first the princess's lonely isolation after Theseus's departure and then the arrival of the youthful Bacchus whom she will mistake for Hermes, the spirit-guide she expects to conduct her to the underworld and to death. After the opera there is to be a firework display; and word has just come from the Master of the House that, as an intermezzo between the two, there will be a brief Harlequinade from a Commedia dell'Arte troupe: a cheery piece about inconstancy in love presented by Scaramouche, Truffaldino, Brighella, Harlekin and the soubrette Zerbinetta (a name Hofmannsthal borrowed from Molière's Italianate piece about Scapino's tricks, *Les Fourberies de Scapin*). The troupe's arrival backstage is the cue for confusion and perplexity, coupled with indignation and heartache on the part of the opera's earnest composer (whom Strauss saw as a teenage Mozart). More perplexity erupts when further word arrives that, to speed things up before the fireworks, *Zerbinetta and Her Lovers* and *Ariadne* must be performed *gleichzeitig*, simultaneously, so populating Naxos not only with a Cretan princess, her Echo, a Naiad and a Dryad but with five jaunty comedians as well.

And so it comes about in the short opera-within-an-opera which follows. *Seria* scenes and scenes *dell'arte* alternate. Ariadne laments at the mouth of her cave. The male Masks express a limited, ineffectual sympathy with her at a distance, but it takes the bold and brilliant improviser Zerbinetta to leap the barrier between the two plots and confront Ariadne directly in a virtuoso show-stopping aria, 'Grossmächtige Prinzessin'. In this she sympathises with the princess, the more profoundly since—or so she assures us—she too has had her Naxos moments. For her, however, they are passing episodes. After all, there are other men out there: a new god comes along; she surrenders without a word—and Ariadne should too. The princess cannot bear such talk and retreats into her cave. Zerbinetta returns to the *buffo* plot, flirting with three of the Masks and then flitting with Harlekin just as the boat of the young Bacchus comes into view. Assuming him to be her Hermes, Ariadne reappears, and the two mythical figures have a grand scene of mutual incomprehension (or is it transformative recognition?), fascination and growing love. As they withdraw together, Zerbinetta steps back on stage for a confidential final word with the audience. You see? A new god comes along; the lady surrenders. QED.

Among twentieth-century operas, only Harrison Birtwistle and Stephen Pruslin's *Punch and Judy* of 1968 draws as vividly on Commedia dell'Arte's symbolism as does *Ariadne auf Naxos*—and Mr and Mrs Punch of course are not 100 per cent Commedia figures. (The adaptations of Gozzi with scores by Sergei Prokovief and Hans Werner Henze, *The Love of Three Oranges* and *Il Re Cervo* [*King Stag*], both downplay the Commedia elements in their originals.) And symbolism is now very much the operative word, for what the operas of Puccini, Busoni and Strauss latch onto, beyond Commedia's attractively vivid theatricality, is what the mode and its performers have by 1910 come to symbolise: an approach to life—Nietzsche might have called it a Mediterraneanised approach—which encourages a bright, bold, accepting, unblinkered, no-nonsense, yea-saying view of things, as opposed to a mystical or religious or subjective or sentimental or tragic view.

It is a symbol that could strike different people in different ways. It is far from certain, for instance, that Hofmannsthal and Strauss understood precisely the same thing by it when collaborating on *Ariadne*. At the end of the opera is the Commedia world rejected as trivial, as Hofmannsthal seems to have believed, or is it held in a kind of dialectical synthesis with the *seria* world, as Strauss's setting of Zerbinetta's last words seems to suggest? (Daviau and Buelow 1975:148–54, etc.) What *is* certain is that a Commedia trouper who found herself on that Greek island three centuries before Zerbinetta—Virginia Andreini, the Florinda of the Fideli company—would have been amazed at the twentieth century soubrette's presuming to critique the heroine's tragic-idealistic mood. Not that Florinda-Virginia would necessarily have been shocked by Zerbinetta's philosophy. After all, 'accept the ardour of such ardent men as come your way' is advice quite as libertine as Zerbinetta's, and that is the moral of *Il Ballo delle Ingrate*, the dramatic ballet with song which was Rinuccini and Monteverdi's other contribution to those Gonzaga celebrations: a piece in which Florinda-Virginia again took a leading role, this time as a lady condemned to eternal subterranean darkness for her prudishness on earth who implores her sisters in the audience to learn to yield to their men. ('*Apprendete pietà, donne e donzelle!*') Nor would Florinda-Virginia necessarily have been baffled by Hofmannsthal's games with theatricality, metatheatre and the blending of genres. She may well have discussed similar notions at the breakfast table with her husband Giovan Battista, who, as several of his plays show, was very interested in such things. (Molinari 1998: 147–50) Rather it is that, as a *prima donna* with particular professional skills, she would have held that the new theatrical mode of opera, much admired by her husband, was worthy of her straightforward and serious assistance. It was not her job to use it to advertise a stance of her own, to embody an antithetical force in a dialectic, or to present the Commedia world she came from as symbolic of a particular philosophy.

Such ideas were for the future: a future which, as it happened, showed very early signs of arriving just nine years after *L'Arianna*. In 1617, Ben Jonson has the Spirit of Delight at the beginning of his masque *The Vision of Delight* sing in '*stile recitativo*' of fantastic pleasures in the offing; and what does Delight summon up to typify them? Those six Burratines and six Pantaloons. That way symbolism lay.

References

Abert, Hermann (2007) *W. A. Mozart*, Stewart Spencer (tr.), New Haven: Yale University Press.

Bianconi, Lorenzo and Georgio Pestelli (1998) *Opera Production and Its Resources* (Part 2, Vol. 4 of *The History of Italian Opera*), Lydia Cochrane (tr.), Chicago, US: University of Chicago Press.

Daviau, Donald and George Buelow (1975) *The Ariadne auf Naxos of Hugo von Hofmannsthal and Richard Strauss*. Chapel Hill, US: University of North Carolina Press.

Fabbri, Paolo (1994) *Monteverdi*, Tim Carter (tr.), Cambridge, UK: Cambridge University Press.

Green, Martin and John Swan (1993) *The Triumph of Pierrot: The Commedia dell' Arte and the Modern Imagination*. University Park, US: Pennsylvania State University Press.

Hammond, Frederick (1994) *Music and Spectacle in Baroque Rome: Barberini Patronage under Urban VIII*. New Haven, US: Yale University Press.

Jacobs, Gabriel (1993), "The *Commedia dell'Arte* in Early Twentieth-Century Music: Schoenberg, Stravinsky, Busoni and Les Six", pp. 227–46 of D. J. George and C. J. Gossip, eds, *Studies in the Commedia dell'Arte*. Cardiff, UK: University of Wales Press.

Kelly, Michael (1975) *Reminiscences*, ed. Roger Fiske. London: Oxford University Press.

MacNeil, Anne (2003) *Music and Women of the Commedia dell'Arte in the Late Sixteenth Century*. Oxford, UK: Oxford University Press.

Molinari, Cesare (1998), "Actor-Authors of the Commedia dell'Arte". *Theatre Research International*, 22/2, 142–51.

Murata, Margaret (1981) *Operas for the Papal Court 1631–1668*. Ann Arbor, US: UMI Research Press.

Nicholson, Eric (2013) "Sing Again, Sirena: Translating the Theatrical *Virtuosa* from Venice to London", pp. 373–89 of Margaret Shewring, ed., *Waterborne Pageants and Festivities in the Renaissance*. Farnham, UK: Ashgate.

Pirrotta, Nino (1984) *Music and Culture in Italy from the Middle Ages to the Baroque*. Cambridge, Mass., US: Harvard University Press.

Weiss, Piero (1984) "Venetian Commedia dell'Arte 'Operas' in the Age of Vivaldi". *Musical Quarterly*, 70, 195–217.

29

CLASSICAL BALLET AND THE COMMEDIA DELL'ARTE

Influences

Barry Grantham

The Academie and the Italian Players

The scene is Paris in the last decade of the seventeenth century. Louis XIV no longer dances himself, but still keeps an eye on the Académie Royale de la Danse that he founded in 1661, insisting that his courtiers are proficient in the social requirements of the dance. He also keeps an eye on his Italian Players who give performances three times a week at the Hôtel de Bourgogne. They are at the very apogee of their popularity, and it might be argued in the 'Golden Age' of the long history of the Commedia dell'Arte.

Caterina Biancolelli, the Colombina of the day, is at the height of her powers, and is so popular that the improvised plays include her role in the title – *Colombina, Advocate For and Against* and *Colombina, a Woman's Revenge*. A similar honour is accorded to the Arlecchino of Evaristo Gherardi: *Arlecchino, Emperor of the Moon* and *Arlecchino, Doge of England, w*ho in spite of being lowest in the status pecking order, brought most bums on seats. Or was that Tiberio Fiorilli, who in his adoption of Scaramouche, dispensed with the mask and appeared '*en farine*'? He was acknowledged as the finest actor of all France – to say nothing of his dancing and acrobatics. But for the Italians the axe was about to fall. Unwisely, in 1697 they advertised a piece called '*The False Prude*'. The King's Mistress, Madame de Maintenon, thinking she was about to be lampooned, put down her pretty little foot and crushed the Italian Players. It was seventeen years before they were permitted to perform again in Paris. But they were not to be forgotten.

Taking advantage of Commedia's popularity, other performers, French as well as Italian, took on the Masks, and performed in the less exalted venues of the fairs and boulevards. In these venues, as dialogue was prohibited, the performances became limited to dance and dumb-show, and a new tradition of mime/dancers replaced the speaking Masks of the true Commedia dell'Arte, though it could not yet be identified as ballet as we understand it.

A Chacoon and the new curious school

Around 1700 Monsieur Feuillet published his *Chorégraphie,* which introduced the Feuillet/Beauchamps system of dance notation and over the next few years a great many dances, both for the ballroom and for the stage were offered to the public. The greater part of these were in the '*Noble*' mode – elegant with erect stance, graceful arm movements, and above all, feet turned out, but among those for the stage, were a few in eccentric or what was known as the *Grotesque* manner – the word derived from the recently discovered paintings in the grottoes of Pompeii. Here, the intention was comic and the execution eccentric and misbalanced, frequently using turned in positions of feet and knees. Among them is: 'A Chacoon for a Harlequin – with all the Postures, attitudes, motions of the Head and Arms and other gestures proper to this character. – Composed, Writ in characters and engraved by F Le Roussau, Dancing master London 1730.' (Beaumont: 1926) In addition to the Feuillet notation, we are given neat little drawings of Harlequin in characteristic poses, showing us an early example of a Commedia Mask making the transition to the dance stage.

From a few years earlier we have an even more interesting publication: *The New and Curious School of Theatrical Dancing* by a Venetian ballet master called Gregorio Lambranzi, originally published in Nuremberg in 1716 (Lambranzi 1928). The document was found, by the ballet critic and writer Cyril W. Beaumont, in 1926 when researching music in the British Museum. Lambranzi declines to use the Feuillet notation, and instead offers a series of engravings depicting the various curious dances, heading each with an example of the music and adding a few suggestions for suitable steps, but leaving it to the performer or ballet master to create his own choreography. Among the plates are examples devoted to Arlecchino, Scaramouche, Mezzetino, Scapino, Pantalone and The Doctor. They are masked, dressed traditionally and appear before appropriate stage settings. The problem of the lack of female characters is solved by giving each Mask a partner dressed in a female version of traditional costume, who is merely referred to as his 'wife': the only one to be given a name is Pantalone's partner, Pandora. Most interesting are a number of plates devoted to Scaramouche, dressed in the Tiberio Fiorilli manner and certainly inspired by the great comedian, and showing several of his known steps and sequences.

Weaver and Noverre

Now we should introduce two celebrated dancing masters, John Weaver, (1673–1760) an Englishman, and Jean-Georges Noverre, (1727–1810) a Frenchman. David Garrick, who brought the latter to London, was at pains to assure his English audiences, in view of the hostilities between the two countries, that

> The first entertainment that appeared on the English stage, where the representation and story was carried on by Dancing, Action and Motion only, performed in Grotesque Characters, after the manner of the Modern Italians, such as Harlequin, Scaramouche, &c, and was called The Tavern Bilkers. Composed by Mr Weaver, and first performed in Drury Lane Theatre, 1702.
>
> (Beaumont: 1926)

If his claim is correct (there is some doubt) we have not only the first 'ballet' but one on a Commedia dell'Arte theme. However, Noverre is more generally accepted as the creator of what we would understand as 'ballet'; *'ballet d'action'* as he called it. It should be noted that the word 'ballet', had been used since 1550, for performances also containing song and declamation, but these might equally be classified as masque, pantomime, burlesque or opera. Had Noverre been more sympathetic to Harlequin and his fellows (in over a hundred works he created, not one suggests a Commedia connection), Commedia might have played a more significant part in subsequent productions.

Harlequin in England

As the eighteenth century proceeded both Commedia dell'Arte and ballet were finding their feet (sorry!). In Paris dancers like Mlles. Camargo, Taglioni and Sallé (whose uncle had been Francisque Moylin, a renowned Harlequin) were busy transforming the Baroque technique into a ballet one. From the mid-sixteenth century the Italian Players had been trying to gain a foothold in England with little success, but it seems that by around 1730 the British public could not get enough of Harlequin (lately anglicized) and a limited number of his colleagues. They appeared in often-lavish productions, usually described as pantomimes, but what did the word mean? One must, of course, free oneself from any similarity to the British pantomimes of recent years. In the 1700s, it indicated a classical (Roman/Greek) story told largely in mime, dance, and spectacular stage effects, remembering that in London only the two patent theatres, Drury Lane and Covent Garden, were allowed to use dialogue. Most famous of these were those presented at the Lincoln's Inn Fields Theatre by John Rich (1692–1761). Rich, under the pseudonym Lunn, appeared as Harlequin to great acclaim in his own productions and as mime, acrobat and skilled dancer he would have been influential in the development of the dancing Harlequin of later pantomimes and ballets. So you may ask how on earth Harlequin and Co. fit into a Roman or Greek spectacular: they did not: the story in progress was interrupted at one or more points for a completely unconnected Commedia scene, usually in a rural setting. Sometimes the Commedia troupe would wander onto a classical set, depicting, for example, a ruined temple in a sylvan forest, just vacated by nymphs and fawns. This was the cue for Harlequin to use his bat, now invested with magical powers, to initiate a transformation scene; temples would be turned into cottages, statues into wheelbarrows, grottoes into haystacks and colonnades into barns, conveniently presenting a bucolic scene for the antics of Harlequin in pursuit of the village maid Columbine. This remained popular until early in the next century when the theme gradually changed from the classical to folk and fairy tales with titles like *Mother Goose, Tom Thumb, Babes in the Wood*, which became suitable for children and also established the theatrical Christmas season. At the end of the Victorian period the Commedia interlude was placed at the end of the pantomime proper, and firmly established as the Harlequinade with its dancing Harlequin, Columbine, Pantaloon and Clown.

The Tivoli

A legacy of the earlier pantomime/ballets may still be seen on the stage of the pretty Peacock Theatre at the Tivoli Gardens, Copenhagen. The theatre designed by Vilhelm Dahlerup was opened in 1874, and the scenarios of the pantomimes are from about that date. An example concerns Cassander (Pantaloon), an old man living alone with his beautiful daughter Columbine, and attended by a single servant, Pierrot. The bane of the old man's life is Harlequin; a charming scoundrel with little money to his name but who is deeply in love with Columbine and often well connected to a friendly sorcerer or fairy. The production at the Tivoli is about fifty per cent mime and fifty per cent dancing and all the cast are trained in ballet. The comedy element raises smiles rather than laughs and is geared towards an audience of children.

Fokine's 'Carnaval'

In the early nineteenth century Paris the sun-loving characters of the Italian cities were right out of favour. The Romantic Age had dawned and nothing suited the taste of the town more than a good haunting; there must be ruined castle, mist shrouded graveyards, haunted lakes, mad maidens, and any number of spectres. Devils were popular, to say nothing of *Ondines*, *Wilis* and *Sylphides*. Paris, then the centre of the ballet world, looked to Germany and the British Isles, especially Scotland, for themes. The surviving *Giselle*, *Sylphides* and *Swan Lake* show the persistence of the genre. However, by the end of the nineteenth century the bespangled dancing Harlequin and his Columbine were still common currency throughout the western world; for example, appearing among the clockwork toys in the Petipa-Ivanov *Casse Noisette* (1892), and would have been familiar to the young choreographer Michael Fokine.

This brings us to the most familiar of all Commedia dell'Arte inspired ballets. After a charity performance in Saint Petersburg, *Le Carnaval* was first given in Diaghilev's second Paris season of 1910. The cast included four Commedia characters: Harlequin, Columbine, Pantalon (sic) and Pierrot. As far as the scenario, representing a ball of circa 1830, it would seem that the cast are guests in 'fancy costume'. But Fokine, who set the ballet to a piano suite by Schumann, gives them traditional Commedia moves and attributes. Cleverly, the ballet takes place, not in the ballroom as one might expect, but in an anti-chamber, through which the characters pass as they go to and from the main attraction. Other characters include Papillon – a social butterfly – whom the infatuated Pierrot tries to catch in his hat and then there are Eusebius and Florestan, not as one might have thought, *innamorati*, but characters showing the two warring sides of Schumann's own often fevered imagination. Cyril Beaumont saw both the original production, and praises Adolph Bolm as Pierrot and Nijinsky as a somewhat malevolent Harlequin, and the revival with Idzikowski (London 1918) more as a boyish tease.

Massine and 'Pulicinella'

As we see, the ballet borrowings from the Commedia dell'Arte tended to select the debased nineteenth century Harlequinades as a source and I know of only one attempt to really come to grips with the vivid and powerful Masks of seventeenth century Italy. Leonide Massine had now replaced Fokine as company choreographer. In 1919 he was on holiday with Diaghilev (having also taken Nijinsky's place as the impresario's lover) when they conceived the idea of using an actual Commedia scenario for a ballet. Massine was sifting through the unpublished scenarios in the Naples Collection and selected one entitled *Quattro Policinelli Simili* (why there were 'four' is not at all clear, but it may be noted that Pulicinella has a tendency to clone, i.e. the Tiepolo drawings). Massine seems to have studied the material extensively and as Beaumont tells us, had a good grasp of the subject. He was entrusted with writing the scenario for the ballet. Beaumont gives a blow-by-blow account in his *Complete Book of Ballets* (1937). The account does not read particularly brilliantly, but his previous works, particularly *La Boutique Fantasque* and *Le Tricorne* showed that he was the right choreographer to take on the task. The cast list is enlightening for both Commedia and ballet buffs. The cast is ideal, with Massine the greatest character dancer of the time, as Pulcinella; the beautiful and witty prima ballerina Karsavina as his partner, Pimpinella; Idzikowski and Zverev as the rather more comic than traditional innamorati; Tchernicheva and Nemchinova as the *innamorate* (again nearer to *servetti*, with a penchant for emptying slop basins over their suitors heads); and we have the great Italian ballet master, Enrico Cecchetti (who in his youth was the first 'Bluebird'), as Il Dottore.

In the meantime, Diaghilev had been searching for suitable music, and had found some compositions, thought to be by Pergolesi, in the British Museum, which he strung together and handed to Stravinsky to arrange for a large orchestra. What did Stravinsky come up with? He interpreted the instructions somewhat liberally and created a piece for three singers and a small chamber orchestra. Difficulties were experienced as Massine was in Monte Carlo and Stravinsky elsewhere. Stravinsky would send single rather inadequate piano transcriptions for Massine to work from, and these were to sound little like the final version. There was also trouble with Picasso: Massine did not like Picasso's design for the set. It showed an elaborate false proscenium framing a simple screen-like structure representing, in minimalist fashion, the traditional Commedia houses. Diaghilev did not like it either; a rather undignified scene is recorded in which Massine in *Tricorn* mode danced a furious *Zapateado* on the offending production. In the end the false proscenium was rejected and a practical set developed by the great scene painter Vladimir Polunin from the inner drawing. This had to include practical doors and upper windows from which the innamorate were to empty slops on their gallants below. Picasso's original drawing was used to decorate the programme cover and some of his powerful costumes designs remain. The ballet was first produced at the Paris Opera in May 1920. Alexandre Benois, one of Diaghilev's first supporters and designer of *Petrouchka,* was enchanted with the ballet: with Stravinsky's music and Picasso's designs, and he praises Massine's choreography as outstanding and marvellously executed by the dancers. Though well received at the time it has never established itself with the ballet public. Some years earlier, Massine had produced *Les Femmes de Bonne Humeur,* from a play by Goldoni.

'Commedia' dance in films

Ballet films as opposed to filmed ballet are rare enough and those related to Commedia almost non-existent. However, there is one example that is worth our attention. In 1954 Gene Kelly, brings us, at last, a Commedia theme told in dance terms. It is to be seen as the second feature in his well-intentioned, but failing *Invitation to the Dance*. The sequence is entitled 'Circus' and is set in a nineteenth century fairground. It features Igor Youskevitch as The Aerialist, Claire Sombert as The Dancer and Kelly as Pierrot. The curtain of a small booth draws back to reveal Kelly as a Jean-Louis Barrault look-a-like, soon to be abetted by Sombert as a sort of Columbine (carrying a Greek style theatre mask) and Youskevich as a long nosed, brightly clad lute-playing sort of Coviello. They then proceed to perform a pale imitation (though in glorious Technicolor) of a similar scene from '*Les Enfant du Paradis*'. The all-American macho Kelly is, alas, no Jean-Louis Barrault, and mercifully the booth curtain soon closes. The next sequence is much better. A group of unaccredited male dancers and acrobats, masked and colourfully dressed (though not recognizably as specific Commedia characters) dance and perform acrobatic feats. Kelly's choreography is splendid, the performers first-rate and the comic business amusing. While not accurately duplicating the Commedia dell'Arte past, they are true to the spirit of the genre and would have entertained the 1950s cinema audiences as their predecessors would have entertained the crowds in the Piazzas. Now to the main crux of the matter! Dancer Claire Sombert, now oddly dressed in a modern pink practice leotard, has only eyes for The Aerialist Youskevitch, now in black practice gear. They treat us to a series of classical *Pas de Deux* and solo variations, watched by the unrequited yearnings of Pierrot. Showtime! The Aerialist mounts onto the platform, high above the fairground. The crowds below cheer vociferously as he embarks onto the wire. As he performs the crowds gasp incredulously; The Dancer looks on nervously and adoringly; Pierrot looks at The Aerialist enviously and at The Dancer adoringly. Soon the entertainment is over. The crowds, apart from a few stragglers, disperse. So what will happen? Pierrot must try his luck up on the high-wire. Yes, he is going to fall onto a conveniently placed red cloak – symbolizing blood. And then he dies as the hands of the two lovers unite. So ends a brave attempt to bring Commedia dell'Arte and ballet together.

Les Enfants du Paradis

I think one must return *Les Enfants du Paradis* to the times of its production: 1943 in German occupied Paris, and see it as a fairly faithful attempt to recreate the Fonambules Theatre where the renowned Jean-Gaspard Deburau performed and the Paris Boulevards and not blame it, and certainly not the brilliant Jean-Louis Barrault, for the endless mime artists trapped in the Barrault/Marceau mould or the rash of one-eye weeping Pierrot dolls and figurines that proliferated over the years. Watching the film today, in spite of all the elegant skill, the set scenes may appear over sentimental and unlikely to have kept a rowdy Boulevard audience amused. They rate, certainly, not as dramatically interesting as the 'Parade' scene involving the stolen watch. It is interesting to see the renowned mime teacher Étienne Decroux as the Deburau Père.

Capriole D'Arlecchino and the Pas de Scaramouche

So the influence of the old Commedia dell'Arte has not been as fecund as one might have believed. Whereas, Spanish and Oriental movement, for example, has found its place in the *divertissement* of many a ballet, and has evolved its own particular balletic form, it is my opinion that there are no steps, sequences, positions of the limbs, head, or torso, originating or inspired by the Commedia dell'Arte and its Masks, that have become a standard part of classical repertoire or training. There are two particular moves that do have a connection, but it is as likely they developed in the other direction: from ballet (or at least dance) to Commedia. The first of these is the familiar Harlequin leap, the *Capriole d'Arlecchino* (goat leap) which as far as we can ascertain was performed by making a vertical leap into the air, while keeping the knees bent and crossing (and possibly re-crossing) the feet at the ankles. It would start and finish in third position *demi-plie*. This was modified, possibly by Fokine for *Le Carnaval*, into the balletic form, by bringing the toes of the feet together, forming a neat diamond space between the legs. The starting and finishing position of this leap is in first. It can also be performed *elancé* (travelling) like a *Cecchetti assemblé porter de côté* (a sideways leap, landing on both feet, usually in 3rd or 5th position). This movement is used by other characters, especially the Jester of the Soviet Ballet. The second is the *Pas de Scaramouche*, an eccentric step performed by Tiberio Fiorilli and his imitators (illustrated in the *New and Curious School*, Lambranzi 1928) The performer slides into a forward split and then pulls up onto the front leg. By repeating this on alternate legs he is able to cross the stage in a few moves. It requires considerable strength and is more for the acrobat than the dancer.

Debased characters

So we see that only three characters from the Commedia dell'Arte made any serious inroads into the classical ballet, and of these the Harlequin in ballet is derived only from the dancing Harlequin of the fairs and pantomimes, certainly not the earthy Zanni Arlecchino of the Italian improvised theatre; Columbine is only the vapid daughter of that wretch Pantaloon, not the witty, plot-saving *servetta* of many a name – Franceschina, Spinetta, Lycetta and, occasionally, Colombina of old scenarios; and Pierrot, is a late French implant to the canon of Masks. The balletic roles of both Harlequin and Columbine offer little to the artist in the way of character interpretation: all that is required is that they should be pleasing and technically proficient. And Pierrot – Ah, let us admit that, in spite of suffering at the hands of many a tyro he can, on occasion, become more than two dimensional. From the early nineteenth century performances in the Paris fairs, the mime dramas of Deburau showed that it was possible to transform a half-witted zanni to a creature of dark shadows, introversion and longing. In more recent times it is Glen Tetley's Pierrot Lunaire, largely performed on a sort of climbing-frame, to music by Arnold Schoenberg, which makes a glorious exception to the dearth of Commedia inspired ballets. The work brilliantly embodies the moonstruck Pierrot, but also delineates the comic potential of the role in his encounters with a black-clad Brighella, and a Columbine personifying 'woman' as innocent, mother, and vamp. The premier was staged in New York in 1962 with Glen Tetley taking the title role. There is a recording of Christopher Bruce in the part in the Rambert Archives.

While not taking a Commedia dell'Arte theme or featuring any of the stock Masks, there are a number of ballets that project character and employ traditional comedy techniques. These and several *lazzi*, inherited perhaps via the silent cinema, may owe something to the professional Commedia players of sixteenth and seventeenth centuries. Examples of this might be Frederick Ashton's *Fille Mal Guardi* and *Cinderella*.

Possibilities

That the classical ballet so rarely sought inspiration from its sister art, the Commedia dell'Arte is surprising, but it does mean that there are opportunities enough for the future: a family oriented ballet in the manner of *La Fille mal Guardi* or *Cinderella*? Or one based on the vibrant engravings of Jaques Callot, or the dream-world paintings of Watteau and Fragonard, or the earthy series of drawings by Domenico Tiepolo depicting the Life and Death of Pulchinella?

References

Beaumont, Cyril W. (1926) *The History of Harlequin*: London: C.W. Beaumont.
——(1937) *Complete Book of Ballets*: London: Putnam.
Feuillet (1700) *Chorégraphie*: Available online at http://publicdomainreview.org/collections/ collection-of-dances-in-choreography-notation-1700/ (accessed 21 August 2014).
Lambranzi, Gregorio (1928) *The New and Curious School of Theatrical Dancing*: London: C.W. Beaumont.

30

IMAGES OF THE COMMEDIA DELL'ARTE

M. A. Katritzky

Introduction

Images add a rich dimension to theatre historical studies, which have traditionally been dominated by the literary perspective. This is particularly true for the Commedia dell'Arte, whose patchy textual record reflects its reliance on brief scenarios rather than extant play-texts with fully-scripted dialogue. From its sixteenth-century beginnings, the Commedia dell'Arte's mixed-gender performances, distinctive costumes and gestures, and slick professional acrobatics, comedy and magic routines captured the attention of artists of every stripe. Their depictions range from reliable records of the appearance of staged events and actors, to imaginative evocations unrelated to any specific performance or performer.

The interpretation of Commedia dell'Arte images falls within the challenging field of theatre iconography. 'Challenging' because this study of the theatrical relevance of images perches precariously across modern disciplinary boundaries. Traditionally, theatre historians have viewed the visual record as historical documents, a repository of easily read evidence concerning the stage and its performers (Duchartre 1929; Nicoll 1963). Art historians, by contrast, have always regarded the stage as a potential source of subjects for artists, who can draw on it to create images not necessarily connected to actual stage practice (Leik 1996). This disciplinary frontier is central to an understanding of Commedia-related images, which are as profoundly shaped by iconographic conventions and cultural influences, as they are by the stage itself. Drawing from theatre studies and art history, theatre iconography recognizes that visual images are both aesthetic works of art in their own right, *and* historical documents which encode valuable evidence concerning past events (Hallar 1977; Hansen 1984; Katritzky 1987a and b; Katritzky 2006).

Commedia dell'Arte related images are more effectively interpreted in groups than in isolation. An awareness of the impact of visual precedents is integral to understanding any one specific depiction, and its relationship, if any, to the stage practice of its time. Even more than reflecting what they imagine or see on stage, their artists are influenced by other art. They look not only to their subject, but habitually also to the cultural discourse surrounding it, in conjunction with earlier art, to inspire them. Theatre iconographers bear in mind that such works reflect and inform ongoing borrowings and interchanges between performance practice and the visual arts, popular traditions and social attitudes of their time.

From the start, Commedia drew on and inspired a broad spectrum of other performing traditions, at every level from court festival to street mountebanks, eventually transcending the theatre to play key roles in music, dance, circus, literature and art. This mixed heritage is increasingly reflected in its iconography. Not just initially, but at every stage, the visual record suggests give and take between the distinctively costumed stock characters of the Commedia dell'Arte, and mystery and mummers' plays, scripted comic drama and popular farces, charlatan and other street and marketplace theatre, and court and carnival entertainments. Disentangling these various interrelated iconographic sources and influences in specific images can be challenging, inconclusive, even controversial. For example, grave doubts have been expressed concerning the authenticity of two tempera paintings I attributed to Ambrose I. Francken (Katritzky 1987a: 97–8). According to Leik 'the suspicion here is that we are dealing in both cases with nineteenth-century pictures, that may owe their origins to the initiative of a *Commedia dell'Arte* enthusiast, perhaps inspired by Maurice Sand's book of 1860' (1996: 157n388). Satisfactory resolution of such questions is often further impeded by the disappearance of the original images into private hands, leaving only low resolution scans for scholarly contemplation.

The early modern period

Depictions of Commedia-related performers, stock stage situations, roles and costumes in non-stage contexts (Figures 30.2–30.4, 30.7, 30.8, 30.10), or of charlatans or carnival masks, often dismissed as peripheral distractions in text-based considerations of the Commedia dell'Arte, are integral to its visual record. Correctly evaluated, the iconography has the potential for clarifying Commedia dell'Arte costumes, gestures and stage practice. This task, complicated by the Commedia's reliance on cross-dressing, is even more difficult with respect to actresses than actors. Men playing men dominated the Renaissance all-male stage, where many of their roles were distinguished by easily recognizable stage costumes. During the course of the sixteenth century, male Commedia dell'Arte stock roles rapidly developed stylized stage names, costumes, masks and other distinguishing characteristics that aided their visual identification, even outside obviously theatrical contexts. In contrast, early actresses honed their skills in arenas requiring less overtly theatrical costume, such as the marketplace, oral tradition and festivity. Images of female performers, whether playing the maid or young lover (Innamorata), suggest that, even in stage contexts, they habitually wore less stylized costumes than men (Figures 30.1–30.3, 30.5–30.8).

From the publications of Tomaso Garzoni and others, we know that the main contexts for Commedia-related costumes in late sixteenth-century Venice are carnival, and professional performances by acrobatic dancers, actors, charlatans, and *buffoni*. These last were comic performers who played solo, or banded together in predominantly male duos or troupes, to offer a repertoire relying heavily on music, mime, acrobatics and visual humour; all of them also important elements on the Commedia stage. This is entirely compatible with the now widely accepted view that the Italian professional stage was pioneered by such *buffoni*, and by itinerant charlatans using theatrical means to market medical or pseudo-medical products and services. The extent to which, as the sixteenth century progressed, not just actors, but also charlatans and *buffoni*, staged performances that fall within the definition of the Commedia dell'Arte, is less clear, although the visual record suggests a considerable overlap in stage practice and costume.

In the 1920s, Agne Beijer, then a curator at the National Museum, Stockholm, discovered a bound volume in the reserve collections containing sixteenth- and seventeenth-century prints of actors and performances, including a section of the scattered and largely lost Recueil Fossard collection. Recognizing them as a uniquely detailed visual record of the early decades of the Commedia dell'Arte, Beijer jointly published them in 1928 with Pierre-Louis Duchartre, whose introduction to the Commedia dell'Arte and its stock roles was first published in 1924. Despite his palpable historical unreliability, Duchartre's pioneering approach to visual material attracted a wide readership of artists, theatre practitioners and enthusiasts, as well as academic specialists, and over the next five years his book went into several editions and was translated into English. Later editions supplement its unprecedented wealth of rare Commedia dell'Arte related images with excellent – and easily accessible – illustrations of many of the Stockholm Recueil Fossard prints (Duchartre 1966: 315–38). Six Recueil Fossard woodcuts depict performances starring the Italian Harlequin Tristano Martinelli with the troupe of the renowned French actor Agnan Sarat, who contributed significantly to the development of the professional stage when he signed the contract allowing his touring troupe to become the first to act on the stage of the Hotel de Bourgogne, in Paris (Katritzky 2007: 194–201). A much larger series of Recueil Fossard woodcuts, depicting onstage Commedia dell'Arte performers, provides invaluable information on their staging, props and costumes (Figure 30.1; Hallar 1977: 33–46; Katritzky 2006: 107–20, 161–5).

As well as inspiring numerous derivative paintings, these Stockholm Recueil Fossard woodcuts, thought to have been created around 1585 by Netherlandish printmakers in Paris, shed significant light on other images. One such is the woodcut illustration to the *Divels Legend*, a polemical pamphlet printed in England in 1595 (Hallar 1977: 146). Long cited as proof that Elizabethans were familiar with images of Italian stock roles, its status is challenged by my discovery of an illustrated French edition of its companion pamphlet, also dated 1595, previously known only in an unillustrated English edition. The provenance of these two pamphlets' texts is French, and the appearance of the 'Pantaloun', 'Zanie' and 'Harlequin' they depict is stylistically similar to their counterparts in the large Recueil Fossard woodcut series (Figure 30.1). Thus, it appears that the two 'English' woodcuts were produced not in England, but in Paris (Katritzky 2006: plates 310a, 310b). By contrast, another anonymous undated series of nine Recueil Fossard prints are in fact the work of an Italian engraver. The whole impression I located in the British Museum indicates that they are nine scenes cut from one print of around the 1590s, by the printmaker Ambrogio Brambilla (Figure 30.2; Katritzky 1987b: 248–51; 2006: 114–17).

Figure 30.1 Pantalon and Zany serenade Donna Lucia, woodcut, 24 × 28 cm, *c.*1585. National museum, Stockholm (Recueil Fossard, f.13, NM2211/1904).

Figure 30.2 Ambrogio Brambilla, Che diavolo e' questo, signed in monogram in the plate, print, 39 × 48 cm, *c.*1590s. British Museum, London.

Outside the realms of popular prints and portraiture, the Italian creators of Europe's most visually distinctive form of theatre had little impact on the early modern visual arts of their own country. The Commedia did, however, inspire an important category of genre painting in early modern France and Flanders, whose significance was recognized by the French art-historian Charles Sterling in the 1940s. Later publications reproduce and discuss many more examples, by Flemish masters such as Jan Bruegel, Louis de Caulery, Ambrose I. Francken, Sebastian Vrancx, Lucas van Valckenborch, Marten de Vos and Lodewyk Toeput, by French masters, and by an outstanding Italian exception, the Veneto painter Leandro Bassano (Hallar 1977: 27–33; Katritzky 1987a; Katritzky 2006: 120–75; Leik 1996: 145–220).

The Commedia also provided a fertile source for frescoes and grotesque interior decoration in German-speaking Europe, notably those created for Prince Wilhelm of Bavaria (Figure 30.3). Wilhelm's 1568 Munich wedding festivities mark a significant watershed for the Commedia dell'Arte north of the Alps (Katritzky 2006: 44–83). Its masquerades featured stock Commedia costumes; professional Italian actors in the roles of Pantalone and Zanni (the master and his manservant) repeatedly performed short comic routines together, and at least once, on 8 March 1568, a full-length Commedia dell'Arte play was staged by male courtiers, including the renowned Netherlandish musician Orlando di Lasso. Wilhelm introduced the Italian fashion for Commedia dell'Arte performances at court weddings to northern Europe, as a prestigious badge of international cultural sophistication for elite patrons who could

Figure 30.3 Alessandro Paduano and Friedrich Sustris, near lifesize commedia dell'arte fresco (detail, Wall South 4), *c.*1579. Narrentreppe (Fools' Staircase), Burg Trausnitz, Landshut, Bavaria.

both understand and afford it. This fashion was resoundingly endorsed two years later, when court festivities celebrating the marriage contracts of the Habsburg princesses, Anna and Elisabeth of Austria, featured performances by two of the most successful early Commedia troupes, respectively led by Alberto Naseli and his wife Barbara Flaminia, and by Giovanni Tabarino and his wife Apollonia.

In 1575, bankruptcy forced Wilhelm to sack his Italian court players. Soon after, he commissioned two major fresco cycles commemorating them in the new Italian wing of his country seat, Castle Trausnitz in Landshut, Bavaria. As the Commedia dell'Arte's most substantial early modern iconographic record, the thirty-two walls of life-size frescoes of the so-called 'Fools' Staircase' (Figure 30.3; restored after the fire of 1961), and sixteen scenes on the ceiling frieze of Wilhelm's adjacent study (destroyed in this fire), represent an unprecedented visual record of sixteenth-century Commedia costumes and performance practice (Hallar 1977: 46–9; Leik 1996; Vianello 2005; Katritzky 2006: plates 19–23). The castle is now administered by the Bayerische Schlösserverwaltung, whose virtual tour of this six-storey cellar to attic staircase, closed to the public to protect its fragile condition, evokes something of its exhilarating feeling of being jostled by Commedia dell'Arte performers at every turn (www.burg-trausnitz.de/deutsch/virtuell/index.htm; accessed 31 October 2013).

Not until the mid-eighteenth-century was there another decorative scheme of comparable scale: in the ballroom of Český Krumlov Castle, in Bohemia (now the Czech Republic). Its vast walls are entirely painted with scenes by Josef Lederer, featuring actors and courtiers. They wear Commedia-inspired pantomime and masquerade costumes, some of the originals of which survive in the castle's collection of theatre props (Lawner 1998: 150–6; Chilton 2001: 34, 41–7, 52, 88, 102–3, 222–38). However, more modest painted iconographic cycles incorporating Commedia motifs soon followed the Fools' Staircase. Late sixteenth-century grotesque ceiling friezes painted on wood were commissioned for a Nürnberg patrician's house, and a castle in Graz. Important Italian equivalents include the grotesque friezes of late sixteenth-century fresco cycles discovered in the late 1990s, during the restoration of two Mantuan palaces. The audience looking down from the painted windows and balustrades above the stage of Sabbioneta's 1590 Teatro all'Antica includes a figure variously identified as Zanni, Pantalone or Magnifico. Grotesque frescoes (c.1563) of a Palladian villa at Poiana Maggiore, and of similar date at the Villa Moneta, at Belfiore near Verona include isolated small-scale Commedia dell'Arte figures. Good starting places for discussions and reproductions of such decorative schemes, and references to specialist literature on them, are the monographs of Angelika Leik (1996: 40, 88–90, 96–8, 103, 243–8) and Danielo Vianello (2005: plates 45–59).

Extensive frescoes in the Villa Il Pozzino, at Castello near Florence, include grotesques of 1619 with several scenes of professional acrobats. The villa was purchased by descendants of Antonfrancesco Grazzini, some three years after the playwright's death in 1583. They commissioned Piero Salvestrini of Castello, whose elaborate fresco cycle was influenced by the prints of the French engraver Jacques Callot, whom he perhaps met during the period 1615–17, when Callot was a Medici court artist. Carnivalesque acrobatic figures also feature in the *Balli di Sfessania*, Callot's suite of twenty-four prints dating to around 1620 (Figure 30.4; see also Hallar 1977: 59–71; Kellein 1995: 23–6; Katritzky 2006: plates 2–5). Despite a

Figure 30.4 Jacques Callot, Balli di Sfessania, series of 24 engravings, each 7 × 9 cm, *c*.1620. Private Collection.

consensus that they depict *moresca* (carnival sword dance) performers, they continue to attract diverse interpretation. Only rarely are they still cited without qualification as a source for Commedia performance practice. Some scholars reject any connection with the Commedia dell'Arte beyond the role names in their titles. Others regard them as imaginative capriccios, unrepresentative of either actors or dancers (Leik 1996: 254).

Another possibility is that Callot is depicting multi-skilled professionals, capable of performing both *moresche* and Commedia plays. Writers such as Garzoni indicate connections between the Commedia dell'Arte and *moresche*, especially pantomimic, acrobatic, armed dances of the type often introduced by way of *intermedi* into plays and generally performed by professional *buffoni* and matachins, such as the armed 'matachin' dances, or the acrobatic displays known as the 'antics' or Forze d'Ercole. Such connections receive significant support from the pictorial record. Regardless of whether Callot's performers are amateur or professional, actors, dancers or acrobats, his series represents an iconographic watershed, a widely circulated and imitated visual repository that influenced virtually every Commedia dell'Arte related image postdating 1620.

Official festival books, the formal reports of invited guests, and the informal travellers' tales communicated by their socially diverse retinues, disseminated news of Commedia dell'Arte performances at court festivals far beyond their host courts. The northern European fashion for Commedia dell'Arte was further fuelled by numerous colourful depictions of performing quack troupes, brought back from Italy in the friendship albums of German noblemen, students and journeymen. During the period 1570–1620, hand-painted costume series of pictures of men and women of different ranks in the dress of foreign lands or regions effectively demonstrated the sophisticated education and travels of album owners. Venetian and Paduan costume series often feature one or more depictions of Commedia dell'Arte costume (Figure 30.5; see also Hallar 1977: 12–14; Katritzky 1998; Katritzky 2006: plates 248–61; Katritzky 2007: 67–9, 221–30; Katritzky 2012: 215–43).

Figure 30.5 Pantalone and Zanni, coloured drawing, 1586. Friendship album of Jacob Praun, Nürnberg, Stadtbibliothek, Solg.Ms.14.8o, ff.66v-67r (reproduced by kind permission of Dr Werner Wilhelm Schnabel, Nürnberg Stadtbibliothek).

When album images are compared with each other, the strength of their shared iconographic traditions becomes apparent. They place a markedly more pedestrian emphasis on Italian street entertainment than early modern textual records, rarely indicating exotic animals or complex spectacle or magic, but giving detailed, although not necessarily literal, insights into professional street performers' costumes, their trestle stages and audiences, and their routines. Although often dismissed as depicting mountebanks, charlatans or carnival revellers, some undoubtedly depict comic actors. Interpreting album pictures does not merely involve quibbling over definitions of the term Commedia dell'Arte, but an enrichment of our understanding of the phenomenon itself.

Similarly naively painted, and even more theatrically informative, are the 100 illustrations to the Corsini manuscript collection of Commedia dell'Arte scenarios. Each recreates, often demonstrably independently of the text it ostensibly illustrates, an onstage scene (Figure 30.6; see also Nicoll 1963; Hallar 1977: 57–9; Katritzky 2006: plates 243–7). The Recueil Fossard, whose Stockholm section is discussed

Figure 30.6 The Two Slave-Girls, coloured drawing. Corsini album (frontispiece illustration to Commedia dell'Arte scenario 16), Biblioteca Corsiniana, Rome.

above, was originally compiled during the later seventeenth century by a French court musician. By then, Paris had consolidated its status as the pre-eminent centre for early modern theatrical print production: for programmes, performance souvenirs, almanacs, frontispieces and book illustrations, and portrait series of performers and theatrical roles (Guardenti 1990; Kellein 1995: 27–32). Numerous examples of seventeenth-century Commedia dell'Arte related portraits and other prints, from Paris and elsewhere, are represented in another substantial section of the Recueil Fossard, now in Copenhagen (Holm 1991).

From Jean-Antoine Watteau to Lucien Freud

By 1720, the Commedia dell'Arte's impact on northern European court and visual culture was increasingly being mediated by French actors playing in the Paris tradition of the Comédie Italienne (Hansen 1984). Eighteenth-century Paris saw the completion of a major stage in the tortuous process of development from 'traditional' Italian Commedia dell'Arte, through assimilation of its stock characters into diverging theatrical forms, to self-conscious pan-European cultural codification and revival. The masks became more rigidly formalized on the stage of the Théâtre Italien, and there was a new awareness of their symbolic possibilities as meta-theatrical types. The fulcrum for this fundamental transformation was created not by a theatre practitioner, but by a painter.

Watteau's *Gilles* (Figure 30.7), the supreme icon of the Commedia dell'Arte, dates to around 1720, soon after the return of the Théâtre Italien to Paris (Kellein 1995: 12–14, 33–44). In Watteau, the masks found a great artist capable of expressing their symbolic potential as the non-biblical, non-classical heroes sought by the 'age of reason'. Having disappeared into a series of private collections soon after it was painted in around 1712, Watteau's little painting *Pierrot Content* has, since 1977, been in the Thyssen-Bornemisza Collection, and is currently on public display in their Madrid museum (inv.nr.432.1977.75). Its blissfully innocent Pierrot, basking securely in the warm companionship of his friends, has become rudely awakened to the threat of 'les jaloux'—Harlequin and Scaramouche. As emphasized with far less subtlety in Edme Jeaurat's print after the painting (Figure 30.8), they skulk in the background bushes, heralding undertones of Harlequin's kinship to the comic medieval stage devil and his association with the realm of hell and death, with Pierrot as his sacrificial victim.

For Watteau, the masks are no longer straightforward actors playing a part, or ordinary citizens borrowing the temporary *persona* of carnival costumes. Nor, like other artists of his day, did he use them as an excuse for picturesque rococo titillation, or domesticate them into the garden statues or porcelain banquet table ornaments favoured by aspiring patrons of live acting troupes (Hansen 1984; Lawner 1998; Jansen 2001; Chilton 2001). Far more than stage practice, *Pierrot Content* summarizes a major stage in Watteau's meditations on human love and jealousy. Its squinting carved stone satyr again presides over his most important canvas. Tragic and naive, the idealized self-portrait of Watteau's life-size *Gilles* is an ambiguous, contemplative outcast who casts larger than life shadows over Parisian culture and far beyond, from the pastoral Commedia paintings of Jean-Baptiste Pater and

Figure 30.7 Antoine Watteau, Gilles (Pierrot), oil on canvas, 184 × 149 cm, *c*.1720 Paris, Louvre.

Nicolas Lancret, and Giandomenico Tiepolo's wryly imaginative everyday scenes from the offstage 'life' of Pulcinella (Kellein 1995: 45–52, 113–17; Lawner 1998: 137–42; Clair 2004: 76–81), to Picasso's stage sets, or *Les enfants du Paradis* (Figures 30.7 and 30.8).

One of the first writers on the Commedia dell'Arte to show an historian's concern for the pictorial evidence was Luigi Riccoboni, better known by his stage name 'Lelio'. The printmaker François Joullain, a collector of Commedia-related images (such as Jeaurat's original copperplate for Figure 30.8), was commissioned to illustrate Riccoboni's *Histoire du théâtre italien* of 1730–1. His engravings depict the comic actors as they were to be seen in Riccoboni's own troupe on the Paris stage of his day. Nothing in the least original about that, but unlike other theatrical costume series of his time, of which many are illustrated by Gunther Hansen (1984), Renzo Guardenti (1990) and Bent Holm (1991), Joullain also added some historical counterparts. *Habit de Pantalon moderne*, for example, is paired with *Habit de Pentalon ancien* (Figures 30.9b and 30.9a respectively), based directly on the Pantalone in Jacques Callot's series of engravings *Les trois Pantalons* of *c*.1618.

Joullain's much copied series inspired that most influential nineteenth-century series of Commedia characters, the fifty portraits of stock roles of the Commedia dell'Arte and Comédie Italienne of Maurice Dudevant's two volume book *Masques et bouffons*, published in 1860 under the pseudonymous surname adopted by his

PIERROT CONTENT.

Figure 30.8 Edme Jeaurat (after Watteau), Pierrot Content, engraving, 35 × 43 cm, 1728.
Private Collection.

mother, the novelist George Sand (Sand 1860). The spurious authenticity of Maurice
Sand's attractive coloured prints is bolstered by their unreliable dates. *Pantalone
(1550)*, for example, is none other than a revamped twin to Joullain's *Pentalon
ancien*, and thus ultimately based not on a model of 1550, but on Callot's picture of
c.1618. Lack of historical rigour notwithstanding, the enthusiasm of George and
Maurice Sand's circle for the Italian comedians encouraged a new curiosity for their
historical development. The demand for scholarly information stimulated closer
scrutiny of the visual record, and an increasing interest by painters, poets and
performers in the Commedia, its characters, and its images, as a potential source for
their own creative art.

Symbolic resonances crystallized in the work of Watteau or Tiepolo, and
sentimentalized through the eighteenth and earlier nineteenth centuries by lesser
artists from Pater, Lancret and Giovanni Domenico Ferretti to Jean-Leon Gérôme,
Jules Chéret or Carl Spitzweg, were again brought into sharp focus by Paul Cézanne.
His *Mardi Gras* (1888) realized the full potential of the visual appeal of two iconic
Commedia servants (Kellein 1995: 64, 131). This powerful and influential painting,

a   HABIT DE PENTALON ANÇIEN   b   HABIT DE PANTALON MODERNE

Figure 30.9a-b François Joullain, Habit de Pentalon ancient, Habit de Pantalon moderne.
Luigi Riccoboni, Histoire du théâtre italien, depuis la decadence de la comedie
latine, 2 vols, Paris: Chardon, 1730–1, plates 3 and 4.

ostensibly a representational portrait of Cézanne's son and a friend, Louis Guillaume,
costumed as Harlequin and Pierrot for the Paris carnival, made a profound impression
on some of the greatest artists of the following generation. Painted as a child in
Commedia costume, Jean Renoir demonstrated his adult fascination for the
Commedia dell'Arte in his film, *Le Carrosse d'or* (1952). Pablo Picasso repeatedly
painted both himself and his son Paulo as either Pierrot or Harlequin, and his early
oeuvre, including his great designs for the Ballet Russes, draws again and again on
Commedia motifs (Kellein 1995: 69–75, 136–43; Lawner 1998: 6, 178–81; Clair
2004).

Italian comedians and the characters they inspire are still relevant today, and
continue to profoundly inform and influence European visual culture, from the
whimsical Pulcinellas of David Hockney (Kellein 1995: 176–7; Lawner 1998: 192)
or Richard Shirley Smith (Figure 30.10) to Lucien Freud's *Large interior W11* of
1983. Freud's magisterial canvas poignantly reinterprets Watteau's *Pierrot Content*,
the then recently acquired painting chosen by Baron Thyssen-Bornemisza to feature
in the background of his portrait of 1982, by Freud. On 5 November 2013, Grayson
Perry gave his fourth and final BBC Reith Lecture on the stage of the Platform
Theatre of Central St Martins. For this, the Turner Prize-winning potter created a

Figure 30.10 Richard Shirley Smith, Pulcinella Archaeologist, acrylic on paper, 72 × 51 cm, 1993. Private Collection, (c) Richard Shirley Smith.

new variant of his long-time alter-ego Claire (in whose persona he delivered the first three lectures and, in January 2014, received his CBE at Buckingham Palace), wearing a knowing post-modern pastiche of a Commedia-inspired costume, 'a kind of satin Pierrot outfit' (http://downloads.bbc.co.uk/radio4/transcripts/reith-lecture-usm.pdf: accessed 6 November 2013).

The Commedia dell'Arte proper has its origins in performing configurations in which the stage dominance of all-male professional *buffoni* is challenged, transmuted and eventually usurped, by women. Actresses gave the Commedia its defining onstage nucleus, which is to be sought not merely in the servant-master duo promoted by traditional scholarship (Figures 30.2 and 30.4), but in the characteristic Zanni-Pantalone-Innamorata trio (Figures 30.1 and 30.2). While this trio is central to many of the Commedia's most important early images, the later iconography increasingly diverges from stage practice. Inspired by the vision of Watteau and Tiepolo, artists explore and exploit the Commedia dell'Arte stock servant (and especially Pierrot and Pulcinella, whose costumes have stayed truest to their humble Zanni roots) as Everyman: an unpredictable hybrid of the bestial, the mundane, and the superhuman.

Throughout Europe, amateur performers and masqueraders, emerging professional theatre, and itinerant troupes drew heavily on the Commedia dell'Arte for costumes and other visual elements. Our knowledge of pre-photographic performance practice is fundamentally dependent on a broad overview of relevant depictions. During recent decades, the systematic base of identified and investigated images available to scholarship has gathered substantial momentum. Publications such as those listed below (and their bibliographies) put specialists, students and practitioners in an increasingly informed position to assess the iconographic record: with respect to the activities of Commedia performers, and from the wider perspective of the diverse manifestations of their cultural heritage, in and beyond Italy.

References

Chilton, Meredith (2001) *Harlequin Unmasked: The Commedia dell'Arte and Porcelain Sculpture*. New Haven, US and London: Yale University Press.

Clair, Jean, ed. (2004) *The Great Parade: Portrait of the artist as clown*. New Haven, US and London: Yale University Press.

Duchartre, Pierre Louis (1966) *The Italian Comedy*. New York: Dover (unabridged reprint of the 1929 first English edition).

Guardenti, Renzo (1990), *Gli Italiani a Parigi. La Comédie Italienne (1660–1697). Storia, pratica scenica, iconografia*, 2 vols. Rome: Bulzoni.

Hallar, Marianne (1977) *Teaterspil og Tegnsprog: ikonografiske studier i commedia dell'arte*. Copenhagen: Akademisk Forlag.

Hansen, Günther (1984) *Formen der Commedia dell'Arte in Deutschland*. Emsdetten, Germany: Lechte.

Holm, Bent (1991), *Solkonge og Månekejser. Ikonografiske studier i François Fossards Cabinet*. Copenhagen: Gyldendal.

Jansen, Reinhard (2001) *Commedia dell'Arte: Fest der Komödianten*, 3 vols. Stuttgart, Germany: Arnoldsche.

Katritzky, M. A. (1987a) "Lodewyk Toeput: some pictures related to the commedia dell'arte". *Renaissance Studies*. 1.1, 71–125.

——(1987b) "Italian comedians in renaissance prints". *Print Quarterly*. 4.3, 236–54.

——(1998) "Was Commedia dell'Arte performed by mountebanks? Album amicorum illustrations and Thomas Platter's description of 1598". *Theatre Research International*. 23.2, 104–125.

——(2006) *The art of commedia: A study in the Commedia dell'Arte 1560–1620 with special reference to the visual records*. Amsterdam: Rodopi.

——(2007) *Women, medicine and theatre, 1500-1750: literary mountebanks and performing quacks*. Aldershot, UK: Ashgate.

——(2012) *Healing, Performance and Ceremony in the Writings of Three Early Modern Physicians: Hippolytus Guarinonius and the brothers Felix and Thomas Platter*. Aldershot, UK: Ashgate.

Kellein, Thomas (1995) *Pierrot: Melancholie und Maske*. Munich, Germany: Prestel.

Lawner, Lynne (1998) *Harlequin on the Moon: Commedia dell'Arte and the visual arts*. New York: Harry N. Abrams.

Leik, Angelica (1996) *Frühe Darstellungen der Commedia dell'Arte: eine Theaterform als Bildmotiv*. Neuried, Germany: ars una.

Nicoll, Allardyce (1963) *The World of Harlequin: A critical study of the Commedia dell'Arte*. Cambridge, UK: Cambridge University Press.

Riccoboni, Luigi (1730–1) *Histoire du théâtre italien, depuis la decadence de la comedie latine*, 2 vols, Paris: Chardon,

Sand, Maurice (1860) *Masques et bouffons*, Paris: Levy Frères.

Vianello, Daniele (2005) *L'arte del buffone: maschere e spettacolo tra Italia e Baviera nel XVI secolo*. Rome: Bulzoni.

31

THE OLD MAN'S SPECTACLES
Commedia and Shakespeare
Andrew Grewar

Shakespeare's direct references to the characters and methods of the early Italian Commedia dell'Arte, together with the many distinctly Italianate elements of his early comedies, lead one to speculate about the nature of his acquaintance with the Italian popular comedy. Although it is widely acknowledged that he drew on contemporary Italian plays as a source for incident and plot, a purely literary analysis of the debt does not adequately explain his access to this source material. Although his ultimate sources may have been ancient Roman drama or the recent Italian *Commedia Erudita*, Shakespeare's immediate dramatic model appears to have been the Commedia dell'Arte, with its reworking of both classical and neo-classical materials.

Many of his plays, particularly the early comedies, *The Comedy of Errors*, *The Taming of the Shrew*, *The Two Gentlemen of Verona*, and *Love's Labour's Lost*, contain elements that can only be accounted for by knowledge of the Commedia dell'Arte. These 'theatregrams', to use Clubb's handy catchall term (Clubb 1989: 1ff.), can be seen throughout his work, in the history plays, the later comedies and romances, and even in the great tragedies. Resemblances of character and incident to their earlier manifestations in the Commedia dell'Arte are too numerous to be coincidental and cannot be due to knowledge of written Italian plays alone. If Shakespeare used the erudite Italian drama and all the other 'sources' that have been suggested for his plays, he must have read very widely indeed, in several languages, and have had access to manuscripts or publications from Italy, France, Spain and Germany. It is far more likely that his knowledge of contemporary Italian drama was not through the printed page, but via the Commedia dell'Arte.

Between 1550 and 1600, Italian Commedia troupes travelled widely, not only throughout the peninsula, but in France, the Netherlands, Germany, Spain and even England, where their activities can be traced in court records, private diaries, literature and pictorial works. The first notice of them in England is in the Norwich Chamberlain's Accounts for the years 1546 to 1547, which refer to 'certen Spanyards & Italyans who dawnsed antycks & played dyvers other feats' before the Mayor. Within a few decades their visits had increased. There are records of performances by Italian players in London and the provinces on at least ten occasions between

1573 and 1578, and on four of these they entertained Queen Elizabeth herself, playing at court, and following her progress to Windsor and Reading in July 1574 (Lea 1934 II: 352--358).

The Queen's annual summer progress through the provinces to pay stately visits to the various great families at their country estates was always the occasion for great pageantry. She was fêted all along the way with orations by dignitaries and citizens, poems were recited in her honour, elaborate masques and mock battles were staged, and every type of entertainment provided. One of the most elaborate of these occasions was the 'princely' festival of entertainment at Kenilworth in Warwickshire in July 1575, presented for Elizabeth by her suitor and favourite, Robert Dudley, the Earl of Leicester.

Lasting almost three weeks, the Kenilworth festival included recitals and 'devices' prepared and performed by some of the outstanding poets and writers of the day, including several by George Gascoigne. There was 'a magnificent display of fireworks [that] may have been engineered by the Italian pyrotechnician recommended to Leicester... in May' (Lea 1934 II: 354). The highlight of the revelries was the staging on 18 July by Leicester's Men, of the *Device of the Delivery of the Lady of the Lake*, with verses by William Hunnis and George Ferrers, and with Henry Goldingham playing Arion (Chambers 1923 IV: 61–62). The performance took place on the lake in the park and Arion was to be seen riding on the back of a dolphin, carried on a boat in which a consort of singers was concealed (Wickham 1963 II: 367). As Kenilworth is only twelve miles from Stratford-on-Avon, it is quite possible that the eleven-year-old William Shakespeare was among the spectators.

One of the performers at Kenilworth that summer was a highly skilled Italian acrobat and vaulter who has been identified as Soldino of Florence, the leader of a Commedia troupe that the Earl of Lincoln had seen performing in Paris two years previously (Lea 1934 II: 354–355). The Italian entertainers, with their extraordinary range of skills, must have attracted widespread attention from the general English public, apart from that of their noble patrons, not to mention their English counterparts. One can imagine that they played at every possible market place and town hall in all the countries and provinces through which they journeyed, as this was their profession.

The last half of the 1500s was, of course, a crucial period in the development of English drama. The cultural renaissance of the time was broadly European, after all, and England's university scholars, like those on the Italian peninsula, followed the great humanist pursuit. As in Italy before them, it was the university wits who wrote the first English plays of the time, as well as translations and adaptations of the Italian Commedia Erudita. The English professional players also flourished under the patronage of the educated aristocracy, despite fierce opposition from civic authorities and puritanical church leaders. Chambers (1923 II: 1–246) gives a detailed account of the boy and adult companies employed as entertainers by various members of the English nobility, such as the Earl of Leicester or Lord Strange, to mention only those that will be encountered again in this discussion. Throughout her entire reign, the most notable of these companies gave special performances for the Queen every Christmas season in London at her palaces at Richmond, Whitehall or Greenwich, as had been the practice since the times of Henry VIII.

The manner in which Italian stagecraft was adapted by the English actors must have been one of fairly gradual, broad imitation and transfusion, as is the way with fashions. English travellers to France and Italy were well aware of the latest European trends and brought home accounts of theatrical performances they had seen abroad. The rapid proliferation of companies and playhouses and the astonishing number of plays written, performed and published during Elizabeth's reign show that drama was definitely the 'in' thing, particularly in that great metropolis, London. The theatre had become the most important form of popular entertainment and social networking of the time, equivalent to our modern day films, television, Facebook and Twitter. Aside from using earlier English staging methods, the English companies and their managers also adopted the many other essential features of theatrical production developed in Italy over the previous century – the spectacular effects using stage props such as artificial body parts, stage furniture and machinery, trapdoors, curtains, smoke and mirrors to represent executions and bloody murders, ghosts, demons, witches and other apparitions, and offstage sound effects, fireworks, cannons, guns and swordplay to present duels and battle scenes. These, together with songs, dancing, musical accompaniment by an orchestra and the gorgeous costumes and military uniforms handed down by their wealthy masters and patrons, all added to the novelty and attraction of their plays.

Elizabeth and the Lords of her Privy Council clearly had a great taste for the new English drama and the Italian Renaissance theatrical forms that inspired it and, like the Gonzagas and Medicis in Italy and France, were generous patrons of the theatre. They also employed many Italian musicians as household entertainers, such as the Bassano family, originally from Venice, who had been musicians at the Tudor court since the 1540s (Lea 1934 II: 369–371; Wikipedia n.d.). In fact, in the same way that Massimo Troiano and his compatriots staged a Commedia play at the Bavarian court for Duke William in 1568 (Lea 1934 I: 5–12; see also Katritzky 1996), Italians musicians at the English court appear on occasion to have given amateur dramatic performances. The Lord Chamberlain records that on 27 February 1576 an amount of £10 was paid to 'Alfruso Ferabolle and the rest of the Italyan players' (Chambers 1923 II: 262 IV: 150). The player named was undoubtedly the Bolognese musician, Alfonso Ferrabosco, one of the Queen's favourite musicians, who was in her service from 1562 to 1578 (Lea 1934 II: 355f). It is interesting to note that, within the same week of February/March, £10 was also paid 'to — Burbag and his company servauntes to the earl of Leicester' (Chambers 1923 IV: 150). The player named here, of course, was James Burbage, leader of Leicester's Men, who that year built the very first theatre in England, famously known simply as 'The Theatre'.

The clearest trace of professional and well-known Commedia dell'Arte players in England comes two years later. In January 1578 'Drousiano' Martinelli and his company were given permission by the Privy Council to perform in London (Chambers 1923 II: 262–263; Lea 1934: 356–357). Drusiano and his more famous brother, Tristano Martinelli, played with various companies, notably the Accesi, under the patronage of Vincenzo Gonzaga, the Duke of Mantua (Duchartre 1966: 92). Apparently, both Martinellis played the part of Arlecchino, and they may have been co-creators of this, probably the most famous of all Commedia dell'Arte masks. The earliest records of the activities of their troupe have been found not in their native Italy, but in Antwerp. They appear to have performed in Antwerp and its surroundings from about March to August 1576. In mid-October of that year they left Antwerp for Paris, probably spending the following year in France (Schrickx 1976; Katritzky 2005: 127–128). Whether the entire company, including Tristano, went to England in late 1577 or early 1578 is not known. Drusiano, as the older brother and leader, is the only one named in the London records. It is possible that the Martinelli troupe played before Elizabeth and her court in London, for the Chamber Accounts for 1577–1578 include payment for 'a mattres hoopes and boardes with tressells for the Italian Tumblers' (Chambers 1923 II: 262; Lea 1934 II: 357).

It is clear that Shakespeare knew of the Commedia dell'Arte at the very outset of his career as he refers directly to some of its stock characters in his earliest plays. The word 'zany' is found in *Love's Labour's Lost* (V.ii.463) (1594–1595), for example, where it is used to indicate a foolish servant or follower, clearly a reference to the zanni of the Commedia dell'Arte. There are clownish servants or zanni types in many of the plays, from the Dromios to Grumio, Launce, Speed and Launcelot, to Peter in *Romeo and Juliet* and even the porter in *Macbeth* and the gravediggers in *Hamlet*. There are plenty of military braggarts from Falstaff downwards, any number of young lovers, and several pedants too, such as Holofernes in *Love's Labour's Lost*, who bears a close resemblance to the Gelosi's Dottor' Gratiano of Bologna in his fondness for absurd Latinisms.

We find Pantalone first mentioned in an unusual stage direction in *The Taming of the Shrew* (1590–1591) where Gremio, the unsuitably elderly suitor to Kate's sister Bianca, is referred to as a 'Pantalowne' (I.i.45). Later, during Bianca's 'music' and 'grammar' lessons, the young lover Lucentio again calls Gremio 'the old Pantalowne' (III.i.36). And Jaques, in his speech on the 'Seven Ages of Man' in *As You Like It* (1599–1600), directly names '... the lean and slipper'd Pantaloon, With spectacles on nose and pouch on side ... (II.vii.158–159). This mention of the old man's spectacles tallies with the earliest iconographic evidence of the Commedia dell'Arte in the frescoes at Schloss Trausnitz in Bavaria (*c*.1576) or the French woodcuts and engravings in the Recueil Fossard (*c*.1580), where Pantalone is shown wearing spectacles for comic effect (Lea 1934 I: fig. 5, opposite p. 6; Duchartre 1966: 324).

There is another Pantalone with spectacles in the Elizabethan 'stage plot' of *The Dead Man's Fortune*, which, like Shakespeare's *Taming of the Shrew*, is believed to date from the early 1590s. A number of these stage plots were discovered in the Dulwich College Library during the 1700s. They must at one time have been in the possession of the Lord Admiral's Men, whose leading actor, Edward Alleyn, founded the College. The 'plots' give only a brief outline of the characters' names, the order of their stage entrances, and the props for each play, set out on a sheet of card that could be hung up back-stage for reference during performance. In the plot of *The Dead Man's Fortune* (see Greg 1931 II: Figure 1) we find the following scene, part of a comic sub-plot to the main tragicomedy:

Enter pateloun & pesscode = enter asspida
to her validore & his man b· samme
to them the panteloun & pescode wth spectakles.

Besides the Pantalone figure, what we can discern of the action immediately reminds us of the Commedia dell'Arte. All the basic types are here: the old man and his manservant with the suitably clownish and suggestive yet English name, Peascod, the young wife Asspida and her maid, Rose, and the young lover who visits, with his boy, Sam. Like his counterpart in some of the early Italian scenarios, cuckolded by his wife with the help of the servants, this Pantaloon appears to need spectacles to see the lovemaking between Asspida and Validore going on right under his nose!

Other details of the sub-plot should be noted. There is the intriguing scene:

Enter panteloun whiles he speakes
validore passeth ore the stage disguised
then enter passcode to them asspida to
them the maide wth pesscodds apparel. (Greg 1931)

Later, Validore is disguised as Rose, and the scene includes two 'flaskets of clothes', which immediately reminds one of the trick played on Falstaff by Mistress Page and Mistress Ford, when he is smuggled out of Ford's house hidden in a buck-basket of soiled laundry (*The Merry Wives of Windsor* III.iii; III.v). As the plot's sequence shows, the musical interludes between acts, marked by X–X–X–X, may have helped the lovers in their deceptions.

The main plot also deserves some attention. It is a tragicomedy that can be analysed as follows: the two stubborn old fathers, Tesephon and Algerius, in typical patriarchal fashion, insist on marrying off their daughters to the unsuitable suitors, Carynus and Prelior. But Alcyane and Statyra are in love with Laertes and Eschines, and when they defy their fathers, the old men go to the extent of having the girls imprisoned. Their hateful suitors visit them there and 'here the laydes speake'. Eschines then disguises himself as Bellveile and gains entry to the prison with Laertes. The fathers also go in disguise to the jailer, with poisoned meat. Their murderous plot is foiled somehow and the magician Urganda, who from the start has been on the side of the lovers, falsely informs the fathers that their daughters are dead. Next, he visits the false suitors with a looking glass, 'accompanied wth satires plainge on ther Instruments'. This confrontation drives both Carynus and Prelior 'madde'. In Act Five, the King Egereon is about to have the wicked old fathers executed when there is a magical *deus ex macchina* that seems to involve some fairly complex staging:

musike plaies & there enters 3 faires dancynge on after another. The firste takes the sworde from the executioner & sendes him awaye the other caryes a waie the blocke & the third sends a waie the offycers and unbinds allgerius & tesephon & as they entred so they depart.

(Greg 1931)

We then have the joyful reunion of the lovers, overseen by the magician Urganda, where Laertes and Eschines enter 'to them', 'leadinge their laides hand in hand'. The characters of the sub-plot then enter in pairs and the final scene resolves the entire situation when the 'Dead Man's Fortune', presumably a dowry, is at last revealed: 'Enter the Panteloun & causeth the cheste or trunke to be brought forth' (ibid.).

The Dead Man's Fortune bears striking resemblances to the contemporary Commedia, with its mixture of farce, romance and lurid tragicomedy. Not only the stock types, disguises and other forms of gulling of the sub-plot, but all the features of the main plot, with satyrs playing instruments, a mad scene, dancing fairies who magically resolve things, the King who is brought in as final authority, the pair of old fathers, the pairs of true and false lovers and the powerful magician were to be found in the infinitely varied repertoires of the Gelosi and their fellow improvisators. They will also be curiously familiar to any student of Shakespeare.

An especially interesting feature of *The Dead Man's Fortune* is the direction:

Enter *Tesephon* [&] allgerius wth atendantes
& others to them Burbage [&] a messenger
to them Euphrodore = Robart lee & b samme.
(Greg 1931)

This refers to none other than Richard Burbage, who only a few years later was to become the leading actor in the Shakespearean company. Five years younger than Shakespeare, he had started his acting career at the age of fifteen with Leicester's Men, whose leader was his father James. He is thought to have played the part of the magician Urganda in the main plot of this revival of *The Dead Man's Fortune*.

Who were the other actors in this anonymous play with its curiously Italianate characters and themes? Unfortunately, they are not named. But a very similar stage plot, *The Second Part of the Seven Deadly Sins*, dating from the same time (1590–1591?) and in the same handwriting, lists in its cast not only Burbage but most of the actors who from 1594 were to work with Shakespeare as the Lord Chamberlain's Men. They include Thomas Pope, George Bryan, Richard Cowley, William Sly, John Duke, Augustine Phillips and John Sinkler. In about 1590 they seem to have been playing as Lord Strange's Men, probably in a company combined with the Lord Admiral's Men. Unfortunately again, two crucial names are missing from these early documents: those of the clown, William Kemp, and William Shakespeare, actor and playwright. Despite this, the mention of Richard Burbage is a definite link between actors of the Shakespearean company and the plot of *The Dead Man's Fortune*, this early English experiment with Commedia dell'Arte types and situations. There is also the interesting coincidence of the name Pantaloon in *The Dead Man s Fortune* and *The Taming of the Shrew*, with both plays being dated at about 1590 or 1591.

We shall return to the stage plots later in this discussion. But first I wish to look more closely at three of the Shakespeare comedies I have mentioned for other traces of the Commedia dell'Arte.

The Two Gentlemen of Verona, one of Shakespeare's earliest comedies (*c.*1590–1591), provides clear examples of parallels with earlier Commedia productions, such as are represented by Flaminio Scala's, *Il Teatro delle favole rappresentative* (Venice, 1611). There are several interesting similarities between Scala's scenarios and Shakespeare's plays (see Tim Fitzpatrick's chapter in this book; Salerno 1967 Appendix: 395–413). In this case, not only the characters of *Two Gentlemen* but the main plot and its surprising denouement might have been modelled almost directly on Scala's *Flavio Tradito* ('Flavio Betrayed'), which contains the essentials of the

Valentine-Silvia-Proteus plot. In outline it tells how Flavio is betrayed by his best friend, Oratio, who falls in love with Flavio's beloved, Isabella, just as Proteus betrays Valentine by pursuing Silvia. Oscar Campbell (1925: 54–56) long ago noted that this sort of three-handed contest of suitors was commonplace in the Commedia dell'Arte. The often-repeated comic devices of dropped love-letters and overheard conversations are also found in both *Flavio Tradito* and *The Two Gentlemen of Verona*. Scala's play also ends with the traitor being forgiven by the betrayed lover as an example of the triumph of friendship over love.

The Taming of the Shrew also contains evidence of Italian origins for the characters as well as the main elements of the plot. We have noted the appearance of Gremio, the Pantaloon. That Shakespeare thought of the old men in the play in terms of the stock Italian types may be seen not only in his reference to the Pantaloon but from Biondello's description of the 'ancient Angel' about to be lured into Tranio's plot as a substitute for Lucentio's father, Vincentio: '...a Mercantant or a pedant, I know not what, but formal in apparel, In gait and countenance surely like a Father' (IV. ii.63–65). Here both the *mercante* and the *dottore* of the Italian scenarios are conflated in their typical role of father to the *innamorati* (see Wells and Taylor 1987: 172). Furthermore, the characters and the setting of the main action of *The Shrew* could not be more 'Italian'.

The very 'English' setting and characters of *The Shrew*'s Induction, the trick played on the drunken tinker, Christopher Sly, on the other hand, accentuates the Italianate quality of the play-within-the-play. This is performed for Sly by a group of travelling players, and Shakespeare seems to emphasize its Italian qualities. There are an unusual number of Italian words and phrases in *The Shrew*, and the presence of the 'Pantalowne' surely indicates that Sly is meant to see a typical Commedia dell'Arte presented *all'improvviso* by an Italian troupe.

In considering *Love's Labour's Lost* (1594–1595), we are immediately struck by the resemblance of the persons in the sub-plot to the character types in the Commedia. I have already mentioned the play's verbal reference to the 'zany'. In Act Five, scene two, Berowne refers scathingly to the French lord Boyet as 'Some carry-tale, some please-man, some slight zany', for having helped the Princess and her ladies trick the King and his companions. According to the Oxford English Dictionary, this is the earliest use of the word 'zany' in English. Another familiar English word first used by Shakespeare in *Love's Labour's Lost*, and which probably also comes directly from the Commedia dell'Arte, is the word 'pedant'.

This brings us to a very interesting feature of *Love's Labour's Lost*. The word 'pedant' occurs in both the Quarto and Folio versions of the play, as a stage direction at the start of Act Four, scene two: 'Enter Dull, Holofernes, the Pedant and Nathaniel.' At the start of the next act, the direction is, 'Enter the Pedant, the Curate, and Dull.' Again, in the last scene (V.ii.581), during the 'Pageant of the Nine Worthies', there is the stage direction, 'Enter Pedant for Judas, and the Boy for Hercules.' And in the Quarto version (1598), the word 'Pedant' is used as a speech heading throughout the rest of the scene, instead of 'Holofernes', the character's name. In many of the speech headings and stage directions, the name of a stock type is used in place of that of a character: Don Armado and Moth are referred to as the 'Braggart and his Boy' (III.i.1; V.i.29). Costard is almost always 'Clowne' and Nathaniel is the 'Curate'.

Dull is called 'a Constable' at his first two entrances, and Jaquenetta is simply 'Wench'.

In drafting his plays, therefore, Shakespeare seems to have thought of at least some of his *dramatis personae* as types resembling those of the Commedia dell'Arte, so that the generic titles 'pantaloon', 'pedant', 'braggart', 'clown', 'boy' and so on came to mind more readily than the names of the characters. This would hardly be surprising if he was using plays derived from the Italian comedians. The characters would have come with the plots, so to speak.

That these types stem from the Commedia dell'Arte and not from the types of classical comedy may be seen from the fact that Don Armado is undoubtedly a Spanish braggart soldier. As Campbell (1925: 32ff) argued, the Spanish captain, his boy page, the pedant, and his parasite, the curate in *Love's Labour's Lost*, are all drawn from the Italian popular comedy as it might have been played by the Gelosi. The verbal acrobatics of the braggart and the pedant in particular are reminiscent of the *capitano* and *dottore*. Don Armado's fantastic language is just like the type of stage rhetoric for which Francesco Andreini's Capitan' Spavento was renowned. As noted earlier, Holofernes, with his Latin phrases and his pedantic insistence on dubious pronunciations, is a close cousin of Dottor' Gratiano, and the 'lessons' in Latin and grammar that Dull receives from him (IV.ii) were a common *lazzi* of verbal confusion in the Commedia dell'Arte.

Linguistic confusion is always a great source of fun. The *comici* used it constantly in portraying the different masks with their regional origins and dialects and the misunderstandings created by Pantalone's Venetian, the Doctor's ultra-educated Bolognese dialect and neo-Latin vocabulary or Arlecchino's peasant Bergamese. Shakespeare made similar comic use of different languages and dialects with the Welsh accents of Fluellen (*Henry V*) or Sir Hugh Evans, and the French one of Doctor Caius (*Merry Wives*). Another example is the English lesson that the French Princess Katherine is given by her maid Alice, with its delicious, 'unintended' *double entendre* (Henry V. III.iv). The most common form of verbal confusion is the puns that the clowns are so fond of:

SPEED: How now, Signior Launce. What news with your mastership?
LAUNCE: With my master's ship? Why it is at sea.
SPEED: Well, your old vice still: mistake the word.
(*The Two Gentlemen of Verona*, III.i.77–79)

Working as a close-knit team with his fellow actors over the years, Shakespeare clearly created his plays with their talents in mind. Baldwin argued that each of the Lord Chamberlain's Men specialized in a particular 'line' or type of role. He makes some interesting conjectures in this regard, although, curiously, he overlooks the similarity of such a practice to the working methods of the Commedia dell'Arte actors (Baldwin 1927: chapter 9, 229ff).

The physical characteristics of the company's players, both men and boys, were certainly used for comic purposes. John Sinkler, for example, was exceptionally skinny, and so played Slender, the pathetically inept, naïve suitor to 'sweet Anne Page' in *The Merry Wives of Windsor* (I.i; III.i; III.iv). He probably also played the role of Doctor Pinch in *The Comedy of Errors*, who is described by poor, confused Antipholus of Ephesus as:

> a hungry, lean-fac'd villain, a mere anatomy, a mountebank, a threadbare juggler, and a fortune teller, a needy, hollow-ey'd, sharp-looking wretch, a living dead man … [who] took on him as a conjuror, and gazing into my eyes, feeling my pulse, and with no face, as t'were, outfacing me, cries out I was possessed.
>
> (V.i.237–244)

Will Kemp, on the other hand was probably more portly, as he seems to have played Falstaff, the fat, braggart and cowardly knight in *1 Henry IV* and *2 Henry IV*.

As far as can be deduced, Kemp's other roles appear to run along the lines of the serving-man and clown, very like the part of the zanni. So it is interesting to speculate on the possibility that he had had personal acquaintance with his Italian counterparts. This takes us back to the Earl of Leicester's Men. From the little we know of the travels of English actors abroad, it seems there were three actors in particular who may have had a chance to meet Italian players in Europe, namely, Will Kemp, Thomas Pope, and George Bryan. Kemp is first heard of in November 1585, at Dunkirk, France, as one of Leicester's players, when the Earl was the leader of the unsuccessful English campaign against the Spanish in the Netherlands. In March 1586 Kemp was in Utrecht, where he is referred to in a letter by Sir Philip Sidney as 'Will, my Lord of Lester's jesting plaier', and where, in April, the company performed a feat of strength known as the 'Forces of Hercules' (Chambers 1923 II: 90–91). Kemp was then recommended by Leicester to King Frederick II of Denmark, and he and his fellows, Thomas Pope, George Bryan and four other members of Leicester's Men were employed at the court in Elsinore (of all places!) from July to September 1586 (Chambers 1923 II: 90–91, 272–273).

Now of course, the names of Pope and Bryan are next found in the plot of *The Second Part of the Seven Deadly Sins*, performed in about 1590, by which time all three players had probably joined Lord Strange's Men. Kemp had published several of the rhyming jigs for which he was so popular and that he danced as after-pieces to the plays (Chambers II 1923: 325–327; 342–345). Earlier references to him by Thomas Nashe indicate that he was well known in London by about 1590 (Chambers 1923 II: 325f.; IV: 24).

Nashe calls Kemp 'Jestmonger and Vice-regent general to the Ghost of Dicke Tarlton' (Nashe 1590: Preface) and he seems to have taken over not only Tarlton's popularity, but some of the characteristics of his role as a rural clown. Richard Tarlton, said to have been the Queen's favourite clown, originally a member of Leicester's Men, was one of the elite company of the Queen's Men from its formation in 1583 until his death in 1588. He was the author of at least one play, *The Second Part of the Seven Deadly Sins*, the 'plot' of which is considered above, prepared for its revival in the 1590s by the Admiral's/Strange's Men, which records the names of so many of Shakespeare's fellow actors.

We know that in 1592 Shakespeare was just such an actor-cum-playwright. Pitifully little is known about his activities between 1585, when his twin children were born at Stratford, and 1592, when Robert Greene first recorded his presence in London. These 'lost' seven years have given rise to much speculation, but they certainly included his first active involvement in the theatre.

Besides the actors he met, Shakespeare's knowledge of the Commedia dell'Arte may also have come from personal acquaintance with Italians in England, particularly those such as Giovanni (John) Florio, who were connected with the households of his patrons and employers. Florio compiled the first Italian-English dictionary, and has been identified as the target of the satirical portrait of the pedant Holofernes in *Love's Labour's Lost*. Shakespeare may have met him at the home of his patron, the Earl of Southampton in 1595, when Florio was closely associated with both Southampton and the Earl of Essex (Rossi 1993: 113). A close friend of Florio was Vincento Saviolo, a well-known master of arms in London, who published a treatise on swordsmanship that Shakespeare may have referred to in writing and staging *Romeo and Juliet* (ibid.).

Rowse believed that through Southampton Shakespeare also met Emilia Lanier, daughter of Baptista Bassano, the Queen's musician, and that she was the Dark Lady and Southampton the Fair Young Man of the Sonnets (Rowse 1989). Rowse points out that Shakespeare used every scrap of information that came his way, and it is therefore no coincidence that the names Emilia and Bassan(i)o occur in *Othello* and *Merchant of Venice*, the two Venetian plays, as the Bassano family was from Venice and may have been secret Jews. Baptista, of course, is the name of the father of Katherine and Bianca in *The Shrew*.

I said earlier that Shakespeare used Commedia 'theatregrams' throughout his plays. Many further examples can be found of the way he used the stock Commedia characters in particular. Pantalone, for example, seems to be reincarnated not only in a character such as Gremio, but also in Baptista Minola, Shylock, Polonius, Desdemona's father Brabantio, and even King Lear, all of whom have trouble with their daughters. Ophelia's madness may have been inspired by the displays of *pazzia* that were such a popular feature of Isabella Andreini's role as the *innamorata*. (We remember, too, the mad scene in *The Dead Man's Fortune*.)

When it came to female roles, Shakespeare also quickly grasped the value of giving the *inamorata* a serving maid as a companion, allowing the women's point of view of a masculine world to be more readily revealed. How many well-known maids there are! From Princess Katherine's maid Alice and Juliet's Nurse, to Portia's Nerissa, Desdemona's Emilia, and Cleopatra's Iras and Charmian, they all provide the heroine with a natural feminine foil. The girl disguised as a boy provided the same opportunity for women's views to be presented. Both of these roles, of course, originated with the Commedia.

It appears then that, as Oscar Campbell (1925: 30–31) argued, it was not the Commedia Erudita but the Commedia dell'Arte that was the primary source of his knowledge of Italian drama:

> Of the two sorts of Italian comedy one would expect the Commedia dell'Arte to have the more definite influence upon English drama. Only those few literary comedies which were translated into English could have exerted any pervasive influence. The appeal of the Commedia dell'Arte, on the other

hand, was largely independent of language ... Its appeal was striking, picturesque, unique. Such plays, once seen, would be held securely in memory and all their comic devices cherished.

An outstanding feature of Shakespeare's drama is the frequency with which types and situations are 'recycled', with slight variations, in more than one play. In the early comedies we have looked at we have seen examples of comic devices that Shakespeare was to use time and again in his later plays. In many cases, these were gags and other forms of lazzi that had previously been used by the improvising Italian players. His playful use of the stock types, and his manner of combining them in creating his characters show a profound influence from Italy that he made uniquely his own.

One can argue that Shakespeare had served an 'apprenticeship' of sorts in the school of Italian improvised comedy, and that this gave him a tried-and-tested way of making a play. It gave him a stock of comic situations and devices with which to propel a story on stage, and a basic but variable cast of character types that he made free and inventive use of. He clearly found the Commedia masks a fertile source for his imagination. We shall never know the full secret of Shakespeare's creativity, but I do not think the role of the Commedia dell'Arte can be ignored in a study of his dramatic genius.

Footnotes and additional background information can be found by searching www.academia.edu, for Andrew Grewar.

References

Baldwin, T.W. (1927) *The Organization and Personnel of the Shakespearean Company.* Princeton, US: Princeton University Press.

Campbell, Oscar J. (1925) '*Love's Labour's Lost*, Restudied'. *Studies in Shakespeare, Milton, and Donne.* Ann Arbor, US: University of Michigan Publications. 1: 3–45.

Chambers, Sir Edmund K. (1923) *The Elizabethan Stage*, 4 vols. Oxford, UK: Clarendon Press.

Clubb, Louise George (1989) *Italian Drama and Shakespeare's Time.* New Haven, US: Yale University Press.

Duchartre, Pierre Louis (1966) *The Italian Comedy: The Improvisation, Scenarios, Lives, Attributes, Portraits and Masks of the Illustrious Characters of the Commedia dell'Arte.* Randolf T. Weaver (tr.) reprinted with a supplement, New York: Dover.

Greg, Walter W. (1931) *Dramatic Documents from the Elizabethan Playhouses: Stage Parts, Actors' Prompt Books, Vol. II: Reproductions and Transcripts.* Oxford, UK: Clarendon Press.

Katritzky, M.A. (1996) 'Orlando di Lasso and the Commedia dell'Arte'. *Orlando di Lasso in der Musikgeschichte. Bericht über das Symposium der Bayerischen Akademie der Wissenschaften München, 4–6 Juli 1994*, ed. Bernold Schmid. Munich, Germany: Bayerische Akademie der Wissenschaften.

——(2005) 'Reading the Actress in Commedia Imagery', in *Women Players in England, 1500–1660*, ed. Pamela Allen Brown and Peter Parolin, pp. 109–143. Aldershot, UK/ Burlington, VT, US: Ashgate.

Lea, Kathleen M. (1934) *Italian Popular Comedy: A Study of the Commedia dell'Arte, 1560–1620, with Special Reference to the English Stage,* 2 vols. Oxford, UK: Clarendon Press, republished 1962, New York: Russell.

Nashe, Thomas (1590) *An Almond for a Parrot.* Preface. London: I. Charlewood for Thomas Hackett.

Rossi, Sergio (1993) 'Duelling in the Italian manner: the case of *Romeo and Juliet*', in Michele Marrapodi, A.J. Hoenselaars, Marcello Capuzzo and L. Fanzon Santucci (eds) *Shakespeare's Italy: Functions of Italian locations in Renaissance drama,* pp.112–124. Manchester, UK/New York: University of Manchester Press, St. Martin's Press.

Rowse, A.L. (1989) *Discovering Shakespeare: A Chapter in Literary History.* London: Weidenfeld & Nicolson.

Salerno, Henry F. (tr.) (1967) *Scenarios of the 'Commedia dell'Arte: Flaminio Scala's 'Il teatro delle favole rappresentative.* New York: New York University Press.

Schrickx, Willem (1976) 'Commedia dell'Arte Players in Antwerp in 1576: Drusiano and Tristano Martinelli'. *Theatre Research International* 2: 79–85.

Wells, Stanley and Gary Taylor (1987) *William Shakespeare: A Textual Companion.* Oxford, UK: Clarendon Press.

Wickham, Glynne (1963) *Early English Stages, 1300 to 1660,* 2 vols. London: Routledge & Kegan Paul.

Wikipedia. n.d. http://en.wikipedia.org/wiki/ (accessed March 2013).

32

SHAKESPEARE'S CLOWN CONNECTION

Hybridizing Commedia's Zanni

Sara Romersberger

Commedia dell'Arte and the plays created by Shakespeare shared many common roots, despite evolving into distinctive and separate beasts. Their creators were educated in the emerging neo-classical tradition, and were among the first early modern theatre professionals in Europe, literally making up the rules as they went along. These rules were highly influenced by local and national politics, the country-urban divide, the power and relationship between church and state, as well as many local cultural factors such as high days, feast days, local carnival and midsummer.

All of these influences were subsidiary, in the minds of the practitioners, to the business of making a living from theatre. Both Commedia actors and Shakespeare's actors used whatever stories and tricks they had up their sleeves to entertain the wide range of social classes that were becoming their audiences. They both exploited the humour through immediately recognizable repertoire defined by the fools, clowns, dupes, gulls, braggarts, windbags, pedants, pantaloons and, of course, zannis, the lowly, clever servants of Commedia. This chapter presents arguments for similarities and differences between Commedia's servants, and the clowns and fools of Shakespeare's plays.

In Italy the artisan-actors of the Commedia dell'Arte developed professional physical comedy with improvised texts. Each performer was responsible for not only his or her character traits, as in Elizabethan theatre, but also for the words they spoke on stage. Eschewing the unifying vision of a singular author in favour of collective efforts, Commedia dell' Arte became *the* popular theatre of Italy and across the continent. The same period of theatrical development in the UK is still commonly referred to as Shakespearean: "Native English invention and literary models take precedence but do not eliminate the possibility of the influence of the classic New Comedies or that of the foreign professional who exploited the same Renaissance types." (Lea 1934: 405)

Commedia's first and second zanni, have clear-cut cousins in Shakespeare's clowns. Shakespeare certainly knew of the Italian comedians, and refers to them frequently. What is interesting to us here is how these two similar groupings relate.

The potential hybridization of these two streams, both sharing some common roots in Plautus' plays and Plautine neo-classical derivatives, is of major interest. It has implications both for the study of historical performance, but also for providing options when creating a contemporary *mise-en-scène* for the text based Shakespearean clowns.

In the 1800 years between Plautus and Shakespeare, many comic archetypes, such as the slave, the old man, the parasite, the lovers, the baud or courtesan, and more, remained in contemporary stage use. The changing nature of government and societal order, however, changed the way these fixed types were represented on stage. The history and politics that separated the writings of the classic new comedies and the early modern period of Shakespeare and Commedia dell'Arte dictated that, as in the former, the servant or slave could no longer drive the action. The clown in the early modern period was a serving man, but no longer the clever slave and the chief mischief-maker who manipulated the outcome of the story.

The Roman comedy classic slave was instrumental in advancing the plot, usually involving intricate comic machinations designed to ensure the young lovers' union against the wishes of the father. Shakespeare, on the other hand, used the clown's relationship *to*, or physical business *with*, his master to develop or reveal the personality, idiosyncrasies and needs of the character he served, rather than furthering the plot. The clown/fool commented on the action or, in harmonic scenes mirroring the major story developments, explicated the plot intrigues and enlivened the dramatic action.

For example, in *The Merchant of Venice*, the considerably dim yet unabashed manipulator, zanni-esque Launcelot Gobbo enters stage right to enliven the subplot. In addition to an embedded *lazzi* with his blind father, he had several zanni-like actions: he set up and yanked the chain of his master Shylock the tight-fisted, possessive father, left the service of his Jewish master to enter the employ of a gentile, and by Act Five spewed anti-Semitism against Shylock's daughter while he cleverly corrected his new master on the proper use of language involving serving dinner. Launcelot splashed around in *Merchant* without influencing the ultimate "pound of flesh" climax.

The Plautian slave-zanni-servant-clown employed in Shakespeare's first two comedies, *The Comedy of Errors* (Dromios) and *Taming of the Shrew* (Grumio and Tranio) were replaced with clowns possessing a more home-grown persona. English audiences recognized the featured clown as the leader of the revels, or the comic master of ceremonies of seasonal festivals or akin to the enormously popular churlish, quipping, rhyming rustic clown, Richard Tarlton, who entertained at venues as sophisticated as Queen Elizabeth's royal court banquets as well as at corner pubs.

As Shakespeare developed as a playwright, his star clowns grew away from the Plautian slaves and second zanni Commedia model, and became closer to that of the English court fool. The Italianate archetypes emerged in Shakespeare's final Jacobean comedies with the appearance of the fool and Robert Armin as the principal comedian. In *The Winter's Tale* (Autolycus with Clown and the Old Shepherd) and *The Tempest* (Trinculo and Stephano with Caliban) the clown teams returned with Italian names, Italianate style lazzi and zanni-centric relationships. The interest is always how the English and Italian streams interact.

English indigenous types

With over 100 religious holidays on the early sixteenth century English calendar, the city and country folk alike enjoyed those festivals along with the touring theatricals—with minstrels, comedians and comic acrobats in tow. (Ghose 2008:146) Even for the casual reader, the titles of Shakespeare's comedies signal a link between the holidays connected to the English Festivals (May Day, Midsummer's Eve, Twelfth Night…) and Shakespeare's comedies. The Medieval Vice, the Lord of Misrule and the Festival Fool were the usual comedic suspects, either elected or paid to guide the festivities.

The Medieval Vice was the central mischief-maker in the Morality Plays. Man, as the central character, was advised or enticed by personifications of Good (Mercy, Good Deeds, Beauty, Strength, Discretion) and Evil (Mischief, Folly, Fancy) with the goal of choosing a godly life over an evil life. The Vice as comic centrepiece of the play was the devil's advocate and a personification of Iniquity. This diabolic figure was also the bridge between the audience and the onstage action: keeping the audience focused on the moral dilemmas portrayed. In the late medieval period and early Renaissance, these Tudor theatrical entertainments were known as "interludes" and were still playing across England when Shakespeare was young.

The Lord of Misrule, dressed in improvised regalia, was initially the ugliest, poorest, and stupidest member of the community, and as a local was the inadvertent figurehead for the event. Elected or following his father, this country rustic took the role of a fake leader and manipulator for the duration of seasonal festivals. Vehicles for release and renewal, the early festivals were *inversionary*: topsy-turvy events in which the low class assumed the roles of town leaders or lords while the rich landowners took on the duties of the serving class or working class. Whether voted in by the community or later hired to make those festive events successful—the latter more civic minded—the Lord of Misrule had a great deal of power over the local politics and populations. Through plays written specifically for the seasonal events, Lords of Misrule had license to criticize unfair rulers and social despots through parody. There were limits, however: those who used their leadership position in the May Games as a pulpit for criticism that uttered slander, or stirred the populous to riot or mayhem, were fined, potentially whipped and given jail sentences. Shakespeare would have known that as long as the butt of the criticism was not specifically named, no one, including the festival leaders, could be accused of libel, as in the Dymoke case of 1601. (Barber 1959:40)

The Festival Fool was an imitation rustic idiot or professional fool, mimicking the behaviour of a Lord of Misrule. He was a professional outsider brought in specifically to entertain. The Vice-like character wore a fool's coat, which was a special costume kept year to year just for the role. He might be required to read a scripted part but could fill in extemporaneously, but with no malapropisms. As a Festival Fool he would also dance outside the formation of the Morris performers, poking fun at the dancers who missed steps (Wiles 1987:163).

The Medieval Vice, the Lord of Misrule, and the Festival Fool carried out very different functions, but through time their distinctions became less defined. By the end of the sixteenth century their unique personas blended with each other or with new characters, or disappeared entirely as both professional and amateur performers usurped their functions and roles. Shakespeare, familiar with all these comic manipulators, borrowed aspects from each: comic anarchism, disorder, and inversion, and used them to pass comment or debunk authority humorously.

For example, Shakespeare transformed the Vice role from the Morality Plays to a fool or clown that questioned the leading character's own human strengths and foibles, rather than controlling and questioning the moral actions of the audience. Like Commedia's zannis, these clowns would often occupy a space on the stage between the audiences and the action, and address the audience directly. This functioned more as exposition or personal storytelling, rather than audience manipulation. The Lord of Misrule also changes within this context. Previously as a leader of local festive comic rites, in Shakespeare's plays he becomes a rabble-rouser and party animal, as personified by Sir Toby Belch in *Twelfth Night* or as Falstaff himself, incidentally also embodying the braggart or cowardly tendencies of a Commedia Capitano. The Festival Fool also got a Shakespearean makeover, giving way to the Court Fool: one who knew "that through parodying normal men, could point up the follies of normal men" (Wiles 1987:163).

Shakespearean comedy and Commedia dell'Arte: farce or comedy?

Shakespeare wrote comedies, not farce, although this issue has been hotly contested in the case of *The Comedy of Errors*. Shakespeare gave his clowns, especially when playing the servants and rustics, many of the trappings of farce, both in how it was performed and what was performed: surprises, incongruities, mechanical patterns of repetition, duplications, sequences, reversals, interruptions, delays, as well as comic devises, dramatic irony, sub-plots, subordinate episodes or meta-dramatic sequences. It is part of Shakespeare's craft that within these trappings and technical accomplishments, something deeper, more human and certainly more focused on humanism emerged.

There are many sections in Shakespeare that might as easily have come from a Commedia performance as from his pen. In *The Comedy of Errors*, speaking of being beaten by Antipholus of Ephesus, Dromio of Ephesus says, in comic despair:

When I am cold, he heats me with beating; when I am warm, he cools me with beating. I am wak'd with it when I sleep, rais'd with it when I sit; driven out of doors with it when I go from home; welcom'd home with it when I return; nay, I bear it on my shoulders, as a beggar wont her brat; and, I think when he hath lam'd me, I shall beg with it from door to door. (IV, iv: Shakespeare 1974: 5)

Likewise we see it in *The Taming of the Shrew* in the play between Petruchio and his servant Grumio as he struggles with the double meaning of "knock":

PETRUCHIO: Here, sirrah Grumio; knock, I say.
GRUMIO: Knock, sir! whom should I knock? is there man has rebus'd your worship?
PETRUCHIO: Villain, I say, knock me here soundly.
GRUMIO: Knock you here, sir! why, sir, what am I, sir, that
    I should knock you here, sir?

PETRUCHIO: Villain, I say, knock me at this gate
  And rap me well, or I'll knock your knave's pate.
GRUMIO: My master is grown quarrelsome. I should knock
  you first, And then I know after who comes by the worst.
PETRUCHIO: Will it not be?
  Faith, sirrah, an you'll not knock, I'll ring it;
  I'll try how you can *sol, fa,* and sing it.

[*Petruchio wrings Gurmio by the ears*]

GRUMIO: Help, [masters], help! my master is mad.
PETRUCHIO: Now, knock when I bid you, sirrah villain!
                    (I, i: Shakespeare 1974: 6)

Shakespeare enlivened his plays with embedded lazzi or implied physical business with prescribed props or instruments such as: Trinculo, Stephano and Caliban under the gabardine in *The Tempest,* (II, ii), Autolycus pickpocketing Clown's money bag in *The Winters's Tale* (IV, iii), and the taunting of the starved and sleep deprived Katherine and her subsequent beating of Grumio in *The Taming of the Shrew* (IV, iii). Additionally the pick and shovel of the Gravedigger and Sexton in *Hamlet,* tabor playing by Feste, and the tipping of him by Viola in *Twelfth Night* (III, i), the bauble of Lear's Fool and the Spanish sword and drum of Parolles in *All's Well That Ends Well*—all have textual set-ups for physical play that reveal possible Commedia similarities. Shakespeare's text prescribed the business and the clown actor brought the lazzi to life and rendered it funny while making it appear improvisational.

   Even if Shakespeare lifted the slave character (Dromio) and the braggart captain (Don Armado, Toby Belch, Falstaff) from Commedia dell'Arte, the physical business or lazzi embedded in the work, could as easily have been appropriated by an English theatre company as from an Italian company or vice versa. If Shakespeare viewed, or heard, from other professionals, and then imitated Commedia performances and documented the style in his texts, could we now interpolate backward to find details on Commedia traits within his play texts? Italian comedians certainly performed in England between 1573 and 1578 (Smith 1912:170–199), and Drusiano Martinelli's company may have even performed on Burbage's stage in Shoreditch as his company had the a grant from the Privy Council "to plate within the city and the liberties" (ibid.: 175)

Definitions: what is a clown and what is a fool in Shakespeare's theatre?

Simply put, clowns and fools are both *clowns*. The clowns were difficult to play and thus required that the company's principal comedian take on such important roles, similar to the demands on actors playing zanni in improvised theatre. The only character listed as a fool in the *dramatis persona* was Lear's fool. The remaining characters described in the body of the play's text as a fool are listed as "clown" in the character breakdown. Thus "clown", in the Shakespeare's playhouse, is a theatrical term identifying the principle actor-comedian, in other words "the actor a company employed specifically to be its clown" (Wiles 1987: 61). Feste, Olivia's fool (*Twelfth Night*), Touchstone, the fool in the court of Duke Frederick *(As You Like It)* and Lavatch, the fool for the Countess of Roussillon (*All's Well That Ends Well*) are all listed in the *dramatis personae* as "a clown".

The term clown is also interchangeable with the word "rustic", signifying a person ignorant of courtly behaviour, not urbane, acting as working or lower class and not knowing or following the rules of the polite world. Whether a bondsman (Dromio), a servant (Grumio), a clown (Costard), or a clownish servant (Launce), many of the early Shakespearean characters who are described as rustics or clowns have the same characteristics as the naïve second zanni: a disenfranchised rustic trying to make sense of the big city. The genesis of the term clown is presented in David Wiles' *Shakespeare's Clown: Actor and Text in the Elizabethan Playhouse*. "The word entered the language because it expresses a new concept: the rustic who by virtue of his rusticity is necessarily inferior and ridiculous" (Wiles 1987: 61).

Will Kemp, Shakespeare's first star clown

William Kemp, the foremost "theatrical clown" in Shakespeare's plays replaced, but did not quite equal, Richard Tarleton, Queen Elizabeth's favourite who died before Shakespeare's time. Dubbed the "vicegerent general to the ghost of Dick Tarlton" (Nashe 1590: preface), Kemp was not *a* clown but *the* clown: the actor hired to play the principal comedian role. Kemp joined the Chamberlain's Men, after *The Comedy of Errors* (Dromios) and *The Taming of the Shrew* (Grumio), marking the beginning of the *star clown* roles. After that he played as a full member of the acting company. By joining he carried with him a significant comedic reputation as a highly gifted performer throughout England. Like the zanni, Shakespeare's clowns were professionals, not boys hired for the smaller comic parts. "Boys and students had neither the technical skills nor the years in the public eye needed in order to project a clown persona-a persona distinct from and interacting with roles written into individual plays" (Wiles 1987: 63).

Kemp was, by all reports, a powerfully built, agile actor, who excelled in leaping, Morris dancing, creating jigs, improvising in prose and rhyme; had a rustic "plain man" persona, not a *gentleman* and no wish to be one and, most importantly, a former occasional Lord of Misrule, known for improvising while on stage (Wiles 1987: 24–5).

The rustics like Launce, Launcelot Gobbo and Costard are not court fools, and therefore do not have licence to speak with impunity. Yet they are defined by their ignorance and avoid punishment out of sheer stupidity. They say and do many things outside the accepted rules *because they do not know any better*. They are always endearing for their foibles and although clowns, they have human needs and emotions. They use the wrong word, or mispronounce, or simply say something inappropriate or inopportune. Even with incorrect usage, the malapropism might be comically appropriate.

The Shakespearian fool stands at a crossroads where all these elements come together, a point where the dramatic traditions of the Tudor Vice and the Folk-drama fool are renewed and where European culture shows at its best the mixture of medieval and humanist concepts of folly.

(Mullini 1985: 98)

A fixture in many royal households, in addition to being an entertainment, and sometime serving man, the fool had nothing to profit from the outcome of what his ruler said so had license to speak with impunity. This lower class subject was summoned to court to speak the truth or simply be a voice of reason. Robert Armin, Kemp's replacement, was skilled at mimicking and was a master of the clever court fool's quick and witty banter. His monologues were written as vehicles for virtuoso mimicry, with language that gave the pretence of "a logical mind" even if, when picked apart, his reasoning would not be valid. This quintessentially English court fool character had fewer characteristics in common with those of the Commedia second zanni. But in Robert Armin's hands, the fool as star clown often sparred or jested with other characters, similar to the antics of a first zanni. While rustic clowns were retained in Shakespeare's plays, the fool exploited the clown's inferiority and ridiculousness for fun and profit. One could look at Touchstone toying with William in *As You Like It* to see this happening:

TOUCHSTONE: It is meat and drink to me to see a clown: by my troth, we that have good wits have much to answer for; we shall be flouting; we cannot hold.

(V, i: Shakespeare 1974: 9)

Shakespeare, using the fool's voice, had license to comment upon courtly behaviour at all levels of English society.

Displaced and fired fools—First Zanni or Brighella

In the later part of Shakespeare's canon after 1600, Pompey (a bawd) and Autolycus (a rogue) in *Measure for Measure* and *The Winter's Tale* respectively are principal comedians who fall into the category of "displaced fools". The "displaced fools" were clever low characters that claimed to have served as court fools but, as in the case of Autolycus, were "Whipped out of the court" (IV, iii), and were now living as bauds, pimps, rogues or thieves. They are clever manipulators who are divisive, but yet not a medieval "vice", devilish but not evil. Though they live on the street and speak in prose, they do not fall into the category of rustic half-wit, adrift in a city. They have evolved one more step: they pretend to be a clown to fool others for their own gain. A great deal of their humour comes in tricking or cleverly outwitting other characters. They verbally spar with rustics, and generally get the better of them: Autolycus with Old Shepherd and Clown in *The Winter's Tale* or Pompey with Abhorson, an executioner in *Measure for Measure*. Although they do not have *carte blanche,* they are literate, and they know the workings of the court and have developed the skills necessary to save their own skins. They are wise enough to play the fool to avoid trouble and well-justified punishment. These are apt descriptions of Commedia's Brighella or Scapino or Mezzetino.

Commedia, the clown and extemporaneity

After *The Comedy of Errors*, Shakespeare's clowns always spoke in prose rather than verse, outside of their songs or occasional rhyming couplets. The actors playing the clowns had well-known clown personas before joining Chamberlain' Men. When the actor, as clown, entered the stage, he appeared to be improvising, taking license with the written material and not following the rules of decorum. The extemporaneous quality of the delivery created the illusion that the actor invented his text in the moment. It may be argued that the featured clown actors invented or collaborated with the author and that only after the performance was the text documented to reflect Shakespeare's authorship. Perhaps Shakespeare framed the story and created sections to highlight the virtuosity of his star clowns. What is sure is that audience laughed at the clown and at the actor playing the clown.

There are large sections of Shakespeare plays with plots paralleling Italian scenarios with Commedia style characters. There is incontrovertible evidence that the Commedia troops travelled to England and the continent and played to provincial, city and court audiences while Shakespeare was living and writing in England. Perhaps Will Kemp, Shakespeare's first principal comedian; the actor who created most rustic clown roles, discovered many of his devices on his own but…

> Cut off from all contact with the Continental stage, it is quite conceivable that Kemp and his associates should have discovered for themselves the effect of the delayed entrance, of bursting into tears, of weeping over an onion, of bringing food or animals on to the stage, of the direct address to the audience, of the use of dialect, mistaken works and parody, and that they should have taught themselves how to exploit the comedy of greed, sleepiness, stupidity, feigned death and mock wooings, but the belief that any or all of these devices were within the scope of their invention does not damage the supposition that, given the chance, they would avail themselves of the short cut of imitation.
>
> (Lea 1934, 405)

The bard's characters "defy the bounds of rigid classification" but investigation of Commedia, especially of the zanni, offers great insight for a player to use action in designing his character and the business called for in the text. The historical congruity between the styles allows a contemporary theatre-maker to see possible choices of action for clown or fool. Knowledge of the roots of Commedia and how the zanni played can create a strong, informed base from which to shape the physical life and staging routines of Shakespeare's clown characters.

Shakespeare wrote for the popular audience. Was it Shakespeare's intention to both employ the Commedia archetypes and also retain the same physical energy and ways of provoking laughter of the great improvisers of the Commedia? We will never know for sure. But it follows that he would not intend to lose the physical play that made the Commedia dell'Arte so popular throughout Europe in the Renaissance, only "refine it somewhat", and amend it to fit the tastes of his audiences, texts and locations. Shakespeare was always trying to draw on what was popular and use it to his advantage.

References

Barber, C.L. (1959) *Shakespeare's Festive Comedy: A Study of Dramatic Form and its Relation to Social Custom*. Cleveland and New York: The World Publishing Company.

Ghose, Indira (2008) *Shakespeare and Laughter: A Cultural History*. Manchester, UK: Manchester University Press.

Lea, K.M. (1934) *Italian Popular Comedy: A Study in the Commedia dell'Arte 1560–1620 with Special Reference to the English Stage*, (2 vols.), Oxford, UK: Clarendon Press.

Mullini, Roberta (1985) "Playing the Fool: Pragmatic Status of Shakespeare's Clowns." *New Theatre Quarterly*, 1, 98–104.

Nashe, Thomas (1590) *An Almond for a Parrot*. Preface. London: I. Charlewood for Thomas Hackett.

Shakespeare, William (1974) *The Riverside Shakespeare*, 2nd edn. Volume II. Boston, US: Houghton Mifflin.

Smith, Winifred (1912) *The Commedia dell'Arte: A Study in Popular Italian Comedy*. US: Columbia University Press.

Wiles, David (1987) *Shakespeare's Clown: Actor and Text in the Elizabethan Playhouse*. UK: Cambridge University Press.

33

WRITING FOR THE ELITE
Molière, Marivaux, and Beaumarchais
Elizabeth C. Goldsmith

In the court and capital of France, the world of theatre in the century leading up to the French Revolution was one that catered to the increasing literacy and sophistication of elite audiences. It was also a world that had to contend with a tightening of official mechanisms of censorship. Actors working in the Commedia dell'Arte tradition found themselves regularly targeted, most dramatically in 1697 when the principal troupe of Italian players in Paris were expelled from the city. But the vernacular culture of slapstick, fairground entertainment, and physical comedy retained its popularity with even the most aristocratic of audiences. The high classicism of tragic drama was only part of the picture in the development of French theatre in the age of Louis XIV. Elite audiences remained open to popular culture, and their increasing fascination with the visual theater of everyday life created opportunities for actors and playwrights to give new depth to the familiar masked characters from the Commedia.

Molière

The author we know as Molière was baptized Jean-Baptiste Poquelin, on January 15, 1622. Molière's fame came during his lifetime, but he was admired as an actor as much as a writer (for his works see Molière 1981, 2001). He always performed the central comic roles in the plays he wrote for his troupe of actors. Molière's career in the theatre began when he decided to abandon the training in law to which he had been committed by his father and join a group of itinerant players led by Armand Béjart and his family, who called themselves "The Society of the Illustrious Theater." Molière and other members of the troupe drew up a contract and rented a space in Paris, opening in 1644, but, soon debt-ridden, the troupe decided to leave Paris and tour the provinces.

This was the beginning of a thirteen-year period that the Illustrious Theater spent playing for villagers and provincial nobility across France. Molière became the leader of the troupe as well as its principal actor, and he began writing short farces inspired by familiar Commedia scenarios. Encouraged by their successes on the road and new patronage offered by the king's brother, Philippe d'Orléans, they returned to Paris in 1658 and were granted performance space in the Petit-Bourbon Theatre, a stage that they shared with the Italian players then in residence in the French capital. Despite his abiding ambition to make a name for himself as an actor in tragedies and tragicomedies, viewed as superior to lowly farces, Molière soon saw that even his most elite audiences preferred to see him in comic roles. When the troupe gave a royal performance of a tragedy by Corneille, attended by the young king Louis XIV and his mother, Anne of Austria, they also added to the program Molière's short farce *Le Dépit amoureux* (The Scorned Lovers), performed in mask in Commedia style. His audience loved it.

In 1659 Molière decided to produce a comic play that would parody provincial women who were coming to Paris and trying to copy the style and tastes of the elite. *Les Précieuses ridicules* mocked the ladies' efforts to immerse themselves in popular romance novels and imitated the affectations of a new generation of women intellectuals. The role he assigned himself was that of a wily servant, Mascarille, played in mask, who disguises himself outrageously as a Marquis and all too easily fools the gullible and admiring provincial newcomers. The play was a great success and Molière decided to take the next step in his career and commit it to print, although in his preface to the play he expresses great anxiety about making the move from actor to published author.

Molière's attention to performance and staging and to the improvisational traditions of the Commedia remained paramount in his plays, even as he developed an increasingly sophisticated vision of the comic genre. His greatest achievement as an author was to have invented a "comedy of character" that introduced psychological depth to stock comic situations, in the process drawing on traditions from popular farce and more serious drama. Beginning with *L'Ecole des femmes* (The School for Wives, 1662) he wrote five-act comedies in verse, as well as *comédies-ballets* combining music, dance, and poetry with the clownish elements of Commedia dell'Arte. His comic characters often have a single dominant trait or "mask," suggested in many of the titles of his plays, as in *L'Etourdi* (The Bungler, 1655) and *L'Avare* (The Miser, 1668). They also portray the social obsessions of Molière's elite audiences, as in his satirical portrait of educated women, *Les Femmes savantes* (The Learned Ladies, 1672) or in his penetrating portrayal of salon society, *Le Misanthrope* (1666).

Molière's audiences understood from the beginning that he was trying to invent a new type of more 'serious' comedy. His first five-act play, *The School for Wives* provoked a literary quarrel and inspired Molière to write another play mocking his critics, called *The Critique of the School for Wives* (1663). Critics had objected to what they saw as the inconsistency of the character Arnolphe, who seemed both tragic and ridiculous. Molière's mouthpiece in *The Critique* argued simply for the psychological realism of the role. This was a formula that would continue to inspire Molière to create characters of increasing complexity operating in a recognizable social setting.

Having secured the favor of the young king Louis XIV, Molière undertook to fight, from the stage, the attacks on the theatre being mounted by radical religious parties of the Catholic reform movement. A first version of his play *Tartuffe*, portraying a religious hypocrite who deceives his gullible and devout host and attempts to seduce his wife, was staged in 1664. It was immediately banned by the Church censors and attacked in print by Molière's former patron Conti, among others. Molière withdrew the play, but continued to press for its revival, at great personal risk, until a final version, that included a flattering panegyric to the king, was produced under royal protection in 1669. Meanwhile he composed and produced *Don Juan* in 1665, a disquieting and innovative version of the story of the legendary seducer of women, who in Molière's version is a libertine and an atheist, a modern, educated nobleman who has lost his moral bearings. Still, both Tartuffe and Dom Juan, and even more clearly the characters Orgon, Dorine, Cle'ante, Elmire, and Sganarelle, are rooted in Commedia traditions and the stock figures of Pantalone, Columbina, Il Dottore, Brighella/Scapino, La Signora, and Zanni.

Throughout the first decade of the reign of Louis XIV, Molière produced plays commissioned for court spectacles, many of them on short notice, in which he also played the principal role. His *L'Impromptu de Versailles* (1663) gives us an amusing inside look at his own troupe at work attempting to rehearse a play that Molière had not had the time to finish. *George Dandin* (1668), with a simple plot taken from a standard Commedia scenario involving a clever wife who outwits her dull drunkard of a husband, was first performed at Versailles, thickly embroidered with ballet and musical *intermèdes* written by the composer Jean-Baptiste Lully. *Le Bourgeois gentilhomme* (The Would-Be Gentleman), a *comédie-ballet* also produced in collaboration with Lully, premiered at the castle of Chambord in 1670. The play mocks a foolish middle-class man who cannot manage to learn the behaviors and graces of a gentleman. In a series of scenes blending music, dance, and parade, the play explores the hazy frontier between mask, performance, and reality. In a finale that takes on the aura of a dream sequence, the ridiculous Monsieur Jourdain is treated to an elaborate ritual fooling him into thinking he has finally turned into the gentleman he has been trying so ineptly to become.

Molière died on February 17, 1673, after collapsing during a production of his play *Le Malade Imaginaire* (The Imaginary Invalid), in which he, at the time seriously ill, was playing the title role of a hypochondriac. In this play the psychological obsession of the principal character with mask and disguise results in a blend of comedy and nightmare. Denied burial on sacred ground because of his profession, Molière was finally interred, secretly and at night, in his parish cemetery by special permission of the king. The manner of his death has become part of his legacy; students of the theatre regard him as an iconic figure, devoted to the stage, whose work bridges the gap that so often divides the play as text and performance.

During the period in which Molière troupe was performing in Paris and at court, the Italian players headed by Tiberio Fiorelli had been given official status and royal authorization to remain permanently in the French capital. With the royal order establishing the Comédie Française in 1680, only one troupe was authorized to perform plays in Paris. The street performances of the fairgrounds and the Comédie Italienne were exceptions to this new monopoly, but they were not allowed to produce lengthy written works or plays by authors of tragedy and serious drama. In Molière's heyday, the Théâtre Italien had enjoyed some freedom from royal supervision – since they did not typically use printed scripts, they were not easily subject to censorship, and even the increasingly vigilant members of the French Academy seemed to take the view that low comedy could be allowed its subversive functions.

The "Italians," as the actors from the troupe who had shared the stage with Molière were known, gradually introduced an increasing amount of French into their Paris productions, and French writers including Regnard, Lesage, and Dufresny wrote plays designed for them to perform, with these plays eventually being printed. With success and the prestige of authorship came closer scrutiny by Louis XIV's increasingly sophisticated system of state censorship. When Evaristo Gherardi published a collection of Commedia scenarios 1694, the Biancolelli troupe of Italian actors petitioned the king to have it suppressed, arguing that the printing of their work was damaging to their success and reputation (Radulescu 2012: 78–9). Indeed, there were consequences of these developments that Molière, had he lived to see them, might have predicted. In 1697, after performing a play called *La Fausse prude* (The False Prude) that was viewed as a satire of the king's pietistic second wife Madame de Maintenon, the Italian actors were banished from the French capital. It was a moment that would be memorialized and bemoaned by French artists and playwrights, and depicted most famously in a painting by Antoine Watteau.

Marivaux

Marivaux was born Pierre Carlet, son of a Le Havre port official, on February 4, 1688. The family moved to the city of Riom in the Auvergne region of France, and young Pierre was eventually destined, like Molière before him, to a career in law. This he pursued with little enthusiasm. Leaving law school, he moved to Paris in 1713, throwing himself into the social world dominated by salon women such as Anne-Thérese de Lambert and the Madame du Deffand, who would become important patrons of his work. At some point along the way he took the name Marivaux. He frequented theatrical circles and argued vigorously for the "Moderns" in the cultural debates over classicism known as the "Quarrel of the Ancients and the Moderns," debates that were dividing the French literati during the last years of Louis XIV and the early phase of the regency of his brother Philippe d'Orléans. Marivaux favored new, innovative genres and he quickly became known as a journalist and novelist as well as a dramatist.

In the world of the stage, Marivaux never abandoned his attraction to Italian comedy, remaining loyal to those traditions, and arguing for their incorporation into modern theatre, despite academic disapproval. Immediately following the death of Louis XIV in 1715, the Italians were recalled from banishment. Under the regency, the strict severity of the court that had restrained cultural productions and social behavior during the last years of Louis XIV disappeared. In 1716 the Italian players were reinstalled on their own stage in the Hôtel de Bourgogne. Marivaux's early career coincided with this official rehabilitation of the Commedia in France, and he along with other playwrights collaborated on early stagings of new comedies designed for the Italians. Despite initial setbacks he persisted in his allegiance to the Italians and in 1720 his *Arlequin poli par l'amour* (Arlequin Polished by Love) was received enthusiastically. For the next twenty years Marivaux worked in close collaboration with the Italians. The Italian actors, unencumbered by the stylized mannerisms that still dominated the training of French actors performing on the stage for the Comédie Française, were able to convey the blend of social parody and emotional subtlety that Marivaux was aiming for in his comedies. The leader of the Italian troupe in this period, Luigi Riccoboni, played many of the principal roles in Marivaux's comedies. His wife Elena Balletti, and another actress Giovanna Benozzi, played most of the female leads. It was Benozzi who would first perform Marivaux's Silvia characters, the character for whom the playwright became most famous. Silvia, a sensitive and intelligent young ingénue, has been permanently associated with Marivaux in the French repertoire since his successful production of *Le Jeu de l'amour et du hasard* (The Game of Love and Chance) in 1730. In the play Silvia disguises herself as a servant to try to unmask the true character of her young suitor, but she does not know that the young man has in turn disguised himself as a servant in an attempt to achieve the same end. Confusion ensues, not only on the level of plot but in the distress of the characters, who attempt to examine the reasons for their emotional responses to each other.

Marivaux invented a particular style of witty dialogue combined with elaborate attention to refined sentiment, stemming from stock comic situations, especially ones involving disguised lovers and confused identity. The style quickly was dubbed "marivaudage," a term that is still current today. He achieved a difficult synthesis of sophisticated linguistic expression, refined psychology, and stock situations and characters from Commedia. For him, the most fascinating of the types would always be the lovers. He did not try to elevate comedy to the level of tragedy through imitating the classical form of five-act plays in verse, rather, he focused on a style of prose drawing on psychological realism, wit, and what his critics would view as hair-splitting attention to the finer sensibilities of young love (for his plays see Marivaux 1993–4, 1997).

Leading up to *The Game of Love and Chance*, Marivaux had produced a series of successful comedies drawing on Commedia traditions including *La Double Inconstance* (The Inconstant Lovers), first performed in 1723, *La Fausse suivante* (The False Maid) in 1724, *L'Isle des esclaves* (The Island of Slaves) in 1725, and *La (seconde) surprise de l'amour* (The Second Surprise of Love) in 1727. After *The Game of Love and Chance* he turned his efforts increasingly to staging plays for the Comédie Française, and with the help of the ever-present Benozzi in the lead female roles he had some success. But his successes invigorated his critics, who returned incessantly to objections he was never able to quite shake, all relating to the triviality or excessive lightness of his theatrical vision. Marivaux turned his attentions as a writer increasingly to experimental novel forms and journalism, which gave him the opportunity to articulate his theories of the modern spectator, and the role of the philosopher in a world governed by masks and human duplicity. He argued for the moral purpose of theatre and philosophy, which was only achievable because of the innate goodness in human beings. In his long memoir novel *La Vie de Marianne* (The Life of Marianne) he was able to explore at leisure the character of a young woman who resembles the ingénue type he had perfected in his plays but who engages in more elaborate adventures and sentimental escapades, overcoming adversity through irrepressible light-heartedness and belief in the generosity of others.

After he finally received official approbation in the form of election to the Académie Française in 1742, Marivaux's creative inspiration seemed to decline. Although he continued to write plays, none were successful. He became a spokesman for moral social engagement, giving away almost all of his personal wealth to philanthropies and falling into debt. He died on February 12, 1763 at age seventy-five.

Two hundred years later Jean-Louis Barrault, the great French actor and spokesman for the life of the theatre wrote a letter to the author of a book on Marivaux, expressing his gratitude for the role the book was playing in creating an audience for Marivaux outside of France. "Let serious people criticize and denounce marivaudage… it remains true nonetheless that we all would want to live with the world he managed to create," he writes. "There is no vaster problem that that of love… and Silvia! We all carry her in our hearts…" (McKee 1958: xiii–xv).

Beaumarchais

Pierre-Augustin Caron (the name Beaumarchais was one he gave himself later) was born in 1632. By the time he was a young adult, with the exception of Marivaux and a few others, authors were drawing less and less on Commedia scenarios in the design of dramatic plots. Most of the plays being written and printed in France were to some degree engaged with the new dramatic theories of "serious" or "sentimental" comedy espoused by Denis Diderot. Also called "tearful" or "bourgeois" comedy because they aimed to make audiences weep over the middle-class domestic crises that were portrayed onstage, the new drama blurred the traditional distinctions between comic and tragic genres in theater.

The young Pierre-Augustin frequented Parisian theatre and admired the new plays that he saw, but he initially followed in the footsteps of his father and became a clockmaker, while also cultivating his business and political talents as a legal negotiator and trade representative at foreign courts. In 1767 he decided to try his hand at playwrighting, producing his first play, *Eugénie*, the story of a young woman seduced and abandoned. The play failed, as did his next attempt, *Les Deux amis ou le négociant de Lyon* (The Two Friends or the Tradesman from Lyon), a drama staging a bankruptcy. Returning to what was becoming an increasingly adventurous career as an international intriguer and spy for the French court, Beaumarchais went to London, then Vienna, where he found himself imprisoned briefly as a spy and only released through the efforts of the French ministry.

Meanwhile, inspired in part by his own itinerant and adventurous lifestyle, and also by his abiding fondness for Italian comedic traditions, Beaumarchais wrote the first of his three plays about an ambitious and clever servant named Figaro, *Le Barbier de Séville* (The Barber of Seville) (for his plays see Beaumarchais 1965, 1993). This play was successful, and in his prologue Beaumarchais promised a sequel to the adventures of his determined hero who declares in *Le Barbier* that "I must force myself to laugh at everything, to keep from weeping" (I.2).

It was his second Figaro play, *La Folle Journée ou Le Mariage de Figaro* (The Mad Day or the Marriage of Figaro) that created the greatest stir in Beaumarchais's career and would be his lasting legacy. The play premiered at the Comédie Française on

April 27, 1784. It had been long awaited. By this time Beaumarchais was a celebrity because of his outlandish life, multiple public lawsuits, financial speculations, and career as a spy and not-so-secret agent. He also had read and circulated his play in the private salons of Paris and gone to great lengths to combat, and satisfy, the royal censors. King Louis XVI himself had declared the play to be dangerous, but he reversed his interdiction under pressure from members of the court who had viewed it in a private performance. Queen Marie-Antoinette demonstrated her own support for Beaumarchais by personally performing the role of Rosine for a production of *The Barber of Seville* in her private theatre.

The Marriage of Figaro at one level draws heavily on theatrical situations that were popular and certainly safe to put on the stage. The play has its share of dialogues between lovers reminiscent of Marivaux, and the character of the beautiful Countess Rosine who tearfully learns of the wayward ways of her formerly ardent husband would have been pleasing to the admirers of the new "serious" comedy. The comic devices employed by the enterprising and clever Figaro and his fiancée Susanne drew on the stock situations of the Commedia, as did the farcical bedroom scenes involving the jealous Count, characters hiding in closets, and confused identities followed by joyous recognition scenes.

But the play was troubling on other levels. Figaro confronts his master Count Almaviva when the count attempts to invoke an ancient privilege permitting him to sleep with his servant's fiancée. Not only does he use his cleverness, collaborating with Susanne, to outwit their master, he also gives impassioned speeches denouncing the arbitrary privilege of the aristocracy. At times, there is an almost surreal aspect to Figaro's blend of character traits from stock comedy along with his lengthy monologues expressing his ambitions as a self-made man. It is clear that Beaumarchais identified personally with this character who declares his fondness for intrigue, his hatred of an arbitrary judicial system, and his determination to succeed despite the corruption of the aristocratic establishment. Figaro's determined gaiety in even the direst situations keeps the play in the safe realm of the comic, while also managing to suggest real risk-taking and even the potential for vengeance. Early productions of *The Barber of Seville* had Figaro masked, in Harlequin costume. But this Commedia scenario of the servant/barber wielding a razor over his noble customer in the chair would soon be seen as more sinister: a prophetic overture to the cataclysmic events of the French Revolution.

References

Beaumarchais, Pierre-Augustin Caron de (1965) *Théâtre de Beaumarchais: Le Barbier de Seville, Le Mariage de Figaro, La Mère coupable*, ed. René Pomeau. Paris: Gallimard.

——(1993) *The Barber of Seville; The Marriage of Figaro; and the Guilty Mother*, trans. Graham Anderson. London: Oberon Press.

Marivaux, Pierre Carlet de Chamblain de (1993–4) *Théâtre complet*, eds. Henri Coulet and Michel Gilot. Paris: Gallimard.

——(1997) *Marivaux Plays: Double Inconstancy; False Servant; Game of Love and Chance; Careless Vows; Feigned Inconstancy; 1-Act Plays*, trans. Donald Watson, John Bowen, John Walters, Michael Sadler, Nicholas Wright. London: Methuen Drama.

McKee, Kenneth N. (1958) *The Theatre of Marivaux*. New York: New York University Press.

Molière (1981) *Oeuvres complètes*, 2 vols., ed. George Couton. Paris: Gallimard.

——(2001) *TheMisanthrope, Tartuffe, and other Plays*, trans. Maya Slater. Oxford, UK: Oxford University Press.

Radulescu, Domnica (2012) *Women's Comedic Art as Social Revolution*. Jefferson, North Carolina, US and London: McFarland & Co.

34

GOLDONI AND GOZZI

Reformers with separate agendas

Mike Griffin

The two eighteenth-century writers, Carlo Goldoni and Carlo Gozzi, agreed on one thing during their careers: Commedia dell'Arte was in a state of decay. However, despite their shared opinions on Commedia's condition, these two writers had conflicting philosophies concerning the methods needed to revive Italy's national drama. Goldoni wanted to reform masked comedy, without masks and improvisation, creating a new style of Italian comic-realism, while Gozzi wanted to restore the traditions of Commedia, by merging the elements of Commedia and fairy-tale, creating his unique *Fiabe*. Their passionate opposing ideals on the treatment of Commedia dell'Arte drove them into "one of the most famous literary feuds in Europe, Gozzi versus Goldoni" (DiGaetani 1988: 4). Throughout this chapter, I will look at each playwright and their connection to Commedia dell'Arte, the feud created by their conflicting ideas, and the new theatrical styles that they generated. (For their works see Goldoni 1892, 1958, 1961, 1963, 1969 and 2001; Gozzi 1951, 1958, 1988 and 1989.)

Carlo Goldoni is often remembered as one of Italy's most famous comic dramatists. At an early age, while reading ancient and modern comedies, Goldoni came to the realization there was no national drama in Italy like there was in England, France and Spain. In his *Memoirs*, Goldoni confesses:

> It was with pain I saw that the nation which was acquainted with the dramatic art before every other in modern times, was deficient in something essential. I could not conceive how Italy had in this respect grown negligent, vulgar, and degenerated. I passionately desired to see my country rise to the level of others, and I vowed to endeavour to contribute to it.
>
> (Goldoni 1877: 68–69)

He saw a need for the richness of Italy's theatre to be written down, documented, and preserved: something to which he dedicated himself, creating over one hundred plays in his career.

During Goldoni's life, Italy was in a state of change. With the theories and philosophies of the Enlightenment came new ways of thinking, questioning the traditional structures of religion, politics, science, and class. Goldoni embraced this sense of looking forward and recognized that with the changing world, theatre needed to change as well. However, on the Venetian stages one saw nothing but "indecent harlequinades, dirty scandalous intrigue, foul jests, immodest loves" (Kennard 1935: 76). The vulgar comedy that had once entertained audiences was no longer effective—their tastes were refined, their expectations higher. Theatre "was no longer credible, while in his [Goldoni's] opinion it absolutely should be" (Fava 2007: 31). Goldoni wanted to raise comedy to the same respected level of tragedy but in order to do that he had to make some changes.

One key to Goldoni's reform was his desire to remove the masks. He believed the actor must "possess a soul; and the soul beneath the mask is like fire under ashes" (Goldoni 1877: 314). Goldoni felt that the mask limited the actor's abilities for expression as "the same features are always exhibited" (ibid.). He also wanted to move away from stock types and towards unique individual characters. For in his comedy, he desired a sense of realism, with characters that were more human and credible than Commedia's fixed types. Goldoni was reaching towards a depth in his characters that was very different from the two-dimensionality that we see in the traditional types. Though Goldoni would not have used the word "psychology" when discussing his creation of characters, he was clearly incorporating "the psychological uniqueness that is in every human being onto his characters" (Fava 2007: 31). With these methods of psychological characterization Goldoni even "opens the doors for the psychological theatre of the future" (Fava 2007: 32).

Goldoni wanted to "hold a mirror up to nature" and show real people in real situations (Holme 1976: 79). He was writing from the perspective of the bourgeoisie, a rising class in Venice throughout the Enlightenment, who "felt itself to be firmly established and wished to see its own virtues, problems and defects represented on the stage" (Cervato 1993: 10). The middle class had for so long been ridiculed on stage it was now time to give it a voice. Goldoni's plays "glimpse every aspect of life, catch the spirit of every social rank, show his love for the homely classes and his condemnation of the Venetian aristocracy" (Kennard 1935: 77). His focus was not to demoralize the aristocracy, though subtle ridicule was often involved; rather, he wanted to show the middle class a reflection of themselves in order to educate them. By showing "the correction of vices, through ridiculing them" Goldoni was "forcing the public to recognize them for what they are" (Cervato 1993: 11).

Another change was the incorporation of written scripts over improvisation. Goldoni wanted to create plays that could last through the ages and stand as a representation of Italian culture, not just scenarios. However, Goldoni recognized that his actors were used to a tradition of improvisation that was two hundred years old and that his potential reforms would have to come gradually. Although Goldoni was asking his actors to develop the new skill of memorization, which would have "necessitated serious changes in the way that his actors worked, there is no indication that he wished the reform of their performance style" (Callan 1997: 40). The Commedia actor's technique was still very important in Goldoni's plays:

Nothing so entertaining was to be found in Italy until Goldoni began fusing the dell'Arte acting techniques to comedies of character, intrigue, and satire, thus providing a vehicle for the formless, unliterary Commedia, and set-down parts for the players, who had hitherto improvised.

(Steele 1981: 40)

Therefore, up until 1750, his comedies were "no more than a part set down for the central character, with occasional scenes of dialogue, while the rest of the play was left to the improvising talents of the zanies" (ibid.: 47). Examples of his early scenario-based plays are: *The Man of the World/L'Uomo di Mondo* (1738), *The Bankruptcy/La Bancarotta* (1740), and *Harlequin's Son Lost and Found/Il Figlio d'Arlecchino Perduto e Ritrovato* (1741). Not wanting to become trapped writing in the Commedia style, he "proclaimed his allegiance to a newer and more literary form of comedy," therefore writing "a kind of hybrid play" (ibid.). The most important of his early plays was *The Servant of Two Masters/Il Servitore di Due Padroni* (1745), which was originally just a scenario but written into full script years after its first production, incorporating elements which Antonio Sacchi, the famous Truffaldino, had developed throughout the run. *The Servant of Two Masters* became "a perfectly constructed half-way house between Commedia dell'Arte and the new comedy of character containing, it could be argued, the best of both worlds" (Holme 1976: 91). The plot follows the wily Truffaldino who, in hopes of earning double wages, becomes servant to both Florindo and Beatrice, soon finding himself madly bluffing his way through numerous tricky situations, juggling both positions as he attempts to serve two masters—without them knowing.

Goldoni's reforms began to progress as he focused on a naturalistic representation of the common people in plays like *The Artful Widow/La Vedova Scaltra* (1748) and *The Respectable Girl/La Putta Ororata* (1748), "the two plays that first distinguish him as the creator of a national comedy" (Chatfield-Taylor 1914: 150). *The Venetian Twins/I Due Gemelli Veneziani* (1747) was also an important play in a unique comedy of identity where the talented Cesare D'Arbes played both twins "one quick-witted and the other simple-minded" (Holme 1976: 103). It was a play based on Plautus' *Menaechmi*, similar to Shakespeare's *The Comedy of Errors*. The 1750–1 season was one for the history books, as Goldoni produced sixteen new plays, an ambitious feat he had proposed the year before. However, this was also the season where Goldoni's reforms would take full force. This started with *The Comic Theatre/Il Teatro Comico* (1750), a play about a company of actors in rehearsal, which served as a vehicle for Goldoni to outline his reforms, a kind of prologue of what was to come. Of these plays, one to note is *The Liar/Il Bugiardo* (1750), a hilarious comedy of character surrounding Lelio, a lover who becomes tangled in a web of his lies, only to be found out in the end. Goldoni was inspired to write *The Liar* after seeing a production of Corneille's *Le Menteur*, in Florence in the 1743–4 season. Goldoni admittedly borrowed plots from Molière, Rousseau, Corneille, and Samuel Richardson for the 1750–1 season. *Pamela*, another borrowed plot, was a monumental work in Goldoni's season of sixteen. Here he removed the masks entirely, dropped the scenario, and strove towards creating unique, realistic individuals. In *Pamela*, we start to see Goldoni exploring comedies centreed around women, also seen with *The Mistress of the Inn/La Locandiera* (1753), one of Goldoni's best known plays about Mirandolina, a beautiful innkeeper who is pursued by three noblemen, only to choose her servant Fabricus in the end. From the 1750–1 season we see Goldoni saying goodbye to much of the Commedia and developing his new form of comedy, which took many shapes, including comedies of characters, comedies of manners, comedies of intrigue and sentimental comic-dramas.

Where Goldoni was inspired by the changing society around him, Count Carlo Gozzi was not. The Count's "political and philosophical views were those of a conservative and religious aristocrat who felt that God had ordained certain classes to rule and others to be ruled" (DiGaetani 1988: 5). Gozzi was disturbed by Goldoni's creation of intelligent lower class characters who showed intelligence superior to that of the nobility. He complained that Goldoni "frequently charged the noble persons of his plays with fraud, absurdity, and baseness, reserving serious and heroic virtues for personages of the lower class" (Gozzi 1890b: 122). In Gozzi's eyes, the aristocracy was not to be played as comic or foolish and neither were the lower classes to play heroes; everyone had their place in the societal hierarchy and to disturb that was to create disorder. These kinds of philosophical differences became the foundation for the feud between Goldoni and Gozzi. Being familiar with Goldoni's plays, Gozzi was very vocal about his concerns with Goldoni's reforms of Commedia. However, at this point, Goldoni was already established; in fact, by the time of the feud "Goldoni had become the theatrical revolutionary and literary lion of Venice with his realistic and comic innovations in natural style, common diction, and social comedy that were his theatrical characteristics—all of which Gozzi thoroughly detested." (DiGaetani 1988: 4)

The feud officially began after Gozzi's publication of *Tartana degli Influssi per l'anno Bisetile/The Tartana of Influences for the Leap Year* (1757), a verse almanac, where he criticized Goldoni for vulgarity and bad style. In response Goldoni published a poem, *Al Illustrissimo Signor Avvocato Giuseppe Alcaini*, defending himself and his plays. These two documents spiraled into a series of written accusations back and forth that lasted four years. Gozzi, and the Accademia dei Granelleschi whom he was associated with, charged Goldoni with writing too many plays, which were "mediocre, dull, and linguistically impure", and claimed that Goldoni was "destroying one of the greatest examples of Italian traditional theatre, the Commedia dell'Arte, and not providing a viable substitute for what he had destroyed" (DiGaetani 2000: 102). Goldoni returned the attacks, writing that Gozzi was a "verbose word-monger" and insisting that Gozzi and the Accademia dei Granelleschi were "puritanical pedants... who want to stop all development of Italian theatre in any new forms that might be possible" (DiGaetani 2000: 102).

As "a commentary upon their own tastes, and a reflection of their personal philosophies of life", these two playwrights were ready to

> defend their theatrical theories with grim seriousness because they saw them as part of such larger issues as the purity of the Italian language, the traditions of the Italian theatre, the traditions of their greatest actors, and the image of society.
>
> (DiGaetani 1988: 6)

Finally, Goldoni gave Gozzi a challenge that he could not refuse: "It is one thing", Goldoni said "to write subtle verbal criticisms, another thing to compose dramas which shall fill the public theatres with enthusiastic audiences" (Gozzi 1890b: 128). If Gozzi thought that better plays could be written then he should do it himself. Gozzi took to the challenge, stating that he could gather a larger audience than Goldoni by putting "an old wives' fairy-story of the *Love of the Three Oranges* upon the boards" (Gozzi 1890b: 158).

So, Gozzi took up the pen to write *The Love of Three Oranges/L'Amore delle tre melarance* (1761) to prove the vitality of the Commedia dell'Arte. It is the tale of Prince Tartaglia, a melancholic hypochondriac who has been cursed by an evil witch, causing him to fall in love with three oranges and making him unable to rest until he finds them. The play was written out in scenario form, leaving room for improvisation from Antonio Sacchi's company who performed the piece. Gozzi was vigilantly opposed to Goldoni's realism; however, he, like Goldoni, also recognized the decline of Commedia and that some modifications had to be made. So he decided to combine Commedia with the style of the fable. *The Love of Three Oranges* would be the first of ten plays, the *Fiabe*, which he would write in this style, introducing additional elements of tragedy along the way. Gozzi drew inspiration from Italian and Oriental fairy tales like the *Tale of Tales/Cunto de li cunti* by Giovambattista Basile, which were very popular in Italy in the seventeenth and eighteenth centuries.

The play turned into a literary satire against Goldoni and Chiari (a contemporary playwright and rival of both Goldoni and Gozzi) with "the doltish magician and the wicked fairy represent[ing] Carlo Goldoni and Pietro Chiari" (Beniscelli 2006: 179). The war between these two magical figures represented the battle the two playwrights had for the Venetian stage; however, regardless of the interference of Fata Morgana and Celio (Chiari and Goldoni), "Truffaldino (the commedia dell'arte) succeeds in making Tartaglia laugh, and cures him" (Emery 1989: 4). In one critic's words, "the older comedy is funny, while the plays of the reformers are not" (Emery 1989: 4). The happy ending of *The Love of Three Oranges* can also be attributed to the action of Truffaldino and Pantalone, the representatives of Commedia, as they find the pin in the dove's head, removing it and transforming Princess Ninetta back to her human form, enabling Prince Tartaglia to marry his true love, a happy ending that could also be Gozzi's representation, or prediction rather, of a triumphant future for Commedia. *The Love of Three Oranges* is seen as "the most artistically perfect of the ten *Fiabe*" (Gozzi 1890a: 163). Here we see Gozzi's strongest example of harmony between fable and masks. Experiencing success with *The Love of Three Oranges*, Gozzi recognized that fairy tales had multiple purposes beyond entertainment; they also could be used for "conveying moral lessons under the form of allegory, and mingling tragic pathos with the humours of the masks" (Gozzi 1890a: 147).

Gozzi wrote solely for the Sacchi Company throughout his career. At the time of writing *The Love of Three Oranges*, the company had four very popular masks (Antonio Sacchi, Truffaldino; Atanagio Zanoni, Brighella; Agostino Fiorelli, Tartaglia; and D'Arbes, Pantalone) and so it was quite natural that Gozzi included those characters in his play. Gozzi was, after all, the self-proclaimed "protector" of improvised comedy and masks. However, even Gozzi did not focus solely on the fixed types associated with the Commedia. He relied on the familiarity of the masks to attract his audiences but then introduced many new characters as well, including witches, wizards, and the King of Hearts, a monarch of an imaginary kingdom, costumed like the playing cards.

Gozzi was opposed to "mirroring" society in his plays, as Goldoni strove to accomplish. Rather he wanted to uphold the social hierarchy in his plays, differentiating class in his characters through use of verse or improvisation. The nobility spoke in verse, without improvisation, and the lower classes had the freedom to improvise using a common tongue. Noble characters were most often serious, leaving the comedy for the Commedia dell'Arte characters. Similar to the way Goldoni introduced reforms, Gozzi slowly reduced the amount of improvisation in his plays. Even in *The Raven/Il Corvo*, the second of Gozzi's fables, he was writing for all of the characters, serious or comic, except Truffaldino and Brighella, though their roles were very clearly outlined. However, he did still give them room to play with incorporating many bits of comic action, or *lazzi*, within the text.

Through Goldoni's reforms we see Pantalone change from a "lecherous, shameless buffoon" to "the ideal middle class tradesman" (Farrell 1997: 4). He loses his lusty miserly qualities and, as we see in *The Liar*, Pantalone becomes an honest and respectable father figure. He now is the one who helps to solve problems rather than being the cause of the conflict. Gozzi often criticized Goldoni for his treatment of the traditional masks; however, when looking closer at Gozzi's portrayal of the masks, "often they do not accurately reproduce the traditional stereotypes" (Emery 1989: 5). For instance, Gozzi's Pantalone, like Goldoni's, lost the lusty fiery ways of the old Commedia and traded vulgarity for virtue, becoming more senile. Where he was once in the spotlight, he is now advisor, tutor, admiral, and supporting character to the higher-class kings and princes. Goldoni's Dottore, like Pantalone, becomes more of an honest father figure, losing his long-winded, nonsensical speeches along the way while Gozzi removes the mask all together.

Goldoni's servants become recognizable as a class of workers rather than just fools. Brighella, who started off as "the cunning servant of the Commedia", now becomes "in Goldoni's comedies the honest servant of his master" (Steele 1981: 69). Now Brighella's "skill at intrigue was directed more at serving his master's interests than his own" (Holme 1976: 80). We see this behaviour in *The Liar* as Brighella does everything he can to help out his master Florindo, or in *The Servant of Two Masters* when Brighella becomes a faithful friend to Beatrice. Gozzi's Brighella also loses some of his cunning and becomes more of a simpleton. Gozzi's Smeraldina loses some of her bite and charm and Gozzi stretches her role in his plays making her "a good mother or nurse, sometimes a shifty waiting-woman, sometimes a blustering amazon, sometimes a bad wife or would-be virgin" (Gozzi 1890a: 154). Goldoni's Arlecchino still plays the role of the simple servant but he is less dim-witted than his traditional self. With Arlecchino we see a rounder character, "the coarse old lazzi are diluted (though not entirely eliminated), the obscenity and violence are gone, and the action begins to take on an increasingly formal correctness and decorum" (Steele 1981: 69). Gozzi's Truffaldino stays fairly consistent and thrives in Gozzi's plays, showing a chameleon-like nature to adapt to any comic situation, likely as a result of Sacchi's skill and position as manager in the company.

Gozzi's combination of Commedia/fable called for changes in locations. Instead of the streets of Italy he turned to imaginary kingdoms in far off lands, or Chinese kingdoms, as in *Turandot* and *The Blue Monster/Il Mostro Turchino* (1764). The change in location coupled with the fairy-tale style established the opportunity for exciting bits of new stage magic that gave quite a modern approach to Gozzi's staging. He believed that

> When the stage effects became magical enough...the audience would certainly be mesmerized by the splendors occurring there, and the spell would compound, in turn, their fascinations with the complexity of both characters and dramatic situations (and possibly a complexity of ideas) to provide added enjoyment from the play.
>
> (DiGaetani 2000: 131)

Elements of this kind of magic would include appearances and disappearances, like those of the witches and wizards in *The Love of Three Oranges*, or transformations as we see in *The King Stag* where King Deramo turns into the stag, an old man, then back into his own body; both Tartaglia and the magician Durandarte experience transformations as well. Another strong example of transformation can also be found in *The Serpent Woman* where Cherestani is turned into a serpent until Farruscad saves her with a kingly kiss.

With *Turandot*, Gozzi changes his style. His writing becomes less magical and more about real human characters. In the character Turandot, he creates "one of the most fascinating characters in the entire history of Italian theatre" (DiGaetani 2000: 124). Turandot, who, despises men and does not want to be married, has convinced her father, the King, that she will marry anyone who solves three riddles; however, the men who do not solve the riddles will be killed. Here Gozzi, for the first time explores a heroine, a strong figure who becomes "an 18th-century spokesperson for modern women's liberation" (DiGaetani 2000: 125).

By the time Gozzi writes *The Green Bird/L'Augellino Belverde* (1765), his work has turned into tragi-comic fables with a philosophical agenda as he voices his opinions on the Enlightenment through the play. Gozzi saw *The Green Bird* as one of his most daring plays as it engaged a new variation of characterization and dealt with a deeper level of philosophy and satire. The fantastical and dreamlike quality of his work has also been seen as an early link to surrealism.

The feud between Gozzi and Goldoni lasted until Goldoni's self-exile to France to work with the Comédie-Italienne. Though he may have had many reasons to leave, Gozzi's antagonizing being one of them, Goldoni had reached his goal during his time in Italy; he created a new realistic form of Italian Comedy that is still recognized. Many of Goldoni's plays have experienced a long life and are still being produced today. *The Servant of Two Masters* recently experienced a revival with Richard Bean's adaptation of Goldoni's play into *One Man, Two Guvnors* (2011). The show met with great success both in London and on Broadway. Not to mention Piccolo Teatro di Milano's famous production of *The Servant of Two Masters* (1947), directed by Giorgio Strehler, which ran for over 50 years, the longest running play in Italian history. Of Goldoni's later plays affected by his reforms, *The Mistress of the Inn, The Fan, The Liar, The Venetian Twins* and *The Holiday Trilogy* hold as his most popular, many of them still being produced by colleges, universities, and professional companies abroad.

Throughout Gozzi's ten *Fiabe* we see quite a range of work. Even though he might have started as the protector of the masks, creating Commedia scenarios with a fairy-tale twist, the Commedia elements realistically became less important along the way, establishing a new style of fairy-tale mixing comedy, tragedy, satire, and philosophy. Gozzi's works have experienced many re-stagings, especially in parts of Europe. By the end of the eighteenth century, Gozzi was "…less esteemed in his own country than abroad" (Emery 1989: 1). Today he perhaps is best known for his inspiration of other works, especially operas. *The Love of Three Oranges* inspired Mozart and Schikander's *Die Zauberflöte/The Magic Flute* (1791) as well as Prokofiev's opera using Gozzi's title. Wagner's first Opera *Die Feen* (1834) was largely based on Gozzi's play *The Serpent Woman* (1762). *Turandot* is often thought of as Gozzi's most famous play as it has been adapted the most, inspiring works by Schiller, Goethe, Busoni, Brecht, Vakhtanghov, and of course Puccini's famous opera (1926). In America, Gozzi is best known from Julie Taymor's Broadway version of *The Green Bird* at the New Victory Theatre.

Though both playwrights had differing opinions about how to treat Commedia, they both were able to take the inspirations of Commedia and use them for their own purposes, creating two new, unique styles of theatre. Through their works, albeit different in many ways, the spirit of the Commedia still lives.

References

Beniscelli, Alberto (2006) "Carlo Gozzi" in Joseph Farrell and Paolo Puppa (eds), *A History of Italian Theatre*, London: Cambridge University Press, pp. 176–185.

Callan, Guy (1997) "Marivaux's La Fausse Suivante and Goldoni's La Bottega del caffe as Physical Theatre" in J. Farrell (ed.), *Carlo Goldoni and the Eighteenth Century Theatre*. New York: Edwin Mellen Press, pp. 37–54.

Cervato, Emanuela (1993) *Goldoni and Venice*, A. Thompson (tr.), Hull, UK: University of Hull.

Chatfield-Taylor, H. C. (1914) *Goldoni: A Biography*. London: Chatto and Windus.

DiGaetani, John Louis (1988) "Introduction to the Life and Works of Carlo Gozzi" in J. L. DiGaetani (ed.), *Carlo Gozzi: Translations of The Love of Three Oranges, Turandot and the Snake Lady, with a Bio Critical Introduction*. Connecticut, US: Greenwood Press, pp. 1–12.

——(2000) *Carlo Gozzi: A Life in the 18th Centrury Venetian Theater, an Afterlife in Opera*. North Carolina, US: McFarland & Company, Inc.

Emery, Ted (1989) "Introduction: Carlo Gozzi in Context" in *Carlo Gozzi: Five Tales for the Theatre*, A. Bermel and T. Emery (eds.), Chicago, US: University of Chicago Press, pp. 1–19.

Farrell, Joseph (ed.) (1997) *Carlo Goldoni and the Eighteenth Century Theatre*. New York: Edwin Mellen Press.

Fava, Antonio (2007) *The Comic Mask in the Commedia dell'Arte*. Illinois, US: Northwestern University Press.

Goldoni, Carlo (1877) *Memoirs*, J. Black (tr.), London: Hunt.

——(1892) *The Comedies of Carlo Goldoni*, H. Zimmern (ed.), Chicago, US: David Stott.

——(1958) "The Servant of Two Masters" in E. Bentley (ed.), *The Servant of Two Masters and Other Italian Classics*, E. J. Dent (tr.), New York: Applause Theatre Books, pp. 79–169.

——(1961) *Carlo Goldoni: Three Comedies*, A. Colquhoun (ed.), C. Bax, I.M. Rawson, E. Farjeon and H. Farjeon (tr.), London: Oxford University Press.

——(1963) *The Liar*, F. H. Davies (tr.), London: Heinemann.

——(1969) *The Comic Theatre*, J. W. Miller (tr.), Lincoln, US: University of Nebraska Press.

——(2001) *Four Comedies: The Venetian Twins, The Artful Widow, Mirandolina, The Superior Residence*, F. Davies (tr.), Harmondsworth, Middlesex, UK: Penguin Books.

Gozzi, Carlo (1890a) *The Memoirs of Count Carlo Gozzi; Volume the First*, J. A. Symonds (tr.), London: Nimmo.

——(1890b) *The Memoirs of Count Carlo Gozzi; Volume the Second*, J. A. Symonds (tr.), New York: Scribner & Welford.

——(1951) *The Blue Monster*, E. J. Dent (tr.), Cambridge, UK: Cambridge University Press.

——(1958) "The King Stag" in E. Bentley (ed.), *The Servant of Two Masters and Other Italian Classics*, E. J. Dent (tr.), New York: Applause Theatre Books, pp. 171–249.

——(1988) *Carlo Gozzi: Translations of The Love of Three Oranges, Turandot and the Snake Lady, with a Bio Critical Introduction*, J. L. DiGaetani (tr.), Connecticut, US: Greenwood Press.

——(1989) *Five Tales for the Theatre*, A. Bermel and T. Emery (eds and tr.), Chicago, US: University of Chicago Press.

Holme, Timothy (1976) *A Servant of Many Masters: The Life and Times of Carlo Goldoni*. London: Jupiter.

Kennard, Joseph Spencer (1935) *Masks and Marionettes*. New York: MacMillan Company.

Steele, Eugene (1981) *Carlo Goldoni: Life, Work, and Times*. Ravenna, Italy: Longo Editore.

35

COMMEDIA DELL'ARTE AS GROTESQUE DANCE

Decline or evolution?

Domenico Pietropaolo

This chapter was presented as the keynote speech for the Windsor University, Canada, Commedia Dell'Arte symposium, in February 2013.

By the beginning of the eighteenth century, mainstream Commedia dell'Arte was showing signs of tiredness everywhere. All but the few stars of the first magnitude that commanded everyone's respect were subjected to increasingly frequent accusations of ineptitude and disinterest. The Commedia dell'Arte was definitely going through its silver age and had a very uncertain future.

In Paris the Italian Commedia superstars who controlled an institution in their own right within the Parisian artistic field, had fallen prey to the trap of self-referentiality, in a desire to maintain their regular but dwindling audiences. Their former performance vigour and openness, implicit in improvisation and a wider audience demographic, was on the wane. Scripted plays in French and an increased reliance on scenic effects became their staple stage offerings, pandering to current taste rather than leading it.

However, its slow demise within the confines of its genre and on its own stage was accompanied by its importation into a series of other artistic domains, including the new one of scenic dance which was then coming into quick prominence. The Commedia dell'Arte made a sudden ingress into scenic dance under the label of the comic grotesque.

During the late baroque period, the term *grotesque dance* was used in a general as well as in a specific sense. In its general sense, it could refer to all stage dances grounded in the idea of stylized buffoonery; in its specific sense, it designated comic dances based on the stock characters and comic routines of the Commedia dell'Arte tradition, raised to a higher level of refinement by the new aesthetic context. In both senses, grotesque dance refers to a form of narrative dance that intentionally undermines the exclusive right of serious dance to artistic status, while remaining itself validated by serious dance in its own vindications as a respectable aesthetic practice. At the root of the phenomenon we find three factors: the old baroque fascination with the principle that the arts can fruitfully cross each other's boundaries, the growing interest in the early Enlightenment idea that historical development involves inherent progress, and, finally, the desire of Commedia performers to re-professionalize their art for the aristocratic entertainment market of theatrical dance. The purpose of this chapter is to sort out the main issues involved in the metamorphosis of the plebeian grotesque that is at the heart of the Commedia tradition into the stylized grotesque of theatrical dance. This way, upper class audiences allow onto their stage a suitably gentrified view of the Commedia dell'Arte, while the refined art of scenic dance makes room for a stylized and muted version of its performances into its aesthetic domain.

The issues involved in the emergence of Commedia dell'Arte characters and motifs on the dance boards of the early eighteenth century were first brought into focus by John Weaver in England and Gregorio Lambranzi on the Continent. Weaver was then the principal dance master and dance theorist of the London stage, where he worked with Esther Booth, his brilliant partner in the role of Arlecchina, to make room for the Commedia dell'Arte in a dance form that would eventually evolve into British pantomime. Lambranzi was a Venetian emigré dance master who transformed the grotesque movements of Commedia performers into spectacular narrative dances for German audiences. Relevant materials on the geometric stylization of Commedia scenic action in the first decades of its existence as dance are offered by William Hogarth, who studied the the physical vocabulary of Commedia-based performances as they developed after their initial acceptance into the genre. By that time the Commedia dell'Arte had been made suitable for the aristocratic and upper middle-class constituencies of the entertainment market. These audiences were themselves developing a taste for what we might call the aesthetics of courteous transgression, that is to say representations of infringement that have been suitably divested of confrontational designs and neatly separated from the offensive coarseness of their origins in poverty and farce. In such an aesthetic purview, virtuosic skill stands unchallenged at the centre, while the thematic repertoire, deprived of ideological bite, remains on the canvas as the necessary background. The Commedia dell'Arte, Weaver thought, lent itself perfectly to this perspective and to the new art of scenic dance, for no one could rival Commedia performers in their "grimaces, posture, motions, agility, suppleness of limbs, and distortion of their faces" (Weaver 1712: 168).

Following the lead of Lucian of Samosata, John Weaver refers to the ancient myths of Proteus and Empousa as allegories of the lives of two highly skilled pantomime artists, the ideal prototypes of all performers who use rhythmical movement as a means of representation (Weaver 1728: 122; Lucian 1905: vol.2, para.9; Elyot 1962: 72). The androcentric nature of western culture has kept Empousa shrouded in obscurity, but has enabled Proteus to become famous, so much so that the adjective *protean* enjoys currency in various modern languages. In Weaver's view, Proteus and Empousa must have both been such skilled imitators that, in the poetic fables inspired by their performances, they could easily figure as being capable of actually transforming themselves into the things they mimed, including, as Ovid tells us, the trembling of leaves and the wind itself (Ovid 1970: 8. 726–737). In positing Proteus as the male ideal of this art, Weaver was no doubt pointing to himself, narcissistically, as the legitimate heir of Proteus on the London stage. In referring to Empousa as his female counterpart, he was probably thinking of Esther Booth, who, in 1717 so dazzled him with a performance of his Venus at Drury Lane that he considered her "the most graceful, the most agreeable, and the most correct performer in the world (Weaver 1721: 56).

Mrs. Booth's legendary beauty and graceful manner notwithstanding, the mythical Empousa was a perfectly grotesque character. According to Aristophanes, Empousa's normal appearance was that of an old hag with a leg manufactured out of bronze and the other transplanted from a donkey. A monster of human, mechanical, and animal hybridism if there ever was one, Empousa, as noted by Aristophanes (1998: *Frogs* 288ff, *Ecclesiazusae* 1094f), is a figure that transgresses formidable boundaries in both nature and culture to emerge as a species of the comical demonic. On the eighteenth-century stage, such ideas of hybridism found an easy parallel in the *lazzi* of the Commedia dell'Arte, many of which were meant to be performed by means of a composite physical language, derived from basic patterns of human and animal motion.

To understand Weaver's reflections on how narrative dance might draw on the virtuosic potential of the Commedia dell'Arte, we must consider the basic principles of his dramaturgy. Weaver explored the genre of narrative dance on two fronts, which he called serious and grotesque. The nature of serious dance is intuitively clear and requires little commentary. It is narrative dance whose characters are taken either from classical literature or from history, and are always represented with decorum and verisimilitude. The performance of this category of works requires what Weaver calls "a nice address and management of the passions and gestures" (Weaver 1728: 56). Aside from the qualifier "nice", which refers only to the refined nature of serious dance and to the degree of technical precision that it presupposes, the terms "address" and "management" suggest analytical concepts that are applicable to all types of physical narratives, comic as well as serious. *Management* is a compositional term that describes the dancer's control of the physical vocabulary required to execute the dance. The meaning is crystal clear: its primary background reference is to the performer's mastery of his art in his performance of signifying gestures. *Address,* on the other hand, is a performance-related term that designates the performer's way of presenting himself to the audience while executing the gestures and movements required by the dance. Serious entertainments elicit recognition as works of dignity, while comic entertainments elicit acknowledgement as works designed to subvert such claim to dignity, with the approval and complicity of the audience. The dancer's mode of address refers to the performance decorum appropriate to each dramatic form, whether in the production or in the debunking of dignity. Unlike management, it is a multiply ambivalent concept, and it is in its ambivalence that its critical utility resides. Mode of address refers at once to the performer's acquaintance with the audience's understanding of acceptable comportment, to his perception of their anticipated response to the dance, and to the artistic skills and techniques that he has to employ in order to elicit that response.

These two concepts of address and management are very useful aids in the analysis of Commedia's transition into the world of scenic dance. They are the dance equivalent of the ideas of point of view and narrated action in literature, and of the notions of self-presentation and imitative representation in the performance of spoken drama. But it is the concept of address that enables us to understand the magnitude of the development undergone by the Commedia dell'Arte in the silver age of its history. For the mode of address that requires acquaintance with, and collusive participation of, upper class audiences is rooted in the notion of gentrification, in the transformation of the humble and vulgar traits of the Commedia dell'Arte into aesthetic expressions appealing to the very class that Commedia had sought to debunk in earlier stages of its history.

In the eighteenth century the Commedia dell'Arte discovers its potential for upward mobility, and disengages itself from the dramaturgy of confrontation in order to pursue the complete professionalization of the art demanded by social advancement. The mode of address that had to be learned by Commedia performers who crossed the boundary into the world of scenic dance, or that had to be assumed by conventionally trained scenic dancers in their appropriation of Commedia materials, is the single most important distinguishing feature of the re-emergence of Commedia as the grotesque scenic dance of the European stage.

In his works on the history and theory of dance, Weaver distinguishes the grotesque from the serious genre in relation to the management of physical action:

> By Grotesque Dancing, I mean only such Characters as are quite out of nature; as Harlequin, Scaramouch, Pierrot, etc. tho' in the natural sense of the word. Grotesque, among Masters of our Profession, takes in all comic Dancing whatever: But here I have confin'd this Name only to such Characters, where, in lieu of regulated Gesture, you meet with distorted and ridiculous Actions, and Grim and Grimace take up entirely that Countenance where the Passions and Affections of the Mind should be expressed.
>
> (Weaver 1728: 56)

We may consider the distinction between serious and grotesque dance in three ways: (i) in relation to the fictional characters represented, (ii) in relation to the dancers representing them, and (iii) in relation to the performance style with which they do so.

As far as the fictional world of the dance scenario is concerned, grotesque characters are unnatural rather than natural, gesticulate without regard for social norms and use primarily the physical vocabulary of the old Commedia tradition. As far as the stage impersonation of these characters is concerned, the performers are skilled in the management of that vocabulary, weaving it into elegant designs of physical distortion and disequilibrium that signify the unfolding of the story in the scenario. Finally, as far as performance style is concerned, the grotesque representation of the events in the scenario is intended to appear as the subversion of regulated gestures; the transformation of countenance into grimace, in a stylized lowering of the serious into the ridiculous. On the aesthetic plane, the grotesque enables the performers to signify social and physical degradation without ever leaving the plane of their own artistic elegance.

In his description of scenic action by the Commedia dell'Arte characters, Weaver presents the physical language of grotesque dance as a displacement of the language of serious dance. His procedure may be taken as symbolic of the working assumptions that governed the practice of the art of grotesque dance as well as its perception. The fundamental principle is that the Commedia dancer starts with the design of a serious action, not only in performance but also in theory and training, and then proceeds to achieve the aesthetic effect of the grotesque by subjecting the serious to a degrading process. Conventional baroque dances are thus recontextualized by Commedia-based dancers by means of a performance language that conspicuously alludes to the language that it deforms. The perception of grotesque dance in the Commedia dell'Arte tradition necessarily raises the image of the dance forms that it parodies. Exaggerated gestures and contortions are intelligible as something more than apparently awkward designs only if their dramaturgical management also summons to imaginary presence the models that they intentionally debunk. It follows that the grotesque performance text of Commedia characters is designed to raise in the perceiving consciousness of the audience a will to be disengaged from serious dance on the interpretative plane, since the grotesque forms to which it has recourse seek to undermine the classical stateliness on which serious dance is dependent. At the same time, however, grotesque dance performs its will to be conjoined with serious dance on the plane of aesthetic judgement, because it is only by being adjacent to it, as if together with its invisible complement, that it can achieve intelligibility and fullness of being as a work of art worthy of its audience.

Given everything that grotesque dance must achieve in a non-grotesque setting, it is clear that the level of virtuosity that it presupposes is considerably greater than the one required by serious dance. Weaver provides a way of assessing the technical difficulty of grotesque dance by rational argument and scientific theory. His *Anatomical and Mechanical Lectures Upon Dancing* (1721), a treatise in biomechanics *ante litteram,* incorporates into the discourse of dance recent advances in physics, anatomy, and geometry. Various principles distilled from these sciences are brought to bear on the study of the human body in motion in the controlled context of scenic narrative. The complex motion of grotesque dance can be segmented into elementary phrases and analysed with scientific rigour. Significantly this operation creates space for the Commedia dell'Arte in the dignified discourse of higher learning. At crucial moments of his argument, Weaver calls to his aid Newton's *Principia mathematica* (1687) and Alfonso Borelli's *De motu animalium* (1685), respectively the most sophisticated theory of gravitational and biological mechanics in contemporary science. All human motion, including the antics of dancing Commedia characters, can be examined in terms of the natural tendency of the body to maintain itself in perfect balance with respect to the line of gravity. Stage movement can then be analysed in terms of the performer's dramaturgical management of the curvature and alignment of his body as he shifts in and out of physical equilibrium. Serious scenic dance and mime are based on the stylization of directions of motion, types of curvature, inclinations from the vertical, and degrees of muscular exertion governed by the principle of natural gravitational balance. Grotesque dance is instead based on unnaturalness and disequilibrium. The dramaturgical management of its physical vocabulary consists in the controlled distortion of the actions of serious dance. Its misalignments, extreme curvatures, and muscular contortions are calculated to undermine the body's natural balance without allowing it to precipitate into a state from which it cannot possibly realign itself with gravity.

In grotesque performance the dancer must display the mode of address of a virtuoso, in order to ensure that laughter is elicited by the dance, rather than the dancer. To do so he requires, and must make visible, great strength and ability. It is much easier for a dancer to cross the stage without having to pretend that he is not moving freely on a flat plane than it is for him to do so configuring his body as if he were climbing a ladder or moving down a steep hill, or walking like an insect, or imitating a woman about to give birth, or even pretending to give someone an enema—the latter lazzi being suitably purified of offensive realism by a high degree of stylization. This reading of the lazzi is the central point of Nicoletta Capozza's book, that is to say the decorum of a virtuosic mode of address and the subversion of the conventional management of physical language, are logical implications of the nature of grotesque dance as a calculated deflation of serious dance (Capozza 2006).

When they are considered in the context of their dynamic existence on the dance stage, the stock characters of the Commedia dell'Arte tradition are clearly distinguished by the movement designs that typify them, as the gestural equivalents of their costumes. The individual dancers that impersonate them manage the repertoire of movements in ways that are peculiarly their own, as a physical idiolect that carries the mark of their training, skill and imagination; but the movements themselves remain recognizable as the distinctive features of the stock character. One can recognize the Commedia characters of the dance with almost complete certainty by the positions assumed by the dancers and by the trajectory of the actions that they perform in impersonating them. The performance literacy of the audience of theatrical dance includes sufficient familiarity with the physical style of Commedia dell'Arte characters to be able to recognize it on stage. It makes no difference to recognition that the style may be subjected to considerable variation, in accordance with the practice of allowing dancers latitude of invention within the parameters of a given dance—that is what is left of the venerable principle of improvisation as the fundamental compositional practice of the Commedia dell'Arte. In his dance manual, *Nuova scuola de' balli theatrali,* of 1716, Gregorio Lambranzi suggests that these positions must reflect the "peculiar characteristics" of each character as known to the audience from other areas of cultural history, including, we expect, iconography and the spoken drama (Lambranzi 1716: 1). Whatever the variation, each dance is compounded of elementary segments of motion, just as sentences are made up of words and words of syllables. The units of action preferred by one character in phrasing narrative comprise, we might say, his unique movement vocabulary. William Hogarth made a careful study of the physical language of various Commedia dell'Arte characters articulated by eighteenth-century dancers, and his observations are revealing. Harlequin's actions, for example, consist of "certain little quick movements of the head, hands and feet" (Hogarth 1753: 149), elementary units of movement brought together into the narrative sequence governed by the logic of the plot. The narrative development of Harlequin's movement cannot proceed other than as the juxtaposition of short angular phrases, quickly produced and configured in order to express the nervous dynamism of the character. However, staccato, fast-paced, and angular action is not natural to anyone's body other than that of the virtuoso (Humphrey 1959: 98). Our natural tendency is to produce action that is curved, uninterrupted, balanced, and phrased as legato units, because that is what offers the least resistance to gravity and does not require the body to compensate for disequilibrium. When such action is produced with appropriate thematic design and with an elegant mode of address, the result is the movement of serious dance. In order to generate grotesque motion, the performer must work against the natural inclination of his body and in opposition to the style of serious dance, which it must destabilize.

From the perspective of the audience, it is clear that the uniqueness of an action so constructed is that it induces the spectator into thinking that the line traced by the dancer in impersonating the character is inseparable from the character himself, almost as if it were the geometric projection of his being—his movement signature, as it were. Hogarth noted that in the Commedia-based dances of British pantomime, Harlequin's dramatic actions seem to "shoot out as it were from the body in straight lines or are twirled about in little circles" (Hogarth 1753: 149). These units of action appear to shoot out from his body, or else to twirl themselves around one of his limbs, for the duration of the dance because they are nothing but a geometric extension of his being that is perceivable only when his body is in motion. As objects of aesthetic perception, the phrases of his dance are continuous with his body. In scenic dance, Harlequin is recognizable with almost total certainty from his style of movement, even when he conceals his characteristic costume by wearing another one over it, as sometimes occurs in plots of mistaken identity. In such plots, the mistake is made by other characters and not by the audience. The performance of angular gestures for the expression of changing states of mind, and the achievement of design by means of staccato phrasing, fall within Harlequin's stylistic range, whatever his costume, producing a physical effect rather like a distinguishing accent and timbre of voice in speech.

By the same token, Scaramouche is identifiable as a character whose actions consist of unit movements of unnatural length, conceived in direct opposition to those that typify Harlequin. Scaramouche communicates by means of large gestural strokes that represent a pantomimic equivalent of his propensity for bombastic self-aggrandizement. In Gregorio Lambranzi's manual, the Scaramouche step is described as a stride so long that the dancer virtually touches the floor with his thighs (Lambranzi 1716: 23). It is so difficult to execute that it cannot be easily imitated by dancers trained to represent other characters (Lambranzi 1716: 1). The designs that typify Pierrot's stage actions consist instead of "perpendiculars and parallels" (Hogarth 1753: 149), since his pattern of movement has been conceived as a dynamic extension of his costume, the folds and long sleeves of which form vertical parallels that suggest a natural propensity to remain in a state of rest, not far from gravitational alignment. The unique geometry of Pulcinella's actions is governed by gravity to an even higher degree, since he makes use of the gravitational pull of his body to undermine any suggestion of elegance of gait or posture. He raises his arms and his legs and lets them fall at the same time in parallel directions, as if he were incapable of normal articulate motion, his joints, as Hogarth noted, being rather like the "hinges of a door" (Hogarth 1753: 149), which does not allow variation of the line of motion (Pietropaolo 2010: 53–66).

The focus on the virtuosic skill involved in the dramaturgy and in the craft of grotesque dance marks the beginning of a new chapter in the history of the Commedia dell'Arte, a chapter in which progressive acceptance into the world of higher art meant increasing remoteness from the conditions of its birth. In their appearance, the stock characters of the Commedia dell'Arte continue to display their social and cultural background, but in their conduct and social relations they have replaced confrontation with sentiment, and coarseness with feigned awkwardness. The Commedia dell'Arte kept pace with the changing social and economic conditions of Europe, preferring adaptation and evolution to demise. It thereby survived in the collective consciousness of later generations, to whom the confrontational manner that fills the pages of the earliest chapters of its history would have been all but meaningless. The performers who impersonated the stock characters either accepted the need to re-market their products to suit the taste of their new audiences or else were left to carry the torch of the old Commedia dell'Arte on its own stage. Their number, however, was destined to become smaller and smaller, as the genre slowly approached its final demise and could look forward only to the prospect of nostalgic revivals.

References

Aristophanes (1998) *Frogs, Assemblywomen, Wealth,* ed. Jeffrey Henderson. Cambridge, Mass., US: Loeb Classical Library.

Capozza, Nicoletta (2006) *Tutti i lazzi della Commedia dell'Arte.* Rome: Dino Audino Editore.

Elyot, Thomas (1962), *Book of the Governour* (1531), ed. S. E. Lehmberg. London: Everyman's Library.

Hogarth, William (1753) *The Analysis of Beauty.* London: Reeves.

Humphrey, Doris (1959) *The Art of Making Dances,* ed. Barbara Pollack. New York: Grove Press.

Lambranzi, Gregorio (1716) *Nuova e curiosa scuola de' balli theatrali.* Nuremberg, Germany: Pushner.

Lucian (1905) "Of Pantomimes" in *The Works of Lucian of Samosata,* trans. by H. W. and F. G. Fowler. Oxford, UK: Clarendon Press.

Ovid (1970) *Metamorphoses,* ed. A. S. Hollis. Oxford, UK: Clarendon Press.

Pietropaolo, Domenico (2010) "The Logic of Gestures and the Dramaturgy of Movement in John Weaver's Theory of Pantomime and the Commedia dell'Arte Tradition", in *The World of Baroque Theatre/Svet barokního divadla* 2007, ed. Pavel Slavko and Jiri Blaha. Český Krumlov, Czech Republic: Baroque Theatre Foundation.

Weaver, John *(1712) An Essay Towards an History of Dancing.* London: Jacob Tonson.

——(1721) *Anatomical and Mechanical Lectures upon Dancing.* London: J. Brotherton et al p. x.

——(1728) *The History of Mimes and Pantomimes.* London: Roberts and Dod.

36

THE MYTH OF PIERROT

Mark Evans

Pierrot and Pantomime: from Deburau and Le Théâtre des Funambules to Georges Wague.

By the end of the eighteenth century, the Comédie-Italienne, which had for many years sustained the Commedia dell'Arte tradition in France, had lost much of its popularity and its scenarios had become dated and old-fashioned. The traditional slapstick and improvisation, historically associated with Commedia, had gradually been replaced by scripts, story lines and characters that appealed to a more refined audience taste. The popular traditions of the Commedia dell'Arte were, by the start of the nineteenth century, more evident in the entertainments presented at the Paris fairs, such as the Foire Saint-Germain and the fair on the Place Saint-Laurent. The fair performances variously included popular plays, comic operas, tumblers, ropewalkers, trained animals and puppets. Recurring periods of censorship had meant that most of these performances had developed silent pantomime or song as a mode of communication that might avoid the historical restrictions placed upon them not to employ dialogue. Whilst the Comédie-Italienne eventually joined with the Opéra-Comique to present light, musical theatre, it was the silent pantomime tradition of the fair grounds that was to prove the most lasting influence on French and Western theatre practice.

Following the introduction of new laws by the National Assembly in 1791, business initiatives were no longer so tightly bound by the restrictions of guild practices or government intervention; one result of this change was a rapid expansion in the number of theatres. Censorship was also more lenient and popular tastes were more actively catered for. This offered an attractive opportunity for those providing popular entertainment to expand their business. In 1816, Nicholas Bertrand adapted his booth theatre on the Boulevard du Temple in Paris, which had up until then been used to present animal and acrobatic acts, into the Théâtre des Funambules. Amongst the new acts that Bertrand signed up was a family of Bohemian tumblers and ropewalkers, including a young acrobat, Gaspard Deburau (1796–1846). Annette Lust relates how Deburau at first was kicked about on stage by his father, who was exasperated by his son's clumsiness (Lust 2000: 45). According to Rémy, Deburau's career was transformed when an old Italian mime from one of the Paris theatres agreed to give him lessons in pantomime (Rémy 1954: 31). The character Deburau used to give expression to his new skills was that of Pierrot. Pierrot is a particularly French variant on the original servant role of Pedrolino, a servant or valet character who is young, personable, and trustworthy (Duchartre 1966: 251). Pierrot occurs in Molière's *Don Juan* (1660) and so had clearly made the transition with the other Commedia characters that had migrated from Italy to Paris in the seventeenth century. Giacomo Oreglia claims that the creator of the Pedrolino mask was Giovanni Pellesini, a member of the Gelosi company, and that 'the most famous interpreter of the part was the Ferrarese actor Giuseppe Geratoni, who made his debut in Paris in 1763' (Oreglia 1968: 65). This implies that the crossover between Pierrot and Pedrolino was a slow transition, a process of gradual cultural evolution. The traditional Pierrot costume is based on that of Pedrolino – it is close fitting and the character is heavily powdered and played without a mask. Deburau's innovation was to place Pierrot at the centre of the drama, displacing the traditional central characters such as Arlechinno, Pantalone and the lovers. He also used a looser, baggier costume, with large buttons, closer to the costume described by Duchartre for Pagliaccio (a character related to, but different from, Pedrolino/Pierrot) (Duchartre 1966: 258). His final change was to use a tight black skullcap instead of the traditional white hat.

Deburau's Pierrot became the star of the show at the Théâtre des Funambules. His success was built on silence; instead of words, he used his extraordinary agility and physical inventiveness to entrance his audience. Duchartre relates how 'he would invent a new dance almost every evening, sometimes eccentric, sometimes burlesque, but always charming' (Duchartre 1966: 260). We know very little about how Deburau's Pierrot was performed. Jacques Lecoq, the French mime and movement teacher, summarised his own conclusions:

> Deburau was big and tall, both physically and facially. We know that his entrance on stage at the Théâtre des Funambules was on his hands and that he exited via the window with a jump called *de fenêtre* ('via the window'). We also know that he achieved a degree of expression that could communicate all of the nuances of the soul, far more effectively than the spoken word. It is said that Deburau hardly moved during his expressive performances. It was in his 'reactions' that the subtlety of his emotions became apparent, especially in his face, as 'action' engaged the whole body.
>
> (Lecoq 2006: 32)

The use of silence, coupled with the romantic storylines, inevitably evoked a degree of sentimentality that clearly appealed to Parisian sensibilities at this time. Allardyce Nicoll suggests that Pierrot appealed because of his lonely reflective qualities, and his hopeless love for Columbine (Nicoll 1963: 93), all of which gave the character a wider resonance that also possessed a spiritual element.

Deburau's legacy survives most vividly in those whom he inspired. The visual image and gestural language he created for the character of Pierrot were strong enough to extend the character into a range of roles and situations, through which it was able to capture both the popular imagination and the creative interest of other theatre artists. Lecoq states that, 'Jean-Baptiste Gaspard Deburau was not a mime but rather a performer in the tradition of circus clowns and tightrope walkers who had not yet achieved a true mimed language' (Lecoq 2006: 34). The 'scenarios' for his performances included mention of *lazzis* – the traditional term for improvised slapstick routines in the Commedia tradition (see Deburau 1833: 72). Deburau did, however, begin the development of a sophisticated gestural language that was to continue for over a century and a half. Lecoq refers to this gestural language as *pantomime blanche* – a recognition of its association with the white faced, white costumed character of Pierrot.

As was typical for the time, the performance of the Pierrot character was handed down through a succession of father-son and teacher-pupil relationships. It is possible to trace this lineage from Deburau to his son, Jean-Charles (1829–73), and then from Paul Legrand (1816–98) to Louis Rouffe (1849–83). Nonetheless, by the end of the nineteenth century the Pierrot tradition in Paris was in decline, and public interest in *pantomime blanche* had waned considerably. Whilst popular enthusiasm for Pierrot remained strong in the South of France (and in Marseilles in particular) the situation in Paris was more uncertain, and probably as a result the acts became either darker and more violent (for example, *Pierrot sceptique* in 1881) or more refined. The situation in Paris was eventually such that by 1888 a theatrical society, the Cercle Funambulesque, had been founded in order to revive and restore the art of pantomime. The Cercle was partially successful, but its tendency was towards supporting productions that were uncontroversial, thus limiting its impact and drawing the Pierrot show into the salon theatre and towards a more elite audience.

Séverin (1863–1930) was one of the last of the traditional Pierrot performers (Rolfe 1979: 70). A pupil of Louis Rouffe, he had watched Jean-Charles Deburau perform when he was a child. Séverin saw himself as part of a tradition that went back at least as far as Gaspard Deburau, and even back through Commedia dell'Arte to the Roman mimes, but in which each mime was an artist for his age. This line of traditional Pierrots draws to a close with Georges Wague (1874–1958), who reacted against the development of precise codes of gesture and movement. Wague encouraged a more modern concept of pantomime where gesture expressed emotion and where economy of movement was more effective than grand gesture, '*Le minimum de geste correspond au maximum d'expression*' (Rémy 1964: 27). For Wague, the error lay in trying to translate words into gestures rather than using mime to capture feeling and mood.

The success of the Pierrot character and the championing of pantomime by some intellectuals during the nineteenth century is in part indicative of a rejection of the 'classical' style of nineteenth century Parisian theatre. Pierrot seems to have served as both a 'social' hero – 'the ancient slave, the modern proletarian, the pariah, the passive and disinherited being who witnesses, glumly and slyly, the orgies and follies of his masters' (Champfleury in Davidson 2013: 49) – and also as a more refined figure – 'He is essentially a gentleman right to the ends of his long sleeves, of which there is not one flick executed without the manners and ways of the court' (Sand in Davidson 2013: 49–50). This ambiguity, whilst problematic in terms of identifying a specific audience, seems to have enriched the character's historical appeal, enabling him to speak to both rich and poor, intellectual and illiterate, alike. Pierrot was a parody of the hero figure, someone whose actions always failed, but through this he paradoxically achieved a form of popular nobility and almost mythic status. In this respect the character became emblematic of 'an attitude towards the pains and joys of life' (George and Gossip 1993: 141). This ambiguity is caught in the following description by British poet and art critic Arthur Symons (1865–1945), which goes some way to explaining Pierrot's sentimental appeal to the nineteenth century sensibility:

> He feels himself to be sickening with a fever, or else perilously convalescent; for love is a disease, which he is too weak to resist or endure. He has worn his heart on his sleeve so long, that it has hardened in the cold air. He knows that his face is powdered, and if he sobs, it is without tears; and it is hard to distinguish, under the chalk, if the grimace which twists his mouth awry is more laughter or mockery. He knows that he is condemned to be always in public, that emotion would be supremely out of keeping with his costume, that he must remember to be fantastic if he would not be merely ridiculous. And so he becomes exquisitely false, dreading above all things that 'one touch of nature' which would ruffle his disguise, and leave him defenceless. Simplicity, in him, being the most laughable thing in the world, he becomes learned, perverse, intellectualising his pleasure, brutalising his intellect; his mournful contemplation of things becoming a kind of grotesque joy, which he expresses in the only symbols at his command, tracing his Giotto's O with the elegance of his pirouette.
>
> (Symons in George and Gossip 1993: 141–2)

The decline of Pierrot and the development of Commedia and mime through the work of Jacques Copeau

With the advent of Modernism, much of the sentimental appeal of the Pierrot figure diminished. Early modernists were instead attracted to pantomime and to traditional Commedia because of their potential for the transformation of people, objects and spaces, and the use of various levels of representation. For modernist artists and theatre practitioners, Commedia was interesting as a theatrical form closer to more primitive approaches to performance, to animal and ritual aspects of life. Commedia also exposed and celebrated the mechanisms of theatre making and of acting. At the same time Modernism placed value on natural physical efficiency and the analysis of movement's expressive potential (Evans 2009), both of which gave cultural status to more subtly expressive pantomime acts such as those of Wague.

As Pierrot became a more serious figure, and as pantomime practitioners sought for more cultural respectability, the tensions between codification and fossilisation, between exaggerated and restrained gesture, and between artistry and archness, became more marked (Gates 2011). Pierrot was in danger of becoming little more than a symbolic figure, detached from the thrust of theatrical innovation. The advent of Modernism led to intense debates over the value and nature of the 'natural' in art. In this context, French pantomime struggled to reconcile its historic techniques and forms with the interest in movement that was, at least in certain respects, more authentic and modern. Lecoq suggests that Pierrot effectively died in 1925, the year of the International Exposition of Modern Industrial and Decorative Arts in Paris, an event that marked the arrival of a truly modern sense of art, design and culture (Lecoq 2006: 35).

But if the character of Pierrot struggled to survive the cultural turmoil of the early twentieth century, the spirit of the Commedia was still strong and vibrant enough to find new champions and a new relevance. John Rudlin relates how, in 1910, Charles Dullin (1885–1949) 'created the role of Pierrot in Saint-Georges de Bouhélier's *Carnaval des Enfants* at the Théâtre des Arts' (Rudlin 1994: 185) – in doing so connecting with the long tradition of French Pierrots. Only three years later, as change started to sweep across Europe, Dullin joined Jacques Copeau's new theatrical enterprise, the Théâtre du Vieux-Colombier – a project that Copeau (1879–1949) intended as a break from the traditions of the nineteenth century Parisian theatre. The activity of the new company was curtailed by the outbreak of the First World War in 1914; Dullin enlisted and was sent to the trenches on the frontline, but he remained in correspondence with Copeau and in some of his letters he is clearly enthused about the possibility of starting a new Commedia troupe after the War. In a separate set of letters to his mistress Elise Toulemon, Dullin also records how he has

> discovered a genuine actor and three improvisers, two of whom descend in a direct line from fairground performers. I give them a scenario and they improvise anything I like. They sing, clown, do Japanese, Spanish, and Italian dances, speak gibberish that sounds just like foreign languages! Evoke for them one word in some foreign civilization about which they know nothing and it's enough to trigger the most unforeseen and droll fantasies. The eighteenth-century and fairground theatre survives in these blokes intact!
>
> (Rudlin 1994: 18)

Dullin also wrote to Louis Jouvet (1887–1951), another of the founding members of Copeau's company, outlining 'characters for a new Commedia, part circus-, part *commedia dell'arte*-based' (Rudlin 1994: 188). He wrote passionately about the kind of actors he thought were right for this kind of work:

> I would like them to be as near to the people as possible – simple folk – artisans – this genre is incompatible with aestheticism and rhythmical and other chinoiseries. Our farceurs would have to be dancers, acrobats, jugglers, musicians, but with the natural ability of clowns and fairground acrobats. They would have to be *alive*, good drinkers, tellers of jokes and tall stories, good to be with… In order to effect such an education, we must forget that we are actors, forget there ever were such things as actors or plays. Wipe any concern for the farceurs of the Middle Ages from our minds, forget Molière lock stock and barrel… Start from nothing in order to arrive at everything. One of the essential conditions, I think, would be great camaraderie and, if possible, living a virtually communal life.
>
> (Dullin in Rudlin 1994: 189)

Copeau, who was invalided out from the military in 1915, clearly shared Dullin's enthusiasm for reviving the spirit of the Commedia without the baggage it had inherited over the last century. He made various notes on characters and traits that he observed with a specific view to the creation of new comic characters. Rudlin mentions a Pedrolino/Pierrot derived character that Copeau describes in his letters to one of his other collaborators, Roger Martin du Gard (1881–1958):

> An *adolescent boy* whose name I have not come up with yet and whom I imagine with the traits of Suzanne [Bing – Copeau's leading actress and principal collaborator in the Vieux-Colombier School] because we have spoken of it together and she has given it some thought. This character is often very quiet. I have one scenario in which he does not utter a word.
>
> (Rudlin 1994: 179)

Martin du Gard and Copeau saw Commedia as an important antidote to the tired conventions of the boulevard theatre. Commedia seems to speak to societal and cultural needs after times of war – as if it touches a desire for a sense of common humanity, humour, spontaneity, and simplicity. Although Copeau and Martin du Gard did not in the end work together on this project, Copeau was inspired to continue with longer term plans to produce actors capable of working in this kind of way.

The ideas, experiences and correspondences circulating between Copeau and his colleagues during the early years of the First World War meant that by the time he came to organise the 1917 tour of the Théâtre du Vieux-Colombier to America he was already excited about the possibility of exploring the spirit and practice of the Commedia dell'Arte. He saw in the Commedia a model for a theatre that was popular, improvisatory, vibrant, rhythmically and physically expressive, and that worked as an ensemble. As part of the tour he presented a production of Molière's *Les Fourberies de Scapin*, which drew on the old Commedia traditions but re-invigorated them through a return to simple staging, improvisation and physical expression, (Evans 2006: 85–116). For Copeau, Commedia embodied a spirit of joyful play in the physical practice of acting; asked why he liked 'Canary Cottage' (a musical comedy he saw in New York whilst on tour in 1917), he proclaimed that he liked it 'because it was fun not only for the audience, but for the actors too. There was joy in it' (Copeau 1990: 151).

Copeau's determination to rejuvenate the art of theatre led him, in 1920, to establish a school attached to his company. Here the students experimented with games, masks, circus skills and silent improvisation, under the guidance of Copeau's assistant, Suzanne Bing (1885–1967). The school provided Copeau with an environment within which he could further explore the creation of new character types. He encouraged his students to develop the externals of the character first and then extend them through the use of bodily isolations and improvisation (Rudlin 1994: 182). In 1924, Copeau abandoned his work at the Vieux-Colombier to take a group of his actors, students and their family members to Burgundy in order to pursue this work with fewer distractions. The group adopted the name Les Copiaus. Their daily work included the making of masks, the development of gymnastic and acrobatic skills, the integration of dance, music and song, and the development of skills in mime. Copeau believed that the creation of a new theatre lay in returning to the roots of theatre – the chorus, ensemble creation, and the physicality of the Commedia dell'Arte. He envisaged a company made up of actors who would each create their own new character types, in the style of a new Commedia, which he titled the *comédie nouvelle*. Copeau's nephew and assistant Michel Saint-Denis (1897–1971) created the character of Oscar Knie, a tramp-like half-masked figure, who emerged through a process of improvisation and experiment. Knie was to become the central figure in the Copiaus' devised production, *La Dance de la ville et des champs* (1928), which integrated song, dance, music and masked characters. Amongst the group of pupils who studied at the school before the move to Burgundy was Etienne Decroux (1898–1991). Decroux was fascinated by the early explorations of silent improvisation led by Bing. Although Copeau was interested in Commedia as a popular form that might help re-invigorate the contemporary theatre, he was less interested in pantomime and silent improvisation as a form in itself. It was Decroux, inspired by this early experience, who worked intensively to (re)discover the techniques of mime and to firmly establish it once again as a silent art.

When the Copiaus disbanded in 1929, Saint-Denis and a few other company members felt strongly enough about the progress they had made in creating new characters and developing a physically expressive form of theatre to continue the work on their own. They formed the Compagnie des Quinze in order to continue with the work; however, the pressures of communal living, international touring, and a persistent lack of funds meant that they eventually disbanded again in 1935. From this point on, the strands of silent mime, masked improvisation and devised comic performance spin out in various directions through: Saint-Denis' work as a teacher and director in the United Kingdom (see Evans 2013: 119–22); the work of Jean Dasté (1904–94, Copeau's former pupil and son-in-law) as director of the Comédie de St Etienne and with his company Les Comédiens de Grenoble; Decroux's mime school in Paris; and the pedagogy of Jacques Lecoq (1921–99, who worked with Dasté and met Copeau in 1948).

Conclusion: Copeau's legacy and Les Enfants du Paradis (1945)

Copeau, together with his collaborators and disciples, sought to create a theatre that took its inspiration from the improvised comedy and ensemble playing of the Commedia dell'Arte, and that also aimed beyond historical reconstruction towards a new improvised comedy. Copeau and his disciples took the techniques and skills of the old pantomime traditions out of the salons and theatrical societies and re-invigorated them. From a tradition that, in France at least, had become codified, self-referential and tired, Copeau created a new sense of the theatrical effectiveness and cultural worth of Commedia. Much of what Copeau (re)discovered through his exploration of Commedia – the value of actors living, working, playing and creating together; the power of the silent gesture and of the mask; the importance of the ensemble – has affected theatre practice throughout the twentieth century, up to and including the work of Complicité, Théâtre du Soleil, Footsbarn and Kneehigh.

There is, finally, one fascinating point at which so much of the subject of this chapter comes together. In 1945, during the last period of the Nazi occupation of France, the French film director Marcel Carné made a film, *Les Enfants du Paradis*, which aimed to celebrate the French theatre of the early nineteenth century. The film's plot centres on the love four men for a courtesan. One of the suitors is Gaspard Deburau, played by Jean-Louis Barrault (1910–94). Deburau's father is played by Barrault's teacher and collaborator Etienne Decroux. Of particular interest are the pantomime scenes, in which Barrault performs routines in the style of Deburau. Barrault had spent an intense period with Decroux developing the techniques of corporeal mime; however, for some of these routines he was advised by Georges Wague, who of course represented a form of professional descendent from Deburau himself. In this manner, the film encapsulates both the past and future of the Pierrot, of the art of pantomime, and of the French Commedia dell'Arte variants and developments, and indicates something of the mythic status that Pierrot has in the history of French theatre. Barrault, a seminal figure in French twentieth century theatre, openly admitted his own sense of affinity with Baptiste, the Pierrot character he plays in the film (Lecoq 1987: 69).

For Commedia purists the nineteenth century history of Commedia in France and in particular the rise of Pierrot and the technique of pantomime is a digression from the essential line of Commedia. Yet such a perspective denies the flexibility that Commedia has demonstrated, its ability to open itself to the needs and cultural nuances of particular places and particular times; and it denies the rich and multi-faceted nature of its appeal. Certainly through the strand that leads from Deburau to Copeau and Decroux, and later to Lecoq, we can see connections to some of the most important innovations in actor training of the twentieth century.

References

Copeau, Jacques (1990) *Copeau: Texts on Theatre*. John Rudlin and Norman Paul (eds and trs), London: Routledge.

Davidson, John (2013) *Clown: Readings in Theatre Practice*. Basingstoke, UK: Palgrave Macmillan.

Deburau, Jean Gaspard (1833) *Deburau. Histoire du théâtre à quatre sous, pour faire suite à l'Histoire du théâtre-français. Vol. 2*. Paris: Librarie de Charles Gosselin.

Duchartre, Pierre Louis (1966) *The Italian Comedy*. London: Dover.

Evans, Mark (2006) *Jacques Copeau*. London: Routledge.

Evans, Mark (2009) *Movement Training for the Modern Actor*. New York and London: Routledge.

Evans, Mark (2013) 'The French ensemble tradition: Jacques Copeau, Michel Saint-Denis and Jacques Lecoq' in Britton, John (ed.) (2013) *Encountering Ensemble*. London: Bloomsbury/Methuen.

Gates, Laura Purcell (2011) *Tout Bouge [Everything Moves]: The (Re)Construction of the Body in Lecoq-based Pedagogy*. University of Minnesota (unpublished doctoral thesis).

George, David and Gossip, Christopher (eds) (1993) *Studies in the Commedia dell'Arte*. Cardiff, UK: University of Wales Press.

Lecoq, Jacques (1987) *Le Théâtre du Geste: mimes et acteurs*. Paris: Bordas.

Lecoq, Jacques (2006) *Theatre of Movement and Gesture*. David Bradby (ed.), London: Routledge.

Lust, Annette (2000) *From the Greek Mimes to Marcel Marceau and Beyond: Mimes, Actors Pierrots, and Clowns*. Lanham, Maryland, US and London: Scarecrow Press.

Nicoll, Allardyce (1963) *The World of Harlequin*. Cambridge, UK: Cambridge University Press.

Oreglia, Giacomo (1968) *The Commedia dell'Arte*. London: Methuen.

Rémy, Tristan (1954) *Jean-Gaspard Deburau*. Paris: L'Arche Editeur.

Rémy, Tristan (1964) *Georges Wague: le mime de la belle époque*. Paris: Georges Girard.

Rolfe, Bari (ed.) (1979) *Mimes on Miming*. London: Millington.

Rudlin, John (1994) *Commedia dell'Arte: An Actor's Handbook*. London: Routledge.

37

SPEECHLESS SPECTACLES

Commedia pantomime in France, England, and the Americas during the eighteenth and nineteenth centuries

Matthew R. Wilson

The 500-year-long tradition of Commedia dell'Arte is like a tree with many branches, some of which grow far apart and bear little resemblance to one another.

This chapter is about pantomime, one of the distant branches of the Commedia dell'Arte tradition that, to purist practitioners, may seem to be a mistake or a misinterpreted divergence from the Renaissance style. It was balletic, not boisterous; refined, not rustic; elegant, not earthy. In eighteenth-century pantomime, Tristano Martinelli's poor, patched Arlecchino was replaced by John Rich's prim and patterned Harlequin, and the bawdy and boisterous multilingualism of sixteenth-century improvised speech was silenced in favor of wordless wonders set to music or song. The everyday, domestic situations of Renaissance humanism were exchanged for fantastical myths, epic adventures, and fairytale settings. Harlequin transformed from a simple servant to an impish miracle-maker—a sorcerer, a traveler, a dreamer, or a mythic creature hatched from an egg—and his mundane slapstick became a magic bat. He remained a relatable Everyman, but his story was no longer confined to the urban street corners of Serlio's comic scene. Fantasy, mythology, and spectacle were the hallmarks of pantomime, and the theatrical style would likely never be lumped with traditional Commedia dell'Arte were it not for the familiar names that peopled its stories: Harlequin, Columbine, Polichinelle, Scaramouch, Pierrot, and Pantaloon.

These characters were born in Renaissance Commedia but lived on in the Harlequinades of the eighteenth and nineteenth centuries. These Harlequinades were staged under two distinct conditions. On the one hand, they might be brief, bare-bones knockabouts in which the characters engaged in simple dances, slapstick routines, and lively chase sequences. These were popular entr'acte entertainments to rouse the crowd between headlining performances at legitimate theatres, and they also served as clown interludes at circuses, fairs, carnivals, and equestrian events. At the other end of the spectrum lay blockbuster spectacle shows in which the unassuming Commedia characters populated high-tech stages with impressive scenic transformations, large orchestras, and an array of special effects to round out

355

mythological or fairytale stories. These plays featured the Commedia characters translated into other roles as distinct as Dr. Faustus or Robinson Crusoe.

Both the simple Harlequinade knockabout and the elaborate fantasy spectacle may seem at odds with the traditional, Renaissance Commedia dell'Arte, preserved in extant *scenarii*. Pantomime's style may feel closer to circus clown and street mime on one end, or comic opera, ballet, and mythological spectacle on the other end. The history of Commedia dell'Arte has frequently jumped over the pantomimes of the 1700s and 1800s in an attempt to connect twentieth-century Commedia revival movements directly to the so-called "Golden Age" of Commedia in the 1500s and 1600s. Pantomime has been dismissed as a degeneration when compared with "original" Commedia dell'Arte practices, but it was one of the most popular forms of dramatic entertainment in England and North America throughout the eighteenth and nineteenth centuries, making pantomime a worthy field of study in its own right.

It is also crucial to recognize the history of pantomime in order to properly understand the twentieth-century revival movements that Giula Filacanapa has dubbed "Neo Commedia dell'Arte" (Filacanapa 2012). Although historians and practitioners of the 1900s described themselves with reference to their Renaissance forebears, the work they produced was heavily influenced by eighteenth- and nineteenth-century pantomime. For example, Edward Gordon Craig (1872–1966) is remembered for helping to bring the Commedia aesthetic back to the modern stage, and yet Craig's landmark 1901 production *The Mask of Love* employed "a chorus of Pierrots as unwilling marionettes manipulated by another chorus of Harlequins" (Fisher 1989: 255) in a way that bears little relationship to Scala but makes perfect sense as a continuation of the poetic pantomime aesthetic. Similarly, the Harlequins popularized by Picasso and the Pierrots made famous by Meyerhold or the French film *Les Enfants du Paradis* all represent a Commedia dell'Arte style that is more nineteenth- than sixteenth-century.

Any history of Commedia, then, cannot be complete without reference to the developments in pantomime that came about after the "Golden Age" but that preceded and influenced contemporary attempts to understand Commedia dell'Arte and to employ it on the modern stage.

Appropriations of Commedia dell'Arte in France and England

The Commedia dell'Arte that was born in mid-sixteenth-century tours throughout the Italian peninsula quickly made its way into Europe, arriving in Spain, France, and England by the early 1570s. These tours continued throughout the "Golden Age" of Commedia dell'Arte, as Italian players became some of Europe's most celebrated theatre artists.

In France, the Italian Commedia found fertile soil, and Italian players made Paris a frequent sojourn. Between 1662 and 1697 Paris was a permanent home to Tiberio Fiorilli and Dominque Biancolelli's troupe, and their work had a profound impact on Molière, who borrowed heavily from the cache of Commedia's characters, conventions, and plot devices.

This "borrowing" from Commedia was commonplace across Europe, even as early as the late sixteenth century. The tropes and techniques of these Italian players became familiar to local audiences and were appropriated by theatre artists as part of a larger European exchange of what Louise George Clubb has called "theatregrams" (Clubb 1989: 6; Henke 2008: 19–34). Louis B. Wright has described how Shakespeare's clown Will Kemp may have had occasion to meet and trade secrets with Commedia players on tour (Wright 1926: 516), and Shakespeare himself is indebted to Italian forms, which he applied and appropriated to his own ends (Salingar 1974: 77). From the early decades of transnational Italian tours, then, Commedia materials made their way into the theatrical life of other countries where they were not merely imitated but were also appropriated, amalgamated, and transformed.

In some cases, the resultant appropriation merged with local theatrical traditions. For example, Kemp no doubt took aspects of Italian Commedia and incorporated them into the already vibrant tradition of English clowning; Molière blended Commedia concepts with traditional French farce or new forms like the "comedy ballet." In many cases, the Commedia characters were translated into different, local types, but sometimes the characters retained their traditional names—albeit in Gallicized or Anglicized versions. Molière specifically utilized the Commedia names Pierrot and Scapin (from the Italian Scapino). Meanwhile, around the same time in England, Edward Ravenscroft gave the Franco-Italianate characters an English twist with his play *Scaramouch a Philosopher, Harlequin a School-Boy, Bravo, Merchant, and Magician; A Comedy after the Italian Manner* published in 1677. Ravenscroft was the first English playwright to place these characters in an English setting and to give them additional characteristics such as "philosopher" or "school-boy" beyond their traditional social roles. Aphra Behn's 1687 *The Emperor of the Moon* employs the Commedia characters Scaramouch and Harlequin as traditional servants but continues to show the evolution of the characters, by way of France, into the farcical dancing jesters that will populate the later stages. The association between Commedia dell'Arte characters and dancing is further seen in the fact that dancing master Thomas Jevon performed the role of Harlequin both in Behn's farce and in William Mountfort's *c.*1686 *The Life and Death of Doctor Faustus* (Martinez 2009: 151). Although the character names remained, the specialties necessary to perform them had begun to change. The traditional roles of Arlecchino and Scaramuccia had been made famous by Italian comic improvisers such as Martinelli and Fiorilli, and the Italian style influenced English and French clowns like Kemp and Molière. However, in the translation of Arlecchino to Harlequin and Scaramuccia to Scaramouch, French and English traditions in the late 1700s began to dedicate these leading comic roles not to renowned clowns but to virtuosic dancers. The shift from Renaissance Commedia dell'Arte to eighteenth-century pantomime was underway.

The French re-birth of pantomime: history meets necessity

By the mid-to-late seventeenth century, Commedia's characters were solidified in popular culture. Meanwhile, even legitimate theatres began to see a greater emphasis on music and dance. Operas and operettas became popular, as did the "ballet comedies" that Louis XIV had commissioned from Molière and Jean-Baptiste Lully. The stage was set for the creation of a new genre, and theatre practitioners who both looked to the past for inspiration and found contemporary solutions to obstacles in their own time developed pantomime.

Ancient inspiration contributed to eighteenth-century pantomime as a result of what Franklin J. Hildy calls "applied theatre history," that is "the use of knowledge gained from the examination of the theatre of past eras to create new theatre forms" (Hildy 2012: 4). The new theatre form in this case used concepts gleaned from Roman pantomime in which masked performers enacted stories through dance, embodying a variety of characters from history or mythology. The performers did not speak dialogue and often utilized full-face masks without mouth openings. These dance-theatre pieces were set to music, often with the pantomimic artist himself wearing bells or cymbals, playing pipes, or stomping his feet, frequently accompanied by other musicians, including solo or choral singers (Csapo and Slater 1994: 370, 378–85; Vince 1984: 79). Eighteenth-century historiographers did not fully understand the Roman pantomime, but they nonetheless cited this ancient tradition as the source of their new, contemporary pantomime. In 1728, dancing master John Weaver published *The History of the Mimes and Pantomimes* in which he not only provided "an Historical Account of Several Performers in Dancing" dating back to Roman times, but also added "a List of Modern Entertainments That Have Been Exhibited on the English Stage, either in Imitation of the Ancient Pantomimes, or after the Manner of the Modern Italians" (Weaver 1728).

This "modern" phenomenon of the early 1700s, however, was not merely a work of historical fancy. It also solved present-day problems for the French performers who first developed the pantomime style. By 1700, two theatre companies held duopolistic control over all Parisian theatre: the Opéra, which had been formed from Lully's Royal Academy of Music and Dance, and the Comédie Française, created by a royal decree that joined the late Molière's company with that of the Bourgogne (Brocket and Hildy 2008: 195). Officially, no other performers were permitted to stage theatrical productions; however, enterprising artists—as they always do—found ways to skirt these prohibitions. By exploiting ambiguities in the definition of "theatre," rival companies staged operas and fairground performers began to specialize in dance theatre that was wordless or sung. In short, pantomime developed in France as a tactic for unlicensed artists to claim that, because they did not utilize spoken dialogue, restrictions covering "theatre" should not apply to them.

While French fairground performers were using the pantomime to subvert the Parisian duopoly, a similar theatrical duopoly existed in London, as two royal patents were held by the companies of William Davenant and Thomas Killigrew. Ironically, by the end of the 1710s pantomime would be so popular in London that it would be regularly staged by London's royal patent companies alongside the legitimate fair that they were licensed to produce.

The evolution of pantomime in eighteenth-century England

The French fairground performers who reinvented the pantomime in Paris brought their balletic brand of Commedia dell'Arte to the "night scenes" they performed in London in the early 1700s. Within a few years, these performances were being copied by the dancing masters at the two London patent companies (Senelick

1995: 837). Weaver's *The Cheats; or, The Tavern Bilkers* appropriated the Franco-Italianate Commedia characters and the fairground style to an English setting. In his own words the piece was, "The first Entertainment that appeared on the English Stage, where the Representation and Story was carried on by Dancing, Action and Motion only, was performed in Grotesque Characters, after the manner of the Modern Italians, such as Harlequin, Scaramouch, &c." (Weaver 1728).

As the pantomime developed in England, it exploited the dynamic opposites between high art and low comedy. On January 24, 1717, at Lincoln's Inn Fields, John Rich staged his *Amadis; or the Loves of Harlequin and Columbine*, which was the first known play to combine "the mythological, operatic part with the grotesque, mute harlequinade" (Martinez 2009: 157). The "mythological part" had been present in the Roman pantomimes of old and was also a common feature of Early Modern court masques. The comedic counterpoint was provided by the Commedia dell'Arte characters whose unassuming knockabouts were juxtaposed with high classicism. Weaver was conscious of this juxtaposition in his *The Loves of Mars and Venus*, which he later claimed was "an Attempt in Imitation of the ancient Pantomimes, and the first of that kind that has appeared since the Time of the Roman Empire" (Weaver 1728).

As the pantomime continued to develop in the early 1700s, the dancing Commedia characters found themselves further carried away into mythological, classical, and romantic plotlines. At Drury Lane and Lincoln's Inn Fields (later Covent Garden), these epic stories were told through the aid of the latest scenic technology. Scenic spectacle had previously been utilized to great effect by Commedia troupes in Italy and France (Scott 1989: 180), but the pretense of magic and mythology allowed for even more spectacular effects in the eighteenth century. The 1723–4 season saw rival productions of Commedia-based pantomime *Faust* stories, with Harlequin himself cast in the role of Dr. Faustus, his familiar diamond costume still visible underneath the scholar's robe. Both productions took advantage of numerous, impressive scene changes involving magical forests, ancient palaces, the mouth of hell, and a "Poetical Heaven." Meanwhile, the Commedia characters Harlequin, Scaramouch, Punch, and Pierrot mixed with a cast that included "heathen deities," angels, demons, and even "a Dragon."

At Lincoln's Inn Fields, the title character in *Harlequin Doctor Faustus* was played by Company Manager John Rich. Rich's Harlequin character became known as "Lun," clear evidence that the term "Harlequin" had begun to describe a character type rather than the name of the character himself. Rich's antics were later eulogized by David Garrick:

> When Lun appear'd, with matchless art and whim,
> He gave pow'r of speech to ev'ry limb;
> Tho mask'd and mute, convey'd his quick intent,
> And told in frolic gestures all he meant.
> (Pedicord and Bergman 1980: 405)

Despite Garrick's affection for Rich, he was at best ambivalent toward pantomime, as is clear from his own "anti-pantomime" *Harlequin's Invasion; Or, A Christmas*

Gambol, which premiered at Drury Lane in 1759 (O'Brien 2004: 219–31; Chesley 1987: 83–134). By the end of the eighteenth century, English critics complained that the artistry seen in Rich's early pantomimes had been replaced entirely by scenic spectacle and senseless choral numbers. The epic or dramatic counterpoint present in the earliest English pantomimes had been lost, and the subject matters moved from mythology and classicism to adventure and fairy tale.

At the turn of the nineteenth century, pantomime in England continued to lose touch with its Commedia roots, as the white-faced clown took center stage, relegating Harlequin, Columbine, and Pantaloon to supporting roles. The most famous clown and the "father of modern clowning" was Joseph Grimaldi, the star performer in Thomas Dibdin's *Harlequin and Mother Goose; Or, the Golden Egg*, which premiered at Drury Lane in 1806 and affirmed a new trajectory for pantomime away from it Commedia origins and toward the holiday frolics that would be reborn in the twentieth-century British "panto" (Stott 2009: xv, 325–43).

Harlequin in America

The first fully documented play in New York City (that is, the first for which we know the title, location, and the date) was a pantomime entitled *The Adventures of Harlequin and Scaramouch, or The Spaniard Trick'd*. According to an advertisement in *New York Weekly Journal*, it played on Greenwich Street at Holt's Long Room on February 12 1739 and boasted perspective scenery of "the most noted Cities and remarkable Places both of Europe and America." The advertisement was an overstatement, as Holt's Long Room was likely nothing more than a converted hall, devoid of the impressive scenic technology one would find in London. While England was producing elaborate, full-length Harlequin pantomime plays, Harlequin in America flourished more easily in entr'actes, afterpieces, and circus knockabouts.

One of America's most famous Harlequins also claimed to be its first, native professional actor. In 1785, John Durang danced his way into Lewis Hallam, Jr.'s Old American Company, where he played supporting roles but also made a name for himself through dances and Harlequinades. His fame became so great that his entr'acte performances were advertised alongside the legitimate headlining titles. At first, Durang played Scaramouch to Hallam's Harlequin in the company's pantomimes, but he was later hired as the chief Harlequin for Rickett's Circus on tour through the eastern United States and Canada, a trip which he describes with panache in his *Memoirs*. Durang's circus Harlequinades featured dances, acrobatics, slapstick, and equestrian routines—common fare for an early nineteenth-century Harlequin. The character had evolved since Martinelli's Arlecchino, and he was known for his iconic white hat, black mask, colorful diamond-patterned jumpsuit, and magic bat, all of which are evident in Durang's watercolor self-portrait of himself in the Harlequin role.

As in England, Harlequin and his compatriots continued to be re-appropriated in the nineteenth century. The white-faced clown, popularized by Grimaldi, also appeared on American stages, especially in Christmas-time fairy tales. The most famous American clown was George "Laff" Fox, whose 1867 *Humpty Dumpty* became the first pantomime to have "a full evening to itself" on the New York stage

(Senelick 1999: 138). In evocative photos and line drawings from the production, Fox's white-faced clown outwits the aged Pantaloon while Harlequin and Columbine dance romantically.

The rising popularity of white-faced clowns corresponds also to the period of black-faced minstrel performers, and, not surprisingly, the Harlequin character—depicted with a black mask since his birth as Arlecchino in the late sixteenth century—found his way into a few minstrel shows in the US and England. Even prior to the advent of the American minstrel show, two British pantomimes, *Harlequin Mungo; or Peep into the Tower* (1789) and *Furibond, or Harlequin Negro* (1807) featured a black slave who was magically transformed into a Harlequin and participated in the customary slapstick, chase sequences, and eventual happy endings on his way to marrying Columbine. An 1819 lithograph entitled "Four and Twenty Hobby Horses" includes a figure whose dress and "magic bat" are pure Harlequin but whose face appears not to be masked, but rather blacked, with exaggerated eyes and lips resembling a black-face performer. In 1836, British performers imported the now-famous American figure Jim Crow and fused him with the Harlequinade tradition in *Cowardy, Cowardy, Custard; or Harlequin Jim Crow and the Magic Mustard Pot* (Gates 1987: 53–60; see also O'Brien 2004: 117–37).

While minstrel shows and fairytale clowning are at a far remove from Renaissance Commedia dell'Arte, they nevertheless became part of the cultural field in which Commedia dell'Arte characters existed in the nineteenth century. In George Fox's *Humpty Dumpty*, Harlequin traveled via railroad throughout the American Old West, a great distance from Arlecchino's Parisian origins.

Pantomime's influence on twentieth-century "Neo Commedia dell'Arte"

The History of the Harlequinade (1915) was the title given to the English translation of Maurice Sand's 1860 *Masques et Bouffons*. The work was one of the first major histories of Commedia dell'Arte and certainly one of the first to appear in English. It is no mistake that the English edition was sold as a history not of "Commedia dell'Arte" but rather of "Harlequinades." In many respects, Sand's book—and most early twentieth-century historiography of Commedia—claimed to seek out original, Renaissance practices but retained significant assumptions drawn from the familiarity of the pantomime aesthetic.

The images of Commedia dell'Arte flourished again in early twentieth-century popular imagination as modernist artists revolted against the dictates of realism (Green and Swan 1993: 7). Nevertheless, the Harlequins painted by Picasso more closely resembled Durang's nineteenth-century self-portraits than the Recueil Fossard images of early Arlecchino. Meyerhold first learned of Pierrot through the circus, and Craig fell in love with Commedia thanks to seaside open-air performers. Even as Craig revitalized the historical study of Commedia with his journal *The Mask*, his own productions bore little resemblance to the "original practices" of the Renaissance.

It is no surprise that Commedia continues to inspire, that its wide and diverse tree branches continue to grow. When questioning what is "original," "authentic," or "historical" in Commedia dell'Arte, it is important to ask "Original to whom?", "Authentic where?", and "Historical when?" It is not enough to say, "Arlecchino looked like this or walked like that," for he adopted a variety of looks and dispositions on his travels through Italy and France, into England, and as far as the American Old West. The pantomime theatre of the eighteenth and nineteenth centuries is not, strictly speaking, Commedia dell'Arte, and yet it embodies the continued adaptability and allure of Commedia's characters. Its lavish presence in the tradition continues to color contemporary assumptions about what Commedia dell'Arte was, is, and can be.

References

Brockett, Oscar G., and Franklin J. Hildy (2008) *History of the Theatre*, 10th ed., Boston, US: Pearson Education.

Chesley, Brent Douglas (1987) *The Faces of Harlequin in Eighteenth-Century English Pantomime*, Ph.D. diss, University of Notre Dame.

Clubb, Louise George (1989) *Italian Drama in Shakespeare's Time*, New Haven, US: Yale University Press.

Csapo, Eric, and William J. Slater (1994) *The Context of Ancient Drama*, Ann Arbor, US: University of Michigan Press.

Filacanapa, Giulia (2012) "Giovanni Poli's Neo Commedia dell'Arte: An Example of Renaissance *La commedia des Zanni*," a paper presented at Passing on the Commedia dell'Arte Tradition, February 18, 2012, at Glendon College, Toronto, Canada.

Fisher, James (1989) "Commedia Iconography in the Theatrical Art of Edward Gordon Craig," *The Commedia dell'Arte from the Renaissance to Dario Fo*, 245–75, Lewiston, US: Edwin Mellen Press.

Gates, Henry Louis (1987) *Figures in Black: Words, Signs, and the "Racial" Self*, New York: Oxford University Press.

Green, Martin Burgess, and John Swan (1993) *The Triumph of Pierrot: The Commedia dell'Arte and the Modern Imagination*, University Park, US: Pennsylvania State University Press.

Henke, Robert (2008) "Border Crossing in the *Commedia dell'Arte*," *Transnational Exchange in Early Modern Theater*, Burlington, US: Ashgate.

Hildy, Franklin J. (2012) "The Theatre of Shakespeare's Time," unpublished manuscript.

Martinez, Marc (2009) "The Tricks of Lun: Mimesis and Mimicry in John Rich's Performance and Conception of Pantomimes," *Theatre History Studies* 29: 148–70.

O'Brien, John (2004) *Harlequin Britain: Pantomime and Entertainment, 1690–1760*, Baltimore, US: Johns Hopkins University Press.

Pedicord, Harry William, and Frederick Louis Bergmann, eds. (1980) *The Plays of David Garrick, Vol. 1*, Carbondale, US: Southern Illinois Press.

Salingar, Leo (1974) *Shakespeare and the Traditions of Comedy*, Cambridge, UK: Cambridge University Press.

Scott, Virginia (1989) "*Junon descend du Ciel sur un Poulet d'Inde*: Spectacle in the Commedia dell'Arte in Paris in the Seventeenth Century," *The Commedia dell'Arte from the Renaissance to Dario Fo*, 178–208, Lewiston, US: Edwin Mellen Press.

Senelick, Laurence (1995) "pantomime, English," *The Cambridge Guide to Theatre*, 837–8, Cambridge, US: Cambridge University Press.

——(1999) *The Age & Stage of George L. Fox, 1825–1877*, Iowa City, US: University of Iowa Press.

Stott, Andrew McConnell (2009) *The Pantomime Life of Joseph Grimaldi*, Edinburgh, US: Canongate Books.

Vince, Ronald W. (1984) *Ancient and Medieval Theatre: A Historiographical Handbook*, Westport, US: Greenwood Press.

Weaver, John (1728) *The History of the Mimes and Pantomimes*, London: printed for J. Roberts, and A. Dod.

Wright, Louis B. (1926) "Will Kemp and the Commedia Dell'Arte," *Modern Language Notes* 41, no. 8: 516–20.

38

FROM MEYERHOLD TO EISENSTEIN

Commedia dell'Arte in Russia

J. Douglas Clayton

From Barcelona to London, from Paris to St Petersburg, images and themes of Commedia dell'Arte (CDA) permeated the international arts movement at the turn of the twentieth century, as Martin Green and John Swan have shown (Green and Swan 2001). The images of Harlequin and Pierrot can be found in visual arts (Picasso), music (Schoenberg's *Pierrot lunaire*), poetry (from Jules Laforgue's *Complaintes* to Eliot's *Prufrock*), in theater (Benavente's *Los Intereses creados*), in opera (Leoncavallo's *I Pagliacci*), in film (Chaplin) and even in fashion (the slicked down hair of the Duke of Windsor, reminiscent of Pierrot). CDA as an international phenomenon was composed of different strands: itinerant Italian street comedy with improvised texts and masks was only one. Mime played a role from when the Comédie Italienne was forbidden to use speech by Mme de Maintenon and the *théâtre forain* appeared in the early eighteenth century. By the 1900s, marionettes and puppet theater had become popular and were to figure to some extent in the new manifestations of CDA, and the proliferation of cabarets and studio theaters was to provide a fertile new environment for Pierrot and Harlequin. Moreover, the related world of the circus with its clowns was called on to participate in the new efflorescence. CDA meant liberty: the twentieth century with its search for new beginnings and change was to embrace it with enthusiasm: it was dangerous, subversive and uncontrollable.

Much of Green and Swan's book is taken up with CDA in Russian art. Russia was not only susceptible to the cult of CDA imagery and themes as they developed in the West: Russian theatrical culture in particular integrated them deeply into its theory and praxis. To a greater or lesser extent they also permeated poetry, ballet, music, painting, and eventually film. Indeed, they were key to the revolution in Russian theater, ballet, and film that took place in the first three decades of the twentieth century. The initial impulse for the cult of CDA in Russia came from the revival of Russian poetry as part of a larger movement away from realistic prose and philosophical positivism towards a new aestheticism. By the early years of the twentieth century, this counter aesthetic had penetrated almost all aspects of artistic life. French symbolist poetry served as a point of departure for Russian symbolism.

The first generation of Russian symbolists had been oriented towards mysticism, and the belief in an ideal world beyond the tawdry realities of everyday life: a *realibus ad realiora* (from reality towards the more real). It was the second wave of poets and artists that became interested in the images and themes of the harlequinade, especially Aleksandr Blok (1880–1921) and Andrei Belyi (1880–1934) (Soboleva 2008). They took from French romanticism the simplified "Pierrotic" version of the CDA images, developed in the nineteenth century by Deburau and lauded by Gauthier. For Blok and Belyi the Pierrot-Harlequin-Columbine triangle seems to have served as a poetic shorthand for the tortured relationship between the two poets and Blok's wife, Liubov' Mendeleeva. Key to their poetry was also, as Olga Soboleva has shown, the notion of the mask as a doubling of the personality.

This initial phase was to bear extraordinary fruit in one of the most important theatrical productions in the history of Russian theater, namely the play *Balaganchik* (*The Little Showbooth*, 1906), written by Blok as an expansion of a poem with that same title, with Vsevolod Meyerhold, who directed it, playing the central role of Pierrot (Jones 1993: 190–1). The title of the play had a double meaning, referring both to the temporary theater booths (*balagan*) erected during Shrovetide and offering trashy, popular entertainment, and also in general buffoonery or even scandal, something accentuated by the affectionate diminutive ending. The intention was to affront bourgeois theatergoers' taste, which it succeeded in doing. The playtext is layered, incorporating elements of the Russian Petrushka, or Punch and Judy show, in the clown who cries out that he is bleeding cranberry juice (a standard feature of these shows). Moreover, there was an important metatheatrical element in the interventions of the "Author," who was constantly objecting to the liberties the actors were taking with the text, the exit of Harlequin through a paper backdrop, and the way Meyerhold as Pierrot confronted the audience at the end. The production was programmatic in that it pointed the way to a non-realistic theater that would draw attention to theatrical conventions instead of seeking to make them unobtrusive.

Balaganchik was the first harbinger of a plethora of productions and plays based on CDA that was to last into the early 1920s. The ballet *Petrushka* was presented by Diaghilev's Ballets Russes in Paris in 1911, with music by Igor Stravinsky, choreography by Michel Fokine, and sets by Alexandre Benois. It retained the triangular plot, but with Petrushka as a Russian Pierrot, danced by Nijinsky, and a dark-skinned Moor replacing Harlequin. The fact that it was wordless hearkened back to the *théâtre forain* of the early eighteenth century when pantomime became part of the CDA tradition (Clayton 1993: 25). At the same time the change of name from Pierrot to Petrushka, as well as Alexandre Benois's decorations, placed the ballet firmly in time and space: the city is St Petersburg, the time is a nostalgically recalled past celebration of Shrovetide (as depicted in Benois's memoirs of childhood), and the characters are the puppets of the Petrushka puppet show who come to life. *Petrushka* thus Russified the Pierrotic tradition (as well as contributing hugely to the cultural myth of St Petersburg) and resulted in one of the great moments in the history of world culture.

Russian interest in the harlequinade grew prodigiously in the fifteen years or so after *Balaganchik*, taking on distinctive emphases and tendencies. Many Commedia plays were staged, some in prestigious theaters, such as Meyerhold's CDA styled productions of Molière's *Don Juan* (1910) and Lermontov's *Maskarad* (1917). Others were in clubs, improvised theaters and cabarets, such as Kuzmin's *Venetian Madcaps* (1914) or Evreinov's *A Merry Death* (1908). There was also a considerable effort to research the history and evolution of the phenomenon. This resulted in the appearance of a book on the history of CDA from the fifteenth to the eighteenth century by Konstantin Miklashevsky (1885–1943). In a seminal article of 1912 titled "Balagan" ("The Fairground Booth") Meyerhold rejected the actor who simply "reads" dialogue and called for a grotesque, anti-realistic theater, incorporating the *lazzi* of the CDA, acrobatics, and metatheater. Then, in 1914 Meyerhold founded a journal *Love for Three Oranges: Doctor Dapertutto's Journal*, which published papers on the history of CDA, reviews and analyses, as well as translations of plays (e.g., Ludwig Tieck's *Puss in Boots*). The title of the journal was, of course, in homage to Carlo Gozzi's play of that name.

The interest in CDA in Russia was part and parcel of the nostalgia for the eighteenth century among Russian aesthetes – both for eighteenth-century St Petersburg, a city in the culture of which Italians had played such a role, and for Venice, the Italian city with which the Northern capital has a special affinity, thanks to its architecture and its canals, hence the heightened interest in both Gozzi and Goldoni as the two great Venetian expositors of CDA. As Victor Zhirmunsky wrote in the journal: "Gozzi's tales transport the audience into marvelous, fantastic lands [...] where in life wonders happen so unlike life, where everything can happen that cannot happen on earth" (Zhirmunsky 1916: 86). Meyerhold did not produce any plays by Gozzi, although his choice of title – *Love for Three Oranges* (one of Gozzi's plays) – for the journal speaks volumes as to his predilection for this most theatrical of writers, whose plays offered room for improvisation. It was, in fact, a student of Stanislavsky, Evgeny Vakhtangov (1883–1922) who directed a celebrated production of Gozzi's *Princess Turandot* (1922). In the production, Gozzi's play was less important than the metaplay in which Venetian street actors are presenting the tale, the opening scene showing the distribution of roles. Vakhtangov died the year the production opened, but it remained in the repertory for many years and became a Moscow legend deeply engrained in the history of the theater that bears his name. Goldoni's tightly scripted plays did not allow the same possibilities of theatrical play as Gozzi's; nevertheless, at least four of his plays were staged in Russia during this period. The Venetian theme was also present in a play by Mikhail Kuzmin: *The Venetian Madcaps* (1912). The play is a love intrigue in the Goldoni/Marivaux style, but with a twist: the triangle is a homosexual one: the sexual ambiguity of the Commedia masks resonated with the gay component of *fin-de-siècle* aesthetic culture (Golub 1994: 55).

Another source of Commedia motifs for the Russians, especially Meyerhold, who was ethnically German, was the work of German Romantic ironists, specifically Ludwig Tieck and E. T. A. Hoffmann. Again, it is Zhirmunsky who points to a key moment in the history of CDA as an international phenomenon: "Carlo Gozzi owed his world-wide fame to the German Romantics" (1916: 85). Tieck was important for metatheater and the questioning of the theatrical sign between representation and presentation. Hoffmann's grotesque fantasies were an important strand in the cultural context of the first decades of the twentieth century in Russia and elsewhere. Moreover, Hoffmann's name was linked to that of seventeenth-century French artist

Jacques Callot (1592–1635), who spent some time in Florence and produced a series of prints of CDA street players called *Balli di Sfessania*. Hoffmann had titled his first cycle of stories "Fantasias in Callot's style," and reproduced some of Callot's prints as illustrations. These offered Meyerhold an important ingredient for his version of the CDA, namely the grotesque.

Callot's drawings of the twisted gesticulating masks evidently inspired the biomechanical exercises Meyerhold invented for his actors, which sought to produce a grotesque deformation of the human figure rather than the statuesque stance of the actor as a declaimer of text. The second element that Meyerhold found in Hoffmann was the figure of Doctor Dapertutto. Dapertutto was a diabolical character in Hoffmann's story "Adventures of New Year's Eve." In 1908 Meyerhold had begun to work as a director for the Imperial Theaters. Since technically he was not allowed to work elsewhere, he chose the name of the sinister Doctor Dapertutto as his pseudonym for his activities in the House of Interludes (Dom Intermedy), an experimental studio-theater. The name was no doubt an ironic comment on his role as director: in his production of *Columbine's Scarf* (1911), an adaptation of a pantomime by Arthur Schnitzler, Meyerhold had played the role of the sinister Kapellmeister (music conductor) manipulating events onstage. The cult of Hoffmann on the stage reached its culmination in Russia in Tairov's famous production of *The Princess Brambilla* (1920), a stage adaptation of Hoffmann's story of that name.

One of the most striking figures associated with CDA in Russia was Nikolay Yevreinov (1879–1953), actor, director, playwright and even composer of incidental music. Yevreinov wholeheartedly embraced CDA. Spencer Golub writes: "He saw in Commedia's reliance upon masks, conventions and *plastique*, a dramatization of the human condition – man pushing up against his finiteness, his mortality and the limitations he imposes on himself" (Golub 1984: 11). Yevreinov was implicated in numerous theatrical undertakings, including being artistic director at the Crooked Mirror theater, a cabaret that put on farcical playlets and parodies. He was also instrumental in the creation of the Ancient Theater, which did reconstructions of works from past theatrical periods – only a medieval cycle and a Spanish cycle came to fruition, although harlequinades were also planned (Golub 1984: 109). Evreinov wrote two short one-act harlequinades: *A Merry Death* (1908) and *Today's Columbine* (Clayton 1993: 187–8). The former is based on the traditional love triangle. Harlequin is on his deathbed, and is due to die at midnight. He affirms his desire to enjoy life to the end. Columbine is cheating on with Harlequin. The play ends with a love scene between them, but Death enters and conceals the couple. The play is inventive and designed to critique the fashionable morbidity of Maeterlinck (Clayton 1993: 150–6). *Today's Columbine* was a traditional harlequinade pantomime except for the ending, when Pierrot, shocked that Columbine should deceive him with an African-American, kills himself with a gunshot.

In his many writings Yevreinov developed the idea of the theatricality of life and the innate theatrical instinct: man realizes himself in theatrical play. It was this philosophy that lay at the heart of his most ambitious endeavor, the play *The Chief Thing* (1919). In this complex, Pirandello-like text the characters are divided into actors who play multiple roles in order to do good to naive characters who do not change and are the denizens of a boarding-house. The latter serve, as it were, as an unwitting audience in the different deceptions. CDA metatheater has thus become integrated into the plot. The central character is one Paraclete, who is equated to the Holy Ghost and has the actors perform deeds on the naive to comfort them. The fourth act is a harlequinade in which the boarding-house has turned into a Shrovetide *balagan* and Paraclete is Harlequin. The play is the most ambitious text to emerge from the Russian harlequinade, and reflects Yevreinov's inversion of Harlequin as a Christ-like savior, not a sinister figure, as in Blok's *Balaganchik*. Unfortunately, its complexity and Evreinov's crackpot theory about the application of theater to life as a healing force make it little more than a curiosity today (Clayton 1993: 175–81).

What astonishes, looking back at the evolution of Russian theater at the beginning of the twentieth century, is the speed with which it evolved. Only eight years after he had played Treplev in the historic Moscow Art Theater production of Anton Chekhov's *Seagull*, directed by Stanislavsky, Meyerhold directed and played Pierrot in Blok's *Balaganchik*, which was the antithesis of Stanislavsky's method and conception of the theatrical spectacle. Twelve years later, in the middle of the civil war that followed the seizure of power by the Bolsheviks, a young man serving in the Red Army was studying how to stage plays, many of them harlequinades by Goldoni, Gozzi, and Benavente, and writing his own harlequinades (Clayton 1993: 209). His name – Sergey Eisenstein – was to become world-famous with the release of his film *Battleship Potemkin* in 1926 – only twenty years after *The Seagull*. Eisenstein's films are to be understood as the continuation of Meyerhold's experiments with CDA. He was a student of Meyerhold, and his famous article "Montage of Attractions" was actually written about theater, not film, and had to do with the structuring of the work. He did, however, apply in film principles developed in studying theater. The first is montage: the editing together ("mounting") of a series of discrete events (as in *Balaganchik*) or theatrical signs, rather than telling a narrative (Clayton 1993: 211–12). The second is what he called, in a Franco-Russian coinage, *typage* – the choice of characteristic faces to provide instant meaning to the viewer, the way CDA masks do (Eisenstein 1949: 9 fn.). The third is the grotesque deformation of the human body. Most important of all is perhaps the disruption of the single perspective of realism, so that we can speak of Eisenstein's films as *balagans* (Clayton 1993: 218–224). Interestingly, Eisenstein even looked to CDA for a method to structure the rhythm of his films. In his notes on *Potemkin* he writes:

> In the foreground is a common compositional variant: an even number of persons is replaced by an uneven number. Two replaced by three. This "golden rule" in shifting the mise en scène is supported by a tradition that can be traced back [...] to the practice of the *Commedia dell'Arte*.
> (Eisenstein 1949: 117)

Thus the CDA continued in post-revolutionary Russia, but underwent a significant change: the masks of the Dottore, Pantalone, Capitano, became the "types" of the factory owner, the government stooge, and the strike breaker in *Strike* and *Potemkin*. The suffering workers were the equivalent of the *inamorati*, the "straight" characters of tradition. This was also true in the plays of Vladimir Mayakovsky – *Mystery-*

Bouffe, *The Bedbug*, and *The Bath-house*: structured like CDA, with mask-characters, but with a new socio-political content.

Nowhere did CDA have a stronger impact than in Russia: works of previous playwrights were translated and staged; the forms, images, and characters were studied in all their evolution. In Russia, as elsewhere, CDA was far from being a spontaneous popular phenomenon, the intellectual elite of St Petersburg having adopted it as a "top down" phenomenon to effect a transition in Russian theatrical practice. The devices and motifs of Italian improvisational theater played a central role in overcoming theatrical realism and naturalism and formed a basis for a new and expressive theatricality, metatheater, and play within the play. Coalescence quickly occurred with the indigenous elements – Petrushka, and the *balagan* or theater booth of the Shrovetide amusements. On the fringe there were other themes and related phenomena, such as circus with its acrobats and clowns, stressing the physicality of Commedia. Before the revolution the aesthetic had been directed at the overthrow of bourgeois values and the tradition of realistic theater. Bisexuality and hints of "illicit" or interracial sex added spice to productions. After the revolution CDA was embraced and transformed by the avant-garde – Meyerhold, Eisenstein and Mayakovsky – to fit the new circumstances. Later still the entire aesthetic in which CDA flourished was labeled "decadent" by the Soviets and suppressed, although some elements lasted a considerable time, an example being Vakhtangov's production of *Turandot*, which ran for many years after his death in the theater that bears his name. It is fair to say, however, that in Russia, CDA contributed to one of the most brilliant and innovative periods in the history of world theater.

References

Clayton, J. Douglas. *Pierrot in Petrograd: Commedia dell'arte/Balagan in Twentieth-Century Russian Theatre and Drama*. Montreal and Kingston, Canada; London; Buffalo, US: McGill-Queen's University Press, 1993. Print.

Eisenstein, Sergey M. "Montage of Attractions," *The Film Sense*. New York: Harcourt Brace, 1948. 230–5. Print.

——*Film Form*. Ed. and trans. Jay Leyda. New York; London: Harcourt, Brace Jovanovich, 1949. Print.

Golub, Spencer. *Evreinov: The Theatre of Paradox and Transformation*. Ann Arbor, Michigan, US: UMI Research Press, 1984. Print.

——*The Recurrence of Fate: Theatre and Memory in Twentieth-Century Russia*. Iowa City, US: University of Iowa Press, 1994. Print.

Green, Martin, and John Swan. *The Triumph of Pierrot: Commedia dell'Arte and Modern Imagination*. University Park, PA, US: Penn State University Press, 2001. Print.

Jones, W. Gareth. "*Commedia dell'Arte*: Blok and Meyerhold." *Studies in the Commedia dell'Arte*. Ed. David J. George and Christopher J. Gossip. Cardiff, UK: University of Wales Press, 1993. 185–97. Print.

Meyerhold, Vsevolod, "The Fairground Booth," in *Meyerhold on Theatre*, trans. and ed. Edward Braun, New York: Hill and Wang, 1969. 119–43. Print.

Soboleva, Olga Yu. *The Silver Mask: Harlequinade in the Symbolist Poetry of Blok and Belyi*. Oxford, UK: Peter Lang, 2008. Print.

Zhirmunsky, Viktor. "Komediya chistoy radosti." *Lyubov k tryom apelsinam: Zhurnal doktora Dapertutto* 1916, 1. 85–91.

39

GIORGIO STREHLER'S *ARTE*

A Commedia master directs Shakespeare

Mace Perlman

> Full fathom five, thy father lies;
> Of his bones are coral made.
> Those are pearls that were his eyes.
> Nothing of him that doth fade
> But doth suffer a sea-change
> Into something rich and strange
> (*The Tempest*, I. ii. 397–402)

In early December, 2005, a cargo ship carrying masks, costumes and scenery of the Piccolo Teatro di Milano's production of *Arlecchino, Servant of Two Masters* was caught in a winter storm off the coast of Faial Island, one of the Central Group of the Azores. Local sailors struggled for weeks to rescue the ship; but another, more damaging storm was to strike before year's end, making any rescue impossible. Buffeted night and day, the ship rolled shoreward, and released its precious cargo to the waves.

From the shore, a local group of amateur actors watched as bits and pieces of the show emerged from the ocean – here a mask, there a corset, now a shoe… A trunk containing make-up and more masks, intact, washed ashore; and the actors gathered up their new-found treasure and began to play along the sands… They found the Piccolo Teatro's address inside the trunk and wrote to the company to tell them of their miraculous discovery. They planned a production in the masks; and received the former owners' blessings from Milan to make full use of the gifts of the shipwreck…

Eight years had passed since the death of *Arlecchino*'s director, Giorgio Strehler, in December, 1997; and following its US tour, the show seemed to follow a will of its own, making an unplanned stop in Portugal – with or without the consent of its actors and technical crew. At the time of this writing, the show has toured the globe for some sixty-six years, sixteen of them without Strehler's physical presence. Yet Strehler's presence, his artistic and spiritual presence, is embedded in the very fabric of the show and its actors; and just as surely, the show insinuated itself over the course of a lifetime into the very fibers of Strehler's being.

In the fifty years of Giorgio's Strehler's theatre-making career at the Piccolo Teatro di Milano, the Commedia dell'Arte was ever-present; and Strehler's productions of Carlo Goldoni's play provided an ongoing conduit for that relationship. In transforming *The Servant of Two Masters* into *Arlecchino*, changing the servant's name from Truffaldino to the more familiar – and indeed iconic – Arlecchino, Strehler set out to "rediscover" the Italian tradition of Commedia dell'Arte; but in truth, he, his actors, and Marise Flach, his Decroux-trained movement coach, were re-inventing it as they went. In that act of re-invention, Strehler was assembling a palette of theatrical tools that would reach far beyond the mask-characters of Goldoni. These tools constitute a kind of universal poetry of the theatre; and they represent the true gifts of the Commedia dell'Arte in Strehler's theatrical career with the Piccolo Teatro.

While the Strehler I knew in the late 1980's often liked to play down any claim to Goldoni's text, or the *Arlecchino* he and his actors had created, as "great art" (he often lamented the fact that this was the play and the production for which he would likely most be remembered), he also understood that the play was somehow a fundamental touchstone to his entire life in the theatre. Rediscovering the necessity for the half-face leather mask and how to use it; learning to fulfill the special demands it made upon the actor physically, vocally, and rhythmically; learning to play to audiences around the world, who responded to the actors' words as music, cadences of the characters' souls: all these taught Strehler and his actors, over the course of decades, certain skills fundamental to the art of playing and storytelling-in-character.

This practical knowledge of theatre-making, like the masks and costumes of the Portuguese shipwreck, would wash up on the shores of other Strehler productions, and particularly in his 1977 production of Shakespeare's *The Tempest*, i.e. *La tempesta*. Just as surely, the lessons learned in *La tempesta* would continue to nourish *Arlecchino*, a show that has grown over the decades as a living organism. If one may consider the master-servant relationship as foundational to the making of Commedia, one may observe in *La tempesta* an exploration of the varieties of servant and servitude through tools native to the players of Commedia. These tools include: (1) rhythmic gesture and repeated gesture to enhance meaning; (2) verbal improvisation around the text in which cadence and the sounds and connotations of extra-textual language amplify meaning; (3) stage props (trunks, masks, bottles) conceived and deployed in a manner emblematic of characters and character relationships; and (4) the body's expression of emotional states, status, and occupation in life with a subtlety and specificity only made possible by the lessons of masked acting.

Stephano and Trinculo are the professional servants of *La tempesta*; and it seems natural to identify them with the first and second zanni of the Commedia tradition. Even in his 1947 production, Strehler sensed that Stephano, the "drunken butler," might be a northern first zanni, a close relative to Goldoni's Brighella. In the play's only moment of Italian speech, when dragged before Prospero and publicly exposed, Stephano offers Caliban the empty consolation, "*Coragio*, bully-monster, *coragio*." (V. i. 257–8) Impressed by the single "g" in the text reminiscent of a Veneto regional dialect, Strehler heard the voice of Brighella's native land. (In fact, in the first folio text, we find the variant "*Coragio* Bully-Monster *Corasio*," which gives an even more Veneto-sounding touch to the end of the line, confirming Strehler's intuition.) As for Trinculo, his "O Stephano, two Neapolitans 'scaped!" (upon their first meeting in Act II, scene ii, 112–13) confirms him as a Neapolitan, which together with his designation as a jester, made Pulcinella a natural choice. The fact that he has been to England, showing off wonders of nature to holiday fools for payment in silver serves to confirm Strehler's notion of Trinculo as a traveling player and mountebank-barker typical of the Commedia, a Neapolitan who had toured as far abroad as England.

Caliban, on the other hand, son of Sycorax, rebels against his servitude; and the porter in Goldoni's play, also native-born and proud of his parentage, proclaims, "I live as a porter, to my misfortune; but I am son to a man of manners … My father… skinned lambs in the city." (Goldoni 1954: vol. 2, 25, author's translation) Dismissed by Florindo as mere madness, the porter's plea for respect is heard by Goldoni, and heard by Strehler, who has always insisted on the dignity of the role. It also receives emphasis through the comic *lazzo* which follows, an insistent and repeated demand for payment, to which Florindo complies twice and no more, giving him a kick in the rear as a final reply. As a coda to the sequence, Florindo comments in an aside, "What airs they put on! He was positively waiting for me to mistreat him." (Goldoni 1954: vol. 2, 25, author's translation)

Strehler's genius was to invent a concrete, scenic solution to express the specific nature of each of these servants, and the nature of their relationship to the master. The oversized log which Caliban drags on his back as fuel for Prospero's cell – indeed, as a necessity to his master's very life – recalls the ever-present trunk – Florindo's life, Beatrice's life – on the porter's back. Even when Arlecchino replaces him under that trunk, the porter's body is unable to adjust: time is required for him to slowly raise himself up and visually discover, while he speaks, that his burden is no longer there. In Goldoni's porter, a wage slave whose source of income has deformed his body, we cannot help but be reminded of Caliban's deformity as well. Strehler understood from the Commedia dell'Arte that we are what we do in life; that our social status is written into our spines; and that nobility of spirit often resides in a character whom the master dismisses as deformed by nature or somehow naturally lacking in humanity or intelligence.

Caliban is, of course, neither lacking in humanity nor deformed by nature. He is a servant against his will, enslaved by the outraged Prospero after a failed attempt to "educate" him. Yet we may also think of him as the deposed Prince of the island, its rightful heir. His sensitivity to music – the music of nature – and his poetic expression of that experience contrast with the crass materialism of Stephano and Trinculo, the two zannis washed up from Naples, from the world of so-called "civilization."

Although Strehler understood these two to be mask-characters, he chose to give them simple fabric blindfolds with cut-out eyes, creating masks so featureless that, in relation to the soulful, half-face leather masks of *Arlecchino*, these masks seem hardly to exist. They contain no character, and are more or less interchangeable. They are empty screens, which on the one hand allow the actors playing Stephano and Trinculo to invent their roles, to write their characters as they play; while also leaving them free to play a type since their costumes clearly identify them as a northern first zanni, in olive livery, and a Neapolitan Pulcinella, all in white. The blankness of their masks is both childlike, evoking the spontaneous creation of that first and simplest of masks, a mere covering of the face; and also somehow impossibly weary, as if after the long exercise of their profession, these performers could no longer be bothered to don a more soulful expression of character.

Caliban, on the other hand, is a soulful artist of instinct. The animal skin on his back presents a mask indeed so soulful that Trinculo confuses it for Caliban's true identity; and he bears a staff whose elements have been gathered from the island. It both reminds us of Prospero's staff – though the master's is more austere – and it speaks of Caliban's animism, and his maternal heritage. His ankle-bracelet of shells produces music with his every step; and everything he wears, including the mask of sand he is about to fashion, is created to solve a need.

In the contrast between Caliban's entrance into Act II, scene ii and Trinculo's, and in the contrast between their responses to the storm, we see two kinds of mask-theatre, two very different forms of Commedia dell'Arte. Caliban, the slave, shows us the birth of the zanni, an atavistic, animistic character; and Trinculo is the latest development of this role and what it has become at the court of Naples. Not just Alonso's jester, Trinculo comes perhaps from a long line of jesters. His gestures are those of an Italian stage-performer, and despite their artfulness, they are over-emphatic and immediately recognizable from centuries of Italian theatre. Caliban's gestures are invented before us, and give an impression of simplicity, of childlike innocence.

Tracing a circle in the sand – actually, in the rice dust – so recently occupied by Prospero, Caliban wields his staff in defiance of Prospero's, his magic in defiance of Prospero's magic, his theatre-making style in defiance of the theatrical art of "the master." Each time he hears the storm, he shakes his islander's staff to ward off what he perceives to be a threat from Prospero. Though believing himself overheard by Prospero's spirits, he cannot help but curse. Upon voicing that need ("*ma io debbo maledire*" "And yet I needs must curse" (Shakespeare, Lombardo and Strehler 2007 DVD; *The Tempest*, II, ii, 4), Caliban crouches down, head in the sand, and rubs the very stuff of the island into the contours of his face, widening his already expressive eyes with circles of sand, as if he had incorporated Prospero's magic circle into this newly fashioned form of battle-armor. His is a mask created in self-protection from the hardship and pains he is suffering under Prospero's reign; and with it, he reclaims the island as his own.

Trinculo, on the other hand, fairly bounces on stage from the ocean. Unlike Caliban, who has incorporated the island itself into his body to create his mask, and whose rage at Prospero and terror of his master's punishment are deeply felt, Trinculo-Pulcinella wears his mask lightly and his fear of the storm is capable of vanishing in the wink of an eye, giving way to a tight-rope-walking lazzo. He is fearful of the new storm as he was fearful of the last storm at sea – which he shakes off his pant-leg as he crawls onto the platform. The brisk rhythm of his repeated gesture and its light delivery allow us distance from his fear; and when he loses his balance, almost falling, his search for a shelter suddenly transforms into a game of tightrope-walking, upon which he laughs, surprised by his own skill, his *arte*. No sooner has he reached the end of the platform – and with it, the end of his make-believe tightrope – than a new concern stops him dead in his tracks: if the thunder should return, where can he hide? As if speaking on cue, the thunder bellows its reply. Trinculo-Pulcinella, startled, calls out the name of the Madonna (*"Maronna mia!"*) in Neapolitan; but he does so without addressing anyone or anything in particular, with the automatic tone of one for whom the name of the deity has lost all meaning.

Instead, he addresses the storm-cloud directly, as if speaking to an unruly member of the audience, up in the rafters. Shakespeare's "Yond same black cloud, yond huge one... yond same cloud cannot choose but fall by pailfuls" (II. ii. 20–4) becomes "That cursed cloud – no I'm not talking to you, you've got nothing to do with it – move over a little, will you, I'm talking to the other one, the big one, yeah, yeah, that's right, the pregnant one there... if she bursts open, she'll send down pailfuls!" (Shakespeare, Lombardo and Strehler 2007 DVD, author's translation) Both Caliban and Trinculo experience other subjectivities, other voices in their island surroundings; but only Caliban speaks their language. Trinculo's lazzo of addressing the storm-clouds is particularly comic because the language and tone he adopts are those he would use to speak to two Neapolitan matrons: he reads the landscape with the eyes of an urban jester.

He may be unable to converse with the threatening cloud, but the thought of her "pailfuls" brings Trinculo to sit for a moment on Caliban, whom he still has not discovered. Running in horror from the strange sensation of "something" under him, Trinculo turns and calls out, *"Scorfano!"* In an inspired moment of verbal invention, the actor offers us a classic image from Neapolitan life: *scorfano* is a kind of bottom-dwelling scorpion fish, or rockfish, which also refers to a very ugly person. This one word, an improvised epithet for Caliban, will usher in the whole next part of the scene; and indeed, all ensuing relations between Caliban and the Neapolitan court zannis.

Under Strehler's direction, such a bold intrusion into Shakespeare's own text is never undertaken lightly. In the term *scorfano*, we find a confusion between a piece of the mineral landscape, a bottom-dwelling fish, and a frighteningly ugly human being. The sound of it, too, contains the 'sk' sound which in Italian so often connotes unpleasantness, added to the word *orfano*, or orphan. Caliban will spend the rest of the play at the feet of the other two zannis, drinking from Stephano's bottle. Following his first unsuccessful "education" at the hands of Prospero, he will now undergo a second one even more disastrous than the first. The epithet of *scorfano* may deliver us the idea of "orphan" only subconsciously as a sound-image, but the image is fitting nonetheless, an example of meaning enhanced not logically but through sound, in a manner typical of the Commedia dell'Arte.

Stephano's first entrance, through the waves of silk, is preceded by his bottle. Using the prop to lift himself up to the platform, we might say that the bottle indeed steps on stage before Stephano does. Right from Stephano's first appearance in the play, Strehler has placed the bottle foremost in the scene: when Stephano first approaches the strange, two-headed creature, it is to heal his fever with a drink from the bottle. Later, Trinculo steals the bottle for a taste; and when Stephano swings the bottle by his side, Caliban will be mesmerized by the motion.

Once again, Strehler concretizes the nature of relationship, and the nature of servitude and mastery in a stage prop, which takes on a life of its own. Like the porter's trunk and Caliban's log – and, of course, Arlecchino's slapstick – the bottle is practically a part of Stephano's body. Always between him and Caliban, it is the agent by which Stefano can maintain the illusion of his mastery over Caliban for so long. To Stephano and Trinculo, it is a pleasurable catalyst for stage-business and play; while to Caliban, it contains "celestial liquor." (II. ii. 117) Stefano exhorts Trinculo to "swear by this bottle" and, more than once, to "kiss the book" (II. ii. 130, 142), riffing on the idea of furnishing it later with "new contents." The bottle is thus conflated with a book, indeed a holy book.

Strehler highlights these meanings from Shakespeare's text by having Stephano intone the words "If thou bee'st Trinculo, come forth!" (II. ii. 103) as *Se Trinculo sei, alzati e cammina!* ("If thou art Trinculo, stand up and walk!"), a clear reference to Jesus raising Lazarus from the dead. And when Caliban swings his head back-and-forth in synchrony with the bottle at Stephano's side, we are not only witnessing his attempts to "read" the bottle's contents, as if it were a book displaying its pages of text, we are also watching the movement of a pot of incense – a censer, as it swings forward and back in a motion both unmistakably familiar and highly evocative to anyone raised in a Catholic country.

This proliferation of meanings, which is the genius of Shakespeare's multi-layered text, is made possible by the deployment of all the theatre's tools, so many of which Strehler discovered over the years through the trials and errors – and most of all the triumphs – of *Arlecchino*. When Stephano intones in priest-like fashion, the sound itself generates meaning for the audience, independently of the words – a gift from *Arlecchino*. When Caliban swings his head to follow the bottle, he is the beneficiary, through Strehler as intermediary, of Marcello Moretti's painful and hard-won discoveries about how to see through a mask, i.e. that the entire head must follow a character's line of sight. At first incredibly awkward – Moretti felt paralyzed on stage by his lack of peripheral vision when wearing the Arlecchino mask – this amplification of eye-movement becomes an incredibly expressive tool, visible from the back row of the theatre. It is a tool for following the actor-in-character's consciousness, whether that consciousness is fixed on a fly, whose every movement we follow, along with Arlecchino; or whether that consciousness is fixed on a bottle, which Caliban believes to be heaven-sent, and along with Stephano, dropped from the moon.

The mask, in the hands of a sensitive actor and director, is thus a tool for poetry – for the revelation of a character's human condition – no less than the bottle, no less than the trunk. These stage-objects are the nexus in which human lives, masters' lives and servants' lives, are joined. The highest example of this poetic deployment of a simple, theatrical tool is in Strehler's use of a wire-and-harness to give his Ariel flight. Long were the hours for Giulia Lazzarini, the extraordinary interpreter of the role; and many were the false starts and failed attempts. Little by little, however, a stage language grew out of the actress', and her director's, struggle, a language which made possible a whole new range of physical expression for emotional states, through a spine, now lifted, now collapsed. Gravity has new meaning when the illusion of weightlessness is possible; and Ariel's moments of slumped disappointment are as remarkable as her flights of pure joy. Both are sublime expressions of human states, and are also other-worldly and uniquely theatrical, giving new meaning to the moment when he/she tells Prospero that she would be moved to pity the conspirators, "were I human." (V. i. 119)

When Ariel is at long last set free, she must discover what it is to live as Ariel without the constraint of the wire, that is to say, without both the soaring power of Prospero's art and the obligation it imposes upon her to return, again and again, to execute his wishes. In the moment before Prospero releases Ariel from the harness, he holds her to his chest and she rests there, her head half-abandoned upon his shoulder, with a kind of tender attachment, expressing all the ambiguity of their relationship. It is an image reminiscent of Abraham upon the point of sacrificing Isaac. As he releases her, she takes in an enormous breath: her last as his servant; or her first taste of freedom? Exploring the feel of the air with her upper body and the new sensations in her legs, she slips under his outstretched arm, barely sensing a caress; then moves, bit by bit to the downstage lip of the platform, and turning, eases herself over its edge, waving to him as she goes; but the weight of her body takes her too quickly for her to complete the gesture – her farewell is cut short by the unexpected speed of her passage from this life into another – and now she has "passed" from Prospero's world, and is reborn among us, the audience, running up the aisle in her first earth-bound flight among the mortals.

Prospero's release of Ariel's harness to the heavens produces a disturbing metallic clang, not unlike the descent of a guillotine. Upon breaking his staff following the sprite's departure, Prospero sets in motion a series of collapses in the structure of Strehler's set – a staged destruction of the theatre. Having freed Ariel and pardoned his brother, an artless Prospero now begs our prayer and applause to release him from confinement. The master, having relinquished all, is now our servant; and real as the collapse was only a moment ago, the theatre now recomposes itself in response to our applause.

Arlecchino's final words to the audience, "*Mi, non sarò più servitor de do patroni, ma sarò servitor de chi me sente*" ("I'll no longer be the servant of two masters, but the servant of whoever hears me") (Goldoni 1954: vol. 2, 1203, author's translation) hold out the promise that as long as there is an audience to listen, he will continue to serve. Just as Prospero's intention is, after all, to please, and the audience's applause and goodwill can magically recompose the theatre; so, too, Arlecchino's final words ask only for a willing and compassionate ear, to enable him to continue in his own enterprise of serving. Ultimately, all theatre is an act of service – it is created for the pleasure of an audience.

In the many editions of his ever-evolving *Arlecchino* and in his mature revisitation of *La tempesta* (Strehler 2002), Giorgio Strehler demonstrated a lifelong commitment simply to keep getting better and better at making theatre: "*fare meglio il teatro,*" as he often liked to tell us, by always improving one's technical skills, always with a little more life-experience, a little more humanity. This is his living legacy, an artisan's approach to the craft of theatre-making which links his work to centuries of Commedia dell'Arte – to the *arte* of yesterday's *comici* – and challenges us in today's theatre to carry this commitment forward into the theatre of tomorrow.

References

Goldoni, Carlo (1954, 3rd ed.) *Tutte le opere* a cura di (edited by) Giuseppe Ortolani. Verona, Italy: Arnoldo Mondadori Editore.

Shakespeare, William (1974) *The Riverside Shakespeare* (edited by) G. Blakemore Evans *et al.* Boston, US: Houghton Mifflin Co.

Shakespeare, William, Agostino Lombardo, and Giorgio Strehler (2007) *La tempesta tradotta e messa in scena 1977–78: Un carteggio ritrovato fra Strehler e Lombardo e due traduzioni realizzate da Lombardo per il Piccolo Teatro di Milano* a cura di Rosy Colombo. (*La Tempesta* translated and staged 1977–8: A rediscovered correspondence between Strehler and Lombardo and two translations by Lombardo for the Piccolo Teatro di Milano, as recorded for RAI television by Carlo Battistoni in 1981, edited by Rosy Colombo) Rome: Donzelli Editore.

——(2007 DVD) *La tempesta tradotta e messa in scena: il DVD dello spettacolo realizzato da Giorgio Strehler per il Piccolo Teatro di Milano nella ripresa televisiva della Rai.* (*La Tempesta* translated and staged: live performance DVD of Giorgio Strehler's production for Piccolo Teatro di Milano, as televised by RAI) Rome: Donzelli Editore.

Strehler, Giorgio (2002) "Notes on *The Tempest*" translated by Thomas Simpson *Performing Arts Journal*, vol. 24, no. 3 (PAJ 72), 1–17.

40

GIOVANNI POLI

The missing link

Giulia Filacanapa

Translated by Eileen Cottis

Peter Brook, in his book *The Empty Space*, focuses on the training of the contemporary actor in what he calls "The Deadly Theatre"; more specifically, for the great English master, "after he reaches a certain position the actor does no more homework" (Brook 1996: 32). Therefore, he continues, "building a career and artistic development do not necessarily go hand in hand" (Brook 1996: 32). The reason for this is simple because often actors who succeed in building a real career in the theatre no longer have time to undertake personal artistic research; to develop in their practice; actors need to go further and deeper, to explore "what really comes hard. But no one has time for this kind of problem" (Brook 1996: 32), and the problem remains precisely there, that is, in the time that is available for in-depth artistic research.

The Venetian Giovanni Poli (b. Crosara di Marostica, 1917 – d. Venice, 1979) had identified this problem and as a teacher/director he decided to pursue his theatrical research, particularly into Commedia dell'Arte, outside the professional system in the amateur theatre. That is why he has long remained unknown to the general public. But after examining the archives accumulated during the course of his career, we can affirm that he was at the origin of the rediscovery, or even the reinvention, of the methods of the Commedia dell'Arte, the traditional theatre of the West which declined after Goldoni's reforms in the eighteenth century. In its decline this tradition was lost within the history of Italian and European theatre, leaving us orphans in the search for the complex identity of this form of theatre. Some of the many groups that are working on Commedia in Europe today are essentially undertaking a work of quotation and homage, whereas others are devoting themselves to real creative research in which tradition joins experiment. Giovanni Poli, who can be considered as one of the voices in the rediscovery of the acting tradition of the Commedia dell'Arte and its use in contemporary theatre practice, is a typical example of someone using the legacy of the past inside new forms (as, for instance, Copeau was in France). In this context tradition becomes "the fuel for contemporary research" (Nosari 2008: 199), which is one of the principles on which I base my research. In an interview in 1966, Poli said:

> The true theatre is the old one. Each moment of theatrical renewal has never been anything but a return to its sources. Our aim is to create a theatrical movement which is inspired by the old one.... To take the essential elements and adapt them to the demands of the modern stage. It is a matter of inspiration... not of imitation.
>
> (Poli 1966)

For Poli the challenge is not the imitation of a lost tradition but rather the invention of a new tradition, which we can call by the neologism 'Neo-Commedia dell'Arte'.

Neo-Commedia dell'Arte: an invented tradition

Poli, who dedicated his whole life to the study of the history of the Commedia dell'Arte, based on original documents and the limited number of books available at the time, had a pretty clear vision of this phenomenon; a conception largely shared by historians of today, but which for the time was totally revolutionary. Indeed he says, in a typed document (5 sheets), unpublished and found in the Poli archives, dated after 1962:

> The Commedia dell'Arte is something lost in time. There exists no literary document, only brief outlines ('canevas'), a few documents of figurative art. Nothing else. But it is something that all the great masters of the twentieth century stage have put forward as the model of a theatre that has freed itself from the artistic and scenic limits of nineteenth century naturalism.
>
> (Poli post 1962)

Thus, we must face the fact that the Commedia dell'Arte no longer exists today. Time, as Poli tells us, has erased its traces; it has been lost in the history of stagecraft. The documents we have in our possession, the traces that the actors of the sixteenth century have left us are not enough to recreate this theatrical practice.

Researchers around the world, especially the Italians, have delved into this Western theatrical tradition, and have revealed certain basic structural elements essential for understanding its operation; such as the repertoire of plays, the structure of the companies, and the life and fortunes of certain actors. But we can never grasp their stagecraft, nor the "secret" of their acting in all its complexity. So the theatrical practice that we inaccurately call "Commedia dell'Arte" today is no more than an "invented tradition" (Hobsbawm and Ranger 2006): a tradition reconstructed over a short period, and which can be dated fairly precisely. I cannot expand further here upon the precise "duration" of this phenomenon, since it is still going on; however, I would say that in Italy its origins lie just after the Second World War. The Neo-Commedia dell'Arte arose after a time of significant social and political upheaval, and a profound artistic and cultural transformation which led in the theatre community to the rise of the director (which happened very late in Italy) and the abandonment of the nineteenth century tradition of the great actor.

As an "invented tradition", in Eric Hobsbawm's phrase, it seeks to establish continuity with a historic past, but it is obvious that this continuity is largely fictitious. Indeed it is important to note that the idea of the existence of a "Commedia dell'Arte as a well-defined theatrical tradition, with a style that has been able to be learned or renewed" (Taviani 2005: 119), is totally false, and that the mythical image that has come down to us (in France, but also in Italy) through the engravings of Callot, the pictures of Gillot or Watteau or later Théophile Gautier's novel 'Le Capitaine Fracasse', has very little or nothing to do with the real theatre practice of Italian companies of the seventeenth and eighteenth centuries.

Giovanni Poli himself was well aware that he was in a process of reinvention, to the point that he situates his flagship show outside historical Commedia, saying:

> The Comedia degli Zanni, rather than being a real Commedia dell'Arte (as there is no real improvisation), is constructed according to a particular way of understanding the sixteenth century 'theatre of masks', which is relived and reinvented according to the demands of the renewal of the modern stage.
>
> (Poli 1960:15)

It is a way of understanding a lost tradition, a personal interpretation rather than a reconstitution, and one which is still fed by this mythical fantasy, in order to confront the contemporary avant-garde theatre.

Italian theatre after the Second World War: a fertile triangle

This form of theatre has returned to the stages of the twentieth century, influenced by the avant-garde and enriched with new meanings. Italy, Padua, Venice and Milan were the cities where the revival of Commedia dell'Arte took place. Strehler's production of *Harlequin, Servant of Two Masters* springs to mind, but this was not all, since it was in Padua that Gianfranco De Bosio (b. Verona, 1924) established the University Theatre (active from 1946 to 1953) with the aim of producing shows based on the rediscovery of the figure Ruzante, linked to the tradition of Commedia dell'Arte actors, which he introduced to the public at large by presenting them in their original language. He was also the one who introduced Amleto Sartori, who discovered and redeveloped the iconography of leather masks, to Jacques Lecoq, who invented an original way of teaching theatre based on French mime; later he arranged for these two artists to meet Giorgio Strehler. Through this meeting the second production of *Arlecchino Servitore di due Padroni* came about in 1952, in which, for the first time, the famous leather masks designed by Sartori were used.

In Venice in the same period, Giovanni Poli founded the University Theatre of Ca' Foscari in 1949 and thence travelled to all the stages of Europe with his best-known show *La Commedia degli Zanni*. The Ca' Foscari Theatre, "the first Italian example of a stable and permanent student theatre" (Poli 1959: 9), was started with the stated aim of carrying out show-based research to free the participants from "traditional patterns of the naturalist theatre of the 19th century" (Poli 1959: 9), and to develop forms which better use the means available to theatre. Therefore, after the experience of the University Theatre, Poli turned professional when he took over the direction of the Palazzo Durini in Milan in1962. However he was disappointed by the market system of the professional theatre, and returned to Venice, where he set up his own theatre: the Theatre a l'Avogaria. His was a lifetime entirely devoted to the theatre and in particular to the Commedia, but always in the background, away from the spotlight and especially from the Italian stage. Indeed he acquired his reputation more in France and America than in Italy, where he never achieved the recognition afforded to other Commedia theatre greats, such as Giorgio Strehler and Dario Fo. His major interest was in teaching theatre rather than producing it, although he staged dozens of plays.

The Zanni at the centre: the implementation of a poetics of theatre

Poli became known, and established his Neo- Commedia dell'Arte on the international stage, with his collage show *La Commedia degli Zanni*. The show, first put on at the Festival of University Theatres at Thessaloniki in 1958, was to have a very long life and much success thanks, notably, to the prize he won for the best director in 1960 at the Théâtre des Nations in Paris, a festival dedicated above all to exploring various international traditions. In an article in the Parisian press, a critic gives us some idea of the show's success during the International Festival:

> The season at the Théâtre des Nations closed with one of the finest performances that I have ever seen. The Commedia dell'Arte, as conceived by the actors of the Theatre Ca 'Foscari, is like an extremely gentle dance where calm gestures slowly glide. This is far from the exaggerated French gesticulation where vulgarity and disorder are the only resources. Italians dance their emotions in soft and graceful movements that never clash with the elegance of the body.
>
> (Théâtre des Nations 1960)

The actors' unusual style of gesture drew the attention of this reporter, from the Parisian magazine *Arts Spectacles*, who managed to grasp Poli's aesthetic intentions, taking his research towards an aesthetic diametrically opposed to that of the nineteenth century: the scenic expression is the transfiguration of reality through the abstraction of "the spoken word", which must take on a universal value, beyond linguistic boundaries. "The voice", the director explains, "is a tool, to guide gesture which becomes a ballet, and to suggest the frequent mimed actions" (Poli 1960: 35). The need for the renewal of theatre is thus supported by constant and continuous work on three main elements that make concrete the somewhat abstract concept of theatre as "pure art": first, speech-music which requires a vocal range giving a melody more pronounced than in normal conversation; then movement-ballet, the rhythmic relationship of vertical lines in movement; and, finally, light-colour, the very basis of his scenography.

Thanks to a video-recording made in 1969 by the television programme *Sapere*, for the opening of the Theatre de la Commedia dell'Arte in Avogaria directed by Poli in Venice, we get a glimpse of what his work was like at that time. The abstraction of the gestures and movements of the Zanni clearly recall the dancing positions of the characters of Jacques Callot (b. Nancy 1592 – d. Nancy 1635) which obviously inspired Poli, as the prints, *I Balli di Sfessania*, were long regarded as a fundamental source for reconstructing the acting. The "interpretation" offered by Callot highlighted the gestural, physical, musical, dancing, acrobatic character of the actors, even though today we know that in reality, there is no evidence that these are "scenes" or sketches from the Commedia dell'Arte, they are, rather, imaginary duos, where characters confront each other without there really being a dramatic situation, at least in the foreground characters. Perhaps knowing this would not have changed Poli's interest in these images, because in his work of rediscovery of the old forms of acting in Commedia, he was fascinated by the "anti-realist" power expressed by the masks – as objects but also as physical posture – which goes back to the idea of an aesthetically pure theatre. The mask, according to the author:

> Frees the theatre from all misunderstanding of the imitation of the real [...] the mask can put aside the expression on stage of the ties of time and space in order to project it into the absolute and turn the characters into moral and social symbols of humanity, according to the psychological classification that gives rise to fixed typologies.
>
> (Poli 1983:13)

Returning to these forgotten forms, to these masks that are both "mysterious and terrible", allows him to make use of fixed typologies and their dynamics while examining their validity on the twentieth century stage. "These changeless and ecstatic faces" are intended to provoke laughter from the audience and lead us, according to Giorgio Strehler, "to the edge of theatrical mysticism, where the demons rise up and bear us to the very sources of dramatic art" (Strehler 1983: 5).

But the fact of wanting to return to the past implies – in the "neo" – a sense of nostalgia for a lost past, an idyllic world, a paradise lost. In fact it may be noted that the show *La Commedia degli Zanni* opens with a prologue in which a certain nostalgia is expressed for Italian masks, described as a "magnificent example of colour" (Poli 1983: 37), the expression of "the exaltation of human nature" (ibid.) as against the grey humanity of modern times. As the curtain opens and the masks emerge from manuscripts discoloured by being forgotten for centuries, the offstage voice says "It is with nostalgia that we gaze at these masks with the sentiment we have for things lost forever, we who have fallen into an era of grey banality, completely devoid of bright colours" (ibid.).

But this "nostalgia" does not prevent our author from continuing his work on masks and ancient dramatic texts. On the contrary, his artistic research feeds on this feeling of melancholy mixed with a deep need, shared by his contemporaries, for the renewal of stage practice.

Poli's theatrical teaching: a syncretic method

Poli explained his theatrical theories a decade after his staging of the Zanni, during a round table discussion focused on the actor's physical expression, organized by the Venice Biennale in 1969 and directed by Jacques Lecoq.

Invited as a specialist in the Commedia dell'Arte, Poli explained how the crisis, which the theatre faced in those years, led him to feel the need for a return to physical expression, with the aim of communicating with the public outside the limits imposed by the word, which he perceived as meaningless. So he declared that "today only gesture can express real emotions" (Poli 1970: 18–19), a gesture that can be expressed through pure forms like those which, according to Poli, characterize the Commedia dell'Arte. The actor must therefore search for the pure gesture beyond mime, and it is in this sense that "the tradition, which goes from Decroux to Lecoq, is a tradition that must be renewed, since it still contains elements of mimesis and of imitation of reality" (ibid.: 19). Poli's theory builds on the appropriation and reinvention of the abstract forms of Commedia in order to leave behind the imitation of reality, thus achieving the long-awaited renewal.

Through his directorial work with student actors, Poli built up a teaching method to teach his own form of Commedia dell'Arte. The stylized forms of the Italian comedy were achieved through relaxation and concentration techniques theorized by the masters of the Russian avant-garde, particularly those of Stanislavski. Poli worked out his method through thirty years of activity, and in 1974 he founded, at his Venice theatre, a drama school with a two-year course where students could be fully trained, for free, in the art of the stage.

Poli's method is based on the actors' perfect mastery of psychic and emotional activity, with self-control of the various muscular systems. To achieve this, the psychosomatic experiments conducted by Schultz through "autogenic training" are of extreme importance.

Thanks to the archival work that was carried out at the Poli family residence, a video-recording was found of a training session in Commedia dell'Arte led by him, in the Summer of 1975, for students of the Conservatoire d'Art Dramatique du Québec et Montréal. To one of the Québecois students who asked him "How did you manage to reconstruct a precise method of training in the Commedia dell'Arte since it is an oral tradition?" Poli replied in a very significant manner, saying that man is for him a "historical man" (Poli 1975) who carries within himself a whole tradition and atavistic experience, and it is this ancestral knowledge that has allowed Poli to guess what the movements of the masked actors were from the iconography of Callot. According to these images – which we now know are not a faithful reproduction of the Commedia dell'Arte but only a fantastic vision by the French engraver – Poli developed his very personal idea that all Commedia masks are disguised Zannis. Thus he declared: "Everyone is zanni [...] There is the old Zanni who becomes rich: the Pantalon; the Zanni who has been to the war; the Captain" (ibid.) and so on. The Zanni is thus the main character of Poli's theatre, and tribute was paid to him by Poli calling his manifesto-show *La Commedia degli Zanni*.

This extremely important video gives us not only the opportunity to enjoy Poli's unique method in all its complexity, but also allows us to compare it with that of Carlo Boso, who, in 1965, before joining the School of the Piccolo Teatro of Milan, was a pupil of Poli's. Thus the circle closes. The teaching and artistic sensitivity of Carlo Boso, today considered one of the masters of the Commedia dell'Arte (co-director of the Académie Internationale des Arts de Spectacle in Versailles), is based on two schools that justify its originality. Officially from Strehler's school, where he returned in 1964, Boso has had a mixed training based, on the one hand, on the invaluable teachings of his master Giorgio Strehler about directing and acting, and on those of Paolo Grassi, who taught him the meaning and importance of theatre in society. On the other hand, as regards his actual work on the Commedia dell'Arte and its characters, of considerable importance is his participation in 1965 in the play *La Venetiana* by Giovan Battista Andreini, directed by Giovanni Poli at the Teatro La Fenice in Venice as part of the Biennale of Theatre. This show, derived from the work of the famous "*capocomico*" of the Compagnie dei Fedeli, was acclaimed by the critics as a real discovery, and bears witness to the long process of reinvention and reinterpretation of the Commedia dell'Arte carried out by Poli and developed by Boso.

Poli's artistic commitment was intended to reverse the trend of realism that dominated the whole Italian stage, but did not leave real traces in the history of Italian theatre, which itself was too much engaged with the novelty of directing for professional companies to focus on the experiments of amateurs carried out away from the cultural capitals of the peninsula.

However, it is on the other side of the Atlantic that Poli is recognized as a leader in Italian avant-garde theatre. In 1971, in the programme of the Théâtre du Rideau Vert in Montreal, Poli is thus introduced to a large audience: "His theatrical research attempts to define the link between the avant-garde theatre and what Poli considered as its source: the Commedia dell'Arte." (Théâtre du Rideau Vert 1971: 3)

Forms and methods from the "old" Commedia dell'Arte stimulate, encourage and enrich contemporary research that gives rise to new theatrical forms, but their permanence in contemporary production transforms them and inevitably turns them away from archetypes to make a new tradition, or indeed a new part of the history of contemporary theatre: the "Neo-Commedia dell'Arte", that is to say, the actors' theatre.

References

Brook, Peter (1996) *The Empty Space*. New York: Touchstone.

Hobsbawm, Eric and Ranger, Terence (2006) *L'invention de la traditio*. Vivier, Christine (tr.) Paris: Éd. Amsterdam.

Nosari, Pier Giorgio (2008) "La legge di Lavoisier alla prova. Maschere e figure animate nel teatro italiano contemporaneo", Commedia dell'Arte. Annuario Internazionale. n°1, Ferrone, Siro and Testaverde, Anna Maria (dir.), Florence, Italy: Leo S. Olschki.

Poli, Giovanni (1959) *Dieci anni di teatro universitario. Cronaca degli avvenimenti scenici e delle ricerche estetiche del Teatro Universitario Ca' Foscari*. Venice, Italy: Emiliana.

——(1960) *Le Maschere Latine, La commedia degli Zanni*. Collana del Teatro Universitario Ca' Foscari. Venice, Italy: La Tipografica.

——(post 1962) Prefazione a Micha. Document dactylographié (5 feuillets) inédit, Archives famille Poli, Venice, Italy.

——(1966) "Le vrai théâtre, c'est l'ancien". Presse. 3 April 1966.

——(1970) "Ritorno all'espressione fisica dell''attore", *Acts of the international round table of 19 September 1969, Venice*, Sala degli specchi di Ca' Giustinian, *La Biennale de Venice (dir.)*, XXVII International Festival of Theatre, Venice, Italy: Fantonigrafica, (pp. 18–19, 33 and 38).

——(1975) Unpublished video of a Commedia dell'Arte workshop in Venice with some students from the Canadian National Conservatory of Theatre Montreal, (Poli family archives, Venice, Italy).

——(1983) La commedia degli Zanni, documenti rinascimentali sulla commedia dell'arte. Collana del teatro all'Avogaria, 7. Venice, Italy: La Tipografica.

Strehler, Giorgio (1983) "Préface" in *L'art du Masque dans la commedia dell'Arte*, Sartori, Donato and Lanata, Bruno (dir.). Malakoff, France: Solis.

Taviani, Ferdinando (1985) "Position du masque dans la commedia dell'arte", *Le masque du rite au théâtre*. Picon-Vallin, Beatrice (dir.) Paris: CNRS éditions.

Théâtre du Rideau Vert (dir.) (1971) "Giovanni Poli", Programme of Barouf à Chioggia, Season 71/72, Vol.12, 2, 29 October 1971, Montréal, Canada.

Théâtre des Nations (1960) "Le théâtre de Venise : l'un de meilleurs spectacles du Théâtre des Nations". Paris: Arts Spectacles.

41

ARLECCHINO APPLESEED

Or how Carlo Mazzone-Clementi Brought Commedia to the New World

Joan Schirle

We might wonder how Commedia dell'Arte came to the New World. Was it through the characters of Harlequin and Columbine in the nineteenth century pantos, or through Italian troupes that set off for gigs across the Atlantic, as so colorfully envisioned in Renoir's *The Golden Coach*? Was it via the Golden Age of silent film comedies? Or did Commedia attach itself like a flea to the clothes of some Italian immigrant looking for a new life? Carlo Mazzone-Clementi was certainly an immigrant Paduan pilgrim in 1957. He was also a pioneer and a poet. With the spirit of a poet he spread seeds of Commedia dell'Arte in the New World. With the spirit of a pioneer he stayed on to tend those seeds. "No roots, no fruits." (Mazzone-Clementi pers. comm. 1978) Author-teacher John Towsen wrote that Carlo "single-handedly brought commedia to the United States starting in 1958." (Towsen 2011)

Paduan

Carlo Alessandro Luigi Mazzone-Clementi was born on December 12, 1920 in Padua, in the shadow of Galileo's tower, across the street from the sixteenth century birthplace of Angelo Beolco, Padua's great actor-dramatist who wrote in peasant dialect under the name "Ruzzante." Carlo died 80 years later in his adopted home in Northern California, having sowed seeds of Commedia dell'Arte from coast to coast, ignited a movement that became known as New Vaudeville, established a company a la Copeau and the Copiaus/Quinze (Baldwin 2012: 8) and began the first training center in North America dedicated to the work of the actor-creator.

Yet... it would be misleading to say that Carlo's approach to life, to art, to Commedia, was in any way orderly and well-planned. His life was full of accidents, surprises, contradictions, and improviso. His teaching was never academic, never formulaic, and above all he valued spontaneity, as befits his larger-than-life, in-the-moment personality and the spirit of Commedia inside him. From his arrival on the East Coast of the United States in its biggest of cities, to his settling on the West Coast in one of its smallest—a town of 1200 people, behind the redwood curtain of Northern California—he was thought by some to be a genius, and by others to be a madman. "What others call my retreat, I call my advance." (Mazzone-Clementi 1973)

Growing up in Padua, Carlo heard many tales from his grandfather Girolamo Clementi, who spoke "Ruzzantino," about the enduring customs of the hill folk immortalized by that nobleman-playwright. Carlo's father was Neopolitan, his mother Padovan. Her father Girolamo was one of Carlo's primary inspirations and natural teachers of Commedia dell'Arte, "My grandfather *was* Commedia. I would not have survived my childhood without him. He was a story-teller and impersonator, with tremendous elocution and clever imitation. He could imitate birds, animals, or humans." (Rolfe 1981: 5)

With an ear for dialects, including his mother's Padovan hill dialect, Carlo eventually spoke French, Spanish, could read Greek and Latin, as well as play in the dialects of Bergamo, Tuscany, Naples, Venice, and more. His father, a military sharpshooter and fencing master, put a sword in Carlo's hand at the age of five. Known as "the earthquake kid," he loved climbing trees and jumping from them. He learned to run fast to escape beatings from his parents, creating such strength in his legs he was able to sprint 100 yards in 11 seconds, competing against the best runners from the USA in 1945.

His five years of army service commenced in 1939 while Italy was in control of the Fascists. In the last years of WW2 during the German occupation, he joined the Resistance. The dialects came in handy—he was once caught by a band of German and Italian soldiers. Noting that some were Tuscan, he conversed with them in Tuscan dialect. They were convinced he was "one of them" and let him go.

Poet

In 1944 Carlo discovered he was an actor and a poet. His formal acquaintance with the history, characters and atmosphere of the Commedia dell'Arte began as a member of the Teatro Universita Padova. He had briefly attended University of Bologna but did not return after the war, much more excited by the artistic and political atmosphere in Padua. He joined the democratically oriented Action Party (*Partito d'Azione*) and in 1945 met Gianfranco de Bosio, director of theatre at the University of Padua, which was one of the leading opponents of the city's Fascist regime. Carlo took part in radio broadcasts from the Voice of Padua University—he was one of two "voices"—performed in revues and sketches and was one of the five-member nucleus of the Padua University Players, directed by de Bosio.

Until this point in time Carlo had no formal knowledge of Commedia dell'Arte.

I didn't know I was doing Commedia because until I entered into this group I didn't realize the importance of Commedia. Some of us went to Paris, came back and said, "Wait a minute, we have this tremendous tradition and don't even know we have it!" I was involved with poetry, with soccer, with silent movies as a kid, with watching my grandfather—then all of a sudden all these things came together, at Padua University. It's like you pass in front of the church all the time and never go into it. People come from 6000 miles and say, "Here's the famous church" and you say "What?" And suddenly you belong, you participate, you recognize.

(Rolfe 1981: 10)

It was de Bosio and associate Lieta Papafava who went to Paris, first bringing back Marceau in 1947.

> Marceau was interested in Commedia, so he came to Padua because Padua was known as the origin—he knew more about Commedia than we did! Marceau wanted to do a show—he'd just been doing the character of Bip two months, and he chose me from among the others to be his partner. We toured Italy in 1947... Then the next year they came back with Lecoq. And we began doing Commedia with him.

(Rolfe 1981: 20)

Carlo became Lecoq's assistant in his work with the Padua Players.

> I was the only one of the actors who spoke French. Lecoq decided I was going to follow; every night I was taking him home and he was giving me notes about what he did that day in class and what he wanted to do the next day, from 1948 to 1951.

(Rolfe 1981: 11)

In 1948, sculptor and fellow Padovan, Amleto Sartori, began teaching mask work to the Players. When Carlo emigrated to America, it was with ten Sartori masks that he began his proposal of Commedia in the New World. One of the masks was "Zan' Mazzone," made by Amleto, just for Carlo.

In 1949 Carlo received a scholarship to attend EPJD (Éducation Par le Jeu Dramatique) in Paris. His work with Barrault, though brief, was deeply affecting. As Commedia dell'Arte became re-discovered, re-invented, re-newed and re-vitalized after WW2, the strongest support for Commedia as a living form was coming from France, from mimes. Lecoq, Marceau, and Barrault: this "tripod" of influences would guide Carlo for the next 50 years, his knowledge and conception of Commedia forever inseparable from the idea of mime.

He acted for Eric Bentley, who directed for Padua University Players the first Brecht play in Italy, *The Exception and the Rule* (1951). Bentley would later assist Carlo to establish himself in the US as a teacher and performer. De Bosio also brought musician Jimmy "Lover Man" Davis, who participated with the Players in *Arte Negro Americana*, a revue of poems and songs from blues to gospel, plus Langston Hughes' *The Mulatto*, with masks by Amleto Sartori. Carlo experienced what he came to call "America's Commedia"—jazz, tap dancing, and musical theatre.

In 1951 Carlo struck off for Rome as a mime artist, with about $15 in his pocket, to try his hand at the now-booming Italian post-war film industry. He got a few film parts, did street pantomime with a guitarist partner, did mime sketches at The Night Owl, a club where cabaret style revues took place. "I did one or two characterizations of Commedia life, but they weren't so good—I'm not proud of that. I was alone, I was the only Italian, and it taught me comedy is partnership." (Rolfe 1981: 22)

He spent 1953 as an actor with the Teatro Nazionale d'Arte Italiano, directed by Vittorio Gassman. In 1954 Lecoq invited him to Milan to work in Company Parenti-Fo-Durano's satirical revue *Sani da legare* (*A Madhouse for the Sane*) at the Piccolo Teatro. Carlo's entrance was a jump from a high platform above the stage to announce the show's title (Cinecitta Luce 1955). Four years later, after a great leap across the Atlantic to New York, another stage jump would determine his future career.

"I decided to have a studio, a laboratory, and to be realistic about working with what I learned from Lecoq, in my talent and my background in Commedia. The only place I could do it was in Rome." His classes drew mostly American actors.

> I had Italian actors also but they were not very consistent. The Americans were dedicated and enthusiastic. I was impressed. So when they started to say "Carlo should go to New York," well... I had a friend who wrote 75 letters to the United States and 25 said "Come right over!" So I said, "Stupid, why am I staying here in Rome to battle to become TV or commercial or non-commercial or having engagements and doing stunts involving risking my life? So the letters from America inviting me... and so I crossed."
>
> (Rolfe 1981: 63)

Pioneer

Carlo and his first wife, Vivien Leone, arrived in 1957 in New York. He enrolled in English classes, and found work through the Models Guild as a "mime model." He created his first mime show for US audiences, and devised *Six Characters in Search of Commedia*, the piece that would introduce in living color the traditional characters and masks of the Commedia dell'Arte to the actors and directors of the American theatre.

> *AN INVITATION* [1958] From: Carlo Mazzone, Studio 42, 58 W. 57th NY 19

> Won't you join a small group of professional theatre people in my studio, and let me try to recreate for you some of the characters and atmosphere of the Commedia dell'Arte?
>
> I am a Venetian actor (recently "The Cock" in "Cock-A-Doodle Dandy"), made my Mime debut with Marceau in '47 and have since done about twenty films and some 8 years of European repertory, particularly in the field of Commedia restorations pioneered at Padua Univ. Theatre and The Piccolo of Milano by my Maestro, Jacques Lecoq, a Barrault protégé who has become the outstanding French rehabilitator of Mime.
>
> Ever since I arrived in N.Y. last year to teach his method, bringing with me ten leather Commedia masks, I have been surrounded by lively curiosity about the Italian comic tradition.

Because I believe an acquaintance with the art of these humble players to be fundamental to all who yearn for more style in the technically brilliant age of American realism, I have combined masks, costumes and dialects of the most popular of the stock characters into a one-man sketch-with-commentary, booked on the college circuit this year. Yet I would like most to show it privately to people like you, for since these men were the inventors of the *professional* theatre, they are really *your* ancestors.

And because they are also, most particularly, mine, I hope I shall not betray them—or you.

R.S.V.P. Vivien Mazzone, Circle 5-4468
[original invitation, emphasis in original]

Carlo designed the costumes, and in Sartori's masks, played Dottore, Brighella, Pantalone, Arlecchino, Capitano, and Pulcinella. Scaramouche was added as a link, plus an "invisible" Columbina. "I did Scaramouche as a fencing master, without words…. '*scaramouche*' means 'skirmisher'—hit and run, a disturbance, a guerilla…. He's a bother, he's a flea, even the elephant doesn't like a flea, right? That's the idea, a skirmish, a disturbance. I was inspired as much by Duchartre, a lot of Lecoq, and I invented this scenario from my own knowing the tirades and dialects and lazzi." (Rolfe 1981: 24) Bentley's agent Toby Cole booked the show across the country.

Fall of 1958 was a turning point. He was cast as The Cock, a non-speaking role, in the world premiere of Sean O'Casey's *Cock-A-Doodle-Dandy* in Toronto, followed by an Off-Broadway run in New York. "Of all the hardy, outspoken company there is one other who deserves special mention. Carlo Mazzone impersonates the title role with dash and spirit, a solid symbol of the production's solid symbolism." (Herbert Whittaker, Globe and Mail review October 2, 1958)

In November, the production opened at the Carnegie Hall Playhouse, directed by Philip Burton, starring Will Geer. Carlo's role was physically demanding.

I was practicing. Every night I would warm up because I had one difficult thing: I would jump into the audience in the dark from 12 feet in the air and crow, 'Cock-a-doodle dandy!' I had not much space to land, *boom*. I had to do it in the dark or it would spoil the whole thing. I was scared every night so I had to warm up as if I was in a competition.

The warm up was real athletic stuff and one night I was jumping downstairs in Carnegie Hall, under the hall they built a little theater. I was jumping on the grids, I didn't realize it was old-fashioned ironwork, probably it was defective or rusty or whatever, but—Bu-dum!—I went two stories down to the basement.

I was wounded, but luckily I was survivor. [In both knees] my cartilages were injured. Of course I sued Carnegie Hall, and of course I still did the show anyway—sitting there in the dark I went "Caw-caw-caw," and I finished the show.

The doctor said, "You have a choice: Operation and you can be better, or operation and you can be worse. Or you can lecture, you can teach

Commedia and so on." I come from a town of surgeons, and the surgeons, they told me, "Please, if you can avoid, avoid!"

(Doran 2000)

So Carlo turned primarily to teaching and demonstrations. He toured *Six Characters* for another two years, revealing to America what the traditional stock characters looked like, talked like, and moved like. On his 1959 West Coast tour, another seed was planted with the San Francisco Mime Troupe, which began performing Commedia that year. Founder R. G. Davis, a former student of Decroux, recalls: "First we read all the books in English on Commedia we could find—plays, histories—and looked at pictures. Fortunately, Carlo Mazzoni [sic] came through San Francisco and spent a week with me talking about Commedia." (Davis 1975: 31)

On Bentley's recommendation, Carlo was engaged in 1958 for two seasons with the Stratford Festival, to teach the actors, among them actress Julie Harris. He was invited to join the new Canadian Centre for Theatre Arts directed by Powys Thomas, a precursor to the National Theatre School of Canada. He continued teaching and performing in New York, promoting the "new natural French method of Jacques Lecoq."(*Village Voice* advertisement, original clipping, 1959)

He was discovered by Theodore Hoffman, head of the Theatre Department at Carnegie Tech (now Carnegie Mellon) and in 1960 received his first fulltime academic teaching position as Assistant Professor of Stage Movement. In this same year the Piccolo Teatro di Milano made its US debut with *Il Servitore di due Padroni,* and Carlo was able to welcome his old friend, Marcello Moretti. Interest in Commedia dell'Arte was growing; Carlo coached and directed a series of productions and in 1962 assisted another Italian visitor, Giovanni Poli, to direct *The Green Bird* for IASTA.

Among his Carnegie students were his future second wife, Jane Hill, future director Arne Zaslove, and actor Rene Auberjonois [*Star Trek*, *Benson*] who became one of Carlo's biggest fans and supporters. Zaslove became a protégé:

[Carlo] did masks, and he did a one man show about Commedia dell'Arte. I was a freshman and all we knew of such things at that time was Marcel Marceau and that was it. Carlo was this mad, incredibly creative genius, but nobody understood what he said because he was inarticulate despite the fact that he spoke five languages. He was just full of life and energy and philosophy. I never quite understood what he said, but I always understood what he meant.

(Zaslove 2007: 11)

Carlo continued to teach mime in New York and eventually opened a Studio for Modern Mime with Jewel Walker and Tony Montanaro based in the three systems of Delsarte, Decroux, and Lecoq. Carlo arranged an exhibition of Sartori masks at the Donnell Library at Columbia University. Though he tried for several years to produce a US traveling exhibition of 100 masks of Amleto Sartori, gathering dozens of support letters from theatre figures like Joseph Papp, John Gassner and Walter Kerr, he never got the foundation support needed to mount the exhibition.

He coached a Commedia-style *The Taming of the Shrew* in 1964 at the Arena Stage in Washington, DC, directed by Mel Shapiro, with Rene Auberjonois as Tranio, and Sartori masks. Now teaching at Brandeis University, he adapted and directed *The Three Cuckolds* by Leon Katz, with masks by Donato Sartori. His rehearsal schedules list several sessions devoted to "*Improvviso All'Italiana.*" At this point he adopted both family surnames, and was henceforth Carlo Mazzone-Clementi. "Much lauded director Clementi, once Marcel Marceau's sign-holder, trained the actors to move with a precision and style spectacular and never before achieved on the Brandeis stage" (*The Justice*, May 11, 1965, Brandeis independent student weekly newspaper, original edition).

In 1965 he was hired to coach the acting company at the new Repertory Theatre of Lincoln Center, under Jules Irving and Herbert Blau; among the actors were Faye Dunaway and James Earl Jones. He also performed in the inaugural production, *Danton's Death*. By 1966, Ted Hoffman had become founding director of the Theatre Program of NYU's School of the Arts, and brought Carlo to teach, where he met juggler and circus artist Hovey Burgess. The two formed a partnership to stage exhibitions of 30 masks of Sartori in New York and DC. Burgess became one of Carlo's closest disciples as well as the first to incorporate circus techniques in actor training. "In 1966 my teaching was profoundly influenced by three men who taught mime and *Commedia dell'Arte*: Arne Zaslove; his teacher, Carlo Mazzone-Clementi; and their teacher, Jacques Lecoq." (Burgess 1976: preface)

In 1968 Carlo married Jane Hill, who became his partner for 11 years, and with whom he started a family. They translated and staged Goldoni's *The Ingenious Chambermaid* (*La Cameriera brillante*) for University of California Davis in 1967. He had felt increasingly frustrated on the East Coast, where theatre training was dominated by the American Method. Hired by founder/artistic director William Ball to teach the actors of the American Conservatory Theatre (A.C.T.), he and Jane moved to the West Coast. Ball was part of the new movement toward regional repertory companies, and toward integrating mime, movement, mask, and combat training in actor training, as St. Denis had programmed for the Juilliard School. At A.C.T. Carlo encountered the F. M. Alexander Technique, and British-style voice training. As he developed his own pedagogy and finally opened his own school in Blue Lake, he included them in his curriculum along with mime, aikido, and mask, using his own version of a neutral mask—the Metaphysical Mask—made by Amleto.

In 1971 Carlo formed a dell'Arte Troupe in Berkeley; Dell'Arte, Inc. was officially incorporated as a non-profit organization. But like many other urbanites of the time, he and Jane sought a life more connected to nature than could be found in cities or suburbs. With no job and little money, with courage and dreams, they moved north to rural Humboldt County, California. Relatively undeveloped, the area drew everyone from artists to outlaws to "new pioneers." With Jane, Carlo was able at last to realize his dream of a rural company/school, with nature as primary teacher.

Inspired by Copeau, with some of his followers from the Berkeley workshops he began teaching "Summer Workshops in the Redwoods." Jacques and Fay Lecoq, Mamako, and Hovey Burgess visited and taught. There, Carlo directed the Troupe's first show, Gozzi's *The Green Cockatoo,* and took it back to the Bay Area to perform. Jane meantime convinced the city of Eureka, and the deans of College of the

Redwoods, to support a summer festival of Shakespeare, classics, and musicals. Meant to celebrate the comic spirit through "grand comedies," Carlo named it "The Grand Comedy Festival" and then added "at Qual-a-wa-loo," the Wiyot Indian name for Humboldt Bay. From the 1973 playbill, his statement:

About the comic theatre:
It's laughable. Not explainable.
About the individual:

> Our word "person" has a meaningful origin; to the Roman actor, "persona," his mask, was the device in front of his mouth, designed to project his voice to the audience. The individual. He wants to badly to be heard.

About society:

> Funny, but true, what others call my retreat, I call my advance.
>   Carlo Mazzone-Clementi

The "retreat" to Northern California was the advance into the dream of having a producing company plus school: "Humboldt County is to San Francisco as Padua is to Venice, Stratford to London— where the art grows." (Pers. Comm. 1975)

He and Jane worked on several fronts: she raising their family, cultivating a board of directors, fundraising, looking for a building to house a company and school; he trying to keep a group of artists committed to a future with a wild experiment. In 1974, *The Drama Review* (TDR) Special Issue on Popular Entertainments included their essay, "Commedia and the Actor" (Mazzone-Clementi and Hill 1974). They were the first in America to articulate visionary ideals for a movement-based actor training system based in the tradition of Commedia dell'Arte, and illuminated its value to the work of the American actor.

That same year, a building was found in tiny Blue Lake, California (pop. 1200)— a former I.O.O. F. Hall (International Order of Odd Fellows) built in 1911. With work, there would be room for teaching studios, offices, a kitchen and a rehearsal hall.

Carlo's appearance at The First North American Mime Festival in summer of 1974 in LaCrosse, Wisconsin inspired several young students who followed him back to Blue Lake to join his new school. Organized by Bari Rolfe and Lou Campbell, the festival was an extraordinary gathering of international mime artists, many of whom had never met: Lecoq, Dimitri, Mumenschanz, Fialka, Shields and Yarnell, Lotte Goslar, and more.

The Dell'Arte School of Mime & Comedy opened in January of 1975 with 17 students. Master teacher and artistic director, Carlo taught Commedia through a series of improvisations he called The Showers—"because you are never too clean to do them." Assisting him were former students from the Bay Area, John Achorn, Diana Perry, Peter Kors. I met them all when I auditioned for the Grand Comedy Festival in 1975. Noting that I was a certified F. M. Alexander Technique teacher and an actor, Carlo invited me to join the faculty of the school for Fall 1975. In 1976

I was teaching with Carlo, Jane, and Avner (The Eccentric) Eisenberg, a Lecoq grad who departed shortly for a tour contract, but dedicated his show "to Jacques Lecoq, who taught me everything I know, and to Carlo Mazzone-Clementi, who taught me everything else." (Towsen 2011). Jon'Paul Cook, another Lecoq grad and Footsbarn co-founder joined the faculty. The two of us joined Carlo in devising *Allusions*, an original mime and Commedia revue we performed at Grand Valley State Colleges, Michigan in 1976.

Jane and Carlo separated in 1976, just after the final summer of Grand Comedy Festival. College of the Redwoods declined to continue producing the festival. The board of directors had quit *en masse*, there was little money in the bank and only seven students enrolled for our Fall term. Carlo, Jon'Paul and myself vowed to keep going. We founded a new company—The Dell'Arte Players Company—and became our own board of directors, working without salaries until we could get the organization on its feet. We had a small federal grant to produce "in Commedia format, drawing on Indian and pioneer sources" (Original program (playbill) 1975: Artistic Director's Statement, Grand Comedy Festival, Eureka, CA., in the Dell'Arte archives) an original play based on Carlo's excitement about correspondences between the Commedia dell'Arte stock characters and Native American animal spirits: Coyote, Loon, Raven and others. We commissioned Jael Weisman, formerly of the SF Mime Troupe to develop a script and to direct. Called *Arlekkino, or The Force of Credulity,* but toured as *The Loon's Rage,* it was co-written by Weisman, Joan Holden and Steve Most. Toured from Seattle to L.A., it was the debut of the new Dell'Arte Players Company. Michael Fields, a young San Francisco actor hired for the tour, is still with Dell'Arte today.

Slowly things grew more stable. More students came, Carlo and I found grants to pay the company and hire staff. In 1980, our company performed at La Biennale in Venice, with Carlo playing The Undertaker in *Birds of a Feather*, thrilled to participate in the first Venice *carnivale* in 200 years.

Pilgrim

The years after his 1979 divorce were difficult for Carlo. Losing his partner Jane, he lost the main translator of his ideas, for without Jane there would have been no Dell'Arte Inc. (DAI) He now found greater support outside the US, among former students and colleagues, and began a decade as a pilgrim without a fixed home. In 1984 he co-founded a second school with Ole Brekke—The Commedia School—in Denmark connecting the circle with Commedia in Europe and Dell'Arte in North America. Brekke was an early Dell'Arte student in Blue Lake who then completed the pedagogical training at Lecoq's. When his father left him an apartment in Padua, Carlo alternated between stays in Italy, work in Denmark with Ole, visits to Sigfrido Aguilar in Mexico, and visits back to Humboldt to see family and Dell'Arte. At the age of 65, in the Veterans and Masters tournament in Tarvisio, Italy, he won a gold in discus and javelin.

In 1994 he returned to Humboldt to live and resume his connection to Dell'Arte. For several summers DAI offered "Masters Teach" workshops, where Carlo and

Figure 41.1 Carlo Mazzone-Clementi teaching at the Dell'Arte International School of Physical Theatre, Blue Lake, California, 1975.

myself would be joined by some of his favorites—Zaslove, Julie Goell, Brekke—alternating summers of Commedia with Bouffon. In 1997 John Achorn began filming a documentary called *Improvviso*! about Carlo and the international diaspora of Commedia, recording interviews with dozens of artists including Marceau.

In 1999 Carlo attended the memorial tribute to Lecoq in Washington, DC and later that year gave his last workshop at a comedy festival in Austin, Texas. He died in 2000 from complications after heart surgery. The hundreds of tributes sent to his memorial spotlighted what an extraordinary, contradictory, unique, baffling and inspirational man Carlo Mazzone-Clementi was. Someone from whom you learned most just by being around him, as Zaslove says, "I just wanted to follow him around like in that old Jewish saying: 'When you sit at the Rabbi's feet you can nibble the crumbs that fall from his beard.' And that's how you learn from Carlo.... He had the masks and the Commedia dell'Arte spirit which is what he conveyed to all of us." (Zaslove 2007) Brekke says Carlo's underlying teaching purpose was to develop "the creative performer," to reveal the genius in each student. "His exercises dealt with what he called 'the creative matter'—to create something out of nothing, improviso." (Speech at the 2000 Memorial for Carlo Mazzone-Clementi in Blue Lake, CA, transcript from video) What Carlo embodied better than anything was the all-of-a-sudden, the spontaneity in the face of life's daily battles, and above all the humor—"life is 51% comedy."(Pers. Comm. 1979)

Carlo is buried in the Blue Lake Cemetery under a tall redwood tree, a short walk from the center where his life's work has survived and grown to include not only a professional company and school, but an accredited MFA program and annual summer festival. Dell'Arte International is home to the Dell'Arte Company, the Dell'Arte International School of Physical Theatre (now with over 1000 alumni), and the Mad River Festival—the fruit of Carlo's vision and mission to carry Commedia dell'Arte across the Atlantic. The City of Blue Lake officially declared December 12 Carlo Mazzone-Clementi Day. He often described himself as "the wind." "I am the wind," meaning that he was one who stirred things, who got things moving. Many Commedia experts have passed through the New World; Carlo stayed and kept stirring the pot. It is a full-course meal: one part Ruzzante, one part mime, one part grandfather, one part his own genius.

HUMUS HUMANIS HUMILIS

Carlo Alessandro Luigi Mazzone-Clementi

1920–2000

PILGRIM, PIONEER, POET, PADOVAN

Carlo Mazzone-Clementi's chosen inscription for his gravestone.

References

Baldwin, Jane (2012) *Collective Creation's Migration from the Cote d'Or to the Golden Hills of California: The Copiaus/Quinze and the Dell'Arte Company*. Available at www.academia.edu/3262869/ (accessed 21 August 2014).

Burgess, Hovey (1976) "Preface" *Circus Techniques*, New York: Brian Dube, Inc.

Cinecitta Luce (1955) *Nel Mondo della rivista "Sani da legare"*1:32. Available at www.youtube.com/watch?v=FfNUZw0yAeo (accessed 21 August 2014).

Davis, R. G. (1975) *The San Francisco Mime Troupe: The First Ten Years*, Ramparts Press.

Doran, Bob, (2000) "Behind The Mask: Carlo Mazzone-Clementi, 1920–2000", *North Coast Journal* November 16, 2000. Available at www.dellarte.com/about/history/founders/carlo-mazzone-clementi (accessed "online journals", 21 August 2014).

Mazzone-Clementi, C. (1973) Original program (playbill) note, Grand Comedy Festival, Eureka, CA. US, in the Dell'Arte archives.

Mazzone-Clementi, Carlo and Hill, Jane, (1974) "Commedia And The Actor", *The Drama Review*, Vol 18, no. 1, March. (Reprinted in *Popular Theatre: A Sourcebook*, Edited by Joel Schechter, Routledge London, New York, 2003 pp 83–9.)

Rolfe, Bari (1981) Typed transcripts of unpublished interview with Carlo Mazzone-Clementi (1981–3).

Towsen, John, (2011) *All Fall Down, The Art and Craft of Physical Comedy* blogopedia August 6, 2011, post 175. Accessed online 2013. Available at http://physicalcomedy. blogspot.com/2011/08/commedia-actor-by-carlo-mazzone.html (accessed 21 August 2014).

Zaslove, Arne (2007) "Helping Students Get It" *Spectacle, A Quarterly Journal of the Circus Arts,* Editor Ernest Albrecht. Winter 2007, 11–14. Accessed online 2008. Available at www.zaslove.com/PDFs/Zaslove-Spectacle.pdf (accessed 21 August 2014).

Part III

ALIVE AND WELL AND LIVING IN...

42

DESPITE EVERYTHING, COMMEDIA DELL'ARTE IS ALIVE IN ITALY

Long live Commedia!

Fabio Mangolini

Anyone living outside Italy would think the Commedia dell'Arte would have maintained its persistence and constancy in the Italian theatre, even while it was being exported and assimilated into other countries. One could imagine a National Commedia dell'Arte Theatre with a seat in Rome, Milan, or in Venice, perhaps modelled on the National Noh Theatre in Tokyo, with an attached academy, supporting the highly venerated masters as living national treasures. Anyone who lives outside Italy would imagine that the Commedia dell'Arte is taught in every theatre school, in every academy, from generation to generation in this manner as surely as it happened in the sixteenth and seventeenth century. In summary, anyone who lives outside Italy would imagine that the Commedia dell'Arte in Italy is considered on a par with Opera, in theatres that produce and disseminate it, conservatories that teach it, and not least, in the enormous public subsidies that guarantee its vitality. It would create profound disillusionment to anyone living outside Italy to discover that no National Theatre of the Commedia dell'Arte exists; no widespread theatrical seasons; no persistence and constancy in its original forms in the Italian theatre; and, last, none of the powerful vitality of its early forms.

However, one can assert that today the Commedia dell'Arte in Italy enjoys much better health than it did twenty or thirty years ago. This assertion clearly contradicts all that was just declared: how can a genre like this, treated with little consideration, barely recognized by officialdom, thrive in good health?

The vitality exists, albeit not in the aforementioned forms nor in the imagination, but because Commedia is now accessible to the whole world, and not just native Italians. This vitality consists of a wide variety of influences, in the fusions that still permeate a good part of Italian theatre today, as much as in acting practices within the models of the theatrical marketplace, that still today, in many ways, define Commedia. The Commedia dell'Arte in Italy is alive above all because it knows how to regenerate both actors' methods and their professionalism.

Most likely, at the dawn of the twenty-first century, the renewed vitality of the Commedia dell'Arte in Italy derives from finally being freed from the oppressive burden of being the bearer of a theatrical mythology. Certainly, to do this, the Commedia dell'Arte had to overcome an impasse, in which all attempts at exegeses made in the name of the new theatricality, merely recreated the old mythology.

Perhaps to arrive at this result, a secular approach, demystified and uninhibited, was necessary, more matched to the epoch in which we live, in an age that tends to reveal the contradictions of the recent past, and in which it is no longer necessary to always claim the art of the actor as the centre of the theatrical act, as was the case in the twentieth century. This approach demanded that theatre necessarily made itself a tool of political struggle, reclaiming a license of a "theatre by the people for the people", in contrast to the bourgeois or high art theatre. Perhaps this new vigour of the Commedia dell'Arte in Italy was born from the discovery of its bare authenticity at the ideological crossroads that were constantly establishing and re-inventing it. Apparently full of contradictions and opposing forces, especially to outsiders, the Commedia dell'Arte holds contradictions within it harmoniously, like those that even now exist side by side: "improvisation" vs. "written dramatics", or "poetry of the actor" vs. "dramaturgical poiesis".

The ideological *impasse* was overcome in substance by departing from the antiquated history of the Commedia dell'Arte and opening up to the possibilities offered by modern theatre. It was probably this purely theoretical departure from the mythology of the Commedia dell'Arte, existing everywhere from the legendary stories by George Sand to those of Dario Fo, that ensured its new vitality. The Commedia dell'Arte was treated as one of many functional accounts of the innovation of Western theatricality from the middle of the nineteenth century through the twentieth century, despite the development of very different themes and tones within it. This purely historical narration is no longer felt today as being a necessity. The renewed vitality of the Commedia dell'Arte that is presently observed in Italy, in the daily making of theatre, assumes the vindicated power of a *praxis* that it never lost, almost as if it was simply resting amidst the embers, ready to burst again into flame when fed with new fuel. This was the sentiment expressed by the ancient actor Gino Maringola to the director Robert De Simone (Testaverde 2007: VII–XVI).

Certainly, the remote origins, the legend of the dissemination of the immortal knowledge sometimes in direct dynastic form, have for a long time rendered Commedia dell'Arte the disservice of being erroneously interpreted as the result of a mythical art, in order to make up for an improbable philology. It is almost as if Commedia was able to make itself an art set in time and space, capable of surviving itself: a legend that locates its beginnings outside Italy and, more precisely, in the context of the French romanticism – a legend whose purpose was to revitalize the theatre and its processes through a sort of archaeological salvage, proceeded, in reality, to sterilize the phenomenology.

From the nineteenth century, the Commedia dell'Arte has been rendered a well-defined theatrical form within a mythical horizon, adaptable to all passing and contemporary schools of thought tending to excess, whether of the pseudo-realistic stereotypes or from the great naturalistic model. The masks, the improvisation, and the popular scenic styles become the key factors within many programmes of theatrical renewal, and also within numerous lines of experimentation involved in the research for a new performative language. The obvious paradox is that in creating a salvaged mythical world idealized in an ostensible "Golden Age" of theatre from the Commedia dell'Arte, while at the same time salvaging its theatrical features and endowing it with singular morphological features often recreated in arbitrary form, the Commedia becomes inflexible and erroneously yields incorrect paradigms.

To quote Roberto Tessari:

> What, without a shadow of a doubt, never existed is an abstract concept of a monolithically strong Commedia dell'Arte: always the same in itself through any alterations of time and of space (truly just like *2001: A Space Odyssey*; and, like that, endowed with the same power of fascination that belongs only to mythological entities). And it never even existed, in reality, some normative model of the Commedia dell'Arte, with its own invariable performance schema, with a permanent system of fixed roles with uniquely determined improvisation, and supported by a normative code of tedious small gestures and of canonical vocal intonations stylized in some way. It is now due to clear the piazza of all forms of uncritical enthusiasm (as well as base commercialization as an end to itself) that they have heaped on, and are able to continue to heap on the theatrical phenomenon in question. And it is likewise due to demand that the Commedia dell'Arte be considered – forever – a *prismatic plexus* of many facets: a body of abundantly variable phenomenologies, as in the course of time as in relation with diverse dynamics which were conditional upon and subject to all of the their concrete manifestations *in vivo*, to appear as individual historical vicissitudes.
> (Tessari 2013: VIII)

"Clear the Piazza" is what Tessari strongly urges us to do: eliminate all the dross that obstructs the sight of the Commedia dell'Arte. It should not be treated as if it is a complex geometric figure able to radiate various clarities. There does not exist, then, "one" Commedia, "one" phenomenologic system, "one" normative code (admittedly, this last one would have never existed). Thus, there does not exist "one canon".

The vanguards of the form established the masks with meaning, types, corporal schematics, and improvisation. Unlike today's protagonists, they did not heed as much what is reconsidered essentially the phenomenology in question: the behavioural and typical products of its exponents – for example, a nomadic touring lifestyle, the mode of composing a repertory, routines of some improvisational forms – that continue to distinguish parts of the theatrical *routines* today.

It is a change of perspective from that which presupposes an ancient and embedded knowledge. Still, if only in terms of how many have regard for the Commedia dell'Arte in Italy, it succeeded in being recognized, almost paradoxically, for restoration, through the invention of a tradition, as Eric Hobsbawm instructs:

> "Invented tradition" is taken to mean a set of practices, normally governed by overtly or tacitly accepted rules and of a ritual or symbolic nature, which seek to inculcate certain values and norms of behaviour by repetition, which

automatically implies continuity with the past. In fact, where possible, they normally attempt to establish continuity with a suitable historic past.... However, insofar as there is such reference to a historic past, the peculiarity of 'invented' traditions is that the continuity with it is largely fictitious. In short, they are responses to novel situations which take the form of reference to old situations, or which establish their own past by quasi-obligatory repetition.

(Hobsbawm and Ranger 1983: 1–2)

The Commedia dell'Arte has therefore been re-invented, through the invention of actual tradition inserting itself, against its will, into that misleading mythology of street theatre: of *Théâtre de Foire*; of clowning; of *bouffonnerie*; of the "Super-Marionette" of Edward Gordon Craig; of Meyerhold's *Balagan*, of a corporality located in the "base" or "low"; of the carnivalesque; of the analysis produced by Mikhail Bakhtin, as well as that created by twentieth-century theatrical anthropologists. There are, sadly, many contemporary workshop practitioners offering their students an "authentic" Commedia experience.

In Italy, the re-invention of the tradition is accompanied by the evolution of the methods of production and diffusion. While performance styles were lost, other practices were not abandoned. The practices of rehearsing and producing theatre that leaned towards a pragmatic and professional approach and being ready to perform on the spot, regardless, kept on emerging from time to time. These last features are from a truly typical Italian "theatrical system", and have always coexisted in the "touring companies": both within the master families in the northern area (I Rame, I Carrara, I Sarzi) and the Neapolitan region (Petito, Scarpetta, De Filippo), and are even part of the tradition of the great actors and the actress-divas (Eleonora Duse, Marta Abba, etc.).

Therefore, it is in the light of the following themes that we must look at the staging, by Giorgio Strehler for the Piccolo Teatro of Milan, in 1947, of *The Servant of Two Masters* by Carlo Goldoni: the historical value of re-invention and of insemination, together with its position at the fundamental crossroads of an artistic and impresarial regeneration. For that masterful show, he touched upon a double stroke of good fortune. By assuming the role of staging a Renaissance model of acting styles and expressive forms of the Commedia dell'Arte, and by being able to diffuse and circulate this particular theatrical craft, he opened up new markets both in Italy and abroad. Strehler *interpreted* a text for his time, taking advantage of the author's own adaptations; Carlo Goldoni *reshaped* the lesson of a theatrical knowledge of which they were custodians for the original purchasers of the text: Antonio Sacchi and his troupe.

Strehler knew that his artistic and entrepreneurial project was not "the" Commedia dell'Arte, but the very successful result gleaned from researching with a group of actors that he then led. They were devising the repertory of a company that wanted a *stabile* (stable theatre company) in an Italy left in ruins after the end of the Second World War. On the other hand, the expectations of Strehler and, in particular, those of Marcello Moretti, the extraordinary interpreter of the mask of Arlecchino, were aimed at re-inventing a tradition that, based on the mindset of the style of play or game, had been lost. Strehler and Moretti did not have at their side a great Arlecchino that would have been able to unfold the continuity of the tradition to them; similarly, they did not possess any literature in regards to technique. They did not have a traditional repertory that would indicate to them the gestures, vocals, and the scenic rhythm: the *style de jeu* which they both sought.

Marcello Moretti recognized how, in the original masks of the Zanni, the eyeholes were of a very small diameter, and these eyes bestow on the mask an interesting animalistic characteristic: they removed, or limited in large part, the actor's peripheral vision. From this arose the need, in order to execute the movement in the minimum space and time, for rapid successive movements arranged in a sequence roughly like this: take possession of the visual field of action; look to your feet to continually keep your movement focussed and not run into any obstacles. Given these needs, this resulted in a jerky gait, and many leaps, highlighted by an almost mechanical movement of the limbs and head. To these movements, Marcello Moretti gave both rhythm and order, so the character crystallized itself within a precise architecture, where every detail was assessed and brought back to the universal, to which he added his prodigious intuition. Amleto Sartori, the sculptor at the birth of the regeneration of the tradition of the mask of the Commedia dell'Arte (See Chapter 15), wrote on the subject:

> Dealing with him and thinking back on it, we found the validation of that intuition in the ancient prints and generally in all the Arlecchinesque iconography. Indeed the character is continuously caught in movements similar to stills of a dance whose inheritance had been sensed by Marcello. He always proceeded how I believed the master artisans of the Renaissance proceeded in their illustrious studios. You were always put through a strict apprenticeship, and he wanted to have an entirely precise cognisance, well researched, and at times fastidious. This phase finished, he set to work with the same consciousness and with the security and with the dignity of someone who had seriously set to and resolved every problem of craftsmanship. Then, that almost without noticing it, he sunk into that vital role as if everything had been a forgone conclusion and inevitable conclusion.
> (Strehler and Grassi 1962: 21, 22)

In this sense, therefore, the revival of master-craftsmanship, resting on the Strehlerian experiment, became a historical landmark for the re-invention of the Commedia dell'Arte in Italy. Simultaneously in the same year in Padua the experiments of Gianfranco De Bosio (1945) were born and in Venice (1949) those of Giovanni Poli, both within the universities of their respective cities. These were intense, very substantial years, that also witnessed the arrival of the young Jacques Lecoq (summoned by De Bosio himself) to collaborate at the Teatro Universitario di Padova. Lecoq carried into Italy the Utopian ideals of Jacques Copeau, through the experiences of his daughter, Marie-Hélène, and of Jean Dastè, his son-in-law, with whom he collaborated in the war years at Grenoble. In Padua, Jacques Lecoq met Amleto Sartori, a meeting that will forever be associated with the rediscovery of the mask. Also, in the first years after the war the Company Fo-Durano-Parenti was born in Milan. A trio of extraordinary actors, among whom Franco Parenti was the most experimental: the *Brighella* to Moretti's *Arlecchino* in the Piccolo Teatro's *Il servitore di due padroni*. They also collaborated with Jacques Lecoq and with Amleto Sartori. This original nucleus of artists, researchers, and teachers, at first only collaborated with each other, but later they did so with other artists from other geographical areas: Vito Pandolfi, Alessandro Fersen and Leo De Berardinis, and these collaborations became the roads along which Commedia dell'Arte spread through Italy in the twentieth and twenty-first centuries.

Particular attention should be paid to the figure of Carlo Boso, formerly an apprentice from the Piccolo Teatro of Milan, and to the experiments, from 1978 to 1994, of TAG Teatro from Mestre (TAG stood for *Teatro alla Giustizia,* Theatre of Justice, from the name of the road in Mestre where the company was based), situated immediately adjacent to Venice but on the mainland. The company, founded by Alessandro Bressanello, with the direction of Carlo Boso, contributed in a definitive manner to the circulation of the Commedia dell'Arte in Italy and beyond. Producing a series of shows to great acclaim nationally and internationally, (including *Il falso Magnifico* 1983, *L'assedio della Serenissima* 1984, *Scaramuccia* 1986, *La pazzia d'Isabella* 1989) TAG became the genetic nucleus of a good, precise model of production and a focus for actors, directors, and pedagogues.

Parallel to TAG, and in the same period, the Italian company *Les Scalzacani* was born in Paris, also under the direction of Carlo Boso, that would contribute to the diffusion of a model already tested in the sixteenth century, a Commedia dell'Arte regenerated from the post-Second World War experimentation. (The following continental actors, working with Boso in TAG and Scalzacani are also involved in the dissemination of Commedia throughout the world: Eleonora Fuser, Eugenio Allegri, Giorgio Bertan, Adriano Iurissevich, Marco Paolini, Mirko Artuso Enrico Bonavera, Luca Franceschi, Giusy Zaccagnini, Alberto Nasson, Dimma Vezzani, Luca Franceschi, Fabio Mangolini [the author] and Michele Modesto Casarin.)

The regeneration of the *praxis* was accompanied by the ever-growing interest on the part of the academic world: attentive to the productive processes, to the poetics, to the creation of live theatre, not to mention historiographical surveys fed by new ideas, research, and a public and wider interest. This academic interest came from such scholars as Ludovico Zorzi, Umberto Artioli, Paolo Puppa; from the "Roman school", Ferruccio Marotti, Ferdinando Taviani, and Fabrizio Cruciani; from Florence, Cesare Molinari and Siro Ferrone; from Turin, Roberto Tessari and Ambrogio Artoni; from Bologna, Claudio Meldolesi, Marco De Marinis, Gerardo Guccini and Elena Tamburini; and, from Bergamo, Anna Maria Testaverde.

Similarly, and in a widespread manner, starting from the 1990s, major national theatrical academies and drama schools began integrating Commedia dell'Arte training into their *cursus studiorum*. A type of pedagogy is developing that makes the Commedia dell'Arte a cornerstone of the transmission of both an actor's knowledge and of his skills. Commedia dell'Arte was taken on by the schools for its capacity to continue the process of constant revision, and to thwart the sclerotic potential of it simply becoming a museum piece. This tying in to the school training system, seen as official theatrical rectitude, makes the study of Commedia dell'Arte no longer merely the study of a theatricality lost to the world or a mythical and legendary subject for recovery, but a living entity carrying within it the capacity for generation and regeneration. In essence, today the Commedia dell'Arte permeates Italian theatre, which absorbs it, and in turn pervades it in a process of constant osmosis. The experiments carried out in these last few years demonstrate the renewed creativity within so many young actresses and actors, frequently just coming out of important theatre schools, as well as already established actresses and actors. They are all practitioners that rely on the Commedia dell'Arte to offer models of production suitable for contributing to the re-launch of a theatre putting itself back in contact with its audience.

The competition I giovani e la Commedia dell'Arte (Youth and the Commedia dell'Arte) happens every spring in Mantua in the evocative background of the historic Teatro Bibiena. It is, without a doubt, a formidable opportunity to see the work of young actresses and actors, often already associated with companies. The twelve competing submissions include diverse interpretive possibilities, evolutions of acquired styles, extremely striking innovations, both stylistic and dramaturgical, that render the Commedia a "phenomenology" in constant evolution.

In addition to companies that dedicate themselves to Commedia dell'Arte (e.g. Pantakin of Venice, Veneziainscena, Hellequin of Pordenone, Santibriganti of Turin, Fraternal Compagnia of Bologna, TeatroVivo di Ravenna), of great interest is *One Man, Two Guvnors* by Richard Bean, liberally based on *Il servitore di due padroni* (See Chapter 52). Adapting the Goldoni classic for the skills and abilities of the company's actors (who are also singers, acrobats, and musicians), the staging hinges on a serial recombination of forms and visual routines completed, conceived, and physically staged according to a maximum comic-sensual impact. The same business model, then, exists in the character of an established repertory company (in this case the National Theatre of Great Britain), as it does in smaller, bolder groups. With Commedia, a company business model is often as enterprising and innovative as it is traditional. The Commedia dell'Arte in Italy today is developing, not only through research, but also by a kind of continuity that has grabbed hold of the elements of a theatrical phenomenon from a specific place and time in history – that is, mask, improvisation, playwriting, and business – and these elements are all reproduced in contemporary forms of theatricality. In this way, and certainly not merely on the outer surface, the Commedia dell'Arte, though supported by hypothetical and normative codes mostly at random, maintains its vitality.

References

Hobsbawm, Eric and Ranger, Terence (1983) *The Invention of Tradition*, Cambridge, UK; Melbourne, Australia; Madrid; New York: Cambridge University Press.

Strehler, Giorgio and Grassi, Paolo (1962) *Marcello Moretti*, Milan, Italy: Piccolo Teatro edizioni.

Tessari, Roberto (2013) *La Commedia dell'Arte*, Bari, Italy: Laterza.

Testaverde, Anna Maria (ed.) (2007) *I Canovacci della Commedia dell'Arte*, Turin, Italy: Einaudi.

43

DARIO FO AND THE COMMEDIA DELL'ARTE

Antonio Scuderi

The Italian playwright and performer Dario Fo (b. 1926) is one of the most important figures in contemporary world theatre. His career began in the early 1950s and spans over half a century. By the 1980s some were proclaiming him the most widely performed living playwright in the world. In 1997 he was awarded the Nobel Prize for literature, which further advanced his popularity and influence. To date, he is still active as a writer, a performer, and a visual artist. His plays, translated into many languages, are still widely performed today and his influence continues into the new century.

Over the years, assisted by his wife and long-time collaborator, actress Franca Rame (1928–2013), Fo developed a unique and idiomatic way of creating and presenting theatre. His first engagement as a professional performer was storytelling for a Radio programme called *Poer nano* (poor sod). He went on to perform in many different venues (some of which will be mentioned below), almost always performing his own material. His primary modes of performance are the satirical farce, which represents the bulk of his oeuvre, and the *giullarata*, a unique type of solo performance. In the latter, without costumes or props, Fo holds audiences spellbound as he simultaneously narrates and acts, accompanied by his remarkable gestural language. Fo's involvement with theatre goes beyond his accomplishments as a playwright and actor. He directs, designs sets and costumes, and choreographs for his own productions as well as for Rossini operas, which have been produced in various European cities.

Dario Fo has often been associated with the Commedia dell'Arte and many consider him one of the primary torchbearers of the tradition. This is despite the fact that he has rarely performed anything that might be considered pure Commedia. There are, however, a few important exceptions. He has taught workshops on playing Commedia stock characters. In 1985 he donned the motley and played the most famous zanni in a series of sketches he called *Hellequin, Harlekin, Arlecchino*. Throughout the years, he continued to perform sketches from *Arlecchino*. There is also Fo's theatrical versatility to consider, mentioned above, which is also a connection to the Commedia (as well as to other forms of Italian popular theatre). The Commedia was an "actor's theatre," where the actors would participate in all the tasks required for production. Besides these few examples, there seems to be little to directly connect him with the tradition, and some scholars refute this notion altogether (cf. Fido 1995). To this we must add that Fo has been influenced by many European playwrights, as well as by oral and popular traditions. Each instance is worthy of a study in itself. The question of Fo's relation to the Commedia is therefore very complex.

A comedy continuum

In order to understand how Dario Fo connects to the Commedia tradition, his view of Western comedy must be taken into consideration. In Fo's view there is a strain of farcical/satirical comedy that has its roots in prehistoric ritual (the carnival, discussed subsequently) and runs as a continuum throughout European history. From this perspective, the Commedia dell'Arte is but one phase of the continuum that connects what came before to what came after it. For Fo the most important tradition that came before the Commedia is that of the medieval street performers. These were itinerant players who entertained in a variety of ways, including acting, music, dance, acrobatics and so forth. Over the centuries this type of performer was referred to by many names. In this study we will employ the Italian word Fo uses: *giullare* (pl. *giullari*). The tradition of the *giullari* was the *giulleria*. (Since the English cognate "juggler" is too restrictive in meaning, English borrowed "jongleur" from French.)

Fo contends that "there is no way of knowing exactly when the activity of the *giullari* ended and that of the Commedia dell'Arte took over" (Fo 1987: 98). When the Commedia began to fade in the eighteenth century, it informed a number of popular traditions, including pantomime, variety theatre, and circus clowning. Fo groups these traditions together in what he calls *teatro minore* or "minor theatre."

Before we try to make sense of Fo's view of the Commedia, we have to consider two types of historical evidence: written and oral. The end of the Commedia dell'Arte's heyday and its subsequent metamorphoses into various forms of *teatro minore* happened late enough to be well documented. The more difficult task is making sense of what came before the Commedia, especially in traditions that left little or no written record. The Commedia dell'Arte represents a confluence of various performance traditions. For those traditions that were written, the extant textual evidence often provides compelling verification or even "proof" of their influence. Others were passed on from generation to generation in an oral tradition, by mostly illiterate people. The latter presents a problem, because the records we have of them are scanty and indirect, mostly based on: written descriptions of their performances; iconography, depicting performances; and speculation based on the nature of later, related traditions. Let us consider as examples the evidence of both a written and an oral form of ancient Roman comedy: the *palliata* and mime respectively.

The Commedia began during the Italian Renaissance, when many scholars were rediscovering the classical culture of Greece and Rome. An important part of this process entailed the search for ancient manuscripts. Around 1427 twelve plays by the Roman playwright Titus Maccius Plautus (*c.*254–184 BCE) were discovered. The type of comedy Plautus wrote was called the *palliata*, which means "in Greek dress." This discovery was, in great part, the impetus for the tradition known as Erudite Comedy, where men of letters (not necessarily playwrights by trade) would write comic plays, inspired by their classical comic antecedents. There is plenty of evidence from written records that demonstrates that Erudite Comedy was a key element in the formation of the Commedia in the mid-1500s. Therefore, it is no coincidence, for example, that the three principal categories of Commedia characters, *vecchi* (old men), *innamorati* (young lovers), and zanni (servants) line up with the Roman *senes* (old men), *juvenes* (youths), and *servi* (slaves).

Now let us take an example of an oral tradition. A form of popular street performance in ancient Rome was the mime (not to be confused with our notion of mime). Although we have no textual proof that tells us how long the Roman mime continued after the fall of the empire, nor of its influence on the Commedia, there are some uncanny similarities. Like the Commedia companies, the Roman mime was performed by small troupes of travelling players led by a principal actor known as the *archimimus*, similar to the Commedia's *capocomico*. And "like *Commedia dell'Arte* these performances were largely improvisational with a plot outline devised by the *Archimimus*, who would roughly assign dialogue sequences (scenes) for the other players to *ad lib*" (Fantham 1989: 154–5). These scenes often involved cuckolded old men and young lovers, like in the early Commedia. Another similarity is that in the Roman mime women's roles were played by women.

Some scholars speculate that the Roman mime continued in the rich tradition of popular medieval performance, i.e. the *giulleria*, and may be one of the various traditions that informed the Commedia dell'Arte (Beacham 1991: 200). However, with no written evidence or proof of a direct link, it is up to the individual scholar to decide whether or not he or she accepts the similarities as evidence of a connection. This is important because Dario Fo—in great part due to the influence of the Italian Marxist scholar Antonio Gramsci (1891–1937)—is a champion of folk and popular culture. He is convinced that all forms of art originated in popular culture, itself based primarily on the oral tradition. "Official culture," the culture of those in power, appropriated many aspects of folk culture, and claimed them as their own (Fo 1993). Fo is therefore inclined to accept most evidence, beyond extant texts, indicating that various forms of ancient performance continued with the *giulleria* and informed the Commedia dell'Arte.

Whereas many scholars of the Commedia focus on the more famous companies that performed in the noble courts all over Europe, Fo emphasizes its roots in popular tradition. Even at the time of the Commedia, the more refined players looked down upon *giullari* and piazza performers, and calling another player a *giullare* was an insult. But Fo's "preference is for those who adopted a popular approach and performed in the piazza, as against those who adopted a more aesthetic or aristocratic style and accepted invitations to court" (Farrell 1989:318). In fact, Fo states that the Commedia dell'Arte "never existed... in the way it has always been presented to us" (1987: 7). He believes that the Commedia itself had elements akin to popular theatre that many scholars would rather ignore, such as "clowning, horseplay, acrobatic tumbles, and vulgarity that are associated in the twentieth century with low farce" (Farrell 2000: 83).

The same popular-versus-official controversies that surround the *giulleria* and the Commedia hold true for the Commedia-derived pantomime, clowning, and other forms of *teatro minore*. Allardyce Nicoll argues that Commedia-derived traditions—such as the Harlequinade in England, the Pierrot tradition in France "as cultivated by Deburau," and the Pulcinella tradition in Naples—represent "three tattered remnant relics" which do not "preserve more than a faint memory of that from which they sprang." He expresses a certain element of contempt when he contends that certain books of the early twentieth century "submerged the commedia dell'arte within the wastes of pantomime and circus" (1963: 217, 219), whereas for Fo the *teatro minore* is simply a continuation of the Commedia, and he rejects any sense that one is inherently more refined and valid than the other.

Fo's first stage performances in the 1950s were with I dritti (the stand-ups), which included Franco Parenti and Giustino Durano. I dritti performed satirical sketches in the tradition of *teatro minore*, akin to an Italian form of variety theatre known as *avanspettacolo*. The great French mime, Jacques Lecoq, worked with I dritti and coached Fo in performance movement. Later, Fo and Rame worked with the Colombaioni clowns in *Throw the Lady Out* (1967). Thus when Fo employs gestural language (akin to pantomime), *grammelot* (the art of pretending to speak without words), and a host of other techniques and tricks that were passed on from the Commedia to the *teatro minore*, he believes he is connecting directly to the Commedia, to the *giulleria*, and beyond.

The carnival and Fo's theatre

The tradition that underlies and connects the Roman *palliata*, the *giulleria*, the Commedia dell'Arte, *teatro minore*, and other related traditions is the carnival. Early on in his career, Dario Fo was influenced by the works of the Italian anthropologist and folklorist, Paolo Toschi (1893–1974). Toschi traces the Commedia dell'Arte back to the carnival, which in turn originates in prehistoric fertility and propitiatory rites of the original Indo-European people. He argues that the prehistoric celebration at the basis of the carnival was a communal rite of passage meant to assure the return of the sun and a good harvest. Over the millennia it took various forms and was marked at different times of the year, but certain basic principles and shared elements remained. Toschi's seminal work on the carnival, *Le origini del teatro italiano* (the origins of Italian theatre), was originally published in 1955. It is very probable that Fo was also influenced in the 1960s by the Russian philosopher and literary critic, Mikhail Bakhtin. His book *Rabelais and His World* (1984) defines the nature of the *carnivalesque*—the carnival spirit of subversion of social structures and norms—and remains as a primary tool for analyzing the influence of the carnival in the European culture of the medieval and Renaissance periods. Specific aspects of the origins of the carnival must be addressed in order to appreciate how Fo connects it to the Commedia (see Scuderi 2011: 53–76).

A principal feature of the carnival is the temporary suspension of social order. During the carnival period, all the members of a given community were on equal terms. This probably did not present much of a problem for the primary Indo-European societies of prehistoric times, which were most likely egalitarian. Later on, however, in the very stratified society of ancient Rome—with slaves, plebeians, and patricians—suspending the social order became more problematic. Those in power tried to control and regulate the situation by imposing rules and interdicts to keep things from getting out of hand. The Roman carnival was called the Saturnalia, and it was during this period that the *palliatae* were permitted to be performed. Although they were set in Greece as a thinly veiled disclaimer, the *palliatae* presented a rollicking satire of Roman society (Segal 1968: 31–8). Typically the fathers (*senes*) were tricked and their power subverted by their sons (*juvenes*), assisted by their wily slaves (*servi*). This undermined the very basis of the strict, paternalistic Roman social structure.

At the centre of the European carnival is the selection of a Carnival King, who rules over the festivities. He reigns during the suspension of social order, and is the original Lord of Misrule. As a form of scapegoat, he takes on the sins and trespasses of the community, and at the end of the carnival period he is "executed." We know that as late as the Roman period, in certain communities, the execution was real, and that with time it became a symbolic execution. An important point for this study is that, during the period of festivities, the Carnival King is permitted to criticize the community, in essence, to speak the truth.

During the Middle Ages, the carnival, with its suspension of social order, increasingly presented an opportunity for the downtrodden to criticize and vent their anger towards their oppressors. This sometimes led to violent clashes and there were many laws and decrees attempting to control this aspect of the carnival. Certain carnivalesque activities continued year-round, and permission to speak the truth and criticize society passed on to "the fool," a role that was taken on by the *giullare*. This aspect of the *giullare* gave us icons such as the court jester and the fool in Shakespeare. The *giullare*/fool was often a key character in a host of carnivalesque celebrations, such as the Feast of Fools, and carnivalesque performances, such as the *sotie* (Fools' Play), where all characters including kings and popes were presented as fools.

This is essential to Fo's concept of political theatre as a vehicle for social change. As his career developed, particularly as he matured as a playwright and performer during the 1960s, he made an effort to associate himself and his theatre with various aspects of carnivalesque subversion. *Isabella, Three Sailing Ships and a Conman* (Fo 1966) could be considered a manifesto of Fo's intention to contextualize his theatre within a greater carnival frame and give it a new direction. *Isabella* is firmly framed by the carnival. The play takes place during the carnival period. An actor, originally played by Fo, has been condemned by the Inquisition. There is a chance that he may receive a pardon and he is granted the opportunity to perform a play. Using the gallows as a stage, he performs a play about Columbus in order to delay his execution. At the end, the actor is executed, much like the Carnival King, by a carnival/Commedia mask—a Pulcinella, dressed in black. His final performance could be taken as Carnival's last testament (Holm 2000: 133–5), a tradition we still see today in European carnival celebrations. (For more on Fo's carnival manifesto, see Scuderi 2011: 77–95.)

Fo conducted an intensive study of the medieval *giullari*. In 1969 he debuted his unique form of one-man show, the *giullarata*, with his masterpiece: a series of sketches he called *Mistero Buffo* (Fo 1977). Based on traditional storytelling techniques in oral traditions found throughout the world, Fo narrates a tale while acting out all of the parts. He also employs various techniques that connect to the

Commedia, some of which will be discussed below. Fo accompanied his original performances of *Mistero Buffo* with slide shows and discourses, explaining various aspects of the *giulleria*. It was obviously an attempt to associate himself with the *giullare* and his carnivalesque attributes, including leave to speak the truth and criticize society. There is an aspect of Fo's theatre that must be mentioned, but for which space does not permit extensive explication. He is rigorous in his research, but will blatantly *re-present* history in order to give his performances more gravitas. In a sense, his whole career, along with its historical distortions, can be taken as one ongoing performance (Scuderi 2011: 35–52). With this last point there should now be sufficient background for an analysis of how the various strands of carnival-derived comedy Fo draws from connect his theatre to the Commedia dell'Arte.

Playing the fool

If the primary function of Dario Fo's theatre is to deliver social and political satire that challenges the powers that be, then the connection to the Commedia dell'Arte is not immediately apparent. Franco Fido points out that "Commedia actors did not harbor any particular political goals or ambitions, which, among other things, explains their extraordinary popularity at the major courts of Europe" (1995:305). Viewing the Commedia in the usual way, by focusing on the preeminent companies, this statement cannot be disputed. Fo's perspective however, encompasses "what might be called the circumambient 'culture' of the commedia dell'arte, extending from the court performer to the piazza mountebank" (Henke 2002: 2). Considering the Commedia from this comprehensive viewpoint, one does not lose sight of its roots in the carnival, of secondary companies, and of street and piazza players. In all of these there are clown figures with links to the clever *servus* of the *palliata*, the *giullare*, the fool, and of course the zanni—all informed by the pervading spirit of the carnivalesque. Bakhtin states, "Clowns and fools… were the constant, accredited representatives of the carnival spirit in everyday life out of carnival season" (1984: 8). Fo argues that players of the early Commedia and of the less prestigious Commedia troupes were more subversive than their refined colleagues in the famous companies. This may very well be true, but perhaps the more important point is that a stock character, such as Arlecchino, embodies carnivalesque subversion, even if limited to the social and dramatic structures and conventions presented in the context of a given scenario. Fo tapped into this power and developed it as one of the most important components and effective satirical devices of his theatre.

An element of certain zanni, such as Arlecchino, is a calculated type of madness, that of the fool (Fr. *sot*). Pulcinella, for example, is sometimes referred to as a *finto tonto* (fake idiot). We find this register of madness in Dario Fo's most famous play, *Accidental Death of an Anarchist*, based on the circumstances surrounding Giuseppe Pinelli, who died while in police custody in 1969. The central character is Il Matto (It. the madman or fool), originally played by Fo. Il Matto infiltrates police headquarters and through his zany antics he unmasks the absurdity of the official account of the anarchist's demise for the audience. At one point, after trying to reason with him, the exasperated police commissioner defines Il Matto's *finto tonto* nature: "Cut the crap! I'm beginning to believe that you really do have a mania for role-playing, but that you're also playing at being mad when instead you're saner than me, I bet" (Fo 1988: 10). The "role-playing" refers to Il Matto's "histriomania" (ibid.: 7), which allows him to take on various roles at will. This ability to self-transform is akin to the *versipellis* (Lt. skin-changer) quality found in the clever *servi* of the *palliatae*, who "may themselves adopt one of the other stock roles of Roman comedy" (Slater 2000: 12). Fo also attributes this quality to Arlecchino, "who can transform himself into anything: a stupid or clever servant, a judge, a woman, a donkey, a cat" (1986: 35). Like the medieval *sotie* plays, in which authority figures were presented as fools, Il Matto plays the roles of three authority figures in succession: a judge, a police captain, and a bishop. Employing the device of a *sot* playing an authority figure in his plays, Fo has taken on the role of more than one Italian prime minister (such as Amintore Fanfani and Silvio Berlusconi) and even popes—Boniface VIII in *Mistero Buffo* and John Paul II in *The Pope and the Witch*.

Playing the *maschera*

The acting technique of playing a role while remaining a fool is inherent to the *maschera*, the mask/stock character of the Commedia dell'Arte. One of the most intriguing aspects of Toschi's work is his evidence of how the Commedia stock characters—the zanni and the vecchi (taken together as *parti ridicoli*)—derive from carnival ritual. Toschi and other scholars of the carnival point out that in the cosmology of many primary societies, the suspension of social norms also implied the suspension of cosmic order. This allowed for beings of the otherworld to visit during the carnival period. These beings were represented in the carnival rites by community members wearing grotesque and zoomorphic masks. In old Germanic and Gallic languages a masked figure of the carnival was a *talamasca*, from which Toschi and others trace the origin of the word *maschera* (and its cognates, such as the English "mask") (Toschi 1976: 170; Walter 2006: 74–5). Toschi's original publication of *Gli origini* has plates presenting iconographic evidence for the connection of the carnival to the Commedia. The juxtaposition of a prehistoric carnival mask and one of the earliest masks of Arlecchino is striking (Toschi 1955: np, pages with plates are not numbered).

In Italian *maschera* denotes both a physical mask and a stock character, even if that character does not wear a mask. Playing a *maschera*—a character with fixed and often exaggerated qualities and characteristics—requires a certain type of performance. More than "getting into character" (in the Stanislavskian sense), the actor presents the character to the audience. Fo was originally introduced to a similar type of playing by the works of Berthold Brecht and Erwin Piscator, who developed what they called Epic Theatre. Fo later concluded that this type of acting is found in many popular traditions, in Roman theatre (where physical masks were used), and in the Commedia dell'Arte. In an interview he explained his theory of *maschera* acting:

> It's the ability to remain detached from the play: I am an actor who narrates something. I am not a pedestrian imitation, but rather he who tells about a character that is not me. The *maschera* means that inside I am a man. The

maschera is something external, it's fake. Don't you see that I am not a real person? I'm fake. What is real is inside that which I narrate to you.

(Fo 1993)

Fo developed a style of acting in which he never gets into character, thus allowing him, at any moment, to comment on the play. This type of *metatheatre*, for example, was very much an aspect of the *palliata*, where asides and remarks on the play itself were written right into the text (see Moore 1998). In the *palliata* this was done for comic effect. But for Fo it primarily serves the purpose of keeping the focus off the characters and on the story and its political and social messages. This type of acting "breaks the fourth wall"; in other words, the actors play directly to the audience. Viewing the filmed performances of famous Arlecchini, such as Mario Moretti and Feruccio Soleri, one can note this type of performance. By giving credence to the mechanisms of the oral tradition, we may surmise that this technique has been passed on through the generations to later Arlecchini, as well as to *teatro minore*.

Late in his career, Fo demonstrated his skill with a tour de force of this acting method in a satire of Italian Prime Minister Silvio Berlusconi, entitled *The Two-Headed Anomaly*, which was first performed in 2003 (Fo 2004). Fo plays a director who is making a film about Berlusconi, while Franca Rame plays an actress auditioning for a part. Fo and Rame avoid getting fully into character and break character frequently (sometimes indicated in the stage directions), in order to keep the focus on the political message (see Scuderi 2005 and 2011: 15–26). Thus Fo takes a style or method of acting—found in many forms of popular theatre and akin to what we imagine would have been used in the Commedia dell'Arte—and adapts it to his sense of purpose. By not getting into character, but rather playing in a style akin to a *maschera*, he demonstrates how he and Rame can freely move from one character to another.

Improvisation

A defining quality of the Commedia dell'Arte was improvisation. The actors did not memorize a written text, but rather based their performances on a skeletal structure, known as a scenario or a *canovaccio*. Richard Andrews explains that in seventeenth-century France, "improvisation on a scenario was prized in its own right as the supremely Italian art of theatre. It was respectable because it was difficult [and] because it reached a high level of specialist virtuosity" (1989: 146). This admiration for *Commedia all'Italiana*, as the Commedia was originally called, was shared in many other parts of Europe at the time. Since this and related techniques are to be found in oral and popular traditions around the world, the logical explanation for its use in the Commedia is that it derived from oral performance traditions, related to the *giulleria*. Early Commedia players—whether literate, illiterate, or semiliterate—continued a tradition that had originated in street and piazza performances.

Fo learned a great deal about improvisation from Franca Rame's family. For generations the Rames had been puppeteers, and sometime in the 1920s they switched to live theatre performances. In either case the technique of improvisation was employed. In an interview, Rame explained how they would develop and perform a play in this fashion. Her uncle would read a novel and gather the family around to tell the story. The key moments of the narrative, such as—"father meets daughter, acts coldly towards her, remembers death of her mother" were recorded. These were then written on outlines or charts called *scalette* (lists) that were placed in the wings. Each actor would consult the chart in the wing before his/her entrance (Rame 1993). Fo was able to read through the Rame family's archive of scenarios and notes, which for him were a treasure trove. Later, in the 1960s, he collaborated with a company who specialized in Italian folk music, Nuovo Canzoniere Italiano. This experience added to Fo's understanding of oral and oral-derived performances. (For more on oral and oral-derived performances, see Bauman 1984 and Foley 1995.)

The key for analyzing improvisation in oral performance (music, etc.) was provided by the study of Serbo-Croatian epic ballad singers by Milman Parry (1902–35) and his student Albert Lord (1912–91). Parry and Lord's works explore how the oral performer contextualizes preconceived units, originally called *formulas*. (Fitzpatrick 1995 is a study of the use of formulas in Commedia improvisation.)

For the purpose of analysis, the unit or formula must be defined for each type of performance being studied. Taking the simple example provided by Franca Rame, "father meets daughter" can be considered a unit or formula to be contextualized on stage. With improvisation, the results of how the units are contextualized generally vary from performance to performance. The variations can include: the order in which the units are presented; the actual words used to convey the idea; and the length or duration, which is often determined by audience response.

Fo intuited the mechanisms for improvisation in popular performances and employs them skillfully. His virtuosity in improvisation by far was developed in his solo performance, the *giullarata*. With audio and video recordings available, it is possible to compare how different performances of the same play vary as he improvises on preconceived units (see Scuderi 1998: 57–62). His Nobel acceptance speech in Stockholm was in part a demonstration of improvisational abilities. Instead of the conventional and expected scripted text, he handed out a series of drawings (which amounted to his units or formulas). "Then he launched into the speech, extemporizing as he referred to the same pages that the audience was regarding" (Heintz 1997). Once again, Fo employed an aspect of the Commedia dell'Arte but approached it as a quality shared by other related traditions.

Accepting Dario Fo's relation to the Commedia dell'Arte requires a broader view of the tradition in its historical context. It must comprehend the traditions of ritual and theatre that preceded and informed it, in particular Roman Saturnalian comedy, medieval carnivalesque celebrations and performances, and the *giulleria*. Fo's take on the Commedia rejects an emphasis on the loftier, renowned companies, and accepts the validity of the many players who moved freely from minor Commedia companies to smaller popular venues. His view must also comprehend the various forms of Commedia-derived *teatro minore*, such as pantomime, circus clowning, and variety theatre. Accepting this broader scope, in which many of the aforementioned traditions share the techniques and mechanisms of popular and oral performance, one can understand the connection between Dario Fo and the Commedia dell'Arte.

Note: All translations are by the author unless otherwise noted.

References

Andrews, R. (1989) "Arte Dialogue Structures in the Comedies of Molière," in Christopher Cairns (ed.) *The Commedia dell'Arte: From the Renaissance to Dario Fo*. Lewiston, US: The Edwin Mellen Press. 142–58.

Bakhtin, M. (1984) *Rabelais and His World*. Hélène Iswolsky (tr.), Bloomington, US: Indiana UP.

Bauman, R. (1984) *Verbal Art as Performance*, 2nd ed., Prospect Heights, IL, US: Waveland Press.

Beacham, R. (1991) *The Roman Theatre and its Audience*, Cambridge, US: Harvard University Press.

Fantham, E. (1989) "Mime: The Missing Link in Roman Literary History," *The Classical World*. 82.3: 153–63.

Farrell, J. (1989) "Dario Fo: *Zanni* and *Giullare*," in Christopher Cairns (ed.) *The Commedia dell'Arte: From the Renaissance to Dario Fo*. Lewiston, US: The Edwin Mellen Press. 315–29.

——(2000) "Fo and Ruzzante: Debts and Obligations," in J. Farrell and A. Scuderi (eds) *Dario Fo: Stage, Text and Tradition*. Carbondale, US: Southern Illinois UP. 80–100.

Fido, F. (1995) "Dario Fo e la Commedia dell'Arte," *Italica*, 72.3: 298–306.

Fitzpatrick, T. (1995) *The Workings of the Commedia dell'Arte: Oral and Literate Performance Processes*, Lewiston, US: The Edwin Mellen Press.

Fo, D. (1966) "Isabella, tre caravelle e un cacciaballe," in D. Fo, *Le commedie di Dario Fo*, 1966–98, vol 2, Turin, Italy: Einaudi. 2–86.

——(1977) "Mistero buffo," in D. Fo, *Le commedie di Dario Fo*, 1966–98, vol 5, Turin, Italy: Einaudi. 5–171.

——(1986) "Arlecchino è il paradosso," *Ulisse 2000*, 29 (Feb/Mar) 35.

——(1987) *Manuale minimo dell'attore*, Franca Rame (ed.) Turin, Italy: Einaudi.

——(1988) "Morte accidentale di un anarchico," in D. Fo, *Le commedie di Dario Fo*, 1966–98. Vol. 7, Turin, Italy: Einaudi. 5–83.

——(1993) Interviews with Antonio Scuderi, October, Milan, Italy.

——(2004) *L'Anomalo Bicefalo*, in *MicroMega* (supplement), N.2, April–May. Rome: Gruppo Editoriale L'Espresso.

Foley, J. M. (1995) *The Singer of Tales in Performance*, Bloomington, US: Indiana University Press.

Heintz, J. (1997) "Nobel Prize Winner Dario Fo Gives Manic, Unorthodox Prize Lecture," *The Associated Press*, 9 December.

Henke, R. (2002) *Performance and Literature in the Commedia dell'Arte*, Cambridge, UK: Cambridge University Press.

Holm, B. (2000) "Dario Fo's 'Bourgeois Period': Carnival and Criticism," in J. Farrell and A. Scuderi (eds) *Dario Fo: Stage, Text and Tradition*. Carbondale, US: Southern Illinois University Press. 122–42.

Moore, T. (1998) *The Theater of Plautus: Playing to the Audience*, Austin, US: University of Texas Press.

Nicoll, A. (1963) *The World of Harlequin*, Cambridge, UK: Cambridge University Press.

Rame, F. (1993) Interviews with Antonio Scuderi, October, Milan, Italy.

Scuderi, A. (1998) *Dario Fo and Popular Performance*, Ottawa: Legas.

——(2005) "Metatheatre and Character Dynamics in *The Two-Headed Anomaly* by Dario Fo," *New Theatre Quarterly*. 21.1: 13–22.

——(2011) *Dario Fo: Framing, Festival, and the Folkloric Imagination*, Lanham, US: Lexington Books.

Segal, E. (1968) *Roman Laughter: The Comedy of Plautus*, Cambridge, US: Harvard University Press.

Slater, N. (2000) *Plautus in Performance: The Theatre of the Mind*, Newark, New Jersey, US: Harwood Academic Publishers.

Toschi, P. (1955) *Le origini del teatro italiano*, Turin, Italy: Einaudi.

——(1976) *Le origini del teatro italiano*, 2nd ed., 2 vols. Turin, Italy: Bollati Boringhieri.

Walter, P. (2006) *Christianity: The Origins of a Pagan Religion*, John E. Graham (tr.), Rochester, Vermont, US: Inner Traditions.

44

CARLO BOSO

Fear and laughter in popular theatre

Anna Cottis

The last 20 years have seen a huge expansion in the number of theatre schools and universities that teach Commedia dell'Arte as an ordinary core subject that theatre practitioners should know about. It is no longer necessary to go to the Piccolo Teatro School or to Lecoq to meet Commedia masks as part of basic training. However, the relevance of Commedia today is not always apparent to the students, or even to the teachers; it is sometimes taught as a historical Italian curiosity, worth knowing about and entertaining for a short workshop, but not something one can really put into practice.

Carlo Boso's work as an actor, teacher, writer, and director, in the field of Commedia, as well as classical and modern texts, is living proof of the contrary. In 40 years he has given over 120 professional Commedia workshops with more than 4,000 participants, created over 60 shows, and directed over 50 plays by other authors, all from a Commedia base. Early in his career he became fascinated by the capacity of Commedia to create theatre that portrays and appeals to all ranks of society, and through pursuing this became not only an important European Commedia trainer, but a promoter of a popular theatre aimed to be an integral part of democratic discourse. Boso's understanding of the function of theatre in society is similar to the ancient Greeks': theatre is a forum for a debate through story and character about how we should live together as a society. He sees Commedia dell'Arte as representing all social groups and the conflicts between them, and the Commedia actor as serving the public's need to see these conflicts played out and resolved convincingly. For Boso, this Commedia-derived understanding of the purpose of theatre is obviously applicable to non-Commedia texts: to make entertaining popular theatre that addresses our deepest fears and concerns and is, therefore, a necessary communal ritual.

Carlo Boso was born just after the Second World War in Vicenza, Italy, and moved to Milan with his family when he was 14. His father was a businessman, and, like many post-war children, Boso rebelled against parental example and decided to go into the theatre. Having seen their *Arlecchino, servitore di due padroni* with a school outing, in 1964 he entered the theatre school of the Piccolo Teatro in Milan, run at the time by Paolo Grassi and Giorgio Strehler, and in 1967 joined the company. The Piccolo Teatro and its associated artists had a fundamental influence on Boso's work. He worked with the company and its members on and off for over 12 years, in particular playing Pantalone opposite Ferruccio Soleri in his production of *Arlecchino, l'amore e la fame* for seven years.

The importance of the Piccolo Teatro di Milano for modern Commedia dell'Arte cannot be overstated. After the Second World War, Italian society was in crisis. Mussolini's fascism had divided the country and engendered enormous amounts of violence and repression, and, as in any society that has come through a period of civil conflict, a new way of existing together had to be found. For many of those involved in theatre, it was necessary to create a new kind of theatre that could bring together all parts of society, leading, amongst other things, to the founding of the Piccoli Teatri (small theatres) movement, which created the basis for a popular stage in Italy.

Strehler, Grassi and Nina Vinchi, the third founder of the Piccolo Teatro di Milano, wanted to create "Art theatre for everybody": fine productions for as wide an audience as possible. A kind of theatre seen as identifiably Italian that addressed all sectors of society was at hand: Commedia dell'Arte. Grassi, in particular, had an analysis of the purpose of theatre in society that was grounded in Commedia dell'Arte. There was a growing interest in Commedia in Italy: other artists involved at the time were Giovanni Poli, Dario Fo and Franca Rame, Donato Sartori, Jacques Lecoq and Carlo Mazzone-Clementi, to name but the more prominent of all those researching and experimenting. Before the war there were no Commedia troupes to speak of; as in the rest of Europe, there were remnants of Commedia in puppet shows, and some local forms based on one particular character – Pulcinella in Calabria, or Harlequinades in seaside towns in England for example – but no living tradition of Commedia. It is not unreasonable to say that Commedia was reinvented in post-war Italy.

Grassi and Strehler played major parts in this re-invention. Before founding the Piccolo Teatro theatre school in 1951, with Jacques Lecoq, with Commedia dell'Arte as a basic discipline, in 1947 Grassi and Strehler created the iconic Commedia staging of *Arlecchino, servitore di due padroni* for the Piccolo Teatro (still touring the world today). For many thousands of people, this production is their only experience of Commedia dell'Arte.

This was the case for Carlo Boso before entering the Piccolo school. Then, in 1965, as a second-year student, he played a zanni in a summer production of *La Veneziana* directed by Giovanni Poli in the Biennale di Teatro, Venice. Poli was deeply engaged in the recovery and rebirth of Commedia dell'Arte and Boso also began to see Commedia as having huge potential, not only through learning from and observing Poli, but also through observing the audience's reactions to the show and their enthusiasm for it. He also had his first inkling that Commedia had relevance beyond Italy. As at any festival, the artists went to see each other's shows, and Boso was struck by the respect international artists had for Commedia dell'Arte.

> The Living Theatre were there: everybody was talking about them. And then Julien Beck and his actors came into our dressing-room after our show

– they wanted to see the masks. He said that with these, through dramatic action you can provoke laughter – through fear.

(Boso 2013)

This confirmed Boso's emerging view that laughter serves to liberate the audience's fears, and that a mask is a ritual object that helps to evoke these fears.

If Poli gave Boso a vision of Commedia and how it might exist today, Strehler and his Arlecchino, Soleri, gave him discipline and understanding of timing. A few years after the Biennale, Boso was on tour with the Piccolo Teatro, understudying Soleri as Arlecchino and playing the porter, as well as playing in the other two shows they toured. On tour Soleri would continually be re-rehearsing scenes, with Soleri capable of rehearsing a two-minute exchange for three hours until the timing and the use of the mask was exactly right. Boso learnt a great respect for the efficacy of precision mask work for producing a reaction in the audience. The troupe were playing in front of audiences that spoke no Italian, yet still laughed in the same places every night.

This also marked the beginnings of a concern that runs through all of Boso's work, a concern to understand what the public is reacting to when watching theatre and why. Where Soleri's interest was strongest in the technical detail, Boso was led towards dramaturgy and the question of what stories the public wants to see represented.

During the seventies, Boso started to use these experiences to develop his own ideas about Commedia. He was based in Milan, working occasionally with the Piccolo, touring Soleri's Commedia three-hander *Arlecchino, l'amore e la fame* in Europe and Latin America and directing his own shows. At the time, Milan was a very important centre for theatre in Europe according to mask maker Stefano Perocco, then also at the beginning of his career:

> Milan was a huge culture factory, the European capital of theatre. There was Dario Fo, Giovanni Poli, Strehler of course, and Grassi, Franco Parenti... but there was also Grotowski and Tadeusz Kantor. Everyone came to Milan – Brook, Mnouchkine. And there were a thousand little companies. There was an urgency to create popular theatre.
>
> (Perocco 2013)

It was in this hive of theatrical activity that Boso continued to direct shows and started giving Commedia workshops. He began to break with the Piccolo Teatro's highly choreographed style of Commedia and create his own, whilst using all that he had been able to observe from the audience's reactions to Commedia shows whilst touring. From the start he included other techniques in his Commedia workshops such as traditional dance and mime, all the while seeing Commedia as of necessity addressing contemporary issues and presenting the end-of-workshop shows in open public spaces. Initially he used scenes from Ruzzante and Goldoni for the workshops but soon turned to writing his own scenarios. Nelly Quette, the French specialist in traditional dance who has worked with him for over 30 years commented:

> Some people wanted to turn Commedia into something quaint ("folklorique" in the French) but Carlo didn't agree with this. He took the style and the chorus from Poli, the precision from Strehler and set out to rediscover a total theatre. A theatre bodily engaged with the audience. We knew we were pioneers.
>
> (Quette 2013)

This sensation of breaking new ground with Commedia was not unfounded. In 1983, after a workshop Boso gave in Venice, he began his collaboration with Tag Teatro di Venezia, a Venetian company that were already well-known for their Commedia shows. This collaboration of two artistic forces with experience and the desire to push the boundaries of Commedia brought them both international success. With a company of well-trained actors and Boso's skills in Commedia dramaturgy, Tag and Boso created Commedia shows, no longer from fully written texts by Goldoni or Ruzzante, but from *canovacci*, simple plot outlines, by Enrico Gherardi and Flaminio Scala. These shows, such as *Il Falso Magnifico* (1983), *Scaramuccia* (1987) and *La Pazzia D'Isabella* (1989), toured the world. They presented a more flexible vision of Commedia, different from the marvellous machine of Piccolo's "Arlecchino": Tag Teatro actors helped to develop the shows and were allowed to improvise.

This was in line with the view, which Boso shares, that Commedia is an actor's theatre, not an author's or director's. For Boso, the actor should have a certain autonomy: understanding the social situation of the character and what the audience expects and needs, the actor should be able to improvise easily and effectively in character.

During the collaboration with Tag, Boso became the theatrical programmer of the Carnival of Venice, taught large numbers of workshops and directed and wrote increasingly for other companies, both in Italy and abroad. However, Tag's last collaboration with Boso, *La Zingara*, in 1992, was not a success. The company was under-rehearsed, (in part due to Boso's lack of availability), in financial and internal trouble, and the tour damaged their international reputation as well as Boso's.

Boso's expectation that actors be autonomous and that the troupe should be able to understand the process and work without him, conflicted with the need of some of the actors for guidance and direction. This points up a problem with Boso's ideal of a self-reliant Commedia actor and the collective process of the troupe: actors today are trained to work with a text and a director, and learning to improvise and construct a show as a group is not necessarily simple. The troupe must find a way to introduce new members to the process and find ways to make artistic decisions collectively or the group will fail. Tag indeed went into liquidation in 1993, after funding difficulties and the lack of success of *La Zingara*.

However, there were numerous other companies wanting to work with Boso. He had been teaching and directing in France since 1979 and, after his last year at the Venice Carnival in 1994, left Italy for Paris. His range of influence continued to expand: he taught workshops, created Commedia shows and directed plays for companies in France, Italy, Spain and Belgium, and his shows began to be seen regularly at the Avignon Fringe Festival, with one venue, the Cour de Barouf, almost entirely dedicated to his work. These shows often enjoyed popular success, whether Commedia or Commedia-based, and some troupes that he worked with became enthusiastic long-standing collaborators, particularly where a troupe already had an actor-manager to run it. According to Guy Pion, director of the Theatre de l'Eveil, Belgium:

> We created *Arlequin* with Carlo in 1997 – it was a triumph. We played more than 150 times in three years. Since then we've worked together regularly. Carlo has real pedagogical force, and he likes transmitting his knowledge. He has such a profound understanding of the history of theatre, of Greek theatre, commedia, Shakespeare; you're always learning when you work with him.
>
> (Pion 2013)

This capacity for transmission, and frustration with the training of actors he encountered, led Boso to found a theatre school in 2005 with Danuta Zarazik; the *Académie Internationale des Arts du Spectacle* (AIDAS). The programme reflects what Boso considers essential in actor training: a thorough grounding in theatre techniques such as singing, mime, dance and stage-fighting, a large amount of experience in front of an audience and classes from international teachers. Given Boso's reputation as a Commedia master, students are sometimes surprised how little they study Commedia and mask. Boso replies that he is concerned with training professional actors that will be as rarely out of work as possible: "97% of theatre is not Commedia. Commedia trains the actor – you learn that you are there to represent the audience, not your own problems. After, you apply that to all the rest" (Boso 2013).

It can seem paradoxical: a Commedia master who does not teach much Commedia in his own school. Yet this springs from Boso's view of Commedia as absolutely fundamental to Western theatre, rather than a side-track; the importance of Commedia is not in studying a particular mask, but learning an approach to theatre that works with and for the audience as Commedia actors did.

The story of Commedia for Boso functions almost like a creation myth, from which how to make good theatre today can be deduced. As he tells it, Commedia actors and troupes had to fulfil a real need in society or go hungry. Studying Commedia teaches us to understand how a popular theatre works, and the actor's function is to serve the audience. The archetypes of Commedia between them represent the whole of society, and the actors have to evoke conflicts that the audience recognise and fears that the audience has, if they are to keep them involved. This is an absolute necessity for Boso, the raison d'être of theatre: "The audience pays to become less afraid. And laughter is the hysterical reaction to fear" (Boso 2013).

This preoccupation with the audience and the necessity of theatre stems from the teachings of Paolo Grassi and Boso's earliest days with Strehler's *Arlecchino, servitore di due padroni*. The actors were performing on stage – but Boso was watching the audience.

> Carlo became interested in the dramaturgy of Commedia dell'Arte as an answer to the question of how to capture the audience and how to play with

them. He believes in the great emotional charge of great archetypes. The actor is only the mouthpiece for what happens in the public.

(Quette 2013)

So for Boso, good Commedia tells stories that the audience needs to see. And it captivates the audience in non-verbal ways, through the physicality of the acting necessary to make the archetypes exist as characters: "The characters of Commedia are not credible. They are heroic and fantastic, and can only be seen as credible if the actor works hard, with a certain violence, if I may say, to nourish them" (Carlo Boso in Camerlain 1985: 69).

By this, Boso does not mean a uniquely intellectual process, but a combination of understanding of the social position of the character and a physical engagement with the archetype. The social position of the archetype defines their motivations and obsessions, and gives them characteristic ways of moving and reacting which are readable for the audience, and credible as being "in character". And the actor has access to these credible ways of moving, not through an intellectual process but because of their own somatic experience and animality. This speaks directly to the audience without passing through consciousness. As Stefano Perocco, his mask maker for over 30 years, says:

What the public find interesting in Commedia is its poverty: of text, of rationality. It has a lot of dynamism, and a lot of our animal side. You develop aggressiveness in a good way. And then once the audience is paying attention, you can play whatever stories you want. That's what's brilliant.

(Perocco 2013)

This is one of the reasons that Boso does not teach mask technique: he believes that if the actor is engaged physically in the body of the archetype they are representing, they will use the mask well and instinctively. This perhaps comes from his own experience as an actor – he himself has an exceptional physical memory and instinct:

We were with Tag at the Carnival of Venice in Piazza San Marco, doing *A Servant of Two Masters* and the Tag Truffaldino pulled a muscle. Carlo steps in and does it, line and move perfect, at 15 minutes' notice. Incredible.

(Crick 2013)

In his workshops, Boso gives a very brief account of the social situation of each character, and their positions and movements, a few indications of mask technique (such as keeping the head steady and looking regularly at the audience) and then steps back. The participants always discover the mask in situational improvisation, never as a character alone. There are always some people who put the mask on and instantly make it work without analysis, sometimes moving in ways that are not what Boso has told them – this does not matter to him as long as the character has an emotional reality on the stage. Those workshop participants who do not "click" with the mask simply do not play a masked character in the final presentations.

Indeed, Boso is renowned for working from the strengths and around the weaknesses of his workshop participants – one British workshop participant recalls:

> We were amazed by how he could create scenarios from scratch of such quality, and with a group of such variable ability: typecasting hopeless actors into roles that utterly integrated their hopelessness into a seamless dramatic scenario... sheer genius and inclusive to boot.
>
> (Crick 2013)

It should be understood that Boso sees Commedia as less about text than about emotionally charged exchanges of words, less about character than about relationships, less about actions than about reactions: "The body must be capable of transmitting a comprehensible reaction. Gestures are useless if you don't have the emotion. And the words are a sound applied to the emotion" (Boso 2013).

For Boso, the audience is engaged with the body of the actor, more than their words (a view I would argue is borne out by recent developments in neuroscience). But this body is not alone on stage. Boso is even more concerned with the actors working in chorus, whether in choral action, singing, dance, mime or group combat scenes, an interest which began with Giovanni Poli and runs through all his work.

Chantal David, long-time collaborator with Boso, director of the Bel Viaggio company and lecturer at the University of Nantes, France, sees the importance of the chorus for Boso as going beyond the stage:

> Some Commedia directors are very academic, very codified. Others go into the instinct of the mask – they are wild and untamed. With Carlo, what counts is the chorus, the rhythm. He will always push Commedia to create a chorus. In the Piccolo (school), it's the actor, the correct angle, the technique, you sweat a lot. Mnouchkine has something collective, ritual and sacred. But she doesn't enjoy it. Carlo watches you, he cracks up with laughter when you do something funny. But it's always the collective that counts. That's why he creates so many companies.
>
> (David 2013)

Indeed, one of the notable characteristics of Carlo's training workshops and his school is the number of companies that emerge from them, often beginning with a show he has created for them. The AIDAS takes its second- and third-year students' shows to Avignon, performing several shows a day, and the school encourages leaving third-years to form a company and tour the shows; the most successful so far being Teatro Picaro, Les Passeurs and Compagnie Avanti. Boso's idea of Commedia is also an idea of the Commedia actor: training actors to be able to manage themselves, through acquiring a strong knowledge of theatre techniques and an understanding of the function of theatre.

In some instances this idea fails; some years, the company formed does not survive. Some of the existing companies he works with need more support than he is willing to give them and the show does not hold together, as with the last show of Tag Teatro. But many do, particularly where there is an existing troupe that is looking to develop its work beyond working with an internal director, and one or more figureheads who hold the troupe together. In these cases, the respect the actors have for his understanding of the audience and dramaturgy is immense. Alain Bertrand, actor-manager of the Compagnie Alain Bertrand, France commented:

> At first I didn't know how to work with him. We had to manage a lot for ourselves. But once you have a good team that understands, it works like a dream. In our last show, *L'Avare*, there was a whole section that wasn't working. He came for one rehearsal and took out one thing I'd put in. It worked straight away. It took me 20 performances to understand why.
>
> (Bertrand 2013)

Boso has never been part of the established subsidised theatre. It is as though Boso feels that the French audience and establishment need to be trained to expect theatre to be enjoyable, whether with Commedia or other texts. His main motivation seems to be to work with as many companies as possible and spread an idea of popular theatre that is grounded in Commedia. His influence is quite visible in France: in the last 15 years, the number of Commedia shows at the Avignon festival and in provincial theatres has hugely increased, and it is now not uncommon to see Molière plays with masks and polyphonic singing – something that in earlier times would have been "desecrating the text". La Compagnie du Mystère Bouffe, one of the first French companies he worked with, still tours original Commedia shows, and has a workshop programme that teaches Commedia to hundreds of children each year.

For Boso, Commedia is not a separate discipline to be studied; it is the practical foundation of Western theatre. Its function is to portray fears brought about by social tensions and to propose resolutions and ways of living together as a society. This is Boso's popular theatre, and once this is understood, it is no longer necessary to use explicitly Commedia codes: Commedia is in the bones.

References

Bertrand, Alain (2013) Interview (22 August 2013, Grenoble, France) by Anna Cottis, unpublished.

Boso, Carlo (2013) Interview (25 August 2013, Paris, France) by Anna Cottis, unpublished.

Camerlain, Lorraine (1985) "Art de la comédie, comédie de l'art: entretien avec Carlo Boso", *Erudit* numéro 35(2). Available at: www.erudit.org/culture/jeu1060667/jeu1066664/27218ac.html (accessed September 2014).

Crick, Olly (2013) Interview (28 February 2013, Dursley, England) by Anna Cottis, unpublished.

David, Chantal (2013) Interview (24 August 2013, Nantes, France) by Anna Cottis, unpublished.

Perocco, Stefano (2013) Interview (23 August 2013, Montreuil, France) by Anna Cottis, unpublished.

Pion, Guy (2013) Interview (24 August 2013, Mons, Belgium) by Anna Cottis, unpublished.

Quette, Nelly (2013) Interview (21 August 2013, Paris, France) by Anna Cottis, unpublished.

All translations from the original French by Anna Cottis.

45

ANTONIO FAVA

John Rudlin

Antonio Fava was born on the 28 May 1949 in Scandale, a village in the toe of Italy in the province of Crotone in Calabria. Despite the family (including five sisters and two brothers) moving to Reggio Emilia in the industrial north before the end of the year, it was the cultural traditions of his birthplace that were to become the progenitors of his artistic and pedagogical identity. Antonio considers he was "born" into the Commedia tradition, thanks to his father, Tomasso, who:

> worked the villages in the countryside around Crotone in the mask and costume of Puricinedda (a local Pulcinella), playing a guitar which he also beat for rhythm, enlivening local festivals with *lazzi*, songs, serenades, comic sketches, and outrageous comic-epic tales with cynical tragic undertones.
>
> (Fava 2007: xvii)

In Reggio in the fifties, Tomasso no longer played professionally, however, but only on high days and feast days and that with the mask perched on top of his head – as if to signify the cultural alienation that exile had imposed. (This position is commonly used by *comici dell'arte* when rehearsing: the mask is present but not controlling the performer.)

After Tomasso's death, Antonio realised that, in watching his father perform, he had been the unwitting inheritor of an exceptional comedic virtuosity, and that he owed it both to his father's memory and to the Southern Commedia tradition to develop his own one-man Pulcinella show and to play it when and wherever possible. Travelling the world as a director and teacher of Commedia (including France, Spain, Switzerland, the Middle East, Senegal, Lebanon, Japan, Czechoslovakia, Pakistan, the United States, Canada, Australia and Great Britain), he has always made occasion to do so. He calls these solo performances *pulcinellate*, of which there have been four so far: *Vita morte e resurrezione di Pulcinella, Pulcinella's War, Pulcinellata nera*, and *Pulcinella furioso*.

In his foreword to Fava's book, *The Comic Mask in the Commedia dell'Arte*, Simon Callow writes:

Antonio Fava, the great Pulcinella of our day, has brought back to life a whole art form. In his own gloriously funny performance, he embodies the elusive, grounded energy – above all mental energy – that one knows to be central to Commedia, creating a character of precise, articulated logic expressed in abundant and constantly varied physical life. Here he comes, with his rolling self-contented walk, his idly vacant eye, his ever-rumbling belly, perfectly at ease with the world until out of the blue he receives a kick in the bum from his master, he gets caught in the cross-fire between neighbours, a pigeon defecates on his head. His face is fixed into the expression of his mask, but one instantly sees a whole human being, both type and individual, full of wants, problems, anxieties: slothful, starving, ingenious, but not clever, surviving from minute to minute. It is almost unbearable to see him glory in his small triumphs because, as the day follows night, they will be short-lived, and in a second he will be shocked out of his skin, knocked flat, have the food snatched out of his hand and the clothes ripped off his back. We can all, as the saying goes, relate to that. Somehow, too, there is a kind of splendour in his indestructibility: he is Everyman, the lowest common denominator; the basic unit out of which life is built.

(Fava 2007: viii)

The latest *pulcinellata* is, in fact a two-hander with his teaching assistant Cecilia Di Donato. Entitled *La Schiava di Pulcinella* (*Pulcinella's Slave*), in a recent email (Pers. Comm. 1 October 2013) he says of it:

It's a work which is different from the previous *pulcinellate* for two reasons: whilst retaining a very comical format, the dramatic situation and the style of playing are both tragic. I don't like the term 'tragi-comical' and I have made up the word 'Melo-comical', which suits it very well, given the massive presence of music in it (which I composed myself). The première in Reggio was played with an excellent brass quintet... The other thing which distinguishes this *pulcinellata* from the preceding ones is the absence of the scene of the 'pozzo' (well), that I insert into all the pieces where I play Pulcinella. This has a very strong story-line and allows me to monitor myself in the development of an extract throughout the years, as was normal for all the ancient companies.

Fava has extended his performance research into other southern Italian masks: Pasquariello, Coviello, Colafronio, etc., culminating in a production by his company ArscomicA of *Le astusie di Coviello* in 2012.

In August 2013, Antonio was invited back to Scandale to be awarded the Premio Leonia prize for cultural achievement. "The mayor gave it to me in a ceremony which took place in the central square in front of the whole population. It was very moving for me. The older villagers remembered my family, especially my father", he told me in an interview at his home in Reggio Emilia (18–20 April 2013).

He began his own career as a professional performer in 1968 when he joined the Fo/Rama Nuova Scena company to perform in *Grande pantomima con Bandiere e*

Pupazzi piccoli e grandi (Grand Pantomime with Banners and Small and Large Puppets). The youngest in the company, he performed with Fo practically every night for a year, which he found exhausting but immensely rewarding. However, he was still training, not as an actor, but as a flautist, and his musical studies continued until 1973 when he left for France to join the Théâtre National de Strasbourg. There he particularly remembers "a beautiful version of *Le Chant du Fantoche Lusitanien* by Peter Weiss, directed by a Columbian director, Kepa Amouchastegui". It was during its run that he had the idea of forming a company, Le Théâtre de la Jacquerie, along with Alain Mollot, Claire Gernignon, and Alain Blanchard. (A *'jacquerie'* is a peasant uprising.) "The first production was a French version of an Italian play that I had adapted and which we translated together into French" (Interview at his home in Reggio Emilia, 18–20 April 2013). Antonio did not perform in it, however, since he had to return to Italy; but he was soon back and in 1978 came the Jacquerie's major success, *'Tit bonhomme l'est pas très mort*, in collaboration with Jean-Pierre Chabrol. Fava composed the music and co-directed. By then the company had moved to Paris and Fava himself was enrolled in the theatre school run by Jacques Lecoq.

Returning to Reggio in 1980 with three diplomas from Lecoq, he founded, with Dina Buccino, Il Teatro del Vicolo (The Alleyway Theatre) under whose banner he was not only able to play Pulcinella *dappertutto*, but also to mount tours using a variety of comedic genres as well as Commedia. For example, *La Santa Luna degli scampati* (1983) was in cartoon style. On the other hand *Morti di fame, d'amore e di paura* (1981) he considers as having been "pure Commedia" (ibid.), and as such toured Italy, France, Switzerland, Senegal, Mauritius and New Guinea.

In 1985 he opened the International School of the Comic Actor, which is best known for its fortnight-long summer Commedia workshops which are attended by drama students and performers from all over the world. Topics covered include the use and significance of masks, the main individual Commedia Masks and their derivations including function, gesture and behaviour, lazzi and comic acrobatics. The course culminates in the public performance of prepared *canovacci*. In the autumn there is a two-month long advanced course in comic acting which includes Southern as well as "classic" Northern Commedia, together with Roman pantomime and Antonio's own reconstruction of the Atellan farces. In July each year he now also offers an intensive week-long course in leather mask-making.

The creation of his own masks is an integral part of Fava's "take" on Commedia, as being both artistic and artisanal. In drawing and sculpting his matrices he constantly seeks variations on the traditional masks offering, for example, different possibilities for Il Dottore – Graziano delle Cotiche, Balanzone, Plus-quam-Perfectus – and for Il Capitano – Spavento, Bellavita, Matamoros, Meo Squaquara, Giangurgulo and Scarabombardone. The latter was made for the 1996 production of *Le Tremende Bravure del Capitano Bellerofonte Scarabombardone da Rocca di Ferro*, a text from 1596 by Giulio Cesare Croce, discovered in Sicily by Roberto Bruni and Diego Zancani. Pietro Mossa played Zanni Frisetto opposite Fava's Scarabombardone. In this short piece an old Capitano boasts to his servant of his military prowess. Through the latter's reaction it becomes obvious to the audience that his master has never fought anyone, and that all his achievements come from the tavern and the bordello, and that, furthermore, his historical–geographical–

mythological references are mere pastiche. That the pair are variants on Pyrgopolynices and Artotrogus in Plautus' *Miles Gloriosus* is obvious, but Croce adds the touch of ageing Scarabombardone, and the relationship between the bombastic fantasist, who is in reality merely a ragged, hungry, impoverished old man, and his lively young valet points forward to that of Don Quixote and Sancho Panza – and that is why Fava felt it necessary to carve a specific matrix for Scarabombardone's mask.

Less successful, perhaps, was the 1999 essay in creating a "new" Mask, that of "Skinhead Zanni". It is possible that developments in Commedia cannot be driven by the mask-maker but only by the performer served by the mask-maker, who needs an objective eye on what the actor is trying to achieve. The problem is that a mask-maker can get bored (not to say sored – an awful lot of chiselling and hammering is involved) turning out the same "classical" masks over and over again.

Fava's first exhibition of his masks as artefacts in their own right was entitled Maschere, La Commedia Continua, mounted by the Commune of Reggio Emilia in 1994. Subsequent exhibitions have been mounted in Spain, Italy, Switzerland, Germany, Beirut and Dubai.

Fava considers it essential for the twenty-first century performer to be disciplined by staging Commedia on its original platform, ignoring the developments of the eighteenth, nineteenth and twentieth centuries. Interviewed in 1982 by schoolchildren, he said:

> For us *Commedia dell'Arte*, as we play it, is a demonstration of how it was played in the 16th and 17th centuries. Commedia lived through a direct rapport with its audience in the present moment in which the action is taking place; to do that again today therefore requires the discovery of situations that are of today.
>
> You can't laugh at something which is outdated – one can't avoid this direct contact, this comedic immediacy, this critique of what is actually happening now... because laughter is always a critique. The ridiculous, the risible, that which releases laughter is connected with everyday life, whether that of an individual or a whole nation.
>
> (Fava, unpublished autobiographical notes, n.d.)

In basing his work on the *then*, i.e. the first hundred years of Commedia's existence, in order to be free to concentrate on the *now*, Fava argues that one needs to be specific about the when of the then: trying to take on board the entire history of Commedia can only lead to confusion. Placing the white-faced, nineteenth century Pierrot on stage with a primitive Zanni, for example, can only lead to a mishmash of styles. In his opinion there is nothing progressive about Commedia: progress is constructive whilst early *Commedia all'Improvisata* – before it became tamed and sentimentalised by the bourgeoisie, before, in fact, it even came to be called "Commedia dell'Arte" – was furiously destructive, out to destroy the pretentiousness which is in us all. It is this quality which has drawn him more and more towards the Southern traditions of the form: the big Northern companies such as the Gelosi, the Dediosi, the Confidenti and the Uniti were "progressively" drawn to making mega-louis and mega-ecus all over Europe, especially in Paris, whilst in the impoverished south it continued its impolite assault on polite society.

The students next asked:

You sometimes insert something tragic into the laugh-making. Is that a way of making the comedic into a grotesque travesty?

You need to understand the following: tragedy and comedy are two sides of the same coin. When one laughs one makes those on high fall down low and never the reverse. When you make a cartoon caricature of a politician or a professor, if he has a big nose you exaggerate it. You take a detail of a facial defect and you blow it up: that makes us laugh and so this normally serious personage loses his seriousness. You're not afraid of him anymore and that makes us feel comfortable.

Comedy is there to put us at ease, to calm us down and to help us fight against fear. It's a provisional victory over fear, and above all over the great fear that we all have, the fear of dying and not existing any more. In order to be able to laugh at it one needs to subvert the image we have of it... Every time we let out the "hahaha" of laughter, every time we are amused, one can perceive that this joy is a provisional victory over a particular angst. That's the reason why laughter is inescapably linked to tragedy.

How do you explain the renewed interest in Commedia? Is it just a passing phase or something more profound?

It isn't only Commedia that has come back into fashion, but other theatrical forms as well. But Commedia does have a problem, which is that it has no living authors. And when one does happen to come along, and I am such a one, you get asked "who are you creating theatre with?" and I reply "with myself", it doesn't seem right: for most people, the only authors are dead ones.

There are loads of similar ambiguities. An ideological crisis, therefore? No... each time there is a creative crisis one re-discovers things. And if there are things that come back again and again, like Commedia, for example, then that proves that they have universal value. One can return to them, perpetuate them... what is left when fashions have passed on, that is what has permanent value... The comic duo, for example, comes from Commedia, they are a pair donkeys, the stupid one and the clever one, the one who gives the orders and the one who obeys them. They are always a couple, that's important, both to know and to understand!

It's often said that Commedia is a theatre with no written text, a physical form, a theatre where gesture rules the day...

They are complementary, inseparable. The tonality of a voice has a consequent physicalisation. When one asks oneself how a character moves, that begins with the manner in which he speaks. A character is a voice, which is the voice emanating from its body, it cannot be otherwise... they are non-detachable. That's what happens in critical analysis, when you give names to things, isolating text, voice and gesture. If you play a lover with the voice of a Capitano, it doesn't work; if you give him the Capitano's words to speak, it doesn't work either...

One may say that one is making theatre which is not solely textual, where the actor talks and talks... and nothing happens! That is undoubtedly a theatre of ideas, psychological or philosophical but with no action. Neither, though, are we solely making action theatre, or we would be dancing. Nor are we on the side of silent theatre like a mime artist. Our theatre is a bit of all that, well integrated, seeking an appropriate balance.

(Fava, unpublished autobiographical notes, n.d.)

One of the productions in which he sought such balance was *Love is a Drug* for the Oxford Stage Company, which had a national UK tour in 1995. It was based on a Flaminio Scala scenario entitled *La Creduta Morta* (*She Who Was Believed to Be Dead*). In the programme artistic director John Retallack wrote:

The first time I saw Antonio Fava's work it looked as if an ancient engraving of the Commedia dell'Arte had burst into three-dimensional life. The first year students at Exeter University Drama Department were doing a production, in full costumes and masks, at the end of a three week course with Antonio. This noisy, messy, colourful improvisation lasted an hour. The sensation of "time-travelling" was heightened by the incongruity of the ancient masks, slapsticks and costumes all bought to life by students speaking modern English. This combination of ancient and modern seemed to me to be very attractive. It presented a dramatic form that could be simultaneously studied and re-invented for whatever culture it found itself in. The students were excellent [but] I pondered what Antonio might do in six or seven weeks with some of Oxford Stage Company's regular actors.

(Oxford Stage Company 1995: 7)

Retallack invited Antonio to Oxford in the spring of 1994 to take a number of workshops with actors interested in participating in the project. Renata Allen, the writer attached to the project, kept notes:

Antonio was very insistent that he was not looking for specific actors for specific parts. He wanted to find actors capable of being members of a 'troupe' with the ability to improvise and understand a number of roles. To play any of the roles requires considerable discipline – working within a framework of traditional movement techniques and character traits for each stock character... Only by accepting the framework could the actors begin to find the way to merge their own personalities with the character they were playing and thereby find the 'freedom' of the technique.

(Oxford Stage Company 1995: 33–43)

With the added problem of working in a mask, it was hardly surprising, Allen notes, that a few actors declined to come back to the second workshop. "These must have been the most difficult audition/workshops most of them had ever taken part in… having learned what Commedia was all about, they decided they needed more 'freedom' to play a part the way *they* imagined the character." (Ibid.)

When the reduced group of actors learned the basic techniques and began to improvise within the discipline "they created wonderfully comic situations that they could never have pre-planned or thought up rationally. It was then that we all began to understand what the 'freedom' and 'spontaneity' was" (Ibid.). Workshops continued in London where Fava and Retallack decided on a group of seven actors: Jonathan Coyne, Andrew Dennis, Clive Duncan, Kate Fleetwood, Andrew Frame, William Lawrence and Lisa Turner. Fava now departed from the flexible troupe idea by insisting that the casting be finalised seven months in advance of rehearsals so that he could make leather masks to the exact facial measurements of each cast member.

On New Year's Day, 1995, Antonio arrived back in Oxford with a complete set of masks for the cast, a set which he now refers to as "Oxonian". Next, his intervention as dramaturg interpreting La Scala's scenario began with his treatment of the "argument" (written exposition, intended to be read before the action begins):

> In our Oxford version, the scene described in the exposition is staged with a particular sort of pantomime, in which everything is action but not mime. Sounds, words, exclamations, both intelligible and not, become *the sound of the situation*, which is the *sound of the characters*.
>
> (Fava 2007: 85)

He also reduced the original three acts to two, noting that otherwise the play might last four hours and that, although actors have not changed, audiences have. The actors now improvised the scenario, scene by scene, with Allen recording their dialogue and making it up into a script. This script Fava then rehearsed in minute detail, leaving nothing to chance: in his view the *arte*, the professionalism, of the performances could not be left to chance. There were a few windows of opportunity kept available for spontaneity, but they were brief and infrequent. As a result the show was well-drilled and impressive, but the idea of the freedom of the "troupe" was sacrificed to presentational certainty. Retallack also mentioned to me later that the actors felt inhibited by Fava's insistence on coming on tour as company flautist. Well, such opportunities are rare in theatre today, and he should perhaps not be blamed for wanting to savour his own creation.

Fava has also directed various Commedia-influenced operas: Rossini's *Il Turco* and *La Gazza Ladro*; Pergolesi's *La Serva Padrona* and *Liviatta e Tracollo*; Banchieri's *La Saviezza Giovenile* and *Il Festino;* Vecchi's *L'Amphiparnaso*. His love affair with opera has been life-long, beginning when he used to bunk off school and penetrate the Reggio Opera House via one of its unofficial entrances in order to watch rehearsals. On a recent visit to Reggio he told me as we walked past the Opera House:

> In 1962 Pavarotti, who had just won the Premio Achille Peri for new operatic voices, sang the role of Rodolfo in Puccini's *La Bohème* here. In the

second act of this marvellous opera, there is a chorus of kids who want to buy toys. I was one of those kids, so, technically speaking I've sung with Pavarotti! I remember him well: he was big, but not gross, very friendly. He sang and everyone was enchanted. In the opinion of the teachers in the orchestra (they were also my teachers in the music school), we were going to hear a lot more of him. The following year he was back, and I was a flautist in the fanfare in the second act. The maestro Gianfranco Masini had assembled all the best talents of the music school, those who he considered shouldn't stay in the normal classes: there were five of us, and with him we really made music. We analysed the great masterpieces, we discussed their merits, and he made a musician of me.

(Interview at his home in Reggio Emilia, 18–20 April 2013)

When I asked Antonio if there was anything he would especially like me to include in this short monograph, he replied: "You once referred to me as a 'Renaissance Man'. Put that in and you can say whatever else you like" (Ibid.). Teacher, writer, actor, musician, director, composer, mask-maker – in the end what more is there to say? Perhaps only that these sometimes frenetic activities are all bound together by his "mission to keep the traditions of Commedia dell'Arte alive by researching and transmitting its artistic and cultural heritage" (ibid.) – his words, not mine.

References

Fava, Antonio (2007) *The Comic Mask in the Commedia dell'Arte: Actor Training, improvisation and the Poetics of Survival.* Illinois, US: Northwestern University Press, 2007, trans. Thomas Simpson, originally published in Italian as *La Maschera Comica nella Commedia dell'Arte.*

Oxford Stage Company (1995) *Love is a Drug* (programme for the show, which toured from 1995 to 1996). Oxford, UK.

46

HAPPY BEDFELLOWS

Commedia dell'Arte, politics, and the San Francisco Mime Troupe

Claudia Orenstein

Commedia dell'Arte's grotesque masks, stylized gestures, irreverent humor, and comic scenarios seem the very antithesis of everything we might associate with politics. One ideally hopes for the political realm to be one of serious discourse on important issues impacting the lives of many. By contrast, Commedia dell'Arte – itinerant, comic performance – seems to promise nothing more than fleeting entertainment. But in the 1960s, swept up in a US cultural revolution intertwined with political activism, the San Francisco Mime Troupe discovered the latent power of Commedia to galvanize audiences around important social and political issues. The theatrical conventions of Commedia dell'Arte gave the Mime Troupe a set of tools perfectly suited to expressing their grass-roots, liberal agenda not only through content, but also form.

Ron G. Davis founded what would later become the San Francisco Mime Troupe in 1959. The company's early work, inspired by Davis' studies in corporeal mime with founder of the art, Etienne Decroux, was stylistically avant-garde or experimental. The 11th Hour Mime Show, which the group performed in various installments at San Francisco's Encore Theatre, grabbing the stage at 11pm between the striking of one show and the loading in of another, was more in the spirit of "Happenings" than fully articulated theatrical pieces. In 1962, however, with their outdoor production of *The Dowry*, a cobbling together of Commedia dell'Arte scenarios, jokes, and songs, they hit on the form that would set a model for all their future work. Performing in the open air, in an environment that echoed the sixteenth-century marketplaces where Commedia dell'Arte flourished, the Troupe was invigorated by viscerally grasping the Commedia aesthetic. The large gestures, exaggerated masks, improvisational elements all made sense when performing outside in parks to a dispersed audience, free to move on at any time. What united this project and the group's earlier work was performance that relied on strong physical expression. In fact, it is the physical expressivity of the Troupe's style, along with a harkening back to popular performances, from ancient Greek and Roman mimes onwards, which accounts for the continued use of the term "mime" in their name, in spite of the company's loud, musical, and politically outspoken shows.

The Mime Troupe's exploration of Commedia dell'Arte led them to politics and activism. In speaking openly and freely, sometimes bawdily or critically, in the public spaces of San Francisco Bay Area parks, where they were required to get permits from the San Francisco Park and Recreation Commission to perform, the company found themselves testing the limits of free speech. The Commission took the liberty of suggesting changes to the scripts and reducing the number of shows when they thought them too bold. In 1965, they took their first committed political stand with an outdoor adaptation of *Il Candelaio*, a play by sixteenth-century philosopher, scientist, and heretic, Giordano Bruno.

As Ron Davis recounts in *The San Francisco Mime Troupe: The First Ten Years,* after having felt pressures from the Commission in the past, the company went into *Il Candelaio* knowing that it was likely to challenge the authorities. They had two civil liberties lawyers review the script – deeming it to be "a little brutal but not obscene" (Davis, 1975: 66) – before applying for their permit. The Commission granted the company forty-eight performances "on the condition that the production used no obscene words or gestures" (Mason 2005: 11). However, neither Commedia nor the Mime Troupe has thrived on being tame. When the Commission revoked the permit after three performances, the Troupe decided to stage their fourth show as scheduled, in defiance of the Commission's censorship.

A large crowd of friends and supporters gathered in Lafayette Park on August 7, 1965 along with police. Ron Davis turned the arrest into a performative event of its own by coming out in character, dressed as Brighella, and announcing,

> Signor, Signora, Signorini
> Madame, Monsieur, Mademoiselle
> Ladieeeees and Gentlemen,
> Il Tropo di Mimo di San Francisco
> Presents for your enjoyment this afternoon…
> AN ARREST!!!
> (Davis 1975: 67)

As he spoke and made a theatrical leap into the air, the San Francisco police came in and arrested him, fulfilling their advertized role in the drama. With this introduction, Davis openly cast his supposedly unlawful act as one of intentional public disobedience. He demonstrated concretely how Commedia dell'Arte could contribute to political activism, and how theatre practitioners could be forced to choose between conformity and revolution, especially in politically volatile times.

Davis' stand for free speech did not take place in a vacuum. In 1964 the Free Speech Movement had erupted on the UC Berkley campus, just a few miles from Lafayette Park. And, as Davis jumped into the hands of police, the Civil Rights Movement was in full swing, with African-Americans and their supporters taking to the streets in force. Indeed, 1965 was the year of the Selma to Montgomery marches, in which Civil Rights activists walked to the Alabama state capital to seek action against suppression of black voter registration and other civil rights violations. Local police attacked the marchers with clubs and tear gas. Throughout the land of the free, protest actions were revealing public space to be contested space and social and political freedoms to be restricted, still needing to be fought for, not simply enjoyed. Theatre, as a form of public expression, could not ignore or stand immune to the political clashes rocking the nation. The Mime Troupe's Commedia dell'Arte style shows, because they were edgy and outdoors, were right in step with the activism of the times.

The company continued to keep pace with the political scene as students took to the streets to protest the Vietnam War. In 1967, Goldoni's Commedia style play, *L'Amant Militaire*, about Spanish intervention in an Italian civil war, offered the Troupe a theatrical template for critiquing America's involvement in Vietnam. In the Mime Troupe show, simple-minded Arlecchino is tricked into signing up for military service by recruiters Brighella and Espada, who explain how "...everybody *poor*, goes in the army, because for them the army represents a step upward – decent pay, respect... the adoration of women – right?" while the rich can get out of service (Davis 1975: 181). Later, Arlecchino attempts to evade the military duty he was roped into by dressing up in women's clothes, only to be chased by a randy soldier.

Most importantly, the show reveals how the military-industrial complex profits from war. In the play, we see industrialists, represented by merchant Pantalone, conspire with military leaders, here in the form of Garcia, a kind of Capitano figure.

PANTALONE: Generale: I got a lot into this war. I own 51 percent of the shares. I got munitions in Milano, I got weapons labs in Torino, I got banks and pawnshops outside every base – when you end the war, you end the war industry! You murder my markets – you assassinate my economy – you expose me to recession – to depression – to suicide [*Pantalone stabs himself. Garcia pulls out the knife and arranges Pantalone like a general leading a charge—one hand across his bow peering ahead, one hand waving a sword; body forward but head still facing Garcia.*]

GARCIA: Learn to have ideals, senor. Learn to have vision. Learn to think of the future of your country: [*snaps Pantalone's head around to complete picture*] with this Operation Guinea Wrangle we are creating for you one hundred and sixteen thousand empty square miles – a desert. [*Pantalone snaps out of stupefaction into fascination.*]

PANTALONE: ...It's a parking lot!

GARCIA: And you'll have the lease, senor.

PANTALONE: And I'll have the lease.

(Davis 1975: 174)

In iconic Mime Troupe style, the scene uses the comic elements and stock characters of Commedia dell'Arte to express facts clearly and reflect a political point of view. The political message sits within an exchange whose comic rhythm lets the truth of the situation fall, at the end, as a kind of punch line: "And I'll have the lease." Pantalone can be convinced of anything, if he will make a profit. The ultimate goal of war is not any noble cause but pure economic exploitation. The scene and its message are enhanced by the physical stage action.

The Troupe added an irreverent Punch puppet to the show. Set in his own puppet booth at the side of the stage, alongside the human actors, Punch provides an anarchic response to the war and questions the company's pacifist views, expressed in the play's main action. He proposes, as the ultimate effective end to the war, throwing a mortar into a napalm depot to create "BL-O-O-M – *enlightened democracy*" (Davis 1975: 190). Punch also offers useful suggestions for avoiding the draft.

In the end, however, it is Corallina, the clever maidservant, who takes the decisive action that ends the war by simply dressing up as the pope and declaring peace. She tells the audience "Listen, my friends – you want something done? Well, then, do it yourselves!" (Davis 1975: 193). *L'Amant Militaire*'s Commedia dell'Arte plot and characters unmask the machinations of warmongers. The play offers both pacifist and militant alternatives to protesting war, but in the end acknowledges, in Brechtian fashion, that the responsibility for making change in the real world lies with the spectators. Ideally, audience members leave the show feeling empowered by having witnessed the seemingly impossible – ending the war – easily achieved by an ordinary person, even if only in a comic play, where the powers that be are buffoons, facilely derailed from their evil plans.

The Troupe had consciously turned to socially and politically engaged theatre a little before Davis' 1965 arrest, using then, rather than Commedia dell'Arte, an American popular form, the minstrel show, to address civil rights. *A Minstrel Show or Civil Rights in A Cracker Barrel* (1965), which premiered a month before *Il Candelaio*, would become one of the Troupe's most notorious shows, leading to the arrests of many company members as they toured it to university campuses throughout the country (Mason 2005: 11).

The American minstrel show, one of the most (if not *the* most) popular forms of entertainment in nineteenth-century America, seems, even more than Commedia dell'Arte, an unlikely candidate for being adapted to convey a liberal political message. A variety entertainment of sorts, minstrel shows began with comic repartee between two "end men" sitting at either *end* of a circle of minstrel performers. An olio section followed, with musical acts, dance routines, and comic sketches. The shows ended with a longer acted scene, usually about the supposed bucolic joys of plantation life. With its simple-minded, somewhat grotesque, comic characters, the minstrel show popularized and perpetuated derogatory black stereotypes that haunted the African-American community through to the Civil Rights era. It also provided America with some of its most well-known folks songs – *Camptown Races* and *Swanee River*, both by Stephen Foster, are two examples – and folk humor. Scholars, such as Robert C. Toll, Joseph Boskin, William F. Stowe and David Grimsted, have investigated some of the more complex forces at work in the development and reception of minstrel shows, suggesting, among other things, that these entertainments provided white Americans with a non-threatening, theatrical vehicle through which to deal with their very real anxieties about slavery, the growth of urbanization, and other looming issues of the times.

The Mime Troupe borrowed the minstrel show format and its derisive clownish characters in order to tear them apart and trouble audience members. They started by using a mixed cast of white and black actors, all dressed in identical minstrel make-up so spectators could not distinguish black performers from white, immediately unsettling racial divisions. By disrupting a well-known theatrical form, the company hoped to deconstruct the accepted social conventions embedded within it and in the American psyche. They also sought to challenge the all too easy "political correctness" of many liberal spectators, by digging into the more troubling roots of American racism.

For example, in the traditional stump speech, a familiar part of the olio, a black minstrel clown traditionally offers a long-winded, supposedly intellectual discourse on a topic. His language, inadvertently full of jokes and malapropisms, allows the audience to laugh at his ineptitude, along with the comic truths revealed through his mistakes. The minstrel's stump speech is the equivalent of a Dottore monologue, trumping pomposity with imbecility. In the Mime Troupe's show, however, the stump speech, which offered a history of blacks in America, only began in traditional comic fashion. It ended, however, with the minstrel speechmaker abandoning his stump, and with it his comic role, yelling instead for "black power" and "blood in the streets." Rather than remaining the passive butt of the joke, the character turns the tables on his audience, implicating them in potentially more volatile situations. The Mime Troupe blew open the minstrel stereotype to show how years of black oppression were at the root of contemporary black militancy.

Although minstrel shows were performed indoors, they shared significant features with Commedia dell'Arte, including the use of popular humor, songs, comic bits, and stock characters. The minstrel's clownish make-up and attire – a cork-blackened face with heavily outlined lips and eyes, a fright wig, and oversized or tattered suit – resembled the Commedia dell'Arte masks in offering a fully stylized character that the performer must conform to and play through. It was significantly different in circumscribing stereotypes that were destructive to a particular community. After the Civil War, black actors started blacking-up, in competition with white performing groups, hoping to seize a career opportunity in minstrelsy at a time when many American jobs were closed to blacks. In donning minstrel make-up and costume, and submitting to the show's conventional format, they found themselves adopting the pre-set, expected, black stereotypes the minstrel show had popularized.

Ironically, in appropriating popular forms like the minstrel show and Commedia dell'Arte, the Mime Troupe, a progressive theatre company, invests in unsubtle, often problematic, familiar stereotypes. Sometimes they deconstruct or question them, but, through stylized acting and exaggerated costume, they always make them large and apparent, such that the audience cannot ignore them, or take them as natural, but must confront and consider, or reconsider, them. In taking their shows to parks and community centers, the Troupe tries to address a general audience and bring them to think about possibly contentious political issues by first drawing them to images, allusions, and ideas that are recognizable, even if not desirable. Taking on popular culture by playing with the elements of popular culture, is part of the Mime Troupe's political-theatrical strategy.

In a production history of more than fifty years, the Mime Troupe has mined many other popular theatrical forms for their political work as well, including vaudeville, circus, and melodrama, adding to those forms tropes from non-theatrical popular media such as comic books, television sit-coms, and noire films. They have also continued to draw on Commedia dell'Arte as a template for their theatrical style. Commedia's stock pairs of servants and masters, in which the masters in power are more buffoonish than the clever servants who outwit them, fits the Mime Troupe's grass-roots, liberal politics, which seeks to empower ordinary people to take charge and question the machinations of economically and politically powerful politicians and corporations. Identifying ordinary spectators with clever Arlecchinos and Colombinas, who may be in seemingly powerless positions but still manage to outwit their betters, provides a straightforward scenario for grass-roots political empowerment.

Over time, the Mime Troupe has moved from a strict adherence to Commedia dell'Arte conventions to creating their own, updated, stock types, more relevant to their contemporary audiences. In *Mozamgola Caper* (1986), for example, the company used a complex plot, based on tropes from spy films, to show how the US government intentionally destabilizes African nations it purports to help. In the show, the case is broken by Regretta, a washed-up CIA operative brought back to spy work by Debarge, a US official who plans to use her as an unwitting assassin in his own mischievous plan. Disenfranchised or down-and-out characters, like Regretta, who, first reluctantly, then zealously, take up the cause of the people and solve the mystery at hand, unmasking hypocrites and criminals, are recurring figures in Mime Troupe plays. They may appear under various guises, but they operate as stock types, immediately identifiable for their positive role in the action.

In *Factwino and the Moral Majority* (1981), the central character is Sedro, an alcoholic bum living on the streets. He transforms into the super hero Factwino when the Spirit of Information gives him a super power: the ability to spread information and reveal the truth. The catch is that he must remain sober to use his gift. In this play elements are borrowed from comic books. In ridiculous bright yellow tights and red cape, with a red F on his chest, Factwino zaps people who have been duped and confused by right-wing propaganda so that they begin to see the facts of situations clearly. Like Regretta, Sedro is at first reluctant to take up the task, more interested in drowning his past sorrows in alcohol. But he soon realizes that he must use his special powers to save the country from right-wing extremism based on misinformation and becomes not only a hero, but a role model for others.

The hypocritical businessman or political official, like Debarge in *Mozamgola Caper*, has become another stock Mime Troupe type. He represents corrupt powers and, through the course of the action, is publically unmasked. By the end of the show he is, at least temporarily, disempowered. For years actor Ed Holmes played this character in its various incarnations in different shows. Like Commedia dell'Arte performers of the past, he honed and perfected his stock role.

Mozamgola Caper also offers us Bongo, a poor, African hustler, whose street smarts help Regretta get the information she needs to solve the case. He is an up-dated Arlecchino. Although living in twentieth-century Africa, he is still impoverished and relying on his wits to get by. While Mime Troupe characters are contemporary, and not played in masks, they continue to be exaggerated types, played with large gestures, and overdone costuming. Clever, low-status figures – they may not be "servants" per se, but the underclass or disenfranchised – continue to outwit those in positions of power, today politicians and corporate heads.

In spite of the very general "good-trumps-evil" storylines of these shows, like Commedia dell'Arte plots, Mime Troupe plays can become quite complex. Like Commedia, these plays draw from an inheritance going back to ancient Greek New Comedy and Roman Comedy that relies on mix-ups and confusions to create dramatic action. This traditional dramatic movement from confusion to clarification is good for the Mime Troupe's political theatre. It allows seemingly complicated political situations to reveal themselves as manageable after all, especially in the hands of ordinary, well-intentioned people.

It should come as no surprise that popular forms like Commedia dell'Arte have structures that aid in expressing grass-roots interests. Growing up in the fairgrounds of Europe, Commedia had to be responsive to the preoccupations of the ordinary people who made up their audiences, and so, popular forms became the unofficial voice of the populace, reflecting their own concerns back to them. Commedia's stock characters, familiar plot lines, and invitations to improvisation gave it an open structure that allowed for topical events and issues of the day to find their way into performance. This is true of many popular forms, and the Mime Troupe has capitalized on these elements, adapting these generous structures to their own objectives.

They have also appropriated Commedia dell'Arte's joyful spirit, creating, what I have called elsewhere a "festive-revolutionary" model of performance (Orenstein 1998, 2006). Through its visions of a troubled-world renewed through comic play, Commedia and other popular forms reflect an optimistic approach to problem solving, and display faith in the power of the populace, the lowly, to combat evil and renew the world for good. This festive spirit is contagious and buoys up the heavier political messages in the plays. It is an invaluable commodity for invigorating a political movement working against the odds.

Since the eighties, when Americans generally became more politically complacent, the San Francisco Mime Troupe has kept the liberal flame burning in their comic, popular-styled, political musical shows, which continue to tour San Francisco Bay Area parks and elsewhere. The company has its critics, however, who see in their adherence to a once-useful theatrical style a reluctance to re-evaluate theatrical and political strategies and adapt them to America's changed political and cultural landscape. There is great validity to these critiques, and the Troupe has had to give up or redefine many of their ideals over the years as the world has shifted around them. But their 1988 production, *Ripped Van Winkle*, constitutes a response to these criticisms. In this play Rip, an activist hippie from the 60s, having, for some mysterious reason, slept for twenty years, wakes to find himself in the conservative, yuppified world of the 1980s. Through the course of the play, especially in the *Update Bringdown* rap song number, Rip comes to understand how the world has changed: his cool pad is now a fancy restaurant, his hippy girl-friend is a political stooge, and conservative California Governor Ron Reagan has managed to win two terms as US President. Nonetheless, Rip rekindles a revolutionary spirit in those around him, who have become disaffected, energizing them in a protest against the docking of a battleship loaded with nuclear weapons in the San Francisco Bay. At the end of the play, Rip discovers that his mysterious long slumber was the work of the spirit of Liberty Leading the People, from the Delacroix painting of the same name. She has, the Mime Troupe tells us, bottled him like fine wine to unleash his revolutionary spirit in a new time that needs him. Through Rip the Mime Troupe expresses their view of their own position and ongoing mission.

The San Francisco Mime Troupe perseveres in their work, still turning to comedy, stock character types, theatrical stylization, and clear scenarios drawn from Commedia dell'Arte and other popular forms as the basis for creating free, politically engaged theatre offered in parks and community centers around the country. They work to empower audiences to face complex and contentious political issues, from a liberal standpoint, with energy, clarity, and optimism.

References

Davis, R. G. (1975) *The San Francisco Mime Troupe: The First Ten Years*. Palo Alto, California, US: Ramparts.

Mason, Susan Vanetta (2005). *The San Francisco Mime Troupe Reader*. Ann Arbor, US: University of Michigan Press.

Orenstein, Claudia (1998) *Festive Revolutions: The Politics of Popular Theater and the San Francisco Mime Troupe*. Jackson, US: University of Mississippi.

——(2006) "Revolution Should Be Fun: A Critical Perspective on the San Francisco Mime Troupe". *Restaging the Sixties*. Edited by James M. Harding and Cindy Rosenthal. Ann Arbor, US: University of Michigan Press.

47

COMMEDIA IN GLOUCESTERSHIRE
Rural contexts (2004 to 2010)
Olly Crick

For Commedia enthusiasts, even the pragmatic ones, the main question is, "Can it work now?" Antonio Fava states that what was state of the art theatrical entertainment then is now irrelevant. A live performance cannot exist anywhere but in the eyes and ears of a living audience (Fava 2007: xiii). If one chooses to adopt historical performance tropes and perform them now, however deeply one immerses oneself in the subject, there will always be a tension. This tension lies between its historical strengths then, and how they might appear in front of a contemporary audience, now. Some of this can be resolved before one reaches the public, but some will only become obvious when face to face with them. What a performer or troupe should carry with it, is not the tales of Commedia's past success, but what entertains now, and why.

The Fabulous Old Spot Theatre Company (named after a Gloucestershire pig breed and active between 2004 and 2010) owed its genesis and working method to combining Commedia dell'Arte and community theatre practice. The company's aim was to create performances that were recognisably Commedia dell'Arte, and carried a distinctively local and English flavour. This chapter contains some of the company's findings.

The Cheltenham Everyman, a production house theatre in Gloucestershire, produces an annual touring community theatre tour. In 2004 this was offered to an embryonic Old Spot Theatre. Finances dictated that only three actors could be afforded. The learning curve started by solving the question whether the Commedia dynamic (and its implicit fast moving physical comedy) could be generated with only three. Seven three-person scenarios were written, and three of these workshopped with actors in a development week. One was quickly rejected, as not being sympathetic enough to the performers' senses of humour. Of the remaining two, one seemed to stimulate better responses than the other one. This became the company's first show: *Hot Crackling*.

Within a local and community framework, the company aimed to balance historical research with its collective experience in live performance. The aim had to be to create an enjoyable show, but became, in effect, a long experiment. There was always an underlying tension between the desire to create a move-and-gag-perfect show, with a strong sense that some solutions needed waiting for.

The company found it useful to regard each "fact" known about Commedia dell'Arte as no longer fact, but as theory. It was then possible to test why some aspect of a theoretical performance canon may or may not work within the chosen context. It was vital to stick to these theories, as they provided the criteria vital in assessing and evaluating the performances.

This early commitment to local touring defined this company's emergent style. At the start, there was conviction that Commedia dell'Arte would work very well in this context. The company believed that the Masks' greatest strength was reflecting the society that made up its audience, and also that the performance structure was fluid enough to allow the same dramatic story to be enjoyed by audiences of different social balances. The question, therefore, became how to adapt these two strands to create a performance both universally relevant and directly aimed at Gloucestershire audiences. The next question faced was what village hall audiences were like, and did they have an easily identifiable demographic, and a particular sense of humour?

To a relative "outsider" to the county, this information came from three sources: experience from previous local touring shows as writer, talking and listening to neighbours, and asking the Everyman about previous touring shows. From the final source was obtained a detailed account of audience numbers, who did the best cakes, where there were poor dressing rooms, who gave you supper and who would not, and, of course, a firm injunction to treat all audiences according to the Everyman's equal opportunities policy. This was not particularly helpful. From the first, the company discovered that people who take command and organise artistic events in village halls, reflect their own tastes, which are not always the same as those who come to the events. This gave the company clues as to marketing issues. From neighbours it was inferred that Gloucester working people are proud, work hard, love their food and drink, prefer rugby to soccer, are inclined towards making their own entertainment, are gregarious and community minded, protective of their own, and will always give one enough rope, though will, without fail, intervene with great hilarity, moments before one takes the drop. Despite occasional islands, it is a county where local rather than high culture rules. There are outposts of high art in the county (Cheltenham is known for its literature and jazz festivals), but generally in the more well-heeled and urban areas.

What also loomed alarmingly was that less than 10 per cent of people had heard of Commedia dell'Arte, and those that had associated it with Art Deco, rather than comedy. This presented a marketing issue. It did not seem wise to sell the show as Commedia dell'Arte if hardly anyone had heard of it, and those that had, thought it something else other than what the company intended. The word itself, it was opined, would alienate audiences who primarily came to their community venues to enjoy themselves and socialise. Anything redolent of "high art" was out. The phrase "Commedia dell'Arte" was duly barred from all publicity. The only exception was drama teachers who ran school-based venues with captive student audiences. For the first show's marketing, phrases such as "high octane comic theatre", "all age range inclusive theatre", and "Theatre from the Merrie England that never was" were used instead. By the fifth tour even the word "theatre" had been dropped from publicity and "A Good Night Out" used instead. Locals who attended communal village events were far more attracted by the word "entertainment" than "theatre".

This decision affected other aspects of company thinking. Assuming that it is the comedy, the dramatic storylines, the *lazzi*, and the individual actor's skills (and not the power of the name), that attracted an audience, what else about Commedia dell'Arte could alienate an audience? Remembering generic early bafflement with the unfamiliar names and locations in both Shakespearean and Jacobean drama, the option to change the Masks' names was put forward. To what, though, was the question?

Unsurprisingly a local solution suggested itself. Gloucestershire is a county with distinctive social, economic and geographical zones all with separate identities, and long-standing rivalries. One of the strengths of the original Commedia dell'Arte was that the Masks originated in different Italian cities, states and social classes. Could the same be done in Gloucestershire, and the Masks assigned to different classes and areas?

This was attempted, and the immediate results were, luckily, that the Masks naturalised themselves quite happily. All the Masks have "attitude" by the bucketful, and once they found themselves in a specific environment, they found the material to react against. The Masks began to display their local "attitude" with ease. Pantalone's mercantile avarice, for example, translated almost perfectly to a landowning farmer. Once a Mask embedded itself into the local landscape, possibilities spontaneously emerged, including a new name or title. Pantalone became a Berkeley Vale farmer renamed Titus Dallymore.

Each Mask now came from an area that was, at the very least, known by reputation to their audiences, had names that had familiar echoes; and generally behaved like, well, the reprobates from the next village (never one's own). On several occasions comments were cheerfully passed on after shows concerning "bad behaviour" by the Masks. The company was informed that all of this was typical of the "next village": assault, wife beating, robbery, inebriation and incest being favourite (and hopefully unfounded) accusations.

In building up the Mask's back-story, additional weight was added by constant reference to local geography. This permitted a category of in-jokes within the shows: those relating to local knowledge and the landscape. Some of these encouraged an audience's direct relationship with the Masks, owning them as representatives of their county, as well as adding more layers to an unfolding plot. The River Severn, bisecting the county, always seemed to become part of the plot. It became the conduit through which various Pirates or Spanish Armadas invaded, as well as being a barrier to stop the Welsh invading. In-jokes about contemporary events were disallowed, as they undermined the dramatic fiction of the show's "historical" setting.

Early show comments (conflated) ran along the lines of "Your shows look like Shakespeare, but are funny and we can understand the words". This was good news. The company was in the same league and historical bracket as the Bard, and was funnier.

Providing one respects the hierarchical ecosystem, the Commedia dell'Arte pantheon can be transposed to regions other than of its birth, and can be made to appear as if it had been there all its life. All the actors (locally sourced) used in the show reacted positively to these innovations. It gave them a very firm notion of where the action was happening. The "historical" landscape we were evoking was the same one that they, and the audiences, saw and travelled through in everyday life.

There were also local issues with the Mask objects themselves. When contacting local venues the company explanations concerning mask use, created a high percentage of antipathy and doubt from potential bookers. Many reservations were expressed, notably that they might frighten "the children". This view seemed to be shared by many bookers and, despite lengthy conversations, many venues did not feel happy booking a masked theatre company.

This may have been due to the absence of any widespread native masked theatrical or folk tradition use in the UK. It may also be due to over-protective attitudes of predominantly third age village hall committees. Since the 1980s various theatre companies, for example Trestle Theatre Company and The Moving Picture Mime Show, toured and popularised their use. However, masked performance remains not a universally accepted entertainment norm.

Previous experience performing masked Commedia dell'Arte in the UK showed the opposite: people are not specifically bothered by Masks and happily accept them as part of the performance. Whilst those under six may (but certainly not always) be frightened, from eight years up there is a palpable sense of fascination. It seemed, therefore, the obvious course of action, when booking shows, was simply not to mention them at all. This approach was adopted for every new venue the company contacted. No venue ever complained, post show, about not being informed. One needs to be very sure, however, that the shows one presents are of sufficient quality to override this particular well-intentioned sin of omission.

A beneficial side effect line of using Commedia Masks is that a small cast can double up and even triple up on roles. This does depart from the paradigm of "one actor playing one role". In fact, skilled Mask use by actors multi-roling in most shows so effectively disguised who was playing what part, that many delightful comments arose when only four actors came out to take a bow at the end: "Brilliant. The only disappointment was that at the end only four of you came out. I am sure I saw at least twelve during the performance" (Salwarpe Village Hall, emailed "thank you" comment on *A Gloucester Scaramouche*, 2007). This meant that the company could create shows with wider ranging storylines than could be done with three single-role actors. As a rule of thumb, the company evolved an understanding that each actor might be expected to play one major, one supporting, and several choric roles within one performance.

An audience awareness of multi-roling added to the performance's innate theatricality, and to the audience's enjoyment. The company made a feature of sharing how a stage trick was done. The audience was invited, always, to admire a joke or a skilful deceit, and to share in how it was carried out. Multi-roling, consequently, became a company skill and trademark. It did require, however, some cunning and skill when writing a show, in order to keep specific plot strands apart. It would be inconvenient for an actor to have to meet themselves on stage. If this, however, became inevitable, meta-theatrical gags could save the day.

The company took on this exact challenge using the "identical twins" comedy trope. As a meta-theatrical device it can be carried out in two ways: either two highly

446

dissimilar actors are recognised as twins by the cast, or one actor plays both. With the latter set up, the skill of show creation focusses on how the twins' eventual meeting is resolved. In Goldoni's *Venetian Twins* this problem resolves by one twin being fatally poisoned before the other can find them. In Old Spot Theatre's *Pirates of the River Severn* the "twins" not only unwittingly disguise themselves as each other, but finally fight a fatal duel to the death through a gap in the backdrop. As the audience was in on the joke, they both enjoyed the skill with which it was played, as well as being amused by the actor's successful attempts to keep the fiction of twins alive with only one actor.

Two sets of relationships became important as touring started: the relationship between the theatre company and each village hall, and the relationship between the actors and the audience. It became clear that a touring company coming into a village hall is a very different proposition from coming into a fully equipped theatre. Practically, it was necessary to carry our own staging and theatre lights with us including a kettle and coffee making paraphernalia.

Villages are proud of their halls, and are protective and proprietary about them. Any theatre company, even when bringing entertainment, is both outsider and intruder. The company, after discussions, took the approach that an open-armed welcome could not be taken for granted and, despite many temporary issues, the company must be consciously deferential to the village hall committee and those who let us in. The appropriate time to be proud is after a good performance. Playing the opposite of the arrogant arty actor won the company friends and future cooperation.

It also became obvious that an exact "curtain up" time could never be guaranteed. Sometimes everyone arrived early and sometimes everyone arrived late. This made it awkward to start a show in the conventional sense, and to carry everyone into the story. To accommodate this, the openings of all the shows became elastic. The actors, in character, sold programmes and checked out the audience, and songs were sung, thematically related to the show. Recorded music or "house" music was never used. Occasionally impromptu talent competitions occurred. The rationale was always to make the hall a relaxed space where actors and audience could eye each other up and then, and only then, when the feeling was right could the show begin.

The company created and devised the shows in a manner learned, and then adapted, from studying under Carlo Boso. However, one major difference was made to this dramaturgy: the company scenarios were written and decided upon before rehearsals started, rather than having a *Maestro* compose a scenario on the hoof. Whilst it was always a stated ideal to be able to collate and organise all the performer's best ideas into a new performance, the amount of rehearsal time available to do this was always dictated by budgetary constraints.

Each scenario was composed with several necessary key elements: it should be written for the strengths of the actors performing it; it should have a central framing idea or philosophy, and should be composed in a conventional comic three act structure. The "script" then developed to final performance stage in rehearsal, collectively devised by the company, with a director getting the final say or edit.

A three-point checklist ran concurrently in rehearsals. First, communicate the story of each scene; second, communicate the unique reactions to the story of the

Masks involved; and third (and not always) look for the opportunities to perform the first or second in a *bravura* (a monologue or dramatic solo) manner. An audience must be able to follow the story and care for the dramatic personages enough to engage with their predicaments. It was found to be very important not to add excessive local detail at this stage. Any story must work on a universal level before local dressing is applied. A "framing idea" provided the link between the "local" and the "universal".

By "framing idea", a single theme that is explored in various ways throughout the scenario is meant. It is the "what the play is about", whilst the "local" is where the action happens. Commedia dell'Arte is not psychological theatre; it is visceral and immediate, concerning itself with love, money and power, so engagement with the "frame" has to be direct and manifest itself as action. Below are some examples from the company's devised shows indicating framing themes used.

1) Two teenagers coming into their power and awareness as adults (*Hot Crackling*)
2) What a woman wants from a partner: stability or passion? (*Pirates of the River Severn*)
3) Why it is always best to patch up quarrels, however awful, the same night (*A Gloucester Scaramouche*)
4) A county healing in the aftermath of a war (*The Curse of Elverado*)
5) How one copes with a career minded partner (*The King of Spain's Daughter*)
6) Is it hard work or fate that controls our destinies? (*Chancers*)

Many lazzi and comic routines evolved in rehearsal, but some had to be pre-planned. Old Spot always tried to include one major prop or skill based *coup de theatre* in each show: a firing cannon, a naval battle with ship as hats and party poppers as cannon, and frequently a monster or mythical beast. The most common theatrical skill available locally was music. Consequently Old Spot shows had a high musical content, many part songs and much live music.

This became the company strength, and deviated from the accepted practice that Commedia actors must have strong physical skills. It seemed to be enough to start with actors with radically contrasting body types. There is also something indefinably "*Commedia*" about a certain type of musician. Those who busk, who play in the street; those who can learn tunes by ear; those who play with other people; the ones who are used to performing things of a high technical skill in a relaxed way in front of drunk crowds; and those who are used to jamming, and who have good patter between their numbers, all seem to "get" Commedia dell'Arte. The initial shows were successful partly because the first shows contained performers with these skills.

The company is no longer active at the time of writing this chapter due to both "life issues" and the economics of running a company within our self-imposed remit. Whether one is obsessed with Commedia dell'Arte or not, theatre is still a business and must succeed as such.

For most Old Spot shows, after a suitable run-in time, the performances reached a very high standard, with a superb ensemble feel. Village hall venues were where the company was best received, and where they most enjoyed performing. The earned income from these venues, however, only generated a small financial surplus. The business plan for each show was to perfect it touring locally, and then retour the next year or later in National (better paid) venues. This never occurred, as the company could never reassemble a complete original cast for the following year. It was only the original cast, it was reasoned (rightly or wrongly), who could have, for a financially affordable period of time, brought back to life the comic ensemble.

Working locally also brought in the issue of a limited pool of performers from which to work. Partly to solve this, the search for new cast members was not carried through auditions. It was achieved by recommendations from existing cast members: from their friends, actors they knew personally, and professional networks. This worked excellently every time but once. When actors bring in other people they like and enjoy working with, the company reasoned, the standard and feel of a company improves. Sadly, the one time it failed became apparent too late in rehearsal to replace the actor and start again. The tour was cut short by collective decision, as it was well below the standard of previous performances. The company was left without any profit to finance the next show. Theatre is always a business.

To conclude: Commedia dell'Arte can indeed be adapted to suit local needs. The Masks survived the transplant and put down local roots. The implicit social and political hierarchy still communicated itself to an audience and, once localised, the Masks needed no introductions. This is all despite the fact that the audiences were largely ignorant of the term. As a fast and wildly inventive theatre style, it won over both naïve theatre audiences and experienced theatre-goers. It is, however, humbly suggested that when starting up your own company, you have a serious look into the practical workings of the fraternal contracts practised by the original performers of the paradigm. This may be the way forward.

Table 47.1 Mask equivalency chart

Mask	Gloucester Name	Region	Local Characteristics
Magnifico	Phillip II of Spain	Leader of the Spanish Invasion	Foreign king
	George IV of England	Legal father of Prince Rupert and illegal father of Florence Dallymore	Our king
Pantalone	Titus Dallymore	Vale of Berkeley	Farmer and master of having a finger in everyone's pie
Il Dottore	Ignatius O'Reilly	Cheltenham lawyer or doctor	Outsider expert
First Actor	Prince Rupert His Highness the Prince of Wales	London/Germany	Slightly mystified and distant landowner
	Lord Cecil	London	London based agent of governmental skulduggery
First Actress	Queen Florence	Cheltenham/London	Landowner
Second Actor	Jack Dallymore	Vale of Berkeley	Rustic and naïve optimist
Second Actress	Florence	Small town, Tewkesbury or Gloucester	Rustic and naïve optimist
Il Capitano	Duke of Berkeley	Berkeley Castle	Landowner

Table 47.1 (continued)

Mask	Gloucester Name	Region	Local Characteristics
Brighella	Ephraim Scatter	Severnside bar owner and small scale entrepreneur	Poacher, gossip, conduit of all shady information. Always "knows someone who might, for the right price". Cider maker
	Sgt Early	The British Army	RSM and minder for Prince of Wales
Zannis/ Columbina	Clutterbuck	Forest of Dean	
	Seth	Forest of Dean	
	Smiler	Gloucester Docks	
	Groggy	Sharpness (River Severn port)	
	Mrs Clutterbuck	Forest	
Witch	Mrs Hill	Forest of Dean	

References

Fava, A. (2007) *The Comic Mask in the Commedia dell'Arte* (tr.), Thomas Simpson. Canada: Northwestern University Press.

48

I SEBASTIANI

Commedia geeks

Judith Chaffee

Antonio Fava claims that "Commedia dell'Arte is the genre of theatre that expresses the present as it moves… the impossibility of re-covering texts of a particular genre is immaterial to the goal of knowing that genre and making something of it in performance" (Fava 2007: xiii). We know it can work now, for one has only to look at the myriad of creative and successful Commedia troupes in Europe, North and South America, Australia, Asia, and even Africa, connecting to a wide variety of cultures and societies. But what if a group of actors were truly curious about re-creating "traditional" Commedia dell'Arte, improvised and spontaneous, dealing with purely Renaissance issues? Would it, could it work? Venues for enjoying Commedia-like performances are often Renaissance Fairs, or historical theatre performances, such as productions of *A Servant of Two Masters* or *The Green Bird*, or a local theatre group using archetypes to poke fun at contemporary politics or social dynamics. But these are usually rehearsed productions with some improvisations. Could totally improvised performances survive the demands of a paying audience?

A fully improvised scenario, guided by a plot outline, in traditional Renaissance leather masks, connecting with stock characters representing archetypes in sixteenth or seventeenth century society, perhaps passing a bucket at the end of the show, to be divided equally among the company members after expenses had been paid describes i Sebastiani, of Cambridge, Massachusetts in the United States. A troupe of history geeks who are semi-professional actors, they adhere to the improvisational traditions of Renaissance Commedia dell'Arte, in social context, language, costumes, and props. Formed in 1990—June 4 at 7:45pm to be exact—the company evolved because of, and within, a Massachusetts Institute of Technology branch of the Society for Creative Anachronism (SCA), the intelligentsia of all things Medieval or Renaissance. The SCA is "an international organization dedicated to researching and re-creating the arts and skills of pre-17th-century Europe" (Society for Creative Anachronism n.d.). With over 30,000 members around the world, SCA participants dress in clothing of the Middle Ages and Renaissance; attend events that feature tournaments, royal courts, feasts, dancing, various classes and workshops; and promote combat and chivalry, arts and sciences and heraldry of pre-1600 Europe.

The MIT branch of SCA was particularly interested in theatre of the Renaissance, and, while not professional actors, chose to perform the early plays of Shakespeare at SCA gatherings. The MIT SCA club adhered to the demands of Renaissance theatre, and, except for women playing women, used period props, costumes, sets, and music in re-creating historical Shakespeare productions, being challenged by, and struggling with, the language and memorization process. After a demanding Shakespeare performance, one of the members, Jeff Hatalsky, proposed that the club do Commedia dell'Arte because he loved comedy, felt he had a gift for it, and Commedia would be improvised theatre, alleviating the challenge of memorizing Shakespeare. While most MIT SCA members knew little, if anything, about Commedia dell'Arte, they told Jeff if he wanted to do Commedia so badly he should start a troupe. At the next business meeting, he announced just that: he was starting a troupe, had rehearsals scheduled, and invited people to join. That was the beginning.

Jeff's name in the SCA was Sebastian, so it was logical to name the troupe i Sebastiani: "those who are of Sebastian—we are Sebastian's people" (Jennifer Kobyashi from the Crow and Kobyashi interview 2013). Researching and rehearsing bits of scenarios and situations began in 1990, taking inspiration and outlines from the scenario collection of Flaminio Scala: *Il Teatro delle favole representative*, translated by Henry F. Salerno, and published in 1611. According to Kenneth McGee in the forward of Scala's book, this collection of scenarios was predominantly from the Gelosi Troupe, directed by Francesco Andreini, a colleague of Flaminio Scala's, who performed from 1572 to 1604 (Salerno 1967: xvi). The Gelosi were one of the earliest troupes to gain respected recognition for their Commedia dell'Arte performances. Since actors themselves created the characters and the dialogue, it became customary to write out their scenarios upon retiring, wishing to preserve their work (Duchartre 1966: 50). These scenarios of the Gelosi Troupe, while published in 1611, were mostly played before 1600, thus adhering to the SCA requirement for pre-1600 art/theatre.

i Sebastiani's research led to understanding that a scenario typically included a Pantalone, the miserly merchant, father, or guardian; a Dottore, the doddering pedant, sometimes friend or neighbor of Pantalone; a Capitano, the braggart coward, usually Spanish, whose bumbling heroics and jealousies were often part of the comedy of the play; the Innamorati, the young lovers, around which the plot revolved; a maid to the ingénue, and servant to the suitor; and two or more zannis, the clever valets and most physical of the cast. The company uses these characters in their rehearsals and performances. They remain especially true to the importance of the Lovers in each plot development. At the end of a show the audiences should care about the Lovers; i Sebastiani actors feel the Lovers are essential to the sixteenth century ideal. If an audience leaves a performance talking about the tricks of the zannis, or the bumbling fighting of Capitano, rather than the Lovers, the company feels they have failed.

Convincing unseasoned actors to play romantic lovers was the leading challenge for the young company. It was easier for the men to play "wooing a lover" when they had a strong character—someone like Capitano Spavento. Consequently, the characters Pantalone, Spavento, Gratiano, Pedrolino, and Arlecchino received more attention and enthusiasm than the Lovers, Oratio or Flavio. Since the dialogue was improvised, compliments such as "Your hair is nice", or "your eyes are so pretty" fell flat. As Jennifer Kobyashi describes it:

> Like Jane Austen, the lovers' story is a courtship story; it's not a love story. How do you do that and still convey it, to a modern audience? We discovered we'd fall back onto a lot of Shakespeare, and translations of Italian sonnets, and the music of the time, and a lot of metaphors: "Oh how my blood sings when you appear, and the birds fly to my heart". Finding people who can do that and practice that, is what took the longest in terms of starting a troupe.
>
> (Crow and Kobyashi 2013)

The company members eventually embraced the poetry and naïve passions of the Lovers to make them the heart of a scenario.

The company strives to refrain from contexts that scream "modern world," especially with the language. There are colloquial phrases contemporary audiences might recognize and not understand as inappropriate moments, but i Sebastiani continually reinforces awareness of words or phrases that would be anachronistic to the Renaissance. They call these "Swastika" words—words or their usage that have contemporary connotations, as well as historically appropriate words whose meanings have changed over the years. They are to be avoided at all costs. The term "swastika" evolved through understanding a word to be suitably period, but unsuitable in context: while a swastika symbol dates back to Mediterranean Classical Antiquity, and is merely an equilateral cross that represents auspiciousness or goodness, its meaning since the twentieth century has such negative connotations that one would not dare risk using it to symbolize goodness. An important example of a "swastika" word for the company is "okay"—clearly not Renaissance but habitually colloquial: "Try not to say 'okay' for a day!" (Catherine Crow from the Crow and Kobyashi interview 2013).

Other examples of "swastika" words that sometimes creep into improvisations:

- "Relationship", as in we need to talk about our relationship. It is about courting, or wooing, or you are engaged, or in love, or not;
- "Watches" for recognizing time, or looking at one's wrist to tell the time. One would refer to a clock in the tower, maybe on the wall, or a sundial;
- "No way";
- "Totally";
- Things strongly suggesting *The Princess Bride*, the movie from 1987;
- "Inconceivable";
- "Mostly dead";
- Some foods, such as tomatoes, tea, coffee (banned by the church until 1600), cheddar cheese, potatoes, and ice cream (Grun 1991: 265, 279, 305);
- Some everyday items: copper coins, daily newspapers, public libraries, wigs, leather upholstery for furniture, letter boxes, non-quill pens, forks (new to

society in the late 1500s), clear glass windows (Grun 1991: 261, 267, 271, 275, 321);

- Talk of the New World, or America—it was known, but often distracts an audience.

Ways to say "yes" other than "okay" are yes, certainly, certes, indeed, I agree, or decidedly (Jennifer Kobyashi from the Crow and Kobyashi interview 2013).

Most members of the troupe are oriented toward language, and clever with puns and gags. But the Lovers are not to be the brunt of jokes; their flighty metaphors and poetic images should be expressions of sincere passions. There are some triggers to contemporary references, but those are usually timeless. Many modern Commedia troupes use socio-political opportunities of the times to poke fun at the nobility, the ruling class—this is part of the Commedia dell'Arte tradition. But unlike jokes referring to a current president, i Sebastiani poke fun at the Doge, the ruling aristocracy—there were no presidents in the Renaissance.

Improvising text and action is the primary distinguishing feature of i Sebastiani. For safety reasons, they set stage combat moments, and some *lazzi* (the physical antics), such as food fights, but they are free with the direction of a plot, sometimes taking it straight to the point, and sometimes veering a long way around to get to the ending. Most contemporary troupes improvise to find material but at some point fix it; i Sebastiani never fixes its performances. One audience member came to four performances over the course of a week in Boston, and when asked why, she said, "I'm fascinated by it because you really are improvising, aren't you?" They know where the plot is going, but they do not know how it is going to get there. And they certainly have had several resounding flops (Catherine Crow from the Crow and Kobyashi interview 2013).

The company did local performances in the early 90s, but knew it had a venue in the SCA because of that organization's interest in pre-1600 customs, events, and people, including Commedia dell'Arte. Every year the SCA holds a convention of members and "kingdoms" in western Pennsylvania, currently at Cooper's Lake campground, near Slippery Rock, PA. The gathering is called the Pennsic War, for Pennsylvania and Punic War. It is a vast camping event, with groups from all over the world coming together to experience Medieval and Renaissance living for two weeks. The Pennsic War began in 1972 as an intense battle (the SCA has a combat system) between the Kingdom of the East and the Middle Kingdom, but has grown to hosting over 10,000 people. Now, along with the battles, the yearly gathering includes a market, a university offering classes, dance events, art displays, clay ovens to cook Renaissance meals—whatever one chooses to immerse oneself in for one or two weeks.

i Sebastiani took two shows to the Pennsic War in 1993: one commissioned by a particular campsite, and one to be performed in public for the performing arts camp. The smaller campsite performance had an audience of 50–60 people, but the public show's audience of up to 400 people was the largest ever for the troupe. Those presentations cemented their reputation in the SCA and they have since had individual campsite requests each year, including public performances in the performing arts tent. This has also led to other SCA related performances in Montreal, Boston, and other locales. While they do not carry their stages in carts like early Commedia troupes, they have become a traveling troupe of sorts.

Another event, which established their Commedia legitimacy, was the Commedia dell'Austin conference in Austin, Texas in 2001. They took a company of their more experienced actors and found they were performing on the first evening of the conference. Since the early formation of the troupe, Sebastian (Jeff Hatalsky) had insisted they begin each show with an introduction haranguing the audience to get them into the mood, followed by a company tag line. He had a particular shtick about "oh you lucky people! Today you are going to see the most magnificent show. Your children will weep that they were not able to see this production…. Blah, blah, blah, blah, blah… and now, i Sebastiani, 'The Greatest Commedia dell'Arte troupe in the Entire World!'"—the tag line shouted by the whole company. At a conference of Commedia troupes, several eyebrows rose… "Oh really?" (Crow and Kobyashi interview 2013).

After the first performance, they were slated for another show the next morning, but their Arlecchino at the time, Alex Newman, lost his voice, forcing an adaptation in which Arlecchino was mute (cp. Harpo Marx). The same scenario as the previous evening, "Flavio's Fortune", was played, but with a silent Arlecchino, obviously necessitating new tactics and dialogues for the other players. It was skillfully played and highly successful. With congratulations bestowed upon them by critical and knowledgeable audience members who had seen both shows, the company exemplified the true nature of improvisation.

We know professional actors, often playing the same character for many years, were at the heart of Commedia dell'Arte. While trying to adhere to all things traditionally Renaissance, i Sebastiani actors are trained to play an array of characters; company members coming and going necessitate this versatility. The company is a core of six to eight actors, with the remaining troupe supported by six to eight additional actors showing up occasionally, or new to the group. They have some favorite scenarios, which call for twelve to fourteen cast members but recently have been writing their own plots or using outlines from the Napoli scenarios to accommodate smaller casts. The plots from *The Commedia dell'Arte in Naples: A Bilingual Edition of the 176 Casamarciano Scenarios* (Cotticelli *et al.* 2001), were from the seventeenth century, and used stock characters such as Pulcinella, Rosella, Coviello, Tartaglia, and Cinzia, popular in the Neapolitan area. These were scenarios of six to eight characters. The company adroitly adapts the archetypes of the seventeenth century Casamarciano scenarios to Scala's sixteenth century stock characters.

Each year i Sebastiani performs for high school or university theatre history or literature classes. An academic setting lends itself to Renaissance sensibilities because Venice and most of Italy had modern amenities such as universities, banks, a postal system, and elected government. "All university situations are the same: parents complaining about tuition, gambling, asking for money, children not wanting to study because love interests dominate…" (Jennifer Kobyashi from the Crow and Kobyashi interview 2013).

The company enjoys question and answer periods after shows because they learn what works and what falls flat. A poignant question after a particular show was "Do you do real theatre?" After much chuckling, they answered, "If you mean do you do scripted theatre, which many members do, but some do not, the answer for i Sebastiani is 'No.' If you are saying this is not a real art form, then we beg to differ" (Crow and Kobyashi 2013).

Music and dance are brought into performances, depending on the talents of actors on hand. Occasionally they will try to teach a specific skill to the troupe members but primarily use what the actors bring to rehearsals. Qualities that are valued in company members are intelligence, quick thinking, willingness to train and participate, willingness to dress in sixteenth century clothing, and eagerness to leave pre-conceptions at the door.

The company is still going strong, building a new website for the twenty-first century, and often passing the bucket for contributions at the end of a show. Unlike original Commedia troupes, they do not seem to be aiming for widespread, public recognition beyond the SCA. The original meaning of "dell'Arte" means "of the actors' guilds," designating professional actors, and while i Sebastiani include amateurs, these amateur actors aim to mirror professionals. May they remain, "the Greatest Commedia dell'Arte troupe in the Entire World."

References

Cotticelli, Francesco, Heck, Anne G., and Heck, Thomas F. (2001) *The Commedia dell'Arte In Naples: A Bilingual Edition of the 176 Casamarciano Scenarios,* Vol. 1. Lanham, Maryland, US and London: The Scarecrow Press, Inc.

Crow, Catherine and Kobyashi, Jennifer (July, 2013) Interview with i Sebastiani company members. Boston University, US.

Duchartre, Pierre Louis (1966) *The Italian Comedy.* New York: Dover Publications, Inc.

Fava, Antonio (2007) *The Comic Mask in the Commedia dell'Arte.* Evanston, IL, US: Northwestern University Press.

Grun, Bernard (1991 [1975] 3rd ed.) *The Timetables of History.* New York: Simon & Schuster/Touchstone.

Salerno, Henry F. (1967) (Trans.) *Scenarios of the Commedia dell'Arte: Flaminio Scala's 'Il Teatro delle favole rapresentative'* (Flaminio Scala 1611) New York: New York University Press.

Society for Creative Anachronism (n.d.) Online. Available at: www.sca.org (accessed August 2013).

49

COMMEDIA WOMEN ON STAGE— AND IN THE WINGS

Joan Schirle

Don't believe
In their feigned ardors; loves imagined in
Their scenes I've handled with emotions false…
And, as in theaters, in varied style,
I have now played a woman, now a man,
As Nature would instruct and Art as well…

(Andreini 2005: 31)

Like my great inspiration, Isabella Andreini, I have played both women and men. I was never a zanni, though I am a good comedienne. I can play the clever servant, but am usually cast as a *prima innamorata*—my height, my looks, my carriage lent itself to that—but I am arguably not a diva by nature or all the time. I created four masked male characters—based on local types—and ten masked women for my solo show, *Second Skin*. I have played Ridolfo, the owner of Goldoni's *La Bottega del Caffè*, and many other males from mad scientists to punks, sometimes with tongue in cheek, but mostly based on careful observation—I like the audience to be unsure of what they are seeing.

It is easy to imagine that Isabella had to prove herself twice as much as the men in her troupe in order to be taken seriously as an actor, writer, and leader. In living *la vita commedia*—founding a company, acting, writing, producing, touring, improvising in art and life—I had to learn to hold my own with strong male partners onstage and off. "And Commedia, after all, is not a theatrical form, it's a way of life" (Mazzone-Clementi and Hill 1974: 64).

Over 40 years' work I have run into both casual and not-so-subtle sexism directed at women in Commedia: the director whose workshop I observed in Rome complaining to me over espressos how much he hated teaching women: "Commedia is not a woman's form"…. Never finding my name among the lists of US artistic directors (this being as much a prejudice against ensembles as against women)…. Being told by male directors how surprised they were to learn I knew anything about Commedia…. That we women were not supposed to be funny—"just help the guys get their laughs".... Hearing workshop leaders say that women of the Commedia dell'Arte, especially the servants, were all flirty, sassy—near nymphos, really—who would tumble into the sack at a wink. Some shoulder-shaking, a little hip twirling, and there's your character! As in life, sex is one of the incessant drivers of Commedia action, but not the only one, and it comes in many colors. The game of attraction, flirtation, seduction, fulfillment, jealousy, and frustration gives poetry and musicality to the form, not to mention that "feigned ardors" have been employed by women for centuries. The shadings of class, economic status, and place give truth to the human comedy beyond just style, the *contrasto* coming through a range of types and motivations, from splendid bawds to incurable romantics, upstairs and down.

Contemporary research, much of it by women, has opened windows onto the everyday life of the Commedia actresses—some of whom were no doubt "honest courtesans." Period documents reveal the context for their characters' behavior and tell their back story. In the sixteenth and seventeenth centuries, as in most other periods of history, virginity was a closely guarded commodity. A girl who was no longer a virgin would not be nearly so desirable in the marriage market, so girls were carefully guarded and watched. Why else would there be a business in sewing up the hymens of upper class girls who had been deflowered?

Girls matured earlier—marriageable at middle-school age, Juliet was 14 when she became engaged to Paris. Marriages were affairs of business, a contract; thus the many plots about girls trying to escape their fathers' choice of husband. A few years ago I co-wrote and directed, with Giulio Cesare Perrone, a play based on the life of Casanova (*Casanova: Animal Instinct*), who loved and was loved by possibly hundreds of women, and whose memoirs give us a detailed picture of mid-eighteenth century mores. A young woman of class could easily end up in a convent, not because she had a religious vocation, but if she could not be successfully married, if she was deflowered, got pregnant, refused to marry the choice of her parents, or if she was not wealthy enough to secure a good husband. The controls in place to shape the lives of young women were strong enough to make great comedy about those controls being subverted by the young and the willing. The younger *innamorati* desperately want to touch each other—their struggle is the game. Staging them always at least a finger's length apart heightens the tension and offers great comic possibility.

In Casanova's day, if you were a young woman of a certain class forced to marry an old man, it was expected you would be entertaining your lovers on the side, and that when your husband died you would be a rich widow—a strong motivation for a young woman of meager means to attract and wed a rich old man. Some husbands turned a blind eye; others employed all kinds of safeguards to keep their young wives in check. This is the stuff of the comedy as well as the tragedy of life. Pantalone's tragedy is not just that he grows old, but that he must constantly worry about being cuckolded. Even if he wins a young wife, he lives with the gnawing uncertainty: "did I or did I not wed a virgin?"

An old, unmarried man (or married, but his wife ignores him) has young female servants—the girls who do the household laundry, clean up, manage the kitchen. Why would they run around the house flirting with their employers? Was that a means to exert control in the house and to keep the old dog from getting too close?

Or because it was the only way they could keep their jobs—*Nine to Five* in the Renaissance. "Sexual harassment" was an unknown concept, and clever girls not only kept their jobs but kept themselves from being backed into a pantry closet and groped by a lecherous employer. Dodge and feint, bob and weave... smile and run away. In other words, walk backwards while pretending to come forward.

On the other hand, who is to say that all old men are unattractive? By the eighteenth century, Pantalone was a model of the bourgeoisie. A clever servant might hope to advance in a number of ways, depending on how smart she was and how pretty:

- She makes herself indispensable to the master (Moliere's Dorine, Toinette).
- She is flattering, flirtatious but never yielding—Pantalone gets a hand on her knee once a month.
- She knows the old man is attracted to her, and maybe he is not so bad, but she is holding out for marriage (Argentina, Goldoni's "ingenious chambermaid").
- She puts out because she is attracted to him, with no ulterior motive (forget it—this is not the stuff of Commedia!).

Women's contributions to theatre and many other fields, either on their own or to the work of the "great men," were often overlooked by most "his-storians," in spite of the fact that the great man himself often gave credit where it was due. Copeau, for example, acknowledged his great debt to his principal collaborator Suzanne Bing for developing the pedagogy of his school:

> Without her, my plan would probably have never come to fruition. For more than ten years, she took the heaviest share of a thankless task... Through her experiments, constantly performed and developed, she furnished me with the elements of a method of education of young actors.
>
> (Copeau in Rudlin and Paul 1990: 255)

Dario Fo has always credited Franca Rame as his indispensable co-creator and partner, though in many news stories announcing his Nobel prize, she was only mentioned as "Fo's wife, the actress Franca Rame." In 50 years, will the true fact of their collaboration be a matter of record, of history?

The history of Dell'Arte International itself is another case in point. Which of the following is true: Carlo Mazzone-Clementi and Jane Hill founded Dell'Arte; Carlo founded Dell'Arte; Jane founded Dell'Arte? Answer: Yes. Jane Hill never had a pedagogical mission independent of Carlo's, nor would she ever claim to. The seed of Dell'Arte was Carlo's vision and personal mission as the bearer of a tradition and his own genius. Less remembered is that Jane clarified his language, found the money, the building, the supporters, and the image: she made it happen. Could one have done any of it without the other? No. Did they both acknowledge that? *Yes.* Will history? Only if we record it that way!

In 1974 their essay in *The Drama Review* appeared—with Carlo as the author—an important article which articulated clearly for the first time to a US audience the importance of Commedia to the contemporary actor. Carlo always stated that it was

Jane who actually wrote the article based on his thoughts. I asked her why she never put both their names on the article. It was related to marketing and visibility, she said:

> I thought that was the most effective way to accomplish our goals, that a school and company headed by a man—particularly a somewhat exotic, romantic-sounding European man—would attract more attention and be taken more seriously. I convinced Carlo this was so.
> (Hill, personal interview with Joan Schirle, Blue Lake, CA, US, 1985)

Noting how few women today are accorded recognition as Commedia practitioners, I might conclude that this attitude still influences our field.

The utterly essential work of women (and men) who themselves were not carriers of a personal artistic vision has also gone unsung in the histories. Much of the work of feminist historians of the last few decades has been to uncover the stories—from all fields, arts, sciences—that lay hidden in the "official histories." Those of us who work in ensembles recognize the truth of Eugenio Barba's words, "It is in the anonymity of the daily work that we encounter the ceaseless challenge that tests the intensity and the credibility of our motivations" (Barba 2000: 3).

> *"On stage there is only room for the fastest and zestiest zanni—often this character is a woman."*
>
> Carlo Mazzone-Clementi

Among the women from whom I have learned about Commedia, the late Sandra Archer was one of the greats, a truly zesty zanni, loved for "her ability to create a *gestus* (Brecht term)—image/mime/memorable series of poses, demonstrations of thought and feeling. The total body image was enlarged and concentrated, specific and memorable. That meticulous skill along with a clear voice" (Davis 2012). This is what gave Sandy Archer her power performing Commedia with the San Francisco Mime Troupe from 1959 to 1970. During the 80s she taught often at Dell'Arte; from this great actress I learned how to enter and exit, what stories the feet tell, the historical contexts, how Commedia dell'Arte plays in contemporary work. I still use scenes she assigned from Joan Holden's adaptation of *L'Amant Militaire,* set in the Vietnam War. Archer transmitted her expertise to Jael Weisman, who directed and collaborated on most of our company's work for its first 25 years. He brilliantly structured comic business (and never stopped coaching me to separate my gestures from my lines!).

Julie Goell inspired me about the musicality of Commedia, its songs and dances. It was Bari Rolfe's slender but important volumes that were for a long time some of the only available English translations of scenarios and short scenes (Rolfe 1977, 1978). Franca Rame inspired through her spirit, her brio, as one who could act, write, and thoroughly understand comedy. In a 1987 workshop she complained that one of the American translations of their plays was unsatisfactory because, for example, "in this line there are *three* laughs, and this translation only gets two!" For comedy to work as instructive, it must be funny. (She also chided us for the lack of glamour in our feminism.) Jane Hill taught me how to manage, how to market, how to write a grant, deal with creditors, run a festival... and deal with the maestro.

I learned my Commedia on my feet from maestro Carlo, who knew the connections from the pelvis and the foot to the mask and who was expert in the rustic, virtuosic chaos of the early Commedia. More learning came from Ferruccio Soleri, Geoff Hoyle, Giovanni Fusetti, Valeria Campo, and my partners of 25 years, Michael Fields and Donald Forest, whose comic partnership was an inspiration and a challenge, whose riffs off each other always cracked me up. Lecoq's approach and the play of masks was transmitted to me through teaching partnerships with Avner Eisenberg, Jonathan Paul Cook, Ralph Hall, Alain Schons and Ronlin Foreman.

The traditional Commedia masks that have survived into our time did so because of the actors who made their name and because of their status as archetypes. In like fashion, our company makes theatre based on our own strengths as actors, and we stretch ourselves through a range of types, genres, and projects. But in our teaching work, traditional Commedia, masks and stock characters are foundational, and studied as containers of essential human experiences embodied throughout the world. One of my favorite Balinese masks is the *telek,* the sole mask danced by women in a country with a vibrant mask tradition, but where only men play women in the masked dramas. Franca Rame said that the women of early Commedia refused to don a mask, in that "they wished to be finally recognized as women, and not just men in disguise" (Fo 1991: 211). The women characters of traditional Commedia nonetheless often adopted physical disguises to be able to move safely in their world with the same agency as men.

As women in the twentieth century fought for equality and access to areas previously dominated by men, from politics to the military, so the need grew for women to have the opportunity to play Commedia with character masks on their faces. But that meant wearing the masks of male zanni and *vecchi,* whether playing them as men or women. Thus our research began at Dell'Arte School in the mid-1970s to develop masks of women characters. Some were feminine versions of traditional stock characters—a Pantalona, or Arlecchina, for example—and some were new characters. The hope for a new mask is to reveal a true archetype, or stock character. But inventing a new stock character is not easy! A stock character can be born, live on for many seasons and then disappear, just as American stock characters—the country bumpkin, the Toby, the hobo clown—were as familiar as the Bergamasque porter in their day; they arose from specific periods in our history. They thrilled their audiences for a time, and like numerous Italian characters, disappeared into obscurity.

A "new" Commedia character must strike an instant chord of recognition like The Miser, for example, so deeply ingrained in the archetypal memory of the audience that it transcends stereotype or caricatures, even national boundaries, and stands the test of time. The mask and character known as Stupino/Stupina was created at the Dell'Arte School in Blue Lake, California in 1978. The mask itself was sculpted by Gina Bastone, then a Canadian student in our class of 1978. She constructed the papier-mâché mask that became the prototype for all subsequent versions of this slow-witted character, and called it "Coviello," after the long-nosed character pictured on page 44 of Duchartre (1966). We continued to call it "Coviello" for a year or two; but in researching the character, we encountered conflicting information gleaned from different Commedia sources. The students began to get confused. The zanni that inevitably emerged from the play of Gina's mask was slow-witted, naive, gullible, and sometimes shy or dull, depending on what the actor brought to it. "But," students would say, "Duchartre says Coviello is keen, subtle, sly, adroit, supple, and conceited!" Duchartre lists Coviello among the "anonymous, forgotten, or little-known characters," (1966: 291) as does Oreglia, who says the character is "a mask of Sicilian origin, a zanni/Capitano who sings, dances and is acrobatic" (1968: 105). Rudlin says he is from Naples (Rudlin 1994: 157); Perrucci complained about Neapolitan Covielli: "they overstep the line between wit and stupidity" (Perrucci 1699: 151). You can see why students might get confused!

Trusting the actors and the mask, I re-named it "Stupino," not forcing onto it qualities determined by sketchy historical information, but letting students make an organic discovery of what the mask had to teach them. This was consistent with our objective to develop a "human comedy" and an American Commedia inspired by, but not limited to, the Italian stock characters. So "Stupino" and "Stupina" were born and live to this day, an ageless mask that easily lends itself to women or men. The many versions I have seen are mostly based on the original Bastone mask, made by graduates of the Dell'Arte International School of Physical Theatre, whose original exposure to the character was in their training with our mask collection.*

My Stupina story illustrates why you should learn your Commedia only a little from books. Carlo always resisted preaching "The Gospel of Commedia" as though it were something that existed on stone tablets, instead of a fluid, lively, controversial, competitive, chaotic creature invented by Actor-Creators! Honor the energy of the masks themselves, remembering that there are tremendous contradictions within the historical material available about Commedia, most of which was written by a variety of actors, managers, historians, clerics, and scholars, well after the work of the actors who gave life to these masks.

Among those actors were women whose personalities and abilities inspired Goldoni to write so many terrific female roles, such as "Theodora Medebach and Maddalena Raffi Marliani, actresses of the Medebach company with whom Goldoni maintained long friendships..." (Coyle 2006: 60). Having directed his *The Ingenious Chambermaid*, I think they must have been impressive—the lead role of Argentina requires incredible virtuosity, extraordinary timing, and a great sense of fun. Developing contemporary female stock characters can be approached as Goldoni did by finding new twists on the old models, in the Commedia spirit and tradition (Kennard 1920: 134). In 1978 I devised a female detective named Scar Tissue, rooted in the twentieth century American archetype of the hard-boiled detective. Dressed like Sam Spade and using the language of Raymond Chandler, she was popular enough to lead a trilogy of full-length mystery plays written collaboratively by the Dell'Arte Company over a dozen years. I was always surprised onstage by the power of an archetype to elicit instant recognition in the audience. In a twist on the woman-as-victim archetype the Dell'Arte Company adapted Moliere's doctor plays as *Malpractice, Or Love's The Best Doctor* in 1984. Lucinde, a patient nearly killed by the pokes and "remedies" of her bumbling doctors, finds the courage to fight Death and take charge of her own healing. Lauren Wilson's *The Golden State*, based on Moliere's *The Miser*, cast me as Gertrude Hopper, wealthy southern California widow with her millions stuffed in her bra. My servants were the Dorines and

Toinettes of today's California—immigrants from the Ukraine and Guatemala. By glancing off the known as well as the new, we help audiences accept the archetype with a new consciousness. They find delight, even when unfamiliar with the originals, through the richness of the stock characters.

Lucky me, to have made my living for 40 years as a player, writer, teacher and member of an ensemble of actors. I continue to research Commedia dell'Arte for its relevance to my own time, place, and cultural context as a theatre maker. Women are now able to populate the Commedia stage through a full range of types—the smart, the crafty, the gorgeous, the manipulative, old and young, foolish and bright, weak and powerful, masked and unmasked. As a teacher, I try to help women take part not only in the preservation of the form, but in the continuing evolution of our beloved human comedy.

References

Barba, Eugenio (2000) *Sonning Prize Acceptance Speech,* Copenhagen University. Available at: www.odinteatret.dk/media/40334/2000,%20Copenhagen%20Univ.%20-%20EN%20Discurso%20Honoris%20Causa.pdf (accessed September 2014).

Coyle, Margaret Anne (2006) *The Sauce Is Better than the Fish: The Use of Food to Signify Class in the Comedies of Carlo Goldoni 1737–1762.* PhD. dissertation, University of Maryland, US. Available at: http://drum.lib.umd.edu/bitstream/1903/3473/1/umi-umd-3299.pdf (accessed September 2014).

Davis, R. G. (2012) Memorial for Sandra Archer, San Francisco, transcription.

Duchartre, Pierre L. (1966) *The Italian Comedy,* tr. Randolph T. Weaver, New York: Dover.

Fo, Dario (1991) *The Tricks of The Trade,* tr. Joe Farrell, London: Routledge.

Kennard, Joseph S. (1920) *Goldoni and the Venice of His Time,* New York: Macmillan.

MacNeill, Anne, (ed.) (2005) *Selected Poems of Isabella Andreini,* tr. James Wyatt Cook, Maryland, US: Scarecrow Press.

Mazzone-Clementi, Carlo and Hill, Jane (1974) "Commedia and the Actor," *The Drama Review* vol.18, no.1; reprinted in *Popular Theatre: A Sourcebook,* (ed.) Joel Schechter (2003), London and New York: Routledge, pp 83–9.

Oreglia, Giacomo (1968) *The Commedia dell'Arte,* tr. L. F. Edwards. New York: Hill and Wang.

Perrucci, Andrea (1699) *A Treatise on Acting, from Memory and by Improvisation,* tr. Francesco Cotticelli, Anne Goodrich Heck, Thomas Heck, Maryland, US: Scarecrow Press (2008).

Rolfe, Bari (1977) *Commedia dell'Arte, A Scene Study Book,* Berkeley CA, US: Personabooks.

——(1978) *Farces, Italian Style,* Berkeley CA, US: Personabooks.

Rudlin, John (1994) *Commedia dell'Arte: An Actor's Handbook,* New York: Routledge.

Rudlin, John and Paul, Norman H. (eds. and tr.) (1990) *Copeau: Texts on Theatre,* London: Routledge.

* These mask makers, all former Dell'Arte International students, have developed versions of Stupina/Stupino for their own Commedia collections: Newman (*Newman's Commedia Mask Company*); Joe Dieffenbacher, Minna Holopainen (*Nakupelle Masks*); Genessee Spridco (*Genessee Masks*); Wendy Gough Soroka (*Arly Masks*); Michelle Schulz (*Taskmaskers*); Jessica Hart (*Hart Masks*); Todd Espeland (*Commedia Zuppa*, with Allison Williams); Chris Beaulieu; Leslie Pasternack; Tony Fuemmeler; Alice Nelson; and former DAI faculty member Bruce Marrs (*Marzilla Masks*).

50

COMMEDIA COUNTERPARTS
Middle Eastern and Asian connections
Kathy Foley

Since the early twentieth century Western exponents of Commedia style performance have been drawn to Asian genres as part of their investigation of the mask as a theatrical tool. Consider that Copeau who helped jumpstart European masks and Commedia in contemporary Western actor training, felt his school's 1924 production of *Kantan* was its zenith, stating: "This Nōh... remains for me one of the jewels... of the Vieux Colombier" (Leigh 1979: 47). (André Gide showed a more traditional Eurocentric bias when he countered that Copeau "terrifies me when he declares he was never nearer to the attainment of his goal than in the Japanese Nōh... a play with no relation to our traditions, our customs, our beliefs" [Leigh 1979: 48].) Ron Jenkins (1994), a translator of Dario Fo to the English-speaking world, has researched Balinese mask performance since the 1970s and undertaken a number of collaborative projects with Balinese *topeng* dancer I Nyoman Catra (b. 1957), while the Blue Lake, California school of Dell'Arte's master teacher Joan Shirle (2009) has taken Western actors to Bali for work in *topeng* with Ida Bagus Anom and shadow master I Wayan Mardika (see Shirle 2009). Attraction goes in both directions: *kyōgen* artist, Shigeyama Akira (b. 1952) became interested in the work of Commedia master Alessandro Marchetti (b. 1929) of Italy/Switzerland and the Swiss clown Dimitri (b. 1935) in the 1980s. Nomura Mansai, scion of another *kyōgen* family, on a fellowship in England in the 1990s met Lecoq-trained Simon McBurney of Theatre de Complicité with whom he has collaborated on a number of acting/directing projects.

In the last fifty years significant research has become available in European languages on forms that use masks such as Japanese *nō/kyōgen*, Korean mask dance genres, and Indonesian *topeng* (mask) forms. To a more limited extent forms that use set types but not masks—Turkish *orta oyuni* (play in the center), Iranian *ruhowzi* (stage over the courtyard pool), and Indian improvised theatres such as the comic *bhavai* (expression of life) of Gujarat—have been compared to Commedia. As more performers are trained in Asian mask traditions, questions of how these genres may relate to Commedia's historical background or may help revitalize contemporary Western mask theatre arise. Western artists who may begin learning Commedia have developed intercultural productions that meld Commedia with selected genres. For

464

example, *Bird in the DMZ,* a 2005 production of Aristophanes' *Birds* set in the Korean DMZ (Demilitarized Zone), mixed Commedia clowning and Korean mask dance as developed by Eli Simon of the University of California, Irvine and Kim Suk-Man of the Korean National University of the Arts (Simon and Kim 2005). The innovative *kyōgen* actor Shigeyama Sennojō (1923–2010) presented the "3 G" Project (3 Greats/3 Geezers) with Commedia-artist Alessandro Marchetti and clown Dimitri (Japan Foundation 2009).

Western artists who come to Asia in search of training in stylized theatres have increasingly become embedded in Asian mask or comic genres as researchers, scholars or performers, for example, Jonah Salz (2001; Iezzi and Salz 2007) leads an English language *kyōgen* group Noho (founded 1981) with Shigeyama Akira in Kyoto; Camencita Palermo is an Italian whose research and performance work has supported the rise of women's *topeng* (previously, an all-male genre) in Bali; and Komang Martin, a Belgian, performs regularly with the comic mask dance (*topeng bondres*) group of I Nyoman Durpa from Bayuning, Buleleng, Bali. Cultures have crossed.

Have the many improvised theatres of comic types evolved independently on the Eurasian landmass or is there a historical connection, and, if so, has influence flowed west to east, east to west, or has it—as in the twentieth and twenty-first centuries— boomeranged back and forth? This brief discussion will not answer historiographical questions, but will briefly address selected issues by discussing selected analogous theatres.

Middle Eastern and Asian theatres of set characters—forms in which performers improvise narratives according to rules of type, conventions of oral formulaic composition theorized by Lord (1960), using music and dance, iconic costumes/makeup/masks, and scenarios selected at the top of the show—are old and widespread. These theatres use dichotomies of class (master–servant/high–low) and ethnic specificities (accents, behaviors) to fuel humor. The genres are closely related to conventions of storytelling and puppetry—characters portrayed, stories presented, and performance techniques overlap within geographic/linguistic spheres. Some genres, especially in Asia, continue to the present, serving as potential models for Euro-American artists seeking performer-generated improvisatory theatre of masks/types.

Older scholarship on Commedia, for example, Duchartre, traces origins of Commedia to Greece via Roman *atellanae* (1966: 25). But it is feasible to argue the Commedia of Renaissance Italy was influenced by performances from further east: Fulchignoni argued Eurocentrism has obscured the non-Italian roots of Commedia and saw it as arriving in Europe via Constantinople: "Is it possible, for instance, without resorting to the East to explain the sudden apparition of the 'black leather mask' (a typical, thousand-year-old product of shamanistic ritual in Central Asia) in the West at that particular time?" (1990: 35–6, see also 29–41). Fulchignoni believes that mask practice moved from India with Buddhism through China, Korea, and Japan, and was carried by the Turks from China into Anatolia. Savarese (2010: 78–86) criticizes Fulchignoni's simplistic diffusion model, but agrees Constantinople was the crucial transition point. Savarese critiques European dismissal of Islamic culture as "anti-theatrical" despite evidence of many improvised genres found from

Turkey to India, suggesting lack of written documents and research on Islamic theatre has limited understanding of historical processes. Though many have referenced the 10,000 Indian performers supposedly coming to Persia at the time of Bahram Gaur (480 BCE), this story was only first cited in Firdusi 1011 CE but the poet affirmed their descendants, *luri* or *luti*—often conflated with the Gypsies—were active as performer-singer-entertainers in Persia in the twelfth century. Such remarks lead contemporary Western artists or scholars to wonder about links back to Indian forms and of course association of Rom (gypsies) and India and performing arts (dance, puppetry, acrobatics, etc.) have been explored.

Meanwhile, inspired by the twentieth century European work in reviving Commedia dell'Arte, Asian researchers are looking for pan-Asian roots and relations too. Japanese *kyōgen* master Nomura Mannojō (1960–2004) sought to explore the arrival of mask performance in Japan in the eighth century from points west. In 2001 he created *shingigaku* ("new" *gigaku*—a Japanese Buddhist mask processional genre of the seventh to thirteenth century). Mannojō studied masks of China, Tibet, Bhutan, Uigur, and Korean groups to find possible roots of Japanese comic/mask arts (Fukushima 2005: 249–68). Meanwhile, Javanese mask dancer/comic Didik Nini Towok has explored Southeast Asian–Japanese connections (Ross 2005: 214–26) as has scholar-performer Margaret Coldiron (2005). There is no doubt that whatever the real history of older connections either across Asia, or between Asia and Europe, contemporary mask training is forging new bonds between Euro-Anglophone Commedia of today and forms of the Levant and Asia. This chapter will discuss only selected forms of the Middle East, South and Southeast Asia, and East Asia.

Middle East

In the Middle East the major theatres with analogous features are the Turkish *orta oyuni* (play in the open air [see Turkish Culture Foundation n.d.]) of the Ottoman Empire (1259–1924) and the Iranian/Persian *ruhowzi* (planks above the pool drama, see Haery 1982). Both genres are only vestigial at present. Some scholars state that Western influences explain the similarities (Martinovitch 1968: 14 sees Greek mime and Italian Commedia as sources for the Turkish genre). At its height, during the late Ottoman Empire, simple screens formed the backdrop for the open air Turkish performance. Drums (*chifte nare*), a reed (*zurna*), and other instruments provided music. Pishekâr (Clever Man) orchestrated the performance, carrying his bat. Kavuklu, the clown sported his high fez. The Zenne (Woman) was traditionally played by a male, while Zampara was the dandy. Other characters represented Ottoman diversity—Adjem, the Persian trader; Ermeni, an Armenian jeweler; Laz, the Black Sea Georgian; Iahudi (Jew); Frenk (European), etc. A dialogue between Pishekâr and Kavuklu was followed by an improvised comic story. This theatre of types paralleled *karagöz* (Turkish shadow theatre)—Karagöz corresponds to Kavuklu and Karagöz's companion Hacivat resembles Pishekâr.

Persian *ruhowzi*, staged over the pool in a house courtyard is an analogous form. Here the straight man is Haji, who has made his pilgrimage to Mecca: his interests are love and money. The clown is the soot face character Siah (Black Face), sometimes called Mobarak after the black clown of *khemeih shab bazi* (string puppetry). Siah criticizes the Haji's status quo. At least one Zenne (Woman) played by a female impersonator was needed. Sholi, son of the Haji, and Shah (Emperor) would be added. Beeman (1982: 104) traces the *ruhowzi* to *taqlid* (imitation), an entertainment in which one or more clowns would improvise comedy using accents and behaviors of different ethnicities. The form has overlap with *naqali* (solo storytelling), the greengrocer's play (*baqqal bazi*) and *pahlavan kachal* (glove puppetry), as well as string puppets. Related forms are reported from the seventeenth century, though the references to *luti* (fifth or eleventh century) are seen as early proof to this comic theatre. In the nineteenth century *ruhowzi* was in its current form with distinctive costumes and ethnic figures presenting simple improvised stories (Floor 2005: 57–61). Haery writes: "The Syah [Siah]'s relationship; with his master, the Haji, is based on the Haji's opinion that his servant is an inferior human being. This... breeds the comic struggle of Ru-howzi" (1982: 72). Haery sees *ruhowzi* linked to Commedia and Indian *bhavai*, a "pan-Eurasian development" (1982: 149).

South and Southeast Asia

India has a multitude of Commedia-like forms, but few use actual masks. Here again there are parallels between storytelling, puppetry, and improvised theatres in which clowns are foregrounded. For example, *bhavai* is attributed to Asaita Thakar, a fourteenth century outcaste Brahmin. The genre is performed for Navarati, a nine night festival honoring the mother goddess. The major character is the Ranglo (Clown) and Brahmin, Tailor, Potter, Scavenger, Moneylender, etc. are satirized (Richmond 1997: 82; Gargi 1966: 51–71). Stories, called *vesa* (costume), may be mythical or historical, but improvised humor is the core. Music and dance are normal. Many other genres with different names, especially those of North India are associated with wandering musician-performer-dancers who may be called *bhand*, *bhat*, *dom*, *baul*, etc. (See Emigh 1996: 210–11 and Pamment 2008).

Documentation of Javanese and Balinese forms grew exponentially over the twentieth century with many Western artists interested in mime or Commedia exploring *topeng*, mask, genres from the 1970s to the present. Emigh (1996: 105–205), Foley and Sedana (2005: 171–98), and Dibia and Ballinger (2004) provide information on Balinese genres that remain lively to the present. A mask dance is needed for completion of Balinese religious ceremonials, so top *topeng* performers are in strong demand to the present. I Nyoman Kakul (1905–82), Ida Bagus Anom (b. 1953), and I Ketut Kodi are among the top artists of the late twentieth or early twenty-first century. Performers generally come from the lowest of the four Balinese castes, but are considered priestly in that their performance of the mask of semi-demonic old man Sida Karya (Completing the Ritual Work) is needed.

Topeng pajegan is a ritual, solo performance, but mask dance can also be presented as entertainment, called *topeng panca* (five mask dancers) where performers group together and divide the various roles (major masks are the prince, female, minister, and two clowns, or *panasar*). Kartala is a boastful loudmouth, while Wijil is a witty fool. The clowns act as narrators/commentators/comics in a way that reminds us of the *dalang* (puppet master) in the *wayang kulit* (shadow puppetry) which is a linked genre (some *topeng* dancers do both mask dance and puppetry). A wide variety of inventive additional comic characters called *bondres* (comics) may enter to provide levity. Stories are improvised in a mixture of archaic Kawi language (for noble characters), while the clowns provide translations into colloquial Balinese.

In contemporary performance, stories are being overtaken by the *bondres,* whose comic impersonations of the sexy woman, the tourist, or buck-toothed fool evoke constant laughter. *Topeng* is traditionally all-male but Western women have been studying the genre since the 1970s, and since 2003 Balinese women have created an all-female troupe (Palermo 2005). The deep and rich performance culture of Bali has inspired many cross-cultural collaborations and innovations.

Meanwhile, on Java, rich mask genres flourish in Cirebon where Pak Kandeg, Pak Sujana Arja and Ibu Sawitri were major artists of the twentieth century (Foley 1990). Madura, Central Java, and West Java are other areas where mask dance theatres of type abounded until recently. Clowning on Java is often the purview of the clown Semar, most customarily a black-bodied, hermaphroditic high god of the universe who has descended to the world to serve the righteous princes as a servant/advisor/ clown. Semar is accompanied by his sons who have characteristics of the straight man (Petruk) and the fool (Gareng/Bagong). Parallels between the *topeng* mask genres and the puppet forms (*wayang golek* rod puppetry in West Java [Sunda] and *wayang kulit* [shadow puppetry] in Central and East Java/Madura) are clear. Stories are drawn from the *Ramayana, Mahabharata,* and tales about Panji, a prince of East Java, along with other histories and legends. Performances were traditionally staged outdoors on temporary stages for rites of passage ceremonies. Dialogue is improvised following an agreed upon outline, with patterns established by puppet theatre (*wayang*). Performance is accompanied by gamelan orchestra, primarily made up of gong chimes and percussive instruments.

East Asia

Shamanism and Buddhism lie behind the Korean mask theatre that goes by different names in different areas, and is believed to have come from China, perhaps with Buddhism, achieving its current form in the nineteenth century (Cho 1988: 15–16). Many Korean mask genres are now listed as national Intangible Cultural Properties (CP). Commoners were performers and lower class views and critique of Yi Dynasty (1392–1906) structures are preserved in the mask, puppet, and mime traditions. All performers were male until the early twentieth century when women began to play novice monks and young female roles. Masks are of gourd, wood, or paper. Costumes and colors for each character are set. Genres fall into three regions. Northern traditions include Bongsan *talchum* (CP 17, 1967), a genre that has the most virtuosic technique: the red-faced, dancing, lusty monk has become a national tourist symbol. Bukcheong Lion Dance (CP 15, 1967), Gangnyeong *talchum* (mask dance, CP 34, 1970), and *Eunyul talchum* from Hwanghae Province (CP 61, 1978) are other northern examples. (All numbering from Cultural Properties Administration 2001.)

A number of performers, originally itinerants or foreigners settled in the central Seoul region during the Joseon Dynasty (1392–1906). Performers were associated with the Confucian shrine at Sunkyungkwan University where they created offerings and were butchers. These lower class performers presented elaborate performances for New Year celebrations and visits by the Chinese envoys, when a raised stage (*sandae*) was constructed—this term (*sandae*) often appears in Seoul genres' names. In the seventeenth century fundamentalist elements and fiscal problems in the Confucian country caused the court entertainment bureau to be disestablished. Thereafter these artists wandered as *namsadang* performers (CP 3, 1964)—presenting puppetry *(ggoduk gaksi noreum)*, mask dance, acrobatics, and percussion music, and practicing homosexual prostitution on the side. This *namsadang nori* genre resembles the "hundred entertainments," antecedents of Chinese drama. In time, locals emulated performances of these comic wandering groups and in the eighteenth century major mask troupes operated in the market at Songpa on the Han River with their *sandae nori* (CP 49, 1973), and at Yangju on the route to China with its *byeol sandae nori* (CP 2, 1964). Yangju was a stopping point where Chinese envoys were entertained by these minor government officials who emulated characters, scenarios, and music of *namsadang nori*. (All numbering from Cultural Properties Administration 2001.)

In the south, Hahoe village *byeolshin gut talnori* (ritual shamanic mask performance, CP 69, 1981) in Andong region, masks dance was an exorcism presented every eight or ten years. The narrative shares features and characters with the northern and Seoul area mask genres, but this was a rite done by local villagers until the 1930s. *Ogwangdae* (five directions/clowns) from Tonggyeong (CP 6, 1964); Goseong (CP 7, 1964); and Gasan (CP 73, 1980), as well as various *yaryu* (field plays) from Suyeong (CP 43, 1971) and Dongnae (CP 18, 1967) were modeled on *namsadang* performance styles, but done by local farmers with ritual purpose, including rainmaking. (All numbering from Cultural Properties Administration 2001.)

Though there are many variations in stories, the overall pattern is constant. Mask dance is a theatre where the elite and powerful are ridiculed and the servants show sense and a sense of humor. For example, in the Hahoe village *byeolshin gut talnori*, Gakshi (Bride) collects offerings from villagers. Yangban (Aristocrat) and Seonbi (scholar) vie for the affections of Bune (a young widow) while their servants Choerangi and Imae expose their bosses' hypocrisy. The butcher (Baekjong) sells bulls testicles as an aphrodisiac and the lascivious monk (Jung) pursues Bune. The old woman (Halmi) weaves. Comic episodes rather than an ongoing narrative predominate. Though traditionally improvised, government inscription of genres as intangible cultural objects has led to freezing of the forms since the 1960s. Documented in early twentieth century practice, training centers now often replicate rather than encourage innovation and change. However, during the political struggles against the dictatorial government of Pak Jung-Hee [Pak Chung-hee] in the 1980s, mask dance style was often used in improvised political-critical theatre called *madang guk* (open air performance) and today young artists have started to develop new pieces, tapping aspects of the genre for new creative work.

Japan's *kyōgen* (wild words) is the comic counterpart to *nō* and the genre passed down in family lineages and traced back to Chinese and Korean sources (Brandon 1997). The art was low-class *sarugaku* (monkey music) associated with Buddhist shrines until it received aristocratic patronage in the fourteenth century, supported by samurai families. After decline in the Meji period, the art stabilized in the early twentieth century and has advanced in the post-World War II period where it has proved more flexible for change than *nō*. The two most important groups today are the Shigeyama family in Kyoto and the Nomura family of Tokyo (Teele 1984). The Izumi lineage in Tokyo has in the past decade been the first and only *kyōgen* family to include female performers.

Though many elements of improvisation are involved, the primary repertoire is 260 plays of the fifteenth and sixteenth century that poke fun at human foibles through puns, onomatopoeia, and physical action. Many scripts are relatively compact, requiring only three actors. *Kyōgen* performers also play minor roles in *nō*, and the *kyōgen* actor in *nō* often clarifies plots in language that is more accessible than *nō*'s archaic texts. This use of a clown as translator, explicator, and comic interpreter of the action corresponds to South and Southeast Asian practices.

Many *kyōgen* plays portray a lord who is outwitted by his two servants—Tarō Kaja and Jirō Kaja. Female characters are played by males with comic exaggeration and stylized feminine dress. Masks are usually reserved for animals or gods, but the unmasked face is less about personal expression than presenting stylized *kata* (gesture patterns) to represent emotion (laughter, sorrow, confusion). Vocal delivery is sonorous with pitch and rhythm learned from early childhood. Dance (*komai*, small dances) shares stylization with *nō*, but is now comically exaggerated. The drum and flute accompaniment is analogous, but often parodies *nō*. Extensive training in *kyōgen* has been available to international students, for example, Sekine Masaru gives regular sessions for Italian students and adapts works such as Shakespeare's *Twelfth Night* (Suzuki 2007: 278–84) for them. The Theater of Yugen in San Francisco, founded by Yuriko Doi, uses *kyōgen* and *nō* to do traditional plays and create new fusion work. Ondrej Hybl is co-founder of the Little Kyogen Theatre (Nagomi Kyōgenkai Czech) in Prague and works with the Shigeyama family. In the 1950s *nō* was already a declared heritage form and its comic partner *kyōgen* was later included when both parts (serious and comic) were recognized as *nōhgaku* to be inscribed as Intangible Cultural Properties of Japan in 1967 and, in time, *nōhgaku* (including both *nō* and *kyōgen*) was named as a Masterpiece of the Intangible Cultural Heritage of Humanity by UNESCO at its first inscription in 2001. In 2013 four *kyōgen* actors were listed as current "Living National Treasures" of the Japanese government (Wikipedia n.d.). The twentieth century has been a rich and creative period where traditional artists have explored and expanded the boundaries of the form.

Conclusion

While this brief survey only scratches the surface of these rich performing arts, I will conclude by noting some ties with Commedia and some differences. The forms are all comic genres where character type and improvisation—linguistic or physical—rule. While texts may now be set for *kyōgen* or Korean mask genres since inscription as Cultural Properties, this was not always the case. In South and Southeast Asia as in the Middle East text is/was improvised. Movement and music are central. Masks are often used, but, even where there is no mask, a set costume and persona make the character immediately transparent. Training and performance practice trump "rehearsal" and psychological interpretation. Actors often specialize in a particular role for life, making that character a well-known second self. Plots or improvisations often deal with issues of class structure, wealth, and power, with the servant-clown, while "low" and "impoverished," normally giving the rich, the religiously ensconced, or the educated master his comeuppance.

Unlike in much contemporary Western theatrical thinking where lines between storyteller, mask actor, puppeteer, and unmasked actor tend to be demarked, in many of these genres there is great overlap and artists might move from form to form. The major clown is often *most clearly articulated* in the puppet theatre, a genre where the puppet master has two authoritative voices: the omniscient narrator who reviews the action from above and the clown who provides a more comic and contemporary commentary from below. The first voice speaks nobly and eternally, making it semi-divine, while the other is comic and contingently human—it is the clown. However in puppetry and storytelling, these are really two sides of the same voice—they both go back to the same performer/storyteller/puppet master. These two viewpoints in one performer may be better articulated to the present in the pan-Asian world than in Western Commedia (where it also existed). This overlap in Asian genres may continue to give non-European clowns a more authoritative voice.

This dualism in one presenter might explain another important difference that may be discerned—the Commedia clown is historically more linked to the demonic: Erlkonig (Halequin) we may be told is a medieval devil. Asian clowns are more apt to be linked to the divine or zennish paths to enlightenment. While this brief report does not allow space to fully develop the "god-clown" theme, the mythology of the god-clown is most transparent in the theatres of Southeast Asia (Indonesia's Semar is thought to be Asmara, the god of love). Archaic patterns of *pasupata* Saivism (king of the beasts/breaking the animal bonds—medieval Shiva cults) or some branches of Vaishnavism (Vishnu worship) may inform some of these arts. These cults advocated radical rejections of societal structures and used singing, dancing, and tantric paths to enlightenment which saw the body—low, sexually fraught, and full of appetites—as the only and best tool to achieve enlightenment in medieval India (Bhhattacharyya 1982: 49–79; Dasgupta 1962; Lorenzen 1972). Ideas from these groups were transmitted into medieval Buddhism moving into Central Asia, North Asia, and Southeast Asia. Similar ideas arose into Islam and were carried by dervish-like members of Sufi orders wandering through North India, the Middle East, and Southeast Asia.

As a sample of how clowning, performance and religion mixed in Asia, I sketch a brief outline of Lakulisa, believed to be a manifestation of Shiva. He founded a cult, perhaps in the second century BCE, which was very popular in India by the seventh to the ninth century CE, especially among merchants and lower classes. Lakulisa's followers seem interrelated with the spread of tantric ideas and performing arts in the medieval period as practices jumped from Saivism to other religion strains—performance traveled with Vaishnavite Hinduism, Buddhism and Sufi-Islam throughout Asia and dervish-like groups in the Middle East. Lakulisa ideology is linked with the *kalamuka* (black face) sect and involves yogic ideas and rejection of hierarchical structures. Lakulisa's *pasupatas* and *kalamukas* broke with conventional ideas of social structure and hierarchy. Their doctrines clearly appealed to lower and disenfranchised groups by advocating a Bakhtin-like (1965) revisioning— enlightenment as accessible to all and in this life.

Though the Iranian Siah's black face today is often explained as an African slave in the Persian court, I sometimes wonder if the revolutionary black face clown that may even have given us our Harlequin is not really another permutation of Lakulisa— who, while a corpse being cremated on the burning ground in Gujarat, "woke up" and to the surprise of viewers, rubbed the black soot from the corpses upon his face. He picked up a bone, and then took his act on the road and using humor, sexuality, and other radical strategies of laughter as he paired with the dancing girls. He and his followers sang songs, danced dances, and used humor as a tool to transport followers from this ephemeral world to the reality of things. Lakulisa's bone/club, is both the Saivite phallus and the slapstick—a tool to awake us to the reality of being via music, dance, performance, improvised theatre and the last laugh that comes from the deep core.

Peculiar behaviors, ragged cloths, with triangular or multicolored patterns, and sacral symbolism pop up in odd places in Asia: Central Javanese court performance/ ritual behind the female dance, Bhutanese mask dance where monk-gurus are the improvising clowns. These patterns could help explain why the clown of many Asian puppet and mask genres is said by performers to be a god, why masks are sometimes treated with special care, fed incense or given offerings. One puzzles if or how an Asian tantric god-clown, which gives the comic theatres of Asia extra force, might relate to the familiar European clowns with their distinctive costumes and seemingly old roots. Were our clowns once divine but became amnesiacs on joining the Christian fold? Connections will probably remain conjectural, but links tantalize both Western and Asian artists who engage in joint contemporary explorations of roots and meanings. As we don the visage of Harlequin with his black face, we sometimes wonder who it is we channel as we hit our comic marks.

References

Bakhtin, M. (1965) *Rabelais and his World,* trans. H. Iswolsky, Cambridge, US: MIT Press.

Beeman, W. O. (1982) *Culture, Performance and Communication in Iran,* Tokyo: Institute for the Study of Languages and Cultures of Asia and Africa.

Bhhattacharyya, N. N. (1982) *History of the Tantric Religion,* New Delhi: Manohar.

Brandon, J. R. (1997) *Nō and Kyōgen in the Contemporary World,* Honolulu: University of Hawai'i.

Cho, O.-k. (1988) *Traditional Korean Theatre,* Berkeley, US: Asian Humanities Press.

Coldiron, M. (2005) "Lions, Witches, and Happy Old Men," *Asian Theatre Journal* 22, 2: 227–48.

Cultural Properties Administration, The Republic of Korea (2001) *Korean Intangible Cultural Properties: Folk Dramas, Games, and Rites.* Elizabeth, NJ, US: Hollym International Corp. (also Seoul: Hollym Corp.)

Dasgupta, S. B. (1962) *Obscure Religious Cults,* 2nd ed., Calcutta, India: Firma K.L. Mukhopadhay.

Dibia, W. and R. Ballinger (2004) *Balinese Dance, Drama, and Music: A Guide to the Performing Arts of Bali,* Singapore: Periplus.

Duchartre, P. L. (1966) *The Italian Comedy*, New York: Dover.

Emigh, J. (1996) *Masked Performance: The Play of Self and Other in Ritual and Theatre*, Philadelphia, US: University of Pennsylvania.

Floor, W. (2005) *The History of Theater in Iran*, Washington, DC: Mage Publishers.

Foley, K. (1990) "My Bodies: The Performer in West Java," *The Drama Review* 34, 2: 62–80.

Foley, K. and I. N. Sedana (2005) "Balinese Mask Dance Drama from the Perspective of a Master Artist: I Ketut Kodi on *Topeng*," *Asian Theatre Journal* 22, 2: 199–214.

Fukushima, Y. (2005) "Masks, Interface of Past and Future: Nomura Mannojō's *Shingigaku*," *Asian Theatre Journal* 22, 2: 249–68.

Fulchignoni, E. trans. by U. Crowley (1990) "Oriental Influences of the Commedia dell'Arte," *Asian Theatre Journal* 7, 1: 29–41.

Gargi, B. (1966) "Bhavai," *Folk Theatre of India*, Seattle, US: University of Washington Press.

Haery, M. M. (1982) *Ru-Howzi: The Iranian Traditional Improvisotory Theatre*. Ph.D. dissertation, New York University. [Ann Arbor, US: University Microfilms International].

Iezzi, J. and J. Salz, (eds) [Kyogen Issue] (2007) *Asian Theatre Journal* 24, 1.

Japan Foundation (2009) "Shigeyama Sennojo: Artist Interview: Cross-over Kyogen Master Sennojo Shigeyama's Quest for a New Form of Global Comedy Theater," *Performing Arts Network of Japan*. Available at: http://performingarts.jp/E/art_interview/0906/1.html (accessed November 2013).

Jenkins, R. (1994). *Subversive Laughter: The liberating Power of Comedy*, New York: Free Press.

Leigh, B. K. (1979) "Jaques Copeau's School for Actors: Commemoration of the Centennial of the Birth of Jacques Copeau." *Mime Journal* 9–10.

Lord, A. B. (1960) *The Singer of Tales*, Cambridge, MA, US: Harvard University Press.

Lorenzen, D. (1972) *The Kāpālikas and Kālāmukhas: Two Lost Saivite Sects*, Berkeley and Los Angeles, US: University of California Press.

Martinovitch, N. (1968 [1933]) *The Turkish Theatre*, New York: Benjamin Blom.

Palarmo, C. (2005) "Crossing Male Boundaries: Confidence and Crisis for Bali's Woman Mask Dancers," *Inside Indonesia* 83. http://www.insideindonesia.org/feature-editions/crossing-male-boundaries (accessed November 29, 2013).

Pamment, C. (2008) "Mock Courts and Pakistani *Bhānd*," *Asian Theatre Journal* 25, 2: 344–62.

Richmond, F. (1997 [1993]) "Bhavai," *The Cambridge Guide to Asian Theatre*, ed. J. R. Brandon, Cambridge, UK: Cambridge University Press.

Ross, L. M. (2005) "Mask, Gender, and Performance in Indonesia: An interview with Didik Nini Thowok," *Asian Theatre Journal* 22, 2: 214–26.

Salz, J. (2001) "Beckett in Kyogen Style: Lessons in Intercultural Translation," in Watson, I., ed., *Performer Training across Cultures*, 133ff., Amsterdam: Harwood Overseas Publishers Association.

Savarese, N. (2010) *Eurasian Theatre: Drama and Performance between East and West from Classical Antiquity to the Present*, trans. R. Fowler, ed. V. A. Cremona. Holstebro, Denmark: Icarus Publishing.

Shirle, J. (2009) http://joansbaliblog.blogspot.com/ (accessed November 2013).

Simon, Eli and Kim, Suk-Man (2005) *Bird in the DMZ*, http://drama.arts.uci.edu/internationalbirds.html (accessed November 29, 2013).

Suzuki, M. (2007) "The Drunkard's Revenge and Love's Labor" [review], *Asian Theatre Journal* 24, 1: 278–84.

Teele, R., ed. (1984) *Nō/Kyōgen Masks and Performance: Special Issue of Mime Journal*. Claremont, US: Pomona College Theatre Department, Claremont Colleges.

Turkish Culture Foundation (n.d.) "Traditional Theatre: Ortaoyunu," www.turkishculture. org/performing-arts/theatre/traditional-theatre/traditional-theatre-ortaoyunu-288.htm (accessed November 2013).

Wikipedia (n.d.) "Intangible Cultural Heritage Lists," http://en.wikipedia.org/wiki/UNESCO_ Intangible_Cultural_Heritage_Lists and www.unesco.org/culture/ich/index.php?lg=en& pg=00011&RL=00012 (accessed September 2014).

51

COMMEDIA FOR THE CONTEMPORARY THEATRE MAKER

Davis Robinson

The vitality and spontaneity of Commedia dell'Arte as an acting style, and the tradition of performing with masks, has applications to many contemporary theatre forms far beyond the traditional scenarios normally associated with Commedia. One need not wait to be cast in a revival of *The Servant of Two Masters* or *Scapin* to find that Commedia training is a useful tool for the contemporary actor.

At its root is the disciplining of the impulse "to play." Underlying the passions of the stock characters are appetites familiar to both the audience and the actors. The hunger for money, love, and food serve as the foundation for all play in Commedia scenarios. These characters are also played with tremendous physical energy and clarity because of the discipline imposed by working with masks. No matter what scenario is used, good players are able to develop dialogue and action based on the known rules of the Commedia universe that frame character decisions: the lovers want to elope, the parents want them to marry someone else, the fathers do not like to part with money, the servants are hungry and must find ways to trick their masters to get food or money, etc. Audiences can relate instantly to these actions because they reveal universal human traits. The collision of these strong needs makes it possible for actors to improvise with full force, using basic human themes of hunger, sex, love, vanity, and survival to riff on. By knowing what buttons to push in the characters and what weaknesses to exploit, common human faults can be amplified on stage to provide a wealth of opportunities for the players.

Implicit in the ability to play well and on the spot is the ability to *stay present*. Nothing is more important in Commedia work than being a good listener whose own physical engine is completely alive and responsive to the other players, the space, and the audience as they pursue their actions with vigor, commitment, and little warning of what comes next. While dialogue and action are playing out on the stage, the actors backstage listen for opportunities to sense which direction the play is heading. Good players know exactly when to enter or exit, how long to explore a *lazzi*, when to develop the main plot line further, and when to introduce a new complication. Interruptions like babies crying or unexpected street noise become fodder for the *Present Actor* to acknowledge on stage and fold into the narrative, building an even stronger bond with an audience admiring their inventiveness.

A third aspect of Commedia training that is relevant to other acting forms is the volume of acting demanded by mask work and the embodying of larger-than-life archetypes. When Jacques Copeau set up his Vieux Columbier theatre school in France in the 1910s and1920s, he engaged Suzanne Bing and others to help him develop training exercises that made actors total performers, able to play with more vigor, passion and honesty than the current theatrical practices of the time. The mantra of the day articulated by the great actress Elenora Duse was that "in order to revive the theatre, we must destroy it" (Rudlin 1986: 36). A large part of the pedagogy they developed was based on children's games, animal exercises, gymnastics, music, studies of nature, and the search for a more universal physical starting point as actors through the use of masks: in particular the noble or neutral mask. This became the foundation for work with other expressive masks, Commedia masks, and a re-discovery of what might have been the acting styles of Greek tragedy, Commedia, Elizabethan drama, and French neo-classical drama.

A major influence on Copeau's vision of a new theatre was E. Gordon Craig's idea that the theatre building itself could be stripped of unnecessary scenery and returned to a more classically Greek ideal of open space and simple platforms. Unadorned screens and pure architectural lines became the new ideal. This affected the design of Copeau's productions and the underlying focus of his training program, putting the emphasis on the skills and strengths of the players rather than on elaborate scenery, costumes, and artificial acting mannerisms. This holistic approach to, and empowerment of, the actor on an open stage had a profound impact on the pedagogy of the next generation of theatre schools that began to appear in England, Italy, France, and the United States. Former Copeau company member Michel St. Denis helped to establish a training program at the Old Vic, The Julliard School, and what was to become the Royal Shakespeare Company. And Jacques Lecoq, who was influenced by Copeau's ideas when he worked as an actor with Jean Daste's acting company in Grenoble, combined his own training as a sports therapist with Copeau's ideas on theatre to develop a school in Paris that became a mecca for training in clowning, Commedia, and physical theatre.

Lecoq's innovations in the field began when he was hired by Giorgio Strehler and the Piccolo Theater to help set up a theatre school in Milan. Lecoq lived in Italy for eight years where he worked with Dario Fo, the mask maker Ameleto Sartori, and with the actors of Piccolo Theatro on shows such as *The Servant of Two Masters*. After watching the actors struggle with cardboard masks, Lecoq realized that the actors needed stronger masks that could handle the heightened physicality of Commedia. The flimsy paper masks had to be replaced by something more durable and flexible. The solution was leather, and he partnered with mask maker and sculptor Ameleto Sartori to perfect a method for making traditional leather Commedia masks. Lecoq and Sartori also went further into the world of character masks and perfected several other masks including the neutral mask (inspired by Copeau's "noble" mask), now a fundamental part of the training program at Lecoq's school in Paris to this day. Commedia mask and movement training became part of a larger pedagogy that begins with all actors learning to work in neutral masks, then moving onto larval masks, expressive masks, Commedia masks, and eventually the tiniest of masks, the red nose of the clown.

"*Le jeu*" is a key part of the vocabulary at Lecoq's school. It is a necessity for bringing masks to life and for creating believable relationships on stage. *Le jeu* (finding the play) is closely related to one of the defining elements of Commedia: the lazzi. Actors trained by Lecoq have gone on to develop a wide range of contemporary work, often distinguished by a willingness to embrace physical choices and imaginative problem-solving that grows directly out of the school's playful and actor-as-inventor approach. Every script handed to an actor is called "a play," and groups arising out of Lecoq's school often take that word to heart.

These concepts of play, presence, and vigorous physical clarity have direct application to many contemporary productions, whether characters are masked or not. Many contemporary plays involve archetypal characters with strong physical needs. Actors trained in mask work and Commedia often have a good head start stylistically over actors trained only in naturalism and realistic movement. The main adjustment Commedia actors need to make is to the discipline of working from a prepared script, which traditional actor training methods can help. Ionesco, Beckett, Brecht, and some of the more fantastical work of writers like Tennessee Williams or Charles Ludlam are full of characters with recognizable Commedia characteristics who live in highly theatrical universes. In the play *Waiting for Godot* Vladimir and Estragon are not masked, but their world is driven by primal human needs as rich and as focused as Capitano's and Arlequino's. Pozzo and Lucky have their own "masks," a warped model of a classic servant/master relationship. The language is perfectly laid out on the page for actors to follow, and a vital and spontaneous physical acting style is required to bring it to life. Actors who have had some training in Commedia or mask work will have an easier time finding some of the lazzi spelled out in the script and making it believable. Bert Lahr was a successful Estragon in one of the earliest productions. Though the writing can be played in more cerebral and minimalist ways, Beckett had vaudeville clowns like Laurel and Hardy in mind when he wrote Godot.

As contemporary theatre makers, the Beau Jest Moving Theatre company, directed by Davis Robinson, relied heavily on Commedia's sense of play, presence, and physical clarity to create and perform its production of *Krazy Kat* in 1995. *Krazy Kat*, the play, was adapted from the early twentieth century comic strip by cartoonist George Herriman. For over twenty years Herriman explored existential themes in a surreal desert setting called Coconino County, an enchanted landscape where backgrounds continually shifted and characters defied the laws of gravity, romance, and grammar. The poetic graphic design of the strips is complemented by a folksy and playful use of pun-filled language. Considered by many to be the greatest comic strip of the twentieth century, poet E. E. Cummings once referred to *Krazy Kat* as a "meteoric, burlesque melodrama" (Herriman 1946: 7).

When the three main characters sit on a log and watch one leaf on a tree in silence for six panels, waiting for it to fall, it is hard not to see parallels to Godot two decades later.

As with any Commedia scenario, *Krazy Kat* was full of strong character archetypes and colliding physical needs in a playful universe, exploring endless variations on universal themes. All of the primary source material was recorded in a two-dimensional format (a daily comic strip). Both Lecoq and Dario Fo say that when you enter the world of Commedia you have to reinvent it for yourself as, really, nobody knows how it was actually performed. Every expert has his or her own opinion, drawn from the same, few written accounts of bystanders and the drawings and paintings of Commedia players that have been passed down through the ages. There is no film or video footage. The remnants of text left by playwrights who tried to capture the language of the original players can only hint at the acting style and energy of the first Commedia performers. In *Krazy Kat*, the challenge was similar. The daily black and white strips and the Sunday color strips gave us over twenty years of characters in two-dimensional poses. The poetic gramalot that Herriman invented for his characters read well on the page, but what would those drawings look like in action? What would their voices sound like? How did they actually play when brought to life? How much language would they actually use? How much physical energy?

The company was presented with a complete, albeit somewhat surreal universe set in the mystical land of Coconino County (inspired by Monument Valley and the Four Corners region of the American Southwest). The three main characters are a cat (Krazy Kat), a mouse (Ignatz), and a cop (Offissa Pupp). Many Commedia teachers emphasize the animal aspects of each stock character. Like their Commedia counterparts, each Krazy Kat character had a strong, singular point of view, a specific way of moving, and an obsession that conflicted with the other characters. This led to endless comic and cosmic variations on a theme. Offissa Pupp loves Krazy Kat and does everything to protect her/him (gender was never defined). Krazy Kat loves Ignatz Mouse and does everything to pursue him. Ignatz Mouse throws bricks at the cat, runs away, and does everything to avoid being caught by the cop.

Ignatz is a close relative of Arlequino, with ingenious pranks and frequent run-ins with the law, a fast-mover with comic entrances and exits. Krazy Kat has elements of Dottore in its use of language, Zanni in his/her logic, and a Lover who drives the actions of Offissa Pupp and Ignatz Mouse. Offissa Pupp has elements of Pantalone and Capitano. All three live in a universe that is closely related to the silent film comedians who were popular when the strip was first written, especially the surreal world of Buster Keaton in its chases, moving scenery, inside jokes, and actions that broke the frame of the comic strip itself by going outside the margins of the boxes and breaking all the conventional rules of comic strip art. In making our adaptation for the stage, we found the closest parallel was the timeless set up and follow through of physical business embodied in Commedia lazzi and in their twentieth century relative, the Looney Tunes cartoons of Bugs Bunny and Daffy Duck.

The main engine for the strip is the endless attempts by the well-meaning Kop (Offissa Pupp) to arrest the mouse for throwing bricks at the cat. Krazy Kat sees each brick as a token of love from Ignatz, and confuses Kop with double speak and puns, confounding his unrequited love for Kat. Sound like Commedia? Our months of rehearsal to find movement patterns, character voices, and bits of business drew heavily on Commedia training. And the sad, surreal, and somewhat existential ending with echoes of Godot made perfect sense as a natural evolution for those character archetypes, who now exist in a more god-less universe. Without each other, they have nothing.

In the Theater Styles course at Bowdoin College, one of the biggest challenges is the unit on playing Commedia. Actors who have wonderfully developed instruments are often at sea, which is why I think Commedia training is so valuable. The physical clarity, the large bold choices, the full body commitment to actions, the ability to whipsaw from pain to pleasure in a split second, the awareness of hierarchy and power struggles, the freedom to play, the in-the-moment-awareness of the situation and where it is going – these are valuable moments to experience on stage. Removing the actor's reliance on the script plunges them into a very present awareness of the situation, their partner's actions, and their own needs. Actors accustomed to working with scripts often find it very disorienting to suddenly be put in front of an audience with no net and no script, and that is the point. More than just building a new generation of actors who can faithfully recreate a classic Commedia scenario, the real value of Commedia training is to empower actors to think on their feet, to play boldly and physically, and to be ready to make use of unplanned or spontaneous moments that occur in any play, scripted or not.

People's eyes light up when those classic characters come to life. It may begin with a cross, a monologue, a stare through the mask, or a bit of business that gets everyone involved in their dilemma. Somehow, with a little adjusting, each generation of students is able to find that Commedia wavelength, and as they put their own individual spin on it, it feels like these universal types are on the edge of our universal consciousness, ready to be called back to life. And when they do appear, it is Pantalone or Arlequino who is doing the talking, not the students. That is a kind of magic that has endured for several hundred years, and it shows no signs of disappearing...

References

Herriman, George (1946) *Krazy Kat*. Introduction by E. E. Cummings. New York: Henry Holt and Company.

Rudlin, John (1986) *Jacques Copeau*. Cambridge, UK: Cambridge University Press.

52

ROOTS AND ROUTES

One Man, Two Guvnors

Didi Hopkins

Charted by Didi Hopkins, with Ninian Kinnier-Wilson of Commedia Works, in conversation with playwright Richard Bean.

Commedia is a visual language, it uses the body not the mouth. Body language is more precise and honest than verbal language.... the masks spoke in dialect so that no one person understood everything... it has always operated on a pictorial level.... The Charivari (*folk tradition*) depicted an old man who had married a young woman being placed on a donkey backwards and paraded through the town. This was to symbolise the threat to the fertility of the community. We should remember that Commedia was often played to a largely non-literate population.

(Ninian Kinnier-Wilson in an interview with
Dr Malcolm Knight, Scottish Mask
and Puppet Centre, 2009)

The Servant of Two Masters

The Servant of Two Masters by Carlo Goldoni starts with a murder. It is a rollercoaster through deceit, disguise, debate, lies, misunderstandings, marriage, parental power, love, accidents, patriarchy and social climbing. It is full of intrigue, madness, and mayhem that would grab an audience in any century. Goldoni captured Commedia as it was dying, diluted and disfigured, to record for us the essence of the oral tradition in *The Servant of Two Masters*. He wrote the dialogue, recorded the rhythmic system, the rhetoric and construction. It is a perfect introduction to the world of Commedia and the characters that populate it. *The Servant of Two Masters* holds keys to unlock techniques of rehearsal, construction and performance that make Commedia such a success. If we peel away Goldoni's words, what is revealed represents the scaffold on which the architects and storytellers of Commedia built their improvised scenarios.

Carlo Boso came to London with mask maker Stefano Perocco in 1981 to run a Commedia dell'Arte workshop. In the workshop Boso introduced Goldoni's *The Servant of Two Masters* as a vehicle to understand the mechanics of Commedia and through which he demonstrated how Commedia worked. Boso, then and now, uses Goldoni's architecture as a blueprint to recreate scenarios collected by Flaminia Scala, and as a blank canvas on which actors create new stories into which they bring themselves to make work that has currency for a contemporary audience. It was at this workshop where Ninian Kinnier-Wilson, John Broadbent and I met. We were hooked. Inspired. We continued to train and work with Carlo and his team over many years in France and Italy, and to develop English Commedia with our own companies. Ninian began his extraordinary work as mask maker, making masks for the company he ran with actor and scenario writer John Broadbent: the Unfortunati. I began to teach and direct Commedia using Ninian's masks and eventually the two of us teamed up to teach and pass on our Commedia knowledge together. To do this we had to deconstruct and reconstruct the physical training that had given us everything. The flame Boso had lit in us needed codifying in order to pass it on: Commedia for us was the DNA of all theatre. We needed to devise a simple system to introduce and distil the world of Commedia for actors, teachers and students. For over twenty-five years we worked together. Ninian's Commedia masks are beautiful and used worldwide. He became the scholar of our trio. His extensive research brought him to the Kabbalah in which he found the key to explain Commedia – through the tree of life diagram. It is this diagram we use to introduce people to the world of Commedia (see Figure 52.1). It represents society from the bottom to the top, shows the positions of the main characters, their position in society, the geography of a city, and even the part of the body the character leads with. It is an experiential and physical map, where the body makes sense of the knowledge.

I met Richard Bean to talk about Commedia as he embarked on his adaptation of *The Servant of Two Masters* for the National Theatre (NT) in 2011, transporting it from Venice 1743, to Britain in 2011. I showed him the masks, and shared the diagram to introduce the characters, masks and world of Commedia as Ninian and I see and understand it (see Figure 52.2).

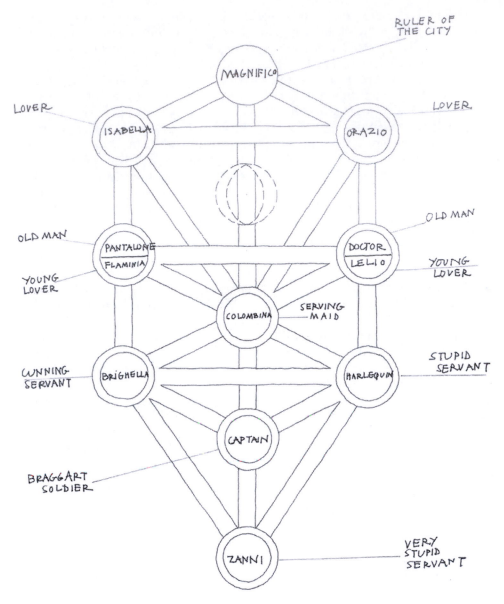

RULER OF
THE CITY

MAGNIFICO

LOVER

ISABELLA

LOVER

ORAZIO

OLD MAN

OLD MAN

PANTALONE

FLAMINIA

DOCTOR
LELIO

YOUNG
LOVER

YOUNG
LOVER

COLOMBINA

SERVING
MAID

STUPID
SERVANT

CUNNING
SERVANT

BRIGHELLA

HARLEQUIN

CAPTAIN

BRAGGART
SOLDIER

VERY
STUPID
SERVANT

ZANNI

Figure 52.1 Commedia Masks mapped onto the Kabbala Sephirot, a step by step plan
illuminating a "Divine" plan of life.

Diagrams: reformatted by Didi Hopkins from diagrams that are copyright Ninian Kinnier-Wilson, 2011.
Used with kind permission of the estate of Ninian Kinnier-Wilson. For illustrative purposes only, not for
further reproduction.

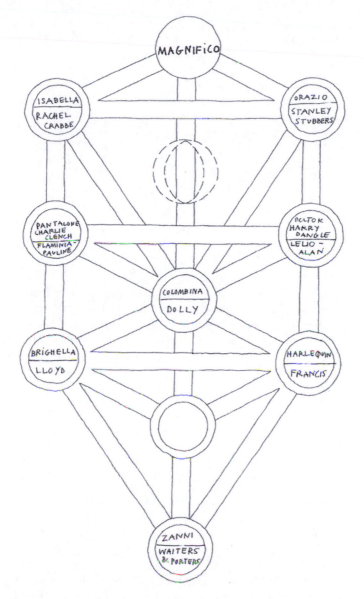

Figure 52.2 One Man, Two Guvnors' characters mapped onto the Commedia Sephirot.

Diagrams: reformatted by Didi Hopkins from diagrams that are copyright Ninian Kinnier-Wilson, 2011. Used with kind permission of the estate of Ninian Kinnier-Wilson. For illustrative purposes only, not for further reproduction.

One Man, Two Guvnors

London 2013: I meet again with Bean and ask him to share some of his observations of turning something old into something new.

Richard Bean has a baby gurgling on his lap.
His other daughter is on the computer downstairs. We are sipping tea.
The tape recorder is running. We start to talk:
Let's talk about One Man, Two Guvnors:

Background (Richard Bean speaking)

I first worked with Nick Hytner, the director of the National Theatre on my play *England People Very Nice* in 2009. I was in the rehearsal room a lot. It was an original text and needed to be worked on as rehearsals progressed. Then he called me to do some textual revisions on Boucicault's *London Assurance*. My first attempt was to elaborate it. I did too much and spoiled the restoration… made it too modern. The central character is utterly pretentious, basically a Pantalone type and a similar plot: he's got to marry his son off. In the original there were very long speeches, and Nick was very specific about which bits to cut. Use full stops! I was able to take a very tricky and difficult text and make it simpler. I got what Nick meant by full stops. I think the reason I got the Goldoni gig was as much to do with *London Assurance* as about the other plays of mine he'd directed. I had also written a version of Moliere's *The Hypochondriac* for the Almeida Theatre.

I wasn't in at the beginning of the Goldoni project, but Nick had played Truffaldino at school and knew the play really well. He was looking for vehicle for one of his favourite actors, James Corden whom he first directed in Bennett's *The History Boys*. Corden's career had taken him into TV, where he wrote and starred in his own hit TV show, *Gavin and Stacey*. Corden had become a popular and well-known actor on the British scene, and wanted to do some theatre again.

When I got the call from the NT, I hadn't read the text or seen the show, ever. There was a version I owned by Lee Hall and I knew of one by Barry Rutter's very successful *Northern Broadside*. I was determined not to read them at first, but after I started my version, I read them both – a very useful exercise as I knew what to avoid and where. I worked from a literal translation by Francesca Manfred. I wanted to know the real bare bones of the plot, and know the characters, but not much about them, so I could do my own thing, and that worked for me. Initially I saw *Servant of Two Masters* happening after World War Two, in the 1950s, with food rationing and hunger as a great drive, but Nick was very clear and saw it positioned with the energy, colour and music of the 60s. He was right.

Updating time and themes

The main problem was to find a new central framing. What needed to change in order for the play to have currency for a modern audience? Where would people run away to in the 60s? Brighton… a sort of weekend retreat for mods, where you would find gangsters, crooks, a seedy underworld, violence, death and gangs. Finding Brighton unlocked the picture.

How did arranged marriages fit into the 1960s? … If the dead brother was gay, and had an arranged marriage for appearance sake, a lavender marriage they call them, when a gay man marries a straight woman to mask his true identity… that works. And if Charlie Clench owed Rachel's dad something, and if the dad was in a position to send Charlie Clench back to prison, then the stakes are high for the marriage to go ahead, and for Charlie Clench to protect himself. The threat of prison also became a running strand… Parkhurst.

The new back story

This was the most difficult part of the writing because it needed so much exposition. That's the hell of playwriting – there's so much exposition in the first scene. Chekhov didn't worry about that – he takes three pages to talk about what he's doing in Gdansk… (*Richard improvises Chekhov…. 'I was the doctor to your father and I came here by carriage from Gdansk….'*). But in the first scene you have to rattle through the expo to get Francis Henshall onstage. Quite difficult when it keeps getting cut/cut/cut. So scene one, in its first incarnation, was twice the length it is now. Perhaps a bit too cut, because if you interview people at the interval and ask what the relationship is between Pauline and Rachel, I bet a lot of people will struggle to explain it. I think they know there was a deal of some sort for two people to get married, Roscoe (the dead one) and Pauline, and that her heart is elsewhere. The plot of the play is part of the joy, but no one will leave this saying 'what a fabulous plot'… but they will leave saying 'great performances' – but just from vanity of a writer, I *would* like them to get the plot line clear.

Working the original

The next challenge was how to stay true to the text structure, which has great architecture. The original play has three acts. Mine has two. I stuck to the structure and the scene sequence, but at the interval the play was already running at 1.5 hours… and I discovered that you could move Act 1, scene 2 to the second half! If you think about that in any other play, it would really blow the storyline, but somehow it works! So the opening of the second half is actually Act 1, scene 2, when Alan Dangle goes to Charlie Clench's house and threatens to kill him. Opening with a mad actor is a great way to start the second half. I think of Alan Dangle as based on the Commedia Captain, swishing swords – although in the diagram he is the second actor – but he is a bit of a show off, and of course we don't use swords, but someone wielding a penknife from Woolworths, and it's quite nice not to open it with Truffaldino/Francis.

The audience

In this version I tried to do something different. In the second half you see Francis has a direct address to the audience talking about how this play works. I like that. That's how this play works. I love that. Talking to the audience – we're just doing a play here, we hope you're enjoying it, let's hope you are, and...

...You will be saying to yourselves 'If the Harlequin, that's me, has now eaten, what will be his motivation in the second act... My character, Francis, has to find a new base motivation to drive his actions in the second half. Your job is to try and work out what that might be.'

I loved all that. I guess all our imaginations are pretty similar: you imagine market day, a cart rolls up, there is a bit of music, the curtains go back, there are a couple of lovers on stage, the crowd's there against the stage. And the idea that there's not a bit of groundlings saying 'give her a kiss' is ridiculous. It's an old play, and you've got to do a little bit with it! None of us have actually seen Commedia dell'Arte in its first incarnation.

Most of my plays have hummus in them somewhere and a hummus sandwich was the very first idea I'd had for this play. I'd spoken to you, and you'd talked about improvisation and talking to the audience. I imagined James Corden going into the audience, and because now you can take drinks into the auditorium at the National, drinking half a pint of someone's lager, and just letting him talk and be himself. We went for 'Has anyone got a sandwich?' and someone offers him a hummus sandwich. People are still blogging – 'the night I was in someone had a hummus sandwich'... (*he laughs*). The hummus moment – it hasn't gone stale.

The dinner scene

When we sat round a workshop table to read my version of the first two acts, it all worked. Except for the dinner scene. It was full of stage directions. Waiters coming upstairs, going down, bringing different foods. Reading the directions is a very dry way of bringing something to life. But something very important happened in that workshop for the dinner scene. At the end of the day we had a discussion about why it didn't work. Everyone was very rational and objective. Then someone suggested we could break the whole form, and get someone from the audience to cut the trout... And from that came Christine Patterson. She wasn't in the first draft. We all had a giggle about the audience... 'you couldn't do *that* with a member of the audience' and 'you couldn't do *thaaaat* with a member of the audience!' We all went to extremes of what couldn't happen to a member of the audience, and then someone said 'but we could if it was an actor!' So that success, not my idea, but a true collaboration, came from the failure of the dinner scene in the first script.

Comic business

I'd written two or three physical *lazzi*, sat at home, written in my head, without trying to do them. One was Francis trying to get the trunk into the pub – (*Richard demonstrates with objects on the table*). Francis tries to pick it up and realises it's heavy. He succeeds and starts pushing it, it gains speed, and he goes over the top and flies through the doorway, out of sight of the audience. Then later, he's got two trunks. He's got to do it twice. So basically it was a trunk being pushed along like a wheelbarrow by two men, Francis and the second waiter, who, standing one behind the other, run at the door. When the trunk hits the door threshold the trunk goes vertical and the two men go up with it and get stuck in the doorway, against the top of the doorframe, with two pairs of legs sticking out. I thought that would stop the show! I thought that was the most brilliant lazzi! I thought if anyone could make this happen it's the National Theatre's props department. I thought I had created a real coup de theatre, with four legs sticking out of the doorway... but the props department hadn't built the door. I suggested rubber. Foam rubber? But on walking and talking it through, it became apparent it was far too dangerous. Again, at that read through, someone suggested we get a couple of people from the audience to help in the trunk scene. It tells the audience 'this is different from other plays', like working with children and animals: anything can happen – it's out of our control. So the failure of my extraordinarily brilliant lazzi was part of the reason we could do something simpler: get two guys up to help.

Actions matter

I'm basically a gag writer. I was a stand-up comedian. There are few verbal gags in Michael Frayn's *Noises Off*, and the comedy comes out of the situations the actors find themselves in. I wrote too many gags, or verbal lazzi. Nick said: 'They're all very good. There are a hundred gags, let's cut ten per cent'.

The play was very overwritten in rehearsals. I found it easier to write Stanley Stubbers than Francis Henshall. I struggled with who Henshall was. He had three autobiographical speeches cut, some quite surreal stuff that just didn't work. I was struggling to get them to work. Corden was struggling to get them to work. I'd be going into rehearsals thinking... 'Uh-oh, he's going to do those monologues, they don't work. What am I going to do to make them work?' They only got cut a week before the tech week. But the history of this play is about cutting it, and letting the story and actions mature.

When they put together the publicity, they often use quotes. Nick asked me for my favourite three lines, and put his in too. The one that went into the brochure was Nick's favourite line, and by the time it got the first transfer, it had been cut from the script! Which just goes to show and emphasise that sometimes words can get in the way of actions. Like if someone is driven to get to room A when they're en route to room B, that's all you want to see.

Different every night

The actors were fabulous, the casting was spot on, and there was great crossover between the original Commedia types on the diagram and the players, which gave the actors space to bring more of themselves to the script and make it their own. And we learned that something's always going to go wrong – and it doesn't matter! We'll work with it! One night the door handle came off and James Corden said something like 'Are there any decent joiners in the house coz the ones at the NT are rubbish'. And one night one of the trunk guys (from the audience), his trousers split. The audience thought it was another set up. But at the interval he went backstage and wardrobe sewed up his trousers. Another night one of the cast broke her ankle and her understudy had to go on, which took a costume change, so Rufus Hound who was then playing Francis Henshall led the audience in a chorus of *Goodnight Irene*.

Where else do you go to the theatre, where whatever happens, if it is a surprise or unexpected, it is commented upon because it is real, it happened? It's a gift. It's given me aspiration to push the form, because what really works is the tricks, the fooling around, it's like a magician. Look at the set-up of Christine Patterson: you prove to the audience that she is a genuine member of the audience and then you do stuff with her that is untenable. It's the best acting in the play: she doesn't stand in the right place, she can't get her head through the cut-out hole, you can't hear her, and she's not tall enough. Brilliant.

This play has taught me what I already knew from watching magicians, but I never knew a playwright could use the same kind of tricks. The power is really unexpected.

It works!

Before the technical week, Nick invited about eighty school kids in to the rehearsal room, sixth formers, to see a run. They went completely bonkers for it. I thought, Bloody hell, this is really working! And it had none of the tricks – the stairs for Alfie to fall down, or the fun slapsticky stuff – it was basically the words and the performance of the actors that were making those schoolchildren go nuts, and that was the first time I felt any pride.

Usually I hate intervals. As a playwright, you go to the loo and people are commenting on whether or not they are getting it or want to go home, are they having a good time… and it can be depressing. You don't want to hear. Normally I run out of the theatre at the interval. But it's the best moment to go to the loo with this show! Everyone is shocked. They're trying to work out if Christine Patterson is real. It's terrific. They are talking and thinking about something they have seen, and they don't know if it's real or not.

That's really playing with the form.

May 2011. The National Theatre, London.

Enter – the audience… Onstage: The Craze, a skiffle band – a washboard, a double bass and two guitars, dressed like mods and playing a pastiche of contagious and popular upbeats of the British music scene circa 1960. Grant Olding's blend of rhythm and blues, rock and roll, and the simplicity of the early Beatles create a carnival-like atmosphere. Members of the audience are dancing in their seats. This musical prologue frames the energy and sets the pace of what is to come. The audience are primed and ready…

If the roots of original Commedia are alive and kicking in *One Man, Two Guvnors*, then we can assume that Commedia must have been a spectacular success. Richard Bean has transformed what was, for some, an arch, archaic and antique tradition into something that now has currency for a modern audience. He has resurrected Commedia and offers a new template for the twenty-first century. The genius of Bean's *One Man, Two Guvnors* has put popular theatre back on the map, and put Commedia centre stage to reclaim its rightful position as a fundamental pillar of European theatre.

No mean feat.

53

COMMEDIA IN A NEW WORLD CONTEXT

The comedy and poetry of survival

Katrien van Beurden

As a young girl on my way to high school one day, between the crazy, loud, staccato noises of morning traffic jams I heard a rasping sound from a saxophone. I turned and saw a homeless man playing the sax lying on a bench in the park. From that moment we started daily conversations about our struggles and joys in life. One morning, on a very cold winter day, he paused in the middle of a sentence and started looking around, searching for something. "Where is it?" he asked. I had no idea what he meant. Then he saw his white plastic cup of beer on the ground, and shouted happily "There it is!" He quickly picked it up, put it to his ear like a phone and said: "Hello?" and went silent for a few moments. He turned to me and said softly "Excuse me, please, it's God calling." He got back on his "phone" and continued: "So great to hear from you! ... What? ... You've got the flu? ... You would like me to take over your job for this week?" Hearing the great news that he would become the leader of the world for a week made him jump up. On his bare feet, he started pacing back and forth with large steps. In a deep voice he asked God: "So, you want me to call the United Nations and end all wars, tell the rich to give money to the poor and create more beer? Consider it done. Go to bed and take a rest. I'll do the job down here!" He hung up, turned to me and said: "Sorry, duty calls" and proudly walked off.

This man made me laugh and moved me at the same time. This incident showed me in a very vivid way how people can use their imagination and ingenuity to survive in a harsh world. He turned reality upside down by turning a simple cup into a phone. Using his imagination he transformed himself from a social outcast into the most powerful man on Earth with a hotline to God and in charge of beer production.

I always longed for a theatre where actors could use imagination and ingenuity to create characters that were larger than life: characters struggling to survive in comic, tragic and mad ways – *just* like the homeless man. Even though I studied at a four-year acting conservatory, the moment I participated in a three-day workshop in the Commedia dell'Arte, I was immediately blown away by this form of actors' theatre.

I discovered a theatre in which an actor could – by using just one mask – transform and create a whole universe in one instant. A universe filled with characters constantly using their ingenuity in order to survive. As an actor this form of theatre offered tools to discover all scales of emotion, thought and rhythm. It showed me how masks could awaken virtuosity within actors. With these techniques and our imagination we could create a tragic-comic universe that touched and showed humanity in all its complexity. For me as an aspiring actress, Commedia dell'Arte offered everything I wanted.

I decided to dedicate my professional life to this theatre. I started learning as a student and eventually developed a modern actors' training method. These workshops are inspired by the Commedia and attended by actors and filmmakers from around the world. This training includes physical transformation, acting emotions from the smallest to the most extreme possible expressions, and the psychology of the body. We work on the imagination, musicality, playfulness and timing of acting. The essential element is the mask. The mask unlocks the creativity and imagination of the actor. Putting on a mask makes the body speak. Every action, thought, word and emotion is immediately seen. Working from the body the actor can fill his work with a visceral reality that emanates life. Since the actor is stripped of props and décor he must create everything through mime alone. The audience must understand perfectly and believe where the character is, what he is doing and what is happening. Therefore, this art creates great technical skills and pushes the actor to extreme precision. But the effort to be precise inevitably leads to mistakes. And it is these mistakes, these moments of being lost that are a gift. The actor re-trains himself to play with his own mistakes and incorporate them into the character. This leads to fully alive actors and characters, with all their passions, needs and flaws.

The intensity of responses to the Commedia workshops triggered the realization on a profound level that this theatre does not only consist of actors playing archetypical characters, but also of spectators having archetypical reactions. Masks can transport the spectator instantly into another realm of experience and awaken within him his own memories, associations and stories. I had mainly focused on teaching these techniques within the walls of institutions and theatres. Now I felt the urge to step out in to the world and find out where these characters live and survive in today's world. Through the masks I wanted to search and perform today's stories around the world.

Out of this urge the international theatre company Theatre Hotel Courage was born. With our team of actors, directors, and filmmakers we tour around the world. In each country we visit, we train and explore with local actors, students, refugees, tribal people, and townspeople from different backgrounds. Together we create performances based on the question: "If the world were a hotel, what would be your place and position in this hotel?" In New York a group of actors said: "We would debate in a conference room full of Dottores and decide how the world should be. Then we would open the windows and give a press conference." In India, a young actress who played with the Harlequina said: "I would live at the hotel secretly without the guests noticing. Early in the morning I would go into each room and put flowers next to all the beds, while the guests are sleeping." In a township in Ghana they answered: "We wouldn't have a room in the hotel. We would be the servants fishing off the coast. That evening the fish would be served as the cook's own freshly caught specialty."

One day while giving a workshop in Memphis, TN, an actor wearing the mask of the Old Man, turned towards the audience and a young student immediately broke into tears. I asked him what had moved him and he told me he had served in Iraq.

> When the actor turned and I looked into the eyes of an old man, I suddenly found myself back in a battle in an Iraqi village. In the middle of that battle, I turned my gun towards an unexpected sound and looked into the eyes of an old Iraqi man. He was very confused and was looking for his wife and children. He was so completely desperate and lost that he didn't seem aware that he could easily be hit by all the gunfire. I had to push him to the ground for his own safety, but he just kept staring at me with tears in his eyes. When the actor turned towards me I remembered that moment.

Command of the mimetic and physical skills of Commedia can lead an actor to greater success in playing and improvising with scenes. An example of this was an improvisation in which the actor playing a general obsessed with war re-created his last great battle. Wearing the mask of Capitano, he proudly enters his beloved battlefield, salutes the student audience, and says: "Pay attention and learn about the art of war." He mimes making a small bush, hides behind it and waits for the enemy. At one point the Captain whispers, "Make the sound of the wind to create some tension." The audience joins in and whistles like the wind. He raises his head from behind the hill and mimes binoculars. He looks slowly to the left and to the right, but when he looks ahead his whole body stiffens. "The great enemy is approaching!" he exclaims. He crawls to the front and mimes perfectly how he digs a hole, picks up a huge landmine and buries it in the middle of the stage. Suddenly, he looks up and his eyes become bigger as he sees that the enemy is very close now. He quickly takes out a grenade and throws it in the direction of the enemy, the audience. His excitement rises and he throws another one. All of a sudden someone in the audience throws a grenade back at him. In a reflex the General catches it, to his own surprise and dismay. He looks at it, looks back to the audience to share the state of shock and screams in a very high voice. He then throws it up in the air, dives behind the hill and holds his helmet in anticipation of the blast. Then the actor does something that shows his virtuosity even more. With his body he mimes the impact of an enormous explosion by pretending he is launched five feet up in the air. At the same time he mimes he is holding on to his helmet that is flying off his head. On top of that, while he is flying through the air he creates a hilarious expression of total bewilderment about what is happening to him. Then the actor takes a moment, looks at the audience and decides to raise the stakes further. The General composes himself and challenges his enemy to hit him again. The now fully alive audience responds by throwing more grenades. The General starts dodging the attacks, hiding his hands behind his back, turning his hips and body like an expert bullfighter. He starts moving in a very staccato rhythm, faster and faster. Eventually he starts clapping his hands and creates a rhythm out of the war noises created by the audience. His movements transform into an extremely fast and highly energetic flamenco dance during which his hands alternate between clapping the rhythm and returning fire. But all of a sudden he freezes. The actor has realized he has stepped on the mine he placed at the start. In a very high pitch he says "Click". The Capitano looks to the mine and then back to the audience, knowing he cannot escape his fate. He clears his throat and starts a big farewell speech. He compares himself to his soulmates, Napoleon and Caesar. He then explains in minute detail the kind of statue that should be made for him. Then he looks at the student operating the lights and says: "This is my last order. Kill the lights."

In the world of Hotel Courage we explore as many countries as possible. Together with the local actors, we create symbolic hotel rooms representing their stories. We do not impose what stories to tell. Every group develops its own vision on the archetypical characters in their own social and political context. In 2016 the different casts will come together to build and perform the imaginary *Hotel Courage* that will have its world premiere in Amsterdam. Last year we travelled to countries such as Ghana, Palestine, India and the United States. I would like to share with you our journey so far.

During our travels it is interesting to create characters in different countries who have the same archetypical behaviour. We approach the masks not from a historical perspective, but using the archetypical associations that the masks evoke. Pantalone, for example, represents the Old Man, clinging on to life because he knows death is around the corner. Dottore is the one who thinks he knows everything, but in reality knows nothing. The Capitano is the one who pretends to be everything that he is not. The mask makers create their masks so well the essence of the historical archetypes still remain. The actors in each country where we work learn how to play the archetypical mask and then create their own characters and stories. For instance, an actor from Los Angeles created a Capitano who was the excursion tour guide for the hotel. He gave a speech about the greatness of nature and how the craftsmanship of camping is the essence of manhood. In his speech we were offered facts beyond facts. After he had displayed his knowledge, he declared: "I will now give a demonstration in the 'art of camping'. We are starting with the basics: setting up The Camping Tent." Unfortunately, this great demonstration turned into a long and tragic fight with the tent itself. A month later, the same mask was played by an actor in a refugee camp on the West Bank in Palestine. Here the actor played the manager in the hotel. This Capitano had the secret ambition to be the greatest manager in the world. But, since there were no people to boss around, he opened his window to the field of tomatoes behind the hotel and started to tell the tomatoes off for not growing fast enough. This developed into a big, furious speech to all the vegetables in the world.

In Ghana we worked with the actors of Act for Change, a group of townspeople in James Town, one of the poorest neighbourhoods of Accra. Here we rediscovered how the body is already trained by parents, culture and life experience and what happens when the actor puts this at the service of a character. One actress saw the mask of the Old Lady and said "She is like our mothers and grandmothers who are always busy providing food for us and, to keep their spirits high, they sing our tribal songs." The actress put on the mask of the Old Lady and improvised for her fellow actors, preparing food for her family. But during the scene the actress got emotional and suddenly stopped singing and looked away from the audience. The audience instantly looked at the ground. After the scene I asked her and the group what had happened? They told me that it was better to hide one's eyes when getting emotional. The next day she came to the rehearsal and said that she wanted to play it again, but this time looking at the audience. While performing, the actress looked into the eyes of the audience. She experienced for the first time the intimacy that this evoked. While singing and cooking as the Old Lady she started to cry, but kept on singing. Now the town audience experienced the Old Lady, fighting against her tears, singing the tribal song to keep her spirits high. Softly they started singing along.

Last May we created a show with The Freedom Theatre based in the refugee camp of Jenin, Palestine. In many ways this experience made – on a visceral level – very clear to me how powerful the Commedia and its techniques can be in unleashing the energy, emotions and imagination of both the actors and the audience. The Freedom Theatre is a group of young actors using theatre to create a better world while living in a very harsh reality where survival is a daily struggle.

Before we started the workshop I gave the acting students an introduction on the history of the Commedia. The reaction of the students was completely different from the reactions I was used to. When I explained that Commedia originated in the past when women were not supposed to participate in acting, most people had not been exposed to theatre and theatre groups had to be very clever at finding ways to work around all kinds of taboos, one of the actors asked very dryly: "How do you mean 'the past'?"

After the first part of the workshop they took us on a journey through the refugee camp, to find out who the archetypes were in their society. They took us to their families and neighbourhoods. They took us to the cemetery and showed me the graves of their friends and families. They showed us a small restaurant with a very big chief cook with a very big moustache. This man constantly talked about the great food he served, about his skills as a cook. The food was great indeed, but it was an open secret that it was being prepared by a refugee, an old man with no family who lived in the basement of the restaurant. While we were studying, the old man serving the food, and the manager giving a speech to a guest, one of the actors tapped me on the shoulder. This very thin young actor was doing theatre for the first time in his life. He did not speak English and was very introverted. He would often just sit quietly in a corner and did not show any emotion. This time, however, he was very excited. He happily pointed to a huge police officer sitting on a big motorbike. With his hand he imitated the long nose of the Capitano mask, indicating that he would love to play this big police officer with his motorbike bigger than himself, wearing the Capitano mask. The first character of the show had been born.

At the end of this five-week workshop the students developed their story, *Courage, Ouda, Courage*. At the premiere they performed in front of an audience of two hundred young boys living in the refugee camp: boys living in a climate of war, not allowed to go in or out of their camp, facing uncertain futures. For these boys it was the first theatre performance they had ever attended, but they got more involved than any audience I had ever seen.

During the performance one actor performed the mask of Pantalone, the Old Man. He played a refugee named Ouda who we first see walking around the cemetery. He looks at the gravestones and talks to his mother and friends as if they could hear him. The audience is completely silent and fully immersed. Ouda remembers the past, how he was standing on the beach with his mother, listening and watching the sea. The actor asks the audience, to help him make the sound of the sea. The boys in the audience who have never seen the sea, immediately respond. Then he points to another grave and asks the audience: "Whose grave is that?" The boys respond immediately. "My father", "My uncle", "My brother" they exclaim. "Is there anything I should say to them?" he asks. After several serious and moving requests one boy jokes: "Tell my brother he still owes me money, I want it back." Instantly the very intense atmosphere changes and two hundred boys break out in laughter.

Towards the end of the show the two hundred boys unexpectedly help Ouda again. Now we see Ouda when he is young. The actor who played the old Ouda, now plays the young Ouda wearing an Arlecchino mask. We follow him as he flees through the mountains to Jenin. There he lives in the basement of the hotel. He works in the kitchen of the restaurant. He is not allowed to go out of the kitchen into the restaurant or out of the hotel. This particular night there are a lot of important guests coming to eat and the Chef, who wears the Dottore mask, is extremely excited and very stressed. He bosses Ouda around, ordering him to get the chickens, who are sitting in their henhouse in the kitchen, to prepare all the food to make the best chicken soup ever. Ouda is working like crazy but the more he rushes the more mistakes he makes and the more panicked the Dottore-Chef gets. While the Chef is preparing his speech he sees Ouda drop some food. He raises his hand, trying to hit Ouda with a pan. Ouda, on an impulse, opens the door to the henhouse and a chicken flies out. The Chef tries to catch the chicken, but misses. He gets ready to hit Ouda again, but suddenly a boy from the audience supports Ouda by imitating the sound of a chicken. The actor performing Ouda looks at the boy in the audience and starts to improvise that another chicken is escaping from the henhouse, flying towards the Chef. The Chef starts waving his arms about to avoid the chicken. Another boy stands up and imitates another chicken. Now Ouda opens the henhouse door wider and all the chickens fly out. Now all the boys in the audience start to imitate the sound of more and more chickens. The Chef tries to escape the flying chickens and locks himself into a huge fridge. A boy in the audience shouts, "Run Ouda!" The actor playing Ouda looks at the boy and then looks at the forbidden door. Another boy shouts: "Run Ouda!!" Then Ouda hurries to the door, opens it and starts running. He stops for a moment and looks at his friends in the audience.... Instantly, like crazy, the two hundred boys start making sounds of running chickens. Running for their freedom, along with Ouda.

One evening we performed for the Santal tribe, in a rural area of India. During that show an unexpected friendship was born. Our performance was based on a story an old Hungarian lady had shared with us during our visit to Jerusalem. As a child she had been in hiding in a small attic, together with her big sister, for three years during World War II. They were never allowed to make any noise during the night. But when the moon was full they secretly and quietly put on dresses, made themselves beautiful and danced in the moonlight. Just before the end of the war her sister died of exhaustion. In our performance we see a young actress playing a fragile old lady. Tonight when the moon is full the Old Lady puts on her dress, brushes her hair, dabs perfume on her neck and starts looking for her sister. She opens the window, looks up to the sky and sees the face of her sister in the moon. She asks, "How are you doing? Shall we dance?" While she dances the night passes and daylight appears. The face of her sister starts to fade. "Where are you going?" she asks. "Don't go!" she begs "Can I come with you? I don't want to stay. I don't want another day!"

While performing this scene at the village of the Santal tribe in India, when the Old Lady reaches for the moon screaming for her sister, we hear a shout coming from the audience. "Eh!" A very old, small, tribal lady with only two teeth left, jumps up and starts shouting in Santal dialect to the Old Lady on the stage. "Don't move. I am coming." She bounds laughing through the crowd of four hundred Santal tribe members until she reaches the stage. The tribal lady looks deeply into the eyes of the other old lady, grabs her by the hand and says "I greet you, let's go home." And they walk off. Instantly, the scene that originated more than sixty years ago ended in a celebration of long lost sisters in India.

During our tour we have met managers, cooks, cleaners, politicians, secret lovers, refugees, economists, soldiers, travellers, and homeless people looking for a place to sleep. We have seen them working, visiting, escaping, fighting, meeting and remembering in the hotel. We are looking forward to travelling to Japan, Iran and Russia this year. We welcome everybody to The Hotel Courage and eagerly await opening the doors at the premiere in Amsterdam in 2016.

The Hotel Courage tour offers us authentic, beautiful and funny stories from around the world told through the masks. The archetypal characters allow stories to transcend time, space and culture and reveal needs we all have in common, showing us a place where we can laugh and cry about how we try to survive in the world of today. And I hope the homeless man with his saxophone will pay us a visit too. We will offer him the biggest suite on the top floor, where he can make as many important phone calls as necessary.

PART IV

COMMEDIA DELL'ARTE
BIBLIOGRAPHY

BIBLIOGRAPHY OF GENERALLY ACCEPTED COMMEDIA DELL'ARTE LITERATURE

Andrews, Richard (1993) *Scripts and Scenarios, the Performance of Comedy in Renaissance Italy*. Cambridge, UK and New York: University of Cambridge Press.

Beaumont, Cyril W. (1926) *The History of Harlequin*. New York: Benjamin Blom.

Cairns, Christopher (1989) *The Commedia dell'Arte from the Renaissance to Dario Fo: The Italian Origins of European Theatre*. Oxford, UK and New York: Edwin Mellen Press.

Calendoli, Giovanni (1985) *Ruzante*. Venice, Italy: Corbo e Fiore.

Carroll, Linda L. (1981) *Angelo Beolco (Il Ruzante): Language and dialect in Ruzante and Goldoni*. Ravenna, Italy: Longo Editore.

Castagno, Paul C. (1994) *The Early Commedia dell'Arte 1550–1621*. New York: Lang.

Clayton, J. Douglas (1994) *Pierrot in Petrograd: The Commedia dell'Arte/Balagan in Twentieth-Century Russian Theatre and Drama*. Montreal, Canada: McGill Queens University Press.

Cotticelli, Francesco, Anne Goodrich Heck, and Thomas Heck (2001) *Commedia dell'Arte in Naples: A Bilingual Edition of the 176 Casamarciano Scenarios*. Lanham, MD, US and London: Scarecrow Press.

Dersofi, Nancy (1978) *Arcadia and the Stage*. Madrid: Porrua; Washington, DC: Studia Humanitatis.

Dick, Kay (1960) *Pierrot*. London, Toronto, New York: Hutchinson and Company.

Duchartre, Pierre Louis (1996) *The Italian Comedy* (tr. Randolph T. Weaver) Toronto and London: Dover Press. (Originally printed in 1929 by George C. Harrop, London.)

Farrell, Joseph and Paolo Puppa (eds) (2006) *A History of Italian Theatre*. Cambridge, UK and New York: University of Cambridge Press.

Fava, Antonio (2007) *The Comic Mask in the Commedia dell'Arte*. Evanston, IL, US: Northwestern University Press.

Felix, Talia, Scribleruse, Lawrence Langer, and John Davidson (2010) *La Commedia Inglese: English Plays of the Commedia dell'Arte*. Seattle, US and New York: CreateSpace Independent Publishing Platform.

Ferrone, Siro (2014) *La Commedia dell'Arte: Attrici e Attore Italiani in Europa (xvi-xvii secolo)*. Turin, Italy: Einaudi.

Fisher, James (1992) *The Theatre of Yesterday and Tomorrow*. Lewiston, NY, US and Queenston, Ontario, Canada: Edwin Mellen Press.

Fitzpatrick, Tim (1995) *The Relationship of Oral and Literate Performance Processes in the Commedia dell'Arte: Beyond the Improvisation/Memorisation Divide*. Lewiston, US/Queenston, Canada/Lampeter, UK: Edwin Mellen Press.

George, David and Christopher J. Gossip (eds) (1995) *Studies in the Commedia dell'Arte*. Cardiff, Wales: University of Wales Press.

Gordon, Mel (1983) *Lazzi: The Comedy Routines of the Commedia dell'Arte*. New York: Performing Arts Journal Publications.

Grantham, Barry (2007) *Commedia Plays: Scenarios—Scripts—Lazzi*. Shepherd's Bush, UK: Nick Hern Books.

Green, Martin and John Swan (1993) *The Triumph of Pierrot: The Commedia dell'Arte and the Modern Imagination*. University Park, PA, US: Pennsylvania State University Press.

Griffiths, David (1998) *Please Be Gentle: A Conjectural Evaluation of the Masked Performance of Commedia dell'Arte*. Oxford, UK: Taylor and Francis Publishers.

Heck, Thomas (1988) *Commedia dell'Arte: A Guide to the Primary and Secondary Literature*. Lincoln, NE, US: Garland Publishing, Inc.

Henke, Robert (2002) *Performance and Literature in the Commedia dell'Arte*. Cambridge, UK: Cambridge University Press.

Hill, Phillip G. and Paul C. Castagno (eds) (1993) *Commedia dell'Arte Performance: Contexts and Contents*. Tuscaloosa, AL, US: University of Alabama Press.

Johnson, James H. (2011) *Venice Incognito: Masks in the Serene Republic*. Berkeley, Los Angeles, US and London: University of California Press.

Jordan, Peter (2014) *The Venetian Origins of the Commedia dell'Arte*. Oxford, UK: Taylor and Francis Publishing.

Kaplan, David (2012) *Commedia dell'Arte and Moliere*. East Brunswick, NJ, US: Hanson Publishing Group.

Katritzky, M. A. (2006) *The Art of Commedia: A Study in the Commedia dell'Arte, 1560–1620, with Special Reference to the Visual Records*. Amsterdam and New York: Editions Rodopi.

Kennard, Joseph Spencer (1932) *The Italian Theatre: Volume 1*. New York: William Edwin Rudge.

Labalme, Patricia H. and Laura Sanguineti White (eds) and Linda L. Carroll (tr.) (2008) *Venice, Città Excelentissima: Selections from the Renaissance Diaries of Marin Sanudo*. Baltimore, US: The Johns Hopkins University Press.

Lawner, Lynne (1998) *Harlequin on the Moon: Commedia dell'Arte and the Visual Arts*. New York: Harry N. Abrams.

Lea, Kathleen M. (1934) *Italian Popular Comedy, Volumes I and II*. London: Oxford University Press.

Lovarini, Emilio (1965) *Studi sul Ruzzante e sulla letteratura pavana*. Gianfranco Folena (ed.). Padua, Italy: Antenore.

MacNeil, Anne (2003) *Music and Women of the Commedia dell'Arte in the Late Sixteenth Century*. New York and Oxford, UK: Oxford University Press.

Marcia, Alberto (1980) *The Commedia Dell'Arte and the Masks of Amleto and Donato Sartori*. Florence, Italy: La Casa Usher.

Menegazzo, Emilio (2001) *Colonna, Folengo, Ruzante e Cornaro. Ricerche, testi e documenti*. Andrea Canova (ed.). Padua, Italy: Antenore.

Moland, Louis (1967) *Moliere and the Italian Comedy*. Paris: Didier et cie.

Nicoll, Allardyce (1963) *Masks, Mimes, and Miracles*. New York: Cooper Square Publishers, Inc.

——(1963) *The World of Harlequin: A Critical Study of the Commedia dell'Arte*. Cambridge, UK: Cambridge University Press.

Niklaus, Thelma (1956) *Harlequin Phoenix*. New York: George Brazillier, Inc.

O'Brien, John (2004) *Harlequin Britain*. Baltimore, MD, US: Johns Hopkins Press.

Oreglia, Giacomo (1968) *The Commedia dell'Arte*. New York: Hill and Wang Dramabook.

Orenstein, Claudia (1998) *Festive Revolutionaries, the Politics of Popular Theatre and the San Francisco Mime Troupe*. Mississippi, US: University Press of Mississippi.

Pietropaolo, Domenico (1989) *The Science of Buffoonery: Theory and History of the Commedia dell'Arte*. Toronto, Canada: Dovehouse Editions.

Richards, Kenneth and Laura Richards (1990) *The Commedia dell'Arte: A Documentary History*. Oxford, UK: Blackwell Publishing Ltd.

Rolfe, Bari (1977) *Commedia dell'Arte: A Scene Study Book*. San Francisco, US: Persona Products.

Rudlin, John (1994) *Commedia dell'Arte: An Actor's Handbook*. New York: Routledge.

Rudlin, John and Olly Crick (2001) *Commedia dell'Arte: A Handbook for Troupes*. New York and London: Routledge.

Salerno, Henry F. (ed.) (1967) *Scenarios of the Commedia dell'Arte: Flaminio Scala's "Il Teatro delle favole rappresentative"*. New York: New York University Press.

Sambin, Paolo (2002) *Per le biografie di Angelo Beolco, il Ruzante, e di Alvise Cornaro*. Francesco Piovan (ed.). Padua, Italy: Esedra.

Sand, Maurice (1915) *The History of the Harlequinade*. London: Benjamin Blom.

Schwartz, I. A. (1931) *The Commedia dell'Arte and Its Influence on French Comedy in the Seventeenth Century*. Paris: Librairie H. Samuel.

Scott, Virginia (1990) *The Commedia dell'Arte in Paris 1644–1697*. Charlottesville, VA, US: University of Virginia Press.

Smith, Winifred L. (1964) *The Commedia dell'Arte*. New York: Benjamin Blom.

Story, Robert F. (1978) *Pierrot: A Critical History of a Mask*. Princeton, US: University of Princeton Press.

INDEX

sensorial aspects, masks 137–8
sentimentality 347, 349
serious versus grotesque dance 341–2, 344
The Servant of Two Masters (Goldini) 331, 335, 404, 480–1, 484, *see also Arlecchino, Servant of Two Masters*
servants: Brighella as 114–15, 120; *buffoni* as 223; Capitano's 87; Goldoni's reforms 334; Harlequin 56–8; Pulcinella as 112; Renaissance context 13–16, 23–4; San Francisco Mime Troupe 440; scenarios 27; status/stakes 183; Strehler directing 371–2, 374–6; women 91–5, 458–9, 462–3
le servette 91–5
servus callidus (clever slave) 199–200
seventeenth century Brighella 117–18
Séverin as Pierrot 348
sexism 457–8
sexual lazzi 172
sexual references 67–8, 458–9
Sforza, Francesco 210
Sganarelle character 102
Sgarra-Muscia 96–7
Shakespeare, William 300–11; appropriation of Commedia 357; Brighella and 117; clown connection 312–20; *Cymbeline* 258; *King Lear* 84–5, 127–8; Scala and 30–40; scenarios use 22; Strehler directing 370–7; *The Tempest* 371–6; Young Lovers 72
shipping goods 209
The Showers, Mazzone-Clementi 393
silent pantomime 346–7, 355–63
Silvia characters 325
singing 259–61, *see also* music
sirens 246–54
sixteenth century: Brighella 116–17; Europe 356–7
slapstick 185–92
social-class rebellion lazzi 172
social classes *see* class system
social commentary 185, 419
social order: carnival and 411–12; subverting 9–17
social position of characters 424, 481
social power 13–14
social status, female servants 92, *see also* status

Society for Creative Anachronism (SCA) 451–2, 454
soldier stereotype 82–3, 89
sound effects, fights 188
South Asia 467–8
Southeast Asia 467–8
sovereign power 14, 16
space, masks and 130, 132–4, 137–8
Spanish Golden Age theatre 238–45
"spatial" qualities, masks 130
Spavento, Captain 88–90
specialization, actors 111
spectacles: old men 300–11; speechless 355–63
speech-acts, scenarios 24–7, 36
speech-music 381
speechless spectacles 355–63
spies 326
sport 180
stage/life duality lazzi 173
stage properties: lazzi 173, 316, 487; musical props 263–4; slapstick/comic violence 186; Strehler and 371, 374–5; touring companies 236
stages/staging practices: celestial sirens 246–54; early history 229–37; Gozzi 335; performance and 233–5; scenarios and 21–9
stakes principle 182–3
status 65, 182–3, *see also* social status
stereotypes 207, 439
stock characters 53–122; Atellan farce 197–8; Beolco's influence 220; Capitano 82–9; dance 343, 345; Fo's theatre 414; Goldoni's views 330; Harlequin 55–61; i Sebastiani troupe 455; Pantalone/Dottore 62–9; passions 475; Pulcinella 108–13; San Francisco Mime Troupe 440; social positions 481; women 461–3; Young Lovers 70–81
Stockholm Recueil Fossard prints 286–7, 292–3
storytelling and puppetry 471
"straight men" 182
Strauss, Richard, *Ariadne auf Naxos* 273–4
Stravinsky, Igor 280
street performances 75, 179, 229, 292, 323, 409–10
Strehler, Giorgio 145–6, 370–7, 404–5